The History Of Old Durban And Reminiscences Of An Emigrant Of 1850

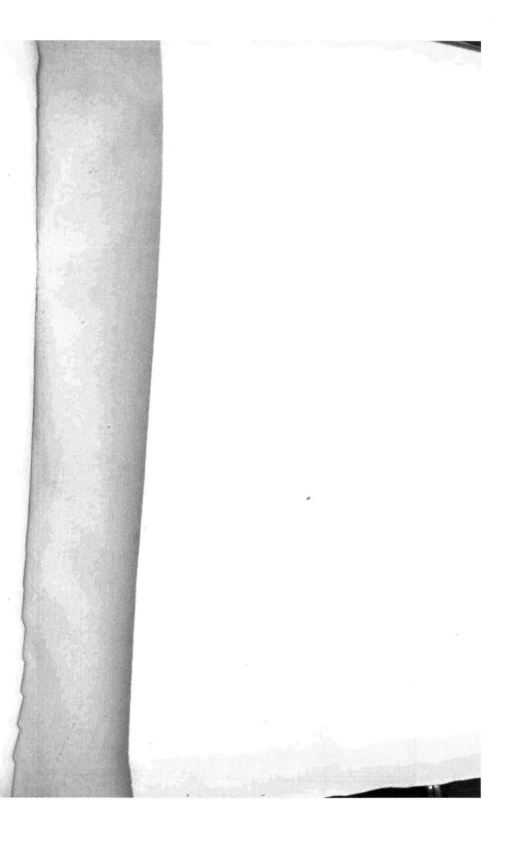

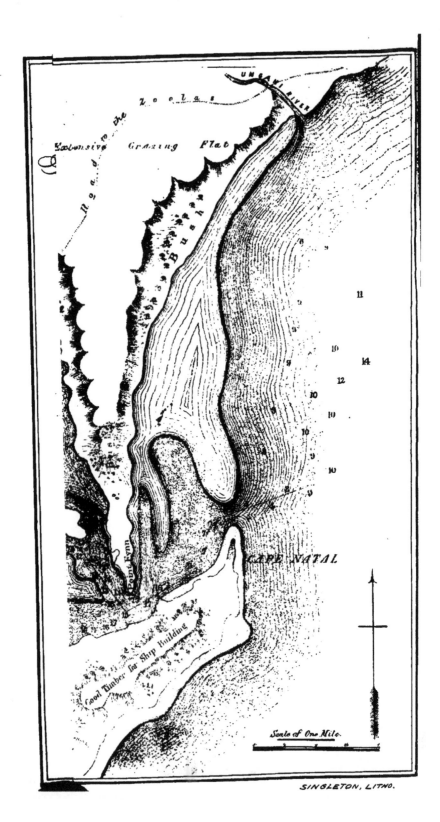

UMGANI RIVER

Road to the Zoolas

Extensive Grazing Flat

Bush

Road to the Zoolas

Point Farm

Good Timber for Ship Building

CAPE NATAL

Scale of One Mile.

SINGLETON, LITHO.

THE

Bistory of Old Durban,

AND

REMINISCENCES OF AN EMIGRANT OF
1850.

[ILLUSTRATED]

BY

GEORGE RUSSELL.

Natal:
PRINTED BY P. DAVIS & SONS, WEST AND SAVILLE STS., DURBAN.
PUBLISHED BY
P. DAVIS & SONS, DURBAN, MARITZBURG, LONDON.

the l
arriv
the
since
the
or s
unfr
rec
gra

shu
of
ha
en
fa
s
i
r

DEDICATED

TO

MY WIFE.

———

THOUGH our families in England were intimate, FRANCES MATILDA SHAW, of that period, would scorn to admit that she was "My sweetheart when a boy!" Nevertheless as years crept on she consented at my instigation to rekindle the latent embers on Hymen's Altar, and to join me in Natal. She arrived as a passenger in the *Early Morn* in 1861: we were married the following year. At her earnest desire I discontinued by Diary, since she had reasonable ground for believing I might record some of the "silly" things we then said, or might touch upon matters personal or social that would call for regret should the effusion fall into unfriendly hands. I have to thank her for this, since it limits my records of Old Durban, for which my readers may be equally grateful.

I dedicate my work to her who has so long and so cheerfully shared my life, its joys and griefs, the births, marriages, and deaths of our children; shedding the love of a refined and sympathetic nature upon domestic cares, business occupations, and daily routine; enlarging the word HOME and rendering it the most attractive centre for an unambitious man. No less is due to her who has patiently shared in this production, and aided my researches, respected my isolation and late hours, tolerated my silence and the enforced relinquishment of neighbourly social intercourse and other pleasures.

We have, as Burns expresses it, climbed life's hill together; now grateful and contented, hand in hand we must totter down, in the sure and certain hope that however apparently wasted have been our opportunities, we shall in a glorified existence in the Great Spirit World, find congenial uses and occupations according to the light that is within us.

GEORGE RUSSELL.

Longlands, Musgrave Road,
    Durban.

CONTENTS.

FIRST CLEARING.

1850.

1851.

1852.

1853.

CONTENTS.

x

PREFACE.

IT will not be amiss to preface this book with a few words of
explanation as to the reasons which induced me to write
the history of Old Durban. Although the task might have
been entrusted to more capable hands, yet I venture to say
that to no one could its performance have given greater pleasure than to me, in its reviving of the memories of those
early days and of my old comrades, when together we
climbed life's ladder.

"Many a true word is spoken in jest!"—A jocular remark
by Durban's first Mayor, the late George Christopher Cato,
led to my assuming the rôle of Durban's historian.

I had the privilege of being on very friendly terms with
Mr. Cato from my first arrival in the Colony, and was indebted to him for many kindnesses and pleasant tales twice-
told. In later years I joined other mutual friends in
begging him to publish the record of his experiences of the
Dutch Emigrant Farmers, and of the first settlement of the
Colony, of Durban in particular. This only resulted in his
snatching from his manifold duties time sufficient merely to
scribble inconsequential letters of a personal character to the
newspapers, relating more to sport than to history. Finding,
as the years passed over me, that this veteran Colonist made
no sign excepting that of advancing age, I ventured again
to urge the necessity while it was yet day, when he stated

sharply and definitely that he had furnished Mr. John Bird
with all his records for embodiment in the ANNALS OF
NATAL, and that, if I wanted anything more, I, being a
" Jimmy," could well do it myself, as Mr. Bird was only
going up to the time of our arrival, or that of Governor
West.   There the matter rested, my own occupations
diverting me from any literary attempts until after Mr.
Cato's decease.

The passing away of other old settlers at length forced on
me the conviction that I was hastening on the same road,
and that if OLD DURBAN's HISTORY was to be done I must
do it myself, as Mr. Cato had recommended.

Thus, albeit with great diffidence and many misgivings,
have I taken upon myself the task of recording the struggles,
the difficulties, and the victories of those early days, feeling
assured that the history of the labours achieved and the
hardships overcome by their fathers cannot but become an
enduring memory and a much prized recollection to our
sons, and our sons' sons, convincing them that, however
meritorious their own share in life's work may be, it is to
those who have gone before them that they owe their present
positions, and the prosperity of the beautiful town which is
their heritage.

In entering upon my labours it has been useful to bear in
mind that quotation from the Masons' Ritual, which states :

" It was customary at the erection of all stately or superb
buildings to lay the first foundation stone in the North-east corner."

The Masons' Ritual, which conveys this information, does
not enlarge upon the necessity of preparing the ground for
the intended structure, but as Colonists we know from experience that bush must be cleared, roads made, and the
ground levelled before permanent operations can be commenced on farm or homestead ; works begun with manly
vigour and brave hearts, in the confident hope that the
eventual outcome will be a stately and superb building for
our declining years.

Entering upon this undertaking as one of the old Colonists, at the earnest solicitation of other Old Colonists—who kindly promised me the support of that most unreliable of history makers, "a good memory," an oft-repeated tale, before memory should fail us altogether—I recollected the advice of another Old Colonist, the late Pastor Cowley, of Durban, in the "Fifties" a master builder in great request for the complicated and excellent construction of Sugar Mills.

His constant axiom was "Never start before you are ready,"—very sound and prudential advice, which I duly laid to heart. To this wise saw I added that of an Irish Schoolmaster of my diffuse youth:—

"If you have anything to say always begin at the beginning."

For these and other reasons I introduce the reader to my

DISCOVERY OF THE SITE.

DURBAN, NATAL, 1898.

" Ncthing extenuate, nor set down aught in malice.''
                              Othello, Act V., Scene II.

OLD DURBAN.

CHAPTER I.

DISCOVERY OF THE SITE.

First Clearing. SCIENCE having proved the Biblical Chronology propounded by Archbishop Usher to be at fault, we must concede that man and other animals were here before the times of Noah or his son Ham.   That the man of the period was in any way related to the Ape may be contested, but certain it is that he was not of the Caucasian family, but decidedly Negro.   Evidence of his intelligent existence is preserved in the stone implements deposited in the Durban Museum.

Tradition and classical writers aver that the Phœnicians circumnavigated Africa.   If so, we will also concede the possibility of their being the first Asiatics or Northernmen to have looked upon our shores.   History, however, credits the discovery of Natal to those bold and enterprising explorers, the Portuguese, who, cautiously coasting along Western Africa in their small and clumsy craft, had finally

reached the Cape of Good Hope under Bartholomew Diaz
in the year 1492, about the same time that Columbus
discovered America for Spain.   Circumstances obliged Diaz
to return to Portugal without actually doubling what he
rightly deemed the Southernmost cape of this great con-
tinent, which, as it presented the possibilities of the much
sought sea route to the Indies, he named the Cape of Good
Hope.

Another expedition was fitted out by the King of
Portugal, and placed in charge of Vasco da Gama (we
assume), with orders to "go East."   After doubling the
Cape, he felt his way up the Coast by cautious soundings
and a bright look-out, until on Christmas Day, A.D. 1497,
he and his people were the first known Europeans to have
looked upon the Bluff, the Berea, the Point, and the Bay
behind it.   Lack of water being one of the shortcomings of
all early navigators, it is safe to conclude that the small
craft of their day, propelled both by oars and sails, easily
came inside the harbour "to water, provision, and refit."
Two hundred years later the crew of a wrecked ship describe
"the river of Natal" as having "a wide mouth and deep
enough for small craft, but there is a sandbank which at
highest flood has not more than 10 or 12 feet of water; this
river is the principal one on the coast of Natal, and has
been frequently visited by merchant vessels."   The inference
is that the Umgeni then flowed through the Eastern vlei
into the Bay, and that Vasco da Gama sent his barges for
water to the outflow of that river somewhere in the vicinity
of that distinguished outlet known as Cato's Creek.   Hence
it may with equal reason be assumed that he and his party
were the first white men to set foot on the site of Durban.

There is no record that this brave explorer landed here,
otherwise we should doubtless have learnt that with the
good Christian feeling of those times he astonished
the natives by erecting a cross, unfurling an embroidered
banner, firing off a few musketoons, with roll of drum and
blare of trumpet, in honour of the country, of which he thus
gracefully possessed himself on behalf of his royal master of
Portugal, and named Natal (Terra de Natal). (*)

---

* The State Records of this Expedition convey the impression
that they simply sailed past that Christmas Day.

Having " careened and revictualled his ships and refreshed his crews," according to custom, he doubtless took with him all he could carry or commandeer, and sailed away northward, naming Capes and Headlands on his way to India. We are not now concerned as to his route, or if he first landed at Ceylon, Goa, or the Island of Bombay ; certain it was, however, that Mauritius was not discovered until exactly 100 years later (1598), that the adventurous Portuguese settled in India, and that their discovery of the route via the Cape was speedily taken advantage of by those equally good seamen and " Voortrekkers," the Dutch. Britain, or England, then, came in a bad third, having her hands full of Protestant succession in Europe and Spanish dispossession in South America and the Spanish Main.

It is, however, on record that Durban was visited by both Dutch and English castaways between 1497 and 1688, who apparently got out of Natal as soon as opportunity offered, but, in the latter year, the Governor of the Cape of Good Hope, at this time a Dutch possession, sent up an expedition to investigate the travellers' tales of the wonderfully fertile country between Delagoa Bay and Caffreland. The officers in command, while at Port Natal, entered into a treaty with the Native Chief of the District for the purchase of the Bay and surrounding land, executing a deed of purchase and sale accordingly, for a consideration of beads, copper, ironwork, and as a general thing good " Hollands."

The burgesses of Durban need have no cause for anxiety as to their title, for, when the Dutch Company returned some years after to take possession, this deed, like many others, was found not to hold water. The Chief in possession said, " My father was dead and buried with his goods, his huts burnt over him, the place fenced in, over which no man must now pass. As to what he agreed to, it was for himself, I have nothing to say to it." This patriotic native no doubt suffered retribution at the hands of the white man, for it is recorded that in 1721 the Dutch established a " Factory," i.e., a sort of fortified trading station, at Port Natal, but soon abandoned it. Possibly this arose from the differences of opinion that would arise between the Native and the European, in consequence not only of the rate of exchange in barter, but by reason of the visits, in the early part of the seventeenth century, of those enterprising mariners of no certain nationality, indifferently classed when occasion arose as Pirates, Privateers, or Slavers, who made their rendezvous Madagascar, and gave themselves out as engaged in the Red Sea trade. The route home from the Indies offered but an indifferent field for piracy when all trading vessels in these waters were heavily armed, and though occasionally conveying gold dust, were not over-burdened with specie. Goods, silks, or spices were cumbersome, so the Bay of Natal became the resort of English slavers, who are recorded as having done good business in that line, no doubt abusing the confidence of the unsophisticated Native, as the more modern " Blackbirders " of the Pacific are said to have done. Durban may consequently have been the site of the slave pen, with its attendant inconveniences, which, I am of opinion, were not until they became illegal, harsher or more brutal than necessary to secure the safe-keeping of · the raw material. After a lengthened experience, I quite concur in the views of the enlightened Boers that a modified form of slavery—or serfdom—is good for the Native African, that is, until he is " tamed." His shipment by these early " Labour Agents " saved him from possible death at the hands of his outraged Chief, or whilom conqueror. There is possibility in the idea that there may flow a commingling of the blood of some of our " Natal boys " in the veins of the " Chivalry of the South," or the Dons of Cuba, as those enterprising Slavers sold in the best markets, notably that of the British settlements in " Ole Virginia."

Tradition carries us over the next hundred years from 1720 to 1820, when we reach solid ground, for, during the interval, Port Natal was visited by waifs and strays of shipwrecked mariners, or by casual hunters and possible traders, in search of the ivory, of which there was abundance. Now, however, a Royal visitor, in the person of Chaka, the organiser of the Zulu nation as a military power, the conqueror of all nations in his world, swept through Natal, " eating up " everybody and everything, and literally reducing the country to a waste almost as far as St. John's River. He ·is reputed, on his locust-like visitation, to have made a temporary settlement upon the Berea

Ridge, in the vicinity of the present St. Thomas's Church, a strategic position commanding views both inland and of the Bay. Certain it is that the remains of much native pottery have been found in the Berea Park, where also human bones are by no means rare. This site must not, however, be confounded with "Chaka's Kraal," a great Military Camp on the lower Umvoti. In the township of Stanger (Dagooza), the mortal remains of this warrior king, nero, and genius, whose cruel ferocity earned from his subjects the appropriate designation of "The Hyena Man," find a permanent residence on the spot where he fell, treacherously assassinated by his brother Dingaan, who accordingly reigned in his stead. "Le Roi est mort, vive le Roi!" Thus human history repeats itself. Chaka, being an African, was to the manner born. He had no opportunity of studying the examples of noble Pagans or knightly Christians. The details of their glorious victories were to him unknown ; he followed a policy strictly his own, conquest and death. The devastation of Natal was complete. The few inhabitants who escaped with their lives into holes, reed swamps, bush, or caves, without food or shelter, had to call upon Nature for their support, living on roots and herbs, or on such small deer as they could snare unobserved. To such an extremity were they reduced in avoiding the ever prowling "impies" of the Conqueror—because they could not cultivate—that many resorted to cannibalism, while the remnants of one tribe, residing on the Bluff, were obliged to overcome their prejudices by subsisting on fish. Old natives compared their existence, at this time, to the life and habits of rock-rabbits.

The overthrow of Napoleon Bonaparte by the Allied Armies of Europe resulted in a readjustment of boundaries, so, by the Treaty of Paris, 1814, the King of the Netherlands formally ceded to England the Dutch possession of the Cape of Good Hope with its dependencies, and, consequently, the British Flag now floated over Cape Town. Governor Lord Charles Somerset gave his consent to Lieut. F. G. Farewell, of the Royal Navy, to establish a station at Natal, of course "for the advancement of trade and civilisation." Farewell enlisted about twenty adventurous spirits, himself, Henry Fynn, and Lieutenant King being the recognised leaders.

Isaacs, Cane, Ogle, and Biggar were among them. They arrived in the brig *Salisbury* in the year 1824—the ship giving its name to the island in the Bav. The newcomers were speedily invited to an " At Home " by Chaka at his residence between the Tongaat and Umhlali. Cattle in thousands and a war-dance of some 25,000 men and women were paraded before the visitors by the self-proclaimed " greatest king in existence." The strangers were doubtless duly impressed, and, though themselves fighting men, pre- ferred for the present to represent the nation of shopkeepers, smiling upon the King of the Zulus and Conqueror of all the world, until, in exchange for brass, copper, beads, and other things, he ceded to them a tract of land 25 miles along the Coast, including the Bay of Natal, and 100 miles inland. In Chaka's deed of grant to Lieutenant Farewell, this district is named or spelled " Bubolongo."

This puts a point to the site of Durban as a British pos- session, squarely traded, bought, and paid for.

So while we, after our kind, abuse Chaka and all his works, let us not, in our self-righteousness, forget that to him is due our right to sit under our own vine and fig tree as the lawful possessors of the finest town in South Africa.

The *Salisbury* on arrival was commanded by Lieutenant King. She was subsequently wrecked, and King obtained command of the brig *Mary*. At St. Helena he made the acquaintance of Mr. Nathaniel Isaacs (*) by whom he was accompanied to Cape Town. Learning at that port that nothing had been heard of his friend Lieut. Farewell and party for nearly two years, he decided to take his vessel up to Natal to seek them, Isaacs agreeing to throw in his lot with him. They arrived in the *Mary* on the 1st October, 1825. She was blown from her anchorage, and in attempt- ing to enter the Bay was wrecked on the Bar.

These gentlemen adventurers now enjoyed what the Americans designate " a good time." Zulu cattle were exchanged freely for " brass." Zulu women were to be had for the asking, ivory and game to be had for the hunting. These primitive men speedily became " fat " in the native sense, and, finding it more convenient each to set up his own

---

* Author of *Travels and Adventures in Eastern Africa.* E. Churton, London, 1836.

empire, instead of continuing in company and minding the shop, possessed themselves of their domain and extended their borders. Farewell elected to build and stockade himself on Durban's Market Square. An old ruin of a house standing between the present Natal Bank and the Town Hall in Gardiner Street was pointed out to me in 1850 as his—it might have been. Lieut. King squatted on the Bluff, above and behind what is known as Shortt's; the land was eventually occupied by Fynn; afterwards by Robt. Boyne, and more recently by Bowers. Fynn established himself at the Umbilo, at the head of the Bay. The other Europeans were either affiliated to these leaders, or lived "convenient" and by themselves. Cane's Camp was in the vicinity of the Botanical Gardens. To the present day indications of ploughed land, near the curve of the Race Course close by, can be traced, but I cannot credit Cane with this, as he certainly would have used women and picks. It was more likely to have been turned up by some Dutchman of a later day.

Isaacs and the rest of Lieut. King's crew named their location on the Bluff "Townsend," where they intended to construct a vessel from the fragments of the *Mary* to enable them to quit the country.

Classical writers need not be quoted to emphasise the facility of the descent of Avernus, but that descent becomes a fall when Englishmen, abandoning all self-respect, drop all disguise and lower themselves to the level of their savage surroundings; not even to plead the advancement of trade, religion, or civilisation can justify them. These friends and whilom comrades, setting themselves up as Native Chiefs, grew jealous of each other, and each aimed at being the "Inkosi inkulu." So to establish their position in the eyes of the Natives and other followers, it became necessary to count in more cattle, more wives, and more ivory. Their camps became the resort of starving refugees from all parts of the country, who crawled in to ask food and protection. These people attached themselves as retainers and henchmen to the several traders, who thus became recognised as the lawfully constituted Chiefs of the Whiteman and Native. These followers were increased by deserters from both the British and Zulu armies, as also by Bastards and Hottentots

from the Cape Colony.   Chaka, regarding his deserters with
lofty contempt, was too great a Chief to require extradition,
saying, " They have gone to my friends, not to my enemies."
Natal thus grew, until there was a respectable array of
trader-hunters and Natives within the Chartered limits,
amounting together to about 3,000 men.   Lieut. King died
on the Bluff, and was buried there, the site of his grave
being named " King's Rest."   Dingaan, Chaka's successor,
commenced his reign by the usual Native custom of cutting
off all the relations and trusted men of his predecessor,
which naturally increased the desertions from his sphere of
influence, and the number of refugees at the Bay.   Dissatisfied with the result of a friendly embassy to the Governor of the Cape at the hands of Cane, Dingaan " invited "
Fynn and Cane to come and be killed in the Zulu country.
They, however, preferred going the other wav, and were
consequently followed as far as the Umzimkulu by the Zulu
impies; who then gave up the chase, and, returning at
their leisure, took back with them all the Englishmen's
cattle they could catch, devastating the Bay settlement as a
matter of course.   Lieut. Farewell, with the other settlers,
had sought to establish an overland route to Grahamstown.
It was just after this event that he was returning with
wagons and goods to Natal, when he and his party were
treacherously murdered in Pondoland, A.D. 1831.   John
Cane and Henry Ogle, who were retainers of the brave and
enterprising Farewell, sorted up his people and what stock
remained, constituted themselves his residuary legatees,
divided the spoil in equal shares, and set up as independent
Native Chiefs of Natal.   Dingaan, apparently dreading reprisals from the Cape Colony, assured the white settlers
that he was perfectly harmless, and invited them to return
and live in peace; they ultimately consented, and, as an
earnest of Dingaan's good faith, asked for the return of
their cattle.   This, however, the latter could not entertain,
but, instead, nominated or recognised Mr. Henry F. Fynn
as " Great Chief " of the Natal Kafirs.   This gentleman,
the last of the dauntless Pioneers, resumed power and
exerted himself for the advancement and protection of the
little community until 1834, when he left Natal to accept a
permanent appointment under the Cape Government.   Ogle
and Cane then assumed direction of affairs, which were any-

thing but pastoral, the Zulu impies claiming free warren over the country in search of refugees from Dingaan, who was constantly claiming somebody's head at the hands of the settlers. These raids were made in circles, commencing inland by the North, and returning by the Coast, killing men and capturing cattle. When these cattle were owned by the settlers, it naturally led to reprisals. In the year 1835, Captain Allen F. Gardiner, of the Royal Navy (known to history as the "Patagonian Martyr," in consequence of his being starved to death in that bleak, inhospitable country), a zealous and devout gentleman, arrived at the Bay, and sought to establish a Mission among the Zulus for "the promotion of religion and industry." He accordingly waited upon Dingaan, but that poor ignorant black man failed to see its advantages, unless Captain Gardiner could teach his Army how to use the musket. So he returned to the Bay without obtaining his object. Here the European inhabitants promised him their support. He accordingly erected a Mission Church on the bush-covered heights overlooking the Bay on the site cleared by Chaka's Army, naming the spot "Berea," paraphrasing St. Paul's reason, "Since notwithstanding any ill success with Dingaan, the Word has here been gladly received." The annexed illustration is a reproduction from his "Journey to the Zoolu Country"—Crofts, London, 1836. The presence and influence of such a pious and evangelical man speedily made itself felt, and the slumbering instincts of civilization were aroused in the minds of the settlers, who were living chiefly in huts scattered anywhere and everywhere, though the Congella seems to have been the favoured locality.

It was here that Captain Gardiner signed his treaty with Dingaan, on behalf of the British residents of Port Natal, by which the Zulu king pardoned all Zulu refugees, claiming them still as his subjects. The British residents promised to give up all Zulu refugees. (*)

It was here, as it is believed, that on the 23rd June, 1835, the first public meeting was held, attended by 17 residents, one of whom was Mr. Richard King, afterwards famous, who passed resolutions as to laying out a township

* It is doubtful if the "Congella" where the treaty was signed was not in the Zulu country, and now spelt Kangella.

to be called D'Urban, in honour of Sir Benjamin D'Urban,
then Governor of the Cape Colony, and establishing a Colony
to be called Victoria, in honour of the young Princess,
daughter of the late Duke of Kent, extending from the Umzimkulu to the Tugela, and inland to the Berg.   The township was to be between the " River Avon," thought to be
the Umbilo, and the " Buffalo Spring," probably the site of
the natural fountain whence the shipping obtained their
water, near the corner of the present Field and Smith
Streets, reserved in the Title Deeds of Erf No. 20, Block D,
for a Public Well.   Lands were appropriated for Church,
Hospital, Cemetery, and public purposes.   A town committee was elected at the meeting and a subscription list opened.
Captain Gardiner, with Messrs. Collis, Berkin, Cane, and
Ogle, were the Committee.   Sir Benjamin D'Urban sent
£50 for aid in the erection of a church, but the British
Government did not recognise the Colony of Victoria, nor
appoint a Governor, though Captain Gardiner, who had
shortly after this paid a visit to England, was on his return
in 1837 invested with Magisterial powers.

The Dutch farmers in the Old Colony, dissatisfied generally with the treatment of the British Government, especially
in relation to the Natives and its unjustifiable interference
with the dispensation of Providence in the matter of slavery,
for which all white men have warrant in the Bible, (*)
renounced their allegiance, preferring independence with the
undisturbed right to follow the example of the citizens of
the United States in their relation to the negro or the
Red Indians, to relegate the Black men as hewers of wood
and drawers of water.   They sold off their farms, often at a
sacrifice, and, loading up their wagons with their goods and
families, driving the live stock before them, they literally
trekked into the wilderness Northward, on the Western side
of the great Drakensberg range.   They fought their way
through the present Free State. driving out the Natives and
occupying the country, which they duly annexed.   From
5,000 to 10,000 people are believed to have trekked out from

---

* The widow Steinkamp, writing in the Cape Monthly Magazine,
September, 1876, to her grandchildren, says:—" Yet it is not so much
their freedom that drove us to such lengths, as their being placed on
an equal footing with Christians contrary to the laws of God and the
natural distinction of race and religion.

the Cape Colony, unopposed by the Government, in different parties during the years 1836 and 1837. The Boer believes he is to be, but never is, blessed. The Free State did not seem large enough for them to settle in. Paradise was elsewhere. They had heard of Delagoa Bay and the Coast country. One party (Trichardt's) went through the present Transvaal, and reached Delagoa Bay, where most of the men died. Their women and children were afterwards rescued, and brought to Natal by sea (in 1839). Meantime, another enterprising party under Pieter Retief, with whom were the well-known families of Gert Maritz—(these two names combined stood sponsors for Pieter-Maritz-Burg)—Uys, Potgieter, Rudolph Landman, and Celliers, sought a pass through the Drakensberg, that they might look for their heart's desire over the vacant country included in Natal, which the Zulu king Dingaan was believed to retain unoccupied as a happy hunting ground and an appendage to Zululand. We are not concerned with the discovery of the various passes of the Berg, or the toilsome road-finding journey down through Natal of the gallant Pieter Retief and party of fifteen men with four wagons as an advance guard, but with the fact that they arrived at Durban in October, 1837, as I was informed, by way of Sea View, their route skirting Cowie's Hill, and closely following the present railway line. Retief was cordially received by the British settlers, who, hearing that a large body of emigrants were likely to follow and occupy the land, half resolved to throw in their lot with the newcomers, and to join their Republic. After a brief rest, with five of his own men, and an Englishman as interpreter, Retief rode on horseback to the Zulu country to negotiate with Dingaan for the settlement of the farmers in Natal. Without waiting to be asked, about one thousand wagons had followed Retief's spoor down the Berg, and spread themselves over the luxuriant pasturage in the upper parts of the Colony between the Mooi River, the Tugela, and the Berg, where they formed patriarchal camps under their different family leaders. Dingaan, who was fully informed of the advent of the white men, received Retief graciously, but, before consenting to grant his request, demanded the restoration of cattle stolen, and compensation for Zulu lives taken, as he alleged, by the Boers. Retief accordingly retired, and, on rejoining his people, found that the raid

complained of had really been made by a Native Chief of
freebooting tendencies residing in the Harrismith district.
This man the Boers obliged to restore the stolen cattle, and
hastened back with them to the Zulu king.   Experience of
Native character had taught the farmers caution, and,
having very reasonable doubts as to the good faith of Dingaan, and the view he would take of their occupation of his
country, the leaders sought to retain Retief, and only to send
a small deputation, which the brave Maritz offered to lead,
saying that two or three farmers were enough to be killed if
Dingaan had that intention.   Retief relied somewhat on
his ability to complete a treaty by which the country would
be ceded to the Boers, especially as he had found the Rev.
Mr. Owen, of the Church Missionary Society, who had come
out with Captain Gardiner on his return from England,
settled, with Wood, an Englishman, acting as interpreter,
both residents in Dingaan's great kraal, and from the fact
that the American Missionaries, the Rev. Alden Grout, D.
Lindley, and others, had been permitted to locate in the
country.   To meet the scruples of his countrymen, volunteers were called for.   Seventy rode out, taking with them
thirty servants, chiefly Hottentots, with their horses, and
reached Umgungundhlovu in the end of January, 1838.
The stolen cattle were restored, and Dingaan was kindness
itself to the farmers, entertaining them in the usual barbaric
fashion in military shows, feasting and dancing.   A deed
was drawn up by the Rev. Mr. Owen in English, ceding
to Retief and his countrymen the place called Port Natal,
together with all the land around from the Tugela to the
Umzimkulu River, and from the sea to the Berg, for their
everlasting property.   To this Dingaan affixed his mark, and
the document was safely deposited in Retief's hunting
pouch.   Saddling up, these brave and gallant Boers were
joyfully preparing to return to their friends and families,
when they were invited to a parting drink of utywala with
the king, but, as it was contrary to Zulu etiquette to go into
the Royal precincts armed, the unsuspecting Boers were
induced to leave their weapons outside.   Wood, the interpreter, guessing from Dingaan's manner that mischief was
on foot, especially as two native regiments armed with sticks
were in immediate attendance on the king, warned some of
the farmers that they might expect treachery.   The brother

of the Hyena-man, himself a sanguinary savage, drank beer with Retief, and, wishing him a pleasant journey to Natal, ordered his regiments to commence dancing. It was the dance of death! They yelled and shouted in unison, encroaching and closing-in, step by step, on the unhappy Boers, until Dingaan gave command, "Kill the witches." A rush, and a thousand clubs laid the heroic band lifeless at the foot of their murderer. Horror stricken, the Rev. Mr. Owen, with Wood, his interpreter, and such of the American Missionaries as were in the country, fled to the Bay. The dogs of war were loosed, as Dingaan at once resolved to make short work of the Boers, and despatched impies to fall upon their several camps unawares. Weenen, " the place of mourning," is named in memory of the massacre at Moord (Murder) Spruit, near Bushman's River, of more than 600 persons, men, women, and children, who sold their lives dearly against overwhelming hordes, which surprised them. Many Boers were away buffalo hunting, others prospecting in small parties, while more were settled just over the Berg. A rally was made, and 350 men, under Pieter Uys and Potgieter, went for Dingaan in the Zulu country. They attacked the Zulu Army surrounding Umgungundhlovu, and, after driving them before them, became involved in dongas and broken ground, and were themselves ultimately driven back with the loss of the gallant Uys, his son, and several men. These disasters, and the hope that while the Zulus were engaged to the Westward with the Boers, the British settlers would be enabled to create a diversion in their own favour, and a little profit to themselves by invading the Zulu country, induced those veteran " Chiefs," Cane and Biggar, to go on the warpath. They could muster 18 white men and 3,000 Natives, 400 of whom were armed with muskets. As Ogle, Stubbs, Joyce, and others, all claimed some authority, questions of precedence having arisen among the Chiefs, they were not quite agreed upon anything, but decided to cross the Tugela near its mouth. Finding themselves confronted by seven Zulu regiments amounting to about 10,000 men, nearly all young warriors—Dingaan himself not appearing in person, but being represented by two notable fighting captains—the settlers surprised a large outpost kraal, killed the occupants, and, relying upon their muskets, boldly attacked the Zulu

forces as they came up.   The "Boys," having to win their
spurs, and flushed with the defeat of the Boers, sacrificed
their lives in gallant style, until they had killed, cut off,
or driven the whole of the Natal army into the Tugela.
Only four Englishmen escaped, and they, with other
refugees, were pursued to the Umhlali, where they only
secured their lives by taking to the bush.   As a reward,
Dingaan sent his impies to Durban to exterminate the
settlers, white and black, root and branch, and to bring back
their cattle.   Many of the settlers, being warned of the
approach, with the Rev. Mr. Owen, Lindley, and several
ladies, encamped for some time on Salisbury Island, obtaining water by sinking wells in the sandy soil.   The Zulu
Army duly arrived and occupied Durban for about ten days,
during which they were taking up a collection on a large
scale, leaving when they returned home nothing but the
mere wattled walls of some roofless houses, and the mutilated
remains of such things as they could not carry.   The brig
Comet was fortunately anchored in the Bluff Channel,
and received all those settlers who preferred to be "Not at
home" to the Zulu king.   (August or September, 1838.)
   The news of these disasters reached the Cape Colony from
two sources; the Boers sent a deputation overland to their
countrymen, appealing for men and means to chastise Dingaan, and to revenge their fallen kinsfolk, while Captain
Allen Gardiner, the Resident Magistrate at Port Natal, as
also private traders at the Bay, gave information to their
friends and to the Governor at the Cape.   The Dutch
responded with 460 fighting men, under the command of
Andries Pretorius and Carl Landman.   This brave band
advanced to the Zulu country by way of the Buffalo River.
At the junction of that river with a stream unnamed, they
formed Laager with their wagons in a strong position in
face of the Zulu Army, which, on Sunday, the 16th December, 1838, rushed upon this devoted band, confident that
the charmed medicine of their witch doctors would ensure
an easy conquest, the extermination of the white man and
the capture of his possessions.   They had to repeat their
rush four times.   The Boers, hunters from their youth up,
sustained their fire for two hours; few of their bullets that
did not find their billets.   They then sallied out on horseback and followed up the flying Zulus, whose blood reddened

the little stream, and earned for it the name of " Blood " River.   More than 3,000 Zulus were slaughtered, while the farmers had only three men wounded by assegais in the pursuit.   This day has ever since been known as " Dingaan's Day," and religiously observed among the Dutch.   Pretorius and his gallant band advanced at once into the Zulu country.   On coming in sight of Umgungundhlovu, they found it in flames, and deserted by Dingaan, who had fled with his women and children into the Umfolosi forest.   On the 21st December, these heroic men surrounded the remains of their murdered countrymen, easily recognised by their hair, and the fragments of clothing covering their bones, and found in the brave Retief's hunting pouch the treaty with Dingaan, which the Rev. Mr. Owen had drawn and witnessed.   After a little more necessary fighting into which they had been trapped by the Zulus, and losing five or six of their men, Pretorius captured and drove in some 7,000 head of cattle to the Dutch headquarters on the Tugela, there to learn, with indignation and dismay that, while they had all been holding their lives in their hands, the British had, in response to the information forwarded to the Governor, sent up a detachment of soldiers, not to aid them, but to take possession of Port Natal, and to put a stop to their war with the Zulus.

On the 6th December, 1838, Major Charters, with 100 men of the 72nd Highlanders and Royal Artillery, arrived by sea, and occupied the Port, commencing at once to erect and fortify a stockade at the Point.   The quarters were built of mangrove poles, reeds, and thatch brought from the head of the Bay.   This they named, in honour of the young Queen, "Fort Victoria."   It was situated on a level patch about half way between the Bay and the Back Beach, approximately the present Alexandra Square, extending over the Point Road.   With Major Charters arrived Mr., afterwards Sir Theophilus Shepstone, known then and since far and wide by his native name, " Somtseu."   After communicating to the Dutch Volksraad, which sat at Pietermaritzburg, the views of Sir George Napier, who claimed them still as English subjects, Major Charters and Mr. Shepstone returned overland to the Cape.   Captain Jervis, left in command, was a wise man, and showed much judgment in soothing the indignation of the farmers at their treatment

by the British Government.   His discretion was justified
by the knowledge that he and his little Army were " between
the Devil and the deep sea."   So as there was no fighting
on hand because of peace (*i.e.*, breathing time) between the
Boers and the Zulus, the object of the expedition, to use
official language, was said to have been accomplished, and
the troops were accordingly ordered to be withdrawn.   The
true reason, however, was the 72nd Regiment having been
ordered home, that routine would have been considerably disorganised had not the little Port Natal detachment
joined their comrades at the Cape.   The British troops
were accordingly withdrawn, and sailed in the *Vectis* on
the 24th December, 1839.   The flag of the Republic of
Natalia was at once hoisted on the flagstaff of the newly
erected Fort Victoria, and the Dutch again reigned in the
land.

The Hon. H. Cloete, in his " Lectures on the Emigration
of the Dutch farmers," states generally that, during this
year, " the emigrant farmers had laid out this township of
Pietermaritzburg, and what is now called the town of Durban.   Landdrosts were appointed to both townships. They
established a more regular system of Government, etc."

Now appears upon the scene a young man of marked
individuality, shrewd, energetic, and independent, in the
person of George Christopher Cato, who became known in
later years as " King Cato," and to his friends and employees
as " G.C."   His marked influence and character were subsequently recognised by the inhabitants of Durban in their
choice of him as the first Mayor of the Borough.   To him
more than to any other person, Durban, if not Natal, must
be for ever indebted.   He arrived, during the eventful year
1838, in charge of the schooner *Trek Boer* from Port
Elizabeth, under the auspices of his employer. John Owen
Smith, whose boating business he had managed, with the
express design of establishing a trade with the emigrant
farmers.   Impressed with the capabilities of Port Natal, he
returned to Algoa Bay, and induced his brother Christopher
Joseph Cato to throw in his lot with him in the Dutch
Republic Natalia.   They accordingly arrived with their
families in 1839, and settled at " Mount Pleasant," at the
N.E. corner of the Bay, close to Vasco da Gama's ancient
watering place.

Incidentally, it may be here recorded, as affecting the eventual laying out of Durban, that Mr. G. C. Cato especially ingratiated himself with the Dutch by reason of his having sailed up to Delagoa Bay, in 1839, and rescued the survivors, chiefly women and children, of Trichardt's party, referred to on a previous page.

Things now went on pleasantly for all parties, the Natives of course excepted.   A Volksraad was established, Prinsloo elected President, and Pretorius placed in the position of Commandant-General.   A regular system of Government was organised, a Customs established, and duties levied. The land was parcelled out into farms and occupied.   The emigrant farmer commenced his homestead, and settled down to enjoy his own.   The snake Dingaan proved, however, to be only scotched, not killed.   With native tenacity of purpose and vitality, he pulled himself together during this peaceful lull, reorganised his army, and, under specious pretences of restoring stolen horses, cattle, arms, and other Boer property, contrived to keep an eye on all the farmers' doings, his intention being to square matters with them eventually. Bullets and buckshot had, however, a salutary effect upon the Zulu native, and a minority of the people, tired of the constant bloodshed at home under their autocratic and man-slaying ruler, concluded they would be safer under the Boers.   These revolutionary ideas having taken shape, were by Dingaan attributed to a somewhat lazy self-indulgent brother, named Umpande or Panda, to whom he at once turned his attention ; but in this instance the Sluggard arose in haste, and escaped into Natal with a very large following of the Zulu army.   He camped between the Tongaat and Umhloti, not far from his father Chaka's old camp.   He at once opened communication with the Boers, who were a long time before they could believe that it was not a plot on the part of the Zulu King.   Convinced at last, they agreed to help Panda in a simultaneous attack on his brother.   In January, 1840, Pretorius with 300 mounted men and Panda, accompanied by his Captain Nongalaza and his Zulu warriors, entered the Zulu country, and in a pitched battle utterly destroyed two of Dingaan's regiments, another regiment deserting to Panda.   Dingaan fled with a few remaining men, closely followed by the Boers, to the Amaswazi Country, whose Chief, glad to pay off ancient scores, made him prisoner, and tortured him to death.

On the 14th February, 1840, Andries Pretorius, in the name of the Volksraad of the "South African Society," claimed all the land from the Black Umfolosi to the Umzim-vubu, and formally installed Panda king of the Zulus. The new king settled the bill with forty thousand head of cattle; the farmers returned to Natal to divide the spoil and resume their peaceful occupations. Masters of the Zulu Country, masters of Natal, from which the British had withdrawn, one would naturally conclude they had reached the Canaan of their hopes, and would invite Peace to reign in the land. But there is always a fly in the Boer ointment, and it usually takes the shape of a Native. The Bushmen, inhabiting the Caves of the Drakensberg, had helped themselves to the Boers' stock, but, as they usually ate what they raided, the farmers could get nothing but the chance of a poisoned arrow by following them; so they did the next best thing in accusing a neighbouring Chief, who had cattle, of aiding and abetting the robbers, and thereupon proceeded to attack and plunder him, killing some 150 of his people and capturing 3,000 head of cattle, women, and children. This Chief was a vassal of Faku, the great Pondo Chieftain, to whom he appealed. Faku, wise in his generation, appealed in turn to the Governor of the Cape Colony for redress against the white men who were eating up his people. Then, again, the original owners of the soil, in the persons of the scattered, hunted and refugee Natal tribes, began to return from the surrounding countries to their old tribal lands. Refugees from among the Zulus also sought shelter in Natal. As we know, the Dutchman's measure of a farm for a single occupant is 6,000 acres. This unwarranted influx of Natives crowding in on their pastoral area created both alarm and suspicion, for then, as now and ever, they wanted the country for themselves. The Volksraad in August, 1841, deliberately resolved that all the Kafirs should be removed from Natal; of course, quietly if possible, but if not, then by force of arms. This kind intention was to be carried out by forcing them on to lands occupied or claimed by Faku. Sir George Napier, the Governor of the Cape, thus appealed to, foresaw without any difficulty that blood-shed must ensue, and, on instructions from the British

Government, proclaimed to its misguided and erring subjects, the emigrant Boers, that Her Majesty's Government
intended to stop the effusion of blood, and to resume
military occupation of Natal, promising at the same time
to respect the rights, laws, religion, and landed occupation of
the farmers so long as they did not interfere with the
Natives, and submitted to the Queen's authority.   The
Intelligence Department of the Service, if it then existed,
must have been lamentably defective, for the British Army
of occupation, Horse, Foot, and Artillery, numbering all
told 237 men under the command of Captain Smith, of the
27th Regiment, from the Cape Colony, were marched overland, principally along the sea shore, swimming rivers and
cutting roads, until at last on the 4th May, 1842, they
encamped without molestation from Boer or Native on the
farm of Mr. Robert Dunn, father of Chief John Dunn, at
"Sea View," near the then charming homestead of the
owner, overlooking the Bay, where "the haughty Dutch
banner was displayed at the Fort as large as life."   Mr.
Dunn is designated in an account written by Bugler Joseph
Brown, of the 27th Regiment, as the "British Agent," and
it is recorded that he smiled to think that this detachment
was to face 1,500 of the best armed men in the Colony, to
say nothing of their Zulu allies.   On the 5th May, 1842,
with guns loaded with grape, and bayonets fixed, the entire
force crossed the Umbilo into the townlands of Durban.
Captain Smith, like a "bold man and true," with an escort
of Cape Corps and Artillery, went for the "haughty Dutch
Banner" on Fort Victoria at the Point, and substituted
that of Her Majesty, after spiking their six-pounder guns.
Returning, he, with his Engineer Officer, planned out a
place for a camp—known to us as the War Department
Lands—which was apparently occupied by the entire force
that night, and there the "Rooibaatje" have ever since
remained.   Bugler Brown states that they "passed through
a small village belonging to the Dutch called 'Kongela,'
but there seemed to be very few inhabitants in it, as they
were all out in the country.   We marched through the
town and came to our Camp-ground."   Owing to the
swamp at the West of the town, the wagon road at that
time was on the flat on the Berea side of the present
railway line. entering the town between Smith Street and

St. George's Street, and winding through the thick bush there known as " Delegorgue's Bush," and over the town by any convenient route; or otherwise along the Bayside at low water to those convenient outlets known to us as Field and Gardiner Streets, both being very swampy. Aliwal Street was generally preferred as it was, in addition, the direct wagon route to the Point. Beyond Bugler Brown's statement, no idea is given us of the line of march, the extent of the town, or the number of its inhabitants. From Captain Smith's despatches and subsequent events, we must infer that the English residents were few in number.

Having now brought my reader through the devious paths of history, ancient and modern, to the embryo of a town in British occupation—a town indeed without a name, for Captain Smith and successive military officers during 1842, head all their despatches from " Port Natal "—we may consider that we have got through our first clearing, leaving the subsequent birth of Durban for future record.

CHAPTER II.

SIEGE AND CAPTURE OF PORT NATAL.

IT is needless to quote Buckle, Max Muller, or other
writers, to prove the difficulty under which historians
and linguists labour in disentangling truth from fiction;
hearsay evidence from documentary; the traditions of the
Fathers from the wonder-loving Romancers.   Ignorance
and vindictive prejudice on one side, political or religious
animus on the other.   The average high-school boy now
knows that the greater number of bad characters of history
have been shown, under the microscope of critical research,
to be not so black as they were painted.

To the unprejudiced mind, the brave old Boer " Voortrekkers " are entitled to the lasting honour and respect of
all South Africans, especially of Natalians, for where should
we have been without them?   They were, as they considered themselves, "instruments in the hands of the Lord."
If not a " chosen," they were a " peculiar," people, whose
chief article of faith, in promoting civilisation among the
heathen, was embodied in the order given to Cromwell's
regiment of " Ironsides," " Put your trust in God, and keep
your powder dry."   Their simple prayer was that of the
American Backwoodsman when in a difficulty with a grizzly,
" Lord, if you won't help me, don't help the bear."   Before
their victorious and sanguinary engagement with Dingaan's
Army at the Blood River, they attempted to bribe the
Lord with a promise of a house in which a day yearly

should be devoted to His worship, if He gave them the victory. Though their Bible tells them, " God is love," yet they are satisfied that He graciously assisted them to avenge Retief, and their slaughtered friends, women, and children. The Dutch Reformed Church on the Market Square, Pietermaritzburg, was built in fulfilment of the terms of the contract, and a " Dingaan's Day " has ever since been observed.

Reader, put yourself in his place, picture yourself with about enough " learning " to be able to spell out a Psalm and sign your name with a pen ; imagine that the main portion of your food and raiment depended upon your gun ; that the only labour you could command would be the little black captives to your bow and spear (whom you duly " apprenticed " when convenient); that you were liable to attack at all times from man, and other wild animals, and could only expect to hold your own by conquest and force of arms. You had helped to hoist your Republican flag, elected your representative to the Raad, and, after settling down on your farm, building a square house, planting fruit trees, getting water led out, land ploughed, your cattle and other live stock kraaled, and your hunting expeditions organised, to be told at this stage that the King of Holland, to whom you had decided to offer the country, was of no account in the eyes of the British Government. That this arrogant Government, after playing fast and loose with you, now sought once more to interfere with your mode of settling Native questions, and thus deprive you of the life, liberty, and land you had won. Deaf to the representations of your Volksraad and not amenable to reason, the jealous and over-officious Governor of the Cape now sought to degrade you further by sending the detested " Rooibaatjes " to take possession of your Port and stop your supplies. Gentle reader, had you been one of them, you would have recollected your flight out of Egypt, with its subsequent hardships, and found, in all this, substantial reasons for violence and resistance. The French proverb declares that " one cannot have omellettes without breaking eggs," neither can we have battles without bloodshed and blunders, with a general letting loose of all the depravities of our nature and the commission of acts of which both sides are afterwards ashamed, but seek to justify by quoting the degrading and dishonouring axiom that all is fair in love and war. ·Byron, who had practical experience, wrote : "Sweet is revenge, especially to women; pillage to soldiers, and prize money to seamen," and we know that, even in this year of grace, a little loot is appreciated. Hence, the events that now follow must be kindly treated and lightly judged, since both parties decided to kill or be killed, and let God defend the right.

The Army of occupation consisted in round numbers of 250 men, with women and children of the 27th Regiment (Inniskillens), Royal Artillery, Sappers, and Miners, and some Cape Corps (mounted). They had sixty wagons, two field pieces, 600 oxen, a few horses, and some 250 drivers, leaders, and native servants. They formed their camp on the site known to us where the Barracks now stand, a dry sandy flat without trees or cover, between the present Umgeni Road and the Back Beach Bush, on the Eastern Vlei. It was surrounded on three sides by swampy porous grounds covered with rushes, which, while affording water for the cattle, prevented them from straying, and also prevented the advance of an enemy. The men obtained their water from a side vlei, and described it as being as black as ink. Hitherto on the march, the command followed the example of the "Voortrekkers," and laagered nightly with the field guns at the corners, but now the wagons were formed up in possibly more extended order into a regular square with a ditch and bank outside, also with proper platforms and embrasures for the artillery, with the tents around the square sheltered by the wagons. The horses may have been inside, but the oxen, and possibly the Native camp followers, were in the open under the protection of the guns. I estimate that their enclosed camp would cover about two acres of ground. On this little spot the British flag was planted, to be afterwards watered by the blood of our countrymen, and sanctified by the bravery and endurance of our gallant troops. It was here Durban took root.

Four days after Captain Smith began making his camp, he compelled an interview with Pretorius, as representing the Emigrant Farmers, who naturally " demanded that the force commanded should instantly quit Natal." The Captain pleaded his orders, and requested on the other hand that Pretorius should disperse his following and vacate Port Natal within fifteen days. The Boer force was increasing daily, and was now believed to be about 300 mounted men. They responded in their own practical fashion by "commandeering" all the provisions they could find in possession of the English residents, and, on the 23rd May, by driving off the greater number of the cattle belonging to the troops. Captain Smith was a Waterloo man, and though it is known that our Army swore dread-. fully in Flanders, it is not recorded how he expressed himself here, under these circumstances, but that they aroused his just indignation and hastened his movements his despatches show, for he decided there and then to give the farmers a lesson and bring them to their senses. Unfortunately he started before ne was ready.

The schooner *Mazeppa*, 90 tons, was at anchor in the Bay, partly unloaded of her cargo of provisions and stores. The brig *Pilot*, Captain Hugh McDonald, with military stores, had arrived on the 13th May, and was also inside, bringing two eighteen pounder guns, powder and shot, engineer tools, beef, pork, biscuits, etc. One eighteen pounder with most of the powder, the engineer's tools, and a portion of the food supply, had been carted to the camp, the other gun had been landed and left at the Point, together with the powder, shot, and provisions already off-loaded, under a guard at the Stockade (Fort Victoria).

The night of the 23rd May, 1842, was chosen by Captain Smith "after mature deliberation," to disband the Boers, and destroy their Laager at Congella. He directed Lieut. Wyatt, R.A., to fit up a howitzer gun in a ship's longboat, with instructions to put it in charge of a sergeant and gunners, who were to float it down the Island Channel at night with the rising tide, and take up a position 500 yards from Congella in support of the main attack, which, when formed, consisted of two six pounder field guns drawn by oxen, four officers, and 134 rank and file, with Captain Smith in command.

The whole force was put in motion at 11 o'clock, the night bright with moonlight, the tide rising. The command marched by way of Aliwal Street on to the Bay foreshore, and headed for the Congella, skirting the mangroves that fringed the Bay, and formed a screen behind which was the open flat crossed by the wagon road to Pietermaritzburg. Smith took this route in the confident expectation that his movements were undiscovered, because he had previously put a picket " to the skirts of the wood in front of our position," which means the thick bush then at the West end of the town; but ten minutes after the Beach had been reached, the Boer scouts had galloped across the flat, behind the mangroves, to the Congella, with news of his advance. The women and children were hurried into a deep glade in the Bush—most probably that overlooked by the present Umbilo Police Station—and the farmers prepared for action, while twenty-five good hunters and crack shots took up position lying on the ground behind the largest mangrove trees, and waited in silence.

The troops came leisurely along, driven in somewhat to the muddy ground bordering the mangroves by the rising tide. They had advanced to within 800 vards of the place they proposed to attack. The boat, with the howitzer, had not at this time, in the opinion of Captain Smith, got within effective range, as it afterwards proved, in consequence of sandbanks and insufficiency of water. Lieut. Wyatt was riding on a gun carriage, and the force was just passing the denser mangrove scrub to a more open place, where they could see and be seen, when, at a distance of about 110 yards, the farmers, with the moon well in their favour, and their targets like a herd of game before them, could resist no longer. A single shot, followed by four others, rang through the still midnight, and poor Lieut. Wyatt fell, shot through the forehead; two men, and one of the trek oxen also fell. The troops at once formed, and returned the fire in the direction of the bushes, without doing damage. A light westerly air carried the smoke of their pieces from them in the direction of the mangroves, thus affording additional cover to the Dutchmen. The guns were unlimbered and opened fire, but men and oxen were falling fast, wounded oxen breaking loose among the men, and adding to the disorder bv upsetting limbers, while no enemy was to be seen or reached. Lieut. Wyatt killed,

Captain Lonsdale and Lieut. Lennard of the 27th severely
wounded, the howitzer with its shells alarming without injuring the enemy, and the other two guns becoming silent
in consequence of the confusion, the Boers took heart,
reinforced their brave comrades, and redoubled their
accurate and destructive fire.   The whole conflict did not,
however, last many minutes, when Captain Smith finding:
"I was not likely to accomplish the purpose for which I
had put the detachment in motion," thought it expedient
to mount his horse and retire to his camp, leaving his men
to follow at convenience.   They followed "at the run,"
leaving   the   two   field   guns, with their ammunition, unspiked, to fall into the hands of the Boers, and to
be eventually used effectively against themselves.   It is
recorded that some of the men got into deep water, and
were drowned, but, as no deep water is to be found a long
way from the edge of the mangroves, I conclude these men
must have imagined a Boer behind each bush, and so waded
a long way out in their attempt to return by the way they
came, or otherwise sought to reach the boat with the howitzer.   Residents describe their return as a flight, many
arriving without their muskets and pouch belts, although
Captain Smith informs the Authorities that "the troops
reached the camp about two o'clock in tolerable order."
Alas! one officer and 17 rank and file were left there dead,
while two officers and 28 rank and file were wounded, and
three missing—total 48.

The Farmers, naturally elated at their unexpected
success, lost no time in following up the game, and, muster-
ing all their forces, reached the British camp about the
same time as the fugitives.   They opened their attack with
their long-barrelled hunting guns, carrying further than a
regulation musket, on three sides of the camp, keeping up
steady independent firing till about dawn, neither side
doing or sustaining much damage; though it is said the
only Boer killed that night was at this camp attack, and
that only in consequence of exposing himself to the range
of an 18 pounder shot.   As he was a single man, Abraham
Greyling by name, he left no widow to deplore his loss.
He died for his country and ours.   The experience thus

acquired by the Farmers saved the camp from capture. (*) It is recorded that the Raad had instructed Pretorius not to attack the Queen's troops, or come in direct conflict with them, but to harass, impede, and annoy, until they quitted the country. The shock and the joy of yesterday's events required deliberation and discussion, so the 24th and 25th May were devoted to this and other purposes by the Farmers and their wives, who, notwithstanding their bitter animosity to the English, behaved with unusual humanity in sending in the wounded and the bodies of the slain to the camp. Captain Smith, in his historical despatch of the 25th May, says, "and to-morrow the sad duty of interring our departed comrades will take place." The spot hastily selected is about 500 yards S.W. from the camp, under a large Euphobia tree. It was eventually enclosed, and became the Military graveyard. The graves of Lieutenant Wyatt and of the other victims of the battle of Congella occupy two separate sites, marked with headstones bearing their names, while, in the centre of the graveyard is constructed on a square base a large freestone cross erected by our townsman, Mr. Thomas Green, to his comrades of the 27th Inniskillens, and the victims of the Zulu War of 1879.

The European residents of Durban at this time .were apparently few in number, the majority of them interested in the landing and carriage of goods. They consequently "hung about" the Point, and chummed up with their new acquaintances of the 27th Regiment quartered there, or, seeking for news of outside civilization, were entertained as guests on board the shipping. The Boers having kraaled the "Rooibatjes" in their camp, determined to keep them there until they were starved into surrender. With this object in view, their deliberations culminated in a resolve to surprise the guard at the Point, and so possess themselves of all the Government provisions and stores. Accordingly 100 men were selected to put this plan into execution. Captain Smith had penned his eventful despatch to Lieut.-Governor Hare at Grahamstown, and

---

* The report of this shot travelled Overberg, reaching Thaba 'Nchu on the 12th June, effectually stopping a Dutch quarrel, which the Boers were then endeavouring to fasten on to the Chief Moroka.

applied to Mr. George C. Cato for native messengers to convey it.   Mr. Cato offered to be the bearer, but the Commandant would not consent to part with so valuable an ally.   Fertile in expedient, as were all Durban men of that age, Cato asked for two horses of the Cape Corps, and undertook to find a suitable white man as express-rider.   Dick King, the Richard King who had attended the town meeting in 1835, under Captain Allen Gardiner, and signed the memorial to Sir Benjamin D'Urban, was visiting on board the *Mazeppa.*   Appealed to by Mr. Cato, he, with the usual readiness of a Colonial hunter to take his life in his hand, and set out for anywhere, with blanket and gun, a handful of biscuit or chunk of biltong, at once consented, his sympathies being naturally with his countrymen, though he had lived for some time at the Isipingo in close neighbourhood with the Boers.   Being from home, he had no opportunity of selecting his clothes, or making any elaborate preparations for his journey of many hundreds of miles, through native tribes and some two hundred rivers.   He is not known to have been of a poetical turn, so his entertainment on board the *Mazeppa* did not suggest his brief reply, "Bring forth the horse," but, Captain Smith having sent his despatches to Mr. Cato, two troop horses, as agreed, were brought forth, and taken to the Point, where at midnight when the tide was low, Mr. Cato, with his brother Joe Cato, in two boats, each towing a horse, crossed over the Island Channel, then narrower than at present, to the end of the Island, shook hands with the brave and deliberate Dick King, the hero of Natal, and if not devoutly, certainly most earnestly, wished him God speed.   The most difficult part of the journey consisted in avoiding the moonlight, after wading the shallows behind the Island, to the Bluff, skirting the Bluff and crossing the Umlaas River without detection or pursuit by the Dutch-men.   That accomplished, and on his way to the Um-komaas River long before dawn, King found the rest com-paratively easy, following the spoor left by the military wagons.   He overcame all risks, including sickness, and on reaching Kaffraria, and the frontiers of the Cape, was kindly succoured and forwarded by the Missionaries on the route, and eventually reached Grahamstown, the Military

Headquarters, a distance of 600 miles, which he accomplished in ten days, thoroughly done up.   Let us hope that Natal, more especially Durban, will mark with some permanent memorial its appreciation of a brave patriot, who, in an unpretentious manner, performed a noble act without hope of honour or reward; an act that any of our sons might be proud to emulate if they are "built that way."

Mr. Joseph Cato returned with the boat to the *Mazeppa*, Mr. George Cato to the Point, satisfied with the success of their enterprise, and the certainty of their friend's ability to accomplish his hazardous task, as he was master of the Zulu dialect, of fine physique, a good shot, a fearless rider, and hunter, known to all the Natives far and wide.   While reporting proceedings and congratulating themselves before turning in, the surprise party of Boers had crept along the foot of the Berea, out of sight of the Camp, and headed for the mouth of the Umgeni, returning by way of the Back Beach to the Point, which they reached, undetected, some time before the dawn of the 26th May.   Creeping "ventre a terre" over the sandy dunes, and through the scrub in a long snaky file, careful not to crack a twig or displace a bough, they posted themselves at a distance of 200 yards around the little stockaded camp and waited for daylight. Your Boer is nothing if not practical.   He knows nothing of chivalry, and less of romance.   Daylight at last dawned on him.   He could see the sights on his gun.   He did not stop to parade his forces, sound his clarion, send forward a flag of truce, and summon the warder to surrender his castle.   Oh, no, he levelled his piece at the unsuspecting grey-coated sentry, followed his movements finger on trigger, and, as he stopped to turn, deliberately murdered him. The alarm being given, the guard, under Sergt. Barry, fired a few rounds of grapeshot at short range, without effect, and replied with musketry, but the Sergeant, finding himself surrounded, and cut off from the well they had sunk for water, in danger of burning, his dead and wounded comrades at his feet, the fire of the farmers too accurate to avoid, the improbability of relief from the camp, and the certainty of being taken if stormed, agreed to surrender on

honourable terms.   Thus fell Fort Victoria.   With it
fell, also, as spoil to the victors, the eighteen pounder gun
and all the Government stores ashore and afloat.   We
may safely conclude there were free drinks all round that
day.   Sixteen soldiers and all the English at the Point
were made prisoners.   The civilians were ten in number,
Mr. George C. Cato among them.   The *Pilot* and
Mazeppa were ransacked, but Mr. Joseph Cato, awakened
by the firing, and discovering the result, anticipated capture
by stowing himself away in one of those mysterious compartments on ship board, known to landsmen as "lockers,"
so escaped, and remained on board a prisoner, though not
a captive.   The prisoners, G. C. Cato, F. Armstrong, S.
Beningfield, J. Douglas, J. Hogg, H. Ogle, H. Parkins, D.
Toohey, F. McCabe, and B. Schwikkard, were regarded as
traitors to the Republic, to which they had promised allegiance.   They and the soldiers were marched off to Congella.   Mr. G. C. Cato, being deemed the headman, was
distinguished by having his hands tied behind him.   On
arrival at Congella, they were placed in the stocks, and
kept there a week, subsequently removed to Maritzburg
where they were imprisoned in the "tronk, chained two
together, and at night placed in the stocks.   The Military
had also been taken to Maritzburg, but were comfortably
quartered and allowed out in the town on parole.   Capt.
McDonald, of the *Pilot*, and the Master of the *Mazeppa*
seem also to have been detained at Congella.   What
became of the other "jacks" is not recorded.

The gloom cast over the little army by this calamity was
deepened that day (May 26th) by the burial of the victims
of the Congella blunder, and brave old Captain Smith
began to realise the gravity of his position now that his
supplies were cut off and in the hands of the enemy.

The good Farmers, desirous of realising their profits and
sharing the plunder, required time to transport what were
now their guns, ammunition, and stores to safe keeping,
without interruption by the eighteen pounder that could
reach the Point, so the following day they induced the
Captains of the *Pilot* and *Mazeppa* to write offering
to remove the troops in their respective vessels, while to
gain time Pretorius proposed an armistice of seven days to

enable the Commandant to come to terms and make his arrangements with the shipmen for the evacuation. Capt. Smith also wanted time, so at once agreed to the armistice. While negotiating terms, he commenced digging himself in, sodding his banks, sinking a well, making embrasures for musketry, and completing the batteries, one for the eighteen pounder, the other for a howitzer, and taking stock of his provisions, which he found little enough.

Pretorius, being master of the situation, dictated terms so outrageous that Captain Smith said, in substance, he would see him hanged first for a rebel, and oroke off negotiations, closed up his fortifications, and put his men on half rations.

Pretorius had also negotiated to some purpose, for they had brought up, mounted and properly enclosed in a sod-made battery, the captured eighteen pounder, also the two six pounder field guns. Following the object lessons of the Sappers and Miners, they constructed shelter trenches for their marksmen. Having arranged matters to their satisfaction, they mustered in force, and opened fire on the Camp about six in the morning of the 31st May, and went at it with a will, actually sending in 122 round shot that day, while keeping up an incessant fire of musketry. The guns of the Camp having knocked over some of their works during the forenoon, they conveniently remembered that there were women and children in the Camp, so, to gain time to repair damages, sent in about noon the Rev. James Archibell, a Weslevan Missionary, who had accompanied the troops from the Colony, with a flag of truce, offering to remove the women and children, and to send in two men of the 27th wounded at the Point. This was agreed to, and the non-combatants had to make so hurried a departure that, among others, the wife and children of wounded Captain Lonsdale left without changes of clothing. They were placed in a wagon escorted by mounted Boers, and taken as promised on board the *Mazeppa*.

These dear encumbrances removed, Captain Smith and his brave men settled down to business, which was resumed that night with fresh spirit on both sides. Troubled somewhat with the large number of camp followers attached to the transport, who had to be provided for, it was decided to kill the few half-starved oxen the Boers had left them, and convert their flesh into "biltong," which was then issued half a pound daily to each man.   The Boers got into good practice with the big guns, and continued making especially at night, well constructed trenches advancing toward the Camp, from which a hot fire was kept up directed against the two batteries.   I never could find the site of the Farmers' batteries, though their "lines on the Berea side of the Camp were long visible.   Their other "lines" were believed to be on the edge of the swamp in the direction of the Bluff, subsequently obliterated by the Umgeni.   Their united lengths were 1,020 yards, average depth 4 feet, width 2 feet, points bearing on the Camp, loopholed.   It has been surmised that their guns were mounted within their trenches, and difficult to reach except by a dropping shot.   Shell is not mentioned in any of the records, so it is probable that the unloaded shells belonging to the field guns, captured with the stores, were used as solid shot while they lasted.   Their shot passed over the encampment through and through wagons and tents, wrecking them, and no man felt safe in showing himself. A main trench or alley-way was dug across the Camp about 5 feet deep.   In this little niches or sidings were cut, where the wounded were placed and attended by Dr. Frazer, with only the shelter afforded by the dried hides of the slaughtered cattle.   The troops were careful not to waste a shot. only firing when the result was likely to be effective.   On the 3rd June they knocked over one of the six pounders, wounding the men working it, but on the 8th a round shot from the Boers broke the carriage of the eighteen pounder in two places, which, however, was soon repaired, and rendered serviceable again.   That night the defenders made a sortie, and destroyed some of the works constructed by the enemy, filling in part of the trenches.

We will for the present leave the combatants to continue the strife, and join the ladies on board the *Mazeppa,* which had been converted into a sort of prison ship, the Farmers having taken the precaution to prevent the thing ("dingus") escaping by bringing her two anchors on to the beach, where they could see them, for she rode in the Channel opposite the Block House.

Mr. Joseph Cato never explained to me how he induced the Boers to allow him to remain on board, where they came and went at all times, when emptying the ship. Possibly, in the absence of the Master, detained at Congella, he overawed them with the astounding averment:—

"Oh I am a cook and a captain bold,
"And the mate of the 'Nancy' brig;
"And a bo'sun tight, and a midshipmite,
"And the crew of the captain's gig."

Remain, however, he did, and received Mrs. Lonsdale and family, with the soldiers' wives and children, together with Mrs. G. C. Cato and daughter Fanny, Mrs. S. Beningfield, with Masters Frank and William, and Mrs. Archbell, the Rev. J. Archbell, and Mr. John McKenzie ("Cragie Burn"). Mr. J. Cato states they were in all 28 people, besides the ship's company, possibly five, total 33. Captain Smith availed himself of the flag of truce on the 31st to urge the escape of the *Mazeppa*, with instructions to seek the assistance of any of Her Majesty's Men-of-War up the Coast, so that the troops might be relieved.

Time, tide, and wind, are factors in these ventures; a combination did not take place until the 10th June. The dew at this time of the year is heavy, so the Dutch guard at the stockade were satisfied daily to see the sails hanging out to dry, and flapping about, while it was entertaining to watch the spider-like shipmen going up the sticks and ropes to tie them up. The women prisoners also did a good deal of washing, and hung their linen on lines around the sides of the ship to dry. The men on board certainly made some noise at times, pulling and hauling, apparently for amusement. All this washing necessitated no end of fresh water, for which they had to use the long boat, so they contrived to get in about four days' extra supply, and as much food as they could accumulate by economical issue.

This day they appeared to have a special "Spring cleaning," for all their clothes, blankets, and bedding were hung around and above the bulwarks, oddly enough on the port or shore side. After so much exertion, it was but natural that they should retire below, and keep the children particularly good and quiet.

c

Mr. Cato, in his capacities of Captain, Mate, and Bo'sun, with the aid of the carpenter, Isaac Craig, had contrived to lead the halliards, sheets, and braces down below.   To keep the women occupied, he posted them to pull on these ropes when the time came, as he should direct.   Realising the situation, they were brave and willing; they knew from experience that discipline must be maintained, and that their turn for duty had arrived. His fore-and-aft sails were kept hoisted, at nights they were loosely bunched in and " stopped.   Now his small fore-topsail and top-gallant yards went up little by little as the women pulled, while he eased off the clews and sheets, and saw to the bracing up.   He had only to cut his stops and sheet home when the wind favoured to be under way. For the sake of appearances, he was obliged to leave his long-boat towing astern.   The time was four in the afternoon, the S.W. wind light, with the tide still running in. Anxiety and responsibility hurried his departure.   He made no display, his only leave taking was to his anchors, but, simply calling on his stout female crew to " sheet home," he hauled in his main boom, and, as the little schooner felt the wind. slipped his cables, and was away on the starboard tack, before the Boers realised the situation ; Cato at the bows conning the ship, old Isaac at the helm. The wind came in puffs, the tide still strong, so she moved slowly down to the sandspit at the corner, while the Boers ran there to find her almost becalmed.   Their harbour defence was a four pounder gun, mounted on the understill of a wagon stationed there.   Soon some eighty men were mustered opposite the Bluff Channel, many of them with huge elephant short-range guns, carrying bullets four to the pound.   The *Mazeppa* became a close target for some time, while hanging off this point, where her sails and rigging were considerably damaged by their shot, but fortunately no one was hit.   The fitful wind freshening, Mr. Cato managed to square his yards, and stood rapidly down to the Bar, which was safely crossed with only the loss of the longboat, waterlogged by the bullets it had received. Having been " offloaded " by the Boers, she was, as the sailors say, " flying light," being without ballast, and drew so little water that she had no need to be particular in selecting a channel.

Once outside, they lay-to about five hours, repairing damages, the nautical portion of the crew knotting and splicing, the women divided between joy and sea-sickness, smiles and tears, the children picking the Dutchmen's bullets out of their mattresses, and counting the holes in their blankets.   Mr. Cato then made all sail with a fair wind for Delagoa Bay, which, as they had no anchor, they passed on the night of the 13th June, and ran on to Cape Correntes, but next day fell in with some American whalers, who, themselves short of provisions, could only supply them with water and an anchor.   As no Men-of-War were reported, they headed back for Delagoa Bay, arriving there on the 15th.   At this period Delagoa Bay, or the Portuguese settlement of Lourenco Marques was, as described by the Americans, a " one horse " place.   Mr. Cato found the inhabitants, as usual, in difficulties with the Natives.   A " battle " had taken place the day previously, and they were in a state of blockade.   He managed to purchase with infinite trouble a little corn, some pork, and a few pigs, nothing else being obtainable, filled up their water casks, took in sufficient ballast to steady the ship, and, finding no cruisers, headed for the Cape Colony.   The women and children were doing as well as could be expected under the circumstances, which is to be attributed to Mrs. Archbell's ever bright and cheerful disposition, making light of all difficulties, relieving pain and anguish, a true ministering angel.   Here we will leave them to work their way down the Coast, until they eventually recross the Bar.

During all this time, the strife around the Camp had been maintained with more or less spirit.   The escape and sailing of the *Mazeppa* were known to the soldiers, but nothing as to her casualties ; indeed, during the whole of the siege, Captain Smith seems to have been kept informed of what was going on around him.   The old residents of that period made a mystery of this, but I have reason for believing that none of them had more than suspicions, the facts being that the Hottentot Drivers and Frontier Natives attached to the troops, preferring something more satisfying than bullets and biltong, absented themselves by degrees, and crossing the swamps, and associating with the resident Natives, contrived by that mysterious system of Native telegraphy to keep up communication with their friends inside, while the Hottentots would easily pass undetected about the Dutch camps, and pick up information together with such spare diet as might be appropriated. Thus the conveyance of a friendly letter, with the prospect of a pannikin of ration rum as a reward, would be a matter of no great difficulty, and of less risk, if it happened to be written in French. Truth obliges us to state that some of the men, with appetites, followed the example of the coloured people, and, though at first reported absent without leave, came to be mustered out as " deserters."

The energy of the Farmers had resulted in their expending their stock of round shot, necessitating their waiting to pick up the tardy British eighteen pounder, before they could return it. They therefore erected furnaces at Congella, where they moulded and cast leaden balls weighing between six and eight pounds each. These they pitched into the Camp, less frequently but with more precision, filling in the intervals, as before, with independent pot-shot firing by their skirmishers. A week after the *Mazeppa* left, the remaining horses of the Cape Corps were ordered to be killed, the flesh cut into strips and made into " biltong," their hides pegged out, dried, and used for roofing. The men had been living on half rations of biscuit dust, alternating with biscuit and rice. Now a general muster of all private provisions was made and taken into store. Finding they had eleven bags of forage corn, no longer required for the horses, they set to work to grind it into meal, and flattered themselves they were quite ready to hold out on this diet for nearly a month. Thus it happened that while their women and children were enjoying roast pork and boiled mealies, these Heroes were existing on dried horse and crushed oats. They added to their larder by shooting some of the crows attracted by the bones of the slaughtered animals around them. The chief drawback to this state of starving contentment, waiting for relief, was the pertinacious pushing forward of the enemy's trenches every night, from which the musket fire became intolerable, so, on the night of the 18th June, a sortie in force under Lieut. Molesworth was made with the object of destroying their works, filling up the trenches, and delaying progress, clearing the way in fact for their own cannon fire.   This was successfully accomplished, the Boers being surprised, and many bayonetted after a short resistance, in which Ensign Prior and two privates were killed, and four others wounded.   This taste of their opponents' quality served to tone down the ardour of the enemy for close quarters.   While maintaining their artillery practice, and keeping a close guard on the Camp, they resolved to resort to other and less hazardous means.

When civilized man asserts his independence, and treks out from the restraints of law, order, education, and morality, brave and self-reliant though he may be, he rapidly reverts to the original barbarian.   The pious, peaceful farmer of South Africa becomes the " Voortrekker," who becomes a hunter, the hunter a freebooter, with a taste for slavery, the freebooter a ruffian, thief, and assassin.   Thus demoralised, ignorant, and lustful, he violates complacently the whole ten Commandments, and degenerates into the " Boer," as we know him.   At this time in our history, a French gentleman, traveller and naturalist, who had spent a long time hunting in the Zulu Country, resided somewhere on or near the present Glebe land, then a magnificent heavily timbered wood, the " Delagorges' Bush " before referred to. '   The undergrowth was slight, and there were many straight tall trees ; the writer has himself seen, beautifully carved on the smooth bark of one of them, two verses in French.   As from this tree a fine view of the Bay could be seen, it may be safely inferred that M. Adolphe Delagorges resided close by, and that his beautiful surroundings inspired the ode.   In his published work, " Voyage dans l'Afrique Australe," he states among other things that his " Villa " was about half way between the two Camps, that the English eighteen pound shot would go hissing over it, and that the Boers used it as a sort of guard house, and when on their way backwards and forwards would hitch up their horses about it, while they smoked their pipes under his verandah.   He writes : — (*)

"About this time, as the Boers were growing tired of seeing that their attempts were ineffectual, because they had not enough

---

* " Annals of Natal," Vol. I., page 722.

of Military science for better measures, too little resolution to act strenuously, an ignoble, cowardly, infamous request was made to me by one of them, after having found that the greater number of the Council had assented to it. This man was ordered to request without assenting—to be prudent and discreet—so that if necessary the thing might be denied, and no one understand the matter. He thought fit to recur to a third person, and chose a German named Krockman, who fulfilled this mission in regard to me as a sort of extra duty. I was to give up to the Boers the poisons requisite for the preparation and preservation of my specimens—arsenic and corrosive sublimate—of which they knew I possessed large quantities. Their object was to throw ten or twelve pounds of these dangerous compounds into the spring near the Camp, which alone supplied more than half of the quantity of water consumed by the besieged; and even if the object of poisoning the troops were not attained, they might at least have the advantage of making them suffer from the want of water, so as to induce them to surrender. It must be superfluous to say how much I was disgusted by such a proposal, but I had enough self-control to conceal my feelings. 'This is a famous expedient,' I replied to the emissary—'I regret bitterly that I have not the means here of producing so powerful an effect. My poisons are at the Umfolozi, where for the great work I have undertaken, the whole quantity might be indispensable.' This was an untruth resorted to as an escape from embarrassment, for there were still at hand by me seven pounds of arsenic and two of corrosive sublimate, which early next morning I hastened to throw away among the rushes, scattering to the wind the white powder, the effect of which if it had been used could not have failed to work disastrous results."

This dastardly proposal led to serious results, affecting the whole future of Natal, rankling in the minds of men, and embittering feelings on both sides within and beyond our borders. It is impossible to extenuate, yet 'tis not set down in malice, since it sustains our contention as to the degenerate Boer, who, being without honour, justifies to the present day the massacre of soldiers at Bronkhorst Spruit, the shooting of British officers under escort during the Transvaal war, the recent use at Mapoch's Caves of dynamite and paraffin, the shooting of a bearer of a flag of truce, with the parcelling out into virtual slavery of the captured women and children. In connection with this, I may record that a quiet, inoffensive German naturalist of the name of Guenzius—whose hut in the Stella Bush I once vacated precipitately on his asking me to " Please zit shtillar on zat box (a rickety gin case), I have therein two goot snakes, and zey may outcome " — was here at that exciting time, absorbed in his vocation.   Events necessitated his leaving in August on a visit to Europe.   His ship, the *Maid of Mona* was forced to put in to Port Elizabeth, and being from Port Natal, he was interviewed by the irrepressible reporter, during a brief conversation with two of his countrymen on the beach.   This irresponsible party forthwith fabricated a spicy article for his newspaper, detailing the proposals made to "Quencias" by the Boer leaders to poison the Vlei whence Captain Smith obtained his water, etc., etc.   This was shown to him on his arrival at Cape Town.   Horrified and indignant at being thus implicated, Mr. Guenzius wrote to the "Zuid African" newspaper (23rd August, 1842) forcibly and positively denying the fact and repudiating the entire article.   Yet we should be thankful for a free press, though occasionally truth is slandered, false history created, bad reputations mended, and good ones destroyed.

Returning to the Camp, let us for a moment contemplate the condition of these half-starved men, shut in behind their sandbank fortifications, burrowing for shelter in holes and corners, the sick and wounded increasing in numbers, under lean-to shelters of hides in their grave-like bunks, without medical or any other comforts, with bad water, and the roughest of cooking, disturbed day and night by their own guns; the shots of the enemy, scattering over them sand and fragments, the stench of the carcases and refuse around them, with the strong language of their weak struggling comrades on duty.   In addition, they had ever in their ears the ceaseless depressing rumble of the surf on the Back Beach, and the nightly din of the sentinel water frogs in the swamp.   Fortunately it was the winter season, dry, and comparatively cool, the bright sun tempered by the haze of that time of the year, the fleecy clouds and the fresh breeze alternating regularly from N.E. over the sea to S.W. over the land, invigorating and refreshing, while the nights, though heavy with dew, were crisp and clear, brilliant stars set in a blue-black sky, and the ever-present emblem of hope in the Southern Cross overhead. Gaiety there was none, though rum was in store, yet the ever-rollicking Irishmen contrived to keep up the spirits of their comrades by their devil-me-care bearing, cheering when

they made a hit, or the enemy a miss, bolting out to secure
a wounded crow, or rushing in the dark with buckets to
the Vlei for water.   Their firewood began to give out,
having burnt all the cattle kraals and spare timber, so
scrambling in the dark for " Bois-de-vache " became a hazardous " divarsion."   A week after the sortie in force,
they began to count the hours, discussing over their
watery stews the possibilities of relief.   Had that despatch
rider reached Grahamstown?   It was more than probable
he was killed or drowned on the way.   No one would get
to know of their condition.   If he did arrive, when, and
how long after, would it take for the men to "get the
route," and a ship to come up here to their relief?   Where
was the *Mazeppa?*   Was she afloat?   She's away   now
fourteen days, and could not have seen any cruisers.   Oh,
if she had only gone to Port Elizabeth, she could have been
back by this time.   Well, blank the odds, boys, give the
blank blanks another shot; the old 27th will see them
blanked first before they surrender. Ready? Fire! Such,
I am informed, was the spirit of the fleshless men, when
the guard was set on the night of the 24th June, for the
Boers were particularly troublesome that evening.   The
sentries, taking in another hole in their waistbelts, tried
to stay their hunger with bites of tobacco, and carefully
peeped through the embrasures in the direction of the
enemy's lines, now comparatively quiet.   A flash of light
in the direction of the sea caught the listless eye of a
sentry, who turned again in his lonely round muttering
" One of them falling stars, I expect."   For lack of interest
on returning, he halted at a loophole to stare again at the
starlit sky over the Back Beach bush.   Suddenly up
sprang a thread of light bursting in a golden shower.
" By God, a rocket, boys!" he shouted, then recollecting
himself, came to " attention," grounded arms, and reported
to the officer of the guard : " There's a ship outside, sir, and
she's firing rockets."   Instantly the Camp was in commotion, as everyone accepted the sentry's deductions.
Capt. Smith immediately ordered answering rockets to be
sent up, but was of opinion that the ship was inside the Bay.
They did not know till afterwards that the vessel was the
schooner *Conch,* William Bell, Master, with the Grena-

dier Company of their own Regiment, under Capt. Durnford, and that their answering rockets were boisterously
hailed by their comrades on board.   All was excitement
and joyful anticipation, since the rockets had wonderfully
diminished the Boer firing during the night.   When
daylight came to the sleepless men, it was evident that
something unusual had happened, for the Boers could be
seen riding in numbers in the direction of the Point.   All
that day (25th June), they were kept in painful doubt and
strained conjecture, hearing nothing, seeing no signs.   They
did not know that, on the previous afternoon, the Dutch
Harbour Master with Pretorius' Military Secretary, the
latter in gorgeous uniform, had boarded the apparently
innocent trading schooner, to be stricken with "ague or
some other disease," Captain Bell says, on climbing over the
side, and seeing the grim Grenadiers "sitting in the main
hatchway as thick as bees," for all red coats had been sent
out of sight as they neared the Bluff.   At that moment
these two men felt that life was indeed short, a halter at
the yard arm might end it; but after begging a drink of
water, hope came again when Captain Durnford directed
them to return and convey a despatch to "General" Pretorius.   This contained a request to be allowed to send
a Doctor with medicines to the Camp, the object being to
communicate with Captain Smith, and acquaint their comrades that relief was at hand.   This latter fact Durnford
was careful to impress upon the Harbour Master and
Secretary, informing them that he would send in a boat
the next day, under a flag of truce, for the answer.

It was this news, and the evidence of the red coats being
actually at their door, that caused the farmers to make a
final effort on the Camp while daylight lasted.   With
night came the cheering rocket the sentry had seen.   All
they knew in the Camp this dreary day was that the wind
was from the S.W., that the enemy had some other attraction, and that no further communication reached them
from the supposed friendly ship; the reason being that
Mr. Bell and Captain Durnford agreed, as a result of the
wind being in that quarter, that they could not force an
entrance into the Harbour with the *Conch*, so instead
they sent in the ship's boat with the Mate, a Sergeant, and

a flag of truce to bring back Pretorius' reply, which, as they expected, was a positive refusal to allow any communication with the Camp.   The boat was not allowed to proceed further than the Bluff Channel, but there they used both eyes and ears.   They found the Boers had cut a footpath up the steep side of the Bluff, and were very busy constructing a shelter trench from about the existing stone Landing Stage to near the Leading marks, where they erected an earthwork, arming it with a four pounder gun, pointing seaward ; also that the four pounder on the Point side—say the *Mazeppa* gun—was being seen to, and protected, for the purpose of sinking any vessel that avoided " Scylla " on the Bluff.   The now safe and happy Harbour Master, who professed himself friendly to the English, asked the *Conch's* crew if they had seen a vessel to the Eastward, for the Dutch guard on top of the Bluff had reported a ship " over there." They, of course, protested they were alone, and knew of no vessel in sight, though they expected a large reinforcement daily.

The boat returned, and on reporting, Mr. Bell went aloft to look for the reputed ship.   After long and careful observation, he saw the glint of the setting sun on white sails, which, then only just above the horizon, were sufficient to satisfy his critical eye by their size and cut that they belonged to a man-of-war.   As day closed, the falling westerly breeze brought slowly into sight the noble proportions of a stately frigate under full canvas, to the satisfaction and admiration of the soldiers, who had cheered Mr. Bell's first announcement of a man-of-war.

Sailors, when associated with soldiers on the water, usually display extraordinary zeal and smartness, born of professional rivalry.   Mr. Bell was well acquainted with the Port, inside and out, inclined for a fight, and brimful of information, which he was anxious to communicate to the Naval Authorities, who, if they had no troops on board, certainly had big guns and men to use them.   Captain Durnford, equally with Bell, growing impatient at the frigate's leisurely progress, decided upon using the schooner's best boat (necessarily a small one) and rowing out to meet her.   They started just after the sun had set, the night fine with a clear blue sky.   They took with them a boat's lantern, and left directions as a guide to their return that Mr. Carrell, the Mate, should fire rockets everv half hour, and pulled away, ultimately reaching the frigate about 8 o'clock, to find her to be the Admiral's Flagship *Southampton*, 50 guns, Captain Ogle, with portion of the 25th Regiment on board under command of Lieutenant-Colonel Cloete.   News exchanged, the visitors were invited to welcome refreshment, and the frigate sent up answering rockets while being guided into the anchorage by the *Conch's* lights.

Captain Smith and the Camp were again exhilarated by the sight of the *Conch's* rockets, which they took to themselves, until the conviction dawned upon them, as they discerned the burst of more distant ones, that there must be a second ship.   Discussion on this point broke into wild joy on hearing the heavy signal guns of the frigate.

All this incited the enemy to hammer away at the Camp, subduing the joyful anticipations of the soldiers as much as possible, for Mr. Bell reports that from the time he left the *Conch* until his return about 10.30 p.m., the firing on shore had been heavy, also that shots continued to be exchanged during the night.   The *Southampton* anchored about midnight; calm with light airs.

Bright and early on Sunday morning, the 26th June, all hands were astir in cheerful expectation.   The wind, as usual at that time of the day and season, had not declared its intention, so the Military Authorities, according to regulation in such cases made and provided, decided upon landing the main portion of the troops on the Back Beach, while the *Conch* was to discharge her passengers into boats, to be pulled in by the frigate's crew, by way of the Bluff Channel.   Colonel Cloete sent for Mr. Bell, who went on board the *Southampton* for his instructions; but the wind by this time had made up its mind, and satisfied the bold merchant skipper that time and tide would enable them to make a less hazardous landing.   He consequently offered his services to take in the *Conch*, when the wind freshened, and pilot the man-of-war's boats. It is to be inferred that his plan satisfied both the Naval and Military Authorities, for he, with the Master of the frigate, presently laid down a buoy to mark the spot where the *Southampton* might safely take up a position. Fortunately, as it proved, Captain Ogle was too prudent to warp his ship up to the buoy, considering it too close to the Bar and Bluff, for the wind, afterwards increasing, settled in a day or two into a gale, obliging the frigate to get away to sea to avoid the land, which she narrowly escaped. Bell, having apparently obtained two howitzers and Artillerymen, returned to the *Conch* and warped her in close to the Bar, which at that time was about 150 yards from the Bluff Point. Lieut. Turner, R.A., had fitted up the howitzers, and was anxious to try the range, so Bell put a spring on his cable, shearing the *Conch* broadside on. The result of the first trial shot is not recorded, but the second shell landed sufficiently close to the Leading marks battery to satisfy one party and scatter the other there assembled. The frigate had by this time got close in, so, swinging herself temporarily into position, she also tried sighting shots from two or three of her broadside guns, throwing shells to the top of the Bluff. It is said no more Boers were seen there after. The sightseers were more than satisfied with the prospect, and cantered back to Congella along the bridle path, cut through the Bush on top, to convey the alarming news. The guard took to the concealment of the Bush on the steep channel side of the Bluff, or hastened by the side path to join their comrades at the foot. The tide having to be waited for, pipes and bugles dismissed the floating Britons to dinner, with the after refrain of "Grog oh," and tobacco accompaniment; while their comrades at the Camp lost all relish for their "Sunday feed" in the conviction that as the firing had ceased, the attempt at relief had proved a failure. Dinner over, duty was resumed. The *Conch's* bulwarks were heightened by yellow-wood planks; when these ran short, sailors' blankets were hung over a line, which, though not intended to stop bullets, effectually prevented the Boers from singling out individuals. A portion of the hold had been set apart for the reception of the wounded, and the Doctor's use. About thirty men of the 25th Regiment were put on board, there not being room for more without obstructing Lieutenant Turner and his guns;

while the Barge and Pinnace of the frigate, with a carronade in the bow of each, the British ensign over their sterns, together with two other boats, carrying in all 85 men of the 25th Regiment, were loaded up.   Blue sailors, armed, at the oars; red soldiers, with cross belts, their firelocks upright between their knees, sat on, or between, the thwarts.   This little flotilla was attached by tow-ropes to the *Conch*.   The two smaller boats, carrying 35 men of the 25th under Captain Wells, were to cast off on near-ing the Bluff, effect a landing, and drive the enemy out of their shelter on its steep sides.

All preparations were completed about 2 p.m.   The frigate beat to quarters, and the gun crews went to their stations, but to the disgust of the impatient men joggling about in the open boats, Mr. Bell insisted on keeping them waiting for another half hour's tide.   By that time a fresh wind was blowing, and William Bell, taking the helm, gave the word to get under way, thus constituting himself Natal's first Pilot.   The sails of the little schooner speedily filled, and, gathering way with the four boats in tow, she dashed at the Bar, which happened to be in a pacific mood, crossing it in safety about 3 p.m.   Bell's cheery shout, "All clear, sir," was the signal for Lieut. Turner to address himself to the Dutch Batteries.   His first report brought shot and shell from the *Southamp-ton* to the Bluff top and the Point, while the carronades of the barge and pinnace made what shooting they could, as they were towed along.   A few minutes sufficed to reach the Leading marks battery, where the now desperate Dutchmen made a brave stand.   Bullets from the Bluff side, the four pounder gun and a breastwork, also from the gun and strong force on, or behind, the sand hills at the Point, forming a cross fire, were showered thickly on the *Conch* and the boats; they were enveloped and hidden in smoke as the soldiers returned a brisk fire, so that Bell could hardly see the Channel.   This he in a measure naively accounts for, as a consequence of a bullet striking the main boom just over his head, ¨at which I made a low bow."   However, he did not lose his head, for on nearing the Leading marks, he cast off Captain Wells, who effected a landing at the Bluff end, and speedily cleared

the enemy from its evergreen side. Our gallant " Pilot" kept
the little *Conch* on her course, handling her sails in this
sulphurous storm, and headed, or, as he would say, "hauled
up," for the Point, scattering iron and lead over the bare
sand dunes on his starboard side, himself narrowly escaping
a shell from the frigate.   Round the Point spit she swung,
to meet resistance from the retreating Boers, even up to
the landing place opposite the stockade.   Here the two
large boats were cast off, Jack putting in his oar, and
pulling for the shore, running their boats on to the sandy
beach.   The troops did not stay to take off their boots,
but, handling their cartridge boxes, jumped knee deep into
the water, and rushed for the Boer Camp with fixed
bayonets.   The boats returned to the *Conch*, which had
now anchored, and landed the long pent up men of the
27th Regiment, under Captain Durnford, who are described
as rushing like bloodhounds into the Bush in pursuit of the
enemy, but, strange to say, though 350 Dutchmen are said
to have been engaged in this defence, Colonel Cloete reports that, though determined men might easily have held
the Point Bush, after landing, not half a dozen were ever
seen.

Events such as these always afford your jack-tar the opportunity he craves of getting into scrapes with a run on
shore.   On the rush of the soldiers to the stockade, the
tars, cutlass in hand, must needs accompany them.   One
man " shinned up" the Boer flag-staff, as the only means
of getting at the Republican flag, to indicate to the frigate
that they were in possession. The tall pole, being without
stays, gave way in the soft sand, under the sailor's weight,
so pole, flag, and sailor came down together.   In their
hurry to rig it up again, they fastened on a boat's ensign,
upside down, which, in nautical sign language, is a token
of distress.   Its being distinguished by the frigate had
the immediate effect of causing her to "cease firing."   The
error was speedily noticed and rectified, then Jack had time
to look about him.   Finding some horses ready saddled
and bridled, they set about securing them, presenting the
best one to Colonel Cloete, who had been landed in one of
the frigate's boats, while others, on being reprimanded for
absenting themselves so long from their duty in the boats,

excused themselves on the ground that they "came athwart" an empty house with a dinner ready cooked and laid out, and lest it should be wasted, they stopped awhile " to stow it away," bringing along as a pretext a prize, or peace offering, a bundle of overcoats which the Dutchmen had left behind them.   The landing was effected with the loss of two soldiers killed, four wounded; two seamen were also wounded.   The Dutch loss was never ascertained. Two four pounder guns were captured at the Bluff and Point, two quarter-barrels of powder, fourteen rounds of ammunition (3lbs. each), with lead balls, weighing 6lbs. and 8lbs.—14 in number.   No other weapons or material were officially returned as prizes.

Satisfied that the enemy were in full retreat, or, as Mr. Bell expresses it, "trying their rate of speed through tne Bush, the "assembly" was sounded and the troops regularly formed up.   Colonel Cloete reports dividing them into three sections.   To Captain Durnford and the men of the 27th he allotted the impossible task of "entering the Bush on the right"—say at Bamboo Square—"and of "driving the Boers before him, while 1 placed myself on a "roadway in the centre "—the wagon bush path — Major "D'Urban (25th Regiment) taking the left along the Har-"bour Beach.   In this order we advanced through the "Bush, the character of which it is difficult to describe."

That Captain Durnford did not carry out his orders is certain, otherwise not a rag of them would have been left, but instead they all reached the open ground—say Winder Street—about 4 p.m., and, guided by the sound of Captain Smith's big guns, who, for the purpose, was probably accelerating the rate of speed of the flying Dutchmen to Congella, marched direct for the Camp.   Strange to say, not a note of music is recorded by any of the actors in these thrilling episodes, but we may safely infer that, when Col. Cloete's bugles sounded the "Advance" for the united column, the joyful hint was not lost on Captain Smith and his brave men, for the Colonel states they " threw out a party," who doubtless hastened to meet their reliefs, with merry drum and wry-necked fife, playing them in with the regimental tunes of the Inniskillens, "The Sprig of Shillelagh," or "The Little House under the Hill," and otherwise welcoming them with that terror to our foes, the Irish howl and the British cheer. What a joyful time they must have had that Sunday night out of prison at last, with something extra to eat and drink, the congenial society of their comrades of the Grenadier Company, with pipes and tobacco, and strangers to talk to! Some of the 25th Regiment, under Major D'Urban, were despatched to Stellar's farm on the road to Congella; others took charge of Fort Victoria. A detachment seized the brig *Pilot* converting her into a prison ship, while the *Conch* was to serve as Hospital, to which 26 sick and wounded at the Camp were afterwards removed.

Natal should ever remember this day as "the glorious 26th June, 1842," the night of which closed in comparative peace and freedom, though the morrow was to rekindle the resentment and deferred threats of the long pent up garrison, leading also to a serious difference of opinion between the new Commandant and Captain Smith.

The 27th June was devoted to clearing up and settling the Camps, and getting stores ashore from the *Southampton*. But on the 28th, the enemy having shown himself in the vicinity of Congella, an advance in force was ordered, and Congella taken without opposition, only a few mounted scouts having been seen at the edge of the Bush. The men of the 27th Regiment were thirsting for revenge, pillage and destruction with fire and sword, desiring to burn homesteads and follow up the farmers inland. Col. Cloete, having his own Regiment under control, insisted upon a less barbarous example to the Natives. But, being short of provisions, and unable to make an immediate advance without oxen, horses, or wagons, he sanctioned only the annexation of a wagon and span of oxen, with such edible recaptured stores as it could carry back to Camp. Though the village had been abandoned, there would be a few unconsidered trifles appropriated by the men, who, having tasted crow, would naturally long for poultry, and every available thing in the shape of vegetables. Fortunately, the force of discipline in the Inniskillens was more effective than that of reason, and restrained Captain Smith's murmuring men from open mutiny; it was indeed a trial of all soldierly, manly qualities, to pass over the bloodstained ground of their former defeat without letting themselves loose on the enemy, or his possessions; but as there were no Dutchmen to go for, and nobody to shoot at just then, better, if not hungrier, feelings prevailed, and the whole force returned to Camp, and resumed the setting of things in order, in anticipation of further strife to come.

Mr. Bell had visited the Camp on the previous day, and says:—" The main entrenchment across the Camp appeared " to have been converted into a hospital.   I found men ' with their legs and arms off, and some suffering from " dysentery; the only shelter they had from the hot sun ' by day and the cold by night was the hides of the horses ' they had just killed for food; the stench from these hides "and the putrid offal lying about was most offensive. Great "credit is due to Dr. Frazer; although in want of almost " everything that was requisite, every amputation he un-" dertook succeeded.   I observed the strips of horseflesh " hanging up to the broken wagons; they were by no " means tempting, the weather had made them quite black. " A poor, half-starved horse, the only one remaining, was " sitting on his hind quarters like a dog, making unsuccess-" ful efforts to get upon his feet."

During the siege, between the 31st May and 25th June, 651 round shot of various sizes had been fired at the Camp, this in addition to a pretty vigilant musketry fire. The casualties to the besieged during that time, in addition to the loss of all their oxen and horses, the destruction of the wagons, tents, and Camp equipage, were one officer, one sergeant, and four privates killed, seven privates, one Cape Rifleman, and one civilian wounded. The loss to the enemy, if known to themselves, was studiously concealed, but, owing to their want of discipline, it is probable that no returns were ever made.   On the occupation of Congelia, a memorandum was found, among cash and papers, in a hut occupied by Pretorius as an office, giving the names of six men killed and six wounded, but as some of the wounds were by bayonet, Captain Smith was of opinion that this only referred to the sortie on the 18th June.

Major Charters, in taking possession of Port Natal in 1838, issued a proclamation of martial law, and defined the boundaries of the area held under military occupation by the British Government as being "A curved line following "the sinuosities of the Bay, every part of which shall be "two miles distant from high water mark of the Bay or "Harbour." It was this Port Natal that Colonel Cloete was ordered to resume possession of, with general instructions to require the so-called rebels to submit to the authority of Her Majesty. The Boers having foreseen their inability to contend in fair fight with white men armed and disciplined, fearing also the probability of the Zulus turning upon them, vacated the proclaimed area, retiring first to Cowie's Hill on their way inland. Thus the Queen's troops were in possession, their banner still flying; the capture of "Port Natal" had been effected, and the siege was at an end.

. . . .

Incidental to the relief, there are certain facts which complete the story. Mr. Bell shortened his visit of inspection at the Camp on the 27th, by reason of a report that a schooner was in sight. Hastening to the Point, he found it to be the *Mazeppa*, which had looked in on passing, but, learning from the *Southampton* that the place was retaken, had anchored with the intention of loading up military stores before going inside. The wind was increasing from the N.E., and blowing fresh, causing their only cable to break. They had consequently to "run for it," cross the Bar, and eventually to pull up by grounding, in some disorder, on a sand bank near the Island. Mr. Bell and Dick King (who had returned as a passenger in the *Conch)* went on board, and satisfied Mr. Joseph Cato and the anxious women and children as to the safety of their relatives. Bell then obtained an anchor and warp from his ship, and properly secured the *Mazeppa.* Thus our Natal Pilot exercised his first functions as Port Captain, a post that was afterwards bestowed upon him for his services.

The night of the relief was very dark; about nine o'clock the sentry on the *Conch* informed Captain Bell that someone was hailing the ship from the water. It proved

to be a boat from the Congella, appropriated by two rene-
gade Englishman, who, taking advantage of the panic
among the Farmers, offered to facilitate the escape of Hugh
McDonald, Master of the *Pilot*, and by conveying him
to his ship, return to their allegiance at the same time.
Captain Bell allowed them to pass on to the *Pilot*. The
deserters were detained as prisoners in considerable sus-
pense, but released next day, and employed to convey
communications from Colonel Cloete to Pretorius. Proclamation was made that all deserters would be pardoned
on returning to their colours, while all British residents
were to give in their allegiance. To this only fifteen
persons responded; add to them the prisoners sent to
Pietermaritzburg, who were shortly afterwards released,
and we arrive at a grand total of twenty-five male persons,
who constituted the Burghers of Durban, or the white inhabitants of Port Natal. An amusing story was repeated
to me by Klaas, a Hottentot wagon driver, of the retreat
from Congella on the night of the 26th June (after the
rockets and guns of the *Southampton* and the report of
the Grenadiers seen on the *Conch*), but I hesitate to
convey in English the equivalent of the "Hottentot
Hollands" in which it was spoken, accompanied by the
grotesque facial expression and sign language, of which
these people are the only exponents.

It was dark, and the "ole vrow" had got out the
children, the "kist," mats, bedding, and pots, with other
household treasures all about the wagon; she ordered him
to inspan at once. "Klaas, Klaas, you must now trek;
we must get far away." Inspan they did, and in a hurry
commensurate with the missus' anxiety, everything was
bundled into the wagon by the light of the Camp fires;
the white children on to the "cartel," the black ones anywhere they could hang on among pots and kettles at the
back. "Then I cracked my whip and off we were; the
first path was sandy and we made no noise, but when we
got on the road to Cowie's Hill, the ole vrow got very
cross. She said she heard the Rooibatjes coming; 'yes,
they were behind, trek hard, Klaas.' I whipped up the
span, and drove fast, and then I got frightened, for I could
myself hear the drums of the soldiers, though a long way

off ; then all would be still ; then I could hear the trumpets, and I knew they would overtake us on their horses and kill me soon, because I looked like a Cape Corpsman. Englishmen don't eat old women and children, so I thought I would jump off, they would not see me in the long grass. But the ole missus was a devil, and some of the children were on the forechest, so I sat still with my neck all crooked. The music didn't come any nearer, and, as we now trekked on the veldt, we didn't hear it any more. We got to the river by Cowie's place, and outspanned to wait for daylight and other wagons to come up. I did not sleep under the wagon, but in a clump of bush out of the way of the soldiers. At daylight I crept out slowly to look for my oxen. When first I found them I swore, then I laughed, and rolled in the grass and laughed, for there was my best after ox, old Blueberg, with his hind foot jammed into the ole missus' ' comfore ' (*), so that was the music we heard, as it went ' Tarra klop, klopperty klop ' along the road. Another soupje, baas, as you blief."

As soon as Colonel Cloete had strengthened his defences, both at the Point and the Camp, the sick and wounded were placed on board the *Southampton* for conveyance to the Cape. He then proceeded with Captain W. J. D'Urban, 25th Regiment, to Pietermaritzburg, to confer with the Boer leaders and the Volksraad, as to their submission to the Queen's authority. The terms of their surrender, accepted by the President and Members of the Council, were ratified by Colonel Cloete, and embodied in his proclamation of 15th July, 1842.

The Colonel, having completed his instructions, shortly afterwards returned to the Cape in the frigate *Isis*, sent here to relieve the *Southampton*.

Capt. Smith was deservedly commended by Sir George Napier to the Secretary of State, not only for his military acts, but for his prudent diplomatic conduct with both Boers, Blacks, and British, in his capacity as Commandant

---

* A brass charcoal brazier, perforated at the top to sustain a coffee kettle. I enquired the use of the first I saw in the Colony, and, being a " jimmy," was told by the jocular clerk that they were " foot warmers," which the storekeeper gravely endorsed, by saying they were used for " smoking hams."

and Administrator of the limited Kingdom of Port Natal
after its reoccupation.   He was promoted to the rank
of Major, and appointed Magistrate, which included Col-
lectorship of Customs, and apparently every other office,
civil and religious.   But he found his honours come too
;hickly upon him, now that he was absolutely Governor,
the armed constituted representative of England, the " Great
Inkosi," for all sorts of questions, facts and fictions, both
black and white, Zulu, Dutch, and Native, were submitted
to him.   Questions as to encroachments, thefts, armed
reprisals, slavery, Zulu refugees, and the still more troublesome one as to the resumption by the farmers of their
land, in fulfilment of the treaty.   Underlying all this was
a ceaseless agitation by a rebellious faction, who would not
consent to be bound by the Volksraad, and so fomented
continued opposition to the British and the Native.   The aspect of affairs, with the threatened influx of freebooters from
behind the Berg, induced Major Smith to look to his guns,
and " take proper precautions."   At his request, the
Governor of the Cape contributed the services of the
gunboat *Fawn*, Lieutenant Norse.   She came into the
Harbour, and by exercising her guns, duly .impressed interested parties that all hope of retaking the Bluff or the
Block House, or of reoccupying Congella, was at an end.

Sir George Napier, duly impressed by Major Smith's
numerous despatches and urgent representations, had to
await instructions from home, and in those slow sailing
days, when the good old *Conch* with mails, took 45
days returning from Algoa Bay, time dragged into months,
until May, 1843, the Honourable Henry Cloete, L L.D.,
Advocate, and Member of the Cape Legislative Council,
was appointed by proclamation, dated 12th May, 1843,
Her Majesty's Commissioner for the District of Port Natal,
to confirm the Act of general amnesty and the treaty of
surrender of the 15th July, 1842, by agreeing with the
Boers as to their land tenure, and laws, and generally as
to their future government under British protection.

He arrived at Durban on the 5th June, 1843, and left
for the Cape, having so far completed his labours, in April,
1844, and a nice time he had of it, for he at once went to
Pietermaritzburg to confront an armed and turbulent mob,

chiefly Overberg ruffians, who, with mulish obstinacy, would neither be led nor driven, threatening all the well-disposed, and promising to burn Pietermaritzburg if the Volksraad surrendered, and did not carry out their Dutch equivalent for "Liberty, equality, and fraternity," with the Kafir left out. He truly held his life in his hand, but did not quail even when a self-elected deputation of rebellious women waited upon him, claimed to have a voice in public affairs, and informed him that, regardless of their craven husbands, they had decided to walk bare-footed Overberg, there to die in freedom, rather than submit; so there! He survived the onslaught, and ultimately succeeded in convincing the Voortrekkers, and by degrees induced them to lodge their claims to the farms and erven—to the possession of which they maintained they had exclusive and special rights by grants from the Volks-raad, purchase, or occupation. He visited Panda in Zululand, and agreed upon a boundary between the two countries, from the sea to the Drakensberg. He inspected numerous farms *en route*, and all over the Colony; investigated the claims of original Native tribes to their lands within our borders, and in fact laid the foundation of a great and lasting work.

The Governor of the Cape at that time was a Napier; a statement than which no greater commendation can be made! Sir George was, however, as good a Statesman as he was a Soldier. He carefully digested the able reports and recommendations of Mr. Cloete, and, with the prover-bial longheadedness of his kin, foresaw and suggested the possible course which the British Government must adopt towards their newly acquired territory. Anticipating its ultimate annexure, and to strengthen the authorities and protect Her Majesty's loyal and dutiful subjects in what was, even then, considered the British Colony of Natal, he sent up in H.M. Steamer *Thunderbolt*, 200 rank and file of the 45th Regiment, with a detachment of the Royal Artillery. They arrived on the 21st July, 1843.

Major Smith was comforted, and was naturally reluctant to disturb his present security by listening to the urgent demands of an irresponsible civilian like Mr. Commissioner Cloete to march his newly acquired forces to Pietermaritzburg for the purpose of overawing the disaffected Boers there assembled. Fortunately, the Volksraad *(male)* formally ratified their submission; the well-disposed returned to their allegiance, while the other kind retreated Overberg to resume life on their own lines. This was accomplished by the sagacious, diplomatic acts of one kindly Christian gentleman in a black frock coat, without the aid of any of Her Majesty's troops. His Secretary (an Attorney from Cape Town) and his Zulu interpreters, D. C. Toohey and Joseph Kirkman, were his personal attendants, while his bodyguard was constituted by the loyal Dutchmen of Pietermaritzburg. Major Smith now placed himself at the head of his forces and, warned by experience, advanced in due order upon Pietermaritzburg. He entered that town by the Camp Drift in the early morning of the 31st August, 1843, followed by two guns and two hundred men of the 45th Regiment, the Band playing "Sprig of Shillelagh" and "Garryowen." The Engineer Officer, Lieutenant C. J. Gibb, selected "a commanding hill at the west of the town," hurriedly commenced throwing up entrenchments, erected a flagstaff, and hoisted the British ensign. Someone named this Camp "Fort Napier," in honour of the Governor. Fort Napier is now a military town, with Horse, Foot, and Artillery to defend the Red, White and Blue Banner, which has never been lowered since planted on its primitive bastion by brave Major Smith and the "Old 45th." The flag was first displayed on two tent poles tied one above the other, and lashed to a wagon wheel. The East bastion was commenced the next morning. The Broad Arrow, with which the Royal Engineers marked this site, practically branded the fair land of Natal as Government property, and constituted Durban a town and port of entry.

Early in the following year, Sir George Napier's term of office having expired, Lieutenant-General Sir Peregrine Maitland was appointed Governor of the Cape. The Ministry in London, having found time to consider affairs at Port Natal, embodied Mr. Commissioner Cloete's suggestions in detailed instructions to the new Governor, and fortified him with Royal Letters Patent, under Her Majesty's sign manual, dated "at Westminster, the 31st day of May, 1844, in the seventh year of our reign," authorising the annexure of the " District of Natal to our said settlement of the Cape of Good Hope as a part and portion thereof." On this reaching the Cape, Sir P. Maitland took time leisurely to make arrangements for a Lieutenant-Governor, and the selection and organisation of an Executive Staff for the new District.

The Farmers, however, were growing impatient as to the survey of their lands and adjustment of their claims; consequently, he hurried up the appointment of Dr. Wm. Stanger as Surveyor-General, and sent him with a poor salary and a small staff of assistants to commence operations, including a trigonometrical survey that would take a lifetime. The Governor defined the boundaries of the new District, and instructed the Surveyor generally as to town lots, grants and reservations, fixing a tariff, and directing that all titles would be prepared in Cape Town and signed by the Governor, pending their ultimate transfer and registration in Natal. By the end of the year the following gentlemen had been selected and despatched to administer the Civil Government of Natal:—

Mr. Martin West, Civil Commissioner of Albany,
to be Lieutenant-Governor.
Mr. Henry Cloete, late Commissioner, to be Recorder.
Mr. Donald Moodie, Acting Civil Commissioner George,
to be Secretary to Government.
Mr. Walter Harding, Crown Prosecutor.
Mr. Theophilus Shepstone, Diplomatic Agent to
Native Tribes.

The Lieutenant-Governor and Staff arrived in Durban on the 4th December, 1845, were duly received by the troops, and welcomed by an address of the inhabitants now swollen to 56 in number, able to sign their names. Pietermaritzburg followed, with 61 on the 12th December, when the Recorder and the Lieutenant-Governor swore each other in. Thus the new reign of law and order began.

Major Smith left the Colony to return to England in the previous August, having been relieved by Colonel E. F. Boys, who had arrived in the meantime with the remainder of the 45th Regiment. He took with him a cordial valedictory address from the inhabitants of Pietermaritzburg. (*)

Note.—The head quarters of the 45th Regiment arrived in H.M.S. *Thunderbolt,* and landed on the 8th August, 1845; the 27th Regiment embarked on the 9th without any casualties.

CHAPTER III.

ROOTS AND BRANCHES.

HAVING now settled down under our flag, and obliterated the Military line of occupation "following the sinuosities of the Bay, two miles from high water mark," let us bid adieu to the Boers, turn our spears into pruning hooks, and, commencing as peaceful Colonists, give our first consideration to Durban as a town. Mr. Commissioner Cloete reported to the Cape Government in 1843, that, in the vear 1840, the Volksraad "appointed Mr. G. C. Cato, " a British resident" [as I have already surmised, at his own instigation], "to lay out a plan of a town along the " North Eastern beach of the beautiful estuary forming the " Port Natal, and which was there alreadv. partially occupied " by a few British settlers, who had built a few cottages " along the beach, and had given their infant town the name " of D'Urban. The Volksraad directed all Lots of ground " to have a frontage of 100 feet, running back to the beach, " and averaging from 5 to 700 feet in depth up to high water " mark. Those British settlers who were in occupation of " some of these lots, were allowed to remain undisturbed " upon their engaging to pay for their respective lots an " average price of what the remaining lots would sell for at " a public sale. With this arrangement they appear to " have been satisfied, and in June, 1840, the first public sale " of these lots took place. About 21 lots along the beach " were then sold, and about 100 smaller lots in several

" squares away from the beach.   The former averaged about
" £18 15s., sterling, and the latter (which were uniformly
" 150 feet long by 100 broad) averaged £3 15s. sterling.
" The payment of these building lots was made contingent
" on the delivery of the title deeds, and these having not yet
" been delivered to the parties up to this date, no payment
" was made by anyone (except by one Ernest Pretorius for
" lot No. 36), and the whole thus remains still a debt due to
" the public by those who have kept and retained possession
" of their respective lots.   In the month of October, 1841,
" a second sale took place of 21 building lots, commencing
" at Lot No. 124 to Lot 144 inclusive, which realised about
" the same average price as before.   The title deeds of
" these also were neither delivered to the parties, nor were
" the purchase prices paid by the latter; and at the outbreak
" of hostilities in May, 1842, very few individuals had con-
" structed any habitations for themselves, but several were
" in the act of collecting materials and laying out various
" plans for their buildings, when they were prevented from
" continuing these constructions by a public notice issued by
" Captain Smith on the 6th August, 1842, and when some
" of them were inclined to disregard such a notice, or actually
" applied for leave, it was peremptorily refused. . . . .
" From such a state of things, it was natural that upon my
" arrival this little town presented nothing but a few miser-
" ably constructed wattle and daub erections, which the
" "inhabitants only kept together as temporary shelters for
" themselves and their little properties, as they had great-
" difficulty in even keeping these huts in repair."

Governor Maitland's instructions to Dr. Stanger say nothing about the area or extent of the Town Lands, but, in
repeating the requirements of the Secretary of State, state :
" His Lordship approves of titles being issued as recom-
" mended by Mr. Cloete to 39 town lots, to which claims
" have been established, under the provisions of the pro-
" clamation of 12th May, 1843, at D'Urban (or the seaport).
" Of these, 31 lots (estimated to contain 38 7-16 acres)
" do not appear to have been paid for; and in their regard
" His Lordship directs that the original purchase money with
" 25 per cent. added shall be paid, exclusive of the expense
" of survey and title deeds.   His Lordship further approves
" of a grant of 150 feet square being made for the Wesleyan

" Chapel at D'Urban in lieu of the 300 feet which appear
" to have been marked out for the purpose. . . . . .
" His Lordship remarks that on general grounds it would be
"preferable that no sales of town allotments take place until
" something of a systematic nature by way of survey of the
" proposed town can be effected; but on the other hand,
" it may be impossible to withstand the pressure of the
" necessity which will probably have compelled parties to
" occupy sites on which to house themselves, and therefore
" sanctions in cases where it mav be essential, and where a
" well defined demarcation of the lots may be made, the
" sale by public auction of town sections of about half or
" quarter of an acre, or of smaller extent, at a minimum
" price of £100 per acre.   At a moderate distance from
" some central point in the town, His Lordship observes the
" lots may be considered as suburban, and he therefore
" approves of their being sold by auction at such upset price
" as may be consistent with the locality, the capability of
" the land, etc., but not less than £1 per acre.   These terms
" and sales previous to a regular survey are, however, only
" sanctioned to meet the cases of persons actually settled on
" the spot, to whom it would be in many cases a hardship,
" and perhaps a public inconvenience to refuse an oppor-
" tunity of acquiring ground where purposes of the first
" necessity may have required.   The area of the village of
" Congella is estimated by Mr. Cloete at 5½ acres, of which
" three remain to be paid for; and His Lordship approves
" of the issue of grants upon the same conditions as the
" town allotments of D'Urban."   In reference to Military
reserves,   " His Excellency desires it to be especially im-
" pressed that no lands near the reserve, whether lots in
" towns or farms, are to be granted or sold until you and
" the Commanding Royal Engineer have agreed upon the
" boundaries, and subject to the approval of the Comman-
" der in Chief; and whenever the Commanding Royal En-
" gineer shall propose any reserve, you will pay attention to
" his suggestions, and you will forward your opinion to His
" Excellency."
      These instructions will be better understood by reference
to the annexed plan (A), which was evidently before Governor Maitland.   It may be referred to as the "Dutch Survey" made for the Volksraad by Mr. G. C. Cato, to whom

A.

Ferriera — A B C 1 — 1
Langetts — 1 2 3 — 2
Ogle — 2 3 4 — 3
Martin — 4 5 6 1 — 4
— 5 6 2 — 5
Swikkenass — 6 7 3 — 6
Wicht or Dapp — 7 4 5 6 — 7
Hogg or Thomas — 8 5 6 7 — 8
Christian — 6 7 8 — 9
Christian — 10 7 8 — 10
Behrens — 11 8 9 — 11
— 12 9 — 12

Godly + — 10 11 12 13 14 15 16 17
Haydon
Morewood
Morewood

Smith Street

Botha — 24 25 26 27 28 29 30 31
McDonald
Gregory
Kronenberg
Dennis
Cogan + Behrens
Short
Dennis
Ogle

Market

archbell — 32 33 34 35 36 37 38 39 40 41 42 43 44
Mission
Perkins
Armstrong
McKenzie
King
Douglas
Cato
McCabe
J.O.S
Cato

Craig

141 J.O.S had possession
before second sale in Nov.
1841 & bought them for £1815 -

142 ditto G.C.C.
143 Granted to G.C.C. for
laying out the Erwen
144 Had Possession in
average price.

therefore belongs the honour of selecting the site, and designing and laying down the original plan of tne town of D'Urban.

This plan was copied by me from a rough sketch in pencil in Mr. Cato's handwriting, which had served him for a draft, to accompany his Report to Mr. Commissioner Cloete.

The accompanying notes seemed to have been furnished to Surveyor-General Stanger, from the original evidence of occupation and balances of purchase prices due, supplied to Mr. Cloete.

Copy of draft of original Report by Mr. G. C. Cato, as to the occupiers of the Erven and prices given when sold by the Volksraad, prepared apparently for Mr. Commissioner Cloete :—

No. 6.—Bought by Phillip Raaths, June 1840, and sold to Ohrtman, 20th March, 1842.

No. 7.—Bought by F. Roos, 7th October, 1841, and sold to Ohrtman, 26th March, 1842.

No 8.—Bought by J. M. Schuper, 22nd June, 1840, and sold to Behrens for £30.

Nos. 9 and 10.—Not occupied or claimed by anyone, but I think Toohey made out a claim afterwards to 10.

Nos. 11, 12, 13 and 14. - Toohey residence. He was allowed to keep the land on paying the average selling price, which was £118 15s.

No. 15.—Mrs. Strydom in possession before the sale of lands sold by Volksraad, 1840; allowed to retain it on the average.

Nos. 16 and 17.—Bought from others and paid them, agreeing to pay the original unpaid sum.

No. 18.—Bought by Badenhorst at the public sale of building lots, sold to P. Raaths, and by him to Botha, 11th November, 1840.

No. 19.—Bought at public sale, 15th November, 1841.

No. 32.—Bought at public sale by Isaak de Jager, and sold to J. A. de Wet, 21st October, 1841.

No. 36.—Bought by P. Ferreira at public sale and paid. Sold to J. J. Steytler, and then to Murison.

No. 44.—Step Combrink occupied before sales. On average price, £7 10s., sold to Ogle, he paying original price.

No. 45.—Purchased by Anna G. Combrink, original £7 10s., sold to Ferreira £22 10s.

No. 124.—Purchased by L. Badenhorst, £9 7s. 6d., sold to C. McDonald, January, 1843, £40.

No. 125.—Gregory had possession in 1839 and agreed to pay average price of Beach lots, which was £9 7s. 6d.

No. 126.—Bought by J. H. Visagie at the sale of building lots held 15th November, 1840, £24 7s. 6d., and sold to Kronenberg for the same.

No. 127.—Granted to R N. Dunn on memorial afterwards.

No. 128.—This lot was purchased at the second sale of building lots by Behrens for £8 5s. 5d , but not paid.

No. 129.—Bought by Short at sale of building lots for £8 5s. 5d., but not paid.

No. 131.—H. Ogle possession. To pay average price, £18 15s.

No. 132.—Bought by J. G. Mocke at sale of building lots, and sold to Archbell, £8 5s

No. 134.—W. Parkins took possession and to pay average.

No. 135.—F. Armstrong the same.

No. 136.—Bought by McKenzie, £11 0s. 6d.

No. 137.—R. King same as 134 and 135.

No. 138.—Bought by S. Maritz for £9 15s., and sold to Morewood for £5 5s. He made over to J. Douglas; he to pay when called on £9 15s.

No. 139.—Bought at second sale for C. J. C. [Christopher Joseph Cato] £11 5s.

No. 140.—Bought at second sale November, 1841, £11 5s. McCabe.

The Dutch Survey and Erven were evidently adopted by Dr. Stanger, who, however, amended the Survey and divided the town into Blocks or Wards, renumbering the Erven. His Surveyors, L. Cloete, Chas. Piers, and Grieves, laid off the Beach Erven during May and June, 1845, and titles to all these granted or passed lands by Mr. Commissioner Cloete were issued by Lieut.-Governor West during 1846 and 7, as the grantees paid up their original purchase prices, with the 25 per cent. fine added.   Thus I find among Mr. Cato's memoranda :—

		£	s.	d.
(142) G. C. Cato.	Cost	18	15	0
	Add 25 per cent.	4	13	9
	Survey expenses	1	10	0
		£24	18	9

		£	s.	d.
(139) C. J. Cato.	Cost	11	5	0
	Add 25 per cent.	2	16	3
	Survey expenses	1	10	0
		£15	11	3

		£	s.	d.
(141) J. O. Smith.	Cost	18	15	0
	Fine 25 per cent. ...	4	13	9
	Survey expenses	1	10	0
		£24	**18**	**9**

After the completion of the English Survey by Dr. Stanger, the first public sale by the British Government was authorised and held on the 22nd November, 1848 (see plan Town annexed). From the evidence at my disposal, I conclude that Mr. G. C. Cato was the Auctioneer. The upset price was £100 per acre, and his notes show a summary of the prices given for Lots bought in for himself and the persons in whom he was interested, viz. : —

		a. r. p.		£	s.	d.
No. 5 A.	W. R. T.	1 1 12. £100		132	10	0
	[? Deposit] 10 per cent.			13	5	0
				£119	**5**	**0**

Survey expenses, £1 10s.

No. 20. L.	G. C. Watts	35	12	6
	10 per cent. £3 11s. 3d.			
	Survey expenses	1	10	0
		£37	**2**	**6**

No. 21. L.	W. Vionnee	35	12	6
	10 per cent. £3 11s. 3d.			
	Surveyor, £1 10s. ...			
No. 18. L.	John Ward	35	12	6
	10 per cent. £3 11s. 3d.			
	Surveyor, £1 10s. ...			
No. 1. L. ⎫	G. C. C.	35	12	6
H. 2. K ⎬	... ...	35	12	6
⎭	[No number or name]	35	12	6

Among the title deeds that have passed through my hands were to be found many bearing the date of that first sale, notably the two Erven Nos. 23 and 24 D., extending from Smith Street to West Street, and fronting Field Street, bought by Robert Pollyblank for £35 12s. 6d. each.   Bequeathed at his death to his daughter, Mrs. Stephen Gee, they are now held by his grandchildren.   The value of this land (without buildings) is now assessed by the Corporation at £15,500.   In January, 1849, the Government issued the following notice : —

No. 2. 1849.

GOVERNMENT NOTICE.

The Lieutenant-Governor directs it to be notified for general information, that in pursuance of the published regulations for the sale of Crown Lands, forty-six (46) allotments varying in extent from 200 to 1000 acres, situated on the sea coast north of the Umgeni River, and adjoining the lands of the Natal Cotton Company, having been duly exposed to public sale at upset prices of 4s and 5s. per acre, may be purchased on payment of the respective upset prices and surveying charges upon application to the Surveyor-General, at whose office plans and diagrams of the lands may be seen.

Five (5) allotments adjoining the Town Lands of Pietermaritz-burg, from 190 to 739 acres in extent, upset price 4s. and 5s., and 80 building allotments in Durban, about one quarter acre each, upset price £100 per acre, may also be obtained on the terms above stated.

Diagrams with freehold titles will be delivered to the respective purchasers upon payment of the purchase money.

By command of His Honour the Lieutenant Governor.

(Signed)   D. MOODIE,

Colonial Office, Natal,   Secretary to Government.
Jan. 8, 1849.

Consequently I have not been able to trace any further "exposure by public sale" of Durban Building Lots, but believe purchasers applied direct to the Surveyor-General, and the Governor issued titles on payment.   In a letter from Dr. Stanger to Mr. Cato, dated July 3rd, without the year, which I fix as 1849, he says : —" With regard to the "discharged soldiers, I do not approve of any of them getting "the best erven.   Armstrong, the blacksmith, can have 9 "Block L, but not one in the front street.   Harley 'cannot' "have No. 8 A., so he need not throw his money away in 'building.   Harley can have as he arranged with me any "number in E. which is not granted."   Lieut.-Governor West was probably influenced by the opinion of the Surveyor-General, but, on his death in 1849, we find his successor, Colonel E. F. Boys, 45th Regiment, temporarily administering the Government, issuing freehold grants to discharged soldiers.   All enquiries have failed to elicit his authority for so doing, and I am forced to the conclusion that the " interests of the Service " induced him to stretch a point in aid of companions-in-arms honourably discharged, who had elected to become Colonists instead of claiming return passages to the place of their enlistment.   Through the kindness and civility of our late Market Constable, Patrick Toohey, who enlisted in the 36th Regiment in Ireland in 1839 at 17 years of age, and volunteered in the 45th Regiment when it left home for the Cape, I have been shown his " Soldiers' Small Book," where it is laid down that, by Royal Warrant of 14th November, 1829, men who enlisted (it was for 21 years then) after 1st March, 1833, were entitled to certain gratuities on discharge, according to service, and, when discharged in any of the Colonies, to a grant of land when available, and subject to the approval of the Governor and Commander-in-Chief.   Acting Lieut.Governor Boys, Commander-in-Chief in Natal, may have assumed the purple, and said in substance, " this shall be your warrant."   Vague as may be our conjectures, it is certain that free titles were issued, and no one has since questioned their validity.   Dr. Stanger, as Surveyor-General, had also to sign these Deeds.   His opinion must have had some weight with the Military Governor, for these soldiers' grants were not of the " best erven " of the period, but on both sides of distant West Street, St. George's Street in the bush, and swampy unnamed Pine Terrace. (*)

It is singular that, in none of Dr. Stanger's letters which I have seen, does he mention the name of any street.   The diagrams, framed by his Surveyor in 1845, describe the boundaries of Lots as :—" By a Street," " Road to Beach," and " Government Reserve."   The urgency for carrying out his instructions centred in the original Beach Erven ; the wilder parts of the town were more leisurely surveyed, and finished by Mr. Surveyor Okes in 1849, for in the letter before quoted Dr. Stanger says :—" I shall send down a " list to Okes as soon as all are fixed, who will point out the " beacons.   I am most anxious to know what Okes is " doing.   .   .   . ·Tell him to write to me by return post,

---

* Government Notice, April 27, 1848.·--Authorises grants of a few town lots in Pietermaritzburg, or lots of 12 acres of arable ground at Howick, Bushmans River, or division of Klip River, to discharged soldiers upon condition of occupation and cultivation.

D

"and tell me what he is about." In 1850 the streets were known by their names, and the Catos were credited with having named them; we may therefore safely conclude that, when the entire survey of the town was completed and accepted by Dr. Stanger, himself, Mr. Okes, and the Catos christened and wrote in the names of the streets on the General Plan. Both the brothers Cato have told me frequently that, in laying out the town, the width of the streets was governed by the length of a wagon and a span of oxen, and the space required to turn in; hence 100 feet came to be regarded as sufficient reserve for that purpose. They also said that Smith Street, being the main street, or high road from the Point to Pietermaritzburg, was named in honour of Captain Smith, of the 27th Regiment, defender of the Camp. Of a certainty the Boers would not thus have honoured it. West Street was named after His Honour Martin T. West, the first Lieut.-Governor of Natal. The Cross Streets were named after Dr. Stanger; Aliwal Street was named in Honour of His Excellency Sir Harry Smith, the hero of Aliwal, who is styled in addition the "Governor General" of the Cape by the *Natal Witness* in announcing his arrival in Pietermaritzburg overland, on the 9th February, 1847 (*); Gardiner Street after Captain Allen Gardiner, who named the town; Field Street after William Swan Field, the first Collector of Customs and Resident Magistrate; Grey Street after Earl Grey, Secretary of State for the Colonies; Russell Street after Lord John Russell, the Premier. Unhappily, another slight was put on Ireland by naming the two last streets after the Saints "George" and "Andrew"; this, however, was popularly corrected in 1850, when that isolated district was known as "Irish Town." It is still more singular that the names of Cloete, Cato, and Gibb were not emblazoned on the roll of fame, when our thoroughfares were named.

Lieutenant C. J. Gibb, the "Commanding Royal Engineer," had availed himself of Sir Perigrine Maitland's instructions to Dr. Stanger, and cut off the dangerous dense bush and the whole of the sand hills extending to the little military post at the Point by a line drawn from the Back Beach to the Bay as a reserve for the Crown under the

---

* Sir Henry George Wakelyn Smith, Bart., Lieutenant General, Administrator of the Government of the Cape of Good Hope.

Board of Ordinance for military purposes. The line of demarcation now known as Rutherford Street, was not defined until some years later. This constitutes what is now known as Addington and the Point.

To protect "The Camp," he centred it in a reservation in the shape of a square, having one point towards the Umgeni, and the opposite one in the Market Place, each face measuring 1,000 yards. He also reserved the Bluff by a line from the head of the Channel to the ocean. He duly beaconed these sites with wooden posts, bearing the mysterious broad arrow and the letters B. ⋀ O., in later years replaced by stone posts, erected by the modern War Department, and marked W. ⋀ D., accordingly. I find the story of Mr. Cato's survey to be all a fable to the veterans of the 45th. "Cato is it? Sure he kep' a store there "beyant, an' sold pipes and tobaccy to the sogers, so he did. "No, sur, its meself that knows it was Mr. Gibbs of the R'yle "Engineers who gave the lines of the town; didn't I see "him surveying many a day, by the same token I was de- "tailed wan of the party," etc., etc. Not even a conciliatory drink would yield the concession that a "Civilian" could have done anything so important, while an officer in the service was to the fore. Yet these circumstantial witnesses are not without justification; for, when the Surveyor-General found that Lieutenant Gibb's square encroached upon his proposed township, these two practical common sense gentlemen courteously met and agreed to remove the corner peg in the Market Place, and cut off from the military reservation the small triangular point which intruded itself beyond the line of Pine Terrace, thus reducing that area to 324 acres. Hence the Ordnance Land has five corner beacons. This short resurveyed line from the Market House to Messrs. Parker, Wood and Co.'s stores may (with other surveys) be the "lines of the town" to which our veterans refer. On the area so relinquished, St. Paul's Church was afterwards built. The title to the Church land granted in 1850 states that it is in the Market Place, and bounded on the north by Ordnance Land.

It only remains for me to account for the deviation from his instructions by Dr. Stanger in fixing the whole width of the Erven at 103 feet instead of 100 feet. This arose,

like many a doubt in the mind of youth, from a conflict
between the real and the apparent.

The veracious Knickerbocker, in his history of New York,
has given us the standard of Dutch weights and measures
at New Amsterdam, but he is not exact as to the size of a
Dutchman's foot, for it appears that the one brought with
them to the Cape, was slightly in excess of the English
standard, consequently 100 feet Dutch measure was found
to be equal to 103 feet and a fraction on the British tape-
line.   But, as Mr. Cato knew that the practical Boer would
consider fractions frivolous, he shortened the business in an
equally prompt and practical fashion by pegging them off at
103 feet sterling.   By applying a T square to his plan, and
extending lines across the sheet, he obtained the width of
all the Erven in the proposed town.   It only remained to
cut the plan into Blocks by streets, when occasion arose.
Practically the width of Smith Street had been laid down
at 100 feet, and the Market Square indicated, but the rest
were on paper when Captain Smith and Dr. Stanger took
possession.   The Surveyor-General accepts the measure
meted out to the original purchasers of 100 feet Dutch for
the width of their Beach Erven, but, in laying off the other
Erven and sub-dividing into Blocks, allowed them only the
150 feet in English length, thus all but Beach Erven are
103 feet wide by 150 feet long.   The only case in which
he may be held to have exceeded his instructions is that of
the lot marked "Chapel" (Plan   ), reserved by the Cape
Governor for the Wesleyan Society, for, instead of the
Governor's 150 feet square, the British rule was placed along
Aliwal Street, and that of the Dutch along Smith Street,
since Lot 2, Block L., is 150 feet long by 154 feet 6 inches
wide, or a frontage to Smith Street of one and a half Dutch
Erven.   Mr. Commissioner Cloete, in his Report, states
that the Beach Erven "ran back to the Beach, and averaged
from 5 to 700 feet in depth up to high water mark."   The
Surveyor-General, when surveying the Lots, preferred to
bound them by solid ground instead of the doubtful mud
and mangrove swamp that constituted high water mark,"
so cut off from their Beach frontages an area which he
marked on their diagrams "Government Reserve."   No
measurement of the width reserved is indicated, but time
and rumour have named this space "Admiralty Reserve,"

and fixed the width as 150 feet from high water mark. Those who know declare this reservation to be one of the "Rights of the Crown," universally applied in British Dominions. The Reverend W. C. Holden, in his History of the Methodist Missions in South Africa, states that he arrived in Durban to take charge of the Mission in the early part of 1847. " At that time there were a few thatched " cottages embowered in the richest herbage. These were " made of poles and wattles with clay walls, having veran- " dahs to protect them, and, being whitewashed, they peeped " out prettily among the shrubbery. The paths to them " wound amidst copse and grass. The streets were not de- " fined, nor were substantial houses erected." . . . . . " There was a small chapel, built in the same style as the " houses, and on my arrival I found a society of twelve " English members, a congregation of 40 or 50 persons, and " a small Sabbath School."

In 1846 the Custom House was a small wattle and daub structure somewhat to the Eastward of the present Alexandra Hotel, for in September Mr. Cato, in conformity with Government Notice, applied for a piece of ground for a temporary Cattle Kraal " below the Custom House, and for a piece of land from high water mark to erect a store and build a jetty on piles." In March, 1847, he again wrote to the Government as to his " temporary stores beyond the Custom House," and obtained permission to build at once on 120 feet, " where my Cattle Kraal stands." This spot was pointed out to him, he says, by Dr. Stanger, Mr. Gibb, and Mr. W. S. Field. He laid claim to this and adjoining sites for Mr. J. O. Smith, by reason of occupation since 1838; and in July, 1877, he asks to have title issued in terms of Proclamations of 12th May, 1843, and 23rd September, 1846. Title was issued to him and Mr. John Owen Smith, and I believe to the representatives of Mr. R. Dunn, for the freehold land now occupied by the " Criterion " Hotel and the African Boating Company, consequently this land must have been conceded by the Military as a reservation to original occupants, when they took over the rest of the lands. This, however, does not apply to the site of the present Custom House. The original Boer Custom House was of stone, and formed a refuge for the few Englishmen when the Stockade was captured on the memorable 26th May, 1842. It stood on the then edge of the Bay, but the ebb-tide current encroached so much on the Point spit, that it was undermined and destroyed. In 1848 what remained of it served as stepping stones for passengers landing, while to-day its fragments have been dredged up in the ship channel, a considerable distance to the Eastward of the present building.

Mr. Chiappini, a Cape Merchant, desirous of extending his trade, obtained from someone—possibly the Governor at the Cape, or the Military Authorities—a concession or stand for the purpose of erecting stores and a Bonding Warehouse at the Point; but this appears to be one of those mysterious conventions of which nobody now knows anything, a sort of transaction that has many sides and an all round profit. Certain it is that, in 1848, our old townsman, Mr. John Dove, Bricklayer, arrived here with a man named Coles, a Carpenter, engaged by a Contractor in Cape Town for the work, and completed a large and substantial structure of brick with slated roof for Mr. Chiappini, which on its completion was let to the Government, and became the Custom House and Queen's Warehouse, with Mr. W. S. Field in possession. A rental of £250 a year was paid to Mr. Chiappini for several years. When his rights lapsed, the property remained vested in the Crown. To protect his property against the ebb tide, a dressed stone wall was constructed by the Government, about 40 feet in front of the building, forming an esplanade, from which stone groins were thrown out at right angles into the Channel. This work was carried out by Mr. John Milne, C.E., and was the origin of the Natal Harbour Works. The men of the 45th Regiment were employed by the Contractor on the building. They also built the Block House on the top of a prominent sand hill near the site of the old Stockade, Fort Victoria. It was constructed of stone, quarried on the Bluff, and roofed with slate. The exterior was rough cast with lime mortar. In size it was about 40 feet long by 18 feet wide, with walls 16 feet high. The basement was used as a store room, and the upper room for the soldiers' quarters. It stood at the left rear of the Alexandra Square, between the latter and the Time Ball Station. A road is now laid off over the site, but the soldiers' well, at this day bricked round, can still be seen at the head of the Square, dry, and partly filled with rubbish. The men of the 45th Regiment were excused military exercises, owing to the necessity for their employment on public works; since, in addition to stockading the Camp, reconstructing ditch and bastions, making Barracks, Stores, and Magazines, they erected a Mess House and Officers' Quarters on the flat to the eastward of the Camp, while the married men constructed shanties in their gardens, on the edge of the swamp at the north-eastern side of the Camp. These buildings, excepting the Magazine, were nearly all of wattle and daub, thatched. The soldiers also bridged, with mangrove poles and sods, a swampy patch crossing the wagon road, through the Bush to the Point. This was known as "Durnford's Bridge," possibly because Captain Durnford's company of the 27th Regiment had first constructed a temporary crossing to allow the stores of the relief to be carted over. They also cut a ditch or water course from the Umgeni to the Camp, from which it followed the line of Boer entrenchments to Pine Terrace, just to the West of the Market Place, to find an outlet into the Bay by the swamp that extended from the end of Field Street. There is much controversy about this work; some say it was done to supply the Camp with water; others, that it was a Royal Engineer's scheme to deepen the Bar by bringing the Umgeni River into the Bay. The *Natal Witness* of November 12th, 1847, states:—" A resident of Durban informs us that progress is being made in bringing out the Umgeni water, and that five men from Lieut. Gibb's department are doing their duty well." The soldiers credit Lieutenant Gibb with it, while the Civilians designate it "Moodie's Folly," asserting that it was paid for out of surplus Colonial Revenues (Customs) voted for Imperial purposes. Be that as it may, the Umgeni did not wait to be brought, but came in person in April, 1848, and wiped out the pretentious ditch, destroyed Durnford's Bridge, and in its fury scooped out a deep creek across land owned by Mr. Cato (Lots 144 and 143) right into the Bay. This water way was then rightfully appropriated, and named "Cato's Creek." The town end of the military ditch is *still* visible from the Camp to the Railway Station.

In the *Natal Patriot* newspaper of the 14th April, 1848, printed and published weekly in Durban by Cornelius Moll, a detailed description of the first known flood is given.

together with an account of how a boat of Mr. Cato's was taken on a wagon to the Umgeni Brickyards, and Messrs. Kirkman and Proudfoot rescued a Brickmaker named Jack Smith (*) and his wife from the roof of their cottage, assisting them with other residents out of danger.   This paper also gives a humorous description of a voyage in the same boat up the Eastern Vlei, past the Camp and the washed-out married men, to the Umgeni and back, by Mr. Cato, Tom and Harry Milner, Sidney Peel and James Gregory. The water along their course averaged from five to eight feet in depth.   It is recorded that the effect upon the Bar was by scour, yielding for a short time a depth of 20 feet, but nothing is said about the effect upon the Bay by silt and deposit.   The Bay, constituting the Harbour of Port Natal, was fringed all round with fine Mangrove trees of both varieties, the red and the white, proving the subsoil to be of a clayey nature, their habitat being on saline muddy shores.   The islands on the south side, with the exception of the largest known as Salisbury Island, were little more than swampy clumps of mangroves, scrub, and marine plants, overflowed by salt water at spring tides.   These were, however, the home of pelicans and the scarlet-winged flamingo, hadadahs, and other wild fowl.   Beyond the vicinity of the Point the waters were seldom utilised, or the head of the Bay visited, except by sportsmen.   The Military and Civilians having cut down all the finest mangroves within reach for stockades, bridges, house building, and firewood, later arrivals had to seek their supplies further afield.   This traffic, with the ever present gun, ultimately banished most of the feathered settlers from our shores. The small island-like cluster of mangroves known to our yachtsmen as "The Cows," was discovered and named about this time.   Mr. Joseph Cato, with a sporting party of townsmen, was sailing in the Island Channel.   They agreed as to a strange object on the surface of the water off the upper end of the island, but disagreed as to what it could be.   F. McCabe, a jovial Irishman (afterwards Landdrost

* Smith had been a sailor. He subsequently removed to a farm near Pinetown, and, in his old age, found with his wife a refuge at Overport Lodge Gates, through the generosity of Wm. Hartley, Esq. He was fond of children, amusing, and well known to the younger generation on the Berea as "Old Daddy Smith."

of Bloemfontein), was positive that the object was a bush, while James Gregory, handling his gun, was equally positive it was a sea-cow, well out in the Bay. Each were confirmed in their opinions as the boat sailed slowly on, with the inevitable result of a wager offered by McCabe, and promptly accepted, resulting in the discomfiture of Gregory, for closer acquaintance showed them a group of young white mangrove trees growing apparently from stranded seeds. A public wager then meant a public carouse, hence the evergreen group was toasted and christened as "Gregory's Cows." Now, Gregory is no more, only "the Cows" remain; they served as a convenient landmark, so their lives were spared.

The Bay then was much shallower than to-day; a large area between the town and the island was covered with a grass-like seaweed, which gave shelter to innumerable creatures with shells and without, and formed the happy hunting ground of various queer fishes as diverse, if not so melodious, as the imps who troubled St. Anthony, the skate, cuttle fish, small sand-shark, and even the turtle being plentiful. It was not until the Harbour piers were commenced that the porpoise ventured to disport himself in the inner bay. The seaweed washed up in heaps on the Bay foreshore, and was utilised by the primitive settler for overlaying his wheel tracks on the sandy roads to and from the Bay, while his wife adopted it for mattress making until she found that no amount of fresh water would remove the ingrained salt. It was possible for a man at low water spring tides to wade across the Island Channel. I have known men to walk across the Bay from Field Street, to their Camp on the Island, wading that Channel with their mouths shut, and their bundles held above their heads.

Commercial intercourse was at this time extending, while the advent of emigrants and passengers gave promise of future recognition and prosperity, for we find the schooner *Douglas*, Captain W. Smerdon, advertised by "G. C. Cato, Agent," as open for freight or passengers to Cape Town and Algoa Bay, while the schooner *Norfolk*, Capt. P. H. Watts, and the schooner *Curlew*, "J. Clarke, Esq., Commander," were advertised for Mauritius.

The first effort in the interests of Agriculture was the following unsigned advertisement:—

"NATAL AGRICULTURAL SOCIETY."

" A meeting will be held at the Commercial Hotel on
" Tuesday, 18th April next, at 10 o'clock, for the purpose of
" attempting to organise a Society. Port Natal, 29th March,
" 1848."

The first " Emigrants " to arrive were 189 Germans in the
ship *Beta*, upon March 23rd, 1848. They all settled at
New Germany, near Pinetown, and became a thriving and
industrious community.

The total number of emigrants from all quarters who
arrived by sea (as reported from official sources) up to the
end of 1849 was 853 statute adults, children under a certain
age not being counted.   The majority of tnese dispersed
throughout the Colony to take up their allotments; the
remainder sought employment in Durban.

The idea associated with the introduction of the Germans
was to grow cotton.   A French gentleman of the name of
Jargal had planted and obtained a good crop from land
near the Umgeni Brickfields.   The overflow of the Umgeni
put an end to his enterprise.   The proof that cotton could
be grown was enlarged upon, and encouraged a beuef that
it would become the staple of the Colony.   This is reflected
in the same newspaper by the characteristic advertisement
of Mr. Samuel Benningfield, one of the Point prisoners, released by the Boers after the relief of the Camp.

"ONWARD NATAL.

" The undersigned seeing the necessity of a Land Regis-
" try's Office being established at this place for the accom-
" modation of Emigrants and others desirous of purchasing
" farms, Cotton, and Indigo Plantations, Building Allot-
" ments, etc., and feeling perfectly convinced that ere long
" the Capitalists and enterprising men of England will turn
" their attention to this highly gifted and rising settlement;
" for—
" Far as the eye can reach or billows roam,
" Survey their empire and behold their home.

" The present magnificent crop of cotton has now established
" beyond all doubt the future success of this young Colony.

" Persons having Property for disposal of the above kind
" will do well to register the same, as no charge will be made
" for registration."

" S. Benningfield,
" Auctioneer and Land Agent."

Two events of importance marked the year 1849—the
death of Lieut.-Governor Martin T. West, on the 1st
August, and the arrival on June 11th of the Reverend William Henry Cynric Lloyd, M.A., who had transhipped at
the Cape to the schooner *Douglas*, Captain Smerdon, to
take up his appointment, under the Crown, of Colonial
Chaplain, bestowed upon him by Earl Grey, Secretary of
State for the Colonies, in November, 1848. He elected to
settle in Durban, where he also acted for a time as Military
Chaplain. He was destined to spend his life in the Colony,
less to the advantage of himself than to Church and State,
and "the beggar at his gate." He died in 1881, aged 80,
and it was said that he had baptised, married, and buried
half the population of Durban. He was a Christian gentleman, genial, courteous, and popular, inseparably connected
with the history of Durban, as I hope to show further on.

CHAPTER IV.

SECOND CLEARING.

HAVING now brought the history of Durban to a period when it became a township under the administration of British officials—to a time when the first European Immigration set in, and people began to qualify themselves as Colonists by taking up the land, and engaging in such occupations as their means or tastes allowed, their inexperience or dire necessities obliged, I am forced reluctantly, for the sake of the story, to introduce a few words of a personal nature, and parenthetically to stray away with my readers, that they may understand how I came to know all that I have here set down, and in order to satisfy them that this superstructure of Durban's History rests upon a tolerably certain foundation, the life-time experience of one who " has been there." To complete my figurative clearing of the ground, I must explain how I was constituted a Colonist; the qualification I brought with me, and the necessities that have since forced me into strange company. When I say " forced," I plead the words of the Poet who says, " There's a Divinity that shapes our ends, rough-hew them as we will!" This I do with greater complacency since the fatalistic motto of my family happens to be, " Che sara sara." (*) My grandfather was a gentleman of Kent, claiming to be a scion of the younger son's branch of the Bedford family, whose arms and crest he bore. He died

---

* " What will be will be."

immediately prior to my father's birth, leaving the latter, the only son, large landed estates and the family mansion, "Longlands," Foots Cray, Kent. My grandmother was young and good looking; a woman, not to put too fine a point on it, obstinately imperious. The accident of my father's birth, or my grandfather's Will, caused her to flout the rest of the family, who of course called in the Law, and landed the whole estate in Chancery, nominally for the benefit of all the minors, period A.D. 1804. Chancery practice was then both good and lasting, so "the parties thereto" kept the ball rolling—*i.e.* round and round—until my Aunts had leave to marry and my father had attained his majority. Then what was left of the estate was duly apportioned after the costs of 22 years had been "adjusted and settled." Thus freed from the custody of his mother and with a restricted income, the young country squire set out to see life, but speedily fell victim to the charms—as they wrote at that period—of Miss Ann S. Barsham, the daughter of a Suffolk Solicitor. The few wild oats he might have possessed having been sown, he married her, and brought his bride home to "Longlands"; sending his masterful mother to Bath, or Cheltenham. The result of these arrangements was myself, born at "Longlands," and christened at Foots Cray Church in 1832. I opened my eyes to this world and its knowledge some years later at Greenwich, where we had a villa and a small estate, in consequence of being told that we were not going back home again, and that little boys should not ask questions about "horses, carriages, and servants before people." After years disclosed the fact that my father suffered from brothers-in-law, all well-to-do men with special gifts, borrowing money on partnership lines being the chief. Inventions, patents, and "safe things" eventually wore away the paternal acres, and left my generous, confiding parent with a diminishing income and an increasing family. He inherited a large Water Mill at East Greenwich, and for some time carried on the business of Miller. The lofty Mill building is still standing, but the Mill ponds are drained, and the place converted into Chemical Works. I was sent to a large Boarding School at Turnham Green, and had George Augustus Sala for a room-mate. (He both wrote and illustrated MSS. Novels even at that time!) De Foe and Captain

Marryat were "our" Authors, engendering in our imaginations a tendency for piracy on the high seas, if commissions in the Royal Navy were not to be obtained for us.   One dear schoolfellow, skilled with pencil and brush, especially in Marine subjects, fire and smoke, illustrated our "engagements" and battle pieces.   He became an artist, but died early.   "Robinson Crusoe" was as much to us as to Mr. Betteridge, while the gymnasium, with its masts and ropes and planks, gave us practical experience in "cutting out," boarding, or nailing the colours to the mast.

After about three years of this, I was removed to Stepney Grammar School, with the view of advancement in the classics, but I knew better than that—sailors did not use the dead languages—so I took my canings with equanimity, devoting my attention to French and Geography, and really struggled hard to acquire Mathematics, as an accessory to Navigation.   I haunted the East India Docks, and took to experimenting with gunpowder and home-made projectiles. I was then quartered on an uncle, one of the brothers-in-law.   His servants proclaimed me a "limb," and I now think the family were right in regarding me as "a young scamp," though of course my dear mother said they did not understand me.   The Council, chiefly Aunts, offered me the advantages of the University, with a view to a professional career.   Dreading more study of Latin, Greek, and Hebrew, I positively refused, and demanded "a life on the ocean wave."   For this I was practically excommunicated, with pious anathemas.   An old sea Captain, to whom my father took me, rather fired than cooled me with his dreadful yarns, notwithstanding that he solemnly assured me, betwixt his pipe and his glass, that I was "like a young bear with all my troubles to come."   I don't know his name, but I remember him as "Count Shucksen" (originally Mr. Chucks in "Peter Simple").   Three or four years in a merchant ship was prescribed, but my mother insisted that it must be in a genteel capacity.   "Midshipmen wanted!" led to my father paying a premium, and my acceptance by the owners of a large East Indiamen as one of their "young gentlemen" with a cabin and mess to ourselves.   Alas, the register ticket that the Merchant Seamen's Act then enforced described me bluntly as "Apprentice."   For a few weeks I enjoyed the felicity of my ambition, swaggering about in loosely cut trousers, gold band and buttons, until I joined the ship.

Then I experienced the ocean wave, and the many strange things that constitute a home on the rolling deep. I served with distinction, as the newspapers say, for four years on voyages to the East Indies, and was finally promoted to be third mate. A difference of opinion with the Captain induced me to leave the ship at Bombay, with the idea of seeing life, and returning home overland with one of our passengers, a young man of fortune. Too late, I found my friend's drafts dishonoured, as he had been sent away on the round voyage for prudential reasons by his guardians, and myself in debt. I wrote home for assistance; my father, incensed at my leaving the ship, sent but a trifle, and I then learnt that, dazzled by the Railway mania of 1846, he had speculated in shares, and lost so heavily that he had decided upon emigrating. He had chosen the new Colony of Port Natal, near the Cape, and I was either to return at once, or join him there. My landlord, having taken all I had, accepted my promises in lieu of balance, and let me go. I joined a brig, whose Captain I knew, and worked my passage home before the mast. Tarry and dirty, degraded and humiliated, I returned to our reduced home in London and forswearing the sea, tried to cheer the gloom that had settled upon my mother and sisters at the prospect before them. My unfortunate father had gathered up the fragments of his fortune, some £2,000, and decided to go out to Natal under what is known as J. C. Byrne's Emigration Scheme, whereby each emigrant received so much land per head, in addition to their passage out, for so much cash down. I found my father had invested all his money in agricultural implements and hardware, so there was but little left for me to superintend, except the final packing and leave takings. The ship *Herald* was laid on, and we could have secured berths, but I persuaded my parents to wait for the next vessel, which was the old East India Company's frigate, *Minerva*, with gun ports on her lower deck, quarter galleries, and stern lights. We accordingly secured a large stern cabin with suitable conveniences and accommodation, loaded up our belongings, and, with about 280 other emigrants, left the East India Docks in May, 1850, anchoring at Natal on the 3rd July, in the same year. On the night of the 4th the ship parted her cable, and drifted on to the end of the Bluff, where she became a total wreck immediately after all on board had been safely landed. We brought ashore what clothes we could carry in our hands and on our persons, and, in addition, a cash box containing £50. All the rest, residue and remainder of my father's estate and effects remain where he left them, and now constitute an integral part of the Bluff foreshore. We were a family of seven, and not insured.

Though so far biographical, the preceding remarks are not set down from vanity, but merely as an instance of the sad experience of hundreds of decayed gentlemen forced to emigrate, whose utter unfitness for the trials and exigencies of Colonial life are only counterbalanced by their proud resolve to do or die, rather than stand dependent and humiliated before their wealthier relatives in the Old Country. Unfortunately, it is the devoted wife and dutiful daughters who suffer most; the boys soon adapt themselves to their surroundings. Yet it is certain many of the children of our fellow-passengers will leave their family names honourably recorded on the roll of fame, as Colonists, and Natalians.   With us were the Coweys, (Durban), Anderson (Pine Town), McLeod (Richmond), Finnemore (Pietermaritzburg), Sam Williams and Jefferies (Pietermaritzburg), Relph and Moor (Estcourt), Waltons (Ladysmith), Questeds (Isipingo), and many others.

So far, all has been plain sailing, but now, like the *Minerva*, I am landed, as I may say, fast aground, for, perhaps from lack of literary method and experience, I do not see how to continue without the apparent egotism of burdening Durban's history with details of a personal character, seeing that, apart from public records, I rely in a good measure for events and dates upon my private diaries, an extension of the log-book habit acquired at sea. But, like our earlier settlers, I will make the best of my circumstances, relying, as they did, upon the sympathy and kindly criticism of friends, who, with me, can look back to those early days of Durban, and can now view with pride the superstructure which each one has borne a hand in erecting. Thus here I complete what I may fairly consider the groundwork of my History.

CHAPTER V.

1850.

AS the Mahommedan dates events from the " Hejira," so the aboriginal settlers of Natal noted events as " before" or " after the Emigrants." The modern descendants of those Emigrants lightly and disparagingly refer to that period as " The year one." To them the stories of England, or of the old family, are but " tales of my grandfather "; to them the tangible present is naturally of more moment than the traditional glories of the past. Yet it is well that history should award to their progenitors the honour and distinction which they earned by their early struggle to create Natal, and thus bring home to the minds of their luxurious, well-to-do children the consideration of the problem, where they would have been without their fathers!

The Emigrants themselves recollect it as the " Pumpkin and Mealies" time. Later arrivals speak of this hallowed, ever-to-be respected, though ambiguous, transitory period as " The Fifties." In " the year one," ships, on arriving from England, generally made the land down south, then stood boldly in to the gap forming the mouth of the Umlaas River, to discover no signs of a harbour, and to find that the prominent headland a little further on was probably the Cape Natal of the Charts. Edging along a safe distance from the shore, the anxious gaze of the Emigrants soon descried the lofty Bluff, with its mass of dark green foliage. The sharp-eyed scarcely considering this as forest, looked in vain for signs of habitation, other than occasional columns of smoke. They noted the rocky shore, light yellow sands, and ever-breaking surf, and would declare they saw elephants, lions, or other invisible game, while the moving ngure of a "black savage" on the beach awakened universal interest, tinged with alarm. Rounding the Bluff, they marked its prominent Cave Rock, its conical rounded extremity, draped in green of various shades, through which patches of red and yellow alternated downward to the dark, rocky foreshore, with its narrow strip of light sand and thundering breakers. The ship slowly folded its wings, and, stopping in what appeared to be a large open bight of the sea, dropped anchor.

There was a small flagstaff on the top of the Bluff, but, as the man in charge was not always at home or awake, the flagstaff at the Port Captain's house, on a low range of sandhills to the South, was used by Captain William Bell and his family to communicate with the shipping at anchor. The Emigrants assembled on deck, and gazed with more complacency and interest than did Vasco da Gama on the same Country, since they were about to occupy and make it their future home. A bright sun, and a sky flecked with fleecy clouds above them, a deep blue sea beneath and around them, gently undulating, with but an occasional splash to mark the swell. A long, low-lying belt of bush ended in bare sandhills at the Point, while beyond and behind this was visible a range of sombre, green-hued hills, apparently covered with forest, which commenced far away to the Southward, and seemed to extend in an unbroken line, without sign of house or vestige of cultivation, right along the Coast on the West, until lost in the haze to the North. A portion of this they subsequently knew as the Berea. The Bluff, bold and prominent, seemed to run back a long way parallel to those hills, while, in the far inland distance, high ground, evidently mountainous, could be distinguished. In the opening, or waterway, between the Bluff and the Sandspit, there were occasional breakers, indicating a reef or a bar, while the whole yellow-sanded shore, as far as eye could reach, was fringed with continuous foam and its attendant spray cloud. A slight indentation in the hills, N.-Westerly, gave promise of a river in their vicinity, while the glimpse of blue water, running in along the Bluff, indicated that a tidal lagoon, or shelter for small craft, lay within, and that, there, the Emigrant might expect to find the inner bay or harbour of Port Natal, a conclusion safely hazarded by the evidence of the masts and yards of a Brig or Schooner, showing over the sandhills beyond the flagstaff. The only other sign of civilised occupation was a white barrack-like building, small and insignificant, prominent on a sandhill, about which a scarlet coat appeared or a bayonet occasion- ally flashed, indicating military occupation by the Queen's forces. No other sign of British possession was discover- able excepting a tall flagstaff away in the Bush inland, flying a large blue and white flag bearing the strange device, " Lloyds." (*) It is a singular fact that, to this day after 50 years' occupation, the stranger driven to our shores would see no outward visible sign, neither fort, flag, bayonet, or scarlet coat, proclaiming our Nationality. Satisfied with what was to be seen, the Emigrant thought of landing; the Captain had been busy signalling with flags, and now an- nounced that a boat would come out bye and bye, while the Doctor was to be ready to certify that they were all well.

Then began the packing up, as everyone intended going ashore in the first boat. The father bundled up the bed- ding and spare clothing, throwing overboard many uncon- sidered trifles, while the prudent mother saw to the final bagging of her saved-up stores of Biscuits, Preserved Pota- toes, Soup-and-Bouilli, etc., with such odds and ends of the children's belongings as could not be got into the boxes in the hold. Late in the afternoon, while the boys, to pass the time, are busy fishing, the cry of " boat coming " brings all hands on deck to see a white whaleboat jumping up and down over the waves on the Bar, then pulling steadily straight for the ship. As it comes within range, the Captain eyes, with suspicion, four nondescript ruffians rowing, with a one-eyed man standing up and steering with an oar. Upon their heads straw hats, embellished with ostrich feathers, veldt-schoons on their feet, and clothing of a bushranger cut on their persons; bearded and swarthy,

* G. C. Cato was appointed agent in July or August, 1850.

they might be honest, but they strangely resembled "long-shore-men," if not released convicts.   The Captain, not caring for them to come on board among the unprotected maidens in his charge, hurls a few nautical adjectives at them to enquire their business.   The man with the steer oar makes believe to touch his hat, and announces that he is a Pilot and Coxswain of the Port Boat, and adds that "Captain Bell, the Port Captain, wants your report, where "you are from, and if there is any sickness on board," etc., etc.   The boat is allowed to come alongside, and its occupants are more tnan stared at, while the Captain and Doctor do what is necessary.   The Pilot leaves again with a remark that it will be all right, and that a cargo boat will come out to-morrow to bring the passengers ashore.   The entire landing and shipping business was practically in the hands of Mr. G. C. Cato, who, seeking to avail himself of his experience at Algoa Bay, had attempted landing cargo on the Back Beach in a similar manner—that is, by lighters or surfboats hauled ashore by means of hawsers running through sheaves at both ends of the boats.   The tidal cross currents, the N.E. winds, damaged boats, lost anchors, and other Natal experiences, obliged him to abandon this plan.   Thereupon, such of his boats as were suitable were fitted with masts and sails to cross the Bar, while in fine weather the open lighters were partly rowed and partly towed out by boats.   As a rule, they went out empty to return loaded.   The getting back was always contingent upon the Bar's caprice, for it would lie sleeping and inviting until you were just smiling "over," when a wave properly called "a blinder," would curl up, "and scatter all the features of your face."   I have myself assisted to row these boats with long sweeps to and from vessels outside, fortunately without accident, though such frequently happened to the crews of sailing boats when crossing.   The sailing cargo boat of the period was between eighteen and twenty tons capacity, with white men for a crew.   The charge for landing averaged about 12s. 6d. per ton.   Arrived alongside, the Emigrants' boxes, furniture, and bedding, were slowly transhipped, stowed at both ends, leaving a space in the centre.   Then the women and children were hoisted out in a chair made from a cask, and deposited in the bobbing, jumping boat with sundry bumps and bruises.   The men and boys essayed to get on board from the narrow side ladder, as the boat rose and fell, but not always success-fully. The boatmen decided when they were loaded, gave the word to let go, hoisted their jib, and, with farewell cheers exchanged with the ship, dropped astern, sheeted home the mainsail, and headed for the Bar; which according to the wind was not always reached without tacking. As the boat neared the white line marking the Bar, the chaff of the youths who disported themselves on the little deck was suddenly quenched on being roughly ordered below, while the hatches were put on. Who can portray or realise the mental agony endured by those frail women and chil-dren (of the men we will say nothing) shut down in a hot, stuffy, dark, and offensive cellar, moving in a topsy-turvy fashion, with just a corner of a hatch left uncovered by tarpaulin to admit light and air, some seasick, others mur-muring a prayer, and children crying, while the emotions of the boldest were tensely strung by the implied possibility of accident and death. The boatmen consolingly assure them it will be only for a few minutes—" just while we cross, to keep yer things dry, in case any water slops on board." Then a gruff order, the hatch is put on, and all is darkness, the boat turns round and round and bottom up. She is surely going down head first! Angry water is heard above and below, while things animate and inanimate are mingled together indiscriminately, one upon another. A groan, a scream, an oath or two, a clutching at infants, a gasp for breath, seemingly half-an-hour's endurance, then God's light and air once more, as a cheery voice, the hatch and stream-ing tarpaulin removed, announces "Only a couple o' seas, missis, and here y'are at Port Natal." The deeply-vowed "never no more" of these occasions have been faithfully kept, for numbers surviving that horror have never re-crossed the Bar, notwithstanding the modern inducements of steam tugs, flags, music, and good company. The cargo boat now on a level keel, its gasping passengers, crouched on their possessions in its hold, glance through the now open hatchway, and feel somewhat reassured as they note the green bushes on the lofty Bluff gliding by. Men get to the deck and, as the boat turns into the harbour shutting out the Bar and the ship from view, are rewarded, refreshed and inspired by one of the grandest sights of their lives, a magnificent landlocked Bay, some $7\frac{1}{2}$ square miles in extent and 12 miles in circumference, presenting one unbroken level sheet of water, fringed all round with trees to the water's edge, where one or two small trading vessels, with a cargo boat or two, are at anchor, and lighters and a few rowing boats resting on the beach.

Slowly rounding the sandy Point on the right hand, the Port Office flagstaff is recognised, while evidence of harbour work is seen in a few groins of stakes and stones built along the shore at right angles to the sandhills; then the Port Captain's wooden cottage, perched on a sandhill and half hidden by bushes; immediately after an imposing gable-ended structure, evidently of brick with a plastered front and a slated roof. It might be a stable or a warehouse, but these irrelevant conjectures are silenced by the sight of the real live soldier in scarlet coatee, with musket and bayonet, doing sentry-go before its front; while an adjacent sentry box gives testimony of the permanency of his occupation. Then the Emigrants learn that this is the Custom House, and are duly awed and gratified, feeling that, though Colonists, they are Britons still. Sail is taken in, and the boat bumps upon the sandy beach opposite a roomy barn-like edifice with its gable to the Beach, built of timber, weatherboarded and roofed with yellow-wood planks, which being tarred present a dingy appearance. This is the Landing Establishment, office and warehouse, of Mr. G. C. Cato, a short, sharp, clean shaved, American-looking man in white clothes and a large Manilla hat worn at all angles on the head, according to the humour of the hour. His clear incisive voice fires orders right and left, and sets the loungers about the beach in motion. The only person not affected is stout Port Captain Bell, who in blue hip jacket and white trousers, with hands behind his back, paces a short quarterdeck walk, with beaming genial face, having an eye for the newcomers, and an ear for information as to the Bar or the ship.

The Natives of those days were primitive and innocent; having no canoes, they knew nothing of boats or their ways, regarding them somewhat as sentient beings, appendages of the white man, equally erratic and uncertain in their movements; hence in boats they were almost useless, but their "main strength and stupidity" were skilfully utilised

in lifting, hauling and pushing about the beach, loading or
discharging.   Employed at this work, they were all but
naked, the "moucha" being tucked up under the arm pits,
when wading out to the boats.   The Emigrants regarded
them with mingled sentiments, their fine physique calling
for admiration, while their light attire was bewildering;
the climax was reached when the boatmen told the new-
comers to "jump on the niggers' backs, they'll put you
ashore dry, they're quite safe."   As the water was up to
the thighs, there was no help for it!   First, a few lads,
then the young men; the Natives laughing and joking,
returned prancing and shouting for fresh loads, to the
scandal of the unmarried women, who persistently looked
anywhere but on shore, and made excuses for delay until
all the rest were out.   The rude impatient boatmen beginning to swear, the maidens accepted their fate, and, with
flaming cheeks, allowed two stalwart black men to carry
them to land, sedan chair fashion.   The moment their feet
cleared the water, down they jumped, and ran indignantly
to their friends.   All goods were carried on shore and deposited promiscuously; things too heavy for one Native's
head were shouldered by two or more; a very heavy package
were entrusted to as many as could cluster round it, and the
chances were even that it was dropped in the water, or
without ceremony on the heavy yielding sands, directly the
feet of the carriers reached land.   Subsequent recovery or
removal was a matter of talk, deliberation, or noisy exertion,
redolent of bad language.

Such was the classical mode in which the majority of the
Emigrants landed in Natal, as the Romans did in Britain,
for no jetty was built for years.   In the case of distinguished personages, the difficulty was bridged over by the
intervention of a row-boat and a stout plank.   Our fore-
fathers were met by the curious crowd which for some
reason always gathers on beaches; one or two stray Custom
House officials; resident wives with their children, wagon
drivers and natives, a Merchant or his Clerks, a "long-shore-
man" or two, and a small party of soldiers from the Block
House, off duty, in dirty white trousers with cotton braces
festooning their sides, grey cotton shirts with sleeves rolled
up, round woollen forage caps with a diminutive brass door
number, surmounted by a bugle, in front, and a little red

tuft on top, clay pipes with brass or wire covers, in their mouths. Courtesies exchanged, conversation and advice became general and bewildering, until at last the Agent of J. C. Byrne and Co. suggested a move townwards. Then were the Emigrants introduced to the two greatest factors in their future lives and fortunes, the ox and his wagon. Men from the Shires joined in deriding the turn-out, exchanging bucolic jokes at the expense of the span of ten or twelve small Zulu oxen, and the tented wagon to which they were so loosely attached. The gentleman looked in vain for a cab, and the town-bred artizan for the carrier's cart. All had to submit to being "loaded up" together once more. The men walked, generally behind, to be out of the way of the driver's twenty feet whip, while the women and children squeezed in on the top of their goods. If the tide did not admit of their coming up by the Bay Beach, the procession wended its way through the sandy bush road, the journey terminating at the Emigrants' barracks. To serve this purpose, a wooden building partitioned off and fitted with bunks had been erected by Byrne and Co. on the open ground occupied by the present Gaol. Here temporary accommodation was afforded, and tents were erected by such as owned them, but the place and its surroundings did not encourage any prolonged sojourn. In theory the Emigrants were supposed to proceed immediately to their several allotments of land, which were sub-divisions of the original farms granted to Byrne and Co., such as "Harmony," "Boileau" —where Richmond and Byrnetown are located—" York," "New Leeds," and the "Cotton Lands," Verulam, and Tongaat way on the Coast, but they found on arrival that the surveys of their allotments had not been completed, and might be indefinitely delayed. Hence arose heartburnings and future trouble. In any case the occupants of the Barracks were expected to move out when the next ship arrived. The Agent and local Manager of J. C. Byrne and Co. was Mr. John Moreland (his wife was a cabin passenger in the *Minerva*.) He was ubiquitous in receiving and locating the people, and in personally conducting them when taking up their allotments, pending survey. He was loaded with all the complaints of the voyage, and freely abused for the want of things which Natal did not supply. He was indefatigable, almost unwearying, courteous, and con- ciliatory. He endured with apparent equanimity the anathemas with which the citizen-emigrant loaded his principals for not supplying those Edens they expected to get for their money, and for the absence of markets which did not exist. Who can say that all this exertion, worry, and abuse did not shorten his life!

It was, however, the men from the Shires, more particu- larly the Yorkshire lads, who viewed their lands with other eyes, and, " full of wise saws and modern instances," set to work to till the land, and utilise the ox and his brother the Native. Adam Smith's axiom, "The country makes the town," should be ever kept before our Colonial Statesmen, notwithstanding the delusive claim of Commerce to consti- tute Natal a Forwarding Agency for inland States.

It was to these early settlers that the towns of Pieter- maritzburg and Durban owe their development and growth. Many and arduous were their struggles and privations to produce enough for their own requirements, and to yield a surplus for the town. After getting the Emigrant to Barracks, the first necessities of life were food and shelter. Some found employment in the growing townships, where considerable building was in progress, though the majority of the structures in Durban of any pretensions were of wattle and daub. Mechanics readily found employment at good wages; they had to put up at canteens and so-called board- ing-houses of a very rough and ready character. But as time advanced, these were made more comfortable, since thrifty wives of steady mechanics would take a house as soon as it was finished, and as many boarders as she could find beds for. Others again erected thatched huts, im- proving on the Native pattern by inserting a frame door about six feet high, and, instead of making the building circular, elongated the structure by combining two huts into one, having two centre poles and a partition, either wattled or of canvas, dividing the sitting from the sleeping room. Into the sides of this were thrust a red gin case, cut in two, for window frames, which in the absence of glass were covered with calico. Some artists, however, constructed movable sashes to open, hung on side screws, which they contrived to glaze with the prevalent window glass of the period, imported for the Dutch trade, in squares

6 inches by 4. In such a well-constructed hut, Mr. John Richardson Goodricke first lived in West Street. In this he commenced and carried on business as an Attorney. Three huts of abnormal length, enclosing a hollow square, constituted the roadside hotel, or "Accommodation House," known as "Carbo Fisher's,' near Camperdown, on the high road to Pietermaritzburg. Natives were employed to construct huts, generally by contract; ordinary huts costing about 10s., while finished huts for Europeans would cost 30s. or 40s. each. The materials consisted of wattles, and the "Konotie" tree-runner from the bush for tying, together with poles for door frames, ridge pole and props; rushes from the swamps; packing-case materials for door and window, with clay and cow-dung for floors. In hut building, as in other things, there can be introduced the refinement of a fine art. Some persons had the thatch of coarse grass, or the usual rushes neatly packed and well pinned in regular rows; Native mats under the thatch, and wattled or reed partitions inside, with a curtain before the inner doorway; the clay floor pounded hard and smooth with stones, and smeared with cow-dung; a good trench cut round outside to carry off the rain water; sometimes with a light trellis porch of reeds in front, a slab of stone for a door step, a scraper of hoop iron, and a second-rate hut for a kitchen. Such constituted, with a few flower beds surrounding, and a contented mind, the happy, comfortable, and primordial home of many English families.

The town settler was much better off than his compatriot in the country in respect to furniture, since tents and huts do not lend themselves to its use, so the general rule was to be content with "bush furniture." Iron bedsteads were not then invented, excepting a massive six-legged folding affair used by the Military in Barracks. Four stumps driven into the mud floor supporting the lid of a packing case, served for the family table; the same outside the hut door, if a log was not available, served as a washing-stand for the members of the family, as also for the pots, pans, and crockery; while the bed was made of six forked sticks hammered level, with a sort of wattled door laid in the forks. Mattresses were usually sacking filled with dry seaweed or grass; planks slung from the roof, ship fashion, served for library and larder, while sticks thrust into the ribs of the hut served for clothes-pegs and the inevitable gun. Lamps of oil were only indulged in by the rich; mould tallow candles and a bottle served the commonalty. When out of stock (for candles were mostly home-made), the kitchen-hut fire met most purposes after dark, as the hard labour of those times induced early hours, and promoted the health, wealth, and wisdom of the proverb. Some persons, taking example from their country friends, tried houses built of sod, but the sandy soil of Durban did not encourage the experiment. Reeds were plentiful at the Umgeni, Umbilo, and Umhlatuzan. They were cut by the Natives, brought on the heads of the women in long bundles, and were readily purchased in exchange for Emigrant biscuit, old clothes, and hoop iron. They were universally utilised in house building in place of laths for partitions and ceilings, for stables, outhouses, and fences, cart and wagon tents. Experience, however, disclosed the unwelcome fact that they were the natural home of the indigenous " B. flat." The general style of architecture was the " Wattle and daub," thatched with " tambootie " or " tambookie " grass. The Bay supplied mangrove posts for uprights; the Berea bush poles and wattles. Daub was composed of clay or ant-heap, tempered with sand and cow-dung, trampled into mud by Natives, and served in balls or buckets to the operator, according to the consistency required, under the generic Native term of " daagah." Daub was usually applied by the hand, in which operation the Native was a proficient. It was only in the finishing touches that any attempt was made to use the plasterer's trowel, or a rough wooden substitute. The doors and windows were made from yellow wood, at first imported, but afterwards supplied through Pietermaritzburg. Windows were generally hung upon butt hinges; wooden floors were rare, the rule being unburnt bricks, or clay and cow-dung; fire places and chimneys were only used for kitchens, and were seldom made of burnt bricks, as these were expensive. Roofs were generally " hipped," on account of the winds, as well as to allow verandahs all round the house, which were utilised for bedrooms, pantry and kitchen, office or workshop. The verandah in front was usually supported by sawn timber posts on stumps, or stone blocks, while an ornamental fascia

board gave a style and finish to the new home, when decorated with a bright green coat of paint.   Thatching became
a trade, of which W. Granger and a man named Petty
were the leading exponents.   The thatch was secured by
lengths of wild rattan sewn on to the wattle (or sawn wood)
battens of the roof, by rope yarns, though in the first
instance "konotie" fibre, or strips of wet bullock hide, had
been in vogue.   The ridge was protected by a plastered
cap of "daagah," tarred and whitewashed.

Bricks were made in several places, Umgeni, Greyville,
and the foot of the Berea (Currie's Fountain), as also at the
back of the Berea (Brickfields).   They were expensive,
averaging when delivered about one penny each.   They
were sold at the yards either burnt or green (i.e., sun-dried);
the cartage was extra, and at the option of the purchaser.
Green bricks were therefore in demand for all inside work,
and may be found in some few of the remaining old buildings.   In the country the settler made his own bricks as
best he could, and I know ladies, now living, who as girls
assisted in that operation.   Lime came with our sugar
from Mauritius (coral lime), though Walter ("Wattie")
Brunton and Chas. McDonald soon supplied the market
from shells dug up from the Bay and burnt in the open air
at Cato's Creek, and at the Congella.   As wall paper was
not, whitewash supplied its place on the unplastered walls,
and, in addition, the exterior was finished off with a sort of
splashboard, skirting or dado, done in coal tar, a mixture of
coal tar, "daagah," and lime being frequently utilised for
the verandah floors.   Ceilings of "bafta" (unbleached
calico) were tacked to battens resting upon the cross-beams
of the house.   Such ceilings are still to be found in Durban
papered over or whitewashed.   They proved to be dust
traps, which, after flapping up and down with the wind,
bagged in the centre, and, as time advanced, became the
playground for rats, who left their marks there.   Rats
were not infrequently followed by snakes.   These houses
were scarcely dry, before the industrious British Colonist
found out the reason for King Solomon's recommendation
to go to the ant and consider its ways, for the ant came to
him and taught him to say things opposed either to Pro-
verbs or Psalms.   However, neither prayers nor poison
seemed to prevail against their clans, white, black, or grey;

so in due time his house became the home of all the insect world and creeping things in Natal, excepting "Cockroach Major," the ship or Indian cockroach, who did not become popular until the introduction of Coolies about ten years later. Some townsmen of a handy turn built themselves frame houses of yellow wood, weather boarded, and floored, with thatched roofs ; when lined with "bafta," papered with illustrated papers, or cheap wall paper, painted, tarred, and white-washed, they were tolerably comfortable, and, being built on stumps of the salt-grown mangrove, were free from the white ant ; many of these can still be said to be standing, if the Irishman's description of the gun he inherited from his grandfather, with only a new lock, a fresh stock, and another barrel, may be applied to them. But as years and the white ant advanced, these gave way to bricks and mortar, affording employment for Emigrant British workmen in all his constructive branches. Iron buildings were a novelty, introduced in England at the Great Exhibition in Hyde Park, but business men had availed themselves of this material before Sir John Paxton erected his Crystal Palace. Mr. E. P. Lamport, representing Lamport and Holt, of Liverpool, had been settled in Aliwal Street, as a Merchant, with a fine large warehouse and dwelling house of corrugated iron, having circular roofs. the idea of the period being that all iron roofs should be arched. Messrs. R. W. and Chas. Dickinson, Dickinson Brothers (now Dickinson and Fisher), had started their ironmongery business in West Street, in such a store, and, when we arrived, doubled our grief by informing us of the extravagant prices they would have given my father for his entire stock, their own being exhausted. Mr. Richard Harwin also had an iron store on the opposite side of the road, for the sale of drapery, and gave employment to T. M. Harvey and, afterwards, to B. W. Greenacre. his successors of to-day. The quality of the iron of that period was excellent, and the corrugations of large size, as may to-day be seen in the sugar warehouse of Mr. John Robertson, Commercial Road, which was an actual portion of Paxton's Great Exhibition building, while St. Thomas' Church, on the Berea, was another product of that early time. As a rule, roofing, other than thatch, was of slates, especially for Government or first-class buildings, but the

erection of the double-storied building by Middleton and
Wirsing, at the Smith Street corner of the Market Square,
in 1850, and the roofing of the same with small sheets of
iron, fluted at both edges, and known as " Morewood's
tiles," led to their importation, and the general use of iron
for roofing, until the present form of corrugated iron
sheets became popular through the introduction of the
" Gospel Oak " brand. Buildings now found with slate
roofs (with 3 or 4 exceptions) may be ranked as of early
Natal period.   Numerous roofs of " Morewood's tiles " still
exist, though sadly dilapidated after wearing for thirty-five
years in our saline atmosphere, proving the good quality
of the early manufacture.

Fifty years of civilization have not brought sufficient wisdom to the intelligent Colonist to enable
him to circumvent the white ant.   This creation
is a blessing in disguise, so far as our decaying vegetation
is concerned. Her enemy, the Black ant, with her brother,
the Brown, or Sugar ant, and the little Red ant, are,
however, far more destructive to substantial structures,
owing to their persistent habit of undermining stone or
brick.   Can Sir John Lubbock, or any other authority,
say that the fall of Babylon, Baalbec, or Ephesus was to
be attributed more to man or earthquakes, than to King
Solomon's referee?   In those early days food was literally
obtained from hand to mouth, and the regularity of the
supply was entirely a matter of conjecture. All was fish
that came to our net, the result being many strange messes.
Python à la Conger eel, Young Monkey, Cane rat, Porcu-
pine, Ant-bear, Inguana, and Sea-cow bacon, all served
their turns, aided by Pumpkins and the Native wild fruits
for pies.   Mealies were abundant and cheap, but were long
in cooking and hard to masticate. Natives crushed them
on stones, while the Dutch showed how they could be
stamped. Milk was procurable from the Natives in clay
pots of their own make, or in calabashes, until they took
to the bottle. From them also were obtained Pumpkins
and Fowls; these last were brought in alive from the surrounding kraals, with their legs tied together, and slung
in bunches, head downwards at the ends of a pole.   Beef
was cheap and plentiful, 2d. to 2½d. per lb. for prime cuts.
Mutton there was none; goat being occasionally substituted

as a delicacy.   I think the price was 6d. per lb.   Flour was imported in 100 lb. bags from the Cape, but it was dear.   Boer meal, though imported, came also from Pietermaritzburg, and served for bread when well sifted or diluted with Cape flour, which was ordinarily reserved for pastry.   Rice was from Carolina, via London, in casks; a little came from Mauritius in bags.   Everybody began to plant vegetables, and to breed pigs and poultry.   The staple articles of food were Beef, Mealies, and Pumpkins, with Rice, Dry Beans, and Eschalots for flavouring, together with Brown Bread and Ship Biscuit (surplus stores).   The Germans produced Rye and Buckwheat, which they had to consume themselves.   They also went in largely for Pigs.   These, however, only found conditional favour with the British Emigrants since the original stock were said to have been brought by the Germans from Westphalia. They were very flat in the ribs, with arched backs, and legs like a greyhound.   Either the climate or the vegetation of Natal did not agree with them, for the race became extinct; Hampshire, Berkshire, and China breeds taking their place.   The Germans, however, soon brought the Sweet Potato into the Market, and it has ever since remained a popular article of diet.   The Irish, or "round" potato, and other garden stuff grown by the Emigrants, with Cape and American flour, Rice and Bacon, Poultry and Eggs, became plentiful after the first year of our settlement.   Butter was not scarce, but it was "very mixed," being Boer-made, and sent down from Pietermaritzburg in hide bags and old casks.   As our trade was chiefly with Cape firms, we received in exchange Cape commodities suitable for the Dutch trade, and to which our Emigrants had to adapt themselves until more familiar articles came to be imported from England.   Coffee was "Blue-bean-Rio," sold as imported "green."   Tea was the rough and coarse article made by John Chinaman expressly for the Cape Market, and known as "Caper," sold universally in 10 catty boxes (about 12 lbs.), a package convenient for the farmers.

The story goes that a Dutch East-Indiaman, homeward bound, was wrecked in Table Bay; her damaged cargo, principally tea, was salvaged, the teas dried, mixed, and repacked.   It was sold cheap, and for years so permeated the Old Colony and its distant homesteads that the farmers' wives acquired the taste, and refused other weak and insipid importations; so the Cape merchant had to yield to woman's influence, and order the reproduction of their cheering cup from China; hence the composition was branded " Caper " accordingly.

In numerous cases the early Emigrants, from want of taste and money, declined the expensive ·· Caper," contenting themselves with drying and infusing an indigenous herb both nutritive and refreshing, which is known to us as " Kafir Tea " (*Athrixia Phylicifolia*) A coarse salt made from sea water was imported from Algoa Bay; this we used for table salt, though the fastidious English housewife would dry and crush it fine, before using. Sugar, brown and yellow, was imported from Mauritius, in bags, the Boers preferring their sugar, like their tea, with some flavour to it. As luxuries, dates and tamarinds also arrived from Mauritius in stodgy masses, packed in sugar bags, while preserved ginger from China, dried raisins, apples, peaches, apricots, and sugar candy in boxes came from the Cape. Other luxuries consisted of Scotch sweetmeats in bottles, jams in earthenware pots, wines and spirits in hogsheads and half aums from the Cape, from whence also arrived, in considerable quantities, transhipped from Holland, gin in square flasks, packed in red and green cases. This liquor, which we knew as " Geneva " or ·· Hollands," is now known throughout South Africa as " Square face." Bottled beer, packed in cases, came from England. Cheese was rare, and for a time only the Dutch " Cannonball " variety was to be had at about 7s. 6d. each. As game was plentiful in the bush surrounding the town, buck-meat was a common article of diet, varied occasionally by bush-pig or blue or green pigeons; but fish was seldom to be had. My first venture was to join some young men, fellow passengers (E. Stafford, of East Griqualand, being one), in purchasing a small boat and a worn-out seine-net, and endeavour to get our living by fishing. The Congella Beach, the site of the slaughter of Capt. Smith's detachment, was recommended us, and we worked very hard, first, to find the fish, next, to capture them, then to get the boat back over the sand banks in reasonable time, and, lastly, in hawking them

around. **Though** prices were good, customers were scarce
and scattered, while the fish, in the first instance, were
never in the place we expected to find them, and did not
stay to be visited. Our hauls were seldom good for this
and other reasons, the badness of our net not being the
least. One or two of the company gave up, desiring to be
paid out. After a spasmodic struggle to earn our daily
bread by using the boat as a lighter, we had to part
company and pocket the loss. It was not until about
fourteen years later that fishing was taken up as an industry by white men, Bone and Owens, on the Bluff. The
death of Bone and the debts of the partnership terminated
the enterprise, the fine sea-going smack tney had built
being converted into a cargo boat.

Coffee, being in the bean, necessitated roasting. Many
and wasteful were the attempts of the inexperienced Briton
at this art, though proper sheet-iron drum-roasters were
sold for the Dutch trade. Frying pans were generally used,
enabling the operator to watch progress, sitting over a
smokey wood fire. Roasted, the coffee required grinding,
the crushing between stones by Natives proving in the
handling both wasteful and distasteful. Little box mills,
with a handle on top and a drawer underneath, were first
used, but the process was slow and unsatisfactory. Then
a larger mill with a handle at the side and two cheek pieces,
enabling it to be screwed to an upright post, came to be
usually adopted, and entrusted to the Native "boy" to
work. The economy of time, as also the contempt for
foreign ways entertained by the average Briton, induced
him to ignore the slow and laborious method of soaking
and stamping mealies in wooden mortars, this being the
Dutch method—especially as it involved boiling them in
milk—neither could he crush them on stones, as did the
Native, but the demands of his children for something
easier to digest than the tough, half-boiled yellow grain,
indigenous to the Country, and called "Kafir mealies,"
induced him to try them through the improved Coffee mill.
A revelation! ' Gigantic Coffee-mills were soon imported
with fly-wheel attached to the spindle, and double bolts to
hold it to tree stump or post, thus establishing the first
conical steel mealie mills. Mealie meal porridge, hot, cold,
fried, or baked, became the staple food of the white man and

E

his family.   The Native servant was permitted to grind his
allowance of mealies in the " machine " in his own time, to
save the delay that their boiling and mastication otherwise
involved.   By degrees, all Native labourers found boiled
mealies disagreed with them, and struck for the more satisfying "Impoopu."   Mealie meal consequently got to be
regularly ground and issued.   As an occasional luxury, a
handful of coarse Liverpool, or Algoa Bay, salt was bestowed
upon the Native, for which they were proportionately grateful.   We are indebted to those quiet, zealous, and unobtrusive men, the American Missionaries, for many things, not
the least of which is the seed of the large white Indian
corn that now distinguishes Natal as its staple, and is exhibited in England as a wonder.   They kindly published
numerous recipes as to Pop-Corn, Mush, Dough Nuts,
Johnny Cake, Hoe Cake, and other good things, with
molasses and without, but the Conservative Briton—tainted
with the same ignorant prejudice that obtained with the
starving Irish people during the first potato famine, when
they stigmatised the graceful donation from America of a
cargo of Indian corn meal as being only food for pigs—has
come to abusing mealie meal porridge, under the name of
" Poop," as fitting food only for Natives and convicts. Hence
to this day, we have but to a modified extent availed our
selves of the hundred-and-one ways of using or utilising the
mealie.   We need not disclaim against the prejudice or
apathy of either Boer or Native, while we continue to import
" Corn Flour," " Maizena," " Semolina," and " Hominy " by
the ton.

According to the Italian proverb, " God sends meat and
the devil sends Cooks."   The Emigrants in the year " one "
were not Cooks.   All things in their new world were out
of joint, few people having ever used wood fires, and fewer
still finding "Bois de vache" a good substitute for peat.
Open air fires, or fires in the mud encircled basin let into
the floor of a Kafir hut, or reed enclosed cook house, did
not lend themselves to the cook's art, but, especially in damp
weather, tried both the temper and the skill of the house
hold; bellows, reed blowpipes, or the ever-ready tin plate
being requisitioned to raise a flame.   With patience, the
kettle, frying pan, or gridiron could be " cooked "; but when
it came to baking, the operation was simply maddening. I

am not alone in having shed cloudy tears of temper, hunger
and wood smoke over that evil, though serviceable, article,
the baking-pot.   Stoves and kitchen ranges were left with
the civilised in the Old Country; here, the Dutch housewife
used the flat-bottomed, three-legged, cast-iron baking pot, or
"Camp oven," which was covered by a movable domed
lid with a little handle on top.   Settling the thing on three
stones to admit stout firebrands underneath, you fired up
while the bread was rising, or the pie being made.   A tin
pan held the baking; this had to be judiciously packed on
small stones, or a zig-zagged piece of hoop iron, to keep it
from the bottom; the lid, replaced, was loaded with such
embers as could be spared, choice chips and pieces being
contributed to build a fire on top.   Then began the struggle,
for so soon as the first firing was going well and pronounced
perfect, the kitchen boy would be wanted elsewhere, and
one or both fires would suffer.   Then storm and smoke,
while both "stupid" and fire were being blown up.   As
meal time approached, the contents were supposed to be
done, but the doubt could only be settled by the skilful
removal of the lid by means of a stick thrust through the
little central handle.   This was rarely accomplished without
cinders and short ends of firewood falling into the pot, while
the "boy," squatting on his haunches, held up the heavy
wobbling lid at the end of his stock.   The "missis," with
skirt between her knees, and hand protecting her eyes from
heat and smoke, inspected the contents, picked out the cinders, and burnt her arm, and, as often, her apron.   Meanwhile the frizzle in the baking pot ceased, the lid was
accordingly hurried on, and the "boy" hurried up with fuel
and bellows.   Too soon, or too late, the burnt or sodden
contents were served up, to be freely discussed, both before
and after grace.   In such manner, and with such food
appliances, did the sturdy Emigrant enjoy "all the comforts
of a home," without dyspepsia or the Beer-shop.

This state of things was improved as soon as the householder settled down, and had time to look about him, when
detached kitchens were built, usually of wood, having brick
chimneys and a raised hearth, the discarded hut being
utilised for the accommodation of the Native.   Water was
obtained from wells sunk in the backyard some six or eight
feet deep, into which casks without heads were inserted one

on top of the other, the top being sometimes protected by
a lid.   The water was lifted by hand with the aid of a cord
and a bucket.   The water of Old Durban was not nice,
but it was preferred to rain water off tarred roofs or dusty
thatch, combined with the flavour of wine or spirit hogsheads used as water butts.   Brick wells were not generally
constructed until the casks had caved in or been converted
into cesspools.   Of public wells, there was only one, Erf
No. 20, Smith Street, until after the incorporation of the
Borough.   Firewood was obtained from the nearest Bush
for the taking, or bought in bundles from Native women at
the door.   It was usually the kitchen boy's employment
on alternate afternoons to go to the bush for the family
supply of fuel.

Fire was obtained from matches " made in Germany " or
Sweden, known as " Tandstickers " (Tandstickor).   They
were silent matches, little round rods tipped with phosphorus
and sulphur, sold in turned wooden boxes with a dab of glue
and sand on the bottom.   They were much appreciated by
horsemen and waggoners in the open air; but, as a rule,
most people carried flint and steel with a cylindrical brass
tinder box, adapted to pouch or pocket.   No Dutchman was
without one.   Darkness was illumined by the primitive
" Home light " of a tallow candle; tin or pewter moulds of
six or more were sold in all the stores.   Tallow was procured at the Butcher's, a twist of cotton wick suspended from
a twig, and the apparatus only awaited skilful manipulation.
Candles, both " Moulds " and "Dips," were regularly manufactured in Pietermaritzburg.   Fortunate was the housewife
who had brought snuffers with her; with most of us scissors
had to serve their place, and in their absence the fingers did
duty.   For drawing-room purposes, imported " composite "
candles were used, though they also required snuffing.
After a time, " Patent Sperm " were introduced, together
with good oil lamps of the " Moderator " and " Camphine "
class.   Paraffin oil was not introduced until 1859.

Having detailed all the first requirements of our Emigrant
in his praiseworthy efforts to take up his possession and
settle himself in the land, the only remaining item that may
prove of interest to his fashionably attired descendants is
that of clothing.   After the things brought with him had
given way to the heat, the tropical rains, bush thorns, and

the native " Wash boy," it was discovered that the children had been rapidly growing out of such things as remained to them ; so mother's ingenuity was taxed to cut down for the boys and let out for the girls. Sewing machines were not invented, and, as time did not admit of much needle-work, advantage was taken of the mildness of the climate to " go light," especially as ready-made articles were not easily procurable. Stockings went first, shoes afterwards, then trousers, and finally boys and girls, not actually living in Durban itself, were commonly seen in the light attire of " Cap and Gown." Father and mother had to adopt the Dutch-made " veldtschoens " and straw hats, or broad brimmed felt. Shirt sleeves were generally worn by the men, while the feminine portion dispensed with superfluities, and adopted the Dutch " Cappie " or sun bonnet for their constant outdoor work. Drab and blue moleskin, corduroy, navy-duck, and drill, " Huis-linen," calico, prints, bafta, and blue Salempore, Coburgs,. and a furniture pattern chintz were sold by the piece as imported for the Boer trade ; but storekeepers soon undertook to supply the newcomers by the ell or yard, which measures were regularly nailed on all counters, and it is asserted that, from force of habit acquired in the Boer trade, some retail shopkeepers would quote prices by the yard and measure by the ell ! (*) I have heard complaints that the stuffs bought in this country did not make up to the same advantage as those obtained when at home, because the yards generally ran short. These materials were toilfully fabricated into the necessary adorn-ments of our first parents, and our first " Colonial born." Locke has defined fashion as the " ostentation of riches." There was no fashion here ; the cut was unostentatious. Inexperienced mothers, before investing the sons with the father's effects, adopted the simple process of unripping them, and cutting out a new garment for the head of the firm from the fragmentary pattern. Ladies as a rule wore jackets descending to the hips, trimmed with white or scarlet worsted braid, belted in at the waist over a skirt, without " gores " gathered into a band ; knitted Polka jackets were also much in vogue.

Labour being the source of wealth, all things had to be paid for, but how ? Consider that the new Colonist had

---

* The Dutch ell is 27 inches, a difference of 25 per cent.

but little coin, that he had to pay for building sites, house material, Native wages, cartage, etc., while at the same time working hard for himself. Artizans earned from 6s. to 8s. a day. There was abundance of jobbing work for a handy man, so a few days' work for another would provide some ready money; credit was given for the balance, which had usually to be taken out in goods. We returned to the first principles of Commerce, "Exchange of Commodities," and, when we had no goods of our own, were content to barter our labour for those of other people. By working overtime and at night, the Emigrant got his own house completed, while his wife and daughters contributed both by direct labour and casual earnings to the family funds. For silver coin we were entirely dependent on the Military chest, and its circulation by the troops. My experience of that period and my frequent enquiries have elicited no clearer explanation as to how the initial start was accomplished, than the honest admission that the settler himself did not know; the general indefinite definition being, "Somehow"! A Yorkshireman said "Me and ma missis just fettled it together; ah thow't if them Blackies could live, ah could da' t' same." While a Scotch lady's secret was, "I just took care ma man die not hae the spending of a' the siller he brought hame." We may safely say that it was the low level of our condition coupled with the bright climate and the sense of "Liberty, Equality, and Fraternity," which induced industry, perseverance, and the bold adaptation of means to the end; the recognition of the value of small things, with the sinking of the pride that is ashamed of honest toil. The general acceptation of our position at this time is embodied in the first of the philosophical utterances of Mr. Sam Weller :— " We shan't be bankrupt, and we shan't make our fortunes; " we eats our biled mutton without capers, and don't care " for horseradish when we can get beef."

The respectable skilled artizan, having some education, force of character, tools, and small capital, soon set up his own workshop. To him necessarily gravitated casuals and later arrivals seeking employment. His permanency secured jobs, upon which he was enabled to retain such men of his trade as offered, and by degrees he developed into a Master-tradesman. In this way regular shops were established for Carpenters, Bricklayers, Blacksmiths, and Wagon builders.   A few individuals found employment as Bakers, Butchers, Boatbuilders, Brickmakers, Painters (Glazier and Decorator), Printers, Saddlers, Sawyers (pitsaws), Tinsmiths (Gunsmith, Brazier, Locksmith, and Engineer), Thatchers, Carters (Carrier), etc.   Many men of enterprise, with an aptitude for the mechanical arts, took to trades to which they had not been apprenticed, since there was no tyrannical Trades' Union to limit their abilities or prescribe their earnings.   Furniture and shop fittings were in great demand. Dry and well-seasoned yellow-wood, flatcrown, knobthorn, stinkwood, and red milkwood were invariably used.   Joiners and Cabinetmakers usually worked on their own accounts, and such first-class solid work did they produce that much of it is still to be found in the Colony, enriched by age and forty years polishing, though too frequently blemished by the incidents of transport, the carelessness of Natives, and the sportiveness of children.   The furniture most in request and made in Durban was bedsteads, tables, drawers, washstands, sideboard-cupboards, settees with arms, wardrobes, bookshelves, and office desks and stools.   Turnery was at first done by the Wagonbuilders, who had lathes capable of taking in a table leg; these lathes were driven from a large band-wheel worked by Natives.   As a natural consequence of his busy industry, the settler had to obtain assistance or cheap labour, and found the Native ready to his hand as a hewer of wood and drawer of water, so his services were at once enlisted, notwithstanding the inability of the contracting parties to converse with one another except in the sign languages.   The Native understood cattle and how to make a fire; he could fetch and carry; that was sufficient for the present.   The sense of right and justice which always dominates the mind of the British workman impelled him to offer the Native wages, food and shelter, according to the custom of the country.   This he found on enquiry to be defined in nautical terms as "Monkey's allowance, more kicks than ha'pence," for the Boers had left a legacy of unbelief in the propriety or fitness of the Native to acquire or receive wages; he should be thankful for the Baas's protection, shelter, with such scraps and cast off things as might fall to his lot.   If he was especially good, it was generally understood that at the end of a year's faithful service he might receive a cow, or even a cow and calf, worth about 25s. or 30s., but it too frequently happened that at the year's end the Baas found it inconvenient to part with either servant or beast.   If the Native dared to remonstrate, his life was made burdensome, with the gratifying result that he retired from active service to his Native bush, leaving the cow behind him, for to take the cow, allotted to him, meant pursuit and possible death.

The native is gregarious, so the allurements of the settlement, the abundance of beef, the splendid knives, hatchets, cotton blankets, picks, steel traps, brass wire, and beads that could be obtained for a few of the English shillings, which were always honourably paid for his goods or labour, induced him to accept service by the month (lunar), while the liberal settler considered that such rough talent would be sufficiently paid at the rate of 5s. per month with food and lodging.   Thus were the "Rights of Man" practically demonstrated to the satisfaction of all parties; but as time advanced, and the Native, without Tom Payne's teaching, acquired intelligence and skill, wages advanced and remained for some time at from 7s. 6d. for kitchen boy's pay, to 12s. for old hands.   The English also offered a cow (value from £1 10s. to £2) as an additional bonus for a year's service, but in practice this proved a failure, since no Native could be induced to remain at work for twelve consecutive months, his instincts and sentimental yearnings usually taking him home on short notice.   Once there, he forgot all about his moral or other obligations to his white employer.   Coins were unknown to the Natives, and required more brain power than they possessed to understand their values.   It was about this period that he named the copper penny "deeblish," and the silver fourpenny and threepenny pieces "pen."   Why "deeblish" I cannot say; but it is believed the designation "pen" arose from the emphatic attempts of the Colonists, when the threepenny coinage was first circulated by the soldiers, to explain with the aid of the fingers that this was "Three pens, and that one pen(ny) more, four see?"   Hence the "pens" sank into the Native's vocabulary.   Subsequently when florins were issued, certain canny Scots passed them off as halfcrowns, hence the Native, on discovering the difference, named the florin "Scotchman" (Imalie ker Scotchman).

The familiarity and mistaken kindness of the Emigrants towards the Natives scandalised the old settlers, and disgusted the Dutch families still residing in or about Durban. Certainly they committed grave faults and many errors of judgment, which were only corrected by experience, for they were diverted and amused, being pervaded by Sunday school teachings as to "A man and a brother," considered the "Nigger" a rum feller, very good-natured if fairly treated; didn't see any harm in him; certainly he was a bit stupid, but rare good fun, etc. So he was received into the house and treated as another child, or a very tame animal. No man is a hero to his valet. Hero worship declined in Natal, and the newly emancipated Native, who had hitherto regarded the white man as a Chief, mysterious and powerful, to be respected and obeyed, learnt by familiarity and intercourse, especially with his employer's wife and children, that the white man was really very ignorant of many things, while it was little use speaking to him, because he could not "hear" (*i.e.*, understand). This loss of respect—almost contempt—has continued from those early days to the present, accentuated by missionary teachings that he has a "white soul," and if good is equal if not better in the eyes of the Almighty than a white man. The respectful salutation of old is but rarely heard in the land, and now in this year of grace (1898) the dressed Native will puff his pipe in your face, and jostle your wife or daughters off the side-walk, while his girl and another sing hymns in your kitchen, or roast your youngest in the sun, flirting with the Native constables; or will mash an unconverted "brother" over your garden gate, while the missis waits.

The Rev. Mr. Holden, writing in 1887, has somewhat confused his periods; otherwise he has correctly described the social condition of the Natives in and about the year "One." He says:— (*)

When I arrived at the Bay there was not a single minister or missionary within ten or fifteen miles of the village of Durban for either white or black; the Wesleyan Minister having removed to Pietermaritzburg a short time before. Within that extent of Country there were thousands of Kafirs, the kraals being numerous, and many men and boys working in the town and on the Beach. But the whole were in a state of perfect barbarism. There was no religious service held

---

*History of Methodism and Missions in South Africa, Part II., Page 431.

for them, nor one person who made a profession of Christianity. They were simply naked barbarians, living and rioting in all the abominations of heathenism. *This was the condition of all the Kafirs.* As to "servants," they were boys so called, varying in age from 15 to 25; but they were all in Nature's undress, with the exception of a few tails of wild animals hanging from the loins. Even those who were employed in European families, or worked on the premises, were in the same condition. These unclothed young men nursed the white children, and did the cooking and washing in English families, so far as these duties were not performed by the mothers and daughters themselves. It was a rare exception to see a man with a shirt on. .The Kafir young women were in a similar state; but as a rule they were not allowed to come and work in the village. In the evenings these wild men had merry times as they assembled, sometimes in one place and sometimes in another, and kept up their singing and dancing until a late hour at night or until the small hours of the morning.

I must pause here to take exception to the use of the cognomen or generic title "Kafir." Mr. Holden was from the Cape Colony, which, according to old geographers, bordered on "Caffre Land," where numerous missions came to be established; consequently all Cape Natives—other than Hottentots and Bushmen—were designated both officially, as by the Dutch and the Missionaries, "Kafirs," and their country "Kafirland." Mr. Holden, in writing his "History of the Kafir Races," was unable to get out of the groove, for he speaks of "Conversion Work among the Natal and Zulu Kafirs." His justification may be that, as the name was originally given by Mahommedan explorers to the East Coast Natives — signifying in Arabic "Heathen or unbelievers"—they *are* Kafirs accordingly. To the proud Zulu and the aboriginal tribes of Natal, this foreign term is a stigma and a reproach implying a people without a Chief, Country, or tribal status, mongrels, slaves. They prefer to be called "Bantu," *i.e.*, "The people," the word, "abantu," serving also as a prefix to the name of the Chief, tribe, or clan (as the people of McGregor or O'Brien). During the recent Zulu war, no greater insult could be hurled at our Native Levies by the Zulus than that of "A'ma Kafoola." It is not generally known that our Natives resent the designation "Kafir," since it is as misplaced as the general term "Coolie" to the Natives of India. We Britons may tolerate our being called "White men," but would make it hot for the Native if he called us Boers.

The difficulty of communication was then, and
and for long after, the great drawback to
Colonial progress and enterprise. We will
consider first the Postal Arrangements, which during 1850
were simple and primitive, suitable for an embryo easy-going
community. The system then followed has by a species of
natural selection developed year by year until it has given us
our existing cheap postage, with house to house delivery,
regular steamer and railway mails, telegrams, and telegraphic
money orders. The first Governmental post between Maritzburg and Durban was conveyed by Contract, the Contractor being paid at the rate of £300 a year, and carrying the
mails on horseback with Hottentot riders twice a week; but
the affinity of the Hottentot for " Cape smoke," and the in-
feriority of the post horses, led to such irregularities that
even the easy-going public remonstrated. The Military
conveyed their own despatches by mounted orderlies from the
Cape Corps. Then the Government, taking example from
the Missionaries, utilised the Native, and mails were thereafter carried by Native Runners or Government Messengers,
who were distinguished by a soldier's second-hand great-coat,
and a wand bearing a tuft of scarlet wool on the top, or a
cleft stick holding an official envelope. They also carried
the assegai and knobkerrie, which on starting was usually
adorned by half a loaf or a raw steak.

Postal.

On the arrival of a ship, the Port Captain obtained the
mail bag. This was sent by Native messenger connected
with the Custom House to Durban, where it was received by
an old Dutch gentleman, by name Schonnberg, who lived at
the beach end of the Erf opposite the present Marine Hotel
(Gardiner Street), one of his front rooms serving for the Post
Office. Here the mails were sorted and the correspondence
pigeonholed. The ship's arrival was soon known throughout
the town, so those expecting letters took an early opportunity
of calling upon the Postmaster. It was customary, to save
time, to ask for the correspondence of your neighbours also;
hence originated the practice of handing out all the letters
you chose to ask for, the objection to this being that you were
apt to receive the correspondence of all the Mr. Browns or
Mr. Smiths not otherwise identified. The only safeguard
at that time was the precaution, adopted in England, of

superscribing "Passenger per ship *Aliwal, King William, Minerva,* etc." Should two vessels with mails happen to arrive together, as sometimes happened owing to the Cape Coasting trade, it was the Postmaster's custom to admit volunteered aid in sorting and distributing, because of the tediousness to him of having to read the address of every newspaper and letter before he could sort them for Durban or elsewhere. The mails for Pietermaritzburg were made up and despatched on alternate days. Postage was payable in cash, stamps not being in use, consequently the Postmaster considered that a vast amount of work was imposed upon him when a ship mail and a local mail had to be despatched together. As a rule, two Native messengers went together to Pietermaritzburg, travelling in the night by short cuts, carrying the mail bags on their shoulders, and well they did it, arriving with tolerable punctuality in the worst of weather at their respective offices. Postage for half-an-ounce was fourpence, under one ounce eightpence; for every additional fraction eightpence. If not prepaid, one half more. Newspapers one penny; letters for England or Cape without reference to weight eightpence each prepaid, newspapers twopence. If the Postmaster happened to be at home and open for business, you walked in and handed him the letters, discussed the news, and settled the postage; taking back any letters or papers which he considered you were entitled to ask for, or were willing to deliver. He felt an interest in clearing his pigeonholes, and, though the system might involve some delays, it was not disapproved, for no one ever expected remittances then. If the Post Office happened to be closed, you simply called again; business hours were from early coffee to sundown.

Transport. Following the Post, as a means of communication and transport, came the ox wagon, that cumbrous and wonderful product of the ingenuity and experience of generations of Boers. Too much cannot be said in its favour as a South African means to an end, inseparably connected as it is with Bullocks and Blacks. The home of the Voertrekker, the pioneer machine of civilization and commerce, it claims a history of its own, and will certainly not remain "unwept, unhonoured, or unsung," now that it has been canonised by both the Dutch Republics by incorporation into their National Coat-of-Arms.

The wagon of the period is known to Colonists as the Tent wagon, such being specially adapted for family use. Its carrying capacity was about two tons. It was drawn by ten. to twelve oxen of the class known as " Bastard Zulus." The Boers arriving up country used the heavy elephantine " Fatherlanders." For the Coast, and Durban in particular, small active enduring " Zulus " were in general use.

It was in such tented wagons that all goods and passengers were conveyed to Pietermaritzburg and the interior, the average time on the road between the Port and City in fine weather being about four days, barring accidents. Family Cap-tent wagons, with a slung ' Kartel " serving for bed, luggage, water keg, and provisions underneath, pots and kettles in the "trap" at the back, lanthorn, chopper, and dishes in the side chests, and only the passengers, white and coloured, travelled light, and at a quick pace, and expected to reach the City in three days.

For mercantile and business purposes, the tent was removed when used about town or the farm. As business increased, and rough goods came to be carried, the highly painted sides were removed, and rough yellow-wood planks substituted, as more convenient and less liable to damage by casks, cases, bar iron, bricks, machinery, etc. Even these sides, together with the bottom or " bed plank " would be dispensed with when carrying timber, which was simply loaded on the " understill." The well known Buckwagon was not then introduced, but came to us later from the Old Colony, evolved by commercial demands from the original trekwagon. I may inform the future historian of the wagon that at this period the original " Reimschoon " of wood was still in use. They were generally complained of, since they acted like ploughs on a soft hill, leaving furrows that became watercourses, ending in mud holes. Durban being stocked with the remains of wrecked ships, their iron " knees " were utilised by the wagonbuilders, and iron " skids " came into general use on the main roads from the Port, until later on the " Block brake " was invented. The oldest authority I have consulted is Mr. S. W. B. Griffin (Willow Grange), a settler from Port Elizabeth, then wagonbuilding at Cato's Creek, who fitted the first brake at the

instigation of the Rev. Dr. Adams, an American Missionary,
but this was applied to the front of the wheels, and worked
by means of a long screw and handle off the wagon box.
It was found to be one-sided, and too good for any but
intelligent minds to use, also too expensive for the ordinary
transport or carrier's wagon.   Then some bright particular
genius, whose name is not recorded, conceived the idea of
applying the brake to the back of the wheels, by the simple
process of a bush pole suspended at each end by a rein,
having an iron rod passing through its centre at right angles,
one end of the rod hooked on to the undersill, the other
tapped with a screw thread and fitted with a handle.   This
tightened or loosened the pole on the after wheels as required.
It cost ten shillings and came to be universally adopted
throughout the Colony, when the authorities prohibited the
use of the locked wheel and skidding reimshoe.   The brakes
of the present day are an elaboration of an old Durban
invention, not patented. (Railway men are entreated not
to exact their "prior rights"). As a general thing it may
safely be asserted that the cart, i.e., the farm or tip-cart,
was not utilised by the Dutchmen. The Emigrants had
brought with them carts of many patterns, but the Scotch
cart predominated.   These were fitted with shafts and
intended for horses, but, as horses of any kind were rare
and expensive animals of a light build and used only for
riding, the settler found himself reduced to the necessity of
substituting a pole, or "disselboom," for his shafts, and of
using oxen, a span of ten Zulus costing little more than one
good horse.   Diverse and manifold were his experiences in
teaching both himself and his span.

The Australians aver that their bullocks will not work
unless sworn at; it is certain that considerable cursing was
engendered at this time, but it did not of itself appear
to have more effect on the oxen or Native "forelouper" than
another curse had on the Jackdaw of Rheims. I have seen
a patient father sitting in his cart, a short thong tied to a
wattle in his hand, his little daughter leading the oxen, to
which he would speak in short snaps of horsey English, as
they crawled through the deep sand of the Market Square,
leisurely whisking their tails, and deferentially keeping
a respectful distance, so as not to overtake the strange little
figure in flapping "cappie" toiling in front of them. The

flicks of the make-believe whip served only to relieve the placid-looking after-oxen of the flies. Under similar circumstances, "stickfasts" in the Durban streets were of everyday occurrence, relieved only by the demoniacal shriek, whistles, and sticks of the ever-ready Native; then, nature asserted itself, and the otherwise capable cattle walked off accordingly with an alacrity that was simply astounding to the Englishman, who, in process of time, relinquished both the driving, leading, and abuse to the Native, whose affinity to the oxen promoted joint and sympathetic action when working together. I may note here that wagon owners only went to the expense of turned yokes for the after oxen, the rest being merely good bush poles of special wood, morticed for the "yokeskeys" and attached to the "trektow" by an iron staple. Trektows were then all made of strips of raw hide, laid up like a rope and well greased. The reim chains used for locking the wheels (by the spokes or attached to the rimshoe) were manufactured by the local blacksmiths, when not home-made. Chains and wire rope were adopted for trektows a long time after, by the self-reliant British "Transport Rider," against the advice of every enlightened Boer, and in the face of a kind Providence, who provides hides for that purpose, since in cases of emergency hides could be cut and the oxen promptly freed.

Conveyance and transport had its gradations. The regular cap-tent wagon, with its appointments and conveniences. The Scotch Cart, fitted with wattle-framed hood, covered with Native mats, over which a canvas cover was secured. The Pack Ox, for riding or bearing loads slung in bags over its sturdy back, adjusted like Gilpin's flasks "to keep the balance true," the animal being led or guided by a thong through the cartilage of the nose.. Last, but by no means the least important, Africa's own original porter, the Native. He was used by traders who went on foot to Zululand or the Pondo Country, taking with them as many carriers as their means would allow. Each Native, in addition to his own personal belongings, carried a load of about 60lbs. in weight, which, however, like Æsop's salt, diminished as he journeyed. It will readily be conceived that the iron cookingpots thus conveyed into the heart of Zululand became articles of virtue which were priced and prized accordingly.

Police.

The majesty of the Law in Durban was entrusted to two or three Europeans, with a few Native constables, and enshrined in a pretty thatched cottage of wattle and daub, surrounded by a cluster rose fence, in Central West Street, having iron bars to the windows (Erf No. 14, Block E). This edifice was known by its Dutch title as the "Tronk." Mr. Thomas Dand, who had accompanied Lieutenant-Governor Pine to the Colony early in the year as personal attendant, was appointed Gaoler, The two front rooms contained stocks, and were reserved, one for Europeans and one for Natives, the back rooms serving as quarters for the European constables on or off duty. Outbuildings at the rear were occupied by Mr. Dand, and were used also for hospital, kitchens, washhouse, etc. All prisoners under sentence wore chains fastened to their ankles by a hook, bent on in a vice by a blacksmith, so as to form an open ring. This prevented running away, and served for prison garb. If the patient became very riotous or unruly, he was duly laid by the heels in the stocks by night. Prisoners were employed on public works, a drain down Grey Street to the Bay being the first work on which I saw them. The white men then employed were run-away sailors, smitten by the charms of the Emigrant girls they did not care to leave behind them. They were guarded, in addition to the great-coated Native with knobstick and assegai, by a European constable armed with a regulation Tower musket. He wore his own clothes and slouch hat, carried a spare ball cartridge in his pocket, and smoked his pipe peaceably in company with his chatty prisoners, seated on a convenient log. The Military method of escorting offenders to justice was with the aid of handcuffs. The Civil method, which we learnt from the Boers, was to drop the loop of a bullock rein over the head of the prisoner, and, secured by a half-hitch at the nape of the neck, thus was he led, or driven, to safe keeping. Country cases had frequently to trot on foot to keep up with the farmer's horse. If, in addition, his hands were tied, the journey was not without its inconveniences. Yet we were not brutal, every European being regarded as his own special constable, and viewing these things in the light of African "custom," just as the Fishwife did the skinning of eels.

Trade. The trade of Durban in 1850 was derived from imports to supply the Dutch farmers settled beyond Pietermaritzburg, and in the Orange River Sovereignty (now Free State), also goods for Zulu traders, from whom were received in exchange hides, skins of all kinds, horns, a little wood, some butter, and considerable ivory and exports. Elephant hunting, which was a regular industry, included also the Buffalo and "Sea Cow" (Hippopotamus). Shortly after my arrival, the last party of Elephants were seen from the Market Square in an open patch on the Berea, close to the site now occupied by the Observatory, near my present residence. About the same time a brick kiln on Mr. Joseph Cato's farm, "Brickfield," at the back of the Berea, was partly rubbed down by Elephants in the night, to the terror of the workpeople in an adjacent hut. Isaacs speaks of "Hyenas and Wolves" troubling Lieut. Farewell's camp on the Market Square, also of his killing Sea Cows at the head of the Bay. Many white men combined trad'ng with hunting, both Overberg and in Zululand, for which purpose they went in well-found wagons with Hottentot drivers and servants, the most prominent at that time being a gentleman known to us as "Elephant White." Mr. Baldwin and the McLeans, I think, came on the scene later. Durban was generally lively for a week or two after the return of one of these expeditions. Among the Emigrants many young men took to Zulu trading, principally for cattle. They went either in wagons, carts, or on foot, whilst others started Overberg to slaughter Buck for their skins, or to trade guns and powder, coffee, sugar, and sundries, with the Boers for skins, horns, cattle, and horses. All exports went to the Cape in payment of the supplies we received. Locally, we produced nothing but hides; this trade was in the hands of the Glendenings, of Cape Town. One or two shipments of cattle had been tried to Mauritius. The price of a "green" hide was from 5s. to 8s.; they were salted and tied up in bundles; dried hides were worth less owing to the crinkled state in which they arrived. After a time, the demand for meat considerably increased. The Butchers, then obtaining large Dutch cattle, were not content to regard a hide as a hide, but required payment by weight; the price then rose

to 2d. per lb.. Nearly all the storekeepers of the period
kept a little of everything in stock, though the Emigrants,
on setting up business, began to open out in special lines, or
trades.

Weights and Measures. The only legal weights and measures
at that day in use were Dutch, and
it may be imagined what conflicts of
opinion arose between buyers and sellers, when 92lbs. Dutch equalled 100lbs. English,
and 24 Dutch liquid gallons only ran to 20
Imperial, the measure being identical with the old Win-
chester or present American gallon. Grain was measured
by the Schepel, four of which went to a muid, while a muid
was held to be three Imperial Bushels. If sold by weight,
a muid of Oats should weigh 104 lbs., Barley 140 lbs.,
Wheat, Beans, Peas, or Mealies 180 lbs. The schepel was
an open box, 14¼ inches square and 8½ inches deep, with
wooden handles on two opposite sides. With this we
measured Mealies, filling, after the Scriptural injunction, and
striking level with a stick; but when it came to bagging
large quantities, the new settlers found that an American
flour cask held just a muid and allowed for " good measure,
pressed down and shaken together and running over "; so
we substituted the cask as a more convenient gauge. The
buying price of Native grown mealies was one shilling a
schepel, selling at 4s. 6d. to 5s. per muid. Machine scales
were mistrusted, and not generally used, the old-fashioned
beam scales, slung from poles or iron standards, being
employed both for counter or yard work, and very troublesome they were with their double sets of heavy cast-iron
weights, Dutch lbs. and British cwts. Unfortunately, when
it came to a close trade with wool, butter, ivory, etc., the
difference between the real and the apparent was not always
in favour of the Dutchman. This was to a degree equalized
by the petty pilferings on the part of the unsophisticated
Boer and his family when sorting up a Storekeeper's stock
during a trade. The Dutch trade, however, soon relegated
itself to Pietermaritzburg, the coast being considered
unhealthy for cattle; from there many were the stories that
reached us " of ways that are dark and tricks that are vain
and peculiar." Though not connected with Durban, I may
be excused for recounting one incident illustrating my sub-

ject. Lead was sold in bars of about 5lbs. weight, and was
much coveted for bullets. A Boer bought half a chest of
tea; subsequently he "annexed" a bar of lead, as he thought
unobserved, which he slipped into the half empty tea chest.
The discreet storekeeper said nothing unpleasant, but, when
closing accounts, carefully re-weighed the tea, and included it
in his bill, which was duly settled.

The "Queen's Shilling" has a fascination for others besides
the recruit, while British gold was historical before the wars
of Napoleon, and although nothing but British coin has been
in circulation in the Cape Colony since 1806, your aboriginal
Boer affects to compute his money in Rix dollars Skellings,
and stuivers, their values being one shilling and sixpence,
twopence farthing, and one and a half farthings respectively
(six stuivers to the Skelling, eight Skellings to one Rix dollar).   The Dutch to this day impose rates, taxes, and fines
on the basis of the Rix dollar, but take payment in British
currency.   I have a clear recollection of an indignant Dutchman refusing to pay a Durban Blacksmith the sum of ten
shillings for making a new iron reinshoe, but readily agreeing
to the apparently reduced price of seven Rix dollars (10s.
6d.)

To illustrate prices and currency, I give copy of an advertisement from the *Natal Witness* :—

FOR SALE AT THE STORES OF G. C. CATO :

Rice,   16 Rixdollars per Bag.
Meal,   30   „   „   Muid.
Flour,   25   „   „   Bag.
Sugar,   20   „   „   100 lbs.
Liverpool Salt, 7 Rixdollars per Bag.
Durban, Port Natal, 6th Dec., 1847.

**Durban
in 1850.**

Durban, when I first saw it in 1850, did
not differ much from what the Rev. W.
C. Holden saw in 1847, excepting that
there was more of it.   Trusting to
my memory, and to that of many old Colonists,
notably the late Mr. Richard Webber Tyzack, I
will endeavour, at the risk of being deemed prosy,
to describe it.   Assuming, reader, that you are an
Emigrant of the year "One," arriving on foot by the bush-
path, you discern open country just before reaching Rutherford Street of to-day, and bear away to the left where two

large red milkwood or "waterboom" trees formed a natural
archway through which wagons drive over the site of the
pretty Scandinavian Church (Winder Street), and describe a
circular course in the direction of the Hotel Metropole (Erf
No. 16, Block O).   This carries you safely over Cato's
Bridge, formerly Durnford's, spanning the Creek, and gives
you the choice of Smith Street, marked by Cato's tall flagstaff, or of pulling up the sandhill to your right over K. Anvil
Aime's Ice Works, and entering at the end of West Street.
The first house to be seen after leaving the Bush was that
of Napoleon Wheeler, formerly a seaman on the *Pilot* during the Boer occupation, who had located himself at the
mouth of the creek named after him, subsequently utilised by
Mr. John Milne, C.E., for his drain.   I believe Wheeler
burnt lime (from shells) and supplied mangrove posts for
building.   There was generally a tent or two to be seen,
also an outbuilding, giving the place the appearance of a
small settlement.   I did not visit it until genial "Wattie"
Brunton took over the lime-burning business.   Mr. N.
Wheeler removed to Pietermaritzburg, where as Market Master for very many years he was known and respected by all
the Colonial world.   This settlement was off the regular
high road, so we will resume our stand in sight of Smith and
West Streets.   The first whitewashed house you sighted was
a long thatched store of wattle and daub known to everyone
as "Cato's."   It stood in an open space shaded and sheltered
by the same grand trees that remained to the date of Mr. G.
C. Cato's death in 1893.   (Erven 10 and 11, Block M.)   It
was the centre of our civilization.   Wagons outspanned
there.   Cattle were tied up or wandered around.   Auction
sales were held there, and on that spot also the Emigrants
piled up in increasing quantities vehicles of all sorts, horse-
hoes, scarifiers, iron harrows, clod crushers, mill-stones, massive iron ploughs, and other heavy things they could not
carry, and hoped to sell.   I believe the remains of some of
these will yet be unearthed there by the antiquarian.   At
the Beach end of this erf there was a roughly built blacksmith's shop with two forges, where C. C. Griffin and Chas.
Hovenden (Griffin and Hovenden) attracted the notice of the
newcomer by the merry clink of hammer and anvil.   Proceeding down Smith Street, the gable end of a wooden building at the back of the next lots (Erven 8 and 9) indicated the

premises of Mr. C. Joseph Cato, afterwards turned into a
mealie and saw mill. Passing that you saw the dwelling house,
large wooden wagon-builder's shop, and premises of Mr. S. W.
B. Griffin (Erf 7), sufficiently indicated by wagons, carts, and
wheels in all stages of construction or repair. Proceeding
onwards to the next Erf (No. 6), you saw a thatched building
belonging to "Dick King," and known to us as the "Pavil-
lion," though I believe it had been relinquished as a Canteen
before we arrived. On the opposite side I think there was
a wattle and daub house, occupied then or later by Mr. Anderson, a Surveyor. Nearly opposite the "Pavilion" there
was a large Kafir-boom tree, which with a stout mangrove
post, formed a gallows on which Dick King suspended and
dressed his slaughtered cattle. A little further on his
brother John King had a house. Trees and foliage formed
the continuation of that side of the street until you came to
the Wesleyan Chapel, wattle and daub, thatched, at the
corner of the Market Square. Continuing from the "Pavilion," you wandered on under some large trees until reaching the Wesleyan Mission Erf (No. 2 M.) I believe the
street face was at that time defined by a sawn yellow-wood
paling, tarred. The snug Mission House, embowered in
trees, was to be seen at the Beach end of a long straight path.
The large wild fig trees, now overshadowing the side walk,
I remember as posts put in to support the fence. A few
paces further on you reached the large thatched store of Mr.
Lloyd Evans Mesham, at the corner of Aliwal Street (Erf
No. 1), which, during 1849, was hired for the Parish Church
and Public Schoolroom, and afterwards used as a Native
School. This, by reason of the white ant, was eventually
pulled down. Mr. Mesham was a Landing Agent, but, on
his appointment to a Magistracy, sold his business to Mr.
J. F. Kahts. Round the corner towards the Bay, there was
a small house occupied, I think, by "Jock" Anderson, Boot-
maker, or Frank Armstrong; possibly there were other
houses. Crossing that street, we have Mr. E. P. Lamport's
new iron stores and dwelling (No. 9, Block I.); next to him
and fronting the Market Square, were Messrs. Henderson,
Smerdon and Co., Merchants—a large wattle and daub building, thatched. This had been known previously as J. A.
Ross's place, and afterwards as Milner Brothers' Stores. The
wagon traffic from the Point by way of the Beach traversed

this road, and left indications of routes in all directions on the shifting sands of the Market Square.   Wandering from the corner by Henderson and Smerdon's, you were liable to be lost.   The Camp could be seen in the distance, while a new brick chapel fronting the Square was being finished; otherwise, look where you would, it was all drift-sand in heaps and ridges, on or about which grew a few date palms and wild bananas with clumps of scrubby bushes, and tufts of a long green whip-like rush.   Presently your eye caught sight of a new double-storied house of brick, apparently of huge proportions about a quarter of a mile further down Smith Street.   Wading through the sand in that direction you sighted a long low thatched building with many doors opening on to the verandah, before which were Native fig trees and a few syringas.   Men lounging about and a sign board proclaimed it as the "Commercial Hotel," by Hugh McDonald; later it was named the "Masonic," now it is known as the "Royal" (Erf 3, Block I.)   Close by on the corner Erf (1, Block I.) was a brick building with slated roof used first as a billiard room by Hugh McDonald, as an adjunct to his Hotel, then as a Library by Mr. Hicks.   It was purchased shortly afterwards by Messrs. John Millar and Co.   I believe it stands to-day incorporated in Messrs. Steel, Murray and Co.'s premises.   Turning the corner of Gardiner Street, there were two humble tenements being put up by Emigrants.   At the Beach end of the Erf was a large wattle and daub thatched building, farmhouse-like in appearance, occupied by the Rev. W. H. C. Lloyd.   Across that swampy street was the Post Office, and a Hide Store at the Beach end (Erf 8, Block H.), owned by Mr. John Daniel Koch, and managed by Mr. George Pay.   On the high ground at the back of these were Mr. Jargal's house and a regular Dutch farm house, owned by the widow Strydom, whose son-in-law, Piet Hogg, looked after the cattle kraal and their joint wagon transport business.   The Durban Club now occupies a portion of that land.   Resuming our position at the Billiard Room corner, the stranger had in front of him the large building that had previously attracted his attention.   It proved to be at the corner of Market Square (Erf 16, Block G.), and was in course of completion as a wholesale and retail store for **Messrs. Middleton** and **Wirsing** (*), and lately occupied by **Messrs. Savage** and **Hill**. Adjoining it in Smith Street was a store of yellow-wood planks, in which the former firm first commenced business, after buying out Mr. G. C. Cato's retail trade. Adjoining this again was the thatched dwelling of Mr. Joachim F. Kahts, Landing Agent, standing well into the street (Erf 14, Block G.). One or two buildings could be seen marking the line of distant Smith Street. Adjacent to the then grand building at the corner in front of us, and facing the Market Square, was an undersized wooden shanty of the mining camp class occupied by a Mr. Jolly as a chemist's shop, afterwards transformed into Agar's Canteen. R. Acutt's was then a vacant space, until you reached George Potter's Saddlery Shop, made out of the fittings of the *Minerva*. Then Beningfield's was not, but the site of their existing Mart was occupied by a lofty storehouse built of yellow-wood and tarred externally, the repository of Mr. J. F. Kahts. A few posts and rails marked the corner of the Erf up to the present Wesleyan Church. This served Mr. Kahts as an outspan and lumber yard. This was known to us as "Kahts' Corner" (Erf 15, Block G.) The Wesleyan Church ground was once a choice garden (Erf 13, Block G.), enclosed by a wattle fence covered with roses, attached to Mr. Kahts' Smith Street house. To this garden the Colony is indebted for many rare and valuable plants and flowers, as also for much experimental experience, which the kindly and obliging owner was always willing to impart to the new settler. It was further renowned for a well with a never-failing spring of good water, to which the success of the garden was justly attributed. A Canteen occupied the site of the Standard Bank. I only knew it by its title "The Mellor Arms," which was not bestowed until the following year. It was conducted by Joe Campbell, an old sailor, who afterwards removed his business to the opposite side of the street. John Smith, an old Whaler, owned the swampy Erf No. 9, Block G. Upon this he had erected a substantial brick and thatched building, then known as the "Britannia Inn." It was not visible from the corner, as it stood back from West Street, and was

---

* Mr. W. H. Acutt subsequently joined; the firm then traded as Middleton & Co.

hidden by Mr. Kahts' fences. I believe that Messrs. Smith and Wraith (Bob Smith), on becoming the Lessees, changed the name to "Family and Commercial Hotel." John Smith did not himself run the hotel until some years later. The "Central Hotel" now occupies this site. The tidal swamp crossing West Street here did not invite further inspection, though several buildings could be seen in progress down distant West Street, and Stephen Gee's Bakery at what is now "The Corner" (Erf 24, Block E., West and Field Streets), was prominent. A winding wagon track through the scrub and grass indicated a thoroughfare, and the line of West Street. Before retracing our steps, we halt at "Kahts' Corner," and glancing at the rush-grown swamp fringed with young mangroves on our left, which extended from the Bay by Field Street to Pine Terrace, we note the gable end of the first double-storied brick house built in Durban, situate in Pine Terrace, and occupied by Mr. W. H. Savory as a Grocer's Shop (Erf 7. Block F.). This building became the property of Barnes and McFie, Butchers, and was occupied for a time by Mr. R. W. Parker, their Manager, and subsequently as a Boarding House. It is still standing. Some four or five small dwellings, other than Huts, could be seen scattered over the face of the sloping ground enclosed between West Street, Pine Terrace, and the Swamp. On the opposite side of the street, where Donald Currie and Co.'s Offices now stand, was a thatched building of brick, owned and occupied by Dr. Chas. Johnston, an energetic and popular medico, who was always prominent at public meetings. Within three months of my first seeing it, Mr. James Pulleyn, a passenger per *Nile*, had bought a portion of the Doctor's Erf (No. 14, Block F.), and built a shop, where he commenced business as "Watch and Clockmaker and Jeweller." "Time" apparently hung on hand, as he ultimately cultivated the newly applied art of photography, and became our premier artist. He subsequently joined Mr. Clark in trading to the Free State, and founded the well-known firm of Clark and Pulleyn, whose reputation for fair trading secured for themselves and Durban a large proportion of Free State business. Looking to the North, behind the Doctor's house we note what is evidently a cutting, a watercourse or drain, leading into the swamp from the far distant grass covered sandy flat.   Facing to the right, and retracing our steps towards the sea, a few paces enables us to distinguish, between sandhills and bushes to our left, the regular formation of a stockaded Camp.   This is "The Camp" of our History.   As "all roads lead to Rome," so all tracks seemed to lead to the Camp.   Later experience proved these tracks to be wind-paths scoured out between bushes and sand ridges, leading nowhere in particular.

Of such was the character of the palm grown Market Square with its clumps of wild date Palms, wild Banana (*Strelitzia*), and what we were told was the vegetable ivory Palm, to say nothing of Amatongoola and other scrub, coarse grass and rushes.   Some three or four clumps of these palms and a few Amatongoola with a wild fig or two, and some scrub of lesser note, increased by time and protection to the rank of trees, and are still growing enclosed in our Market Square Gardens, in which the observant wayfarer will conjecture the state of the original hummocks, when noting the difference of level between the interior and exterior of the Gardens Wall.   St. Paul's Churchyard, then an open space, also encloses a fine clump of Palms that must have been growing there before Chaka was born.   Wandering Eastward, there was no building to obstruct the sight of the Back Beach Bush, so, unless one kept an eye upon the wagon spoor, you were apt to diverge from the undefined limits of West Street.   It was then, and for a year or two afterwards, no uncommon thing to meet in this locality a red-faced Briton in fustian and heavy ancle-jacks, mopping his brow, hat in hand, who would ask civilly and in earnest, "Please, Sir, Sir, whereabouts is De-urban?"   I must, however, add that before the year was out, Mr. H. W. Currie had erected a green-grocer's stall for the sale of farm produce about the centre of the Market Square.

Proceeding onwards, and taking our bearings from Cato's Flagstaff, or the new Wesleyan Chapel (opened 12th May, 1850), fronting the Market Square, we find ourselves entering a regular village.   The house at the corner (Erf 1, Block L) is occupied by Mr. J. Riddle Wood, Notary and Deputy Sheriff.   Next to him is the dwelling of Mr. Jeremiah Cullingworth, at the rear of which was his small printing office, containing an Eagle hand-press, on which the *Natal*

Mercury had its birth on the 25th November, 1852. Next
door to him were the premises of Messrs. Aitcheson
Brothers, Merchants. Their office was built of brick, and
stands to-day altered to serve as the Belgrave Bar. A few
dozen yards away, under a fine large tree, Mr. Edward
Pickering had a noisy Cooperage. On the opposite side of
the way Messrs. Knight and King, Merchants, had a wooden
store, where Mr. Wm. Palmer first found occupation as
Clerk and Bookkeeper. A little beyond them, a thatched
house, fenced off from the Street, was known as Moffatt's
Boarding House. Looking across the street again, as
strangers will do, under a group of fine wild date Palms
(still growing), Mr. John Milne, C.E., had a neat little
cottage (Erf No. 7, Block L). His only daughter, Jessie,
then the Belle of Durban, kept house for him; she subsequently married a Captain Robertson, and went to India.
Next to him was a Bakery, kept by an ill-conditioned little
Scot (A. R. Forbes), about whom more anon. This man
had an abnormal memory. A "refresher" on Sunday
evenings, would ensure his repeating the forenoon discourse
at the Wesleyan Chapel (so far as our poor recollections
would serve) literally word for word, and point by point,
with a gravity, expression, and burr, that was intensely
comic. Mr. John Hannibal Grant subsequently acquired the
land and business. He was our first Confectioner, and a
handsome daughter in the shop drew largely upon our youthful resources for jam tarts and ginger beer. Next to him,.
I believe, Andrew Welch kept the "Ship" Tavern. On
the opposite side of the Street was Mr. James Blackwood's
retail general Store (Erf 10, Block K). He had been
associated with Mr. Tomlinson, but Tomlinson was taken into
partnership by a Mr. Griffiths. They set up the retail
grocery establishment of Griffiths and Tomlinson, between
the residence of Whitehead, a Carrier, now "The Home"
Boarding House, and Dick King's Butchers Shop, at the
corner of King Street. King, owning the Erven (11 and 12,
Block L) right through to Smith Street, had cut out or
laid off "King's Street,' and sold small plots there. Harry
Milner, of Milner Brothers, owning the Erven on the opposite
side (11 and 12, Block K), cut up "Union Street," and sold
the land on both sides in small sub-divisions. It was on

one of these lots that Mr. R. W. Tyzack set up his tent dwelling and tailor's shop. His trim garden, wattled in, extended to Pine Terrace, and it was from this humble abode that he and his wife obtained and distributed relief to the shipwrecked *Minervas*. Up and down Union Street and its vicinity were many small cottages. One was occupied by Mr. John Hunt. Petty, thatcher; Mitchley, thatcher; Rapson, Jacobs, carpenters; Tait, Hobson, tailors; John Dove, bricklayer; W. Horne, gunsmith; Lloyd, artist; Redman, baker; and others, were residents. Here also to the great scandal of Mr. R. Elliott, builder and local preacher, —whose wife kept a temperance boarding house at the West Street corner, afterwards the well-known "St. George's Hotel," situated at the Pine Street end, fronting the Camp and the Emigrant Barracks—was a disreputable Canteen, part canvas, part reeds, known as the "London Tavern," and owned by Messrs. Howell and George, who advertised "monthly balls, first Thursday every month," where fiddling and sing-song by the guests was to be heard upon almost any evening before the Camp bugles recalled stragglers at 9 o'clock. Turning again into West Street, I am told a cottage stood on the site of Mr. R. Jameson's original grocery store (Erf 16, Block K), but I recollect the last building, which is still standing at the corner of West and Stanger Streets (Erf 22, Block K), since it was the well-known Emigration Offices of Mr. John Moreland, previously referred to, conveniently in the vicinity of the Emigrant Barracks. Mr. Wm. Vionnee had not then built "Mazeppa Cottage" on the opposite corner (Erf 21, Block L), neither had Mr. Charles Hovenden built his house on the neighbouring Erf (Erf 17, Block L), now owned by the estate of S. Grant. Mr. Samuel Grant and his wife were both *Minerva* passengers. These houses were built a year or two later.

Such was the Commercial centre of Durban in 1850, promoted and advocated by Mr. G. C. Cato, who either owned or was agent for owners of the major portion of the Erven at what was then designated the "East End of the township." It was his opinion that the proximity of the Point both by water and road would ensure its establishment and prosperity, consequently the prices of those Erven were raised accordingly, and, as the Emigrants flocked in, holders, under his advice and influence, remained firm,. or otherwise would not sell except at what were deemed fancy prices by men who had but little hard cash at their disposal. Leases for a term were certainly offered, but no one cared to build on another's land. As a natural result, new-comers sought ground on the far side of the tidal swamp, dividing Durban into East and West Ends, where most of the old soldier owners (especially along the line of West Street) were willing to sell half their holdings for a reasonable sum in gold. Stories were current that some took out their values in goods, a half-aum of Cape Smoke or a bag of Coffee, but of this I can find no authentic record. I only know of one case where, as a deal between Emigrants, a corner Erf, at the Western end of West Street (Erf 1, Block D) was exchanged for a wagon valued at £60.

Shops and dwellings were speedily started in this quarter. Merchants began to settle, and build handsome brick stores and warehouses, inviting Trade to settle in their midst, to which she graciously acceded, rapidly deserting the East End, while making for herself a permanent home in West Street, West of the Market Square.

From memoranda made by Mr. G. C. Cato, I find that the Bluff Road, following essentially the existing line from West's Jetty to the signal station on the top, was cut through the Bush between the months of April and August, 1850; while the Bluff Signal House and Flagstaff were not erected before October, 1850. The entrance channel was buoyed off in 1849, and it is safe to infer that leading marks on the Bluff were erected at the same time. Cato records also that in 1850 there was a depth of 15 feet of water on the Bar, a circumstance that remains unaltered after 45 years' engineering on Harbour improvements, and the expenditure of tons of money!

Domestic. Mr. David Dale Buchanan, of Pieter-maritzburg, the Editor and Publisher of the *Natal Witness* at this time, was apparently glad to record gratuitously such personal information of a local character as came to hand; thus, under date March 15th, 1850, we find:—

DOMESTIC INTELLIGENCE.

BIRTHS.

On the 3rd inst., Mrs. A. B. Roberts of a daughter.

CHRISTENINGS.

On the 12 inst., at his residence, a daughter of Mr. A. B. Roberts, baptized by the Rev. J. J. Freeman, Sabella Louisa.

On the 12th inst., at his residence, two sons of Mr. D. D. Buchanan, baptized by the Rev. J. J. Freeman, Edwin James and Henry Freeman.

DEATHS.

Edward Prettyman was bathing near the mouth of the Umcomas a few days since and was unfortunately drowned. Deceased leaves a wife and family.

On the 11th inst., at Pietermaritzburg, Mr. Joseph Helman, wagon-maker.

CHRISTENINGS.

May 23rd, at Durban, by the Rev. W. H. C. Lloyd, Colonial Chaplain, a daughter of Mr. Alfred Samuel Raddon, baptized Julia Arabella.

26th, a son of Mr Baseley, baptized Edward.

June 16, at D'Urban, by the Rev. W. H. C. Lloyd, M.A., Colonial Chaplain, a daughter of Mr. S. F. Drake, baptized Charlotte Henrietta.

DEATHS.

June 15th, at D'Urban, Mr. William Smith, Emigrant per *Sovereign*, aged 53.

Marriages are not of sufficient interest to extract from this column, being bare records of Paul M. to Virginia N., with never a flower or feather added.

Officials. The Emigrant Ship *Ballengeich* arrived here on the 26th July, bringing as part of her 95 statute adults, four gentlemen, whose destiny it was in a great measure to originate the Durban of to-day, commercially, socially, and physically. Clubs, Churches, Institutions, Buildings, Lands and Harbour Works all bear the impress of their hands, their energetic organization, and professional ability. I refer to:—

Henry James Mellor (Resident Magistrate).

John Millar (Mayor, and First Member of Legislative Council for Durban).

Hugh Gillespie (Mayor).

Robert Sellers Upton (Architect and Town Surveyor).

It was through them also that my destiny became linked to Durban, enabling me to gain the experience which has encouraged me to become its historian.

To the gentlemen already named must be added Alfred Winter Evans, James Fleetwood Churchill, and John David Shuter, passengers per *Devonian*, arriving in October; W. M. Collins, who became Postmaster-General of the Colony, came in the same ship. The end of 1850 witnessed the results of successful measures instituted by a new Lieutenant-Governor, in the person of Benjamin Chilley Campbell Pine, Esq., who, having acquired experience as Lieutenant-Governor in the West Indies, speedily organised an active administration throughout the Colony. So far as Durban is concerned, the Civil Government was represented by Mr. Henry James Mellor, an English Barrister, as Resident Magistrate; V. A. Schonnberg, his clerk, afterwards replaced by J. B. Roberts; John D. Shuter, an English Attorney, being Clerk of the Peace. Our old acquaintance, Henry Francis Fynn, of the Bluff, acted as Native Magistrate, under the Diplomatic Agent, Theophilus Shepstone; William Swan Field, Collector of Customs; Francis Spring, Postmaster-General; William Bell, Port Captain; G. Archer, W. Hodge, and W. Vionnee, Pilots; Thomas Dand, Gaoler; European and Native Constables; G. C. Cato, Lloyd's Agent.

The upper portion of the new store of Messrs. Middleton and Wirsing, on its completion, was rented by the Government, including a good-sized room on the ground floor, which was utilised as a Post Office. A narrow passage at the end of the building gave access to a steep staircase, leading to the Court Room, and to three smaller rooms used as Offices by the Magistrate and the Officials. Witnesses, or prisoners awaiting trial, squatted in the Corridor, or occupied the floor of the Court Room.

The annexed illustration of this building is reproduced from an oil painting made about 1851, and now in the possession of Wm. Palmer, Esq., the present occupant.

CHAPTER VI.

1851.

Mercantile. Messrs. Millar and Gillespie left England as partners, bringing with them a stock of general merchandise. They acquired part of the Erf No. 1, Block I, at the Gardiner Street corner of the Market Square, and in due time opened as " John Millar and Co., Merchants and General Agents." The ship *John Line* arrived May 3rd, 1851, with 130 Emigrants. Messrs. John Millar and Co. were Agents for the ship. At that time, fishing and other enterprises having failed me, knowing no Dutch, no Zulu, and no trade, I had serious thoughts of returning to the sea, but, reluctant to leave my equally helpless family, I gravitated in spare time towards the Point, looking out for any employment befitting a white man. It was in consequence of my being thus in evidence that the Agents of the *John Line* tendered me the standard wages of 5s. a day to join a gang of men they had collected to go outside and aid in discharging that ship of its Emigrant fittings and cargo. In the language of seaports, gentlemen engaging in this occupation are known as " Lumpers," that is, ship labourers, in no way to be confused with the more professional " Rigger." I believe they consider themselves a notch above dock labourers, though I fear the dividing line is at best but a thin one, represented by a " copper " or two. Thankful for employment, I asked but few questions, pocketed dignity,

and next morning went out in a Cargo Boat with the rest
of the needy men composing the gang, among whom was one
Edward Kermode, a Manxman, who afterwards set up as a
Baker, and eventually owned and laid off Mona Place (Erven
3 and 4, Block M). His son in later years compiled a History of Natal, and retired from business. We accomplished
our task in about a week, towing or rowing an open surf boat
backwards and forwards over the Bar with the lumber and
cargo. I assume that my seeming smartness in ship ways
must have attracted the notice of the Captain, the result
being that Messrs. John Millar and Co. offered to take me
on permanently as their first clerk and general utility man,
at the encouraging salary of £40 a year on which to eat,
sleep, and clothe myself. I knew nothing of Commerce or
the qualifications of a trader. Bookkeeping, taught at school,
was forgotten at sea, but I was quite alive to the fact that
many young men were seeking employment. I accepted
the terms in the light of an apprenticeship premium, and
remained with the firm some nine years, during which I advanced to the position of Chief Clerk and Bookkeeper.

The leading line of the business was that of Wine Merchants, in which the firm was supported by first-class London
Houses. The rest was made up of general agency and goods
on consignment. As an illustration of the average goods
then dealt in by Durban Merchants, I recall our stock at
different times:—Deals (cut and uncut), roofing slates, coal
tar, Kafir picks, pots, beads, brass wire, blankets, and sundries under the generic title " Kafir Truck," Gamble's Oil-
man's Stores, crockery and glassware, canvas, sacks, rope,
junk, sail twine, wall paper, tin in sheets, sheet and bar lead,
zinc, groceries, such as tea, loaf-sugar, currants, figs, raisins,
nuts, flour, rice, soap and candles, bar iron, smiths' coals,
with occasional piece goods and woollens, saddles, boots, birch-
brooms, hairbrooms, brushes, writing desks, work boxes, and
fancy articles. All these goods had to pass through my
hands inwards and outwards, in addition to blending, bottling
and packing, so my experience was varied, and my time
occupied. The primitive and unsophisticated native in the
employ of the settler appealed to Nature to regulate the hours
of labour, and, in his usual stolid fashion, succeeded in establishing the custom of a day's work as between " sun up "

and " sun down." Practically, this came to be modified in wholesale and retail stores, until, by degrees, the hour of closing was fixed at 6 p.m.

This, in the case of wholesale firms, was subject to the accidents of transport; the delivery of goods by wagon from the Point, or the loading up of wagons going inland. As a general thing, business was over for the day at about four o'clock, or earlier, if the tide served. Then the "heads of the people" went on the Bay, sailing, fishing, or shooting (on the Island). Shops opened at 8 a.m. Employers, unless residing on the premises, would arrive about nine, go to lunch at about 1.30, and return again, as chance or circumstances might dictate, that day or the next. Time was by no means frittered away, as there was always business of a public char-acter to discuss, and many social functions to regulate, while the Clerks always found something to do if it was only to "regulate" the Natives, or exercise them in feats of strength or agility, by way of amusement, and though not exempt from the prevailing curiosity as to Native customs, I could always find occupation for my " Boys " in wheeling sand from the billowy heaps in Smith Street to fill up the hollow at the back of the store. This economical and pre-vailing practice was used in evidence against us at the first contested election for the Legislative Council, for an opposi-tion " Squib " asked, among other things, " Who raised his Erf, and that by stealth, John Millar ! " Though but an innocent accomplice, the fact of my recollection proves the sting.

Queen's Birthday. Young as we were in 1851, short of cash and deficient in accessories, we continued to raise our own events, throwing ourselves into them with a force, energy, and determina-tion, worthy alike of our newly-found freedom, and of our old country prerogatives, Magna Charta, and the Bill of Rights. Strange comment upon our radical republicanism, we were intensely British and loyal. Her Majesty's Birthday was not only marked by the usual parade of the troops in garri-son at the Camp, about two companies of the 45th Regiment, with a detachment of Royal Artillery and Sappers and Miners, a salute being duly fired at noon, at which the loose

population of Durban was present, but the loyal inhabitants
made it the occasion of a popular jollification and free show
in the evening by an excellent display of locally made fireworks, exhibited on the open flat, in front of Platt's "Trafalgar Hotel," a double-storied building of wood, situate on
Erf No. 21, Block E (Pine Terrace).   A bonfire always
attracted the Natives, whose singing in unison soon drowned
the fiddles of the gin-drinking Hottentot wagoners, while
soldiers and civilians thronged in and out of the "Trafalgar,"
adding considerably to the "diversions" of the wondering
Emigrant spectators until a late hour.

**Business
Hours.**

The before mentioned primitive Native servants made a further appeal to Dame
Nature, on the question of dietary.   Our
initial difficulties in regulating their hours
of labour have not yet been overcome, notwithstanding half
a century of experience acquired in prisons, garrisons, railways, and mining camps.   Yielding to the demands of the
masterful European, the Native labourer is now obliged to
take his "scoff" at the regulation intervals of breakfast, dinner, and supper.   This is contrary to the health-giving
lessons taught by Nature to both the Native and the Boer,
who make but two square meals a day, i.e., about 11 a.m.
and 6 p.m., or dusk.   It will therefore be understood how
trying and contentious the storekeeper's forenoon was frequently made just as goods arrived or orders had to be
delivered.   Strikes were frequent, nor were they remedied
by blows.   The first line of defence, being boiled mealies,
was overcome by the issue of mealie meal, but this did not
mend matters; as, from fear of witchcraft, or malignant in-
gredients, no Native would eat alone, so if part of your gang
was away, the potful of boiled porridge would remain un-
tasted until all had assembled.   Squatted round it, each
provided with a long spoon, or small wooden paddle, they
shared it fairly per caput, the largest mouth apparently
benefiting most.   With these unsophisticated ones, the
consideration was not so much the hour or the quality as
the sufficiency of the quantity of the repast.   A shin of beef,
a bullock's head or paunch, was held to be a reward of
virtue, and smoothed all difficulties accordingly.

I may here note in reference to the delivery
Parcels   of .goods just alluded to, that, as a general
Delivery.   thing, goods were not delivered.   In the
                  retail trade, you were expected (after the
Dutch custom) not only to take them away yourself, but to
find your own string and paper, flour sack, tin dish, or basket.   A fascinated assistant might "oblige a lady" by tearing a scrap off the original wrapper, or the glazed lining of
a packing case, and keep the charmer talking while he hunted
up a piece of string or sail twine.   If a good country
customer, the storekeeper might go so far as to cut off a
piece of baleing, and bundle up the whole of her purchases
in a portable package, placing it in her wagon at the door,
or handing it over to her attendant driver or forelooper to
carry to the outspan, but I have seen flour in a pocket-hand-
kerchief, butter in a newspaper, nails in a hat, and candles
on a string.

In the wholesale business, a wagon and a span of oxen, or at
least a cart and eight oxen, were required to deliver a hogs-
head of wine, or any single article that could not be carried
by two Natives on a hand barrow.   Durban's sands did not
admit the use of handcarts, or even of wheelbarrows, so
packages were usually shouldered.

                  The first public Ball was announced as a
Public   "Grand Subscription Ball," to be held at
Ball.   Platt's New Family Hotel, originally ad-
                  vertised for the 18th July, and postponed at
the especial desire of His Honour the Lieutenant-Governor,
to the 28th July.   "Gentlemen's tickets, 15s.; Ladies'
tickets, 5s."   Lieutenant-Governor Pine was unmarried, and
a *bon vivant*.   The story of this Ball and the subsequent
proceedings originated personal antagonism in the newspaper
press, and led to Mr. Pine being openly described as a "gay
Lothario," unfit to govern.

                   The plaintive advertisement, calling a meet-
Agricultural   ing on the 18th April, 1848, for the purpose
Society.   of "attempting to form an Agricultural
                   Society," seems to have borne fruit, for we
find that a few gentlemen had constituted themselves a
Society, under the title of the "Natal Agricultural and Hor-

tieultural Society." This, after rejecting a small plot of
ground in the vicinity of the Umgeni, selected and obtained
a grant from the Government of 25 acres of land at the foot
of the Berea, near the site occupied by the kraals and gardens of Chief John Cane's following, who no doubt selected
that locality from the proximity of the ever-flowing water-
holes. This 25 acres was in after years increased to 50,
and is now enclosed in the Botanical Gardens. The Society,
as originally formed, languished for want of practical support
from others than commercial men. The President was Mr.
Hypolite Jargal; Dr. Stanger was Vice-President, and Mr.
John Turner (Blackburn) Secretary. They held their first
Show in the Government Schoolroom, Field Street, on the
9th August, 1850. Though liberal prizes had been offered,
the exhibition was a failure. At a subsequent dinner at
McDonald's Hotel, the Society was virtually reorganised by
the following zealous gentlemen, notably enthusiastic over
flowers, fruit, and vegetables, or anything that could be induced to acclimatise itself to Natal. The President was Mr.
Edward Morewood, of Compensation (whilom Harbour Master, under the Boer Volksraad), a name inseparably associated with Natal's Coast industry, sugar, as he was the first
man to produce that commodity as a marketable article.
Mr. Samuel Benningfield and Mr. J. F. Khats were Vice-
Presidents, Mr. John Turner and subsequently Mr. J. R.
Goodricke, Secretary and Collector, G. C. Cato, Treasurer,
while the following gentlemen were on the Committee:—
Captain Smerdon, E. P. Lamport, A. F. Dawson, A. Jacques,
W. Wood, W. Dacomb, J. Moreland, H. Jargal, John San-
derson, J. L. Fielden, E. B. Herbert, W. T. Sanderson, H.
J. Barrett, A. W. Evans, Leonard Wray, C. Dacomb, J.
Proudfoot, and H. Searle. The services of Mr. Mark J.
McKen, recently from Jamaica (*), had been secured as
Curator, at the inadequate remuneration of £50 a year and
a Hut. The Society in their report of 1851 congratulate
their subscribers upon the event, and also upon the many
valuable plants Mr. McKen had introduced into the Colony
and brought with him to the Gardens. Six acres of the 25
were grass land bordering the flat, the remainder hillside
bush land.

* Ship *Emily*, October, 1850.

Show. On the 1st August, 1851, the Society held its first Show on its own ground.   All Stores were closed during the morning, and the majority of the townspeople found their way by the Pietermaritzburg Road, and over the flat to the entrance of the Gardens, and then on the lowest side between the present St. Thomas' and Sydenham Roads. Here a few poles and ship flags gave animation to the scene, while the exhibits were displayed on rough tables of yellow-wood planks, under an awning of wagon-sails and evergreens. Farmers and visitors were camped with their wagons and families all around, while children's voices and the curling smoke from under the domestic kettle indicated a series of picnics within the shelter of the gardens.   A lively interest was taken in this first most important occasion by the inhabitants generally, who had generously subscribed toward the prizes.

The chief attraction was to be a ploughing match between Colonists, not a trial of ploughs by experts.   It was to take place on the flat grass land just inside the Gardens, and three experienced judges, Mr. H. J. Barrett, Mr. Robert Babbs, and Mr. John Grice, had been appointed, but unfortunately no record can be found of the ploughs, terms, or prize winners.   Mr. John Allison, of Ladysmith, has generally been credited as the winner, but as he tells me he arrived in the *Isle of Wight*, September 26th, 1851, his triumph must have been at the second Show and ploughing match in 1852.

The total area then under cultivation was reported by Mr. McKen as not exceeding four acres.   The means at his disposal were very limited, consequently the clearing of bush was restricted.   He had therefore to plant out young trees in such spaces as were available, with the result that as these exotics took kindly to the soil and throve exceedingly, they had eventually to be cut down to give room for development and later introductions.   The space at my disposal must necessitate the same treatment to this subject, but I cannot sacrifice a list of the prizes and products at this budding stage of the Colony's development, otherwise I should do a great injustice to our townsmen and neighbours, who, with the true spirit of enterprising Anglo-Saxons, had moiled

and toiled to make two blades of grass grow where not one
grew before, and to produce something upon which to subsist
in the present, or to serve as an export in the future.

Prizes of £1 each were awarded to the following:—Mr.
Sydney Peel, turnips; Mr. Brown, mangel-wurzel; Mr. J.
F. Kahts, turmeric, arrowroot, and ginger; Mr. Stockhill,
finest potatoes; Mr. Brooker, bacon; Mr. De Terrason, rice
grown on high land, Pistachio nuts, cambarus, tobacco; Mr.
S. Benningfield, greatest variety of vegetables and fruit; £2,
coffee plants, and coffee; £1, pineapples, and jams; £2 to Mr
Brooker, 2 bales cotton; 10s. to Mr. Henry Shire, sweet
potatoes, underground nuts, Pistachios; 10s. Mrs. Hawthorn,
cheese.   In addition the following were shown:—S. Benningfield, drumhead lettuce, and cabbage, dwarf beans, 2
sorts turnips, 3 sorts cabbage, carrots, colerabbi *(sic)* cassava
Scotch kail, peas, 3 sorts chillies, mountain spinach, broc-
coli, leeks, onions, cauliflowers, 2 sorts eschalots, watercress,
mustard and cress, radishes, endive, 2 sorts celery, parsley,
sage, thyme, cucumbers, sorrel, Kafir beans, parsnips, sweet
potatoes, red beet, yams, broad beans, guavas, pineapples,
lemons, bananas, 3 sorts potatoes, bacon, pork, tomatoes.
Mr. Garrod, 2 samples wheat; Mrs. Bowen, papaw; Mr.
Bottomley, bamboo; Mr. Brooker, one bunch bananas,
lemon, 1 bag white mealies, 1 ditto mealie meal, yams; Rev.
Mr. Lloyd, Mauritius beans, 1 sample potatoes; Mr. Ed-
monstone, potatoes; Mr. John Sanderson, 1 plough, 1 harrow, 1 grubber, 1 Scotch cart, cottage cotton gin, 1 drill
harrow, 1 double-mould board plough convertible into drill
harrow, 1 scarifer or horse hoe; Mr. T. P. James, 2 lion
skins, 1 rhinoceros horn; and Mr. West, 2 water colour drawings, views of Durban.

A single plant of arrowroot, procured by Mr. McKen
from the Royal Gardens at Kew, had reproduced at this
time sufficient to plant out a third of an acre.   This led to
the cultivation of the plant by small Coast farmers, resulting
in several manufactories, and an extensive export, until the
supply exceeded the demand, lowering prices below cost.

Time had not allowed for the yield of the orange *(citrus)*
family, the mango or the loquat, but newly planted in the
Gardens; while the Sugar cane was in an experimental
stage.   But why the homely universal pumpkin was not on

view on this occasion, I cannot account, unless it was deemed a Native product, or otherwise because exhibitors saw enough of him in their daily fare. The sweet potato was also in its infancy, being exhibited in quantity by only one person, Mr. Henry Shire, of Milkwood Kraal, whose experience in Mauritius and elsewhere induced him to cultivate and disseminate these and many kindred plants, for which the Colony will ever be indebted. The absence of flowers, cut or uncut, is a significant proof of the practical earnestness of the original promoters of the Agricultural and Horticultural Society.

This Show was a success, happy and memorable; an occasion to be recollected by the new settler and his wife, who recognised the reproduction of the garden stuff which they believed grew nowhere out of England, and looked with doubtful eyes upon the "furrin thing" they could not be tempted to try, until assured, like their first parents, that it was good for food. We can now afford to smile at this initial industrial effort, and bear with equanimity the ofttold aspersion that we produced nothing but samples. *Finis coronat opus !*

Holidays. Christmas Day was duly observed as a public holiday, of which advantage was taken in the afternoon by the recently formed target club, to practise themselves and their various guns at the range used by the Military on the Eastern Vlei, almost identical with the existing Rifle Range. It was out of the question to work upon the day following, and so was established the custom (said to be of Dutch origin) of making two days' holiday on important occasions; the inducement this time being to witness a much talked-of walking match against time by Durban's only Barber, an eccentric character, who gave himself an English reputation as "The Little Wonder," and challenged any man "fair heel and toe." As a natural consequence, the Army were interested spectators, enlarging the occasion by impromptu sports among themselves.

Pine Terrace. In Mr. Cato's notes I find that "Pine Terrace" was named this year in honour of the new Lieutenant-Governor. It had been previously advertised by residents as "Nelson Street." Even West Street had been miscalled "Russell Street," and is so marked in some old diagrams. .

To attempt to reason upon the motives that
Municipal.   induce emigration is not my province, but
I venture to assert that the British Emigrant
is in advance of his stay-at-home countrymen in spirit, self-
reliance, and independence of character.   He carries with
him his national characteristics, seeking in a new land the
liberty and enlargement denied him in the Old Country.
Our townsmen had barely sheltered themselves and set to
work, before a desire arose to regulate their new possessions.
There was so much to do, that could not be done single
handed.   Accordingly a public meeting was held on the 21st
December, 1850, in the building used as the Government
School Room, Church, and Court House, Field Street, "to
obtain the sense of the inhabitants" as to memorialising
the Government to create a Municipality.   Opinions were
divided on the questions of expense, so a Committee was
nominated to draw up special town regulations to be submitted to another meeting. The *Natal Independent* newspaper was started in Durban just at this time, and gladly
proclaimed local grievances, while private persons cor-
responded on the same subject to the *Natal Witness* or to
the Government, but the latter, like the townspeople, had
many things to do, and little money to do them with.   The
Municipal Committee delayed their report, whereupon the
more active and energetic townsmen, remembering the
fabled wagoner, put their own shoulders to the wheel, and
attacked what was then the greatest drawback to progress,
the swamp across West Street, which virtually divided the
town and hindered all wagon traffic.   Subscriptions were
raised, and a contract entered into to dig a drain and construct a bridge.   Aided by convict labour, mangrove poles
were driven in on each side of a good wide ditch, stockade
pattern, and bridged over with the teak timbers of the old
Minerva, backed with sea-weed, sand from the Market
Square, and a little lowering to the hill opposite Gee's corner
(now Challinor's), the whole covered with sods.   This completed a substantial structure between Erf 8, Block F, and
Erf 9, Block G, and raised Central West Street about six
feet above the swamp bottom.   In after years this drain
was by degrees bricked in.   The line can be traced to-day
from Pine Terrace, through Mark Lane, across West Street,

to the passages by the Central Hotel (formerly Commercial), back of Pickering's, across Smith Street, and out to the Bay through Poynton's Timber Yard.   This was followed up somewhat later by an enterprising man, Esdaile by name, who, for want of employment, conceived the idea of constructing a hardened causeway over the sands of the Market Square.   Subscriptions of about £40 were promised, and he laid a footpath of inverted sods, brick refuse from the kilns, and clay from the Eastern Vlei, along the line of the present Market Square Gardens in West Street, protecting it on the inner side by a wattled fence.   This work stood well for a season, and was highly appreciated by the foot passenger, who, however, expected his man " Friday " to continue his footprints in the sand.   Money being, as I before noted, very scarce, the Government found itself short of funds, and, as a relief, decided to sell, as Crown lands, part of the area reserved by the Surveyor-General for the township of Durban.   Accordingly, 18 Lots on the Berea were surveyed, including some 46 acres at the Umbilo.

The residents, who with much toil and privation had commenced to shape and drain their town, at once took the alarm, declaring they saw " the thin end of the wedge."   A general meeting of householders was forthwith summoned and held on the 6th September, 1851.   In importance, it may be ranked as the Runnymede of Durban.   Mr. E. P. Lamport was in the Chair.   The meeting was a crowded one, and, as it was against the Government, all parties, old Colonists and Emigrants, were united, though speeches were hot and strong.   Mr. John Millar proposed:—" That this " meeting do therefore enter a formal and solemn protest " against any attempt of the Colonial Government at any " time to alienate any portion of the town lands of Durban," seconded by Mr. A. W. Evans, " who urged upon the meeting thus formally to assert the principle that they would not allow the Government to touch one tree or one handful of sand, which was not theirs, but the rightful property of the town."   Resolution carried by acclamation.   Durban's Magna Charta was accordingly embodied in a solemn protest by the Notaries, J. R. Goodricke and George Laurie, and signed by 112 persons, then residents or landowners in Durban.   This document, with the faded signatures of the

sturdy settlers of that time, was framed and glazed, and
now hangs in the Law Offices of Messrs. Goodricke and
Son, Smith Street.   Copies were duly served on the Colonial
Government, with the result that no sale of the Berea Lots
was held.   The Bee may be defined as a busy-body, but the
quidnuncs of the period imitated its habit of indignant
buzzing along after the cause of alarm had subsided.   They
strove to show how the troublesome wedge of the demagogue
had again protruded its thin end, so another public meeting
was got up and held on the 22nd September, to consider if
the town should have some Municipal regulations.   Mr.
John Sanderson was called to the chair, and Mr. E. P.
Lamport made a masterly speech.   As on the previous
occasion, the meeting could not agree, owing to the very good
reason that we, the young men, having no responsibilities,
promoted and patronised these public gatherings and evening auction sales as places of amusement, constituting ourselves "the Gallery," putting up or crying down speakers,
and chaffing the Auctioneers or Purchasers—a sort of
"Smoker" entertainment, without refreshments.   The
motion for a Municipality was rejected unanimously, apart
from the mover and seconder; only one hand was held up,
and that a tipsy one.   The meeting being over, the "gods"
departed, but a few more earnest persons lingered, and,
constituting themselves into a second meeting, appointed a
committee of 20, to revise any Municipal Ordinance the
Government might draft for Durban.   An Ordinance did
appear in the November following, proposing a Mayor and
11 Aldermen, qualification to be £100 freehold, £25 rental,
with power to raise by sale, lease, or mortgage each year
three times the amount raised by rates, main roads of the
District within the Borough to be kept in repair, and half
the cost of the Police to be paid by the town.   A public
meeting was forthwith held on the 21st November in the
Court House, Mr. John Millar in the chair.   Only one
resolution was proposed, and it was carried by a large
majority, to which the "Gallery" contributed : --

This meeting thanks the Committee for the services performed in
watching and reporting upon the Municipal Corporation Ordinance
as proposed by the Lieutenant-Governor, but considering the present
circumstances of the town, and its total inability to bear the expenses
of a Corporation, this meeting contents itself with saying that it is

satisfied with the Municipal Ordinance of 1847, and in more prosperous times the town will avail itself of the provisions of that Ordinance to resolve itself into a Municipality.

Postal.   In the same *Gazette* with the Municipal
Ordinance, appeared another, reorganising
Postal matters. Mr. F. Spring was
appointed Postmaster-General, with headquarters in Durban
(in Middleton and Wirsing's Building, ground floor, under
the new Magistrate's Offices), instituting local money orders,
payable 24 hours after sight, and reducing postage to threepence per half-ounce, not prepaid fourpence. Oversea letters
" according to custom," in addition to local postage. Newspapers local ½d. each, oversea 1d. This was regarded by
the townspeople as a progressive step, and helped to soothe
their suspicions as to the intentions of the Governor.

Funereal.   Shakespeare says, (*)"Hope is a curtail dog in
some affairs," and so our Emigrants found,
for they landed in hope of gaining life,
health, and fortune, and to return in good time to the land
of their fathers, but to many those laudable aspirations were
not to be realised; " the ills that flesh is heir to " terminated
lives on the brink of their enterprise, necessitating a last
home in the land of their adoption. As in conformity with
one law, men must die, so in obedience to another, their
remains must be suitably and reverently disposed of. Though
we have got past arms, provisions, or a holocaust of slaves
as aids to entrance into the other world, yet the sentiments
of the age demand many superfluous habilaments; adorn-
ments in glass, tinsel, or varnish, with good, dry, and picturesque localities in which to consign earth to earth. All
honour to the sentiment that lingers around the memory of
the departed, and to the natural selection by the civilian
settlers of a delightfully cool and shady nook in the dense
virgin forest on the outskirts of the township, for their last
resting place. Here on the edge of the Western Vlei the
graves were out of sight, and not likely to be disturbed. The
first grave was followed, as near as conveniently could be
for the growing trees, by the second, and as fresh space was
demanded, graves were dug by willing hands somewhere near
the previous clearing, but without special regard for uni-

---

* " Merry Wives of Windsor," Act II., Scene I.

formity.   That touch of Nature made us kin; we did not
stop to dispute about consecrated ground, or the articles of
belief adopted by the deceased.   Natives of course did not
present themselves; they usually found a convenient hole in
the Bush.   The good broad net of the Church of England
claimed all the waifs and strays, the poor and the neglected,
the stranger and the outcast; and, under the liberal administration of the Colonial Chaplain, ensured their decent burial.
On assuming office, he found ample work in organising
Church matters, and those offices which fall within the province of Her ministers.   As the Camp burying ground was
exclusively Military. while that at the Point was regarded
as for the use of "Poor Jack," the Rev. Mr. Lloyd induced
the Governor to sanction the reservation of a "God's Acre"
at the West End of the town enclosing the graves already
there, as a General Cemetery.   Inspected and recommended
by Dr. Stanger, an area of 100 yards square was surveyed,
and title issued to the Bishop of Cape Town by deed dated
12th June, 1850.   What the Church organization was, I
am unable to say, but I know that Sunday services were
held in the Government Schoolroom (Field Street); that
what the newspapers designated a Vestry meeting was held
in the "Church Meeting House" on the 25th June, 1851;
that the meeting appointed one Geddes, Clerk and Sexton at
£10 a year, and that thereupon the Churchwardens, Messrs.
J. R. Goodricke and Robert Raw, resigned their offices, under
the influence of the prevailing touchiness.   Thus early did
"the other fellow" obtrude himself into Durban's church
affairs.   Meanwhile, the Rev. W. H. C. Lloyd, bland and
impecunious, had to raise funds and encourage the public to
interest themselves in enclosing and laying out the ground.
The convicts made a ditch and sod bank, while the gates
were contributed by a general parish levy of wood, labour,
hinges, fastenings, and paint.   The gates not being for everyday use, a stile of bushwood was erected at its side.   The
entrance to the Burying Ground was almost in a direct line
with Pine Terrace.   Dr. Stanger was himself buried here;
his monument is placed fronting the main entrance and pathway of that period.

In later years, when the West End Park came to be laid
out and cleared of its undergrowth, certain parallel mounds,

with intervening hollows, attracted attention. They were scattered irregularly throughout the area, previously described as "Delagorgue's Bush." Some visitor of antiquarian tastes compared them to tumuli; hence the report got about that they were ancient graves, whereas in fact they were the remains of saw pits, dug at the instance of one James King-hurst, formerly a ship's carpenter of the brig *Sarah Bell*, who in the dawn of civilization, cut down most of the fine straight yellow-wood trees to be found there, to convert into planks for building purposes.

It is more than probable that the first tenant of the site now selected for the Burying Ground found a nameless grave in an abandoned saw pit. Funerals at this time, and for some years, were conducted naturally in primitive fashion. Coffins were made of plain yellow-wood. The body was brought to the ground in a wagon or ox cart, preceded by the undertaker on foot, and friends following. The coffin, covered by a flag or a pall, was carried to the grave-side by friendly bearers. Those who possessed black coats wore them, but crape was scarce, and the "habilaments of woe" were not then part of the trade. Suitable stone was not to be had, so the graves were marked by wooden crosses, brick-work, or numbered tin labels by the Sexton, to be replaced later by lettered slate or marble slabs from England, or free-stone from Pietermaritzburg.

Natal Almanac. In this year, Mr. Jeremiah Cullingworth commenced the publication of "Cullingworth's Natal Almanac," containing much useful information, price one shilling. His son and successor, Mr. T. L. Cullingworth, has continued the annual issue ever since. This popular production has now assumed the proportions of a book, without enlarging the original shilling.

CHAPTER VII.

1 8 5 2.

Horses. AT about this period riding horses had become a necessity for business men as a means of locomotion. They were imported chiefly from the Orange River Sovereignty, and notwithstanding their liability to sickness on the Coast, and the high price asked for them, their use was becoming general. Merchants, having accounts to collect in Pietermaritzburg, did it in person, usually arranging to ride in couples, carrying an oilskin coat and a valise, or saddlebags, strapped front, rear and sideways to the saddle. This arrangement was adopted on the return journey for mutual protection, as debts were usually paid in coin. In many cases, the money —gold in particular—was carried in rolls, in a silk handkerchief or towel concealed round the waist of the rider. A night was usually spent on the road, unless a led horse was used. Pietermaritzburg being the headquarters of the Cape Mounted Rifles, the best horses necessarily gravitated to Fort Napier, while the townspeople were otherwise well provided and mounted, the climate of Pietermaritzburg being more suitable for stock of all kinds than that of Durban. A few up-country settlers were turning their attention to breeding and dealing in horses, therefore, as a natural result, horse-racing became a favourite diversion and attracted visitors from all parts ; the interest of our Dutch fellow-colonists being always awakened on these occasions by a reasonable expectation that they can excel at a horse-race or a shooting match.

Races. The first Durban Races were held on the 14th and 15th January of this year, after being advertised for several weeks euphemistically as "Annual Races." All places of business were closed after noon, and we went out to the course among the bushes, between the Umgeni Road and the swamp that crosses the present Race Course, where ropes and posts indicated "the straight," while flags marked off the rest of the ground to be run over. A stand called Grand had been erected by McDonald of the Hotel. It was a Bar-room of wood and canvas, about seven feet high in front, roofed with a kind of open staircase of rough deals to serve as seats, which might accommodate about 100 persons; but the majority of visitors preferred to line the ropes in their outspanned wagons, with the wagon sails half removed, the ladies seated therein on chairs or camp stools, while the Native, conveniently handy, "cooked the kettle" for coffee and refreshments. There were bell tents for the presiding officials; a post and inverted packing case for the judge, and a roped space for scales, horses and riders at the end of the Grand Stand. Other canteen keepers had their own booths in convenient proximity. There were no racers at this time; every man owned "the best horse in the Colony." If he had determined to run him, it was fed, groomed, and practised over the Course for days beforehand. The ownership of a horse was no guarantee of horsemanship, so, when it came to business, ambitious owners had frequently to admit that a lighter weight would stand a better chance. Catch weights were allowed, and the services of little monkey-like Hottentots were engaged as jockeys.

They rode well in all the pride and glory of a fancy jacket and cap the first day, but too frequently the second day saw them vainglorious, ready to ride anything with or without a saddle. Their ways and their tricks were both "vain and peculiar." The uncertainty of stakes or bets in consequence led to the banning of coloured riders on the Durban Course. Rarely more than three horses were entered for an event, which they all ran to win. Some classification took place between horses and ponies, and some "weight for age" regulation was enforced with an old-fashioned shot-belt over the shoulder, but I have no recollection of handicapping until a much later period, when men were wiser, and sport became business. A bugler of the 45th Regiment was requisitioned in place of a saddling and starting bell, while some of the men were utilised by their officers as special constables to keep dogs and Natives clear of the "finish."

The waits between events were lengthy, allowing time for refreshment; they were not, however, marred by the voice of the "Bookie" of later growth. The interest manifested in each race was marked by the roar of the throng, consisting chiefly of astonished Natives, who swelled the sound by shouts and noisy imitative gesture, prolonged like a reverberating echo. The weather, though hot, was fine and enjoyable, lending an additional interest to the occasion. The natural excitement and indulgences of the day instigated comparisons between friends, resulting in a challenge of the speed of the horses which they rode. A reference and fee to the Stewards enabled them to try conclusions between the events; thus we had the added diversion of two red-faced white men, handkerchiefs in the place of hats, without coats, pounding their astonished horses round or about the course, which arrived with or without their masters as fortune favoured.

The sports terminated with a Native foot race, for a liberal reward to the first and second runners, the distance being a mile. Any Native on the ground could start, but only two could receive a prize. This afforded much amusement to Natives and Europeans alike. At the given signal, the assembled crowd of laughing, boastful, stick-carrying Natives started with a rush, but as rapidly thinned off, but a score or two reaching half the distance. By twos and threes they fell out, or down, until but half a dozen high-stepping, perspiring "boys" remained when the three-quarter post was reached, and but three or four straggled laboriously on to the end. Sunset closed the proceedings, and dispersed the gathering.

The afternoons of the two days following the races were devoted to running off scratch matches between some of the competing horses; so wholesale stores were closed, and the Course re-visited. Mr. J. Millar's grey pony "Charlie" had astonished the knowing ones, and been challenged accordingly.   He won £5 matches on both days.   In this pleasant manner did we combine business with pleasure.

I have found no record of the persons who officiated at these first races, but a marked feature of the day was the sale by auction on the Course by Mr. S. Benningfield, in what the reporter called " true Tattersall's style," of a stud of horses brought from Pietermaritzburg by Mr. Arthur Walker, an Attorney.

It is evident, however, that the races, in the language of to-day, " caught on," and the results gave general satisfaction, for even Time was taken by the forelock, and the next " Annual " Races held on the 6th August following, the reason assigned being that it would take place at a cooler season.   Matters seem to have been systematically organised ; Captain Griffiths, 45th Regiment, was judge, and the Stewards were the Honourable W. S. Field, Messrs. H. Milner, J. Proudfoot, Dr. Best, 45th Regiment, and Mr. J. D. Koch, Secretary and Treasurer.

It may interest sportsmen to know that on this occasion the last race of the day on the card was a Pack-ox race, three of those active; intelligent animals of the Zulu breed having been entered—Benningfield's " Roman Dutch," Davidson's " Westminster Practice," and Watson's " England." Entrance 5s., with £1 added.   They were ridden by lads, trotted their distance stolidly and arrived in the order named, to the great amusement of the spectators, who appreciated the sly allusion to the conflict of laws then obtaining in the newly-established Resident Magistrate's Court.

Zulu Trade.   I am indebted to my friend, Mr. Thomas Groom, J.P., M.L.A., an Emigrant per *King William,* and original settler at Verulam in 1850, for the details of the Zulu and local trade, during the periods covered by the years 1850 to 1856.   Casual white men were to be hired in the country at wages varying from 2s. 6d. to 6s. per day, while Native lads were content with 2s. 6d., and men with 5s. per month, in cash, or six months' labour for a cow worth 25s., or one month for a goat worth 4s.   Mealies were bought from the Natives by barter at an equivalent of 2s. 6d. to 4s. per muid.   Beans were grown by the settlers for export to

Mauritius, and sold here for 15s. to 17s. per muid. Yellow-wood planks, one inch thick, 12 inches wide, and 20 feet long, were to be bought at 3s. 6d. to 4s. each. Cape flour 30s. per 100 lbs. bag; American, 50s. per barrel. Cash, as I have before noted, was scarce, consequently people in the country bartered Salt, Kafir-picks, Calico, Beads, and odds-and-ends for mealies, green or dry, Pumpkins, Amadoombies (an edible potato-like root), Tambootie grass thatch, Poles out of the Bush, etc. Zulu trading meant a trip into the Zulu Country with cart and goods, extending over six or eight weeks. Some humble traders, however, went on foot with Native carriers. The "outfit," as the Americans term it, consisted of woollen blankets at 9s. or 10s., cotton blankets 4s. to 5s., cotton sheets 2s. each, beads 1s. 9d. to 3s. 6d. per lb. The latter were subdivided into bunches, or made up in strings. Other stock included scarlet woollen night caps, or Comforters, at 7s. 6d. per dozen—these were unravelled, and sold in enticing hanks, to go round a girl's head or waist—Kafir picks 1s. 6d. each, Red Turkey twill cut into strips, Blue Salempore sold at 6d. to 9d. per yard; springtraps, hatchets, sickles, butcher's and clasp knives, finger and arm rings, brass wire, looking glasses, etc. In exchange for such goods as these to the value of 7s. 6d., a beast could be bought (though I have heard of a heifer being given after two days' haggling for two Kafir-picks), which, when it reached Natal, would be sold on an average for 20s., a profit satisfactory even to a modern "Fair trader," since, after all expenses, food, and wages, were paid, a sure return of 100 per cent. might be relied on. Native sheep and goats were obtained in the Zulu Country for goods costing 1s. 6d. to 2s. They were sold in Natal at 4s. to 5s. each. It must, however, be admitted that frequent losses were sustained among cattle brought down the Coast. Ordinary hides and skins were not considered worth the trouble of carriage to Durban, but buffalo hides were in demand for reims. It was but rarely that a trader from Durban brought back Ivory from Zululand. The Elephant hunters and traders, who went a long way into the country shooting and trading, monopolised this trade, which rapidly diminished as the large game acquired a knowledge of fire-arms. Ivory was held to be "doits of the Crown," and any chief or

headman, trading it away, guaranteed it as acquired by
personal gift from the king. The trade price for Elephant
tusks was 1s. 6d. per lb.; they realised 5s. to 5s. 6d. per lb.
in Durban. Guns and powder were in request by the Zulu
king and chiefs. They were supplied principally from
Delagoa Bay, but their possession was not healthy for
common people.

Trade Routes. It may here be noted that the two great
trade routes of the period were the wagon
roads to the Zulu Country, and to the
Orange River Sovereignty, or Free State,
the latter through Pietermaritzburg, over the top of the
Town Hill, crossing the Umgeni on the bed rock at the
brink of the Howick Falls. The starting point of these long
caravan routes was in Durban. Wagons seldom travelled
alone or singly, but usually in small parties for company and
mutual assistance. The open sandy flat bordering the snipe-
haunted Pine Terrace, about a quarter of a mile out from
West Street, was the general outspan and camping ground
of both inward and outward bound traders, and here the
tents were pitched, while goods were conveyed hither to be
sorted up for loading. A jollification among the whites, and
a literal flare up at the Native camp fires of roasted beef,
terminated the day of final preparation, and the early
morning saw those for the Zulu Country wending their
way towards the Umgeni River, over any hard piece of ground
they could find on the grass, or through the bush. They
had to elect from many wagon tracks through the heavy
sand, and found the 4½ miles to the North bank of the
River sufficiently long for a first trek.

They had the choice of two drifts or fords; the lower one
by the River mouth—the direct Zulu road through dense
bush on to Smerdon's Flat—was known as " George's Drift,"
after the resident ferryman. This ferry was influenced by
the state of the tide, and ordinarily was broad and flat,
with a deep channel at each bank, but very uncertain as
to quicksands, holes, and alligators. This uncertainty
extended to the Government Punt and to the Boat, for the
solitary horseman often lost patience, shouting " the Boat"
roundel, when the Ferryman was of opinion that there was
no need to " haste," by reason of insufficiency of water to

float him across, though to the eye the yellow stream, when the tide was in, looked deep. The main or upper Drift, known as "Morewood's Drift," crossed the River immediately above the site of the existing wooden wagon bridge. If the River was at all in flood, crossing by this drift was a hazardous operation for wagon or cart, as there existed a long reed-covered island in the middle, creating two channels. The plunge from the bank on the Durban side brought the oxen into a bunch before the leaders could reach the island, while the water frequently covered the "bed plank," damaging the freight. If no entanglement ensued, the customary whip and yells landed the wagon among the reeds of the dry island, to dip again into the lesser channel on the opposite side, the pull out from which was muddy, but more level. The road passed by the barrack which Mr. E. Morewood had erected for Emigrant settlers, between the late Mr. S. W. Bishop's house and his sugar mill, up the hill at the back, and over Effingham to the "Little Umhlanga" River, thence following somewhat the line of the existing Railway to where the Bridge now crosses the "Great Umhlanga." Here one Watkins then entertained man and beast. From there the road passed the "Phœnix" sugar mill, through Smerdon's Flat, to join the Zulu lower, or bush road, about a hundred yards on the Verulam side of Mount Edgcombe Railway Station.

The Pietermaritzburg, or main high road through the Colony to the Drakensberg, started also from the Pine Terrace Flats, or through Field Street, in the direction of the Botanical Gardens, to avoid a series of sandhills, now levelled, by Alice Street, thence down the incline of the open flat to the head of the Western Vlei, where a Brick Culvert now bridges the race course drain, thence through the heavy red sand into the Berea Bush. The original road to "Brickfields" farm, at the back of the Berea, was by what we now call Leathern, Mansfield, Povall, Silverton and Windmill Roads. But the Military cleared a track, by consent of the Corporation in 1855, through the Berea, along what Mr. G. C. Cato assured me was wrongly called "The Old Dutch Road," right up to the Berea Ridge past the present Toll Bar; thence the road wound down hill to the right in the direction of Sydenham, crossing the head of the Brickfields Swamp, and thence

over the high ground direct to Rooi Kopjies.   The 45th
Regiment had previously lowered the road over the ridge
by the cutting above the Toll Gate, and made other
cuttings along the main road, notably those of Cowie's Hill
and Inchanga.

The " Old Dutch Road " proper ran, as I have before described, out of Durban between Smith and St. George's
Streets, by way of Congella and Umbilo, Sea View, Malvern,
and Pinetown.   From the Umbilo a main road or " trek
path " existed down South through Natal to Pondoland, Kaffraria, and the Cape Colony.   It was the same track that
Dick King followed.   No one used it for hunting or pleasure ; the search for profit kept it open, since it traversed
a country then known as " No-man's-land," afterwards settled
as Griqualand.

**Democracy
and
Finance.**
The faithful historian is always confronted
with the initial difficulty of fixing a period
when things began ; the embryo stage ; the
first movement, which until authenticated by
some available record is likely to escape
notice, causing him unwittingly to pass over the author of
the conception.   The whole Colony at this time was keenly
alive to the necessities of the country and its general development.   The people of Durban, especially, fretted under
circumstantial restrictions on trade, and were keenly alive
to the necessity for expanding their Port and Town.   Even
at this period the ready writer was full of suggestions and
recommendations as to Harbour improvements, while the
removal of the Bar was a thing of easy accomplishment, if
only his suggestions were followed.   Certainly, we all were
in earnest, having our opinions on things in general, and we
dearly liked to ventilate them.   Public meetings were got up
on the slightest provocation, and prudent, clear-headed men
introduced progressive measures ; many and sharp were the
conflicts that ensued, much fine oratory, many frothy de-
claimings, and no end of fun, resulting usually in some practical action, from which Durban stands benefited to-day.
We were truly democratic and familiar.   It was " Dick,
Tom, and Harry " with every man, who was popular or notorious, *vide* " Dick " King, " Tom " and " Harry " Milner,
" Joe " Cato, " Joe " Kirkman, " Bill " Griffin, " Bill " Lea-

thern, "Jack" Smith, "Jimmy" Baxter.   Others were
indicated by nicknames—"G.C.," (Cato), "Father Kahts"
"Indigo Wilson," "Hookey" Walker, etc., while many came
to be universally designated by their Native names, notably
Mr. S. Benningfield, Mr. W. Smerdon, and Mr. H. Gillespie.

We loved to talk about manhood suffrage, and considered
ourselves all equal as "friends, countrymen, and lovers" of
Durban.   But the real thorn in our side was the want of
money.   From this cause grew the issue of that dangerous
epidemic of "negotiable paper," promissory notes, good-fors,
I.O.U.'s, which in after years brought the whole Colony to
the verge of financial ruin.

The "Natal Fire Assurance and Trust Company," of Pietermaritzburg, of which Mr. Carl Behrens was Secretary, was
then in its infancy.   A suggestion had been made that the
Company should issue notes, or that the Government should
do so on the Mortgage of private property of the shareholders, on a guaranteed interest of 6 per cent., that being
the then legal rate.   Bills, though discounted at 6 per cent.,
were charged an additional "commission" of 6, 8, or 10 per
cent. per annum.   Private Bill discounters, however, were
not wanting, who would take the risk at 5 per cent. per
month !   By a side wind the Company's Solicitor obtained
an adverse opinion in Court from the Recorder, the Honourable H. Cloete, as to the legality of their issuing £1 notes
payable on demand, so the matter rested for a time, while
the tradespeople issued copper tokens and printed "Good-
fors" for small change.   This naturally directed the minds
of the leading commercial men to the institutions and available capital of the "Old Country."   The first suggestion
appears in the *Natal Witness* of the 15th July, where
D. B. Scott and Joseph Henderson called a meeting of the
Provisional Directors of the Bank of Natal, in the Library,
Pietermaritzburg.

Though that paper is silent on the subject, it was currently reported that the idea of the promoters was to raise
the necessary capital in London, and to issue notes on the
credit of the shareholders.   This elicited from Captain Walter Glendenning, of the schooner *Gem*. a regular Cape trader,
an advertisement to the effect that he was about to issue
"Shin plasters" for the benefit of the public (and himself),

and offered the names of his cook and steward as additional security. Glendenning's influence and extensive trade connections in the Cape Colony gave sufficient importance to this little skit to stop the flotation of the Bank of Natal. The want of banking facilities for remittances to England were in a measure overcome by the purchase of Treasury Drafts. It has been my duty on many occasions to convey the requisite coin (silver preferred) to the Commissariat Office at the Camp, in exchange for Bills upon London. These were issued in even amounts (round numbers) remitted to Messrs. J. Millar and Co.'s London Agents, who were drawn upon in settlement of balances due to Consignors.

Town Pound. The first recognition of the necessity for a Pound was announced early in January, when Mr. H. W. Currie was appointed Pound Master by the Authorities. The duties and tolls were regulated by Ordinance, the fees went to the Pound Master. This important institution, ancient and honourable, closely allied with commerce and agriculture, noted in song and story, is not to be passed over lightly by the irreverent, since its use and application was, and is, a cherished institution of the Boers, by whom it is known throughout South Africa as the "Schut Kraal." In our case it was a square post and rail enclosure or cow-pen of stout timbers erected at the Field Street entrance to the town, or near what is now Messrs. Pollok and Button' Wool Exchange in Commercial Road. Much business was transacted, for whole spans would get impounded, in addition to the waifs and strays that careless Natives allowed to roam into people's gardens, or enclosures. It was also the practice of the Pound Master to take in cattle to herd on the town commonage, and this proved a great convenience to the Zulu trader. Here did the youth of the village meet at early morning to "see the row," which as often as not ensued between the lawful owner, and the lawful custodian, fanned by a possible claimant for damages. And here did Mr. Currie acquire that knowledge of Municipal requirements, that acquaintance with law and its operation, which qualified him eventually for the offices of Town Councillor, and, subsequently, Mayor of the Borough.

Municipal. Notwithstanding the decisive rejection of the Municipal Ordinance by the public meeting in November, 1851, the committee of twenty, while accepting the thanks, did not regard themselves as dismissed. A quorum appear to have held together, for in April of this year a public meeting was called and held under the presidency of Mr. H. J. Mellor, the Resident Magistrate, in the Court House, " to receive the report of the Committee." The meeting was crowded and cheerful, utterly refusing to receive any report from any Committee, and finally adjourned until the 1st May. We met then, and again on the 10th June, but, beyond the entertainment, nothing resulted for our pains.

A final appeal to public opinion was made on the 3rd July, when the proposal to introduce Municipal Government was again rejected. The so-called minority declined to accept their defeat, so prepared a memorial to the Governor on the subject. As this clearly sets out the position, and is signed by nearly all the burgesses and property holders of the period, I give it *in extenso*, as taken from the *Natal Times* of the 16th July, 1852, since the names subscribed cannot fail to be interesting as a special record of the Emigrant period. It will be noted that the names of the Cato family, the older Colonists, and the young men about town, do not appear.

To His Honor Benjamin Chilley Campbell Pine, Esq., Lieutenant-Governor of Natal. The Memorial of the Undersigned Inhabitants, Householders of the town of Durban sheweth :—That at a public meeting of the Inhabitants of Durban, held on the 1st of May last, a Committee was appointed to prepare the Draft of a measure for the Incorporation and Municipal Government of the town. That the measure so prepared (having been previously published in the *Natal Times* of the 19th of June) was submitted to another public meeting the 3rd of July instant ; but that a majority of that meeting refused to entertain it.

That your memorialists do not consider that result to be a fair expression of public opinion on the subject, but on the contrary are satisfied that the small majority by which the consideration of the Draft was negatived, comprised many persons not being householders, or even inhabitants of the town.

That under these circumstances, your memorialists, believing the measure in question to be adapted, on the whole, to meet the pressing requirements of the community—though' without individually pledging themselves to all its provisions—respectfully submit it to your

Honor's favourable consideration, and request that you will be pleased without delay, to introduce in your Legislative Council, an Ordinance founded on the general principles therein embodied.

And your memorialists will ever pray, etc.—Dated at Durban, this seventh day of July, in the year of our Lord One Thousand Eight Hundred and Fifty Two.

W. H. C. Lloyd, Colonial Chaplain, J. A. Ross, Middleton & Co., Alfred Bell, William Josiah Irons, McArthur & Hunter, Edward P. Lamport, Arthur Searle, R. W. Dickinson & Co., John Sanderson, W. T. Sanderson, John Lennox, John Atherton, A. F. Dawson, Geo. Robinson, Henry John Gale, the mark of M. Haley, George Potter, Edwin Griffiths, James Grundy, J. Millar & Co., J. Millar, H. J. Leuchars, Chas Agar, George Dimock, Jno. R. Goodricke, W. H. Middleton, R. Dickinson q.q., A. Chiappini & Co., Hypolite Jargal, Willson Wood, Hugh McDonald, Robert Acutt, T. P. James, William Acutt, Thomas Dand, Richard Thomas, Edward Smith, Charles McDonald, Alfred George, J. W. Elliott, Peter Hogg, A. Ferguson, W. G. Geddes, G. J. Bottamly, E. R. Dickson, George Bottamly, James Grosvenor, John Prince, James Waal, William Walsh, Samuel Reddish, Stanfell Clewes, Geo. H. Wirsing, Joseph Glover, R. S. Robertson, H. W. Currie, W. Wright, James Pulleyn, Hy. Bennett, Robt. Anderson, Alexander Scorgie, F. E. Jackson, W. H. Savory, Robert Boyne, Geo. Spearman, Peter Steel, James Webb, Alexander McArthur, John Crocker, Jas. Metters, Henry Baker, Joseph Adlam, C. L. Stretch, J. Coles, Thos. Heys, Paul Henwood, Wm. Harrison, George Hicks, M. Penfold, Richard Harwin, Thos. Poynton, J. C. Adams, Francis Harvey, Jas. Dryden, T. J. Shorthouse, John McLaren, William Jones, Wm. Anderson, John Taylor, L. J. Lucas, Thos. Mitchley, Jos. Harris, Thos. Abbott, Samuel Stageman, John Hall, Andrew Welsh, James Willis, E. Kermode, F. C. Salmon, Robert Elliott, James Lloyd, W. T. Petty, William Horne, James Putterill, James Blackwood, J. Cullingworth, Wm. Boast, Thos. Sink, Francis Corbett, Henry L. Greave, Boultbee & Seal, Hy. Cowey, Edwin Standish, Hartley & Handley, Alfred Moore, Emory Roberts, Baumann & Wilson, E. W. Holland, M.D., John Hunt, Robert Nimmo, R. S. Upton, T. Spencer Cope, Geo. Lawrie, Alfred W. Evans, William Dacomb, G. W. Saker, John Granger, Brian Coulson, Patrick O'Neill, Mark Foggitt, John Walker, Sydney Peel, Henry Milner, Edward Snell.

Calamity. In the prevailing goodfellowship of the young community, a sad disaster, which may be regarded as Durban's first public calamity, took place on the Queen's Birthday, observed as a holiday. The attractions of the day were a review of the troops and a Royal salute at the Camp, while picnics in various directions had been organized. A party had gone to the Bluff to inspect the newly-cut path up to the Signal Station, but, when returning in a sailing boat during the afternoon, were caught in a South-Westerly gale and capsized, resulting in the deaths of Mrs. Dawson, the wife of a merchant, and Mrs. Virtue, whose husband was a planter, together with a Native servant. The ladies were young and prepossessing. No business was done on the following day. A gloom hung over the town until the 29th May, when the bodies were found, and buried. The whole community was represented at the funeral, which was most impressively conducted by the Rev. Mr. Lloyd, in the new burial ground, where a tombstone still records the disaster.

Sugar. In June of this year, the *Natal Times* deemed it of sufficient importance to record that Messrs. Hartley and Handley, Grocers, West Street, had lately received 4 cwt. Mollasses, manufactured by Mr. E. Morewood at Compensation, " which were sold off in an incredibly short space of time, and that more was shortly expected." Mollasses it was, for, at that infant stage of the Sugar Industry, treacle was extracted by simple drainage, or filtration. These samples of the productive power of the soil and climate were sufficiently convincing to stimulate the further cultivation of sugar, so in July we find that Messrs. Henderson and Smerdon, with Messrs. Knight and King, had chartered the barque *Jane Morice*, to Mauritius and back, and were advertising the importation for sale of 15,000 cane tops for planting. Morewood's first cane plants were imported by Messrs. Milner Bros. in the *Sarah Bell*.

First Steamer. Our communication with the outer world was by water. Steam communication had been opened between England and the Cape, whence mails and passengers were brought on by any vessel coming our way. She might possibly call at Mossel Bay or Port Elizabeth, or the Cowie (East London), and arrive after a month's passage; but as the trade increased, direct vessels, brigs and schooners of the *Douglas, Mazeppa, Gem, Rosebud,* or *Wanderer* type, ran regularly between Cape Town and Port Natal. Emigrant and other ships direct from England also brought mails; home news therefore reached us months after the event. My diary notes: " 1851, September 10. *Rosebud,* English mail, *via* Cape; October 15, July and August mails arrived; November 2, September English mails arrived; 1852, March 12,

Wanderer, with mail"; hence may be conjectured the keen
interest with which we heard that the Government had been
in correspondence with the "General Screw Steam Shipping
Company," who offered to run their steamer *Sir Robert Peel*,
with the mails monthly from Cape Town.   This vessel they
described as being 250 tons capacity, drawing nine feet of
water, and capable of carrying twenty passengers.

Of course the doubters said it would never pay; not suf-
cient passengers or cargo; and that with average weather
the Brigs and Schooners should satisfy any reasonable man.
They doubted if any serviceable steamer would come inside;
would believe it when they saw it, etc. So some two months
later when it was reported that the steamer *Sir Robert Peel*
had arrived, and would come inside on the following day, the
news was carried like wildfire through the town and neighbourhood.   Everyone decided to see her risk the Bar, and witness the entry of the first steamer on the afternoon of the
16th August.   She was a schooner-rigged screw steamer with
a tall black funnel, and, notwithstanding the flags she displayed, had a generally dark appearance.   She was commanded by Captain J. Boxer.   Her registered tonnage was
234 tons; her horse power is not recorded.   She brought as
passengers Mr. and Miss Fairbridge and servant, Mr. Thompson and son, Mr. Symons, and Lieut. Inglis, R.E.

It was understood that she would come in at high water
about 4 p.m., so after "tiffin" a half holiday was proclaimed,
and stores were closed.   Those who had horses took their
way down by the Bay shore, those who had none made for
the footpath over Cato's Bridge, and through the Sand Hills
to the Back Beach.   Not being acquainted with the habits
of steamers, we anticipated that she might come in at any
time before we could reach the Point, since the depth of
water on the Bar was then, as now, a matter of uncertainty;
thus we could at least secure the advantage of seeing her
cross, or go ashore, as we walked by the Back Beach to the
Point.   Men, so constituted, had brought their wives, while
the elder children were not forgotten.   There was quite a
holiday gathering, enlivened by a pleasant breeze and bright
sky throwing the massive dark green Bluff into bold relief.
The Bar was visible, but not obtrusively so.   Captain Bell
would possibly term it "smooth."   I had reached an ele-

vated position in the neighbourhood of the present "Look-out" when the *Sir Robert Peel* steamed in grandly on a tolerably straight course, while we waved our hats and shouted a distant greeting.   Having no cannon there, we could not fire a salute.   Without venturing to turn round, she anchored in the Bluff Channel, between what is now West's Jetty and the Lazaretto; then deep water.   Here moorings were subsequently laid down, and coasting steamers for years afterwards occupied that berth, the width of the channel opposite the Custom House then being too narrow to allow a "mail" steamer to swing and give room for vessels and cargo boats to sail past in safety.

Gold. Little we thought as we congratulated each other on the success of the arrival, and its eventual advantage to the Colony, that a demon would be let loose with the opening of her mail bags. That night the discovery of gold in Australia was made known to us for the first time. Nothing else was spoken of the following day. The spirit of covetousness and unrest was among us; the germs of the gold fever were circulated, and every scrap of gold news eagerly sought. As mail after mail arrived with confirmatory news, details of rich finds, high prices, and general rush, we grew furious at our isolation and consequent inability to share in the harvest. Single men and unsuccessful settlers drifted away by every ship, and a large party, seventy in all, left here in September for Melbourne direct, in the ship *Hannah*, Captain Weatherall.

In December Messrs. J. Millar and Co. decided to relinquish business in Natal, removing their stock to Australia, and they offered me a very liberal inducement to accompany them, and remain in their employ. Without doubt, we all "had it" badly.   The gold fever gradually deserted those who had no money and could not move, while those who had something substantial to lose thought twice about selling off at a sacrifice, and breaking up their connection and their homes; among these were my employers, Mr. John Millar being somewhat restrained by the result of his marriage with Miss E. Ayres, sixteen months previously.   As the details of Australian news continued to arrive with their tales of nuggets and strife, famine prices, disorganisation,

and individual hardship, we easily satisfied ourselves that
the grapes were sour, so settled down with rekindled energy
to the safer, slower, if more legitimate Colonial trade,
Durban thus benefiting by this determination to "Advance
Natal."

Shipbuilding. In the year 1686, the survivors of the
wrecks of the Dutch East-Indiaman *Staven-*
isse, and the English ship *Bonaventura*
constructed on the Bluff the first vessel built in Natal.
They named her the *Natal Packet ;* she was afterwards
rechristened the *Centaur*, and on the 17th February, 1687,
left with twenty men on board, without chart, compass, or
instruments, to grope their way down to Cape Town,
which they actually reached in twelve days.   One hundred
and forty-two years later (1828), Lieut. King, Isaacs, and
Hatton, chief officer, with the crew of the *Mary*, utilised
the Bluff shore, about the site of the old Lazaretto,
to build a vessel of bush timber, and the materials
of their brig.   This occupied them nearly two
years and a half.   She was successfully launched,
named—Isaacs says—the *Elizabeth and Susan*, rigged as a
schooner, and sailed for the Cape 30th April, 1828, with
Lieut. King, Isaacs, and crew, taking with them as passengers two Zulu chiefs as Envoys from Chaka to the
Governor.   They put in at Algoa Bay, but met with a
cold reception from the authorities, who looked upon the
King with suspicion, and did not desire to extend their
responsibilities even to so great a King as Chaka.   After a
detention of three months the Envoys were dismissed with
a few trifling presents, and, by orders from Cape Town,
were sent back in H.M.S. *Helicon*.   As they refused to
return in the man-of-war without Lieut. King, he consented
to accompany them, Chaka having entrusted them to his
care.   Isaacs having shipped four horses and goods purchased with their ivory, left Algoa Bay in their schooner,
arriving at Natal on the 18th August, and found the
Helicon at anchor.   Lieut. King, who was in ill-health,
came on board; they crossed the bar, and anchored opposite the dockyard.   King grew rapidly worse, and
died at his house on the 7th September, of what
they believed was Dysentery.   He was buried at his Camp ;

the site of his monument must have been marked on his
Chart by Isaacs.   Fynn and Isaacs appear to have
entered into possession.   Chaka lamented his death, but,
expressing himself hurt at King George's indifference to
him and his envoys, began troubling the white men generally as the fabled wolf did the lamb.   He was killed at
this juncture by Dingaan, who was not expected to smile
on his brother's friends and supporters.

The enterprising Europeans concluded to carry out their
original design in building the schooner, and   quit the
country.   Fynn, with others, went Ivory trading down
South.   Farewell, Isaacs, and the crew of the *Mary*, after
caulking the *Elizabeth and Susan*, shipped their Ivory and
other possessions, and crossed the Bar in her on the 1st
December, 1828, arriving at Algoa Bay on the 15th.
Suspicious of slavery, or of Native designs against the
Cape Settlements, owing also to local jealousies, and
inordinate red tape, she appeared in official records as
the *Chaka*, and in that name was, by instructions from
Cape Town, seized and confiscated as being unregistered
and from a foreign port.

Lieut. Farewell met his death returning by wagon.   N.
Isaacs returned to St. Helena.

The chart made by Lieut. King at that time marks the
" Dockyard " on the Bluff. [See Frontispiece.] Another
quarter of a century sees the advent of the first steamer,
and the launch on the same day of the first sea-going
vessel built in Natal under the flag.   The importance of
the steamer's advent, with the ever-prevailing lack of
interest in local productions so strangely marked among
British Colonists, reduced the spectators of the launch, and
tended to obscure the significance of so great an enterprise.
The desirability of fostering a Coasting trade had induced
Mr. Edward Snell, Merchant, of West Street, to construct
a seagoing vessel for that purpose.   The foreshore of the
Bay, between Acutt Street and Beach Walk, was appropriated, and the frame of a small schooner placed on the
stocks.   She was constructed by a man named Willis, who
utilised a good deal of the *Minerva* timber, and I believe
the local talent of the ship-carpenters, Wm. Cooper and
Herman Wackernow. Mrs. Snell, as sponsor, bestowed her

own name, *Leontine Mary*, upon the vessel at its christening. The launch was only partial, as the little craft remained a short way out on the sands, until dug out and floated to the Point to be rigged. Captain Fuller, of Fuller's Flat, took command, and made a first voyage to Port Elizabeth, where she was duly registered as of 28 tons capacity. Port Natal was not a port of registry at that time. She proved a quick sailer and a credit to this Port, making many successful trips coastways and to Mauritius.

Coal. In connection with the shipping trade, it may be of interest to note that, in the supplementary estimates for the year, we find "For procuring and conveying three tons of coal from Compensation to the Custom House, Port Natal, to be put on board the mail steamer *Sir Robert Peel*, to test its quality for steam purposes, £25." Subsequent events disclosed the fact that the coal was of inferior quality, and delivered so broken that the Engineer could not use it; truly a costly experiment. The mine on "Compensation Flat" was shut down, and filled up, and has never since been reopened.

Congregationalists. On the 11th April the first anniversary meeting of the Congregationalists, or "Independents," as they were then more commonly designated, was held in their place of worship, a room in the long, low wattle and daub thatched building, overshadowed by a huge wild fig tree in front (both still standing), on the Beach Erf No. 10, Block A, Smith Street, owned first by Mr. E. H. Hunt, and rented by Mr. Ralph Clarence, who occupied the front portion as a store. The members numbered at that time twenty-six, and Mr. J. C. Adams, a schoolmaster, was the pastor. Messrs. Peter Lennox and R. W. Tyzack, the first deacons, attended at the tea meeting, an additional attraction being the presence of some local American Missionaries. Mr. J. C. Adams was an earnest, unobtrusive gentleman, to whose kindness and ability myself and others are indebted, for he kept an evening school, and helped young persons of both sexes to repair the defects of incompleted education.

To Mr. Ralph Clarence is to be ascribed the merit of introducing the Blue Gum and Eucalyptus family into Natal from the Cape Colony, whence he originally came. He was an enthusiastic horticulturist, introducing many useful trees and plants. He died a Sugar planter at his " Clare " Estate.

Roman Catholics. This year saw the arrival from France of Bishop Allard, and the Rev. Jean Baptiste Sabon. They were members of the congregation of the Oblate of Mary Immaculate, and literally followed the Apostolic steps, travelling without purse and without scrip. The Roman Catholic community were gathered together and a congregation established, who attended the services of these zealous priests in a private building in Smith Street. I believe I was present at the opening ceremony on the 28th March, for the reason that it is so stated in my notes. Application was made to the Governor, and a small plot of land granted to the Bishop for religious purposes, outside the town, where the present Church of St. Joseph now stands. Here Father Sabon was joined by Father Barrett, and they contrived to build a little brick Chapel, having a couple of small rooms at the back in which they resided, with a hut for a kitchen. Mr. John Hunt (subsequently Mayor) was the Contractor. The land, now in occupation of that community extending to Smith Street, was subsequently purchased at auction when the Corporation laid off that extension of the town. Hence arose the naming of Convent Lane.

This new Chapel, plain and unadorned, was opened for service in July, 1853. On this spot Father Sabon ministered for thirty-three years, during which his old Chapel was pulled down, and the existing Church, Convent, and Schools erected, but not before it was dignified by the body of the Prince Imperial of France, killed in the Zulu War, and honoured by the presence of his bereaved mother, the Empress Eugenie. Father Sabon died in 1885. A handsome mausoleum, in the centre of the Roman Catholic Cemetery, marks his burial place. This good priest, by Christian benevolence and simple piety, endeared himself to the townspeople. His was a well-known figure in the streets of

Durban as he toiled through its sands on foot, in rusty cassock and napless silk hat, carrying a green-lined umbrella, to visit the sick and afflicted.   His habits of self-denial were well known, while it is believed that he would barely have existed, had it not been for the pious frauds of his friends in ensuring his attendance at meal times.   The story of his refusing a new coat and hat, lest their splendour should be attributed to vanity, and so give offence, was credited among us as a fact.

Convicts. The year 1852 closed with a popular demonstration in which Durban took the lead.   The success attending their many public meetings had demonstrated the power of the people, and fostered a belief in the right of the Colonists to a voice in their own Government, a conviction to which Durban has always adhered.

The discovery of gold in Australia emphasised the opinion previously expressed by our cousins there, that the reception was no longer desirable of those " Crown Colonists," described by one of themselves at a social function in Sydney, as :—

" True patriots we, for let it be understood
" We left our Country for our Country's good,"—

consequently the British Government was at a loss to dispose of those " true patriots " already under sentence of penal servitude.   However, to the dismay of the Cape Colonists, the transport ship *Neptune*, with a cargo of convicts, arrived unexpectedly in Table Bay, with the design of landing those people for public works.

Mr. Boycott's name had not then been applied to that peculiar institution, but the Colonists, threatening to rise in arms, applied the Boycott principle to the ship.   No communication was allowed, no water,. no beef, no flour, and it was even in contemplation to extend its operation to the Governor and the Garrison.   A compromise was ultimately effected, and the *Neptune* returned, taking her felon crew with her.   Meantime, our busybodies gave it out that the Governor of the Cape would certainly not send these men back to England, but intended· landing them in this Dependency in answer to our repeated demands for harbour improvements, main roads, and public works. Though this may have been "played off" upon us, as the Americans say, yet the possibilities inflamed the public mind, so a meeting was convened for the 6th of December at three in the afternoon, to discuss the situation. Stores were accordingly closed, and a packed house was the result. All classes were represented, as the hour admitted the attendance of people from the country.

The principal speakers were Messrs. Galloway, Robert Babbs, E. P. Lamport, Wm. Campbell, H. J. Barrett, Jas. Brickhill, D. D. Buchanan, J. B. Roberts, Joseph Few, and the Rev. Calvert Spensley. The alarming prospect was presented by these fervid speakers to the imagination of the audience, who were influenced as much by the midsummer temperature as by the energetic denouncements of the orators, who stamped and raved in perspiring periods, encouraged by the cheers of the people and "gallery"; consequently those contradictory persons, found in all states of man, who had ventured a belief in the advantages of convict labour, were submerged by the popular torrent, and the meeting terminated on carrying an unanimous vote in praise of the Cape Colonists, and against any attempt to introduce convicts into Natal, followed by frantic cheers, cordial greetings, and cool drinks.

Durban men of that period still recall the "Great Convict Meeting" in Mr. Francis Harvey's wooden auction room, now replaced by the double-storied building occupied by Mr. John Pardy, watchmaker.

CHAPTER VIII.

1853.

Gold. IT was during this year that the disastrous effect of the Gold discovery became rapidly apparent, as efficient and qualified men of all degrees, renouncing their farms and occupations, began to leave this Colony for the older and more promising Australian settlements. Hope was naturallly excited that this undeveloped country of Natal might prove equally auriferous, while the possibilities of discovery might lie within every one's reach, for did not that glorious hymn of our youth tell of "Afric's golden sands," while the Queen of Sheba was credited with obtaining her supplies on our very coast.

To counteract the depletion of our population, twenty of those resolute Durban merchants who had elected to throw in their lot with Natal advertised early in this year a guarantee of £1,000 reward to the first discoverer of gold in this Colony; unfortunately, in the prevailing scarcity of capital, their "good for" only extended to four months, while the discoverer had to produce gold to the value of £5,000. The proclamation was well meant, but, being somewhat "shoppy" in its terms, created but a passing enthusiasm. Several parties went prospecting in a desultory manner. A Mr. Martin was reported to have sold an inland farm to a party of diggers for £700. A few specimens of honeycombed quartz came in from Cato

Manor Estate;   this quartz, "slightly gilded as it were
by electrolysis" *(sic)* was solemnly treated by Mr. Robert
Raw, chemist, an analysis of the process published, with a
satisfactory explanation how the acids employed had removed all trace of gold!   The editorial comment on "Martin's Diggins"   and Mr. Raw's assay being "Whatever
the indications may be, there is as yet no sufficient ground
for pronouncing Natal a gold colony."   The fact was that
no one knew what to look for, or what to do with it when
they had found it.   Californian traditions were enlarged
upon, and someone kept alive the interest by showing the
model of a   "Rocker"   goldwasher.

Exodus.   In the meantime, Messrs. J. A. Jackson
                  and Co., agents of the brig *Wee Tottie,*
                  150 tons, had laid on that vessel for Mel-
bourne, after fitting her up specially for passengers.

The rush was such that some seventy souls elected to
crowd into this small vessel.   She sailed on the 22nd of
February.   The public devoted the afternoon to the Point,
bidding our friends good-byu, cheering them as they started,
and seeing them safely over the Bar.   Among the passengers were Mr. Thomas Milner, Mr. T. Spencer Cope, L.C.B.,
a gentleman of considerable legal ability, for a short time
partner with Mr. J. R. Goodricke and practising in Durban,
Mr. Geo. Hicks (librarian), who became sub-editor of the
Melbourne Argus,   Mr. Francis Spring, late Postmaster-
General; a large number of mechanics with their families,
and Mr. Geddes, the parish clerk and sexton.

The *Hannah,* was however, the first vessel to leave here,
in 1852 with passengers.   This and other vessels subsequently took away more of our settlers to the New Eldorado.

Natal Sugar   That a conflict of opinions existed as to
Company.   where Fortune was to be found is shown
                  by the fact that, at the time of the *Wee
Tottie's* departure, Durban's business men
in public meeting assembled agreed to form the   "Natal
Sugar Company"   with a capital of £10,000, in 2,000 shares
of £5 each.   A committee was formed, and a Mr. X. R.
Breede elected chairman, and Mr. Edwin Griffith secre-
tary *pro tem.*   Operations were to be commenced on Spring-

field Flat, in which Mr. Henry Milner and J. L. Fielden were interested. The company was duly floated, a mill erected and sugar manufactured; but a subsequent overflow of the Umgeni devastated the estate and terminated the company.

St. Paul's. The limited space in the Government Schoolroom, Field Street, and its unsuitability for Church purposes—the military at that time attending morning service—coupled with a benevolent desire to find employment for those artizans who declined Australia, instigated the Colonial Chaplain to avail himself of the Church erf on the Market Square, and to commence the erection of a substantial and suitable edifice. A Building Committee was formed, subscriptions lists opened, and a general levy made upon the public. Contributions were given of bricks, others of lime, while two young men promised their labour for two days each. The first published list amounted to £292 9s., which was, however, supplemented by contributions from England and Cape Town. With this capital, the ever-sanguine, hopeful and popular Parson Lloyd set about St. Paul' Church. Designed by Mr. R. S. Upton, architect, and estimated to cost several hundreds of pounds, it was, when completed, to be 110 feet long, with transepts and a square tower, but for the present it was decided not to exceed £1,000, excluding the tower, and limiting the length to 70 feet, with a width of 34 feet, to be roofed with slate. A contract was accordingly entered into with Mr. W. P. Downs, builder, and the 17th March selected for laying the foundation stone.

After a special morning service in the schoolroom, a procession was marshalled by Mr. Robt. Acutt in the following order: School children with banners, followed by Mr. R. S. Upton carrying the plans and silver trowel; the Rev. W. H. C. Lloyd, and the Rev. Mr. Jenkins from Pietermaritzburg in cap and gown; Clergymen of the Church of England; the Rev. Wm. Shaw, Superintendent of the Wesleyan Missions in South Africa; Revs. C. Spensley and Joseph Gaskin, Wesleyan Ministers, Durban and Verulam; Rev. H. Wilder, American Board of Missions, Presbyterian (?); Rev. Mr. Grosvenor, Congregationalist; Mr. L. E. Mesham, J.P., Resident Magistrate, Inanda; Lieuts.

Johnstone and Smyth, with Dr. Cunningham, H M. 45th Regt.; the Churchwardens, Sidesmen, Members of Building Committee; and members of the Church of England, two and two. The site was marked by scaffold poles supporting the stone and a few ship's flags.

The surrounding bare sandy space was occupied by the procession and the spectators, the majority of whom were ladies.

The dedicatory part of the ceremony was performed by the Clergy, an amateur choir, with the congregation, joining in the hymns and psalms, the stone in the meantime having been duly laid with the customary forms by Mr. L. E. Mesham, who, being at the time the principal subscriber, had been invited to preside, in the absence of the Lieut-Governor from the Colony, and the detention in Pietermaritzburg of Major Preston, 45th Regt., the Acting Governor. The following is a copy of the document deposited under the foundation stone : —

"The foundation stone of this Church was laid by Lloyd Evans Mesham, Esq., Magistrate of the Inanda location, on Thursday, the 17th day of March, in the year of our Lord One Thousand Eight Hundred and Fifty-three, and in the sixteenth year of the reign of Her Majesty, Queen Victoria 1st.

Lieut.-Governor, Hon. Benjamin Chilly Campbell Pine, Esq.
Chief Judge, Hon. Henry Cloete, L.S., L.L.D.
Colonial Chaplain, Revd. W. H. C. Lloyd, M.A.

Committee for Building the Church—J. R. Scott, Esq., J.P., Treasurer; Lancelot Newton and W. H. Middleton, Churchwardens; Robert Raw, Secretary; J. L. Fielden, L. E. Mesham, J.P., John Millar, Henry Fynn, Robert Acutt, Thomas Dand, Robert Nimmo, W. H. Savory. Architect, R. S. Upton; Builder, W. P. Downs.

At the conclusion of the ceremony the children were regaled with the luxuries of the period, buns and gingerbeer.

A cold collation, tickets 5s. each, was provided for the seniors in Kinghurst's large store in Smith Street, at which ladies were present. The Rev. W. H. C. Lloyd presided with special aptitude. The usual loyal toasts, with complimentary and congratulatory speeches, detained the company until shortly before 6 p.m. Two years later St. Paul's was opened for service, the windows being covered with calico for want of funds to procure glass. The ground was not efficiently enclosed until some years after the opening.

As illustrating our adaptability under pressure of circumstances, the *Mercury* reported that the "silver" trowel used on this occasion was made by Mr. H. W. Currie (who had commenced business as "tinplate worker and engineer"). "It was made of copper, plated with silver, with a handle of native ivory beautifully turned and polished."

Customs. In June the Hon. W. S. Field, Collector of Customs, left Durban on his promotion to an office in the Cape Customs, and Mr. George Rutherford, promoted from the West Indies, arrived some few months later to take over his duties. In July the Colonial Treasurer announced that the public could be accommodated with drafts on the Custom House, free of charge, for sums exceeding £10. This was followed a month later by the Natal Fire Assurance and Trust Company (Pietermaritzburg), advertising drafts on and by their Agent, G. C. Cato, payable at sight in Durban or Pietermaritzburg, at a charge for sums up to £10 of 1s., to £25, 2s., to £50, 2s. 6d.; above that ¼ per cent. This proved so great a convenience, and so profitable a business, that Mr. Cato built his well-known offices on the Stanger Street frontage of his erf with a large fire-proof safe let into the brick walls. This served us for a long time as a sort of Banking Establishment; in fact, it was the precursor of the Natal Bank. The department was presided over by Mr. John Ward, who continued in Mr. Cato's service as confidential clerk until incapacitated by age.

Social. The first of a series of social functions for which Durban has since maintained a reputation was inaugurated in the winter months of June and July; the initial festivity being a Ball given by Mr. H. J. Mellor, the Resident Magistrate, at his residence; the second Ball being given by Mr. John Millar, at the firm's new store, Market Square Corner. The reporter of the period writes of this:—

"The large store was most tastefully fitted up as the ball-room. A line of couches extended along each side, and one end was covered by carpeting; while an elegant piano, pier glass, sofas, lounge chairs, ottomans, etc., gave it all the appearance of a handsome private drawing-room. Here the host and hostess received their guests. . . .

The walls were hung with flags, surmounted with evergreens and
graceful festoons, and arches of evergreens, intermingled with flowers,
were disposed around the room and along the joists of the open roof
in such a manner as to destroy for the occasion the character of the
apartment, and make it appear, not a merchant's warehouse in Natal,
but a noble drawing-room in some 'stately hall of England.'   A set of
chandeliers with a profusion of wax lights suspended from the roof
brilliantly lit up the scene, and thus completed the illusion."

Though Mr. Hugh Gillespie was the principal Architect,
I acted as "stage carpenter," and thus shared the credit.
The Market Square yielded the evergreens and palm
branches.   Cases of gin and wine constituted most of the
"couches."   A large stock of glass tumblers ranged on the
wall-plate and shelving reflected the dazzling rays of the
candles in the primitive chandeliers I had constructed with
a few pieces of plank crossed, having tin sconces at
the ends and hung by the centre, disguised by paper and
flowers.   I also gained some merit and many smiles for
elaborating a Sedan chair from a convenient packing case,
fixing a seat and foot board, adding a little calico trimming
with canvas curtain in front and attaching side poles, to
enable the ladies to be carried over the damp sands by
Natives, after the fashion of the handbarrow to which they
were daily accustomed.   The machine realised the expectation of its designer at the opening of the proceedings, but
failed totally in "the wee sma' hours" in consequence of the
absence of the necessary bearers, who could not be found.
The guests at both these gatherings being, with a few exceptions, almost the same, I avail myself of the aforesaid
reporter to enumerate those at Mr. and Mrs. John Millar's
party :—

Mr., Mrs., and Miss Robert Acutt, Mr. W. H. Acutt, Mr. and Mrs.
Ashton, Mr., Mrs., and (2) Misses Ayres, Lieut. Barnes (45th Regt.),
Miss Barrett, Mr. J. Brown, Mr. and Mrs. Collins, Mr. and Mrs. Clowes,
Dr. Cunningham (45th Regt.), Mr. Dickinson, Mr. Dacomb, Mr. and
Mrs. Durham, Mr. and Mrs. Fielden, Miss Forbes, Mr. and Mrs. Good-
ricke, Mr. Grundy, Mr. and (3) Misses Grice, Mr. Gillespie, Mr. G. W.
Harvey, Mr. Hoffmann, Mrs. Kahts, Mr. J. D. Koch, Mr. Lamport, Mr.
Lee, Mr. and Mrs. Mellor, Mr. and Mrs. McArthur, Mr. George Miller,
Mr. J. B. Miller, Mr. and Mrs. H. Milner, Mr. Millar, senr., Mr. and
Mrs. Middleton, Miss Madigan, Mr. and Miss Munro, Mr. Jas. Proud-
foot, Mr. and Mrs. Roberts, Mr. G. Russell, Misses Robinson (2), Mr.
and Mrs. Snell, Mr. and Mrs. Scott, Mr. Sanderson, Lieut. Smyth (45th
Regt.), Mrs. Smerdon, Mr. and Misses (3) Terrason, Mr. and Mrs. G. H.
Wirsing, Mr. Otto Wirsing, and Miss Willis.

Mrs. John Leyland Feilden, one of the guests at both
Balls, after her return to England, wrote a book, entitled
My African Home, from which I extract this record
as showing a lady's point of view:—

(Page 70; time, June, 1853). Went to a grand ball this month,
which I really must describe, it being so unusual an affair, and so
superior to any yet given in Durban. It was a stroke of policy in one
of the Magistrates to overcome some ill-will and jealousies that had
been growing and talked about. . . . . Leyland told me he had
engaged a bedroom in town for us where we should dress and sleep.
So we got out our dress clothes, put them in a portmanteau, and sent
a caffre straight off with it, took a bite of beef and bread in our fingers,
saddled and were off, Leyland carrying my ornaments in a flat basket
over his shoulder. . . . . We dressed and drove to the ball in the
only van in the place, which was engaged to do duty all night. . . .
I was quite surprised with the elegant and extensive arrangements. .
There were three dancing rooms decorated with flags and wild flowers,
beams across the ceiling were hung with festoons, the windows which
opened to the ground were all taken out, and the wide verandah outside covered in and seated all round, while the music was so placed
centrally that it served equally for all the dancing rooms. Some
of the ladies were very good looking and nicely dressed in pink tar-
latan, white muslin, and silk; one lady in a rich velvet dress.

For such a mixed set of people, and the first ball of such pretensions,
it was surprising how everything went off. One of the prettiest and
best-dressed ladies I recognised as our landlady, who danced all the
evening. . . . . There were all classes of people present even to
the police. One hundred and fifty guests were invited, and where so
many were found I know not. So great was the excitement produced
in Durban by so uncommon an entertainment that one lady, rather
than miss the treat, took her baby of three months old with her,
and kept the child with its nurse in the ante-room until five in the
morning.

(Page 85; time, July, 1853.) Mrs. Millar's ball came off on the
13th. It was held in Mr. Millar's store, instead of the house, and thus
we had a beautiful ball-room and supper-room seated for 80 persons
without crowding.

The long room was lighted by six wooden chandeliers made for the
occasion, fitted with wax candles, and all very brilliant and elegant;
the walls covered with calico and decorated with flags and flowers
and evergreens, etc.

The end of the ballroom was carpeted with sofas for those who preferred watching the dancers, and sundry glees were sung during the
evening. Mrs. McArthur took her baby again as at Mrs. Mellor's ball,
and I found the poor thing in the midst of a lot of shawls at half-past
two in the morning, where it nearly got turned over by the ladies
searching for their shawls to go home. Mrs. McArthur,
who is quite a young woman, is early initiating her poor little infant
into habits of dissipation.

Administration of Justice. Following Nature's own law, we now pass from sunshine to shadow. While these festivities were in progress, the Circuit Court had been sitting in the Government Schoolroom, Field Street, presided over by the Honourable Walter Harding, Acting Recorder, assisted by Mr. Henry Cope, Acting Crown Prosecutor; Mr. J. D. Shuter, Clerk of the Peace; Mr. Theophilus Shepstone, Acting Native Interpreter; and Mr. Edwin Lee, Chief Constable. The Jury list for the Division of Durban embraced the County of Victoria, County and Town of Durban, and numbered 326 men, of whom sufficient had been summoned by Mr. J. Riddle Wood, the Deputy Sheriff, for the purposes of the Circuit. The Court was crowded, special interest being taken in the trials, which lasted three days.

On the first, a private of the 45th Regiment, a bad character, consorting with escaped convicts and thieves, was convicted of " receiving stolen goods, knowing them to be stolen," and sentenced to three years' imprisonment and 40 lashes; while a Native was convicted of an attempted rape on a Corporal's wife at the Camp. He was sentenced to five years and 50 lashes.

The two following days were taken up with the trial of five persons—a white man, a Native woman, and three Native men—for the murder of a notorious character called " Jemmy Squaretoes." They were convicted and sentenced to death.

Saturday, July 2nd, being the day fixed by the sentence of the Court for the public flogging of Private Desmond, and the Native Nohlosela, a large crowd of Europeans and Natives, attracted by an escort of armed constables, the cart and the prisoners, gathered in the Market Square in the early morning after sunrise. The soldier's back looked broad and very white when bared; his arms and legs were lashed to the cart-wheel, so that he stood in the form of the letter X.

The police warder who handled the " cat '"—apparently a flimsy affair, made for the occasion—was an old soldier, and laid it on thick to all appearance, but there is a secret known to Drummers and Bo'sun's-Mates, acquired by a long experience in those arms of service, by which the force of the blows can be neutralised.   Desmond received his 40 lashes without emotion, his back only showing a broad pink patch fringed here and there with a few scarlet dots. When loosed, he took a drink of water and put on his shirt with a grumbling oath or two.

The Native was treated in the same way, but the warder did not extend his art to him, so his back became first white, then livid, and then streaked with blood.   By this time I, like the prisoner, had had enough ; my morbid curiosity was satisfied, and I left the scene without waiting for the Doctor's opinion.   I must admit, however, that, though this was the first time I had seen a white man flogged at the hands of Justice, it was not so as regards the Native punishment, for the verandah of McDonald's Hotel, which adjoined J. Millar and Co.'s store, was the Court of Mr. Henry F. Fynn, the Assistant Resident Magistrate and Administrator of Native Law.   His Native Assistant, or Chief Constable, was Tuta, who for his services was afterwards raised to the rank of "Induna," and with his successor, Mafingo, was for many years connected with the Resident Magistrate's Court.   He had a kraal under the large fig tree, between the present Mosque and the Cemetery, serving as Native Police Camp, where the Post-runners and Government Messengers congregated.   Prisoners for minor offences, master and servant cases, thefts, assaults, etc., would be marched up from the "Tronk" by great-coated Native constables, armed with assegais.   A grassy seat, near by the presence, would be pointed out to them, until their case was called.   Prisoner was then duly haled before the judge, whom he would salute, squatting down a respectful distance in front of him, until ordered by the great man to stand.   Complaint promptly heard, prisoner interrogated, reprimanded, but more frequently condemned to ten or twenty lashes, more or less.   Mr. Fynn gave point to his sentences by producing his snuff box and taking a refresher, while Tuta and his men took the culprit aside a convenient distance, spreadeagled him on the sand, face downwards, and counted out the stripes with a sjambock on his back and shoulders.   Prisoner, on his release, would writhe into his blanket, hold up his hand and shout a respectful " Inkosi " to the dignfied white chief, while walking past to resume his employment.

Thus did the power of justice appeal, not only to his feelings, but to his understanding.   No lingering torture cf
expectation before execution, but " suit the action to the
word, the word to the action," as Zulu law and custom
provided.   The Native knows when he has done wrong ;
his sense of justice is very keen, and he expects to pay the
penalty when found out, even with his life.   Hence the
severance of all his social ties by incarceration in a prison,
with its routine and cleanliness, is particularly distasteful
to him, but it carries with it no degradation, the enforced
labour being regarded simply as a tax paid to the Government.   He would at any time prefer a flogging with
liberty. (*)   The methods of the time were decidedly good
in their results, though influenced by the want of prison
accommodation, the incidental expense, and the absence of
coin from which to enforce a fine.   Except in marriage
cases, or offences between Natives, cattle were rarely taken
or paid.

Scarcely had these two floggings been administered before
those hysterical sentimentalists, who persuade themselves
they are prompted by piety and virtue, began to express
their conviction that such things were demoralising and
degrading, particularly to the white youth of the town.
Hypocrisy and pure selfishness ! for, on the perpetration of
any specially brutal, or cruel outrage, they clamoured for the
life's blood of the ruffian ; the full penalty of the Law, and
if that proved insufficient, were ready to execute justice
themselves.   The culprit caught and punished, they are
comforted and safe, so disregarding the unfortunate victim—
the neighbour suffering by the wayside, they can afford
to pose as good Christians and hold their fingers before their
eyes at the prospect of making a public example of the next
case, with a mental reservation that it must not of course
touch them, their wives, or daughters.   These are the
people who actually promote crime, by encouraging a popular belief in the certainty that petitions will be made against
the due execution of sentences passed on offenders.   The
viler the crime, the greater the interest likely to be taken,

---

* This may be controverted, as the modern overdressed town
Native is said to prefer the velvet glove of prison discipline to the
sharper tooth of the " cat."

thereby naturally enlarging the chances of escape. Justice and expediency demanded that both our Dutch fellow-Colonists, the Emigrant, and the newly-liberated Native should SEE that the law for the future would deal equally with white men as with black; actions speak louder than words.

Murder and Execution. It was on the same ground of public polity, that the old-fashioned practice, which obtained at the Cape, condemned the five wretches left for death to be hanged on the site of the murder. As this was the first public execution "sus : per coll :" at the hands of the common hangman that took place in Durban, a brief description of the crime and its fitting punishment may be noted.

Samuel Harris was a seafaring man of the " Beach comber " class. Crippled by the loss of his toes from frostbite at some early period of his career, he acquired the sobriquet " Jemmy Squaretoes." How or when such men appear in a new settlement or a Pacific Island is seldom noted, but in the year of the Umgeni Flood (1848) there existed in the Back Beach bush on an eminence adjacent to the recent residence of the late Mr. William Brickhill, a den of thieves and prostitutes, known as " Seraglio Point " or " Jemmy Squaretoe's Kraal." In 1852 cattle from the flat, goods from wagons, merchandise left outside stores at night, even pigs of lead, and half-aums of spirits vanished strangely, and were not traced at the time. Squaretoes ostensibly worked at the Point, usually spending his earnings on drink. He lived with a Native woman of Hottentot descent, named Flatta. They had between them a following of demoralised Natives, who brought into community such unconsidered trifles as their talents could supply.

Jemmy sober was not a very despotic chief, but Jemmy drunk became a tyrant. A runaway sailor and thief from the *Sir Robert Peel,* on his release from gaol, sought and obtained refuge at Squaretoe's huts, where he opened up communication with those soldiers from the Camp who resorted there, disposing of such goods as they brought for sale or barter ; of these the convict Desmond was one. A path led from town to Squaretoe's kraal across the vlei, which it entered at a point about 200 yards from the Camp.

It was a watery way, and about midway existed a shallow pool through which it was necessary to wade. The advent of this younger sailor, John Elliott, alias Frederick Cooper, induced the woman Flatta to persuade the other Native refugees that life under the domineering, gun-firing Squaretoes was no longer safe. They accordingly applied to a Native Doctor for medicine to remove him. Paid well, the Doctor supplied an unpalatable, but harmless, herb, which Flatta duly administered, the only result being that the victim complained that his coffee was nasty. A second attempt convinced them that they had been imposed upon by the Doctor, so a resolve was taken for more forcible measures, the man Cooper kindly suggesting that it would be better to keep him drinking until he disposed of himself.

On the day of the murder, Squaretoes had been working at the Point, spending his evening in town. A Military picket saw him about ten at night the worse for liquor, surly and abusive, as he took off his trousers preparatory to crossing the vlei to his home. Arrived there, he turned in on the floor of his hut. The conspirators, Flatta, Cooper, Chinguia, Hants (Flatta's son), and Magyan, were also inside, or about. After complacently watching until they assured themselves that he slept, the signal was given. One Native clutched his throat, another sat on his chest, the third held his hands. The poor wretch was just able to gurgle an inarticulate cry to his countryman for help, upon which Cooper, having done nothing, rushed for the door, but, called back by the woman, turned and held the victim's legs until all motion ceased. The directing genius—the woman—suggested the depositing of the body in the pool, as people would then suppose that he fell in when drunk and was drowned.

The white man and three Natives, each taking a limb, stepped out from their deed of darkness into the silent starlight, carrying the body, which they disposed of as directed. To complete the evidence, they afterwards threw in the trousers the deceased had made into a bundle with his belt in the presence of the Corporal. Then they returned for refreshment, and well-earned rest.

Next morning an Officer's Native servant discovered a white hand and arm above the water. Reporting the matter at the Camp, the body was drawn out, and a sort of drumhead enquiry resulted in a verdict of "drowned while drunk, poor devil!"

One of the murderers chanced to be arrested, and deposited in the Tronk, pending an enquiry as to how he came to be unlawfully carrying a gun. He there disclosed to a convict sufficient to lead the latter to think that his friend Jemmy had been done to death. This man, Fisher—a West Indian negro—used Squaretoe's kraal and surroundings as a place of refuge and entertainment, whenever he felt the restraints of the Gaol, and concluded to work out of the wattle and daub prison. This he effected by escaping sometimes underneath it, and at others through the thatch, taking his chains with him. He at once gave information, and it was owing to the shrewd investigation of Mr. J. D. Shuter, the Clerk of the Peace, that the whole of the culprits, with other residents of Seraglio Point, were arrested, the events described elicited and proved eventually at the trial. Mr. J. B. Roberts, who appeared as Advocate for Cooper, consented to defend the other four gratuitously. He made a very able appeal to the Jury, having little else to go upon; Native lads and a woman, actual witnesses of the murder, with the Herb Doctor, gave such conclusive evidence that no eloquence could persuade a faithful Jury to aid the prisoners in escaping the consequences of their foul and treacherous crime.

The day of execution was fixed for Saturday, the 23rd July, the hour 7 in the morning. The exceptional circumstances, with the prospect of witnessing the first execution in Durban, to say nothing of the morbid or depraved curiosity that prompts people to view the taking of life, induced a large number, myself included, to be present. The gallows was erected on the high ground overlooking the vlei, and was approached from Smith Street, over Cato's Bridge, by an open route following substantially the present Brick-hill Road. I arrived at the spot just after sunrise, and found a number of people present, both European and Native. German families from Pine Town were camped around their little home-made ox-carts (with solid wheels) in social enjoyment of early coffee, cheerfully anticipating the coming show. Townspeople stood about on the

dewy grass in groups, or inspected the remains of the burnt
huts; pointing out the fatal pool and pathway to the Camp.
Persons of all social grades kept strolling up, some with
apologetic, or shamefaced air, others pipe in mouth carrying
themselves as they might on a race course.   The feathered
creatures in the surrounding bush hailed the coming day.
Doves cooed, and "Toppies" answered each other obtrusively, while the hum of bees fell on the strained ear in
intervals of silence.

The sun rose on a glorious day, and had just topped the
Back Beach bush, silvering the gloomy gallows, the verdant
vlei, the Camp, Town, and sombre Berea, in a flood of
cheering, re-invigorating light, as the flash of arms and
colour between us and the curling smoke of the town, indicated the approach of the malefactors, with their guard.

Soon a few men on horseback, and the loose nondescript
crowd, that always precedes a procession, surged up from
the vlei at our feet followed by an advance guard of police,
a span of oxen led by a terrified Native, then the open
wagon in which were seated the convicts with white night-
caps on their heads, the Executioner (a man named Wardle),
and the Revs. C. Spensley and Joseph Gaskin, escorted on
each side by armed policemen and followed by a detachment
of soldiers with bayonets fixed.   Arrived at the foot of the
rise, little time was lost by the Deputy Sheriff.   The prisoners were marched up the steps on to the high platform,
Cooper first, followed by the woman Flatta, and the other
three.   They were arranged in that order under the long
beam that rested on stout uprights at each end.   To this
the halters were already fastened.   The Executioner fixed
the nooses, at the same time fastening their feet together.
The soldiers and police took ground around the gallows,
about 20 yards distant, and stood at "attention."   An
awed silence fell upon the spectators as the ministers followed the prisoners.   Mr. Spensley, standing by Cooper,
commenced reading the beautiful funeral service of the
Church of England.   Some of us reverently uncovered,
while the Natives looked on in grave silence, their arms
crossed over their chests, with their hands grasping their
shoulders, or before their mouths.   As the service reached
its conclusion, the prisoners were asked if they wished to

speak to the people. Cooper was repentant and in tears; Flatta and Chiguia followed each other in a clear voice in prayer, admitting their crime; the other two were stolid and apparently indifferent. The hangman pulled the elastic caps over the faces of his victims, and while the Rev. Mr. Spensley resumed the concluding portion of the service, took the opportunity to light his pipe—a short white clay. Mr. Gaskin, evidently quite overcome, left the platform. A few brief puffs, and Mr. Spensley walked slowly down in front of the culprits, reading the Benediction, the hangman on his narrow gangway at the back of the prisoners keeping pace with him to the head of the steps, as the closing of the book was to be his signal. Giving the Minister time to descend, the Executioner turned, and as leisurely walked back again, pipe in mouth, to the centre, where an iron lever projected. A sudden stamp on this, and, with a crash of falling flaps, the unhappy wretches dropped simultaneously, their head and shoulders remaining visible. For a few moments no one moved or breathed. A wailing of Native women broke the silence. My limbs refused to obey the impulse of my mind; my eyes were fixed on the swaying bodies as the ropes began to untwist, and I have an indelible recollection of that smoking hangman reaching out, and tenderly steadying first one, and then the other. I felt very sick, but could not move. The sharp command, "Fall in," followed by "Unfix bayonets," "Fours, right; quick march," restored impulse to my faculties, as the soldiers marched off. I returned home, but not to breakfast. The bodies were, I believe, buried in one grave on the spot.

Town Improvements. The public improvement of the town was delegated by the Resident Magistrate to the Chief Constable, who made the best use of the small supply of convict labour at his disposal. There were so many things to do, and so few to do it, that efficient drainage was not attempted. Burgesses, growing impatient, resolved, as before, to help themselves. Mr. James Brickhill, described in the Jury List as a "Farmer," who had just settled on one of the newly-sold Umbilo Lots (known later as "Prospect"), appealed to the public for shilling subscriptions, "for the

" purposes of draining the pond, and repairing the road on
" the outskirts of Durban leading to Congella, so necessary
" for their comfort as well as that of all Durbanites, who are
" prevented taking the only pleasant walk about Durban by
" this disgraceful swamp." Tenders were also called for
cutting a ditch " to the spring tide high water mark, 2 feet
deep, 1 foot wide below, and 2 feet wide above." Contributions to the extent of £5 were made, and, with the precise-
ness and method that ever characterised Mr. Brickhill, a
statement was published, at the cost of 10s., shewing that
he had paid one " W. Gordge £4 10s. for cutting furrows
and making bridge across ditto." Thus was the drainage ef
the Western Vlei commenced. The construction of the
drain and bridge in West Street had the effect of concen-
trating the outflow into the hollow in Smith Street, bordering Mr. J. R. Goodricke's new Office. In August we find
him advertising for tenders for mangrove posts and planking
and the making of a bridge across Smith Street. I believe
he was aided by some of the landowners in the vicinity,
though the burden of the bridge and drain was borne by
himself and Mr. E. P. Lamport, as shewn by the statement
of account subsequently published, the total cost being
£33 14s. 10d. One curious item appears—" 9s. 10d. paid
for tobacco and provisions for convicts." All trace of this
bridge has been removed, but it was of sufficient height to
allow his little sons " Dick " and " Johnnie " to hunt fish
and crabs underneath.

Mechanics'
Institute.
The discontinuance of the "Library"
presided over by Mr. G. Hicks, came about
in consequence of the purchase of the building by my employers, the books being
deposited with Mr. E. P. Lamport, who, with commendable
public spirit, entertained the idea of appropriating them
for a future Literary Institution.

Accordingly in 1851 meetings were held and rules
adopted for the establishment of the " Durban Commercial
and Literary Institution," the object of which was " to
provide a place of resort for Commercial purposes, and to
afford facilities for the moral, intellectual, and general
improvement of its members." There was a President
(Honourable W. S. Field), two Vice-Presidents (Messrs.

Samuel Benningfield and G. C. Cato), eighteen ordinary
Directors, one Treasurer, and two Auditors; annual subscription 20s. The birth was premature, its proportions
did not satisfy a public want, so it died early of inanition.

On the 21st of September, 1853, a public meeting was
held in Kinghurst's Store, Mr. A. W. Evans in the chair,
when a committee was appointed to draft rules and regulations for a " Durban Mechanics' Institution," its object to
be " the moral and intellectual improvement of its members
and others." On the 5th October a public meeting confirmed these rules, 12 in number, subscription 5s. per
quarter, young men under 18 and ladies 2s. 6d. per quarter.
The first meeting of members was held on 10th October,
when office bearers were elected.

The Institution dispensed with a Chairman, a member
of the Committee presiding as *locum tenens* at each meet-
ing, General meetings electing their own Chairman. On
this occasion W. H. Savory was elected Treasurer; E. H.
Hunt, Secretary; Messrs. A. W. Evans, R. Acutt, and R.
Raw, Trustees; Messrs. Mark Foggitt and R. S. Upton,
Auditors. The Committee of Management were Dr.
Holland, Messrs. H. W. Currie, W. Campbell, R. Acutt,
Francis Harvey, H. W. Barrett, G. Potter, —. Palmer, Jas.
Brickhill, J. F. Kahts, Jas. Kinghurst, and J. Lumsden.

At the second meeting of the Committee Mr. Kahts
resigned, and Mr. Thomas Dand was chosen by lot in his
place.

Mr. Jas. Pulleyn offered to lease a small thatched wooden
building intended for a shop in West Street (the site now
occupied by the Castle Mail Packets Company, Ltd.), at
£18 a year, payable quarterly, which offer was accepted.
The services of Mrs. Hall were engaged as " Attendant at
the Library " for £12 per annum, with the use of the
rooms and ground at the rear; her husband, John Jervis
Hall, being at the time an upholsterer and mattress maker.
A sub-committee was appointed to canvass for books and
subscribers. War was shortly after declared with Mr.
Lamport for the non-surrender of the books of the old
Library. He stood upon the order of their going; each
side wrote themselves out, and having " vindicated principle," the miscellaneous collection was ultimately sold by

auction (May, 1854) to defray the liabilities of the defunct
Commercial   and   Literary   Institution,   when   the
" Mechanics " became purchasers of a choice selection.

The first committee meeting held at the Institution was
on the 1st November, 1853, and the place was formally
opened to members on the 14th November, when proposals
were made for holding lectures, and for formation of classes,
which were afterwards carried out; the first lecture being
by Dr. Holland, 31st January, 1854, admission free. At
the first half-yearly meeting the Secretary reported 112
members on the list, 409 volumes of books, and 272
pamphlets.   The subsequent successful career of the
" Mechanics' Institute " will be noted later on.

Political Meetings. In October another public meeting was
held in Kinghurst's Store, Smith Street,
ostensibly " for the purpose of obtaining an expression of public opinion
on the recent Government measures." Mr. John Millar
was called to the Chair. Mr. Lamport spoke to a Memorial
that had been prepared, expressing the poverty of the
Colony, and complaining generally of the measures proposed
to be introduced by the Government—increasing taxation,
official salaries, providing for a Trigonometrical Survey,
establishing County Councils, and imposing Wharfage
dues. In reference to the last, the Chairman pathetically
said " it would be but reasonable that they had a wharf
and cranes, before being called upon to pay for them." As
the Government was not represented at the meeting, we
had a good time, and, after the usual contention on the
wording of paragraphs, adopted the memorial as amended.

The other speakers were J. B. Roberts, J. R. Goodricke,
Jas. Proudfoot, J. F. Kahts, Dr. Johnston, R. W. Tyzack,
W. Campbell, —. Galloway, and Savery Pinsent.   The
Lieut.-Governor was directed to send the Memorial to the
Secretary-of-State with the estimates for 1854, and Messrs.
J. Millar, E. P. Lamport, Jas. Proudfoot, A. W. Evans,
Goodricke, John Brown, and John Sanderson were
appointed a Committee to see that he did it, " or transmit
the same to the Secretary-of-State in the event of His
Honour declining to do so."   In this mode were liberty of
speech and the principles of self-government encouraged in

Durban. It is, however, only just to the burgesses of Pietermaritzburg to record that they had already expressed similar views, and with the same license.

Public meetings in these years were usually held in the evening, and in such buildings as were available.   The promoters had to provide the accessories and the lighting.   The Field Street Schoolroom, being used by the Church, had forms, and tin chandeliers for candles, in the form of a hoop, suspended by three or more chains to a central ring; the same pattern, varying in style, paint or perforations, was to be found in most canteens and Auction Marts, from which they were occasionally borrowed on public occasions. Platforms were extemporised from deals, or cases in store, on which a table was placed, backed by a few American wood-seated chairs, a couple of tin, or pewter, flat candlesticks for the Chairman.   Porter bottles held the candles for the reporter's side table or desk, while occasionally some of those peculiar tin candle-holders and reflectors combined, shaped like the letter **L** were hung on nails against the wall; but as a general thing the platform end of the room was sufficiently lit to read by, the rest of the space being left in obscurity.   All that was thought necessary was to see the speakers, *we* could always be heard.   If, however, any "gentleman at the back" ventured a remark, he was immediately requested to "come forward" or to "go up."   Seats were seldom to be had, so the majority of the audience stood, the more fortunate occupying such posts of vantage as window sills, casks, cases, or bales afforded. Smoking was universal.

Amusements. With the exception of public meetings and evening Auctions, the young men of the period strove to be virtuous by force of circumstances.   There being no Reading Room, no shows, no places of social intercourse—excepting the prohibited canteens with their cards, bagatelle tables, and military customers—nothing but sandy roads and no lights, excepting the Moon, there was not any inducement to walk abroad, consequently music became an attraction.   A set of young fellows, who rented a house in common in Union Street, scandalised the neighbourhood by forming a Glee Club, which met on the iron roof of the house in question, the

members reclining on the slope, and reaching over the ridge
to drum time with their hands on the opposite side, as accompaniment to very secular songs. Hymn tunes, common
meter, with the words given out by the conductor, two
lines at a time, were the most popular.   This Club had been
invited to assemble at a building known as the " Growlery,"
on Mr. G. C. Cato's premises, occupied by his younger half-
brothers, Thomas and John P. Cato.   Thomas Cato was
both mechanical and musical.   He had constructed a
" Seraphine " in his spare time, which was the admiration
of all the apprentices and young men of the East End.   As
a consequence, musical instruments were introduced, and we
were welcome to practise there either vocally or instrumen-
tally.   Smoking not being prohibited, it became a social
" free and easy," while we were constituted members of a
regular organized society.   But, as is usual in all musical
circles, someone aspires to be the centre, so, when concerted
pieces were attempted, the smokers and jokers were voted
out, yet being " sturdy varlets," they held their ground for
a time, until excluded by the instrumentalists forming themselves into the " Durban Philharmonic Society," of which Mr.
W. H. Cullingworth was Secretary.   The original members
were, I believe, Thomas and John P. Cato, D. Hull, jun.,
J. J. Chapman, W. Swift, W. Palmer, W. Grant, W. Fraser,
John Cubitt, J. F. Baumann, T. L. Cullingworth, — Thring,
G. J. Cato (G.C.'s son), and W. H. Cullingworth.   I think
that W. Throssel and W. Hart joined later with Bassoon
and Trombone:

The Society took root and flourished, and to demonstrate
its proficiency gave an entertainment on the 10th November
in the store of Mr. Wm. Palmer (late Knight and King),
which was elegantly fitted up for the occasion.   One end
was occupied as an orchestra, the rest by their guests.

The *Natal Mercury* of that date designated it " The
Annual Soiree," and notes that : —

"A pianoforte and a seraphine accompanied, and added greatly to
the effect of the instruments.   At intervals during the evening, vocal
music accompanied by the piano furnished a variety to the entertainment.   A numerous party of ladies and gentlemen (no fewer we
believe than fifty) partook by special invitation of the refined enjoy-
ments of this occasion ; and we must not omit to mention that abundant and elegant refreshments were provided for the company by the

gallant and harmonious hosts, who rightly relying on the 'spiritual intoxication of sweet sounds' did not mingle with it grosser libations of the grape or the grain, but only 'cups which cheer but not inebriate.' The seraphine (at which Mr. Hull, junr., efficiently presided) is the work of Mr. Thomas Cato, one of the members of the society, and the case is made entirely of the woods of this Colony. It is a very beautiful and full-toned instrument, and reflects the highest credit on the skill and taste of the maker."

Trivial as these particulars may appear, this Soiree was both eventful and historical; notwithstanding the absence of stimulants, there was an intoxication, unnoted by the reporter, in the presence of those bright eyes and dainty forms which most of us had hitherto only looked at in Chapel, that fairly turned our heads, resulting eventually in the establishment of six families in consequence of affinities then discovered.

This Society, of which Mr. John P. Cato was the Honorary Secretary, revived the Christmas Waits by organising Carol Singing, vocal and instrumental (if this expression be not Hibernian), from house to house, commencing their perambulations on Christmas Eve, 1853, visiting the residences of the principal inhabitants, who in subsequent years made provision of hot coffee, cool drinks, or a final supper, as the only recompense the minstrels would accept. This practice is maintained to the present time, principally by members of the Wesleyan Community, who, as the Town extended, and roads were hardened, added a hand cart, and cottage harmonium, to enable them to reach the distant Berea, and spare the breath of the singers. There the sweet strains of " Christians arise," breaking suddenly on the close midsummer night, roused both the inhabitants and their sleeping dogs. Thanks and abuse were mingled!

Christmas Festivities. The year 1853 terminated in the good old Dutch fashion with festivities, gun-firing, bell-ringing, and other noises. On this occasion Mr. S. Benningfield, whose house was on the Bay side of his well-known garden, extending from Smith Street, the whole length of Grey Street to the shore (Erven Nos. 1 and 2, Block A.), had invited a few friends to a display of home-made fireworks. These proved a great success, the rockets especially, seen by the natives for the first time, producing cries of admiration or astonishment, from the near vicinity of "Irish Town." Several wagons, bringing Dutch visitors, were outspanned hard by; their Hottentot drivers and leaders, fraternising with town acquaintances, had gathered round the bonfire, without which no open-air function was complete. Always liberal and jocular, Mr. Benningfield, an Essex man by birth, kept up the traditions of the season with the spirit of "a fine old English gentleman"; so the coloured stranger at his gate participated in the good things, their tastes leaning to bread, beef, and "Cape smoke." Their delight at the fireworks and feast was testified by boisterous laughter, antics and guttural exclamations in pure "Hottentot Hollands," culminating, as the fireworks gave out, and the fun became fast and furious, in the production of fiddle and accordion. The music (such as it was) induced the nurse-girls of the visitors to join in, and a regular Hottentot dance (Old Colony style) was commenced. It was to most of us new-comers a novel and extraordinary sight. These yellow-skinned people, small of stature, their round heads dotted with "pepper corns" of wool, ugly in feature, active and agile as monkeys, skipping or strutting about to the tune, leaping, clapping their veltscooned feet in the air, advancing and retiring to their partners, with an occasional lift of one leg and a hissing of the lips, with bright, vigilant eyes, bursting with fun, but not a note of the tongue or muscle of the features betraying anything but the most solemn gravity, gave them the appearance, by the fitful light of the smoking bonfire, of a group of clothed baboons mimicking "humans" until the *pas de grace* was accomplished by a simultaneous flap of one foot on the hard ground, when they disclosed their brotherhood to man by an outburst of merry laughter, and took a drink.

The New Year had reached England before I relinquished tho fascinations of the Old Year to these dancers, with their valedictory and somewhat disjointed salutation, "Goode nicht, Baas."

CHAPTER IX.

1854.

IT altogether depends upon one's *locus standi* how the events of 1854 may be regarded in relation to their importance to the history of individuals and of Durban.

We had the Volunteer movement with its correlative, the Moustache movement. The Early Closing movement. The Advent of the Right Reverend John William Colenso, who, if he did not make Durban famous, is inseparably connected with its history, and did more to make Natal known to the rest of the world than any living man. This year we became an incorporated Borough with a Mayor and Town Council, and lastly, we were blessed with the Natal Bank and paper money.

As the interest of history is centred somewhat in the chronological order of facts, I will endeavour to condense my record on those lines, asking the sympathy of my readers for any looseness in construction.

Crimean War. On the 16th January we heard by overland mail from the Cape that war had been declared on the 1st November by Russia against Turkey, and that British and French fleets had entered the Bosphorus to watch events. It is needless to relate here how they took a hand in the game, or of the Crimean War and its results. But after blows had been exchanged, and the combined armies obliged to sit down before Sebastopol, the good people at home advised

Her Majesty, Victoria I., to apply to a Higher Power for aid; so her Governors throughout the Colonies were directed accordingly. Lieut.-Governor Pine proclaimed the 25th August as a public day of Solemn Fast:—" That we should humble ourselves before Almighty God," and "implore His Divine assistance and blessing on Her Majesty's Arms, for the restoration of Peace, etc." In such case killing is no murder, of course, the Almighty being expected to suspend the Decalogue—as a recent Mayor of Durban did the Bye-laws—for the occasion. Stores were accordingly closed, and the forenoon, at least, treated as a Sunday. Some sinners regarded it as a holiday, while others strayed with rod and gun.

Bishop Colenso. On the 30th January the steamer *Calcutta*, 1800 tons, called, in passing on her way to India, with the English mail of the 15th December. The newspaper remarks:—" She had a remarkably fine run from England (to the Cape) of 35 days. For the first time in the history of Natal, we have had communication with England in 45 days." Her only passenger for this port was the Right Reverend Dr. Colenso, the new Bishop of Natal. His first sermon was preached in the Field Street Schoolroom, St. Paul's being but partly built. His visit was purely one of inspection, but he made good use of his time, visiting the American Mission Stations, Pietermaritzburg, and various parts of the Colony, baptising, marrying, burying, and confirming. He consecrated the Military burial ground at the Camp, and another at Claremont, leaving the Colony again by the SS. *Natal* on the 10th April to return to England, and publish his " Ten Weeks in Natal," before resuming his Diocese, and the thorny paths of a Missionary Bishop.

How far the appearance of the woolly-headed sheep may have affected the shepherd, or influenced him in remonstrating with the Government upon their nakedness, we cannot say, since other decent men had already expressed their conviction that some compulsion should be used with Natives resident in towns. It is certain that, immediately on the Bishop's arrival, a Proclamation was issued that " All Natives residing in or passing through the towns of Pieter-maritzburg, Durban, and Ladysmith, are required to be

clothed with some garment from the shoulder to the knee."
Blankets not objected to. This created a brisk barter trade
in those cast-off articles of European attire, known to the
Natives as "Ingouboos." The men did well enough with
shirts, meal sacks, blankets, or soldiers' great-coats, leaving
their women and girls to forage for themselves. Here
these children of Nature displayed their keen appreciation
of the fitness of things, scorning to clothe themselves in male
attire. They fitted on anything feminine, night gowns,
dressing gowns, flounced skirts, obsolete dresses, from which
the buttons had been cut, petticoats with and without
bodies, shifts, the front and back flaps tied together round
the neck, frilled pantalettes, inverted and improved, to
admit the head and arms, or any other article suitable
for their purposes. Grotesque and gratifying, a step towards civilization, delighting the heart of the Missionary
until the garments acquired a second age, when their presence in Chapel was not insisted upon. Sumptuary laws
are always resented, hence the enforced civilization has not
to this day won the heart of the Native damsel, who, when
at home, dresses *au naturel*, in the belief of our poet
Thomson, that "Beauty when unadorned, adorned the
most."

Exports and Imports. At the commencement of the year, the courtesy of the new Collector of Customs, Mr.
George Rutherford, allowed the *Mercury*
to publish a statement of values of imports
and exports from the beginning, showing the state of affairs
when Natal was annexed, with the very marked progress to
this date; the result not so much of British rule as of
British Emigrants, Capital, and Labour. This accidental
circumstance by imparting information to the people had
important results, for at a later period in the year certain
malcontent Boers stirred up their compatriots in Natal to
memorialise the British Government to abandon this Colony
to them, as we had done in the case of the Sovereignty.
Counter-memorials were formulated by the British settlers,
to which it is said every male inhabitant of Durban subscribed, and these Customs facts and figures were made use
of, with other cogent reasons, to convince the Secretary of
State, that, if we did not own the larger land area, we made

practical use of our opportunities and of our capital and labour. I limit my extracts to intervals of five years; thus, in

1843 the imports amounted to £11,702, and the exports to £1,348.

1847 the imports amounted to £46,981, and the exports to £14,376.

1852 the imports amounted to £103,701, and the exports to £27,845; of which exports £20,164 was Colonial Produce.

Possibly this publication gave encouragement to commercial men, since it showed conclusively the progressive and prospective nature of our trade and transactions, the returns for the last vear (1853) giving Imports £118,000, and Exports £36,458.

Banking. However, early in 1854 rumours of Banking institutions, originating in Pietermaritzburg, were received in Durban with approval, for suddenly the Bank of Natal revived its constitution, got together its provisional Directorate, and in the middle of February published its Prospectus in the *Natal Independent.* The proposed capital was £15,000 in 3,000 shares of £5 each, deposit £2 10s. per share, with limited responsibility to shareholders. Provisional Officers, Jas. Archbell, Chairman; John Macfarlane, Manager; Charles Barber, Secretary; A. B. Roberts, Attorney; Head Office, 30, Market Square, Pietermaritzburg.

A rift in the lute was disclosed at its first meeting, originating, as explained by the Secretary, in over-sensitiveness as to short notice for the meeting, in some of the original Directors. Hence on the 1st March the public was favoured with the following declaration :—

We, the majority of the original projectors of the proposed Bank, hereby make known that we have withdrawn from the same, as at present constituted, and that we are proceeding in the formation of a Bank according to the original intention.

D. B. Scott.	J. P. Hoffmann.	R. Vause.
Jos. Henderson.	P. Ferreira.	J. A. Jackson.

It was on this occasion that these gentlemen first proved their metal, and earned for themselves reputations for doughty deeds and business ability, which remains to them.

Natal Bank. They took thirty days' grace, and at the end of the same month (30th March) published the Prospectus of the "Natal Bank," Deposit, Issue, and Discount, Capital £20,000, in 4,000 shares of £5 each, payable in three years. Provisional Officers, D. B. Scott, Chairman; Directors, J. Henderson, P. Ferreira, J. P. Hoffmann, F. M. Wolhuter, R. Vause, John McKenzie, J. W. Winter, G. C. Cato, Jas. Proudfoot, J. R. Goodricke, Jas. Brickhill, A. W. Evans, and G. H. Wirsing; Attorney, D. D. Buchanan; Hon. Secretary, R. Vause, with a list of 160 subscribers to 3,000 shares, of whom nearly one half belonged to Durban.

The Natal Fire Assurance and Trust Company were both shareholders and promised depositors. The Prospectuses of both Banks were advertised together for some time, and meetings of their provisional Directors were held, until the easy-payment system of the Natal Bank coupled with the backing of the Natal Fire Assurance and Trust Company, and the energy of the Provisional Directors, on whom Mr. G. C. Cato had no mean influence, turned the scale in its favour; so on the 1st May they were able to advertise their establishment, and at a general meeting of shareholders, Messrs. P. Ferreira, R. Vause, D. B. Scott, P. Allen, John McKenzie, T. Puckering, and J. P. Hoffmann were elected Directors; P. Ferreira and G. C. Cato, Trustees; Carl Behrens, General Manager; W. Hutchinson, Cashier; D. D. Buchanan, Attorney. Business *pro tem.* in the Office of the Natal Fire Assurance and Trust Company, Pietermaritzburg. Discount 8 per cent. Deposits three months and upwards 4 per cent.; twelve months and upwards 5 per cent. Certain Durban shareholders objecting to the Trust Deed, it was resolved that the Durban Branch business should not be opened until the question had been submitted to a general meeting. As the history of the Natal Bank will be found in the records of that institution during its successful career from that time to the present, I will content myself with noting that the first Bank Notes issued by them—in August, 1854—were for One Pound value. They were type printed by Mr. Jeremiah Cullingworth; we looked to the signatures for security. In September the shareholders elected five Directors for the

Durban Branch in the persons of Messrs. J. F. Kahts, Jas. Brickhill, W. Smerdon, A. W. Evans, and G. H. Wirsing, who advertised a fortnight later for a Manager and suitable premises.   Mr. G. C. Cato tendered himself as Branch Manager with the offer to build suitable Bank premises on the Erf at the corner of West and Aliwal Streets.   His offer was accepted.   The Branch Bank opened on the 28th November, and Mr. Cato in his capacity as Manager advertised that the Directors would receive applications for discount on Tuesdays, Thursdays, and Saturdays, while deposits would be taken daily between 10 a.m. and 3 p.m. for the present at his office in Stanger Street.

The Bank of Natal continued to call for subscriptions until the 4th November, when a general meeting was held. As they apparently joined the majority, their " subsequent proceedings interested us no more."

Dr. Stanger. It was justly considered that the Colony lost an efficient public servant, and a valued member of society, by the death of the Surveyor-General, Dr. William Stanger, which took place at Durban on the 14th March.   His remains were interred in the new General Cemetery.   The funeral was large and imposing.   The Lieut.-Governor, the local Civil Servants, Officers from the Camp, and 120 townsmen dressed in black followed.   Shops were closed along the route.   The Bishop of Natal, assisted by the Rev. W. H. C. Lloyd, conducted the funeral service in a most solemn and impressive manner. The site of the grave was selected by Lieut.-Governor Pine, under a wide-spreading flat-crown tree, still standing, though sadly decrepid by reason of old age.   He also originated the design for the monument which marks the spot.

Mail Steamers. The progress of our postal, passenger, and steam communication with England and the Cape was of a variable and uncertain quality.   For months Mr. Edward Snell advertised for freight and passengers to Coast Ports and Cape Town, by the Royal Mail Steamer *Natal*, 680 tons, Captain J. Boxer.   In December, 1853, " expected on the 30th "; in January " hourly "; in February " shortly "; in March " hourly."   She was intended to replace the *Sir*

Robert Peel, sadly in need of repairs, and was called "the new steamer"; but alas, when she did finally arrive on the 6th April, it was alleged she had only a new name. She was enabled to cross the Bar without anchoring at low water neap tides, which the *Natal Mercury* asserted was "a satisfactory illustration of the effects already produced by these [Harbour] Works, even in their present comparatively incipient state." The official record on the 14th April was "21 feet spring tides, equal to 18 feet neap tides."

The *Natal* left for the Cape with the Bishop on board, as previously noted, on the 10th April. The *Sir Robert Peel*, Captain Freezer, took our May mail. The *Natal* also returned, came inside, and sailed again on the 14th May. Then those accidents of the sea to which steam machinery, new or old, is liable, happened to both of them. The *Sir Robert Peel* went out of the running, and the *Natal* experienced "difficulty in effecting her repairs"; so the English news she brought, when she did come up, on the 13th July, was no later than that by the direct sailing ship *Queen*, from Liverpool, but she picked up from an Indian steamer, Overland news to the 24th April. This time the state of the Bar detained her "an hour or two" outside, but the reporter cheerfully notes, "We understand the facility with which she entered the Port and its obvious natural advantages struck with surprise and delight the two Admiralty Surveyors on board."

We existed without steam communication until the 10th August, subsisting on crumbs of information from Coasting schooners, and the overland post from the Cape, which was regarded as a missionary enterprise, subsidised and utilised by both the Military and Civil Governments. The "arrival of the *Natal* with an English mail to the 24th May" on the 10th August, was deemed worthy of head lines and heavy type, but even this news came, like tne knowledge of the ancients, from the East by the S.S. *Argo* from Calcutta, which had called at Madras, Ceylon, Mauritius, and Cape Town. Our overland mail from Algoa Bay, where it had been taken by Coaster, reached Cape Town a day too late for the homeward bound *Argo*, so we had to rest satisfied that it would be sent on to England by sailing ship, as regular steam communication with the Cape was interrupted, we were told, by the war.

On the 30th August the *Natal* returned from the Cape, after an absence of seventeen days, with the English mails brought by another new coasting steamer, the *Cape of Good Hope*, placing us in possession of English letters and news " in the unprecedentedly short space of 49 days." On the 29th September the *Cape of Good Hope*, 700 tons, Captain Lowen, arrived after a passage of 18 days from Table Bay, owing to heavy weather, and consequent detention at Coast ports. She did not come inside, though the irresponsible reporter explains " there was ample water on " the Bar, but in consequence of the recent gales the heavy " swells rounding the point of the Bluff had deposited a " narrow bank within the Bar. . . this bank is altogether " a temporary formation. . . It may be worth while to " notice that, when the present Harbour Works are com- "pleted, the tidal current will be so confined and " strengthened that, even under such unusual circumstances " as have lately transpired, no banks of this kind could " possibly be formed."

The fares advertised by the Agent of these steamers were : —

		Saloon.	Fore Cabin.	Deck.
East London	...	£5 5 0	£3 3 0	£2 2 0
Algoa Bay ...	...	6 6 0	4 4 0	3 3 0
Mossel Bay	...	9 9 0	5 5 0	4 4 0
Cape Town	...	12 12 0	7 7 0	5 5 0

Princeza. Whatever temporary formations the Bar had assumed, the Captain of the *Cape of Good Hope* was not disposed to risk its possibilities, having before his eyes the three-masted schooner *Princeza*, 149 tons, fast aground on that unknown quantity the " Lea Bank," where she had arrived in attempting to cross the Bar two days previously. She was from Liverpool, consigned to Mr. Lamport. Most of her cargo of salt and soap was thrown overboard, as the attempt to discharge it into boats proved slow and hazardous, with risk to life, one lighter having sunk alongside. After the lapse of six days she was floated off, warped into the Bluff Channel, and secured, but shortly after broke adrift, and was carried by the outgoing tide to a more convenient spot on the same

Lea Bank, from which she was speedily hauled off and brought to a proper anchorage off the Custom House. Strange to say, her hull sustained no damage.

Fire. Resuming the order of time, the month of May was marked by a calamity, the extent of which may yet be felt by Durban and Colonial families, for on the 12th of that month, during the absence from the Colony of the Rev. W. H. C. Lloyd, the Parsonage on the Glebe land was burnt down; being of wattle and daub, and thatched, it was wholly destroyed, no water being available. Mrs. Lloyd and family, with the assistance of the neighbours, were enabled to save a portion of the furniture and clothing. The Rev. Mr. Cox, acting for Mr. Lloyd, was with his wife occupying a room in the Parsonage, and shared in the loss. The Churchwardens, having now to look into matters, found that the Parish Registers were not in order, and advertised the fact as under :—

NOTICE.

Some omissions having been made in the Baptismal Register for some time back, and there being a probability that part of the memoranda respecting Baptisms were lost in the fire at the Parsonage on the 12th inst., it is therefore requested that persons who have had their children Baptised, will inspect the Baptismal Register of the Parish, and if they find that due entries have not been made there, will furnish such information to the officiating Clergyman as may be required to supply such omissions.

All the Parish Registers may be seen at the Government School room, between the hours of 9 and 12 in the forenoon.

Durban,   Robert Nimmo, ⎰ Churchwardens.
    30th May, 1854.   W. H. Middleton, ⎱

Let us hope that the omissions were corrected, and that no nameless ones will be refused confirmation or burial, for want of conscientious ability to fix a date, or answer a question of their Catechism, " Who gave you this name?"

Bazaar. During July two diverse events happened which bear upon our history. The first was the holding of a Bazaar by the Congregational body to raise funds for the erection of a suitable place of worship. The Rev. Mr. Grosvenor's

H

connection with that Society having largely added to the congregation, preparations had been in progress with ladies' working committees for a year or more. Mr. John Forrest, of the Umbilo, had offered a site, which, however, was declined in favour of the more suitable one given by Mr. Savory Pinsent, an Attorney, and now occupied by the Congregational Church and School in Smith Street, valued at that time at £100.

The American Missionaries had possibly explained the principles of "working bees" and "log-rolling," for the ladies of other denominations, having their own prospective Churches in view, readily co-operated in full assurance of future help; while, this being the first religious trade enterprise held in Durban, general interest was manifested.

The bazaar took place in Breede's Store on the 4th and 5th July. The following ladies presided and persuaded at seven stalls. No. 1, Mrs. M. Penfold, Mrs. Lennox; No. 2, Mrs. Kahts, Mrs. Leslie, Miss Grice, Miss Beningfield; No. 3, Mrs. Grosvenor, Mrs. Cato, Mrs. Dixon, Miss Crowder; No. 4, Mrs. G. Robinson, Miss Robinson, Miss Ward; No. 5, Mrs. Ashton, Miss Ashton, Miss Barrett; No. 6, Mrs. A. W. Evans, Miss Churchill. Refreshment table, Mrs. W. Smerdon, Mrs. Barrett, Mrs. Brickhill. In addition to the matrons and their fair assistants, there were the usual raffles and other diversions. A Post Office, organised by Mr. Jas. Brickhill, was a marked feature, and afforded much amusement. It fell to my lot to write, or get written, the first day's issue, Miss Crowder, the Postmistress, directing the envelopes on demand, and obtaining payment of postage at the window. The second day the young people poured in letters duly addressed, paid and unpaid, taking care those addressed called for them. Mrs. John Cubitt presided at the piano. Mr. Churchwarden Middleton and other gentlemen sang glees, duets, trios, etc. The price for admission was 1s. The place was crowded each evening, Mr. Robert Acutt selling "the remains" by auction on the last. Everyone enjoyed themselves and looked forward to a repetition at the forthcoming Wesleyan Bazaar. The total proceeds amounted to over £200, yielding about £175 to the building fund, a large sum in those days.

The second event happened on the 31st of the month. At dawn someone discovered a large ship, with all her sails loose, looking as it were over the Back Beach Bush, about the end of Smith Street. All Durban rushed to the scene, to find it was a fine American vessel, named the *Ariosto*, 361 tons, from Sumatra to Boston, with a cargo of pepper. The previous night had been fine with a gentle N.E. breeze. There was no sea on, and everything was right except the Master's computation, which led him to think he was some miles outside the Bluff, so his ship calmly continued her course until the watch on deck heard the breakers on shore; they edged her off a little, but too late. She struck, bumped over the outer sand bank, and was carried on to the Beach. Being old, some of her timbers gave way. She became water-logged and settled down to remain. We found the crew, seventeen in all, had effected a landing in their own boat. When they discovered they were not in " Caffreland," but among white men, their language—in the words of their own poet—" was free " at our lack of attention to their signals, for they " had been blazing away all the adjective night, and not an adjective mother's son had shown up before daylight," etc., etc. A singular attestation to our good morals and correct habits at that period, as she came on shore between a Sunday and a Monday. Having no fear of Malay pirates on her homeward voyage, her guns had been stored below with the cargo, so it was long after midnight before they were got up and fired. The sentry at the Custom House, hearing the first and second guns, being deceived by the echo, aroused Captain Bell with the information that the sound came from behind the Bluff. Captain Bell was expecting H.M.S. *Penguin*, so he at once knew all about it; she must be lying off till daylight, dismissed the sentry, and turned in again, but only to be turned out after a brief nap by Mr. Mellor, the Magistrate, whose house in Smith Street, being in the line of fire, received the sound without mistake. He rightly conjectured that it was from a ship in distress, and as soon as he could get saddled up, rode down to the Point, at half past two in the morning, to inform the Port Captain. Firing having ceased just then, and no rockets or other

"Ariosto."

lights being seen, Captain Bell explained the *Penguin* theory, dismissed the Magistrate, put a light in his office window, turned in again for the second time, until break of day, when looking around for the noisy *Penguin*, he caught a flash and report towards the town, that at once awoke the sailor spirit, dispelled all his expectations of early coffee, and sent him, as soon as he could don his boots, with his Port Office retinue, Customs House Officers, Soldiers off duty, and the usual longshoremen, hurrying up to the wreck. Mr. G. C. Cato, the American Vice-Consul, was ubiquitous, and, judging by the fact that the peak of his cap was at the back of his head, in some perturbation of mind, for they were not long in concluding that the ship could not float again.

Preparations were at once made to land as much of the cargo as possible while the weather was fine, by means of the ship's long boat and a raft. Numerous willing hands set to work, tents of sails were rigged up for the Customs Officers, Military Guard, and the Crew; while bags of pepper were packed high and dry on the sands. The property of the crew, and such of the ship's moveables and cargo as were not reached by the water, were landed.

Then the *Ariosto* began to break up, with the result that the Beach was black with pepper corns, mingled with fragments of wreckage. An auction sale was held by Mr. R. Acutt, when most of the washed up pepper was bought by Mr. Wm. Hartley, as a job lot. The hull and cargo were knocked down to Mr. Edward Snell, realising a good price, as 100 blocks of tin were stowed on the bottom. These I believe to be there still, for first, a reward of 10s. a block, increased after to 20s., was offered for their recovery, without result. The shovelling, sifting, drying, winnowing, and carting of this great quantity of pepper gave considerable employment. Stores, outhouses, and back yards were filled. The whole town had a spicy flavour, until it was finally bagged and reshipped, resulting in a very handsome profit to the enterprising speculator. The loss of this vessel, followed a few weeks later by the grounding of the *Princeza*, and the detention outside of the Mail steamers, drew attention, both in the United States and in England, to our earlier records, the vagaries of the Bar, and our facilities as a port for losing ships.

Volunteering. The calling up of the Militia, and enrolment of Volunteer Rifle Corps in England, upon the declaration of war with Russia, combined with the conjectured possibilities of an immediate advance on Durban by some Russian privateer, kindled a flame of patriotic enthusiasm throughout the Colony, and as a first stage in the line of defence a Volunteer Cavalry Corps was mooted—not so much for maritime purposes, as to avoid the conscription of the Burgher Law, with its loose, undisciplined organization—and also to serve as Military Police, in event of any Native troubles.

In this the horsemen of Durban took the lead, with the title of " Durban Rangers." The footmen immediately followed, and distinguished themselves as the " Durban Volunteer Guards." Pietermaritzburg followed suit by establishing the " Natal Carbineers."

The fate of a campaign, and the destiny of individuals, hangs upon the date of a commission; this rule applies to Proclamations by the Governor; hence the honour of ranking as a first Volunteer Corps, not alone in Natal, but in South Africa, might be claimed by the " Durban Volunteer Guard," as their services were accepted by Proclamation dated 27th January, 1855. The " Rangers " had obtained authority to style themselves " Royal." The Proclamation of the " Royal Durban Rangers " was dated 22nd February, 1855, while the " Natal Carbineers " were proclaimed on the 6th March, 1855. When people are in a hurry, there is always a difficulty about " fixings "; so the Volunteers found, for notwithstanding the good fellowship of the 45th Regiment and the Cape Mounted Rifles, the Colonial Government could not induce the Military Authorities to look graciously upon the Volunteers. The utmost concession red tape could be made to stretch was in the shape of " surplus stores," another name for obsolete arms and accoutrements. The " Rangers " used their every day saddles, adapting them with D's and C's, straps and buckles to carrying their blankets, valise, etc. They were supplied by Government with swords and carbines, the latter a heavy article, Brunswick pattern, of two grooves, carrying a belted ball, which had a trick of jambing half way down, necessitating dismounting for a stone to act as a hammer; while the clumsy old Dragoon sabres were practically useless. The recruits on foot, with straddled legs, doing the cuts and points, learnt to hold and use these tools tolerably well, but I have seen many a man fairly lifted from his saddle in giving the final downward cut over his horse's head; while rumour said that both steeds and riders suffered at times from bruises and contusions, the swords providentially not being sharpened to cut.

As it happened that the Volunteer Law was not promulgated until November 21st, 1854, there may be some excuse for the delay in gazetting this and other Corps, since its provisions had to be discussed and accepted by all, though I believe it to have arisen from their "Royalty," as no doubt reference on this grave point would have to be made to the Governor and the Commander-in-Chief at the Cape. But the fact remains that they had formed themselves into a Corps and adopted a dark blue uniform with black facings, which on the "Royal" addition were changed to scarlet. They had moreover been reviewed by their Honorary Colonel, Lieut.-Governor Pine, on the 5th October, 1854, after holding races (we made it a public holiday), given a Ball in connection with it on the 6th October, 1854, and better still sent off in December a detachment of 15 men on active service against the Native Chief Dushani, for which they were thanked in the *Gazette* of 5th January, 1855. Hence the accidental prior proclamation of the "Durban Volunteer Guard" must not be quoted to prove that the "Royal Durban Rangers" were not the first Volunteer Corps of Natal.

Royal Durban Rangers. The original officers chosen on the 13th April were Captain James Proudfoot, Lieuts. Harry Milner, and Patrick J. Maxwell, late Officer in the Austrian service, Cornet Wm. Wood, Sergts. John D. Koch, J. L. Fielden, Corporals Edward Smith, Frank Beningfield, Surgeon W. G. Taylor, Military Instructor Sergt. Robert Tatham, Cape Mounted Rifles. W. H. Savory and —. Cox were subsequently elected sergeants. Of the rank and file I can only recall Jas. Pulleyn, John King, J. B. Roberts, J. R. Goodricke, E. Snell, —. Greenaway, Robert and Charles Dickinson, C. J. Hill, J. C. Field, Arden Fell, —. Moreland, with Bugler Taylor. At a later period we shall find Major Bennett, Captain H. E. Stainbank, Quartermaster Robert A. Smith, Cornet Harry Escombe, Dr. Taylor, and Bugler T. L. Cullingworth; with a squadron raised at Pinetown. In 1858 Captain H. E. Stainbank contributed a handsome Regimental Flag in scarlet and gold richly embroidered, made in England, which, having been duly consecrated by the Bishop of Natal, was publicly presented to the Corps by Mrs. Scott, wife of the then Governor John Scott. It was exhibited at all Regimental parades on the Market Square, and was carried by the Corps on the occasion of their escorting Prince Alfred and retinue from Pietermaritzburg to Durban. The discovery of the Diamond Fields served us instead of Australia, so loyal men hurried away to peg off claims, and carve out fortunes for themselves; sadly reducing the ranks of the Volunteers. In the course of my business, many years later, I became the agent of Quartermaster "Bob" Smith, who settled and died at Kimberley. I took over from him a brass mounted staff, with muster sheets and memoranda, and this Regimental Flag, in a newspaper parcel. Though not actually disbanded, the Corps was at that time virtually "mustered out"; so I relieved my conscience of "the divinity that doth hedge a King," or a Bishop, and handed the consecrated banner to the Rev. Leo Guard, and the Churchwardens of St. Paul's, Durban, for safe keeping in the chancel. It hangs there now out of danger. Ten days prior to the Review and Ball of the "Rangers," viz., September 26th, a public meeting was held in the Court Room, when it was decided to form a Durban Defence Association, or Infantry Corps.

Durban Volunteer Guard. On the 3rd October those patriotically disposed met in Messrs. Jackson's Store to subscribe the roll of the "Durban Town Guard" and elect Officers, when the following gentlemen were chosen:—

Commandant: Honourable Geo. Rutherford.

Lieutenant-Commandant: Christopher Joseph Cato.
Adjutant: Thos. Foster.
Captains: W. H. Evans, Wm. Smerdon, J. F. Kahts.
Lieutenants: Wilson Wood, John P. Cato, H. W.
   Currie.
Treasurer: Robert Raw.
Honorary Secretary: J. D. Shuter.

One hundred and twenty members had subscribed. I
gave in my name and was posted to C Company, Captain
Kahts, Lieut. J. P. Cato. The Regimental Committee met
four days later, and by consent changed the name to
"Durban Volunteer Guard." We were all anxious to get
to work, so the first general muster for routine business and
a little goose step was held in Jackson's Store, on the evening
of the 13th October, when I was elected Sergeant. A Company was supposed to consist of 50 men, but we were
always short of our complement, owing to resignations,
when drill and discipline became irksome. A cheap and
serviceable uniform was adopted, consisting of a hat and
shirt. The hat was tailor-made, of dark blue cloth, with
straight peak, after the pattern of a French "Kepi," chin-
strap of patent leather, with the letters D.V.G. cast in
pewter (by our only brass founder, Robert Bookless) sewn
on in front. The coat was domestically made from a sailor's
blue serge shirt, cut down the front, the collar reduced and
stiffened so as to stand up a little, as a compromise for the
regulation leather stock; red worsted braid served for trimming and chevrons. Every man wore his own trousers,
though grey was supposed to be the uniform, together with
such waist-belts as he could get. Officers and exclusives got
Mr. Geo. Potter, the saddler, to fasten a piratical brass
buckle on to a patent leather band, and we were ready.

Not waiting for uniforms, we drilled in the open on the
Market Square, by squads or companies before breakfast
and after business hours; on Saturday afternoons, General
Parade. None of us knew anything; many had difficulties
with their rights and lefts. For instructors, we obtained
the services of old army pensioners, the most reliable being
Sergt. John Adams, a Dublin man, who retired from the
3rd Buffs with the rank of Sergt.-Major, receiving the
appointment of Barrack Sergeant at the Camp, and a slice

of the War Department Land for life. He resigned his Military appointment some years later, to join the Civil Service as Messenger of the Magistrate's Court, and Field Cornet of Durban. The others were Sergt. Towning, Sergt. Peters, and Shoemaker Sergt. Hart, all burgesses of Durban. It is due to these veterans to record the zeal, I might say the relish, with which they resumed their masterful authority over recruits and squad drill, practising upon us all the devices of their early torments, "goose step," extension motions, counter-marchings, etc., until we complained to our Adjutant, in the plaintive words of Mr. Mantalini, about "having our eyes turned right and left, oh demmit."

The patronising condescension and caustic remarks of these and other old soldiers, lookers on, were only to be endured from a sense of duty, with a belief that we should soon acquire sufficient knowledge to fit us for defensive purposes. So a month after formation saw us mustered under arms, that is to say, every man brought his own gun, double or single, fowling pieces, rifles, rabbit or rook guns, ship muskets, or old carbines; those without arms brought wooden guns, while our old acquaintance Sandy Forbes, the baker, scandalised my company by gravely falling in with a broom stick; his knees inclined inward, his eyes "fronted," immoveable, as his ears took in the jibes of his comrades, and the orders of his Sergeant to get back into the rear rank, an expediency that occurred to me from an old writer's description of the muster of a West Indian Militia Regiment, when the negro Sergt.-Major orders:— "Dem gen'lemans as hab shoes and 'tockings, 'tand in the front rank; you men as hab shoes and no 'tockings, 'tand in the second rank; and dey niggers what hab no shoes and no 'tockings 'tand dar in the rear!"

Forbes meant well, but he smarted under the indignity of public opinion, ceased to answer to his name at Roll call, and scorned us.

Not content with learning how to carry, shoulder, and present arms, we must hurry on to the real thing, so soon began with what the Instructor called "blank cartridge," but as guns were of all sizes and no cartridges were to be had, while very few knew how to make them, we overcame the difficulty by bringing our powder horns and flasks, with paper or rag for wadding in our pockets. A slovenly Carpenter man, standing in the rank between John J. Chapman (spared to be Mayor of Pietermaritzburg) and myself, after firing his fowling piece once or twice, was preparing to "load and prime," when his powder flask was blown out of his hand and exploded.   The shock and scare caused Chapman and myself to feel for our wounds, but, as nothing gory resulted, we descended upon the Carpenter in wrath by way of gratitude.   This incident led to a general order, prohibiting flasks and imposing cartridges.   But our ambition was to complete our Military education by becoming good shots—nothing else. As it was neither safe nor practicable to allow men to make their own bullets, much less to fire them, we applied to the Government, and ultimately there were issued to us a lot of brass-mounted, long-barrelled Tower Muskets, with bayonets, cross belts, and cartridge box, which, rumour said, had been returned into store by the disbanded Native Police of Pietermaritzburg, commanded by Captain Walmsley. A cask or two of blank and Ball cartridge of ancient date, with caps like miniature copper hats, were also received by Lieut.-Commander Joseph Cato for our use.

Debating societies have an evergreen question as to the greater amount of pleasure derivable from the pursuit, or acquisition, of an object.   Band instruments, through the kindness of the Officers of the 45th Regiment had been obtained for our use, so we considered ourselves set up in arms and appointments, and were happy. As a matter of fact, it was now that our troubles began, for the acquisition of these implements of warfare disclosed the humiliating fact that we were not the stuff of which soldiers are made. I have never ceased to wonder how British troops could have used similar equipments, and fought at Assaye, the Peninsula, and Waterloo, cumbered as they were in addition with stocks, head gear and knapsacks.   The musket placed in our hands was long and heavy, with a huge square metal sight at the end, upon which the bayonet was twisted and held, with the aid of a side spring that locked it in place. In firing, this projection literally covered a haystack at 200 yards. To fix and unfix the bayonet was a work of art, combining skill, strength, and care, since you were

supposed to draw the implement with one hand and fix it
smartly with the other; while to unfix, you had again to
change hands, after struggling with " the second jint of yer
forefinger," to release the obdurate spring, perform an
untwisting of the bayonet, then prick the left hand or
thumb with its point while guiding it into the scabbard,
" an' spring smartly back to ordered arms."

The ambidextrous performance must have been a choice
pièce de resistance with military n artinets, as the whole
movements were supposed to be done to time. We got over
the difficulty by climbing up our pieces, so far as holding
them between our knees, and if the right hand man didn't
look along our front to see when we were ready, he •
heard from us, while we heard from the Instructor. Marching with fixed bayonets might look effective, but it was
formidable, especially at the "trail," while "charge
bayonets" was only hazarded in unfrequented spots, and at
very open order.   The cross belts were nearly four inches
wide, of buff leather, pipeclayed. One carried a stiff black
leather cartridge box, large enough to contain a pint bottle
of beer, a packet of sandwiches, pipe, tobacco, and 20
rounds of blank cartridge.   The other supported the long
triangular bayonet and a cap pouch.   The sight of these
scared away many members.   Private J. R. Goodricke, of
my Company, asked if I expected him " to put on that
harness and make an Ass of himself?"   He joined the
"Rangers."   Little men were quite borne down with it,
while the tall ones were hidden.   These trappings were
ultimately discarded, cartridges being carried in the pocket,
while the bayonet was hooked into a waist-belt. But our
vaunting ambition was sorely tried when class firing commenced.   The old soldiers spoke as they knew, putting us
through the lecture course, in loading, of " Handle cartridge," biting off the top, shaking in the vile saltpetre,
pushing in the paper and ball with the thumb, " Draw ramrods," " Ram down cartridge," with two taps at the bottom,
" Return ramrods," " Bout," " Prime." We were drawn up
opposite the target on the Eastern Vlei (used by the
Garrison), which was of iron, 6 feet high, 2 feet wide,
equally divided into upper, centre, and lower.   The centre
had an 8 inch bullseye, distance 100 yards, position stand-

ing. We were told how to sight, and how to pull the trigger. The heavy gun wobbled as the Volunteer tried to see the target over, or on either side of his large sight; pressure, as instructed, was of no avail on the trigger. He had to get a good hold of it and pull. The course of the ball was surmised, but the effect on the shooter was apparent, for he staggered back two or three steps, picked up his hat, and felt first his cheek, then his shoulder Five rounds usually knocked us out of time for the week, and the man whose nerves and muscles enabled him to hit the target twice in succession at 150 yards was regarded as a marksman. Bullseyes were conceded to be chance shots.

Our parade ground is now occupied by the Town Hall and Market House. In skirmishing we extended as far as the Camp. On wet or windy days we drilled in St. Paul's Church, after the floor was laid. On the Queen's Birthday in 1855 we got the hint that her forces objected to our company at noon, so to prove our quality, and avail ourselves of the holiday, we paraded at 7 in the morning, making a gallant show with polished muskets, pipeclayed belts, mensized, band in the rear, officers with such swords (divers patterns) as they could muster, fired a "feu de joie" with precision, presented arms, played "God Save the Queen," gave three cheers and dismissed. This was our grandest performance for the defence of the town, yet volunteering, under the conditions described, was discouraging, since we were without rifles, and could not adapt the musket to Hans Busk's Rifle Volunteer Drill Book. So we melted away until January, 1856, when, at a general muster, the dissolution of the Corps was proposed by Lieutenant-Commander Joseph Cato. I was then Sergeant-Major, and carried an amendment "That the Corps remain in abeyance until the arrival of new Government arms, etc." But it died nevertheless, and the arms, harness, and instruments were returned into store.

Durban Rifle Guard. The "Durban Rifle Guard" was recruited in 1862 from the old members. Mr. Henry James Mellor was Colonel, and I received a commission as Lieutenant and Quartermaster.

Moustache Movement. The exigencies of Colonial life and travel had induced many men to abandon that instrument of fashion, and tax upon time, the razor. Owing to the wretched administration in the Crimea, Military martinets had to surrender the razor to the climàte, and bless Nature for supplying them with hair to protect their faces and lungs. The authority granted to the Army in India, and subsequently to the Police of large cities in England, to adopt the moustache, led naturally to the example being followed by those embryo soldiers the Volunteers, who constituting in civil life "the public" graduaɪɪy and permanently extended the moustache movement. An effeminate fashion gave way to common sense, so, regardless of ridicule, the martial spirit of the time overcame all opposition. The French proverb has it, "'Tis but the first step that costs," so it was at some cost that our Volunteer townsmen allowed the first Sunday to pass without a shave. The newspapers, however, came to their aid. The *Mercury*, to satisfy the ladies on the score of decency, propriety, and Royal approval, published a column and a half from a lecture given at Ipswich in favour of the movement, subsequently complimenting the Captain and members of the "Rangers" upon their improved and martial appearance. After that, what could we do but abandon the razor. Beards grew and flourished in Durban from that time forward, extending even to the exponents of Law, Physic, and Divinity.

Incorporation. The event of the year, and of the age as we then deemed it, was the birth of Durban as a Borough (the French apostrophe had by common consent been discarded, so that a British face might be given to our proper name, thus depriving the D'Urban family of a share in their ancestral inheritance). By many signs we knew that the Government was labouring over this enterprise early in the year, and that whatever was done was intended to apply to all towns in the Colony, when they had grown large enough to bear the strain. The increased prosperity of the Colony, the absence of facilities for doing business, and the positive necessity for local improvements, silenced the active opposition of the non-contents, whose views were, however, taken into account by

the Government in framing the Draft Municipal Ordinance, published in the *Mercury* on the 8th March. This
received the editorial approval as "a measure which, so far
as their Municipal rights are concerned, may be fitly
designated the People's Charter."

My readers will have seen how preoccupied we were at
this period, so could not devote much time to politics, or
controversial questions, consequently the Ordinance, as it
stood, was generally accepted. The newspapers, guaging
public feeling, suggested certain alterations, which were
finally embodied in the Ordinance No. .1, 1854, "For
establishing Municipal Corporations within the District of
Natal," dated 21st April, 1854, and published in Durban
May 3rd.

This Ordinance declared "Whenever the population of
" any township shall amount to 1,000 souls, as aforesaid, the
" Lieut.-Governor shall, by proclamation, declare ·the same
" to be a Borough within the meaning of the Ordinance, and
" define the boundaries thereof, and shall, immediately after
" the first election of the Council of the said Borough, by
" grant under his hand and the public seal, grant and
" convey to the corporate body thereof, such lands, situate
" within and near the town as to him shall seem just and
" proper."

As the Ordinance further provided that the Mayor was
to be elected on the first Saturday of August in every year,
there was plenty of time before us,· so we went on with our
business, our Volunteering, and our Banking. Meanwhile
my employers, desirous of taking advantage of the dry
season, and foreseeing that the Corporation, when established, having to keep the Queen's highway in repair, and
pay half the cost of the Police, would have very little to
spare for other public works, instituted a subscription to
drain the swamp in Gardiner Street, from Smith Street to
the Bay. The Convicts cut a ditch on the West side of
the street, now a brick culvert. The Market Square was
again utilised for sand, and the street raised between
3 and 4 feet, greatly to the convenience of the wagon traffic
from the Point. As the work was almost completed before
the Mayor was elected, the insinuation that it was a bid for

votes was made only after Mr. John Millar had been
requisitioned as a Town Councillor.

In terms of Ordinance No. 1, 1854, the Government
Gazette published a Proclamation by Lieut.-Governor Pine,
dated 15th May, 1854, "that the said township of Durban
" shall be and the same is hereby declared to be a Borough
" within the meaning of the said Ordinance. And I do
" further proclaim and make known that the said Borough
" shall be bounded as follows, that is to say :—E, by the
" Indian Ocean ; N, by the Umgeni River ; N.W., by the
" farms Springfield, Brickfields, and Cato's Manor ; and S,
" and S.E., by the Lots 1 to 11 on the Umbilo River, by
" the Umbilo River, and the Bay of Natal."

Roughly speaking, this contained an area of 7,000 acres,
but there were some among us of Dutch proclivities " giving
too little, and asking too much," who wanted more, though
the Burgesses generally thought we had then more than we
knew what to do with, and manage. The Ordinance, however, had a reservation that lands required by the Crown
were to be defined after the first election of Mayor, so we
let the matter rest for the present. The Proclamation
also divided the Borough into four Wards as follows: Draw
a line from the Bay to the Umgeni through Aliwal Street.
Ward 1 was all to the Eastward of that. Another line at
right angles from Aliwal Street along Smith Street "to
the limits of the Borough," taking in all the Beach erven,
that was Ward 2, Start again at Aliwal Street and draw
a parallel line down West Street "to the limits of the Borough," that included Ward 3, while Ward 4 extended North
from that line to the Umgeni, thus :—

4 | .   Each Ward was to return two Councillors, eight in
3 | 1 all, one of whom was to be chosen by them as Mayor.
2 | The qualification of a Burgess was, that he must be a
male inhabitant over twenty-one years of age, and the pos-
sessor of landed property of £25 value, or a renter to the
extent of £5 yearly. While to be elected a Councillor, he
must own property to the value of £100, clear of mortgage.

By Proclamation of the 23rd May, the Colony was divided
into Counties, by which the newly created County of Victoria was cut off from the Division of Durban. These
Counties were sub- divided into Wards, with the intention

that they should be managed by local Councils. Consequently we were completely overdone with elections. The difficulty of finding representatives, who, as a rule, only consented to stand provided they were put to no expense, limited enthusiasm, placards, party colours, or demonstrations. Conscious of our newly acquired honours, we were all going to play fair, and really carried it out, this time.

The first Burgess Roll was published by the Resident Magistrate on the 1st June, and contained the names of 229 persons. At this time the Field Cornet's official enumeration or "Census" of the population of Durban was:—

ADULTS.		CHILDREN.	
Males.	Females.	Males.	Females.
316.	263.	313.	312. - Total 1204 whites.

It was contended that the Burgess Roll was not correct, as persons otherwise qualified, who were not actual inhabitants, were excluded. Living at the Store, I was not regarded as a renter, or placed on the "List of persons qualified to vote." The gravity of the situation was apparent in the long deliberations consequent upon the abundance of the self-governing principle so suddenly bestowed upon the whole Colony. Hence it was only at the end of June that Ward Meetings were held in town, to consider the position and nominate fit and proper persons as representatives. The meetings of Volunteers had in a measure served in lieu of public meetings, so we gladly participated in all the Ward meetings, on the principle that if not "on the list" we were interested in the Borough generally. There was an earnestness about these meetings that checked any attempts at frivolity, except perhaps in Ward 4, which then acquired the title "Lively Ward." Mr. G. C. Cato accepted a requisition for Ward 1, in a characteristic letter, "it being an honour I neither expected nor desired," but declining "would be inconsistent with my views, that now "is the time that the Colonists, generally, should do something "to advance the interests of the Colony, and thereby help "themselves." The candidates finally nominated were—Ward 1, G. C. Cato, Alexander McArthur, James Blackwood. Ward 2, John Millar, G. H. Wirsing, James Brickhill, Wm. Smerdon; Ward 3, Richard Harwin, A. W. Evans; Ward 4, W. H. Savory, Robert Raw, Charles Johnston, Francis Harvey, Edward Snell, and William Hartley. The poll was fixed for the 2nd August, to be held in the Magistrate's Court Room, between 8 a.m. and 4 p.m. Mr. Thomas Foster, Returning Officer.

On the eventful day I acted as Polling Clerk at McDonald's Hotel, where a Committee Room had been engaged in the interests of Messrs. Millar and Wirsing. My duties did not call for much ability, as there were only 51 possible voters in the Ward, all of whom were personally known to me. We gave a little colour to the scene with bunting, posters, and ribbon favours, with a commendable show of bustle up and down the wooden stairs of the Court House, and in the vicinity of the Committee Room especially, where our voters expected to find refreshments provided. At the close of the poll, the Burgesses gathered outside Middleton and Wirsing's Store until the Returning Officer and Polling Clerks had agreed figures; then the Magistrate, Mr. H. J. Mellor, threw up his office window, and declared the following gentlemen elected:—

Ward No. 1.—George Christopher Cato, and James Blackwood.

Ward No. 2.—John Millar and George Henry Wirsing.

Ward No. 3.—Alfred Winter Evans and Richard Harwin.

Ward No. 4.—Charles Johnston and Robert Raw.

Cheers and counter cheers, congratulations and a general adjournment to the Committee Rooms and Public Bars.

By permission of the Magistrate, the newly-elected Town Councillors met in the Court Room on Saturday, the 5th August, to elect a Mayor. Though the time was in the forenoon, the Burgesses were fully represented in the audience. The first speaker was Dr. Chas. Johnston, who came to be known as the "Combative Member," and who made an onslaught on the Resident Magistrate for not continuing to act as Mayor. Mr. Wirsing was elected to preside as Chairman, then the Doctor objected to voting by Ballot, but came to terms on the proposer agreeing that this secret voting should not form a precedent, stipulating, however, if the present voting was equal, the decision should be by lot.

The Ballot resulted as follows:—

       Mr. G. C. Cato ... ... 6 votes.
       Mr. J. Millar ... ... 1 vote.
       Dr Johnston ... ... 1 vote.

The result, when announced by the Chairman, was vociferously cheered. Applause was resumed on His Worship taking his seat as the first Mayor of Durban.

He returned thanks in a straightforward practical speech, hoping they would all pull together for the good of the town. " The public in the different Wards must not think that their " respective representatives are to be pitted against each other, ' for the promotion of separate ends and interests. The " Council is one body, and must act together for the good of " the entire community. He had long opposed a Munici- " pality for Durban, but the time had come for introducing " the machinery of local Government. We had escaped the " crisis at the Cape, and the town is now advancing."——Mr. Councillor Millar, having an eye to coming rates, gave the first notice of motion, to the effect that they should ask the Lieutenant-Governor to let the question of maintenance of the Police remain in abeyance for eighteen months, or two years. Fixing the 10th August at 6 p.m. for their next meeting, the Councillors adjourned for refreshment to John Millar and Co.'s store opposite.

The first business meeting was held on the 10th August, (Mr. J. Millar absent). Dr. C. Johnston moved the first resolution as follows: —

"That a Town Clerk be appointed at a salary of £50 per annum, whose duties shall be to attend all meetings of the Council, and enter proceedings of same, to collect all rates and dues, and generally to superintend the carrying out of all orders issued by the Council; further that advertisements to this effect be published in the local papers. Applications to be made to the Mayor, from whom further information may be obtained."

Carried unanimously. The question of appointing a Town Treasurer was ordered to stand over till next meeting. Mr. Evans proposed that the Resident Magistrate be requested to allow the meetings of Council to be held in the Court Room, for the first three months, as frequently as necessary, and at such hours as would not interfere with the business of his Court.   Dr. Johnston would ignore the Magistrate (to whom he was always in opposition), so moved an amendment, " That the Lieutenant-Governor in Council be memorialised to grant permission."   Amendment lost by 4 to 2. Mr. Millar's notice of motion was not introduced, but the Mayor got to business with the object of " at once opening correspondence with the Government on the subject of the immediate grant to the Council of the Town Lands in terms of Clause 5 of the Ordinance," with the result " That the Council resolve itself into a Committee of the whole to consider the subject; to meet at Mr. Wirsing's Office on Monday evening next." This terminated the business, but there being a large gathering of townsmen present, the Mayor having had time to think twice on what he did not say on the occasion of his sudden access to office, emboldened also by his popular reception, and doing violence to his natural speech, which may be defined as " short and sharp," seized the opportunity to announce his election as Mayor, and address the burgesses upon their responsibilities as a Borough. That the Council would uphold its dignity, and, while imposing necessary rates and dues, looked to the public for co-operation and assistance. The speech was a long one, but characteristic of " G. C.," replete with humour and practical common-sense, most admirably adapted to blend the views of the old Colonists and the new. He styled himself an " Africander," who had taken the oath of allegiance to Her Majesty the Queen, adding, amid much applause,   that   the   motto   of   the   Council   would   be " Economy."

On the 19th August a sub-Committee for the selection of Town Clerk reported in favour of two candidates, Mr. Foggitt and Mr. Goodricke, recommending that a ballot be taken; result, four votes for each candidate, the Mayor giving his casting vote in favour of Mr. Goodricke, whereupon Dr. Johnstone gave notice of protest against Mr. Goodricke's appointment, on the ground of his not having confined himself to the terms of the advertisement. Mr. J. Millar, another " short and sharp " man, moved " that the above notice of protest be not received.   The *Mercury* report says: " 3 votes, motion lost."

The feature of the meeting, however, was the report of the Mayor, that the Committee of the whole Council had that morning interviewed the Lieutenant-Governor at McDonald's Hotel, when His Honour said that their Memorial for the Town Lands and the Quarantine Laws should have his best and immediate consideration. This short sentence covers much ground. It testified to expediency of working by Committees, as also to the judgment of the Burgesses of Ward 1, in electing so practical and experienced a man as Mr. Cato to represent them ; and of the rest of the Councillors in placing him at their head. A memorial had been adopted by the Town Council, and transmitted to the Colonial Secretary, in reference to the Town Lands. A copy of this Mr. Cato took under his arm. He introduced the members of the Council individually, and presented the Memorial, assuring His Honour that the Council did not seek to bind him by anything that might transpire at that interview, as they were aware that the formal reply would come through official channels. They were only anxious to give His Honour any explanation he might wish to receive. His Honour assured the Committee that the memorial would receive his attentive consideration, and he would give them an answer as soon as practicable. Meanwhile, if anything should render another conference desirable, he would inform the Mayor. The interview then partook of a free and desultory character, much to the relief of the Mayor and newly dignified Councillors ; when it transpired that the innocent object of the Council was to secure the conveyance to the Corporation of the Town Lands of Durban, as originally surveyed, together with the Crown Land on the Bluff, estimated (by them) at 400 acres, "excepting such portion at the extremity, as may be requisite for the public service," for the good reason that in the opinion of the Mayor, the Bluff would form the most eligible place of refuge for women and children, in case of an attack upon the town, and it should therefore be under the control of the Corporation. Then, again, the insufficiency of the grazing land should be taken into account; there really was not 1,000 acres available, after deducting building ground, bush, sand, and Government reserves. This quantity was at present insufficient, and would, as the traffic of the place increased, be wholly inadequate. The prospect of the rapid development of both the interior and the coast trades would further increase the demand for grazing ground, necessitating the wagon trek-ox being driven to feed on private property at extravagant charges, or finding a lodging in the Pound. "By granting a sufficiency of grazing ground, His Honour would, in fact, be serving the whole Colony." His Worship further urged the claim of the Corporation on the precedent of the large grants made to the Dutch farmers, and also the recent grant to the Episcopal Church (Umlaas Location). His Honour thanked the Mayor for placing the matter very properly before him; it was impossible for him then to give a reply; but he really thought that, with improved roads and business, oxen would soon give way to horses, and supposing the Bluff were included in the Town Lands, how would it be if the Corporation cut it up into 10 acre lots, and leased it to forty tenants on a tenure of Military service; thus they would not only form a sufficient defensive force for that promontory, but they would also be able to grow oats for the horses used in the traffic at the Port.

Finding the cogency of this free talk rather too masterful, the Lieutenant-Governor got behind his Commission. "Acting on behalf of the Colony at large, he could not give charge of the Port to one class in it. A Parliament of the people, if such a body existed, would not sanction such a course. His principle must be to give the Corporation the land needed for the proper regulation and improvement of the town, and no more." He mentioned the difficulty he had experienced in obtaining from the late Dr. Stanger a clear understanding as to the Town Lands, and reminded the Council that he must first refer these matters to the Secretary of State, since, if he exceeded his powers by making grants, his acts would fall to the ground, and render the grants mere waste paper. One Councillor enquired why the Ordnance Department required so large a block of the Town Lands; to which His Honour replied, that the Board of Ordnance represented the Imperial Government, and, if their demands were curtailed, Government might withdraw the troops and leave them unprotected. This terrible enunciation toned down

the meeting.   It has since served platform orators, like the
proverbial red rag, to flout in the face of opposition.
Undaunted Cato made some uninteresting though pertinent,
enquiries as to enforcing Quarantine, since it was known
that Cholera had broken out at Mauritius.

After assuring His Honour that " they were inclined (*sic*)
to support the Government as far as possible," the
Lieutenant-Governor graciously replied "they were all in
the same boat, and with honest and able seamen on board,
such as he saw before him, he feared no mutiny." The
reporter says naively :—" The Council then exchanged parting courtesies with His Honour and retired ! "

The *Natal Mercury* containing the foregoing report,
announced that Mr. J. R. Goodricke had declined to accept
the appointment of Town Clerk, "in consequence of the
clamour raised by faction," so at a meeting of the Council
held on the 6th September, Mr. Mark Foggitt was elected
to that office.   On the same day the burgesses elected
Messrs. Alex. McArthur and W. H. Savory, Borough Auditors.   The Council met again for business on the 4th
October, when the new Town Clerk was apparently installed,
for it was resolved " That the Town Clerk make a valuation
of all the rateable property in the Borough, in accordance
with the 73rd clause of the Ordinance."   On the 17th
October the Mayor was requested to express to the Government how greatly the Council was inconvenienced by the
delay relative to the Town Lands.   This brought a reply
to the Memorial from the Colonial Secretary, to the effect
" That the Acting Surveyor-General was taking the necessary
measures for the preparation of a Grant of those lands.
That the land to the ·South of the Line of West Street
.produced to the sea would be reserved to the Crown for the
use of a future Harbour Commission, and that, as the Bluff
lands gave no grazing, their application [for them] could
not be granted."   As the Mayor was absent, and only four
Councillors present at this meeting (1st November), the
business was adjourned until the 14th, when nothing
important was done, as again only four Councillors were
present; so they "Resolved that the Town Clerk examine
and report upon the state and requirements of the Town

Pump, situate in Smith Street [Erf No. 20, Block D], in order that the same may be made available for the use of the public." When the full Council met and considered the Colonial Secretary's letter, there was much indignation. Mr. Evans would not give up an inch of their lands, the present demand was a downright robbery, and he urged that the Council resign in a body rather than submit. Dr. Johnston referred to the extent of the Ordnance and Admiralty Reserves, stating that in addition the Government proposed to reserve 600 yards at the Point measured from the Block House, the Admiralty Reserve being 150 feet from high water mark all round the Bay. They should not submit to this. The Eastern Vlei was the natural course for a Canal from the Umgeni to Cato's Creek, which must not be cut off from the control of the Town as proposed by the new line from West Street; it was the proper outlet for the Town drainage. These two gentlemen proposed and seconded a resolution to the effect that the Council do hereby positively refuse to accept the curtailment, or make themselves parties to a despoilment of the rights of the Townspeople. In addition it was "Resolved that the Local Government be again respectfully requested to convey to the Corporation of Durban the whole of the Town Lands as surveyed by Mr. Okes, with the exception of such portions as nave been alienated or reserved previous to the formation of the Town Council. "

Dr. Johnston further recommended an Englishman's panacea, a letter to the *Times*, and the securing the interest of some zealous Member of Parliament, to take up this and other all-round matters of mal-administration in Natal.

On the 13th December, the *Mercury* announces a Draft Ordinance providing for the constitution of a Harbour Board, to which Board was to be conveyed " Lands adjacent to the Harbour." The Editor viewed this Ordinance with satisfaction, with the exception of the land question, as " the Town Council deemed it an infringement of the rights of the Burgesses." He had moreover committed himself in a long leading article, in justification of the rights of the town, and the Council's contention.

The Town Council met again on the 6th December. Having fired their trenchant Resolutions, they had to receive the "retort courteous" of the Colonial Secretary, who informed them that "The Lieutenant-Governor considered there was " no use prolonging the corresponderce; that he had arrived "at a deliberate opinion by the advice of the Executive " Council, and the report of the Harbour Engineer; he denies "the right of the town to claim any portion of the adjacent "lands, the Government naving the right to retain what it " required for Military or any other purposes." Our fathers knew better and said so; was not their opinion as good as that of any Governor, Executive Council, or Engineer? So they appointed a Committee of four, with the Mayor at the head, to draw up a statement of the claims of Durban to the lands as surveyed by Okes, which they maintained was in conformity with the original reservation made by the Governor at the Cape. Correspondence was now growing serious and heavy, so they terminated the meeting by re-solving "That the Town Clerk be authorised to purchase a Letter Book!" —— The Sub-Committee went to work at once, and submitted a Draft "Statement of Facts" to the Town Council on the 8th December, wherein they showed by figures that the Town Lands should be 7,165 acres, but that after deduction of bush, swamp, sand, building lots, and Government reserves only some 2,000 acres of grazing land was left to them. This the Council accepted, and ordered to be forwarded to Government, with a letter from the Mayor. Beyond minor matters connected with the Town Clerk's duties, this appears to close the Municipal records for 1854.

Laundrymen. From the outset, the difficulties attending the family wash were an added trial to the Emigrant's wife, who, when unable to do it herself, either put it out or left it undone.

The kitchen boy was first employed, but with uncertain results; by degrees, "ring polled" natives (*i.e.*, married men), living near the town at their own kraals, devoted themselves to the industry, and established the "Togt" principle, being paid by results, or in other words by the job. This suited the Native and the European, the first because he was his own master, could work or not as he felt inclined, while the Eurpoean could rely upon some experienced "wash-boy" calling for the clothes during the first days of the week. These washermen, however, declined to take certain specified articles of underlinen at any price; these had consequently to be done by the housewife at home. The gauge of a week's wash was a muid sack packed tight; this he carried to the Umgeni River together with a large bar of London yellow soap, a bucket, and two or three balls of thumb blue. They were taken away without inventory at early dawn, and returned washed, blued, and dry in the evening. This process of washing dates from the time of the Egyptians; the articles were put to soak in the river, reasonable care being taken to avoid their being carried away by the current, the result not always being successful. Selecting a stone, a stranded log, or a board borrowed for the purpose, the clothes were well soaped, kneaded a little with the hands, then flogged on the stone, rinsed in the flowing river, blued and wrung out to be hung on neighbouring bushes, or spread on the hot sands to bleach and dry in the sun. At the decline of day, collecting as many pieces as he could identify, the wash boy refilled his sack, enjoyed a final "snuff," and returned with his load to the "Missis," receiving for his day's work the liberal wage of one shilling, with possibly liberty to sleep in the kitchen boy's hut, and share in their evening meal. By degrees the prices advanced, ultimately reaching 2s. 6d. to 3s. per bag. As it sometimes did happen that neither boy nor bag returned, the necessity for identification called for redress, so in later years the Corporation issued numbered badges to licensed washermen, this system still obtaining, notwithstanding the Indian Dhoby has secured almost a monopoly of laundry work.

Having got the clothes home, the next care was to sort and fold them ready for the mangle or flat iron. In this many of the young fellows about town with domestic leanings acquired some skill by contriving to assist the landlady or her buxom daughters. "Mangling done here" adorned two or three signboards in town, their British proprietors, true to their faith, having brought the treasured mangle with them. I believe they are now obsolete; it was a wooden framework like a railed-in bedstead, on which instead of

mattress was a long box loaded with stones, running on
turned rollers, moved backwards and forwards from end to
end by a sort of bucket windlass with bands and cogged
wheels, turned by hand.   But as payment for the use of
this luxurious article was beyond the means of most of us,
we learnt from our Africander fellow-Colonists the use of the
Colonial mangle, and the application of animal power in the
shape of a native's foot for the purpose.

After sprinkling and folding the clothes to our satisfaction,
they were neatly packed in a square pile on an old sheet or
clean wrapper, pinned or stitched tightly together, then enveloped in a canvas cover, and deposited on a brick floor
or other sure foundation.   The ever-willing-to-play house-
boy was then turned on to stamp them flat; he smilingly
ascended the pile, started a " Hi-gee-gee with a G " song,
and pounded away with his broad beetle-crushing feet in
single, double, and triple bangs until the Missis declared
they were " done," and stopped the perspiring stamping
engine.   The result was generally a satisfactory substitute
for the mangle of history, which Mr. Mantilini was "per-
petually turning like a dem'd old horse in a demnition mill "
until his life became " one dem'd horrid grind."

Wild Animals. Among the lesser events of the year, it may
be recorded that, in July, the spoor of a
lion was traced from the Botanic Gardens
by way of Montpelier on to Springfield Flat, where on a
Friday it killed an ox belonging to John Crocker.   On the
Saturday, it, or another, was heard roaring behind the Berea,
on Cato's Farm, and the same night it killed an ox of Mr.
Milner's on Springfield.   A few weeks previously, two had
been seen at Isipingo, one of which was believed to have
been poisoned with strychnine, and in November the *Mercury* announced that a large black-maned lion was shot by
Mr. J. C. Field, on Mr. Drake's farm, near Pine Town, after
it had killed a mare and foal running there, the property of
Mr. G. Potter.   Mr. J. L. Fielden also took credit for shooting one at dusk in the Stella Bush, which proved, on examination by himself and friends in the morning, to be one
of his own trek oxen!

Snake stories were very prevalent, and the capture of pythons from 14 to 18 feet in length was not uncommon. Several deaths and serious accidents were recorded, caused by alligators in the Umgeni, Umhlatuzan, and Umlaas Rivers.

Powder Magazine.   On the 18th October appeared an Official advertisement, by the Collector of Customs, of the first private Bonding Warehouse, authorising Mr. John Daniel Koch to warehouse gunpowder at the Point. The impetus given to the community by the establishment of the Corporation, the organization of the Mechanics' Institute, the promotion of Church and Musical Societies, and, above all, the Volunteer movement, necessarily reacted on trade, and compelled the Early Closing Movement, so on the 18th October appeared the following advertisement by Retail Shopkeepers : —

EARLY CLOSING.

We, the undersigned, agree to close our respective stores at 6 o'clock on and after Monday, October 16th, 1854., until further notice. H. and W. H. Savory, William Cowey, Richard Harwin, Henry Cowey, Edwin J. Challinor, J. H. Grant, Ann Scorgie, E. H. Hunt, T. Heys, J. C. Adams for A. Jaques, Jas. Fuller, Joseph Mason, Robert Raw, Thos. Chapman, Alexander McArthur, J. F. Baumann, Jas. Blackwood, Alfred Moore, R. W. Dickenson and Co.

Lung Sickness.   At the end of the year, a disease, known as the "Lung Sickness," was devastating the horned stock on the borders of the Colony so the boiling down of cattle for their tallow and bones became an established industry in many localities, chiefly in connection with Durban firms.

CHAPTER X.

1855.

(G. C. CATO, MAYOR.)

THE year commenced and ended in strife. The temper of the Burgesses was bellicose, self-assertive, and contentious; taken as a body they were by comparison young, or men who had not reached the meridian of life; their aspirations were yet to be realised, so they hotly contended for principles, wages, and rights that should descend to the town and their children, and ensure to themselves a properly constituted Paradise.

The Town Council met on the 3rd January, and as no reply had been received to the Mayor's letter accompanying the " Statement of Facts," it was resolved that, as the Lieut.-Governor was in town, the Mayor should enquire if a deputation of the Council would be received, to bring about a final settlement of the Town Lands question. This interview was conceded, and on the 10th January the Mayor read his report to the effect that, as a result of the interview, he had proceeded with Mr. John Milne, the Resident Engineer of the Harbour Works, to the ground and arranged that the dividing line between the town and the Harbour Board lands should be parallel to the proposed prolongation of West Street, but that it should start from the Bay end of Stanger Street, and at right angles to that street, eastward to the sea, so as to secure to the town the outlets of Wheeler's and Cato's Creeks (now defined by the existing Rutherford Street). He concluded his report by notification that His Honour had formally assented to the new line, and in justification of the arrangement proceeded to read a private letter from Mr. Milne, wherein he gave as his reason for recommending the West Street line to the Government, that the town should be restricted from diverting any additional drainage, or flow of water, into the Bay. Up rose Councillors Millar and Johnston in wrath. What had the Council to do with this letter? They objected to its tone and style, which was officious and presumptuous; the Council had not asked for Mr. Milne's opinions and views, and did not want them. It was not for Mr. Milne to specify, or recommend restrictions on the Council's use of the Town Lands. Whereupon the Mayor, "in rather an excited tone," explained that the Governor had stated he would act on the report of the Engineer; as for Mr. Councillor Johnston, he was present at the interview, and appeared then to concur. Dr. Johnston replied, he heard what the Governor had to say, though he did not agree with him; his private opinion was different from what he expressed. He thought the Governor proposed to do everything agreeable, and yet he constantly thwarted the Town Council. "But, no matter! we were likely soon to have an alteration in the constitution of our legislature."

The other Councillors thought the letter should be read; there was no harm in it, it was prosy, but it contained information.

Resolved: "That the foregoing report by the Mayor be "placed on the minutes, and that the Town Lands be "accepted by the Corporation as set forth in such report, "and defined by the line marked A.B. on the plan."

The Borough Debt originated at this meeting, for, notwithstanding that the Town Clerk had formed his Valuation Roll, his salary was in arrear, while books, candles, and sundry small contracts had exhausted the funds and called for payment; so it was resolved "The Town Clerk communicate with the Directors of the Natal Bank, asking for a loan of a sum not exceeding £50 *to the members of the Council* (*) to meet current expenses."

---

* The italics are mine.

The first Borough Valuation Roll affords no criterion as to the real valuation of property in the Borough, for the reason that all buildings, whether occupied by owners or tenants, were rated at their annual value, *i.e.*, their estimated rental, while vacant erven were assessed to their owners "in freehold"; thus G. C. Cato's Beach Erf Stanger Street (11, Block M), on which was his office, is rated at £25.   The adjoining Erf No. 10, on which was his dwelling house, also £25; but the Erf No. 9, John Owen Smith's, vacant, was rated in freehold at £300.   Consequently the total Borough valuation for assessment was :—

					Annual.	Freehold.
Ward 1	...	...	...	...	965	3,228
„ 2	...	...	...	...	1,034	3,778
„ 3	...	...	...	...	1,077	1,665
„ 4	...	...	...	...	1,411	1,615
					£4,487	£10,286

The Council fixed the first assessment at one shilling in the £ on the annual value of occupied property, and four-pence in the £ on the freehold value of unoccupied property, the Town Clerk being appointed Collector at a commission of 4 per cent.   A long and pleasant existence without anything to pay had become so constitutional that the advent of a tax-gatherer was regarded by the inhabitants with distrust, while objections were raised against the rate as being premature and excessive, several appeals being lodged.   As time went on, the Town Clerk reported many defaulters, so Mr. George Lawrie, who had been appointed Town Solicitor, was instructed to sue for arrear rates.   Summons was accordingly issued at the instance of Mark Foggitt, Borough Collector, against Mr. Henry Milner, Merchant, Shipowner, and Sugar Planter, for £4 10s.   On the case coming into the Resident Magistrate's Court, Mr. J. R. Goodricke appeared for the defaulter, and took exception to the summons in all directions, but mainly on the ground that the Town Clerk as Collector had not been properly appointed in terms of the Ordinance, under the "Borough Seal."   As the Council had no seal, the Magistrate held, after a trial of two days, and a lengthy, learned judgment, full of English precedents, that the omission of a seal was fatal in law, and inferentially an injustice to the defendant, so dismissed the summons with costs.   Indignation was rife, and newspaper comments severe.   Mr. Milner, however, upon the opinion of the Honourable Walter Harding, paid the rate, and thus stayed the pending appeal.

The Council, after this warning, invited designs for a Borough seal.   Several were sent in, all more or less regardless of the rules of Heraldry, my own among them. They were exhibited at the Mechanics' Institute, and ultimately that of Mr. C. Joseph Cato was formally accepted.   This represented a view of the Town, Point, Bay and Bluff, with a portion of my design (added by consent), a star over the Bluff, intended as an emblem of the Star of Bethlehem, typifying the Nativity and the East, and the seal was cut in silver by Mr. John Vialls, an engraver.

Attached to a handle of native ivory, to be used as a hand-seal, it was presented to the Town Council by Mr. Cato, the Mayor, surrounded by a silver band recording the fact and the names of the Town Councillors of the year. This seal and specimen of local talent, is preserved with the Archives of the Borough, notwithstanding its use has been abandoned for the more pretentious heraldic design by Mr. Councillor J. Sanderson, now in use.

The five-pointed Natal star was appropriated by the Town Council as a sort of Crest, and used for a time as a trademark to brand all Corporation tools and property.   The

Seal now adopted was in use for years, and fastened upon us the debt for £60,000, for which part of the Town Lands are hypothecated.   It is attached to the 6 per cent. Debenture Bonds repayable in 1906.

The captious critic, or the fortunate Bond-holder, will find on comparing this reproduction of the hand-seal design with the later embossing seal used for the Bonds, that the English die-sinker has made slight variations in the picture.   The Bluff at that time only carried a plain flagstaff, near to which was the signalman's small cottage.   This in the embossing seal might be mistaken for a Martello tower or a lighthouse; as a matter of fact the Lighthouse was not erected until 1864.

Public Health. According to established custom—because the Magistrate ruled the Police and directed Convict labour—certain residents of Pine Terrace, early in the hot and wet month of January, memorialised the Magistrate to effect certain improvements in that locality.   The Magistrate passed it on to the Town Council, who informed him that " that part of the town will have the first consideration of the Council as soon as possible."

The need of Magisterial, or Corporate, consideration is pointed out in the " Mercury " of the 31st January : —

"Pine Terrace is still a *foot* and *fever* trap. On Sunday night during and after the thunderstorm, it was completely flooded in many parts, and gentlemen had to carry their wives on their way home from Church through the slough of despond. The cattle kraals, piggeries, and stagnant pools, reek with filthy steam, foul incense offered to the guardians of the public health."

A correspondent in the same issue ironically advocates abandoning Pilot George Archer's proposed Bathing Stage in the Bay, "and converting the salubrious and centrally situated lake in West Street into Public Baths."

At a Town Council meeting on the 16th February, it transpired that, in grasping at the shadow, the Council had missed the substance.   The Government had notified that the Municipal Ordinance required the formation of a Police Board, half the cost of which was to be borne by the Town, but, in consequence of the delay over the Town Lands dispute, the time had lapsed when trade licenses were payable. The Government accordingly claimed to receive all that revenue in support of the local police.   Resolved on a proposal by Mr. J. Millar "That the discussion respecting the proposition for the establishment of a Police Board, contained in a letter of the Resident Magistrate of the 6th inst., be postponed until the Corporation receive the Title Deeds of the Town Lands, and that the Resident Magistrate be informed of the resolution by the Town Clerk."

Police.
The position and status of our local Police in May of this year is thus noted in the *Mercury* :—

"We believe it is a fact that we have no street police for the protection of this town, by night or by day   The six men who wear blue jackets, with budding tails, at the public expense, with their grave and well dressed superior officer, and his corpulent milk-white charger, are taxed to the utmost of their physical powers in guarding the purlieus of the prison and the Police Court, and in doing official errands.   'The town,' as one of them candidly remarked, 'the town, sir, takes care of itself'   We fear our corporate funds will not bear the expense of a larger number of bluejackets, even without tails, and the milk-white charger must continue to whisk its flowing tail in sober and solitary glory."

The article proceeds to suggest that a military main guard might be posted in a central situation, with outlying sentries for day and night duty.   In this connection I cannot refrain from mentioning that the "grave and well dressed superior officer" was Mr. William Harrison, Chief Constable, vice Mr. Edwin Lee, promoted a Customs landing-waiter.   He was prim and methodical, inclining to corpulence and good nature, leisurely in all his movements, merciful to his milk-white charger, which was never known in the extremest case to exceed a triple.   This pony was a white-eyed animal with a hogged mane, in build like a Suffolk Punch, much over-fed and indulged, Harrison's sympathies extending to a lantern over his manger at night, to enable it to see to eat its food.

Naturally, both the horse and its rider were the cause of merriment and practical jokes; it being a common thing for "a bad young man" to establish an alibi, by arriving at the Chief Constable's destination before him and his horse.

1

But, alas! during the throes of a contested election in the following year, the hearts of the good old man and his equally sympathetic dame were nearly broken by the cruel and dastardly behaviour of some ruffians, in burglariously entering the sacred precincts of the Chief Officer of the Law, and removing the cherished milk-white charger from his comfortable stable. The poor thing had evidently been out all night, for it was found in the· morning grazing on the flat, and ignominiously led back through the town, gorgeously painted in blue stripes like a Zebra, with blue rings round his eyes, blue and white being the party colours. It died in the course of nature from horse sickness, but Mr. Harrison always attributed its decease to the action of the undiscovered miscreant.

From January to June the Town Council was kept very busy, framing Bye-laws, and contending as to the leasing or sale of Berea lands, giving instructions to Town Surveyor as to cutting up Blocks A and Z, with a 100 ft. road, above the Botanic Gardens; also debating whether the boundary road on the Berea ridge should be 5, 30, 60, or 100 ft. wide.

The Town Clerk reported on the state of the Town Pump (Erf 20, Block D, Smith Street), and the Council resolved upon repairs of the well, and purchase of a new pump; on completion this was deemed of sufficient importance for the newspaper to record "The public well in Smith Street, opposite the premises of John Brown, Esq., is now thoroughly repaired, and in perfect working order." In June the first edition of the Borough Bye-laws was "submitted, received, and passed, and ordered to be forwarded to the Lieutenant-Governor for his sanction." On the 10th July, Mr. George Lawrie appears to have resigned his appointment as Town Solicitor, for two applications for that office were before the Council. Mr. J. R. Goodricke was elected. The Burgess Roll for the year 1855 contained 234 names, including my own. I had taken this precaution to secure the franchise, and whatever benefit attached to Burgher rights.

The Government having nominated Messrs. E. P. Lamport and Wm. Smerdon as unofficial members of the Harbour Board, the Town Council at its meeting of the 17th

n and his
the cruel
lariously
he Law,
m his
n out
the
usly
nd
ed
rz-
e

y
g
.

!

1
b-
ned
0th
his
that
was
d 234
tion to
hed to

Lam-
Har-
17th

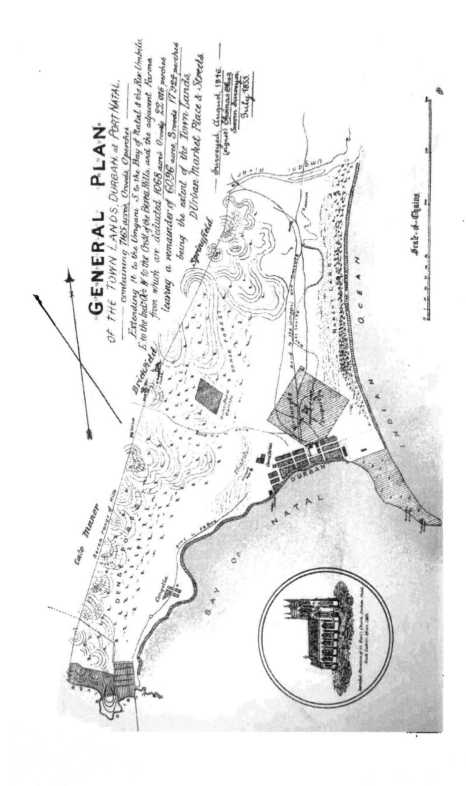

"GENERAL PLAN."
OF THE TOWN LANDS, DURBAN, at PORT NATAL.
containing 7165 acres Streets Opended

Extending it. to the Umgeni S. to the Bay of Natal & the Rev Umhlatuzana.
E. to the Indian N. to the Crest of the Berea Hills and the adjacent Farms
from which are deducted 1068 acres 0 roods 22.016 perches
leaving a remainder of 6096 acres 3 roods 17.924 perches
being the extent of the Town Lands
DURban Market Place & Streets

Surveyed August 1846.
(signed) Thomas Okes
Survey Surveyor
July 1855

Scale of Chains

July protested —"As the promised nomination of two members by the Council to sit upon the said Board, was the chief inducement on the part of the Town Council to consent to the adjustment of the Town Lands upon the present basis." While in this frame of mind, the Acting Surveyor-General submitted (19th July) for the approval of the Council a draft Deed of Grant and Diagram of the Town Lands. The Council requested the Governor to amend the conditions of the Title Deed, by confirming all existing servitudes. This was promptly acceded to by the Government, ånd the receipt of the amended Title Deeds was duly acknowledged on the 30th July by the Town Council.

The annexed Plan is a copy of the original Diagram attached to the Title Deeds. For the sake of identification, I have " hatched " all portions reserved, previously granted, or sold by the Crown. The Town proper, or Blocks of Erven, amounting to 111 acres, though handed over, had been deducted from the gross area of "Town Lands," because many Erven, as I have shewn, were previously granted or sold. The total acreage of Durban Borough is thus shewn as 6,208 acres. I have taken the liberty of indicating the site of the Windmill and Tollgate for future reference.

The first Mayor's Minute, published on the 1st August, by Mr. G. C. Cato, demonstrated the wisdom of his selection ; his natural aptitude in business affairs, and his far-seeing shrewdness, amounting almost to genius ; for his duties expired with his year of office, and hence the necessity he felt for putting on record the work of this initial year. This once accomplished, it became almost obligatory upon succeeding Mayors to do the same, consequently his example has ever since been followed, leaving to the Burgesses, as the years roll by, a continuous and voluminous history of the affairs of the town. Supplemented as they are by the Town Treasurer's Statement of Income and Expenditure, they afford, in the well-ordered records of the Town Office, a mine of wealth for many future historians, to whom I must yield this Treasury of Knowledge for want of time and space, confining myself only to those major issues associated with Old Durban.

This Mayor's Minute and Corporation Balance Sheet showed that the total Revenue (including borrowed money) amounted to £326 0s. 3d., while the total Expenditure was £279 2s. 5½d. Of this the Town Solicitor and Law costs, sueing for rates, took £3 18s. 2d., Candles and Stationery absorbed £5 4s. 2d., while the interest on the Bank's Loan to the Corporation disposed of 10s. The whole rateable property should have yielded £341 18s. 2d., but, it being a novelty and cash scarce, people did not quite realise the necessity of paying up, so at the end of the municipal year there was still £103 1s. unpaid. The drainage of the feeding ground of wild duck and snipe in Pine Terrace by a brick culvert through Grey Street, 700 ft. long, was the chief item of expenditure for the year, costing £131 4s. 2d., more than a third of the Borough Rates. Salaries. Surveys, Pumps, small Contracts, and labour accounted for the balance of Expenditure.

At the first re-election of Councillors, there was only a contest in Ward No. 4, Messrs. Charles Johnston, E. Snell, and R. Raw having been nominated, resulting in the election of the two first named. The new Council consisted of : —

Ward 1. G. C. Cato, James Blackwood.
2. J. Millar, Archibald Ferguson (new).
3. Richard Harwin, John Sanderson (new).
4. Charles Johnston, Edward Snell (new).

On Saturday, the 1st August, Mr. G. C. Cato was re-elected Mayor for the second time by 6 votes, Mr. Millar having 2 votes.

J. R. Saunders. Before proceeding with the acts of the new Council, it is necessary that I digress for a space, in order to introduce a new actor. James Renault Saunders, with wife and child, arrived, via the Cape, in the S.S. *Natal*, on the 23rd October, 1854, and speedily wrote himself into notice, by pointing out in November to the Victoria County Council, and to the Durban Town Council in January of this year, the necessity for a floating pontoon bridge, and the facility with which it could be constructed over the Umgeni. The County Council grasped the idea, and, in imposing a County Cess of three farthings per acre, justified the act by stating that it was "owing to their anxiety to have a Bridge over the "Umgeni"; this resulted in a protest by Durban Land Owners, or Agents of Owners, in the County. Mr. G. C. Cato—among others—declined to submit to the "enormous burden," and threatened to sell out before paying. Mr. Saunders' communication to the Durban Town Council was "laid on the table." However, a month or two later (April) he wrote an attractive letter to the *Mercury* on "Imported Labour," giving a very clear and able statement as to Chinese and Coolie emigration to Mauritius, and the suitability of these people for Natal, which occupied two columns, and was dated from "Itongati," at which place he had settled as a Sugar planter. From it, when in later years he became a member of the Legislative Council, he derived his title, for he was known to the political cartoonist, as also to his opponents, as the "Tongaat Slasher." The impecunious Town Council had ignored the Bridge proposal, because they were at that time negotiating with the Government for the free delivery and control of the Ferry at the Lower Drift—Umgeni Mouth. A tariff of fees was adopted, and tenders invited to rent; and on the 14th August the new Council accepted the tender of William George, who thereupon took over the punt with its gear.

Apparently George transferred his rights to the other tenderer, "for a consideration." This man, to recoup his bonus, set to work diligently while the sun shone, with the result that an appeal was made to the Town Council soon after, to correct his reading of the tariff. A loaded wagon on the river's brim was something more than a yellow wagon to him! First it was a wagon per tariff; then it was oxen per head; then the contents were goods, by weight, freely estimated. The simple wayfarer having complained, the Town Council defined a "loaded wagon" to include the wagon, contents, and the span. These regulations remained in force until the Umgeni itself came down in April following, carried away the punt, levelled up the ferry, and disposed of the contract.

The new Council was much exercised as to the Berea lands, since there existed a conflict of opinion in the minds of the Burgesses as to how they could have their cake and eat it too. The Town Surveyor had been ordered to survey for leasing purposes "the portion of ground marked A on the plan, supposed to contain 14 lots of 5 acres each, leaving roads 100 feet wide." The Government had offered the services of the Military—on the completion of the High road and the cutting through the Berea Ridge, to continue the High road—to clear down through the Bush, and connect with the old Windmill Road at its commencement on the flat near the Agricultural Gardens, this to be done under the supervision of the Acting Surveyor-General. The offer was gladly accepted by the Council on the 14th September, when it was "Resolved also that the Town Surveyor be instructed to open a line on the ridge of the Berea, adjoining the Agricultural Gardens, preparatory to surveying Block Z."

This tampering with our possessions was regarded with so much suspicion that the Mayor called a public meeting to take a vote on the subject. The meeting was held in Mr. R. Acutt's Auction Mart on the 21st September. The question submitted was, "Should a portion of the Town Lands be sold to furnish funds for the Corporation?" An animated, heated discussion took place, for and against, while many present advocated leasing only. The views of the opposition were voiced by Mr. R. W. Tyzack, who "looked upon the present scheme as only an attempt to insert the thin end of the wedge, and warned the meeting against tampering with the inheritance of their children, to gratify the cupidity and ambition of a class." The meeting, having regard to the present heavy rates, and the benefit posterity would derive from an improved town, decided by a large majority to sell. It was on this occasion that an equally enthusiastic burgess, in opposing Mr. Tyzack, amused the meeting and astonished himself by shouting, "What good has posterity done for us, I should like to know?"

Having got so far, the Council appear to have become frightened at their own temerity, or otherwise held the consent to sell in reserve, for, at their meeting four days later, they agreed to issue Leases at an upset rental of 15s. per acre per annum, subject to the erection of a building of £25 value thereon, and to seek the permission of the Government to lease 150 acres on the Berea Range. This consent obtained, the old leaven of suspicion pervaded the Council, for at their meeting on the 14th December, they could not agree as to whether the sizes of the Lots and Leases in Blocks A. and B. should be half-an-acre, 1, 2½, or 5 acres. So the Surveyor rested from his labours.

The Town Clerk's salary was now increased to £80, and the Rate fixed at 1s. in the £ on the rental, and 3d. on the freehold. By the Municipal Ordinance the cost of the Police, as previously stated, was to be shared by the Government and the Town. The Gaol was a central one, being also Lock-up and Police Station; the Police having jurisdiction in town and county. The Government had notified the Council that the Police Board must be constituted forthwith, when the Corporation would be entitled with the New Year to certain Licenses, hitherto collected by the Government. The Ordinance provided that the Resident Magistrate and the Mayor with one Councillor form the Board. On the motion of Mr. Councillor Johnston it was " Resolved that the constitution of the Police Board as part of the Corporation Ordinance is at variance with the spirit and integrity of self-government, introducing an authority for the preservation of the peace and order of the Town other than that of the Town Council.'

Nevertheless they proceeded to ballot for a Councillor to sit at that unconstitutional Board. The lot fell upon Mr. J. Millar.

At the first meeting of the Board (7th January, 1856), the three members were present, and as might be expected, their proceedings were eminently practical and unique.

" Mr. Millar moved that the Mayor be Chairman of the Board, on the ground that as it was strictly a department of municipal administration, the head of the Borough Corporation ought to be the head of the Police Board; seconded by Mr. Cato. Mr. Cope (Acting Resident Magistrate) moved as an amendment, that the Resident Magistrate be President, on various grounds connected with the functions of that office. The amendment not being seconded, the Mayor was duly elected, and the Board having elected the Town Clerk as its Secretary, proceeded to direct returns to be prepared connected with the numbers, expenses, and the duties of the existing constabulary, as a basis for future proceedings."

Notwithstanding an indignant sub-leader against the Acting Resident Magistrate, because he had fined a Native five shillings for omitting to salute him in the street as he rode past to his office, there is evidence that his Worship was of Inspector Buckett's opinion, " that discipline must be maintained," for a " Local " in the same issue notes : —

" The Acting Resident Magistrate has followed the worthy example of his predecessor in providing an ample feast of roast beef and plum pudding to regale the prisoners in our gaol on Christmas Day."

Sugar.   Endeavouring to keep to the sequence of events, we will glance back to the 21st March, on which day a considerable number of the leading Merchants and other inhabitants betook themselves to Springfield Sugar Estate, where Messrs. H. Milner and J. B. Miller were about to start new machinery, and demonstrate the conversion of cane juice into sugar by steam.   The crushing and boiling processes having already been effected ; thus the reporter : —

" The first operation of the new machinery—the beautiful little steam engine (the first introduced into Natal) and the wonder-working centrifugal machine displayed their powers to perfection, and excited the delighted surprise of all present. . . . . A quantity of thick dark-coloured syrup was poured into the inner perforated cylinder of the centrifugal, and in exactly four minutes after the revolutions commenced (of which there were 1,700 every minute) the syrup was converted into a beautiful sample of bright, dry, yellow crystallised sugar, equal to the finest qualities imported from Mauritius. In seven minutes the same syrup was converted into sugar of still finer quality, almost white in colour, and far superior to the imported article. Samples of the sugar made severally in four and in seven minutes may be seen at our office, and any very sceptical person may also see a sample of the original syrup."

Everybody had samples; the firm returned with its pockets full, and I had to make it into packets like Seidlitz powders with the bluest of paper, to distribute, and send to England.

On Saturday, the 23rd June, on the Market Square, Mr. Robert Acutt held the first auction sale of Colonial Sugar grown and manufactured at the " Springfield Estate "; there was about eight tons.   The event partook somewhat of a public character, as Mr. Acutt had advertised that he would give his services gratuitously.   There was consequently a large gathering.   It was put up in gunny bags, enclosed in Vacoa mat bags imported from Mauritius, and sold for this occasion by the single bag, in order that all might have an opportunity of laying in supplies. There were several qualities, but the price averaged 30s. per cwt., which was considered satisfactory, for, at the conclusion of the sale, Mr. Henry Milner thanked the company for their attendance and ordered a basket of champagne for those present to drink success to the Sugar Enterprise. This scene was sketched at the time by Mr. J. Lloyd, our local Artist, and subsequently appeared in the *Illustrated London News*. The Sugar Industry rapidly extended, so that, by the end of the year, the small and defective Cattle-power Mills of Messrs. Babbs, Jeffels, Mack and Joyner at the Isipingo had given place to steam, and were sending in sugar in quantity to Durban Merchants for sale.

Patriotic Fund. The battle of Alma had been fought, and we had the details of this and other engagements before Sebastopol, with harrowing descriptions of the sick and wounded in the Hospitals at Scutari and elsewhere. Her Majesty's "Letter to her people" promoted the Patriotic Fund. This was taken up in the Colonies, with a zeal and enthusiasm only excelled in the British Isles. The influence of a garrison town, the martial air, and sympathetic laments of the men of the 45th Regiment at their long detention in Natal— "shure we're growing blue mouldy for a want of a bating"—stirred the residents of Pietermaritzburg to unwonted action, for, on the formation of their Patriotic Fund Committee, they formally proposed to change their town's polysyllabic surname to "Alma" in honour of the event.

We followed later on the 19th April, when the Resident Magistrate, acting under instructions (*), called a meeting of town and county people, to be held in Durban, to organise contributions to the Fund. Though loyal, we were still keenly sensitive of our Burgher rights and privileges; that the meeting had been called by the Resident Magistrate, instead of by the Mayor, was given as the reason for the absence of the general public on that occasion. However, the Magistrate voted the Mayor to the chair, and those present duly elected a Committee, with the Mayor at its head.

* *Gazette* Notices 31 and 34, 1855.

To put the thing on a proper footing, this Committee convened a public meeting for the purposes of organisation, to
be held in Breede's store (then Mr. E. Smith's) on the 26th
April.   There was a large attendance, and the first at which
ladies were present; also the Band of the Durban Volunteer
Guard, who could be relied on for " Cheer, boys, cheer," the
" British Grenadiers," and " God save the Queen."   A large
" British Ensign, " nailed by its four corners, adorned one
end wall, while other flags were displayed in the Hall, in
which a platform had been constructed.   The Mayor opened
the meeting by reading a portion of the Queen's letter on
the subject of the Fund, following it up with a neat patriotic
speech, from a Colonist's point of view.   The cheers and
instrumental flourish which followed brought Mr. Councillor
Johnston to his feet.   He did not think there was any
necessity for any meeting at all, and he strongly objected
to the manner in which it had been called—(hisses, with
partial cheers)—inasmuch as the whole business should have
been organised by the Mayor, as Chief Magistrate of this
town.   (Cheers and hisses.)   As the Committee seemed to
have all their resolutions cut and dried, he would like to
know what they had done in the way of subscribing.
(Strong cries of disapprobation.)

   The Mayor said that the names of Dr. Johnston and of
all other subscribers would be published in due course, and
called upon the Resident Magistrate to address the meeting.
Several other gentlemen spoke, the patriotic public cheered,
the ladies waved their handkerchiefs, and the Band responded, closing the meeting with a final " God save the
Queen."   Subscriptions followed in liberally in coin, in
goods, and in paper, the Natal Bank having headed the
Pietermaritzburg list with a donation of £50.   The curious
may find the lists in the newspapers of the period.

                      Our Boys have much to be thankful for,
   Education.   by reason of the wise and liberal measures,
                      introduced in the year One for the educa-
tion of their sires, which resulted in a system of almost free
schools, of a high class order, for the whole youth of the
Colony.

We must go back for a little to 1849, when the Rev. W. H. C. Lloyd got together a few adherents of the Church of England, and induced them to constitute a Vestry. No other building being available, they agreed to hire the thatched store of Mr. L. E. Mesham, on the corner of Aliwal Street, as a Church and Schoolroom, at a rental of £70 a year. Pulpit, seats, and fittings were obtained, and Mr. J. R. Goodricke appointed Parish Clerk and Schoolmaster. The Clerkship he soon resigned. The duties were thereupon undertaken by Mr. L. E. Mesham *pro tem.* It transpired, when the Vestry sought Government aid for the public school, that other men, not Churchmen, had also moved in the matter of education, and they learnt that a public schoolmaster was shortly expected, and that on the completion of the new building in Field Street [Pollybank's Erf], the Government would open it as a school. The Vestry thereupon regretted they had been premature, and petitioned the Government for the use of the new schoolroom for Church services. Government consented to allow this when the building was not otherwise required, possession to be taken 1st January, 1850. In the meantime the Government schoolmaster had arrived and been appointed, in the person of the Rev. W. Nesbitt, late of St. John's, New Brunswick, an elderly gentleman, unmarried—salary £150, with £30 yearly house allowance. His rod and his staff were his support, as many a boy still living can testify. As the lease of this building expired in 1855, and could not be renewed, the Government removed the school to a slated brick building on the opposite side of the street with garden attached, the property of Mr. James Elliot, Signalman at the Bluff, where Mr. Nesbitt also resided. The building, now offices, is still standing.

St. Paul's Church. The Parish Vestry having thus got notice to quit, the Churchwardens hurried on the completion of St. Paul's, by substituting oiled calico in the place of glass for the windows, and advertised that they would attend to let sittings in anticipation of the opening for regular services in future. Accordingly on Sunday, the 1st April, St. Paul's was formally opened for service—in so far as the Vestry could go without the ceremony of consecration—by the Rev. W. Nesbitt, acting Colonial Chaplain, who preached the first sermon to a moderately large and attentive congregation, taking his text from Genesis, 12 ch., 8th verse, " And there he builded an Altar," etc., and on Easter Monday, April the 9th, a Vestry meeting was held for the first time in St. Paul's. The Rev. W. H. C. Lloyd presided. Messrs. R. Acutt and W. H. Savory were unanimously elected Churchwardens.

Bishop Colenso. Matters were so far got in order in anticipation of the arrival of Bishop Colenso, his family and party, who were to have left Liverpool in the *Jane Mcrice*, 256 tons, Roper, Master. This ship arrived on the 20th May, crossed the Bar, and anchored in the Bluff Channel. She brought the Bishop of Natal, Mrs. Colenso, and four children, Archdeacon McKenzie, and Miss McKenzie, the Rev. W. O. Newnham, a body of Clergymen, female teachers, and others, completing his Lordship's ecclesiastical and mission staff; among the latter was Mr. A. W. L. Rivett, subsequently ordained and nominated to St. Paul's, who founded Christ Church, Addington. I am indebted for much information to his " Ten Years' Church Work in Natal." Mr. E. P. Lamport, the Agent of the ship, returned in her as a passenger, bringing with him his bride.

A public meeting, called on short notice, was held in the morning of the 24th May (Queen's Birthday) for the purpose of presenting an address by the Bishop, signed by 51 persons, welcoming his return to the Colony, wishing success to his mission, but calling in question some reflections upon the people in Natal made by him in England. Mr. H. J. Mellor, the Resident Magistrate, presided, and, considering it was a public holiday, there was a fair attendance. But before the Chairman opened proceedings, Dr. Johnston wanted to know if it was a public meeting to present an address, or a meeting of the friends of the Church of England. If the latter he should quietly retire; if the former. he considered the address could not be regarded as emanating from the public ; it had been improperly got up, it had not been adopted at any public meeting, and the signatures had only been obtained by a hole-and-corner system of canvassing.　He could not allow it to be said that this was a "Public Address."　The Magistrate appealed to the Doctor's good feeling and sense of propriety, with the result that "a slight personal altercation ensued," whereupon the Bishop asked the Chairman to allow Mr. Johnston to be heard.　Apart from constitutional habit, the true cause of this display of feeling arose out of newspaper reports; rumours, and general assertions, which had reached us of the Bishop's speeches on Mission tour in England.　Dr. Johnston, though upholding the rights of the Burgesses, or the dignity of the Mayor, was equally ready to champion the Colonists generally against mis-statements from whatever source, ecclesiastical especially.　There is no question that public sentiment had been worked up to regard the Bishop's advent as something more than "a terror to evil doers." The liberty-loving, free speaking and thinking Colonist regarded this invasion of Clergy and lay sisters, with their spiritual head, as imposing an establishment upon them, whose tendencies savoured of innovation, possibly Tractarian, or even Puseyite, and, from the incompetency of all the Mission party, certainly dangerous to the Native population and peace of the Colony.　These sentiments rankled, festered, and broke into outrage, resulting in a cancerous sore, which, coupled with later events, permeated the Established Church, and has refused to be healed to this day.

Several gentlemen spoke to the Address.　The Bishop replied fully, answering the objections and explaining the garbled reports of his speeches at home.　Dr. Johnston thereupon apologised for any apparent opposition at the commencement of the proceedings, and assured the Bishop "that he had never been one of that class of the public who had delighted in spreading abroad distorted views of his (the Bishop's) speeches in England.　Having now heard the explanation, he must say that his opposition was entirely at an end.　He was perfectly satisfied with all the Bishop had done, with a view to the best interests of Natal, and it was to be regretted that the more important and more acceptable parts of his speech in England had been suppressed."

Mr. Savory Pinsent asked if it was the Bishop's wish, or the wish of the Government, that the whole of the Kafir Tax should be applied to the support of Church of England Schools, or whether it was intended to divide it among all the different denominations of Christians.   The Bishop replied that in this and every other question he should be guided by the Government.

The Bishop preached for the first time in St. Paul's on Sunday, the 27th May, in the morning, Archdeacon McKenzie in the evening.   Mrs. Cubitt presided at the harmonium, and led the Choir, " Jackson's *Te Deum* being admirably sung."   There were crowded reverential congregations, of whom Mr. Rivett is good enough thus to approve : —" The Church was full, and the congregation might " be considered equal in intelligence and position to those of " any town or city suburb in England."   The impression produced upon myself by the Preacher obliterated the sermon, and minor details of the service.   There was something indescribable in the Bishop's personality,: tall and commanding, graceful and gentlemanly, melodious in voice and dignified in bearing, without " effects " or display, quiet, orderly, and reverential.   One could not but feel that you were in the presence of a refined gentleman and scholar, who spoke direct to the people, and not over their heads, appealing both to reason and understanding.   A man of power held in reserve, who preferred rather to draw us by Love, than to terrify us by threats.   In after years, when persecuted for heresy, his appearance was truly described as " Leonine."   The fascination exercised upon me may be attributed to the influence of mind over matter, but the intelligent congregation admitted his vast superiority to the general run of individuals claiming to constitute Colonial Society.

At a Vestry meeting held in St. Paul's—June 21st—a sub-committee, consisting of Messrs. J. Millar, J. R. Saunders, and Goodricke, reported that in endeavouring unsuccessfully to negotiate a loan of £250, to complete the Church, they had referred to the Bishop, who was already a creditor for £300.   He had at once expressed his disapproval of the means by which the Vestry designed to repay the loan [the mortgaging of the Pew Rents].   He objected to the system of pew rents, and would not advance the money. In a letter addressed by him to the congregation and read at the meeting, he pointed out that the land was vested in the Bishop of Cape Town, and through him (the writer) to Natal, as Trustee for the Church of England; consequently it would not be possible to constitute the Church a Proprietary Chapel. The funds subscribed in England and elsewhere were for a Parish Church. As the Parishioners were unable to discharge their liabilities or finish the building, he undertook to do it on their behalf, relying for re-payment solely on the voluntary offerings of the congregation. "In order to do this, I must take into my own hands the Church of St. Paul's with all its affairs, for the next ten years, or such shorter time as would liquidate the debt, with any additional expenditure, bearing interest at 6 per cent. . . . . I must request the Archdeacon to come down, and be for the present resident among you."

A resolution was carried handing over St. Paul's to the Bishop and Churchwardens, for the temporary and conditional term and purposes specified by him; prefaced by an intimation that they did so by reason of His Lordship having expressed "his objection to the Tractarian movement, and his approval of evangelical and apostolical truth are a pledge to this meeting that these innovations will not be tolerated by him." This the Bishop repudiated.

Another Vestry meeting was held on the 25th June, under the presidency of the Rev. W. H. C. Lloyd. Free discussion took place, and the meeting is said to have been harmonious, though the speakers hovered round Tractarianism, Gown and Surplice, High and Low Church in their observations. Ultimately a resolution, proposed by Mr. L. E. Mesham, seconded by Mr. J. B. Roberts, was carried:—
" That this meeting, having every confidence in the Lord Bishop of the Diocese, instructs the Church Building Committee to make over the St. Paul's Church to his Lordship for the purposes specified in his letter dated 18th June, 1855, anything contained in any resolution passed by the Vestry Meeting on the 21st inst. notwithstanding." The Chairman took an affectionate leave of his parishioners, intimating that his duties would for the future lie in the country.

In terms of this arrangement, Archdeacon McKenzie came to reside in Durban as Incumbent. Mr. Upton, the Architect, called for tenders for the completion of the building, and the work was proceeded with; yet the good churchmen were unhappy. So a Vestry meeting was summoned for the afternoon of October 17th to take into consideration the "Instructions and Regulations" recently issued for the guidance of members and Churchwardens, and also as to certain intended changes in the order of public service.

Strong opinions were expressed on three particulars. First, a declaration of conformity to the doctrines of the Church of England as a qualification to the rights of parishioner. This it was resolved *nem. con.* that the Bishop should be requested to withdraw. Second and Third, wearing the surplice during sermon, and collecting the offertory from seat to seat. The Archdeacon mildly explained, but the meeting insisted they were unnecessary and dangerous innovations, indicating a tendency to practices at variance with the true blue Protestantism of the Church people of Durban, who regarded them as badges of a party. Archdeacon McKenzie was earnestly requested to give way on these points, as the principal parties present declared that they would rather absent themselves, or resist the innovations by withholding their cash. The conduct of the Archdeacon was marked by great forbearance, under circumstances very trying to flesh and blood. Mr. Churchwarden Acutt, after commenting strongly on the dangerous tendency of these innovations, declared that he would be no party to them and should resign.

At an adjourned Vestry meeting on the 30th October, Archdeacon presiding, both the Bishop and Archdeacon disclaimed any intention of introducing Tractarian practices, and urged upon the meeting the advisability of conforming to the Bishop's "Instructions" for twelve months, to test their working, promising to amend or alter them if circumstances warranted.

The meeting, by a large majority, declined to adopt the "Instructions" on the ground that the Bishop possessed no legislative functions and could not make Law, even with the consent of the laity; they were otherwise objectionable in giving the Bishop exclusive and unusual control, thereby depriving the Churchwardens and Vestry of their legitimate powers. The Parish Clerk, in consequence of extra duties, asked for an increase of salary; the Vestry admitted its justice, but passed it on to the next meeting. Both these meetings were of a stormy character, the report of them occupying five columns of the *Mercury*. Archdeacon McKenzie and the Rev. R. Robertson appear to have stood almost alone. Messrs. J. Millar, W. H. Savory, Wm. Dacomb, E. P. Lamport, Robert Acutt, J. B. Roberts, Dr. Holland, Hon. G. Rutherford, R. Raw, T. Dand, J. R. Goodricke, T. P. James, H. W. Currie, H. Gillespie, and J. R. Saunders took part.

These names are sufficient indication to old Colonists of the nature of the strife. Only one man, H. W. Currie, had the good taste to remind the meeting of the obligations they were under to the Bishop, and to move the adjournment of the Vestry until the Bishop could be communicated with. This was rejected, and a resolution by Mr. Millar, seconded by Mr. Gillespie, was put:—" That the Churchwardens call " a Vestry meeting for Tuesday, November 27th, to con- " sider the propriety of petitioning the Government to pass ' an Ordinance legally authorising the appointment of a " Vestry and Churchwardens for the Episcopal Church of " Durban based on the precedents of the Churches at Ron- " debosch and Graaf Reinet [Cape Colony], and at the same ' meeting to receive any communication from the Lord " Bishop." Carried by 17 votes against 1.

In terms of the resolution, St. Paul's bell rang at 3 p.m. on the 27th November, to summon the Vestry. On ar- riving the malcontents were astonished to find themselves the subjects of a " Lock-out," Archdeacon McKenzie, key in hand, like another St. Peter, with the Rev. Robert Robert- son, being outside the door in earnest conversation with Mr. Robert Acutt. The crowd increased, a long and violent altercation ensued on the Archdeacon declaring that he should not admit them until he had first read to them, outside, a letter from the Bishop. Mr. Acutt accused the Archdeacon of obtaining the key from the Clerk by mis- representation. The afternoon was noted as a specially hot summer day, and this may have affected the feelings of the gathering at the Western door, for, on the question being ultimately put to the Archdeacon if he would admit them *after* he had read the letter, he replied "he would not." Tempers rose, and the voice of the people made itself heard over the clang of the "Church-going bell" kept going to drown the voice of the Archdeacon, who, standing on the Church steps insisted on reading the Bishop's letter to the unruly flock.   He retired expressing his intention of carrying out the Bishop's wishes, in preventing the Church being used for that meeting. The indignation of the locked-out found vent in rude words, but, the wolf being gone, Mr. Churchwarden Acutt effected an entrance by removing one of the calico windows, and opening the door from the inside. The crowd then entered and constituted itself a Vestry. with Mr. Acutt in the chair. Mr. J. R. Saunders carried a resolution that the appointment of Vestry and Churchwardens should be the subject of legislative enactment, while Mr. J. Millar carried another resolution to appoint a Committee to draft an Ordinance to that end, on the lines of the Graaf Reinet and Rondebosch Churches.

Mr. Millar suggested that Churchwardens should have a new key made.   Mr. Acutt suggested stopping supplies. Resolved—on motion, by Mr. Millar ; seconded by Mr. Goodricke :—" That in the opinion of this meeting the unwarrantable conduct of the Bishop and Archdeacon in taking possession of the keys of the Church, and refusing to allow the Vestry meeting, legally called, to take place in the Church, is highly reprehensible, and calculated to forfeit the confidence of the members of the Church."

A minority objected to the resolution, as not sufficiently strong, but were ultimately prevailed upon to pass it.

Mr. Churchwarden Savory thereupon resigned.

Proposed by Mr. H. W. Currie, seconded by Mr. Gillespie :—" That a plate be held outside the Church railings " every Sunday, in aid of a Church of England Defence " Association.   It would then be seen if the Bishop's plate " inside, or theirs outside received the largest contribution.' Carried unanimously, whereupon the meeting, which is reported as orderly and business-like throughout, broke up.

Naturally, like sheep, everyone turned to his own way, so that the extraordinary events of that hot afternoon became the talk of the town, and led to an outrage in the cooler hours of the evening, that smirched the fair fame of this maiden Borough, and left a permanent stain upon Colonial Episcopalians.

Burning in Effigy. Some jovial after-dinner spirits, who strangely were never publicly called to account, were moved to testify their zeal for the Protestant cause, by burning Bishop Colenso in effigy. A rude surpliced figure was accordingly prepared, paraded through West Street by men and boys with torches, fastened to a stake in the Market Square above three empty tar barrels, broken fences, and firewood, and there burnt. The flames, and cries of " No Popery," " Down with the Bishop," " No Puseyism," etc., attracted a considerable crowd of Natives and Burgesses.

The Camp bugles had not yet sounded on this evening when the Town Council terminated a meeting; the members on coming out on to the Square gravitated like moths to the light, with the deplorable result that the persons of Councillor Millar and Town Solicitor Goodricke, though both distant spectators, were recognised, and denounced to the Bishop (by a gentleman with a Hebrew name) as aiding and abetting the outrage. As there were no night police and none to interfere, the fire burnt itself out, when the men and boys dispersed satisfied with the senseless little spree.

Miss Boulter. The susceptibilities of the public had been roused to this intemperate pitch by a demented young woman, backed by the gossiping tongue of Rumour, and by the depositions of Joseph Few, a citizen of Pietermaritzburg, and William Palmer, a Merchant of Durban, which were to the effect that on the 23rd of the month Mr. Few was in conversation with Mr. Palmer at his Store, West Street East, when he noticed a young lady clinging by one arm to a post in the road, and an older lady without a bonnet, pulling first at her waist, then at her arms and wrists, apparently in efforts to remove her by force. Seeing them, the young lady asked " Is there no one who will come to my assistance?" Upon

their moving over more or less like true knights to the aid
of a damsel in distress, she enquired, "Is there no good
lady who will take me in? They have been using me very
badly." Mr. Few urged that unnecessary violence was
being used, and enquired if the young lady was out of her
mind, to which the elderly lady replied in the affirmative,
and stated that she had the charge of her. To this conclusion Mr. Few apparently arrived, as the young lady
informed him that "they said they were bringing me to
Durban, but this is not Durban." She consented to remain at her post, until arrangements could be made for her,
and instead of returning to the Rev. Robertson's home,
ultimately accepted the shelter offered by Mrs. J. H. Grant.

On the day after the *auto-da-fé* (28th November), Mr.
J. D. Shuter, Clerk of the Peace, applied for a summons,
not against the raiders, but against Miss C. Barter for assaulting Miss Boulter, both members of the "Bishop's
party." The case came before Henry Cope, Esq., Acting
Resident Magistrate, on the 29th, when Miss Barter appeared on the arm of the Bishop, accompanied by the
Honourable W. C. Sergeant, Colonial Secretary, Archdeacon
Mackenzie, and her brother, Mr. Charles Barter (afterwards
Resident Magistrate, Pietermaritzburg), who appeared on
his sister's behalf. His Lordship took upon himself the
responsibility of what Miss Barter had done, explaining
that Miss Boulter had joined the Mission in England, that
during the voyage out her deportment had called for paren-
tal authority and correction, but, it having now become
evident that her mind was affected, he had decided she
should return to her friends in England under Miss Barter's
charge in the *Lady of the Lake*, sailing on the morrow.
Miss Boulter was called by the prosecution, but Dr. Best,
of the 45th Regiment, deposed that, though physically able
to be present, she was mentally incapacitated as a witness.
Messrs. Few and Palmer, on being called, were reported as
away in Pietermaritzburg, so in the absence of other evidence the Court dismissed the summons.

Unfortunately, the Bishop, having the ear of the Court
in his opening address, and seeing Mr. J. Millar in the
room, was led away to the side issue of the effigy outrage,
and thereupon animadverted severely upon the inhabitants

of Durban, and especially against Messrs. Millar and Good-ricke, as having been present, " aiding and abetting, and encouraging by their concurrence "—thus endeavouring to associate them and others with what is known as " Miss Boulter's case."

By way of interlude, Mr. Millar thereupon informed the Court that the statement regarding himself was utterly false, and that "the Bishop was a disgrace to the cloth." The Court said the Bishop was out of order, and presently that Mr. Millar was out of order, for persisting in further forcible observations after the Court had ordered him to stop, but as this did not stay the loosened flood of vestry-born in-vective, he was promptly given into custody. In the cooler atmosphere of the ante-room, Mr. Millar's good sense came to his aid. He asked leave to return and apologise to the Court; having done so, he was released, while the Bishop apologised for any irregularity in his procedure. The Court had hardly resumed its dignified composure and the " Case," when Mr. Goodricke, having heard of the strife, hastened from his office, entered, and threw himself head-long at both the Court and the Bishop. The Magistrate would not allow him to speak, though speak he did, in snatches, on the ground that the Bishop had been allowed irregularly to attack him, and *they* must be allowed to vindicate themselves, but the Court contented itself with being unable to hear him, and proceeded to close the case.

It transpired subsequently that Miss Barter, indignant at these public proceedings, had declined to go to England, so it was arranged that poor Miss Boulter should go home in charge of Mrs. Taylor, wife of the Captain of the ship.

Electricity was in the air, for shortly after Mr. Good-ricke returned dishevelled to the Court-room to lay information against Messrs. Charles Barter and John Brown for assault, and against Mr. Charles Green for aiding and abetting. The provocation was stated to be disrespectful language, used by Mr. Goodricke in a letter to the Bishop, towards Miss Barter. Defendants were released on bail, and the case heard on the 4th December.

The facts disclosed that Mr. Barter, with his friend Joshua Walmsley, late Captain of the Native Police, who, having been appointed Zulu Border Agent, was in town for the trial of Dalmaine, a trader, for illegally importing two Zulu refugees,—both gentlemen at that time reputed " fire eaters "—proceeded in company as principal and second to look up Mr. Goodricke at his residence, Smith Street. Finding him engaged in his office, Mr. Walmsley remarked that he didn't know who else there was to thrash in town; nevertheless they hastened up to J. Millar and Co.'s store, and entered with a rush, Mr. Barter threatening Mr. Millar with a riding whip. Actual blows were avoided by the interposition of Mr. Gillespie and myself. Angry words and threats drowned Mr. Millar's denial of any knowledge of the letter prior to its publication. Messrs. Barter and Walmsley then withdrew, the latter saying they would at once 'horsewhip Mr. Goodricke. Shortly after Mr. Millar, with Mr. W. H. Evans and Mr. Gillespie, called on Mr. Goodricke, and, while in conversation outside his house, Mr. Barter rode up, dismounted, and asked to speak to Mr. Goodricke; advanced upon him, and, after enquiring the reason for his remarks to the Bishop, struck him a blow in the face with his open hand. Mr. John Brown, from his corner of Field Street, seeing the crowd— for Mr. C. Green and several others happened to be there (six people then constituted a crowd)—hastened to the rescue, as Mr. Goodricke was returning the blows with his closed fist. He endeavoured, he said, to separate them, but was accused and indicted for assisting Mr. Barter by holding Mr. Goodricke, while Mr. Green, ostensibly getting between the combatants, was indicted for holding Mr. Goodricke's head by the hair. Mr. Millar, however, in his evidence, stated that no one endeavoured to hold Mr. Barter, but that he believed both Mr. Brown and Mr. Green were actuated by a desire to separate them. Barter committed for trial before the District Court, Brown and Green dismissed.

It is due to the Bishop to say that, having made further enquiry as to Mr. Millar's presence at the bonfire, he wrote him a very ample apology, giving the name of his informant, who was unable to substantiate his assertion. The Bishop regretted having made the accusation in Court, and felt bound to say he had now no reason to suppose Mr.

Millar had been concerned in the outrage. This was sent by Mr. Millar to the newspapers, and duly published. Three days later (17th December) St. Paul's Vestry met, and the proposed Ordinance to establish a legal Vestry (Rondebosch pattern) was adopted, with the extraordinary amendment that the words "in communion with the Church of England" be struck out, so that the Vestry should be an open one; the meeting pledging itself to pass it through the Legislature as a Private Bill.

The party spirit engendered by these events can be judged from the following "Local" paragraph:—

"On Sunday [2nd December] the Offertory, as announced, was read before the Sermon, when most of the male part of the Congregation left the Church, returning when the collection, which amounted to £1 18s., was over. The 'people's plate' outside the gate received £7 17s."

The state of affairs in the Diocese during the last half of this year is exactly reflected by one of John Leech's sketches in *Punch*, representing two miners of the "black country" looking at the back of a passing gentleman. First Native: "Bill, who's he?" Second Native: "Dunno: stranger." First Native: "'Eave 'arf a brick at 'im"; for the newspapers teemed with letters and articles on controversial subjects, aimed more or less at the Bishop. The proposed ordinance for the education of the native youth; his views on Polygamy; other persons' views on Church government; Auricular confession, etc. Mr. J. R. Saunders was particularly prominent firing church cannons, loaded with Thirty-nine Articles, Homilies, Rubrics, and Biblical texts, intended to shatter His Lordship's "Instructions" and Pastoral Letters, while they thundered in his ears the Laws and practices of the Church of England. Though there is yet much to record in reference to St. Paul's, space will restrict me to the bare and imperfect Vestry minutes; meantime, those of my readers not interested in Church Squabbles may be informed that the majority of the Opposition eventually saw the error of their ways, and lived to rally round the Bishop as his friends and supporters; they had only "started before they were ready."

On the 20th June a public meeting was
Reception held to consider an address prepared by
of the Town Council (the drafting of which
Sir Geo. Grey. was credited mainly to Mr. Councillor
John Sanderson) to be presented to Sir
George Grey, the Governor of the Cape, then on his way
up overland. A discussion took place as to the expediency
of amending it, by drawing His Excellency's attention to
the Sugar Industry, and the necessity for Coolie and other
imported labour.   Notwithstanding that the very able
address traversed the whole requirements of the Colony,
its administration and resources, the meeting directed the
Town Council to amend it upon the labour question.   This
resolution rekindled the aspirations of the advocates of
convict labour; who shortly after prepared a memorial " for
the introduction of a limited number of convicts, not being
ticket-of-leave men, with a sufficient military force, for the purpose of completing, under the Imperial direction and charge,
the improvement of this Port, with a view to render it a
secure harbour of refuge, and to perfect its capabilities for
the increasing commerce of this district and the interior."
The customary public meeting to consider the subject was
held on the 17th October, when a very lively discussion
ensued, *pro* and *con.* A resolution against the introduction
of convict labour was declared carried, but "boys with
sticks" were alleged to have contributed to that majority—
vide Reporter. "The cheering and counter-cheering of
each party claiming the majority prevented the restoration
of order, and in this excited state of feeling the meeting
broke up." Each side cooled off during the week in drafting and subscribing rival petitions to Her Majesty, for and
against this expeditious mode of Harbour improvement.

His Excellency Sir George Grey, K.C.B., arrived in
Durban on November 8th, escorted by the R.D. Rangers
from Pinetown, and some 130 horsemen. He found
quarters at Colonel Cooper's house, near the Camp. His
Excellency received the Mayor and Council with the Town
Address, which he subsequently characterised as an
elaborate State paper, and the most complete document of
the kind that had been presented to him in South Africa
(it occupies two columns of the *Mercury*). In his reply, he
fully concurred in the expediency of introducing Coolies or

white labour from Europe, but he makes no reference to convicts. Only Councillor Johnston is reported as having raised the question in conversation, when it was understood His Excellency had put a decisive veto on the movement.

The Governor visited Springfield Sugar Estate, the Harbour Works, and the Gardens of the Botanical and Agricultural Society. We took the opportunity to constitute the two days during which His Excellency and Suite were here, as public holidays, no business being done. He left in H.M.S. *Hydra* to return to the Cape on the 10th November.

Our Lieut.-Governor, Mr. Pine, had left the Colony in the ship *Hannah* on the 2nd March, it was said, on a visit to Sir George Grey; from him he must have obtained an extension of leave to visit England, and, as a record of the homeward voyage of that period, it may be noted that the steamer *Pacific*, in which he was a passenger, arrived in England on the 18th July, after a 34 days' run from the Cape. The duties of Lieutenant-Governor devolved upon the Officer commanding the troops, as previously shown in reference to Titles to Land.

July 11th. The foundation stone of the Congregational Chapel in Smith Street (Erf 10, Block G) was laid with the usual ceremonies. A procession was formed at the temporary place of worship, before described, headed by the children of the Sunday School with coloured banners, and proceeded to the new site. The Revs. W. Ireland, H. A. Wilder and S. B. Stone, all of the American Mission, assisted the pastor, the Rev. J. Grosvenor, the Deacons and friends (among whom were the Mayors of Durban and Pietermaritzburg) in the ceremony. The building was designed by Mr. R. S. Upton, Architect. The foundation stone, containing a tin case in which were the records, was laid with the customary formalities by Mr. Town-Councillor A. W. Evans, as Deacon of the Church, after the delivery of a very able address.

In the evening a tea meeting was held in the late Government Schoolroom. I made one of the 220 persons said to be present, representing all shades of Protestant opinion. D. Lindley (American) wrote their regrets at being absent. The Bishop of Natal, the Colonial Chaplain, and the Rev. "Mrs. Cubitt presided at the Melodian, an elegant and

effective instrument, recently imported by Mr. Brickhill."
Speeches were made, chiefly by the Ministers present, who,
while they had the opportunity, proposed a Resolution in
favour of the extension of the Voluntary Principle, seconded
by the Mayor of Pietermaritzburg, Mr. D. D. Buchanan,
and supported, with expressions of delight at the proceedings of the day, by Deacon Peter Lennox; it was carried
nem. con., and the meeting broke up about half-past nine
o'clock.

Whether by the influence of " the cup that cheers, etc.," and
the better sociability engendered by these proceedings, or
through the common-sense of the women of Durban, who
intuitively saw that the contentions now arising among
some of their men over St. Paul's were likely to qualify
their Christian Charity, certain it is, and greatly to their
credit, that on this same day they stood forth as " Ministering Angels " and organised the : —

**Durban
Benevolent
Society.**
The Committee consisted of the ladies, R.
Acutt, Kahts, Evans, Goodricke, Millar,
Grundy, Wirsing, Harwin, J. Sanderson,
and R. Anderson.   President, Mr. Robert
Acutt.   Treasurer, Mr. Kahts.   Hon.
Secretary, Mr. E. H. Hunt.   No eulogium is necessary to
emphasise the capacity and capability of woman to manage
affairs in her own sphere, since this society has from that
day carried on successfully its errand of mercy among the
poor and afflicted, until it has now grown to be regarded
almost an integral part of the Borough system.

Typographical.
The difficulties of Printers at this period
of our history is shown by the Jury List
published in the *Mercury* of the 8th
August.   The supply of " caps " being short, all the
proper names of towns and places are printed in the
ordinary " letter," and have now a strange appearance,
though to us at that make-shift time, when stocks of paper
ran out, and substitutes had to be found, it elicited no
unkindly comment; thus : —

Acutt	Robert	durban	auctioneer	owner.
Beningfield	Samuel	england	farmer	owner.
Bishop	George	pinetown	Cap. R. N.	owner.

I am told also that resort was made to many strange devices in order to supply deficiencies in the absence of "fonts" that only a master printer could recognise and appreciate.

August 24th. A difference of opinion that could not be reconciled having arisen between the proprietor and the printer of the *Natal Mercury*—Mr. George Robinson and Mr. Jeremiah Cullingworth—the former gave notice that he had purchased the goodwill and material of the defunct *Advertiser*, and should no longer "borrow pinions from another, but will henceforth speed upon my own wings." Accordingly on this day his newspaper appeared in enlarged form, and at reduced rates, under the title of *Natal Mercury and Advertiser*, published on Fridays, from a wattle-and-daub structure on the site of the existing three-storied "Mercury Buildings," price 6d per copy. Mr. Cullingworth at the same time started the *Natal Star*, at reduced advertising charges, publishing on Wednesdays, price 6d. per copy.

First Cargo to England. August 28th also became an historical date, the occasion being marked by a novelty in the form of a dinner on board the schooner *Siren*. This vessel was consigned to Messrs. J. Millar and Co., who made strenuous efforts to obtain a full return cargo. Arriving on the 7th July, she was discharged and reloaded in the course of two months, sailing on the 5th September, being the first vessel to leave this port with a full cargo direct for England. Thus the Reporter:—

"DINNER ON BOARD THE SIREN.—An event of great importance to this Colony was inaugurated on Tuesday last. The merchants of Durban were entertained at a sumptuous dinner given by Captain Hellyer, on the quarter-deck (*sic*) of the schooner *Siren*, to celebrate the first full cargo of Colonial produce shipped from this port direct to England. The entire mercantile body of the town was present. . . . . John Millar, Esq., the senior partner of the firm of the Agents and Consignees of the vessel, presided over the festivities of the occasion and, besides the body of merchants, the Resident Magistrate of the County of Durban; His Worship the Mayor, and the Post Master General. The usual loyal toasts," etc., etc.

As their wives knew *when* they got home, the reporter did not think it necessary to say *how* they reached the.

town by water, and before dark.   The *Siren's* cargo was
said to form a sort of universal exhibition of the resources
of Natal.   It was estimated as worth £10,874.   The
largest item was wool, of which there were 416 bales.   She
had six tons of ivory, and a large quantity of wood, tallow,
hides, arrowroot, a sample shipment of Natal sugar, with
some miscellaneous produce.   A considerable portion of
this cargo passed through my hands as packer.   Some of
the wool was pressed in Screw Presses, secured by hide
lashings.

**The
Natal Bank**   Announced that they would remove into
the new premises on the Aliwal Street
side of the Market Square, recently erected,
and partially completed by Mr. G. C. Cato,
on the 10th September, and on the 19th October they
advertised for a Branch Manager at a salary of £200 per
annum, including clerical assistance.   He must live on the
Bank premises and find security for £2,000.   Mr. Cato
having resigned, Mr. Jas. Brickhill was appointed Manager
of the Durban Branch.   Mr. Jas. Augustus Rich and Mr.
William Swift were engaged respectively as Accountant
and Teller about ten months later, at salaries of £100 and
£60 per annum.

**The
Durban Club.**   With regard to this Institution, like the
boy who worked the bellows for the organ-
ist of story, I feel that my services have
not been duly recognised.   I have made
no claim, yet I cherish a conviction that my exertions contributed largely to the creation of the Durban Club.   The
sand which I had transposed from the Market Square to
Messrs. J. Millar and Co.'s Erf, was necessarily deposited
immediately in rear of the Store, along its entire length
and convenient to my own rooms.   It was levelled, and,
to secure it from the wind, also to give it a firm surface,
I covered it with sods from the swamp in Gardiner Street.
Time in those days hung heavily on the hands of masters
of vessels, as also of the merchants of the Port, so my yard
was appropriated for an occasional game of Quoits.   Single
contests led to matches, matches to sides, sides to contests
with " a little money on," and ultimately to the formation
of the "Durban Quoit Club," of which all the leading mer-

chants and the Officers at the Camp became members—with
the privilege of free drinks out of the funds.   I had to
relinquish my yard to the claims of Sport.   Iron pegs
were inserted in properly-made clay floors; a space about
25 feet wide was fenced with tall reeds to cut off the wind.
I also constructed rough seats and long narrow tables of
bush-furniture pattern, while provision was made of bottles
and tumblers, water and towels for the general accommodation of members.   This was about June, 1852.   In
November a match for a supper at McDonald's Hotel was
played between married and single members.   Both my
employers were enthusiastic and good players.   The Club
flourished, forming a social rendezvous every afternoon,
weather permitting.   In September, 1854, a Silver Cup
value twelve guineas was specially imported to be contested for, and things went on pleasantly, until those who
failed to score at this game—notwithstanding that all the
smiths in the town had been requisitioned to make the
Discus of classical pattern, of all weights and sizes, while
bright and shining ones, engine turned, modern shape, were
now imported—declared they would give their opponents
points at Billiards, a less violent hand-trying game, and one
more befitting gentlemen.   The answer was "Very well,
let us get out a table!"   Mr. Hugh Gillespie was accordingly constituted Hon. Secretary to a proposed Billiard
Club.   The Scotch element at that time predominated in
Durban, and, on a canvas for subscriptions, the proposal
resolved itself into a shareholding concern, which expanded
into a Proprietary Club, restricted to shareholders, to be
called "The Durban Club."

Its initial success was nearly marred by the irresponsible
and effusive reporter, on the appearance of Mr. Gillespie's
advertisement soliciting subscribers.   The grateful newspaper man, to give it a good send-off, informed the public
that the Club had acquired a piece of ground, and were
about to erect a building for the billiard table, in which
there would be a reading-room, a card-room, and a room
for a bar; whereupon the editor was flooded with letters
from local Chadbands, pointing out the demoralization that
must ensue from the introduction of cards and gambling
houses into our hitherto virtuous community.   The Hon.
Secretary had to repudiate the card-room, and say little

about the "cakes and ale," intimating that the Club was only intended as a place of harmless recreation during the day-time.

Land in Smith Street (Erf No. 6, Block H) was acquired from the widow Strydom, and my Quoit Ground utilised by the contractors, Putterrill and Abbot, to frame a wooden building about 30 ft. by 20 ft., sufficient for a full-sized Billiard Table, a few chairs, and a space at the end to form a "reading-room." This wooden building, having its side to the street, with a sentry-box porch in front, was accordingly erected on the site of the present Club premises, being then on a bank at some elevation above the sandy road. It was thatched and had a short overhanging verandah all round, without posts. It was subsequently enclosed with a post and rail fence. In the turmoil surrounding the Bishop and the Church, the pious declared that the delay, or loss, of the ship *Intrepid*, reported to be bringing the billiard table, was a "special vis'tation"; while admitting the possibility, we welcomed the *Intrepid* on the 3rd June, 1855, after a five months' voyage direct from London, and unpacked the miscreant table eight days later. As the marking board that arrived with it was defective, I was deputed to prepare a scoring slate, whereon games of several hundreds up could be recorded in chalk. I procured, and with much labour ground down to a smooth face, the largest "Duchess" slate to be had in town; then suitably engraved it for the games; had it framed, and saw to its erection. It was used for years, and, though now discarded for modern recorders, the old slate is still to be found on the Club premises. About three months after the opening, the Hon. Secretary advertised for a billiard-marker, whose services would be required " by daylight only." The privacy of Club life prevents my saying anything as to their financial arrangements, beyond the fact that I was long troubled to supply members with silver coin for gold; while the general difficulty experienced in this direction ultimately induced the Club to issue their own coinage. Nickel tokens with milled edges were accordingly obtained from Birmingham, about the size of a shilling, bearing the name "Durban 6d. Club," and on the obverse the legend " Six Pence Natal 1860." These coins eventually became absorbed in the currency of the Colony. The Quoit Club being thus merged into the Durban Club, in 1856 I was enabled to resume the use of the ground for the firm's business.

The success of the Durban Club was established by the fall of Sebastopol, and the Indian Mutiny; the desire for news of those harrowing events, as also of our Legislative and County Councils, to say nothing of Municipal or local matters, brought Officers from the Camp, and planters and professional men to the rooms; lights were introduced with the newspapers, and the premises formed a regular and recognised place of meeting and gossip for all the leading people, thus promoting membership. From a horse-post in front of the thatched wooden billiard-room, the premises extended by a species of natural evolution; first shelter for the beast, then for the man; then entertainment for both, with their servitors, until at this time it has acquired substantial and elegant proportions with all the attributes of a first class Hotel "for gentlemen only." The land and buildings are assessed for rating purposes at some £15,000.

Sebastopol. Sebastopol fell several times during the year with varied results, twenty millions of plunder being about the highest flight of newspaper imaginations, while the losses to the Allies were also reckoned in distressing quantities; but we did not give way to our credulity until the 28th December, when the certain news reached us over-land in 14 days from the Cape, and the flagstaffs of Cato, Lamport, and Milner blossomed with "the flags of all nations." It being Christmas time with a high temperature, we fraternised and found an "excuse for the glass."

Time. We were taught to "mark time" during the year by a semi-official imposition of the Mayor. He had volunteered to hoist a flag on his tall flagstaff a few minutes before nine o'clock every morning; the time, regulated by Ship's Chronometers, was indicated when the flag dropped. Some irregular watches had induced their owners to write to the papers on the loss of a minute or two, and the fining of Jurymen in consequence; so as the old flag became worn out the practice was discontinued, though suggestions were made that Mr. Cato should continue the voluntary principle for

public benefit, by substituting a time ball.   But, there
being no money with the proposal, it did not make the
Mayor to go!

Minor Events.   Among the minor incidents of the year it
may be noted that in the month of August
the adventurous were attracted by Mr.
Wm. Cowey's offer of " £1,000 Reward for the discovery
" of a cheaper and better Boot and Bonnet Warehouse than
" Cowey's, West Street, Durban."   This enterprising
tradesman was of a poetical turn ; or, like Moses and Son,
the advertising merchant tailors of the Minories, " kept a
poet " ; for many strange and amusing rhymes of a topical
character adorn the advertising columns of the newspapers,
where they are now to be found like flies in amber.

At a Circuit Court held on 21st August, a native house
servant was convicted of stealing a considerable amount of
money and goods from his employer ; to impress upon the
native mind the sacred rights of property, he was sentenced
to five years' imprisonment, and a public flogging of 25
lashes on the Market Square—and flogged he was at the
cart wheel accordingly.

Mr. T. P. James, having commenced business as a Landing Agent at the Point, advertises in September :—" An
" extra charge of 2s. will be made for the Landing and
" Delivery of Spirits overproof (sic), Silk and plated goods,
" Gunpowder and Coals in bulk.   Shipping Ivory with
" wagon hire 8s., other goods the usual charge of 6s. per
" ton for Landing and Shipping."

The Town Gang was initiated in August by a resolution
of the Corporation :—" That the Town Committee be and
is hereby authorised to employ one or more laborers when
required."   In 1896 this small beginning had expanded to
658 Natives and Indians, 52 Europeans, 55 horses, and 30
carts.

A practice obtained at this time among men of position
and merchants of notifying their intention of leaving the
Colony, and of calling in all claims for settlement ; these
advertisements were frequent.   In later years it was
sought to confirm this custom by legislation, rendering a
Master of a ship liable in a penalty for accepting a passenger without a clearance, but, with our susceptibilities on

the liberty of the subject, it was never carried into effect, and the practice fell into disuse. As the *Spectator's* friend, Sir Roger de Coverley remarked, "there is much to be said on both sides" of this question; but there is no doubt that we, as a "nation of shopkeepers," are greatly behind the "heathen Chinee," whose great ambition, if not religion, is to owe no man anything on the advent of his New Year's Day. We, however, know better, so carry the balance over and seek the defaulting debtor where he may not be found.

Of Local Manufactures there is little to record apart from the country Sugar and Arrowroot Mills. Mr. Daniel Hull, senior, advertised his make of specially Hardened Mould Candles. Mr. James Brickhill proclaimed the production of his writing and copying ink; while Mr. H. W. Currie also came before the public with an Ink made from an indigenous nut *(exclegaria reteculata)*, an air-tight domestic utensil made of tin, for which he compounded the alarming name of "Chiraphedron"; while his ingenuity extended to a mode of zinc roofing, with overlapping water-proof joints. These roofs were fixed by him on buildings at several Sugar Mills, and served their turn until replaced by imported corrugated galvanised iron.

CHAPTER XI.

1 8 5 6.

G. C. CATO AND EDWARD SNELL—MAYORS.

IN December, 1854, Messrs. Van Prehn and T. Colenbrander, two Dutch Indigo Planters from Java,
arrived with their families and Javanese workmen, their
intention being to settle in Natal, acquire land, and manufacture Indigo. The indigenous Indigo plant flourished,
and still flourishes, in Durban County.

These gentlemen, being men of substance, were induced
by Mr. A. K. Murray, of Pinetown, to commence operations
on lands belonging to him, and to admit him into partnership. Indigo was planted, a "Fabrik constructed, in
which the plant was "vatted" and the beautiful purple
product "caked" for market, on the Umbilo River at the
foot of Cowie's Hill, the site of the present intake of Durban's Umbilo Water Works.

The enterprise was said to have proved unsuccessful;
this was attributed to the climate, fermentation not being
sufficiently rapid; also to the Umbilo water being chemically
defective, poverty of soil, etc., but the real cause was a
suspicion raised in Mr. Van Prehn's mind that Mr. Murray
had mislead him. The works were stopped before the
secret of manufacture was disclosed. An action at law
ensued in which all the members of the legal profession
had a share, occupying the Circuit Court, Supreme Court,

Arbitrators, the public attention, and many columns of the
local papers during the whole of 1856, and resulting in the
departure of Mr. Van Prehn from the Colony after a
judicial declaration in his favour dissolving the partnership.
" Van Prehn *versus* Murray.   Judgment.   Defendant to
" give transfer of land actually his own ; each party to pay
" their own costs, or in default, defendant to repay plaintiff
" £600 with 6 per cent. interest, together with £300
" damages and costs from date of judgment (August 1856)."

Mr. Van Prehn had considerable business with the firm,
the result being that I became very intimate with him,
being enabled to render him some slight services, and to
help him over idiomatic stiles.   My East Indian experience induced him to discuss with me the probable consequences of the introduction of Coolies.   He urged, as an
outcome of his experience, the importance of locating them
outside the European Town, in a village of their own ;
appointing a suitable man among them as Chief or as he
styled him, " Rajah," who would maintain his own Police,
taking an equitable share of the revenue, and an uncove-
nanted " screw," or tribute, for his pay ; with liberty to
administer the Indian quarter after their own congenial
and delectable practices, but subject to the authority of
the Mayor and Council ; no Indian to be allowed to reside
in Durban ; all offenders against the laws to be required at ,
the hands of the Chief, whose tenure of office and emolu-
ments would be conditional upon the aid afforded the Civil
power in maintenance of order and production of offenders.
This system worked well in Java and in other Eastern
States governed by Europeans, accommodating itself as it
did to the Indian character and love of free warren.

At Mr. Van Prehn's request, I wrote to the Corporation
setting out his recommendation, or, as he preferred to call
it, his *warning*.   The letter was received and forgotten.
The explanation verbally given was in substance :—That
the Coolies were yet to arrive ; that they would have to
work at least ten years before they were free ; money was
scarce, the Town Surveyor had other things to do, and
there would be plenty of time to attend to it when the
Coolies did come and wanted to locate in town.

Alas! they had not been here twelve months before
Baboo Naidoo, an Interpreter and " high caste man," opened

a little innocent shop in Field Street for the sale of condiments and other delicacies not included in the " rations ' issued by law; thereupon another caste set up Candasamy Chetty, with subscribed capital, in a shop of Messrs. Evans and Churchill's at the corner of West and Field Streets. The Mohamedans then stepped in, and others followed in quick succession, Mr. Councillor Millar and other Burgesses deriving satisfactory rentals from tenements let to these enterprising people.

The Harbour Works. The Harbour Works were slowly and surely progressing under the patient plodding application of Mr. John Milne, C.E., who, in the existing state of the Colonial revenue, was expected to make bricks without straw. He had to construct a wooden tram-line round the Point of the Bluff to the Cave Rock to obtain the necessary stone, and afterwards boat it across for his works. This was done by two Contractors, William Campbell and Richard Godden, with native labour; and well they did it, slow and sure, for their skilled handiwork is still to be seen embodied in the root of the North Pier, every stone hand-dressed and packed, easily recognisable, at the junction of the modern concrete wall. The thought and research devoted to these works by Mr. Milne, before the commencement of operations, were extraordinary, as shown by his many long letters to the *Mercury* during 1855, and afterwards in the *Natal Colonist.* He was constantly about the Bay with flags, buoys, and Natives, and he gave plenty of exercise to the Port Captain, his boat and crew, in soundings. The crests of the sea at high tides would break over in streamlets from the Back Beach, where the Signal Station now stands, to the Custom House Channel, and it was his aim —the true resort of a scientific Engineer—to compel the forces of Nature to the success of his design. His main project was to carry out a North Pier to the Bar with a short South Pier opposite, gradually narrowing the entrance and facilitating scour. He employed the fragments of labour and funds doled out to him in wattling the sandhills, from Captain Bell's house to the Point, with a series of rough fences divided into sheepfold-like paddocks, to divert and retain the drifting sands from entering the Bay.

These sands were then secured by planting the 'Hottentot fig" and any other runner, grass, herb, or green thing that would consent to grow there.   It was there I first realised the value and importance of his rough-board notices, "The public are respectfully requested to keep off the grass."   His heart was entirely in his work — of him it might be truly said that he was always on duty.   As a rule, he was certain to be found hovering over the sand dunes or lingering around the stone workings, dressed in a long Nankeen coat, and wearing a broad Manilla hat, from under which his grey hair and thoughtful face could be seen as he plodded, long walking-staff in hand, over his "Works," or round the scorching Bluff.   He so identified himself with his undertaking that he was playfully spoken of as " Old Mortality."   He was not permitted to demonstrate the problem he had set himself; so also with all Engineers who succeeded him.   Nature is still mistress of the position; Science, for the present, has yielded to Mechanics, applied in Steam Dredgers.

The Harbour Board advertised in December for a "Secretary and Treasurer to the Board," salary £50 per annum.   " The person appointed will be required to devote the whole of his time to the duties of the office; Security will be required. Apply to George Rutherford, Esq., Collector of Customs."   •

Climate. Though the spots on the Sun may in these latter days be accused of effecting a variation in this world's climate, yet that glorious luminary was capable of imparting as much heat in 1856 as at the present time.   No attempt at meteorological record was made here (the Port Office possibly excepted), but an occasional newspaper reference noted, as I have shown, abnormal temperature and thunderstorms. Thus on the 9th January, it is stated that the temperature in Durban was 95° in the shade at 2 o'clock in the afternoon.   During the summer months this was expected, and with equal confidence we relied on a relieving thunderstorm from the South-West every third or fourth day, and made business arrangements accordingly; that is to say, with regard to goods in the open, buildings in construction, or preparations for a journey.   These storms, with their cleansing rain, undoubtedly saved the swampy, sandy Durban of the period from pestilence. The relieving electrical discharge and cool Westerly breeze came to be referred to as " The Doctor."

Native Education. A Public Meeting, held on the 24th January, unanimously adopted a Memorial to the Secretary of State, praying Her Majesty to disallow "Ordinance No. 2, 1856, for promoting the education of coloured youth in the District of Natal." Mr. Councillor Sanderson was called to the Chair. Mr. E. P. Lamport submitted Draft of Memorial, which Mr. J. R. Saunders seconded. The spirit of the meeting is embraced in the Editorial comment: —

"Some hard hits were dealt at the Bishop, as well as the Government. There will be no peace for us until the latter is placed on a broader basis; and is purged from the suspicion of over-riding, backstairs, ecclesiastical influence."

The Secretary of State did not take our advice, or trouble Her Majesty on the subject, for at the end of the year we learnt that the offending Ordinance had been duly confirmed.

Annabella Bank. The ship *Annabella*, 200 tons, Capt. Louis Wilson, Owner and Master, arrived on the 21st January. She was unable to come inside until the 26th, when she crossed the Bar in charge of a Pilot, with the Master at the wheel, and attended by a steady N.E. breeze. There was said to have been 16 feet of water on the Bar, but, there being a moderate sea on, she touched between the swells, lost steerage way, and drifted on to the Lee Bank, where she was taken aback in an unsuccessful attempt to make a stern board, (*i e*, get off backwards), and so swing round head to sea. Notwithstanding attempts to move her, she hung on the bank all night. The crew were landed, and next morning she was found to have 8 feet of water in her hold. Heavy seas had set in, and, her seams having opened, all hope of her floating again was abandoned, though efforts were made to discharge her cargo of general merchandise, the greater part of which was damaged and passed under the hammer of Mr. Auctioneer Acutt, who disposed of the hull and cargo left on board on the 4th February.

Captain L. Wilson eventually settled here with his wife and family, and became a Burgess of Durban on establishing a Ship Chandler's business at the Point, where he has been succeeded by his son, Mr. L. J. Wilson. The *Annabella*, not so fortunate as the *Princeza*, gave her name to that locality, and the " Annabella Bank " became, in all Harbour Board records and reports, synonymous with the earlier " Lee Bank." The existing North Pier passes over the site of the disaster and marks the grave of the *Annabella*. The Lee Bank has, in consequence, asserted its prior rights, calls Nature to its aid, and continually obtrudes itself in unexpected places to the perplexity of Engineers and navigators.

St. Paul's Church. A letter from the Bishop to the Legislative Council, objecting to the Durban Vestry Draft Ordinance, having been published, and the Bill having been rejected, a Vestry meeting was held on the 25th January to consider this rejection, Mr. R. Acutt occupying the chair. Messrs. Baker, Goodricke, J. R. Saunders, Wm. Dacomb, F. G. Salmon, H. W. Currie, G. Rutherford, and J. Millar compensated themselves for their disappointment by an all-round vilification of Bishop and Archdeacon ; Mr. Goodricke saying, in reference to the Bishop's letter to the Legislature :—" The Bishop does not stick to the truth, but "falsehood, from the beginning to the end, had character-"ised his statements. Dr. Colenso was not fit to be a "Bishop. His filthy pamphlet on Polygamy—(cheers)—" was calculated to do more moral mischief than all the "convicts that could be sent to the Colony. (Cheers)." The Vestry was unanimous, and appointed a. fresh Committee. to prepare another Draft Ordinance for a free Vestry ; to collect documents and affidavits for the presentation of the Bishop* ; to devise the best means of obtaining repossession of St. Paul's ; and to deliberate and act as a

---

* Query—To the Bishop of Cape Town.

Church of England Defence Association. A proposal to brick up the front door, and to hire a Clergyman of their own, and a place to worship in, was not entertained; other measures amounting to a plot to regain possession of the building were, however, discussed.   On March 7th, the *Mercury* announces : —

".We regret to hear that the bell of St Paul's Church was stolen and taken away last night. This is not the way to effect a reform or abate an annoyance ; and we are sure the act has not been done by a genuine Church Reformer."

The Vestry meeting, changed by the Archdeacon at the last moment to Easter Monday after having been announced for Tuesday, and corrected by the vigilance of Mr. Churchwarden Acutt, who sent round a Native with a Bell and Notice Board, was well attended, in pursuance of the design of the 25th January, and lasted five hours, the Archdeacon presiding.   The personalities, insults, and abuse showered upon him by a professedly Christian community are better left unpublished.   The meeting, having declared themselves qualified Church members, outvoted the Archdeacon, and ended by electing their own Chairman, and, on the Archdeacon's retirement, doing as they pleased, with the result that, in direct opposition to their agreement with the Bishop on his taking over St. Paul's, and to his Instructions to Ministers and Churchwardens as to conduct of Church affairs, Messrs. Robt. Acutt and E. W. Holland, the newly-elected Churchwardens, advertised on the 25th March :—" A collection will be made at the Church door " after morning service for the purpose of defraying the " current expenses and clearing off the debt on the Church." Also " that they would be in attendance on the 3rd April " at 3 p.m. for the purpose of Letting the Seats in accord- " ance with resolution of the Vestry."   The Vestry in addition ordered :—" That the Reading Desk, the present " position of which enabled the Clergyman during part of " the service to turn his back to the Congregation, be placed " as formerly and screwed down to the floor."   The Archdeacon protested against these contemplated acts of defiance in a letter to Mr. Robert Acutt, and duly reported them to the Diocesan.   They were more than mortal Bishop could submit to, so he published a notice to the Churchwardens and Sidesmen "inhibiting for a season the performance of Divine Service in St. Paul's Church.' Thus the *Mercury* of 11th April:—

"St. Paul's.—Last Sunday Mr. R. S. Upton, the architect, read the service to about 100 in the morning and 60 in the evening. The Archdeacon with one of the Churchwardens (Dr. Holland) conducted service in 'Jackson's' Store, West Street, number present stated to be between 20 and 60. Handbills were circulated by the Vestry during the week to prove that the refusal of the Archdeacon to conduct Divine Service, under the direction of the Vestry, was an act of *desertion and practical dissent*."

At this Easter Vestry meeting the Archdeacon had refused to admit Mr. J. R. Goodricke and others as qualified Church members, on the ground that they had not signed a declaration of membership, or conformed to other Church regulations of the Rubric. Zest was thereby added to Mr. Goodricke's zeal, and he naturally looked to the Law for assistance, and at a Circuit Court in June applied to the Recorder for an order compelling the Archdeacon to admit him a parishioner. The Recorder asked for the law by which his rights were guaranteed. Mr. G. quoted English authorities and precedents. The Recorder denied they had any force here, and recommended him to seek his remedy from the local Legislature. Application dismissed. As an outcome of this application, a resolution was adopted at an adjourned Vestry meeting on the 15th June to petition the Queen:" to define the rights and privileges of the "laity, as well as give peaceful means for establishing order "and good government in our Church.' It was also notified at the meeting that the Rev. W. H. C. Lloyd had been suspended from his office of Colonial Chaplain. On the 15th August an action was brought by the Bishop in the Resident Magistrate's Court for the ejectment from St. Paul's Church of Mr. Churchwarden Acutt, "for wrongfully and unlawfully retaining possession of the premises." Mr. Advocate A. Walker, of Pietermaritzburg, appeared for the Bishop; Mr. Goodricke for St. Paul's. The latter lodged so many preliminary objections to the summons, that the Acting Resident Magistrate was relieved to find he had no jurisdiction, so dismissed the summons with costs. "A burst of cheering followed the announcement, which was immediately suppressed by the Court," says the Reporter. On September 5th, Mr. Walker, having amended his summons, renewed his action before the Acting Resident Magistrate, who again yielded to a preliminary technical objection taken by Mr. Goodricke. What might be sport for the Lawyers was growing intolerable to the more devout of the Church-going community, so during the month two Memorials, emanating from the congregations of St. Paul's and Jackson's Store, were addressed to the Bishop lamenting the discord, and asking that they might return to St. Paul's, and that the services there might be conducted in the manner to which the petitioners were accustomed in England, so that they might be privileged to worship together in peace and brotherly union. These bore 25 and 14 signatures respectively. The Bishop addressed his reply to Dr. Holland, Churchwarden; it occupied a column and a half of the *Mercury*, and pointed out that their complaint was reduced to four points of difference, and that these were all within the stipulations of the Prayer Book; that the Vestry had defied his authority; and that he regretted he could not comply with their prayer, beyond restricting himself and them to the laws of the Church of England. To this the component parts of the self-constituted Vestry replied in another full column manifesto, asserting that the two memorials emanated from "the small congregation who deserted St. Paul's with the Archdeacon," and might therefore be considered friendly to the Bishop; certainly "they were subscribed by some few of St. Paul's who wrongly imagined peace possible." They repeated all their grievances, with stringent comments on His Lordship's reply, and finally concluded that they could expect but a hollow peace with the Bishop, "who dares in " a printed sermon at St. Mary the Virgin, Richmond, to " talk of our Church as one which to be seen here 'in " ' her beauty must be stripped of those foul ragged gar- " ' ments, which many years of sloth and indifference have " ' suffered to hang about her in England.' " The Bishop's consistency in bringing his Diocese into due form, his general courtesy, personal piety, and force of character apparently reduced opposition to a semblance of conformity, for, after this outburst, public attention is not again called to their affairs in the newspapers.

The inhibition of St. Paul's must have been removed, as the Rev. W. H. C. Lloyd seems to have made his peace with the Bishop, and resumed his duties in that Church on Sunday, the 6th December; the Bishop, however, insisting upon the offertory being continued every Sunday morning, strictly in accordance with the letter of his ¨Instructions,¨ "in defiance," says the *Mercury*, "of the wishes of both the Minister and the Congregation."

Emigrants. The ship *Jane Morice* arrived on the 15th February, and on the Sunday following those who attended the Wesleyan Chapel were interested in an additional occupant of Mr. Richard Harwin's pew; his fashionable attire, debonair carriage, and fresh appearance, indicated that he was the newly-arrived assistant to Mr. Harwin, and, on investigation by the envious youths after service, he was announced to us as "Mr. B. W. Greenacre." As we could not unbend so soon after service to be more than decently civil, we took further opportunity to interview the stranger. His frankness of manner, ready wit, and genial smile broke through our reserve, and, as his speech proved him an East-Anglian, the fact of his not being "a Londoner" (why I can't say) seemed to establish him forthwith as a welcome addition to the *jeunesse dorée* of Durban. The latent jealousy with which his personality at first impressed us has not been effaced by time; his abilities having placed him far above his compeers. He has been Mayor of the Borough, and is now its representative in the Legislative Assembly. In partnership with his fellow assistant, Mr. Thos. M. Harvey, he has acquired a large private fortune. He married the daughter of the ·Rev. Ralph Stott, Wesleyan Minister, and with his wife and ·children is associated in all Durban's Public Institutions worthy of support.

The Flood. Old settlers, in acquainting us with the seasons, told us to expect the "latter rains" in April, when the "dry season" set in; to be broken up again by spring rains in September. After the continuous thunderstorms and showers throughout the summer hot season, our expectations did not extend to anything beyond "decent" showers; consequently on Saturday, the 12th April, we regarded with complacency, bred of custom, a heavy thunderstorm with vivid lightning of a blue tinge and a sulphurous smell, which burst over the town and hovered round the vicinity the whole night, because the atmosphere was thereby cleared, and Sunday morning dawned bright and fresh, with no damage done. " Spirits from the vasty deep" must have been called up by the thunder and lightning, and came bringing with them their contribution to the hurly-burly, for about 2 p.m. the silver-topped cloud-banks, which had been rapidly accumulating to the South-West, rolled on towards the town with darkened faces black and ominous, the advanced scud dropping a gentle even rain soon changing to spiteful squalls, followed by a mad downpour before a driving wind, bringing darkness with it, and literally enveloping us in a watery canopy. Everyone waited with what patience they could assume for this outburst to subside, but the Genii of wind and rain, after saturating everything on that side, apparently resolved to cut off all escape by veering round to the South, and settling down for the night into a steady downpour collected by the wind from oversea-Easterly. Monday brought lamentation and woe, but no cessation. The " Spirits worked " successfully all day Tuesday, when people sat in their huts under umbrellas, piled their children on boxes, thought of The Deluge, and the wherewithal to get fire and food. The elements then took a little breathing time, as if to inspect the damage, and, but half satisfied, resumed on Wednesday by drenching showers and fitful wind squalls, which were maintained with variations until Thursday at sunset, when, having business elsewhere, they retired from the strife, leaving us in a dead calm to emerge from our holes, and look for roosting places and dry clothes. The total rainfall in those four eventful days amounted to 27 inches, which means that, had it frozen as it fell, Durban would have been covered by a solid sheet of ice about the height of an ordinary table !

Having spent Sunday at the newly-erected house of my friends, Mr. and Mrs. Palmer, on the Berea Ridge, I was constrained to accept their kind hospitality and a sofa until Tuesday morning, when I set the rain at defiance, to return to duty and my own quarters at the Store. The survey line through the Berea Bush, recently cut by the military and used as a horse path, was a running stream of red sandy mud and little frothy pools; the overhanging trees agitated by the wind scattered a perpetual shower-bath of pistol-shot drops, so that I had no hesitation in wading up to my hips in the broad expanse of water that covered the head of the Western Vlei (now the Race Course Drain Culvert). On reaching Field Street by the wagon road, the effects of the storm were everywhere apparent in collapsed chimneys and kitchens, wattle-and-daub structures, sod houses and fences; it was "water, water everywhere." A few desperate men, with spades or Kafir picks, were cutting drains about their houses; stockingless white women were bailing out of the back door the water that came in by the front, the roof, or the sides; children and natives were dabbling about or chopping firewood in sheltered spots; while all domestic animals seemed set at liberty to seek their own sustenance like the Royal Marines, " By Sea, by Land." As nothing could be seen from the Berea but rain and cloud, obscuring Bay, Bluff, and sea, I was unaware of the fact that, during the early morning of Tuesday, the Umgeni River had overflowed its banks, and was then pouring into the Bay down the Eastern Vlei; but of this I was soon informed by the almost panic-stricken people, as I took my way to the Market Square prepared to swim West Street if ford there was none. I struck off, by advice, in the direction of the Camp; waded that drain and entered the Square by St. Paul's. It was the fashion at that time for persons, whose walks abroad took them in the vicinity of rivers or swamps, to carry a native-made knobbed staff about six feet long; to the use of my stick on this occasion I was indebted for my safe return home, where I found the Store closed, no one being at business. After food and a change, I hastened down to Cato's Creek. A description of the sight that met my view on reaching Mr. Cato's residence, can only be conveyed to modern readers by modern names. The wagon roads to the Point and to Durnford's [Cato's] Bridge were gone. The Umgeni spread from Farewell Street to the Point Road and Winder Street on your right front; while to the left one unbroken sheet of yellow muddy water extended between Brickhill Road and the Gaol, right up the Vlei as far as the eye could reach, fringed with the tops of rushes, a few bushes—the tops of growing trees—projecting, while towards the Scandinavian Church little islands of bush, palms, and trees, appeared in the still water of that basin. "Wattie" Brunton and his family had been rescued by boat, *via* the Bay, from his residence at Wheeler's Creek. The outfall was concentrated at Cato's Creek, where it flowed in a strong swishing current, with a rolling ripple, into the Bay. It was neap tides, but the Bay itself was full of yellow river water and *débris*, reeds, trees, old huts, pumpkins, mealie stalks, thatch, utensils, animals alive and dead, alligators, snakes, and cane rats. The larger bodies of cattle, pigs, goats, buck and Natives, found their way out to sea, and to the Back Beach, direct through the mouth of the river. The accumulation of trees, reeds, and *débris* generally, remained piled up in masses all along the beach for long after, until the ever-restless sea had time to devour them. The Bay also was filled with mud and rubbish, rendering the Beach road from the Creek to the Point dangerous from "Snags." After a comprehensive glance at the weird scene, my attention was naturally directed to a new schooner, which Mr. G. C. Cato was building at the foot of Stanger Street, only to find that she had been washed off the stocks and carried by the Umgeni well out into the Bay; a premature launch before her completion; having grounded, she was temporarily anchored by her builder, Mr. Charles Povall, and assistants. Shortly after my arrival, Mr. Cato, Captain Smerdon, and others, essayed to get a four-oared boat through the rapids, where the Bridge had stood, to go up to the parent Umgeni. Being desirous of repeating for myself the experience of the bold navigators of 1847, I volunteered to take an oar, but notwithstanding that I waded out on very treacherous ground over my knees, the boat swerved out of reach and I was left lamenting to watch them row away in the direction of the Camp and note the turgid waters bearing past me things living and dead, mingled with fragments of all kinds, wriggling or twisting like snakes or fish; while the imaginations of the onlookers conjectured what they in the boat would see, and what we ourselves saw.

Accuracy of observation in rain squalls cannot be relied upon, but, as the wind was shifting to the East, there was a delusive promise of clearing that enabled me to observe the dark-green line of Back Beach bush, the lake-like expanse of muddy water, shadowed by the dull grey clouds that effectually hid the sun, as they were driven inland; while beyond the Camp the whole was blended in a foggy obscurity. The dreariness of the scene and the prevailing sense of calamity were heightened by the angry roar of the sea upon the Back Beach. Seeing the things floating down the stream, men were disinclined to prospect about, fearing to tread upon the unexpected, yet the thunder of the sea so close had its attractions, and the crowd discussed the practicability of reaching the Back Beach, laudable anxiety being felt for the safety of two brigs known to be at anchor outside, the *Breeze* and the *Portia*. The latter had 80 passengers on board; she dragged her anchors, drifting in toward the Umgeni, where she would certainly have gone ashore, but for the river flood which caught and held her against both wind and sea, until she was enabled to shift her berth with safety. The *Breeze*, having more experience of these latitudes, was better provided, and held to her anchors throughout. When the rain and wind finally ceased, the sun again blessed us with light and heat, and the whole town assumed the appearance of a vast bleaching ground, with goods and garments spread out to dry. The outlook was dismal, disclosing a vast amount of damage, almost overpowering to our townspeople, and the infant Borough. Its swampy condition might have recalled the City of Eden to fever-stricken Mark Tapley, when he announced himself as "Floored for the present, sir, but jolly." The whole of the Corporation drains, roads, and footpaths, were gone or damaged. Communication with the Point was cut off by road, and the only route was by the Bay Beach through a deposit of mud and among roots, holes, and quicksands. The Umgeni was impassable; the punt washed to sea was returned to the Back Beach in halves; the central islands of reeds entirely scoured out. The river was said to have risen 18 to 20 feet above winter level. All Springfield Flat was under water; fortunately the main cane-crop did not suffer, but the sugar mill had 9 feet of water in it, which started the pans in the battery, and injured the building; crushing was, however, successfully resumed in 1857. A spare sugar pan outside and a cane wagon were floated away. It was said that, during the night of the flood, an elephant went floating past the Mill, trumpeting in alarm. The last of the Berea elephants were thought to have crossed the river in a troop by the beach a year or two previously. Having too much respect for the sagacity of the elephant, I am inclined to attribute this story to the general list of wonders which the Natives gave us of the Creatures of the Flood.

A relief fund was afterwards opened, and £110 subscribed to provide funds, food, and necessaries, for those families who were in dire straits. The Rev. C. Spensley was Secretary, and Mr. G. Rutherford, Treasurer.

Durban Corporation. Early in January, Mr. Robert Acutt disposed of what were called "The Berea Lots" — of 5 acres each, situated at Stamford Hill, which were sold in freehold and with few exceptions did not realise more than the upset price of £10 per acre. In February Mr. Acutt advertised the sale of 6 Lots of 5 acres each in Block Z, near the Windmill, and 3 Lots of 5 acres each west of Umgeni Brickfields (Block A)—upset price £10 per acre — terms 15 per cent., and survey fees cash, balance by Bills at 3, 6, and 9 months. The declared object of this sale was to obtain the means of defraying the cost of the New Pietermaritzburg Road. The "Windmill Road" reaches the crest of the Berea between what is better known as the residences of Mr. John Sinclair and Mr. W. Arbuckle. This hill-top range extending to the Toll Bar comprises Block Z. "The Windmill" was a sort of Martello tower of rough stone built with ant-heap standing on the edge of "Brickfields" Farm, and only separated from the Borough by the Ridge Road. The site was on the highest point, the crest of the hill separating St. Thomas's Road from Windmill Road. It was built by a man named Barker, who, after the failure of his enterprise, became a Locker in the Customs. This Mill with its sails was a prominent and picturesque object from the back of the Berea; it was intended to grind mealies, but as the Mill was as inaccessible for the farmers at the back of the Berea as for the townspeople, the cost of cartage, loss of time and inconvenience, tended to limit business, since the custom was to take grain to the Mill, and return for it when ground. By an unfortunate miscalculation of those interested, the winds which were expected to have prevailed there were found to be very variable, and not to be relied on as a motive power, so Barker's Mill was subsequently dismantled and converted into a dwelling, after an ineffectual attempt to establish a Brewery. The "New Pietermaritzburg Road" was an important and progressive undertaking by the Town Council, at the instance of the Mayor (G. C. Cato) and without reference to a public meeting—the ostensible plea being the necessity for improving the road to the Umbilo and the Sugar Estates at Isipingo. The Western Vlei had not greatly benefited by Mr. Brickhill's little drain; there was no road or means of crossing it, except at the ancient Dutch wagon track by St. George's Street end [Blakey the Turner's Shop], which was a quagmire. Smith Street being the main thoroughfare, it was decided to extend it across the Vlei, so as to form the Umbilo Road on higher ground, above tidal influences. On carrying Smith Street in a straight line to the edge of swamp, Mr. Cato demonstrated the simplicity of diverting it northerly, cutting a road through the intervening bush, and so connecting it half-way up the Berea with the road recently cut by the Military, and thus, while making a path to Isipingo, secure a new and shorter route to Pietermaritzburg. Tenders were accordingly called for the construction of an embankment and the erection of a bridge, or brick culvert; the enlargement of the drain being apparently left to the convicts. A contract was entered into with Geo. Drew and J. Grainger for the work, which was commenced in May, and was to cost £144. It was, after many shortcomings and complaints, eventually opened for wagon traffic, and constituted simply a raised causeway across the swamp. What remains of it can be traced from the railway line in the direction of the Berea Road, by which name the "New Pietermaritzburg Road" is now known. Some bush road clearing was undertaken by Mr. John P. Cato, who also had been employed to clear 3½ miles of the boundary line on the Ridge at a total cost of £21 7s. 6d. Sad to say, timber was of such little value that it could not be given away, so was burnt on the spot.

A sub-committee inspected a Fire Engine offered them by Mr. Currie for £20. After much deliberation, the purchase was declined; each Councillor knew that the Garrison owned and kept in order a double-pump hand-power engine on wheels with hose attached. On every occasion of fire in the town, the soldiers had turned out, drawn their engine through the sands by drag ropes, and rendered such efficient service as the scanty supply of water from drains, wells, and water butts would admit.

Among the items passed for payment in July, the end of the Municipal year, was " E. Kermode—clearing bush in " Smith Street from the Market Square, £3. John Prince " —for a pump handle, 7s. Edwd. Coward—repairing road " to Umgeni, £1 10s."

One of the consequences of the Flood was the desire for a reduction in the cost of Municipal management, so a section of the Burgesses decided to organise a working man's platform, and to return fit and proper persons for its support, their battle cry being " No Rates, no Improvements." As a natural result the Lively Ward (No. 4) led the way; with the exception of Ward 2, contests took place in the others, resulting in the return of Robert Acutt; Savory Pinsent, Attorney; John Gavin, Blacksmith; Walter Brunton, Limeburner; Mr. G. C. Cato having retired at the end of his second year of office. The records show that the number of meetings for the Municipal year had been 73, of which the Mayor (G. C. Cato) attended 60; Councillor Millar, 57; Harwin, 41; Snell, 50; Johnston, 59; Sanderson, 62; Blackwood, 47; Ferguson, 70.

The Mayor's Minute, in addition to noting the damage done by the Flood, informed us of contracts entered into with those I have already mentioned, and others, for the sinking of new wells; also that tenders had been called for a new Bridge over Cato's Creek, and that the enclosure of half the Market Square was commenced.

On the 1st Saturday in August the New Council met for the election of Mayor. Mr. J. Millar and Mr. E. Snell were both nominated, the latter being elected, it was said, by the working men's vote. Be that as it may, he did not return the compliment by betraying his trust, for, at the first business meeting of the new Council, the working men proposed:—" That with the exception of the Town Clerk, all the Corporation Officers get a month's notice to quit!" On being put to the vote, opinions were equally divided, 4 on each side, Mr. Snell, as Mayor, giving his casting vote against the motion.

    With the inconsistency that sometimes afflicts adminis-
trative bodies, they admitted the necessity for repairs, if
not for "improvements," by directing that "Tenders be
"called for supply of a cart with span of oxen, with driver
"and leader, at per day of six hours, to cart different kinds
"of material within the Borough. Contractor must be
"prepared to supply one or more carts when required."
In October the Council manifested their desire for retrench-
ment by advertising "That sealed tenders will be received
"at the office of the Town Clerk. . . . from parties
"desirous of holding the office of Treasurer to the Corpora-
"tion. The tender must state the amount of salary
"expected, and the names of two substantial parties as
"sureties." The late Treasurer received £15 a year. There
was no rush of applicants, so in November the Town Clerk
was appointed Treasurer at £15 per annum.

    His Honour John Scott, the new Lieut.-Governor, and
family, arrived on the 30th October, in H.M.S. *Geyser.* and
landed on the 31st in the Port boat at the Custom House
jetty. He was received by Major Shaw with a Guard of
Honour of the 45th Regiment ; the "Royal Durban
Rangers," under Hy. Milner, Acting Captain; the Mayor,
the Acting Resident Magistrate, the Collector of Customs,
Mr. G. C. Cato, and a large assemblage of gentlemen on
horseback, by whom, after the customary Military honours,
he was escorted to Colonel Cooper's quarters, near the
Camp. An address had been prepared by the Town
Council, and submitted (Sept. 5th) to a public meeting,
which ultimately adopted it, after rejecting a lengthy
amendment by Mr. E. P. Lamport, amounting to a dissertation on the past and future government of the Colony,
which caused more than the usual heat in discussion, and
occupied the meeting for an entire evening. The presentation of this address by the Town Council was fixed for the
following day. It was announced in a supplement to the
Mercury, wherein the Editor unconsciously shews the
'Little Pedlington" quality of our politics as follows:—

    "We beg respectfully to warn His Honor against all ear-wigging,
come from what quarter it may. The voice of the people is not to be
gathered through self-constituted media."

    The Town Council accordingly met the new Lieut.-
Governor on the Saturday as appointed; the Mayor (Mr.

Snell) read the address and received a very courteous reply.
His Honour then invited the Council to be seated, and
entered freely into conversation on local and Colonial
affairs, with the usual promises of prompt attention. The
Council and the Burgesses had their ideas and aspirations
considerably encouraged by the announcement that His
Honour had brought with him a New Constitution enlarging the representative character of the Legislative Council,
and that it was possible the Colony would be called upon
to return representatives within six months. The qualification for voters or representatives was the ownership of
property to the value of £50, or of £10 annual rental. The
fly in the ointment was " as there is to be no payment of members, the choice will virtually lie amongst men of property
and leisure, and will therefore in truth lie within a narrow
compass."

By Christmas Day confidence had been restored.* Mr.
C. Joseph Cato announced his intention of cutting up a
portion of his farm " Brickfield," north of the Windmill,
into half-acre lots, so as to form a *Village on the Berea*, on
" the highest part of the Berea Ridge, on a table flat
" having beautiful and extensive views, and suitable for
" garden cultivation." This he eventually accomplished,
and named it " Catoville," the site of Capt. Allen Gardiner's
Mission Church being reserved (now St. Thomas'). The
trading instincts of the Town Council were aroused; fearing to lose customers, and having many schemes on hand,
notably that of drainage, and the erection of a Town Hall,
they obtained Governor Scott's consent to the sale of
sufficient Town Lands to yield them the extravagant sum
of £800. They thereupon ordered the Town Surveyor to
cut up for sale Lots of 2 acres each. The local reporter
states :—

"The site fixed upon is the beautiful ridge immediately above the
Botanic Gardens. The money is required for important drainage
works now in progress ; but we hope there will be a surplus available
for the commencement of a Town Hall."

These lots were accordingly surveyed, marked Block. B,
and sold; thanks are due to the " Working Man's Council "
for disposing of this portion of the birthright of posterity.

---

* See Zulu invasion.

In after years when these Lots were built upon and
occupied, the bordering roads, 66 feet wide, were named
respectively after Mr. H. W. Currie, Mayor, and Sir
Anthony Musgrave, the Governor. With that minuteness
of detail and regard for economy promised by Mr. Mayor
Cato, the Town Council conclude the labours of the year
with " An account due to Mr. Savory for two buckets
" amounting to 12s., was laid before the Council · and
" passed, and the Treasurer authorised to pay the same."

More Emigrants. The ship *Rydal*, from Liverpool, arrived
on the 12th May, bringing as passengers
the Misses E. and M. Gillespie, Rev. F.
Mason, Mrs. Beater and son, W. Lello and
wife, and others. The career of at least three of these
persons is inseparable from the history of Durban and its
Institutions, moral, philanthropic, and social. The advent
of the Rev. Frederick Mason, a Wesleyan Minister, a
delicate-looking, intellectual young man, evidently a gentleman by birth and training, naturally stimulated our
curiosity, while the gravity of his bearing and courteous
manner fostered a belief that to exceptional circumstances
must be atributed his leaving England for Natal. I had
the gratification of listening to his first sermon on the
Sunday following his arrival, the occasion being the anniversary of the Wesleyan Sunday School. The Misses E.
and M. Gillespie were introduced to me at the Store some
days after their arrival, for, owing to the Flood, they had
proceeded, by way of the beach, direct to their brother's
house on landing. One lady became the bride of her fellow
passenger, the Rev. F. Mason; the other was sought in
marriage by Mr. J. F. Churchill (Evans and Churchill),
whose sister consented to fill the void thus created in Mr.
Hugh Gillespie's house, Grey Street, by becoming the
latter's wife. It is superfluous to inform modern Durban
of the many praiseworthy labours and influences exerted
by all these six persons, or of the honourable records vet
being framed by their descendants in the Colony. Mrs.
Beater also took a prominent place in advancing the tone
of Durban's social life. Mr. William Lello settled in
Smith Street West as a builder. He was successful, and

gave his name to the passage through his property into
St. George's Street.

Peace. On May the 30th we received through the
Press our first intimation that preliminaries
of peace with Russia had been signed early
in March. In the same issue, the Corporation, at the
instance of the Government, notify that subscriptions will
be received toward the "Nightingale Fund," for providing
a national testimonial to the noble-hearted Miss Florence
Nightingale and her sister nurses, in recognition of their
services at the seat of war in the Crimea. The news of
peace was confirmed here on the 13th June, when Mr.
G. C. Cato, as on the occasion of the Fall of Sebastopol,
"dressed" his flagstaff and fired his "private artillery" of
ship's canonades, and an anvil or two, in salute. We were
bound to be jolly under the circumstances, but we were
discreet (i.e., not unanimous), so proceeded leisurely with
our

Peace Which were held on Thursday, the 10th
Rejoicings, July, on the two Beach Erven, between
the Streets known to us now as Acutt
Street and Albany Grove, and are thus
described in the *Mercury* of the day : —

"The spot selected is a sheltered grassy area surrounded by bush
commanding one of the most picturesque views of the Bay and
Bluff, with a majestic old tree in the centre capable of affording
shade beneath its spreading branches to a large concourse of people.
It was thought the Gardens [Botanic] would be inconveniently remote, considering the shortness of the days; and the sand in the
Market Square was thought a sufficient objection to that place."

A committee of inhabitants had been organised—subscribers entitled to dine—non-subscribers by ticket, prices
not stated, Mr. R. Acutt being Treasurer, and Mr. E. P.
Lamport, Secretary. They arranged a sort of Sunday
School programme to fit the day, which had been proclaimed as a "Day of Public Thanksgiving for Peace." It
was bright and cool, with a nice Easterly breeze, befitting
a day of Peace. All the places of worship held their services in the forenoon, and on this occasion were well
attended by grateful Christians and other anticipators of
favours to come; the rest of the day was devoted by the

Committee to " the World, the Flesh, and the Devil." Thus the programme : —

"At half-past one o'clock the Military will dine with those inhabitants who have invited them to join in the festivities. At three o'clock refreshments will be provided for the children attending the various Sunday and Day Schools in the town. In the evening a number of oxen will be roasted on the Market Square for the kafirs employed in the town. A loyal address of congratulation to Her Majesty will be proposed for adoption after dinner. . . . . Tickets may be had on application to," etc.

The trees and grounds were adorned with flags; a large booth of sails, tarpaulins, and bush poles, called " a spacious temporary Pavilion," 80 feet long by 20 feet wide, had been erected, tastefully dressed, and decorated with palm branches, creepers, kafir boom flowers, the British and French flags, and having " Peace " and " Victory " at either end in letters 3 feet high, worked in evergreens and flowers. Yellow-wood planks on tressels or stumps served as tables and seats. About 80 of the inhabitants and some 60 men of the 45th Regiment (including others of the Garrison), with Major Shaw, the Commandant, sat down to a very ample collation prepared by Mr. J. F. Bauman, the Confectioner. As beer in hogsheads was not then imported, ale and porter in bottles, with Cape wines from the wood, served for the toasts of the day, which the Committee had condensed into three, namely, " Her Most Gracious Majesty the Queen and the rest of the Royal Family "; " The Allied Armies and Navies ' ; and "His Excellency the Governor of the Cape Colony, His Honour the Lieut.-Governor, and His Honour the Acting Lieut.-Governor of Natal." After the toast of Her Majesty, " the National Anthem was sung in solo, the whole company joining in loud and hearty chorus." The men from the Camp were dressed in their dark trousers, scarlet shell-jackets (green and white facings) and " pork-pie " forage caps; my belief is that only certain branches of the service then wore the white waist-belt, but stocks were still in evidence.

The scene was a memorable one, the dark coats of the townsmen contrasting favourably with the brighter colours of the Military, while the native waiters, in shirts to their knees and perplexity on their shining faces, lent humour to the surroundings and a zest to our enjoyment. Being the guests of the Civilians, and under the eyes of the Major, the Resident Magistrate, and the Mayor, the "regulars" comported themselves with becoming hilarity, freely partaking of the unusual delicacies served up, or within call. Irishmen being in the ascendant, their fun and banter served to console us for the absence of a Band. Fortunately no one was asked to "favour the company with a song." The soothing pipe, grassy banks, and cooler shade, claimed their homage, while the Civilians were discussing the Royal Address, and taking up the fragments.

Later in the day the proceedings were enlivened by Sports got up by the youths of the schools, feats of strength or skill, jumping, sack races, gymnastics, and other "divarsions." At the conclusion of the dinner, Mr. Lamport read, with much gusto, the Address to the Queen from "Your Majesty's loyal subjects of the Borough of Durban, the seaport of your Colony of Natal in South Africa." This advertisement was adopted by acclamation. The cloud of witnesses—nearly 400 children—who had long before entered an appearance with their Banners, Rosettes, and Mottoes, took their places on the grass, while "the brave sojer boys" were enjoying the digestible pipe. The tables were utilised to supply the children with tea, cake, buns, dates, and oranges. After these were disposed of, the Native population thronged the ground by invitation, and, having been addressed by their Magistrate—Mr. H. F. Fynn —as to the reasons for the unwonted liberality of the "white men" in the matter of slaughter oxen, were marshalled in a huge circle—the cattle in the centre—and were let go, in thanksgiving song and dance. A scene strange, wild and novel to nearly the whole of the European spectators, terminating with the shades of evening, by their driving the poor oxen off the ground to be converted into beef at a more convenient spot. The youngsters and the Military had in the meantime shared fully their games and merriment. The Garrison returned to Camp in the evening, with expressions of intense satisfaction with the entertainment and the day's events.

The presence of the ladies of Durban enhanced the proceedings and, as the Reporter said, "protected the celebration from profaneness or excess." Being unable to illuminate, short of gunpowder, and without fireworks of any kind, we let off our latent joys in the evening by a little horse-play round a monster bonfire on the Market Square, but without attempting to burn even a Russian in effigy.

German Legion. It having come to our knowledge that the Home Government contemplated providing a settlement in the Cape Colony for the auxiliary troops raised for service during the war, known as the "British German Legion," we naturally wanted some; so it was at first suggested that advantage should be taken of this celebration to embody our desire in the Address to the Queen. But the general feeling was that the writers of our Petitions had not space to enlarge upon the many special advantages possessed by Natal for military settlers; so a separate memorial was prepared, soliciting that a sufficient number might be located in the Colony.

"We venture to represent to your Majesty, that the District of Natal, with a population of a hundred thousand uncivilised Natives within its borders, and with powerful barbarian nations immediately beyond it, is peculiarly exposed to danger."

This was duly forwarded to the Secretary of State, but, as we had apparently proved too much for the comfort of the new settlers, we did not get any. Those of them who elected to emigrate were located by the Crown in the Cape Colony, where their industry and frugality have brought their own reward.

St. Helena. While this was in progress, we had a vision of St. Helena *via* the *Cape Monitor* newspaper, at the hands of Mr. W. P. Norsworthy. The *St. Helena Herald* of April gave a very gloomy account of the state of the population and the necessity for their emigration, strongly advocating Natal. As the islanders were poor and without a friend at Court, no effort was made on their behalf by those among us who had clamoured for Convicts, Chinese, or Coolies. The German Legion being expected, cheap labour would surely be provided.

Congrega- tionalists. The New Congregational Chapel, Smith Street, was opened on Sunday, June 8th. The Rev. Louis Grout (American) officiated in the morning; the Rev. D. Lindley (American) in the

afternoon, and the Rev. C. Spensley in the evening.   The
opening services were followed by a public tea meeting on
the Monday evening.   Mr. A. W. Evans gave a financial
statement of an appropriate character, showing that the
Chapel, which would accommodate about 350 people, had
been built and furnished at an outlay of £659 15s. 7d., out
of a fund amounting only to £574 14s. 7d., but, as the land
given them by Mr. Forrest, the articles left from the
Bazaar, and that evening's contributions would more than
realise the deficiency, they might regard themselves out of
debt .

Customs Dues.   An increase in the Customs Duty came
into force on the 6th June.   All our
merchants sought at the same time to clear
goods and save duty, but, owing to a deficiency in the
Customs House Staff, it was impossible to get the entries
passed in time, or the goods delivered from the Bonded
Warehouses and removed to town on the 5th; consequently
on that day the Collector of Customs, with the courtesy
and good sense that ever distinguished him, relied upon
the integrity of Messrs. J. Millar and Co., and met the
difficulty by accepting their "Good Fors" for the duty on
such goods as we required to clear.   Cash only being
accepted by this Department, cheques were unavailable.
I noted that I was particularly busy all that day (Friday)
making out Prime Entries which were necessarily dated
back.   I cite this emergency case to demonstrate the condition of business at that time, and prove that, even in a
Governmental Department, where there's a will, there's a
way.

Bank Rates.   July 4th.   The Natal Bank advertise that
they will discount Bills against Drafts on
England at 6 per cent. discount, and 3 per
cent. commission—this being in effect a reduction of 3 per
cent. on previous rates—whereat we were proportionately
grateful.

Piratical.   July 13th.   The Barque *Amigos*, J. Lee,
from China to Algoa Bay and England,
put in for provisions and water.   Mr. W.
Smerdon was appointed her Agent.   He advertised for
sale at his store 500 bags of China sugar of various

qualities, of which he had become the purchaser. The ship took in such supplies as she required, and sailed away on the 22nd July. But in September the lovers of the sensational, especially the ladies, were concerned to learn that a genuine live Pirate had walked and talked with us for a whole week without having his head cut off, and that they were now actually using nice stolen sugar which he had landed and sold to us. As piracy has differential qualities and modifications, like common gallantry, "where the climate's sultry," and as this case developed nothing dramatic or sanguinary, our interest flagged when its piratical character was reduced to that of Barratry, or the running away with a ship and cargo by the Shipmaster; a sort of marine "sneak thief."

The facts reached us from Hong Kong *via* the Cape, and are briefly that the British ship *Amigos* J. Lee, master, sailed from Melbourne bound for Hong Kong in October, 1855, with freight and passengers, Chinese diggers returning to their ancestors. Bills of Lading were duly signed, among others, for a parcel of two thousand sovereigns, which the consignee at Hong Kong never received. After waiting with exemplary patience, he discovered that the *Amigos* had stopped at the Chinese port of Shanghae, and reported himself from Sidney. There he induced his Chinese passengers to land, first borrowing £200 from one of them at high interest, and giving him drafts on his Hong Kong Agents. He then purchased a cargo of sugar at Swatow, and cleared South, it was thought to South America. South he came, and looked in here on the 13th July, 1856, as stated. Whatever was his intended destination he did call at Algoa Bay, and, while trading the rest of his cargo, was overtaken by Nemesis in the shape of a Solicitor from Cape Town, arrested on a charge of embezzlement and Barratry, and lodged in their Tronk, which possibly, being no better than ours, allowed him to break out during the night. His subsequent proceedings must be looked for in Cape newspapers; I cannot recall them.

The Durban County Council. Sued Mr. G. C. Cato on the 8th August (as a representative case) for the amount due on his County Rate of ¾d. per acre. The District Court, in consequence of the non-qualification of some of the County Councillors who made the assessment, gave judgment that the rate had been illegally imposed, and that the assessment could not be recovered at law; consequently those Proprietors who had not paid, did not pay, and the County Council—always unpopular—ceased to exist, it being held that they had "run themselves out" by not complying with the terms of the law providing for their constitution and duration.

The Social Pest. The Social Pest (Native) had thus early on his road to civilisation, called public attention to himself in several cases with young white girls and children.   The newspapers raved about it; the Ministers preached about it; 'while parents wrote about it, one and all urging death, imprisonment, whipping, or banishment, quite overlooking the fact that early in the year a soldier and a native had both been sentenced to a public flogging, against which an equally strong outcry was raised, and in deference thereto the Recorder had ordered floggings in future to be administered in private.   The moral influence was consequently lost upon the Natives.   The continued familiarity of domestic intercourse between the Europeans and Natives gave the latter every encouragement to undervalue the morals, or social customs, of their employers.   Even the cautious *Mercury* voiced public opinion in very strong and forcible terms on the question of Native outrages, domestic servants, and sponging "brothers," suggesting that Lynch-law might be resorted to with advantage; consequently in a local paragraph (November 20th) it takes credit thus:—

"KAFIR DODGES.—We are truly glad that our article on this subject has had the effect of evoking fresh instructions to Tuta, the the Kafir Captain, to make known among the Natives in this neighbourhood that the sponging system will not be allowed, and secondly a notification to white employers that they are at perfect liberty to inflict A SOUND THRASHING on any strange Kafir who intrudes without leave upon their premises."

Natal Chamber of Commerce. After one or two preliminary meetings, this was finally organised on the 19th August, when the Rules were adopted, and the Directorate elected as follows:—A. W. Evans, Chairman; E. P. Lamport, Vice-Chairman; G. H.

Wirsing, Treasurer; Richd. Vause, Hon. Secretary; Directors, J. Millar, J. Sanderson, R. Harwin, Wm. Smerdon. In after years I was appointed Secretary under the Presidency of Mr. John Sanderson. From this commencement the Chamber has maintained its existence in the face of adverse circumstances, commercial depression and calamity, steadily establishing its utility and efficiency, until at the present time it has become not only a well organised local institution, but a strong factor in determining Colonial legislation.

Ship Launch. The afternoon of Saturday, the 30th August, being a holiday, there was a large gathering at Cato's Creek to witness the christening of Mr. Cato's new schooner, prematurely launched by the Umgeni Flood. The day was brilliant with a fine breeze fluttering the flags with which the schooner was decorated, her masting and rigging having been completed. A gangway had been constructed from the bank to the vessel. The ceremony was to be performed by Miss Fanny Cato, the owner's only daughter, and one of Durban's Belles. She accomplished the task gracefully, though with some trepidation owing to the over anxiety of pretty cousins, the officiousness of their cavaliers, and the friendly banter with which Mr. Cato was greeted in consequence of the irregularity of the Launch we were gathered to celebrate. This was the second sea-going vessel built in Durban, and, as it happened, the first to be registered here as belonging to Port Natal. When the interesting ceremony was accomplished, the tide had risen sufficiently to allow the *William Shaw's* removal to the Point, there to load for her first voyage to Mauritius under the charge of Captain Wm. Vionnee, recently a Pilot. The *Mercury* states:—

"This beautiful schooner, the most finished specimen yet produced of our Colonial shipbuilding capabilities, was taken from her berth into the Bay prior to proceeding on her first voyage. The name had been kept a profound and very unnecessary mystery; and the ceremony of 'christening' was ultimately performed by Miss Cato, the daughter of our late Mayor, in a cup of sweetened tea, her father having first addressed a few words to the numerous company assembled to witness the ceremony, which was also inaugurated and succeeded by the discharge of Messrs. Cato's private artillery. The name our readers will be aware is in honour of the excellent Superintendent of Wesleyan Missions in South Africa, the Rev. William Shaw, who first, Mr. Cato informed his friends, taught him to restrict his libations to ' the cup that cheers, but not inebriates.' "

Cheers both hearty and ironical followed, while the thirsty ones proclaimed her as having been christened the " Tea Pot," by which name this smart little schooner of 40 tons was known, and even advertised, long after.

Schooner "Siren."   On the day following (August 31st), the schooner *Siren*, which had made a return voyage from England, discharged and reloaded with a second full cargo for London, sailed out and anchored, until the Captain and Mr. W. M. Collins (late Post Master General) and his family came on board. On the 1st September, the Bar was pronounced too rough to cross. On the 2nd and 3rd it blew a gale from the North-East, and much anxiety, amounting to excitement, was manifested for the safety of ship and cargo, as she was reported to be in a " nasty position," too close in, and confidently expected to come on shore. However, by the aid of springs on her cable, she rode safely to her anchor with 100 fathoms of chain out. On the 4th the wind having changed to the South-West, Captain Hellyer, the Collins family, five bales of wool and sundry live stock were enabled to risk the Bar under the hatches of a cargo boat, and get on board; but as the wind increased in violence, she remained at anchor until it moderated. She got away late in the afternoon of the 5th September with a Colonial Cargo valued at £9,000; such was the order of our going; the time occupied by this departure would have sufficed a modern direct-line steamer to have " doubled the Cape."

Saturday Half Holiday.   Usage had crystalized into custom, but there being no agreement on the subject, no reliance could be placed on its permanency, so, as an outcome of the Chamber of Commerce, the Wholesale Merchants published a notification on the 24th October that in future they would close their places of business at 2 o'clock on Saturday afternoons. This still obtains; long may it flourish.

The Commissariat. The Commissariat called for tenders in December for certain supplies to the troops at Fort Napier and Port Natal for the year 1857. Among other things the daily supply at Port Natal was estimated as follows:— Bread 155lbs., Beef 155lbs., Firewood 690lbs., Tallow-candles 5lbs., Water 150 gallons. Of dry firewood "the maximum weight of any log was not to exceed 200lbs." Candles "must be of best quality and in such proportions of moulds and dips as may be required, Officers and all persons of the Staff being entitled to moulds." "Pure water to be procured daily from the Umgeni River, the Contractor to provide the Casks." The Garrison well and equally convenient swamp furnished water only for washing, stable, and garden purposes. The use of roof water collected in tanks was condemned by the Medical Board for drinking purposes. The troops were therefore daily supplied from the Umgeni with as much purity as the season permitted. Though the Camp was almost surrounded by swamps, the military doctors always maintained that its health standard was higher than that of Fort Napier.

Zulu Country. At the end of November disquieting rumours reached us as to the state of affairs in the Zulu Country, where several of our townsmen and Colonists were trading. Panda, the Zulu King, had divided the government of a part of his dominions between two of his sons, Umbulazi and Kitchwya (Cetywayo). This promoted jealousy and ill feeling, resulting in a determination by Kitchwya—at the instance of his young men—to have all or none. We heard also that Umbulazi with his people and cattle had sought refuge with Mr. Walmsley, the Border Agent. The Natives working in Durban were fully informed of the position and alive to the probability of pursuit and a battle. If Umbulazi or the Colonial forces should be defeated, all their precious stock, to say nothing of their families or tribesmen on the Natal Border, would certainly suffer in the general raiding and slaughter that would ensue; consequently they were very restless, and many, not staying to ask leave, took it with such arms as they possessed and went home. The leading inhabitants, becoming alarmed,

waited on Mr. H. F. Fvnn, the "Kafir Magistrate," who
at once summoned the Natives to an " indaba."

A great body, armed chiefly with sticks, assembled at the
junction of Gardiner and Smith Streets, where about 11
o'clock in the morning of the 4th December he addressed
them from the stoep at the corner of Messrs. Wirsing and
Acutt's Store.

Pointing out the advantages and protection they enjoyed
under the British Government, and the folly and danger of
their embroiling themselves in Zulu affairs, he finally urged
them to remain at work until their several engagements
terminated, and leave the rest to the Government.

Respectful salutations to Mr. Fynn followed his remarks;
the crowd seemed disposed to obey, and were returning
to their employers, but unfortunately the Acting Resident
Magistrate (Mr. H. Cope), who knew nothing of Natives
or their language, felt it incumbent upon him to show his
authority, so ordered the Natives to be informed that if
any of them left the town—employed men or free—he would
arrest and punish them.   This little suggestion was sufficient for the wild lovers of liberty and cattle; the crowd
quickly dispersed, and as quickly collected their blankets
and assegais and went.   Mr. Cope now found his opportunity, and sent an official invitation to the Mayor to
confer upon the situation.   They met and Mr. Cope
announced his intention of calling out the "Royal Durban
Rangers," and swearing in special constables to patrol the
town limits and arrest all Natives leaving.

Mr. E. Snell thereupon summoned a special meeting of the
Town Council, which resolved : —

" Resolved—1st : Tnat in the opinion of this meeting no necessity
has arisen within the jurisdiction of the Resident Magistrate of Durban, and especially of this borough, for the calling in the aid of the
military or swearing in special constables, and that such measures are
imminently prejudicial to the public peace and safety as engendering
disquiet where it did not before exist. 2nd : That in the opinion of
this Council, should any emergency arise on well substantiated information, the Mayor immediately summon the Burgesses for the
purpose of being sworn in as special constables. 3rd : That a copy of
these resolutions be forwarded to Government, and a copy to the
Resident Magistrate of Durban."

This, however, did not deter Mr. Cope from carrying out
his ideas for the preservation of peace.   The " Rangers "

were accordingly ordered out to the Umgeni, on the banks
of which river they passed an eventful night, almost pathetic
in its history, for had it not been for the few arrests they
made, or parties turned back, they were in imminent
danger of being routed by the resident mosquitoes.   Men
and horses suffered until the following day, when they were
withdrawn by orders from Government.

On the 5th December it became known that a great
battle had been fought about seven miles on the Zulu side
of the Tugela, that Umbulazi had been defeated, and was,
with some 3,000 naked, wounded remnants, believed to be
fugitive in Natal.   The town was denuded of "boys."   I
had managed to retain those of my employers by consenting to one going as a delegate for the rest.   Traders and
Europeans also began to return, having lost all their effects,
and had miraculous escapes; among others, my friend
William Grant, son of J. H. Grant, of the East End.   I
called on him that evening, and we gathered at William
Palmer's rooms to meet other companions, J. J. Chapman
and W. Swift in particular, who had but recently returned
from a Zulu trading trip, and knew the people and the
country.   We heard the thrilling blood-curdling account
of Grant's escape "out of the jaws of death; out of the
gates of Hell," subsequently officially confirmed.   I felt
my courage oozing from my finger ends, and became of one
mind with the panic-stricken Burgesses.   William Grant
owed his escape to fleetness of foot and ability to swim;
barefooted he reached the Tugela—which was in flood, and
several hundred yards wide—through thorns, rushes, and
reeds, having kept some distance below the fugitive army
of Umbulazi, with the battle cry of the victors, the thuds
of their knobkerries and clash of shields and assegais, the
screams of men, women, and children in his ears.   The
swollen river with its alligators before him, Natal and safety
on the other side, the only desperate chance was to swim.
Cooling his bruised and torn feet by crouching in the reeds
at the brink, like a hunted animal, he saw the fugitives
drawing down stream towards him followed by the exul-
tant blood-thirsty hunters, who butchered every living thing.
The muddy waters, charged with pink, changed to scarlet,
bodies gyrating among the reeds, the quivering limbs or
gaping wounds too evident for doubt as to what might be

L

his fate from the relentless broad-stabbing assegai of the Zulu warrior.

Alone and without aid, he realised that he must do or die, so, securing his shirt and trousers round his neck, and giving one glance up the river, with its crowd of black heads and waving limbs, sinking or swimming in effort to escape, he plunged absolutely into blood and water, with the dead and dying around him, and, aided by youth and courage, succeeded in effecting a landing on the Natal side, exhausted but safe; with gasping, naked, bleeding wretches crawling out around him along the river bank.

On the 11th December, the *Mercury* published a detailed account of the battle; while sanguinary reports from various witnesses filled all the newspapers. Without doubt, we were like a flock of frightened sheep, and made no attempt at organization to protect our town or ourselves, while suggestions, each more reckless than its predecessor, were offered. We took some comfort in the report that Mr. Theophilus Shepstone (without any escort) was on the Tugela, from the idea that his advice would be listened to by the belligerents, or Panda.

The return of the schooner *William Shaw* from Mauritius gave occasion for the *Mercury* to assert that we were in no immediate danger, but nevertheless required additional troops, and that she should be despatched instantly—*à la* Dick King—to the Buffalo or Algoa Bay, to summon aid. Also, as an act of self-preservation, no Zulu refugee should be allowed by us, at any cost, to enter the Colony.

Being Sailing Master of Mr. J. Millar's boat, I made every preparation to follow the example of older Colonists, and transport the families of Millar and Gillespie to the island, after burying our stock of liquors. Happily all this was avoided, and we resumed our normal courage on hearing that the victorious Kitchwya—declining to risk the swollen Tugela—had divided his army of 20,000 men into three divisions to secure the spoils and hunt Zululand for fugitive relatives and his brother's people. How many fell in that day will never be known. One eye-witness reported having counted 500 bodies in one place. The slaughter continued for some time after of old men, women, and children hunted out of hiding in bushes, reed beds, and ravines. Certain it is that the sea coast for miles, right down to the Umgeni, was strewn with mutilated bodies, and that the Authorities were appealed to to allay the pestilential stench.

The force of the swollen Umgeni apparently deflected such fragments of humanity as came our way, so that, with the exception of a skull or two, they were not deposited on the Back Beach. The Resident Norwegian Missionaries in Zululand afterwards estimated the total number of Zulus " wiped out " from all causes as twenty-one thousand.

Reader, spare your jibes at our weakness; recollect that we were but a handful, and, including the garrison, could not have mustered 600 white men capable of carrying, and, what is more essential, using arms; that our women and children about doubled our number; that our buildings might have been easily fired; that we should have to accept short notice, as the Zulu " impis " could have reached us in four days, and found shelter in the Berea and Back Beach bushes, and that we should then be between the devil and the deep sea ! Recollect also the respect shewn by the Burgesses of Durban to this same Cetywayo some twenty-three years later (1879), when they conferred with General Lord Chelmsford, in the Town Office, as to the expediency of entrenching the town, and constructing bastions from the Eastern to the Western Vleis. When the Point was actually barricaded ; the Gaol and all Government buildings loophooled for musketry ; the parapets of Merchants' stores made defensible by sandbags, and all the Burgesses enrolled as a Town Guard, armed with sniders. Sentries posted ; hospitals and refuges provided, and signal guns arranged ; a Brigadier General, and an Admiral in command ; then say if you can that there was no justification for the blanched cheeks, sleepless nights, and anxious cares of 1856.

Hotels. Early in the year, the " Commercial Hotel," in central West Street (otherwise " Boltons "), passed from the tenancy of Bolton to Spencer F. Drake, a retired sea captain. Under the latter's energetic, genial management, " Drake's " became a popular resort, much favoured by shipmasters, hunters, and traders. In consequence of the death of old

Captain Hugh McDonald, his widow continued to carry on the Hotel Business on the Market Square with indifferent success. She disposed of it in March to Mr. Thomas Galloway, who, in announcing his accession, made no alteration in its name.

New Year's Eve. The Old Year went out with a strong North East wind and sounds of revelry or strife, which, coming so soon after the Zulu scare, aggravated the nervous susceptibilities of the timid; for at midnight gusty bells were rung, and undulating sounds of a general discharge of musketry took place from weapons large and small that had been furbished up to repel the Zulus, whose advent many families—not given to seeing-in New Years—believed was then taking place. The morning's dawn dispelled their fears, and gave presage of a " Happy New Year," without the aid of " First Footings."

CHAPTER XII.

1857.

MAYORS—E. SNELL AND A. W. EVANS.
ACTING—A. FERGUSON AND S. PINSENT.

Meat and Vegetables. THANKS to the practical effort of the Natal Agricultural and Horticultural Society and their annual shows, the "Pumpkins and Mealies" period of the early emigrant was now fast passing away, and vegetables of many varied kinds were hawked from door to door by the small farmers and new tenants of Corporation Leases, who sent out baskets of fruit or vegetables by their native servants. The faithful native, true to his instructions and uncertain as to currency, would not bargain or "break bulk"; a cabbage, bunch of carrots, herbs, or eschallots, was to him so much coin each —you must take it or leave it, nor were you able to sort up your requirements according to your needs, or annex a banana or two extra for the children.

This led to a trade with the Butchers, who also became Greengrocers, taking supplies from the growers, and retailing fruit and vegetables in assorted quantities to suit the economical housewife. The advent of the Corporation obliged the Butchers to remove to proper slaughter-places at the West end of the town, for which a stand license was charged. Richard King had given up his business in Smith Street East, and for a time Mr. James Kinghurst was at the head of the trade. His slaughter-place was on the beach, at the foot of the erf now built upon by Messrs. W. Dunn and Co. He claimed to utilize the Admiralty reserve, but occupied as a cattle kraal a site on the flat to the westward of Albert Street. He relinquished business in 1856, on being elected a member of the Legislative Council for Durban County. Mr. W. Leathern also removed to one of the new stands. Mr. Paul Henwood disposed of his Butchery business to Joseph Mason, who in turn was taken over by Richard Baynes, the latter disposing of his business this year to Robert Surtees. He advertised himself of Field Street (where the Princess Café now is), and specially laid himself out for the sale of Colonial produce, in addition to beef, mutton, and pork. Poultry was apparently disregarded, as every Burgess kept his own stock, while the Natives brought in fowls in bunches, hawking them about.

Millar & Gillespie. At the commencement of the year the title of the firm of "John Millar and Co." was altered to "Millar and Gillespie." As agents of the "Imperial Fire Insurance Company" they advertised that they were prepared to issue Fire Policies "on 1st class risks 5s., 2nd class risks 7s. 6d., Thatch risks according to circumstances." Mr. Millar having developed a taste for sugar, was seeking to purchase an Estate and turn his attention to that promising industry, so the partnership was dissolved in July, Mr. Hugh Gillespie continuing the business in his own name; Mr. Millar settling in Victoria County.

Mail Steamers. The arrival of the first of a long talked of new line of Mail Steamers was announced on the 20th January, when the S.S. *Madagascar*, 500 tons, Captain George Rennie, anchored outside. Mr. John Brown was the Agent. This steamer was from London 18th November, Capetown 14th January. The news which interested us most was that she brought "several thousands in gold and silver" for the Commissariat, but, owing to strong N.E. gales, we did not see the specie landed with the mails and passengers until the 26th; it was then marched off to Pietermaritzburg under military escort 'per ox wagon. We were rather gloomily calculating the time when any of this money would filter down to Durban.

Specie. So the announcement on the 1st February that H.M.S. *Highflyer*, 21 guns, Captain Shadwell, had arrived from England with ten thousand pounds in specie for the Commissariat Department at once relieved the tightness of our chest, and raised sanguine hopes that this plethora would lead us all on to fortune. In the meantime the newspapers, commenting on the *Madagascar's* freight, state that: —

"The scarcity of silver coin has been lately felt most inconveniently; but we are happy to hear that £500 in silver have been received into the military Chest by the late arrivals of specie, £100 of which have been sent to Durban, and the whole will find its way gradually into general circulation."

Public Dinner. On the 23rd January a Public Dinner was held in the store of Mr. E. Smith, Central West Street, to welcome back to Durban Hy. Jas. Mellor, Esq., who, having resigned his office as Crown Prosecutor, resumed his duties as Resident Magistrate. Mr. S. F. Drake, of the "Family and Commercial," was the caterer. The gathering was essentially of a social character, though I must admit the *raison d'être* was less to welcome the coming, than to speed the parting guest. Off the bench, Mr. Henry Cope was generally popular, gave excellent dinners, and proved a genial host. He was essentially a gentleman of taste and refinement, courtly in bearing, though somewhat precise—his detractors said pedantic. He bore about him an old-fashioned air of the Inns of Court, and was afterwards elevated to the Bench as one of our Puisne Judges.

We sat down to dinner, as soon as candles could be lit, about fifty in number, in white trousers and waistcoats, with black coats, patterns various. The Menu may be described as "everything in season." All political topics being avoided, there was but little speech-making, but that little was good, being enlivened by the wit and repartee of the legal, clerical, and medical members, who were well supported by the rest of the guests. As usual, those who could not speak, volunteered songs; from both these afflic-

tions I was spared. We separated at a late hour, and the
following day pronounced this inaugural dinner a great
success; so much so that on the complaint of about twenty
exclusive but repentant subscribers, who had cautiously
absented themselves, the *Mercury* published their names.

Zulu Refugees.
At the end of January the Government
having issued regulations for the allotment
of Zulu refugees as labourers for a period
of three years on very moderate terms, a
large number of these people were accordingly brought into
Durban, and herded like slaves by the Native Police on
the Market Square in the vicinity of the Court House;
while the more marketable articles—the girls—were brought
upstairs—mostly on their hands and knees—into the Court
room, there to be picked over and alotted with the proviso
that families were to be selected together as far as possible.
As the majority of the Refugees had quitted the Zulu country without their wardrobes, the costume of the whole was
very scanty, scarcely a garment among them " from the neck
to the knee "; while the costume of the girls was little more
than a string with a fringe of fibres about three inches
deep, or a bead-trimmed skin apron a few inches square.
The children of both sexes simply wore a coat of grease.
Some of these girls had grass or wire anklets and bracelets;
a very few had blue, or grey calico squares on their
shoulders about the size of a large handkerchief.   They
were all fairly clean, and in good condition, and sat on the
floor of the Court room, crouched against the walls, silent,
wild-eyed, and terrified. I positively noted the pulsation
of their hearts against their ribs, a steady throbbing, while
the native constables in charge leered at them with the air
of victors, and in the masterful manner assumed by native
Jacks-in-office. The allotment and registration of the men,
their wives and families, were duly made, and they were
marched off to their destination, to be invested with a cotton blanket or a yard or two of calico. Whatever great
expectations the farmers might have had, they were doomed
to disappointment, for these people were very wild and very
ignorant (excepting in handling cattle), and proved themselves mere " hewers of wood, and drawers of water." Very
speedily complaints were made to the Government that the

Regulations were insufficient, since many of the allotees could not be induced to work, while others departed in the night to seek their tribesmen in the Locations. The planters remonstrated that they were debarred from the Americans' privilege of "wolloping their own nigger," but had to take them to a Magistrate for correction; while others desired to make the boys and girls useful (and profitable) by prolonging their servitude for five years. Mr. Theophilus Shepstone—the Secretary for Native Affairs—had to answer all these remonstrances, and, owing to his consideration for the welfare of the native population, and the justice due to the Refugees at the hands of the British Government, found a hasty condemnation by the Planters, who characterised these equitable principles as the weak and vacillating "Shepstonian Policy."

Elections. The first twenty days of February were given up to the delights and excitement of a contested election. No trivial Municipal matter, but the honourable position as the premier representative of this borough in the first Legislative Council of the Colony, the constitution of which Governor Scott had given intimation on his arrival. Requisitions were accordingly prepared and submitted, accepted or declined, until they finally settled upon the candidates in the persons of John Millar, John R. Goodricke, and Savory Pinsent, two of whom must be elected. Having no clear notions of what we particularly groaned under, though we desired things many and various, it was absolutely necessary that we should learn the views of the candidates upon things in general, and if possible pledge them to carry out our views instead. The Mayor was accordingly requisitioned, and a public meeting held on the 13th of the month, for the purpose of harrying the proposed representatives. Notwithstanding our desire for entertainment of this character, it is doubtful if the meeting would have been enforced, had it not been that at the very last moment a new candidate was sprung upon the Borough in the person of Mr. Donald Moodie, of Klip River County, formerly Colonial Secretary. Of course it was clearly shown by the opposition that the acceptance of his requisition was "by authority," and after hours; that he was evidently a Government nominee, and equally so that he was designed for the Speakership, etc., etc. His past experience in the Government service both here and in the "Old Colony" essentially fitted him for Legislative honours, and made him a formidable opponent, but the importation of "a stranger" was quite sufficient to arouse the jealousy of Durban men, who at once drew the sword, threw away the scabbard and rushed to the battle. As it is impossible to reproduce the report of this historical meeting, which was long and especially noisy, I must limit myself to the questions put to the candidates, in order to show the range of our requirements, and our belief in the benefits to come from representative institutions. The replies in most cases were guarded, non-committal, vague, or rambling, but very positive on things not asked about. The meeting was held in E. Smith's Store, Archibald Ferguson, Acting Mayor, presiding. Mr. Goodricke was the first to step into the ring and address the meeting, concluding a long and able speech with the observation "that he would only support a loan for the Harbour Works, but for no other object."

Mr. Reddish : Do you support convicts ? (Laughter.)

Mr. Goodricke was sorry to hear the question raised; was it that of the meeting ? (Cries of " No, no !")

Mr. Reddish again asked the question. (Great uproar.)

Mr. Currie : Do you think that all ecclesiastical grants should cease on the death of the present holders ?

Mr. Goodricke : Most certainly I do ! (Cheers.)

Mr. Babbs wished to know what means he would advocate for making up the deficiency in the revenue.

Mr. Bottomly stood up amid immense uproar, and appeared anxious to deliver himself of a speech, which however the meeting would not hear. He asked Mr. Goodricke whether he had ever said that he could not trust the Durbanites on a jury ?

Mr. Goodricke : I never said so ! (Great cheering.)

Mr. Henry Milner asked, in the event of increased taxation, would Mr. Goodricke levy it upon the white inhabitants, or the black population ?

Mr. Babbs wished Mr. Goodricke would state his reasons for preferring the poll-tax. (Groans.)

The Mayor now called Mr. Millar as next in the field. Mr. Millar was received with "great cheering;" spoke briefly, and kept behind his published address.

Mr. M. Penfold wished to know if Mr. Millar was favourable to the introduction of convicts ? (Oh, oh !)

Mr Tyzack rose amid great uproar and confusion. He would pledge himself to be as brief and consecutive as possible. (Laughter.) Mr.

Tyzack's voice was here drowned in the clamour and noise that prevailed; but at last, though often interrupted, he put the question. Referring to Mr. Millar's address, he asked him where he had had the opportunity of obtaining that knowledge of the kafir character which would enable him to take up such a dangerous position as to advocate the breaking up of the Locations?

Mr. Millar appealed to the meeting; question hostile and discourteous.

Mr. Tyzack disclaimed any hostile intention, and said he was himself for "breaking them up." (Immense laughter.)

Mr. Tyzack again rose, and after loud and prolonged interruption, and cries of "Question," said he wished to know what Mr. Millar would do with the present occupiers of the Locations, and how he would break them up without doing injustice to the kafirs. (Uproar.)

Mr. Millar sat down.

Mr. Tyzack still declaiming in his own peculiar oratorical manner,

Mr. Cato (a Voice—"Cato will reason well.") would likewise repeat Mr. Tyzack's question; he also wished to say a few words, but was prevented by the continued interruption.

Mr. Millar replied.

Mr. Tyzack again wanted to know what Mr. Millar's chances had been of learning the native character. (Great clamour.)

The meeting here became very uproarious, and the Chairman had some difficulty in producing order.

Mr. J. Sanderson asked Mr. Millar if he would advocate in the Council Chamber the views and principles he expressed when out of it—would he adopt the view respecting the kafirs which he (Mr. S.) had heard him advocate, that they should all be slaves. (Oh, oh!) Mr. Millar denied that he ever advocated slavery: the law would not allow it. Mr. Sanderson did not want to know what the law would allow, but what Mr. Millar's principles were. Mr. Millar promised not to advocate slavery.

Mr. Pinsent having been called upon, rose amid considerable confusion, which increased his natural hesitancy of speech, and said as he had stated his views at length in his published address, he only thought it necessary to answer any questions that might be put to him.

Mr. R. Baynes wished to know whether Mr. Pinsent intended to plead that the kafirs had more right to the land than the whites?

Mr. Pinsent: Certainly not!

Mr. W. Dacomb: What are the practical modes alluded to in your address to promote a habit of continuous labour among the kafirs?

Mr. Dacomb asked Mr. Pinsent if in his farming operations he had adopted the same means respecting the kafirs as those recommended in his address? (Cries of "No question")

The Chairman considered Mr. Pinsent's farming operations had nothing to do with the objects of the meeting.

Mr. Tyzack said: Is Mr. Pinsent prepared to advocate measures —(awful groans and loud laughter)—for immediately facilitating the completion of the Harbour Works, and construction of a lighthouse?

Mr. Milner: Do you think there is sufficient engineering talent in the country for carrying out improvements to the amount of £100,000—if such a loan were obtained? (Hear, hear.)

Mr. F. C. Salmon asked whether Mr. Pinsent was the writer of the pamphlet connected with the last municipal elections signed " A Burgess"? ("No question.")

Mr. Tyzack: What measures would you advocate with reference to education?

Mr. Currie wished to know whether Mr. Pinsent was in favour of the payment of members, and of a salaried Speaker?

Mr. A. Clarence: Are you in favour of special juries?

The Chairman called upon Mr. Moodie, who on rising was greeted with a hurricane of cheers, groans, and other discordant cries.

Mr. Currie was about to ask a question but was interrupted by Mr. Kershaw, who asked with reference to the kafir policy propounded in Mr. Moodie s address, what means he would advocate for gradually effecting those changes, so as to save the Colony from jeopardy?

Mr. Mason: Are you pledged to the Shepstonian policy of keeping up the Locations?

Mr. Currie: Do you not apprehend as much danger arising out of the changes respecting polygamy, as the breaking up of the Locations?

Mr. Dacomb: Why not give it [Location land] to the whites as well as to the blacks?

Mr. Salmon: Are you disposed to advocate a Location for the poor whites? . . . Have you taken into consideration the number of acres the kafirs occupy? . . . Are you not opposed to curtailing one inch of the Coast Locations?

Mr. Baynes: Are the kafirs now in a more prepared state for improvement than when you first came here? (Cheers.)

Mr. Hartley: Would you advocate a loan for the improvement of the port? . . Would you press for a steam tug at the expense of the Government?

Mr. Baynes: Were not the kafirs in a better state for improvement when the Government took possession than now!

Mr. Moodie said they were.

Mr. Baynes: Would it not be advisable to take immediate steps for increasing the troops, to bring the kafirs under improvement and subjection?

Mr. Moodie: Undoubtedly, and he would advocate the obtaining of more troops. (Cheers.)

Mr. Kershaw: Would you take any steps respecting immigration?

Mr. Lamport: Do you feel yourself under Government influence in consequence of having two sons in the service and one a Government Surveyor? (Immense uproar, and cries of "Cut and dry.")

Mr. Moodie: On his honour, No! (Cheers and hisses.)

Mr. Lamport: Will your resid ince at Doornkop prevent you from advocating the local interests of this port?

Mr. George Robinson: Would you, if elected, accept the office of Speaker if you had a chance? (Great excitement.)

Mr. Moodie would feel it a very high honour. ("Oh, oh!")

Mr. Mason: Would you advocate a speedy and practical plan for ensuring a supply of native labour?

Mr. Baynes: Would you support Sir George Grey's policy respecting giving away Crown lands?

Mr. Lamport: Would you grant St. Paul's Church an ordinance giving it a right to manage its own affairs?

Mr. G. Robinson: Are you on principle and under all circumstances opposed to the interference of the secular power in the affairs of Christian Churches?

Mr. Moodie knew nothing about St. Paul's, and could give no opinion.

Mr. Robinson did not allude to St. Paul's but to all Churches, and demanded an answer.

Mr. R. Acutt: As you are acquainted with the Cape, would you support such an ordinance as has been passed at certain places there, for any Church in this Colony.

Mr. Robinson: Will you do all in your power to place the £5,000 reserved by the Charter for "Native purposes" within the control of the local Legislature? (Applause.)

Mr. R. Acutt wanted a definite reply to his question; the Episcopalians in this Colony labour under great difficulties, &c, &c. Will Mr. Moodie support such an ordinance?

Mr. Moodie would give the subject his best consideration. (Hisses.)

Mr. Robinson reiterated his question respecting the rescinding o the £5,000 reserve. ("Hear.")

Mr. Moodie thought if they want that condition removed they had better say, take away the Charter also! (Hisses and groans.)

Mr. Baynes: Would you advocate a poll-tax of 10/- a head on all able-bodied kafirs?

Mr. Milner: Do you think that the kafirs could contribute £25,000 instead of £10,000 to the revenue without jeopardising the peace of the Colony; for if the taxation is increased it must fall on the kafir?

Mr. Gillespie: Should you be prepared to prevent the Bishop shutting up a Church when he liked?

Mr. Moodie would not interfere with the Bishop so long as he did not interfere with him.

The meeting now broke up after three cheers for Mr. Moodie, and three more still heartier for Messrs. Millar and Goodricke.

The polling was to take place on the 19th and 20th of the month, so on the day following the meeting the friends Millar and Goodricke coalesced, amalgamated their committees, agreeing to stand together and share expenses. Canvassing was taken up in earnest on both sides, and the electors were bombarded with broadsheets, cackling newspaper shots, and placards; while the more homely wits expended their energies in squibs, lampoons, and pen and ink sketches, all more personal than polite. Memories of the famous Eatanswill election, in which Mr. Pickwick took part, were recalled, and plans discussed for the due production, or due suppression of voters, reluctant or willing; while proper preparatory instructions were to be administered to the unsophisticated to ensure his voting "straight." It was held to be very unfair of the Government (*i.e.*, the Charter)—and the *Mercury* complained accordingly—to prolong the contest for two days, the candidates regarding it as more than probable that a voter, primed unsuccessfully to-day, might think of his head in the morning, and go over to the enemy. In this opinion they were justified by the event. Having recently published a code of Villa Signals with the necessary sets of flags enabling communication to be made between houses on the Berea and offices in town, I was requisitioned to prepare the election flags for our party, who had chosen the colours of pink and blue for their favours. Messrs. Moodie and Pinsent adopted white and green. I obtained a 40ft. scaffolding pole, attached block and halliards, and erected our flagstaff at the front door of the store, from which on the day of election flaunted our standard "Millar and Goodricke" in letters a foot high on a pink field, bordered with blue. The Committee had decorated voters' houses, verandahs, fences, and trees, with little pink and blue hand flags of the Sunday School pattern. Thus the newspaper report of these two eventful days:—

"On Thursday morning the early sun shone upon a perfect galaxy of banneas, chiefly pink and blue, the colours of Messrs. Millar and Goodricke; and the people wondered at the industry that had prepared, and so quietly suspended them everywhere. The more populous part of the town, West of the Market Square, exhibited chiefly the colours of this party. It was not long however before large flags of white and green floated from the flagstaffs of Messrs. Moodie and Pinsent's friends, and less pretentious banners of the same colours appeared in various places—the East end exhibiting the chief display of the party. At 8 o'clock a.m. the poll opened, and continued languid throughout the day, each party apparently holding back its strength. Messrs. Millar and Goodricke, however, kept ahead the whole day.

The poll for the day closed at 4 p.m. as follows:—Millar 33, Good-ricke 32, Moodie 25, Pinsent 23.

"Everything was quiet during the first day, though considerable excitement was manifested towards the close. We are sorry to say that instances of undue influence and intimidation occurred, most disgraceful to the parties concerned."

The polling office was at A. Clarence's Auction Mart—late Government Schoolroom—Field Street, in the vicinity of which convenient booths had been erected for the use of the Committees and the "instruction" of voters. Having been appointed scrutineer, I was in attendance at the table from eight o'clock till the close of the poll, and therefore did not see all that the editor complains of; but, nevertheless, had my suspicions. At dawn the following morning I found the excitement of the day had extended to the night, during which, certain jovial spirits, voters for the County, having *three* days at their disposal, testified their opposition to the Borough candidates by cutting away my halliards, and subsequently advertising the colours of their particular candidate (J. Kinghurst, W. R. Thompson, or Dr. Addison) by painting, in alternate smears of blue and white, the shutters, palings and verandah posts of West Street, even flaunting their brushes in the face of slumbering authority, by decorating the gate-posts of the Tronk.

Re-hoisting my flag after laboriously lowering my flag-staff to replace the halliards, 1 resumed my place at the poll, and there learnt in indignant tones from Mr. Millar that, whilst at the Durban Club in the evening, he had been made the victim of his own flag line the "jolly dogs" having utilised it to interlace all the stakes of the wattled fence on either side of the Club steps. Happening himself to be the first to quit the building, he was tripped headlong into the sands of Smith Street. I have reason to believe that one of the Speakers of the Legislative Council could testify to these playful incidents. Resuming the newspaper narrative:—

"Second day—Friday. This morning the polling shortly after its commencement showed great activity, and Moodie and Pinsent came up to their opponents. During nearly the whole day it was a neck and neck race, and the efforts of both parties were very strenuous. It is positively affirmed that the most open corruption was practised . . . . . The excitement was intense towards the close at 4 p.m., when the result was announced by the Returning Officer as Millar 113, Moodie 108, Goodricke 101, Pinsent 97."

Then Babel or Bedlam broke loose, the result being a surprise to most of us. Cheers and counter-cheers and calls for Messrs. Millar and Moodie, who with the defeated candidates had to respond with as much grace as the circumstances admitted. However this election may be regarded by modern experts, we at least did not consider that our mountains of labour brought forth small results. Allowing for the sick, the absent, or the reluctant voters, we polled all in the Borougn that could be brought up, or induced to leave their occupations and distant houses at the Point, Umgeni, Berea, or Umbilo, the only means of conveyance over the sandy roads being on horseback, or by ox cart.

Sir Benjamin Pine. Immediately after these elections, we learnt by overland mail that Mr. B. C. C. Pine, our late Lieutenant-Governor, had been knighted, and appointed Governor on the West Coast of Africa.

Emigrants. On the 25th February, new actors in our local history entered the port by the barque *Admiral*, 215 tons; Glendenning, Master. Her passengers were the Rev. J. L. Crompton, Mrs. Crompton, child and servant, Miss Barter, two servants and Kafir, Miss McKenzie (the Archdeacon's sister), and Miss Cohen; the Rev. J. L. Crompton shortly to plunge into the turmoil of Church strife, and Miss McKenzie to be accused of murder, as will appear in due course.

Crime. Durban was aghast as the news circulated on the morning of the 26th February that Mr. Robert Acutt's Auction Mart had been burgled. His loss was stated to be £700, but when he offered £5 reward for the discovery of the thief, we learnt also that with the exception of a small amount of coin, all the rest was in our current literature, good-fors and promises-to-pay, or Drafts by Peter upon Paul, payment of which were duly stopped by advertisements and notices to the parties interested. The recent robbery of the Treasury Chest in Pietermaritzburg of a similar amount was recalled to our minds, but in this case a native was supposed to have been the perpetrator; the Chief Constable having expressed this conviction, there the matter rested, because he assured us he knew of no bad characters among the Europeans, and without doubt time and circumstances would disclose the facts, and his astuteness. I saw to my store locks and induced the firm to have iron bars fixed to the windows; they remain there to this day.

Wesleyan Church, West Street. The foundation stone of this large and imposing edifice was laid on Monday, the 16th March, by that venerable Missionary among the Amapondo's, or, as we then styled it, "in Fakus' country," the Rev. Thomas Jenkins. The children, Ministers, and friends walked in procession across the Market Square from the old Chapel, with the usual banners, clean frocks and faces, to the site known as Mr. Kahts' garden. The Revs. Louis Grout and Seth B. Stone of the American Mission opened the proceedings, the Rev. C. Spensley, at this time Superintendent of the Durban Circuit, gave an address on the rise, progress, and universality of Methodism, and Mr. R. Harwin read a list of articles, including coins of the realm and the record, to be deposited in a glass jar under the Foundation Stone. The Rev. T. Jenkins then laid the stone with the usual ceremonies, followed by an excellent address, which was listened to by the numerous company, comprising members of all denominations, with respectful attention.

In the evening a tea meeting was held in the Schoolroom, when several Ministers and friends gave addresses, that of the Rev. Thomas Jenkins, who recounted his 37 years' experience as a Missionary in South Africa, chiefly at Palmerton, being of special interest.

Mr. R. Harwin, Treasurer of the Building Committee, explained the financial position, and paid Mr. William Hartley the compliment of being the first originator of the movement, by depositing with the Rev. Mr. Spensley a substantial sum "for Wesleyan objects in Durban." The estimated cost of the new building was £1,200, free from debt. The Aliwal Street Chapel would then be surrendered to the Missionary Society for Native purposes.

While we were enjoying all these good things and hoping for more to come, the Evil One or some other "bad character" was abroad in boots, seeking the hidden treasure referred to in Mr. Harwin's list, for, before the mortar had set, the foundation stone was found to have been rolled away, the bottle shattered and the "filthy lucre" vanished. Great was the outcry caused by this sacrilege.

Legislative Council. The 23rd March found Durban depleted of all its prominent citizens, for everybody who was anybody had journeyed up to Maritzburg to be present at the commencement of a new epoch in the history of the Colony, the inauguration of the first Legislative Council, which was opened by Governor John Scott on this day. However much they may have been impressed by the ceremonial, the military display, the civil uniforms, and the transformation of the thatched barn-like structure from a School to a Parliament House, they were not successful in answering the non-content Burgesses of Durban, when the newspapers reported that the elected representatives of the people had dared to vote a salary to the Speaker and an attendance pay to themselves. It was a breach of promise! The voice of the people of Durban must make itself heard, so the Mayor was requisitioned, and a public meeting held on the 14th April to protest. There was a comforting grumble all round, and many virtuous men repudiated the possibility of their accepting one pound a day; legislators should pay their own expenses "for the honour of the thing." So far as my notes show, the Legislators did not revoke.

Teetotal. I find in my Diary under date May 8th:— "While at tea, Tom Harvey and Greenacre "called to invite me to their quarters; went "and spent a very proper evening; two Harveys, Joel Lean, "Swift, and Grant; broke up at 2 a.m., and home to bed." We must have been teetotallers—or very near it—for on the 9th July appeared an anonymous advertisement by "a few friends," who desired to form a Total Abstinence Society, and called a meeting for the 14th July. Subsequently Thomas Harvey's name appeared as the convener of the Society after its organization. In this I was misled by several creditable witnesses, who at different times gave me to understand that they were respectively the "first man, etc.," notably R. W. Tyzack, Peter Steel, Francis Harvey (T.'s Father), Jas. Brickhill, and Peter Lennox; possibly my memory is defective.

The Durban Auxiliary Bible Society. Seems to have had an existence of which I find no record until the 15th May of this year. The month must have revived memories of the May meetings in the Old Country, for we find Mr. Savory Pinsent calling a Public Meeting of the Society (*sic*) in the Court Room on the evening of the 21st, chair to be taken at 7 o'clock. This serviceable organization still flourishes as one of Durban's recognised institutions.

Durban Mechanics' Institute. Having been elected on the Committee in 1855, I paid regular attendance to the duties of this Department. The old Committee had negotiated with the Town Council for a site on which to erect a suitable building, but, as every inch of land was begrudged, it was not until August, 1855, that we were granted a piece of the Market Square large enough for a cottage. However, before we had raised sufficient funds to permit the erection of the little wooden house, reading room, and Librarian's quarters adjoining St. Paul's, five years had elapsed. The area was then extended to the piece of ground now occupied by the Durban Public Library, but a further period of some 15 years passed before the Government conceded a title to Trustees, the right of the Corporation to alienate land on the Market Square being a vexed question.

At the annual meeting of subscribers in May, 1857, on the resignation of Mr. Joseph Mason, I was unanimously elected Secretary in his place, while Mr. John Robinson (now Sir John) was chosen on the Committee, and promptly put to work, with Mr. Wm. Swift and myself, to write out and re-arrange the Catalogue; this involved the use of much paste and brown paper in restoration of damaged Books, occupying our evenings for a considerable time.

It was on one of these occasions, leaving the Institute late on a wet, dark night, that the future Premier of Natal met with an accident which might have spoilt his career. Like weary shepherds, we were wending our dreary way homewards, sheltered by umbrellas, when, passing Kahts' Corner into Gardiner Street, there was a sudden cry from my companion, a snorting of oxen, and a clashing of horns; I could see only the figures of cattle, but no Mr. Robinson. It then dawned upon me that we must have walked into a team of bullocks, sleeping peacefully, fastened to the trektow of some outspanned wagon. Sounds of lamentation and woe directed me to my fallen friend, who I found prone, hatless, and with shattered umbrella. He was much shaken and bruised, as the particular beast he stumbled upon rose under him, and cast him headlong over its neck. Mr. Robinson—like Byron's " Miss "—was so much alarmed, that he was quite alarming," and I was at some pains to sooth his anxiety, and get him safely to his father's house. The morrow disclosed neither fracture nor dislocation; he was himself again.

Mrs. Hall, the Librarian, having resigned, a Mrs. Harrison was appointed in her place, but before the end of this year Mr. John Vialls received the appointment; later he was succeeded by Mr. Morton Green.　We made special efforts to raise funds for a new building of our own—a Castle in the Air, though designed by Mr. R. S. Upton— which, had our projected ideas been carried out, would have exceeded the Wesleyan Church in cost and accommodation, since we stipulated for a spacious Museum, Lecture Room, Library, and Class Rooms, together with residence. To this end we succeeded in organising many lectures and ertertainments, by which a few pounds were collected; among others we had lectures from Dr. Holland, Rev. H. Wilder, Judge Cloete, Dr. Mann, Mr. Lamport, Dr. Johnston, Mr. Wm. Hartley, and Mr. R. S. Upton. As illustrating the style of entertainment, the mode and manners of the time, I may mention that on the 25th August Mr. E. P. Lamport gave us a Dramatic Reading in the Magistrate's Court Room, which, for its size, contained a large audience. The programme consisted of selections from " As you like it." Reporter says :—

"It was read, we might almost say acted, by Mr. Lamport with great taste and beauty. The reading was introduced by a clever poetical prologue, ' Not by Shakespeare.' The Songs occurring in the play itself were admirably sung (not read) by Mr. Lamport; thus adding vocal music to the evening's entertainment."

The funds of the Institution benefited 20s. 6d. This success induced a repetition on the 28th, in Mr. R. Acutt's Auction Room, when, it having been announced that there would be music between the parts by Mr. Haygarth, there was a crowded attendance, and the Building Fund was further augmented by £2 2s. 6d.

In consequence of the enforced closure of a Committee meeting owing to leakage of rainwater through the thatched roof, and of other complaints, we abandoned Mr. Pulleyn's building as no longer tenable for a Library, or comfortable for a Reading Room, and removed into the adjoining double-storied house, belonging to Dr. Johnston (now Randles Bro. and Hudson). From there we removed, in September, 1860, into our own humble wooden building by St. Paul's—Mr. John Hunt, Contractor. The date of its formal occupation is not recorded in the Minutes. I resigned the Secretaryship in November, 1858, and was succeeded by Mr. John Robinson, who reigned three years. By gifts, endowments, and stipulations, the vulgar "Mechanics' Institution," being deemed out of date and no longer an Institute, was re-named the "Durban Public Library," and this, having always secured the friendly sympathy and material, if insufficient, support of the community, continues, under existing management, aided by a Government subsidy, to be of permanent use and increasing benefit.

Sea Bathing. During last year, Pilot George Archer advertised—unsuccessfully—that he was prepared to erect a Bathing House in the Bay, if sufficient inducement offered. That was not secured until he induced Mr. Mark Foggitt, Town Clerk, to co-operate. The latter took upon himself the venture, and advertised in June of this year that he had completed a Bathing House opposite Mr. Wm. Cooper's residence (Orange Grove) at a cost of £120, and soliciting subscribers—Ladies £2 2s., Children 10s., Gentlemen 10s., yearly. The building was of wood on Mangrove posts, about 50 yards from the dry ground, a sort of shed, with a dressing room on a platform, approached by a plank gangway on the Bay front. A small yard for the bathers was enclosed by a reed fence, which from a boat had the appearance of a large fish kraal. The arrangement was sufficient for ladies and children, and when the tide served was well patronised during the first summer season; but as the depth was only about three feet, the more ambitious men sought a wider range, so availed themselves of a small reed door left in the front to enjoy a swim in the open. They were restricted by the regulations to a forenoon dip, the ladies having the rest of the day. As the outer door was frequently left open in the morning, and neglected by the ladies' bath attendant until the afternoon tide had risen, visions of fair forms in white garments were occasionally obtained, while many high-spirited maidens who could swim would venture out into the open, before closing the door, if no boats were about. Self-respecting ladies objected to this frequent loss of privacy, as also to the discomfort caused by children of all ages, who abused the privileges of the place; hence subscriptions fell off, then children and coloured nurse girls entered into possession. It ceased to be remunerative, fell into disrepair, and was removed to give place later to the existing men's bathing-stage. Wisdom is made the sport of Folly, so the efforts of genius are subjected to ridicule; consequently in our primitive state this well-intentioned attempt to promote health and recreation was known to the vulgar as " Old Archer's *Duck* Pond," or, for variety, " Archer's *Hen* coop."

Postage.   As all legal documents were required to be written on stamped paper, the Government used embossing dies to impress the respective values on the regulation foolscap. These dies had been utilised for postage purposes, and sheets of tinted paper, yellow, green, blue, were stamped all over with the requisite values, then gummed at the back, and issued to the Postmaster General. Stamps were cut off with scissors as required. The *Gazette* contained a notice that, after the 1st June, 1857, coloured postage stamps (obtained from England) and worth 3d., 6d., and 9d. respectively would be issued. This was welcomed as being a great improvement and likely to save much trouble. I believe this first issue of engraved Natal Stamps were not perforated.

Slavers. On the 21st June our local Cutter, the *Herald*, of 10 tons capacity, returned from a trading trip; she was an emigrant-ship's longboat, decked and fitted by our enterprising fellow-townsman, Mr. G. W. Duncan, a gunsmith, who, with his friend Charles Hillyard, a ship-wright, had sought to extend business by trading with the Portuguese, or with their settlements on the East Coast. They left Durban on the 8th May for Delagoa Bay. The published Manifest of the cargo they returned with indicates the nature of the coasting trade at that time:—" 78 elephants' teeth, 13 sea cows' teeth, 26 kafir baskets, 3 baskets rice, 60 bundles tobacco, 20 mats, 40 bags mealies, 2 bags bird seed (millet), 3 bags moss." Mr. Duncan was a man of superior intelligence, observant and enterprising. His report of the state of affairs at Delagoa clearly indicated that the slave trade was in full operation; two cargoes of natives, nominally rebels and prisoners-of-war, having been deported to other settlements during his stay in those waters. He wrote a very able letter on the subject to the *Mercury* in July, in consequence of the arrival here on the 22nd June of a rakish Schooner, pierced for guns, and having an exceptionally large crew, which anchored a long way out, and was duly visited by the Portboat. She was reported to be Spanish, the captain an American or Englishman who gave himself out as an honest trader from Havana to Madagascar with a cargo of rum, in want of provisions and water; he had sent his mate and a boat's crew lower down to buy provisions, but the boat got smashed on the rocks; he had directed them to come up by land to the proper port, and would pick them up, etc., etc. The old salts of the Portboat's crew saw signs which landsmen would not note. Anchored short to a warp, sails stopped, hatches newly battened down, well appointed boats, arm racks in the cabin, and a locker (accidently opened) containing what they imagined to be grape shot. The swarthy Spaniards who showed themselves constituted an extra large crew, without counting those reputed castaways in the boat. As the coxswain informed me, " they smelt a rat," and didn't stop any longer to jaw, but tumbled back into their boat in considerable trepidation, remarking incidentally, to cover their hasty

retreat, that there was a Man-o'-war Schooner inside requiring their services.   So they pulled away for home
without actually ascertaining the name of the vessel ; at
least I can find no record at the Port Office, and equally
strange the newspapers only speak of her as "A Slaver."
When the Mate (who proved to be the Supercargo) and
boat's crew subsequently arrived from the mouth of the
Umlaas, they found their Captain had "cut and run"
directly the Portboat left him ; hence it was concluded
that he took alarm at the apocryphal man-o'-war, and preferred losing his boat's crew and going on short commons,
rather than risk his ship and cargo.   The men were taken
before the Magistrate, who, having served the Queen of
Spain, spoke sufficient Spanish—when the vessel's name was
declared to be the *Menimtonka*, of New York, but the men
being Spaniards were all ignorant of anything more than
their Captain disclosed.   After requisitioning all the Saints
and vowing vengeance against the Captain when they came
within arm's-length of him, they were directed to be sent to
Cape Town at our expense as distressed seamen.

Pine Town and Rome. Mr. Van Prehn and family left Natal for the Cape on the 9th April.   In July Mr. Robert Acutt advertised the sale of Pine Town property, including the Indigo
Fabrick and the Pine Town Hotel known as "Fort Funk,"
by order of the Master of the District Court, in the matter
cf the suit Van Prehn *versus* Murray.   The "Fort" and
adjacent erven were purchased by the Rev. J. L. Crompton,
who converted it into his residence.   He acquired other
lands in Durban, and thus became a Burgess and Parishioner
of Durban, and elector for the County and Chief Ruler of
Pine Town.   But the eye of the Nonconformist Press was
upon him as a suspect, for in June a local showed : —

"ROME UNVEILED.—We understand that the Rev. Mr. Crompton,
who administered the sacrament at Pine Town Church on Sunday last,
made his appearance decorated by sundry little crosses, having also a
large mystical embroidered robe, similar to those worn by Romish
Priests. If such things are tolerated in Protestant Clergymen, what
can our religion by coming to ? "

This performance at St. John's, Pine Town, of which the
Rev. John Walton was then the incumbent, led to a public

meeting of the inhabitants and a general condemnation of the innovation.   The Bishop ultimately induced Mr. Crompton to confine the offending practices to the Oratory he constructed at his own residence.

As Durban and the Colony is largely indebted to the refined cultivated mind, the classical tastes and sound business abilities of the Rev. J. L. Crompton, these incidents are merely noted to connect him with much that comes after in the history of Durban.   If we are judges of what are extremes, let us at least credit him with having acted up to his beliefs as a Christian gentleman and well-abused ecclesiastic.

Indian Mutiny. On August 6th, by the Overland Mail from the Cape, we learnt that news had reached there *via* Mauritius of a hoax believed to have been played on the Ceylon Press by the alleged receipt at Point de Galle (Colombo) of carrier pigeons from Bombay with the report that the native troops at Bombay had mutinied, murdered all the Europeans, and robbed the Government chest of twenty-five millions sterling.   We also heard incidentally from private sources that one or two Sepoy regiments had mutinied and been disbanded, so comforted ourselves with the assurance that if there was ground for the report it must be exaggerated—reduced probably to 25,000 rupees; also that if a widespread rebellion had commenced, it would without doubt be speedily put down, with severe punishment to the rebels.   Our complacency was soon to have a rude awakening, for a month later, on receipt of the English Mail of July 8th, all loyal men held their breath as they realised that our Indian Empire tottered in our grasp, while the Ancient Briton in our nature began to thirst for the blood of the Cawnpore fiends and other murderers of defenceless women and children of our kith and kin.   Selfish though we might be, we were prepared to risk the Zulus without the aid of troops, and to send forward the eager old 45th, who desired to relinquish their long-expected return home, if only they might be sent to the front to avenge their comrades-in-arms.

Though but slightly linked to Durban's history, it is due to that able Statesman, Sir George Grey, Governor of the Cape, to record that, by a masterly assumption of power when the Indian disaster was but too painfully authenticated, he intercepted the transports with troops on their way to China—where, in conjunction with France, we had a little war—and ordered them to proceed to India instead. Their unannounced arrival at Calcutta was looked upon as a God-send, and by some eulogists is said to have saved India.

Education. On the 5th August the Rev. G. Y. Jeffreys and wife arrived per S.S. *Madagascar*, in deference to " a call " from the Congregationalists of Durban.   He waited upon me as Secretary to the Mechanics' Institution in reference to promoting a higher standard of education for boys than obtained at the Government Primary School.   Unsuccessful attempts in this direction had previously been made by private tutors. The question was felt to be of growing importance.   Being an experienced Schoolmaster, his advent and desire to supplement the modest income which his pastorate was likely to yield induced people to consider the future of our boys, and how best to advance them.

" A preliminary meeting of gentlemen interested in the cause of education was held in Mr. Acutt's Auction room on Friday evening last [19th Sept.]   Mr. Sanderson was called on to preside, and Mr. Pinsent acted as Secretary.   A long conversational discussion took place on the defectiveness and insufficiency of the existing means of education, in the Colony at large, and in this town in particular; and various views and suggestions were set forth for remedying the evil. The Rev. W. H. C. Lloyd (Colonial Chaplain), the Rev. C. Spensley (Wesleyan), and the Rev. G. Y. Jeffreys (Independent), and Messrs. Pinsent, Currie, Robinson, Dacomb, Gray, Russell, and the Chairman took part in the conversation, which at length resulted in an unanimous resolution for appointing a Committee to inquire into the whole matter of education at Durban, and to report to a general meeting of inhabitants.   The Committee consists of the Revs. W. H. C. Lloyd, C. Spensley, and G. Y. Jeffreys, with Messrs. Evans (Mayor), Sanderson, Rutherford, Lamport, Pinsent and Currie."

The result of their labours must be looked for later on, as the year apparently ran out without their reporting to a public meeting.

Photography. The first practical use of this newly-acquired art was thus announced early in October of this year:—

PHOTOGRAPHIC LIKENESSES.
Taken by the Collodion Process by
W. H. BURGESS,
Dispensing Chemist,
West Street, Durban, every Monday, Tuesday and Wednesday until
further notice.
Hours from ¼ past 10 a.m. till 3 o'clock p.m.
Terms Cash.

Mr. Burgess eventually removed to Verulam. Mr. Jas. Pulleyn, Mr. Brock, Fry and Co., and James Lloyd followed each other in quick succession as Photographic Artists, but, alas! the collodion process of the period has yielded to our climate, for few of their works survive them; they are now, with rare exceptions, faded ghost-shadows of the persons and scenes they "took," hence I am unable to reproduce them here.

Congregational Church. On Sunday, 25th October, the Rev. G. Y. Jeffreys was duly inducted into the pastorate of the Congregational Church. Recognition services in the new Chapel, Smith Street, were conducted by the Rev. Louis Grout and the Rev. J. Tyler, the Rev. D. Lindley delivering the charge to the Minister. The Revs. S. Pixley, W. Mellin, J. Allison, and H. A. Wilder, all of the American Board of Missions, took part in the services of the day. The Rev. C. Spensley preached in the evening, and we were said to have had a good time. I preferred Monday evening, when a Tea-meeting was held in the Chapel, and about two hundred persons were present. Tea was followed by the usual ministerial addresses, supplemented by speeches from Mr. A W. Evans (Mayor), and Mr. P. Lennox, both Deacons, as also from Mr. Councillor R. Harwin, a visitor. As every lady had of necessity to walk home, the seriousness of the proceedings were afterwards enlivened by escort duty.

An Infamous Trial. As an outcome of the clamour raised against Bishop Colenso, and the supposed unpopularity of his mission, his Clergy and party, a dastardly attempt to benefit by the sentiment was made by a man named Patrick Adrian Carnegy, whom Robinson Crusoe would have designated a "Renegado." On the 27th July he made a sworn deposition before the Resident Magistrate, charging :—"The

Bishop, Archdeacon McKenzie, Miss McKenzie, the Rev. Robert Robinson and his wife, with murder, sodomy, and conspiracy."

All this broadcast was too much for the Magistrate, or Clerk of the Peace; the complainant's gun was evidently overloaded. On further interrogation, he confined his aim to the Archdeacon alone, declaring " he knew of his own knowledge," and produced in support a little native girl who declared she saw the offence committed. Thus Archdeacon C. F. McKenzie was formally charged with the commission of an unnatural crime, the penalty for which, under Roman Dutch Law, was death. The Archdeacon was invited by the Superintendent of Police to attend a preliminary examination before the Resident Magistrate in August. The whole community was horrified; the newspapers denounced the charge and the man Carnegy before evidence was taken. The Court-room was packed. The prisoner *de facto* was allowed a chair at the Attorney's desk. I stood at the railing between him and the witness box, and was much impressed by the accuser, who was evidently a man of education (I learnt in later years that he was well-connected), notwithstanding his brazen umkempt mien, assumed coarseness of language and filthy vindictive utterances. His logical deductions and apt reasonings displayed a more than ordinary amount of shrewd and consecutive mental process. He fairly warmed to the strife on feeling the touch of blades as keen as his own. It appeared from the evidence that the cause of the attack was the conversion to Christianity by the Archdeacon—at his Mission Station, Umlazi (Rev. Robertson in charge)—of one of the native women with whom Carnegy consorted, and her refusal, under the Archdeacon's advice, to return to his kraal. It having come to Carnegy's knowledge that two children, a boy and a girl of his or his woman's acquaintance, had been received at the Mission, and that on an occasion of the Archdeacon's visit to the Station, the boy had slept in the hut usually occupied by the Archdeacon, the prurient imagination and depraved malice of the man conceived this opportunity for his diabolical revenge, so lodged the before-mentioned charges.

If any doubt lingered in the minds of the Magistrate or spectators as to his comprehensions of the force and nature of an oath, he sought to remove it by his reiterated abjuration of the Almighty at every detail of his polluting and disgusting story, which he now sought to improve by declaring himself an eye-witness.   The poor Archdeacon sat there scornfully stern, yet sick at heart and depressed by the filthy deluge of depravity poured out by the infant, baptised Patrick Adrian, "the Child of God, and an inheritor of the Kingdom of Heaven."   I watched him closely, and on my conscience believe, from the occasional movement of his lips and eyelids that he was inwardly praying for strength and grace under his martyrdom.   Native children and other witnesses named by Carnegy were examined, till finally the Clerk of the Peace asked the Magistrate to dismiss the accused, as the charge had not been established in any way, and in his opinion was a base conspiracy.

The informer having oversworn himself so thoroughly, and all his witnesses having failed, the Magistrate very properly ordered his arrest for perjury and conspiracy.   We retired to Agar's Canteen adjacent, to wash the foul taste of the perjured atmosphere and language from our virtuous mouths.

Carnegy was tried at a Circuit Court held on the 26th October before the Hon. W. Harding, Recorder.   The trial lasted the whole day.   Mr. Advocate Goodricke, assisted by Mr. G. Laurie, appeared for the prisoner.   The Indictment is a masterpiece of pragmatic quaintness such as constituted good law "when George the Third was King." The parties named in prisoner's depositions positively contradicted his allegations, and the Archdeacon solemnly denied the charge and all possible grounds for it, with the sole exception of the native boy having slept on the floor of the hut occupied by the Archdeacon on his visit to the Umlazi Station.

Dr. W. G. Taylor having sworn to his belief that the prisoner had acted under a monomania, the jury clutched at the word, which sounded well, and opened a door for their bewildered judgment, so brought in a verdict of "Guilty under a monomania;" but this was informal as to the indictment, so they retired again and cut the knot with plain

English, "Not guilty on the ground of insanity." The
Court ordered the prisoner " to be kept in strict custody in
Gaol, until the Queen's pleasure be known."

St. Paul's Church. The campaign was resumed on January
21st, when another disorderly meeting was
held, the Rev. W. H. C. Lloyd being in
the chair.   The supporters of the Vestry
in opposition to the Bishop, declined to have the offertory
taken up as by him requested, insisted upon raising money
for the purpose of paying off their creditor the Bishop, and
commenced by letting the pew sittings, which he had desired
should be free.   The next meeting is thus reported:—

" On Tuesday last [April 14th] the annual Vestry was held for the
election of Officers, &c. The Rev. W. H. C. Lloyd, Colonial Chaplain and
the minister of the Church, took the chair, and briefly opened the
proceedings. Want of space forbids our giving a full report of these
proceedings; indeed from the character of a great portion of them, it
would be impossible to do so. We can only give a picture rather than
a report; and even that must necessarily be a hasty sketch. The
meeting frequently degenerated into a babel and a brawl, the result
entirely of the constant interruption, speeches, and interpolations of
the Rev. Mr. Crompton—a very pure specimen of the genus Rome—
species Anglican—recently arrived and at present residing among us,
without cure of souls. This gentleman on entering the Church,
reverently bowed to the Altar; (a gentleman sitting near the aisle
mistaking it for a personal salutation, returned the courtesy). · He
commenced his (shall we say delegated?) task by questioning the
Chairman as to whether the meeting consisted only of members of
the Church—that is of those, as he defined the term, who partake of
the Communion at least three times a year, of which one shall be
Easter,—moving a resolution that all but such should be requested to
retire. Dr. Hulme (an interesting neophyte) seconded the motion;
and a long, noisy and confused discussion ensued. The Reverend
mover quoted Canon law to show that his position was a sound one,
and though he was repeatedly informed that the question of eligibility
had long ago been settled here; that in fact none but Churchmen took
part or voted in the Durban Vestry meetings; and that the Bishop
had enunciated a rule of admission different from the quoted Canon
law; he persisted in his course of impertinent and often insulting
interruption."

Mr. Saunders and Mr. Baker severally answered the rev.
gentleman, the latter giving an historical sketch of the
Durban Church affairs to show the irrelevancy of Mr.
Crompton's attempt to disturb the proceedings, and moved
" the order of the day," which was carried by 23 against 3.

Mr. Churchwarden Acutt presented the accounts for the past year, showing an income from collections and pew rents of £50 18s. 1d.   The expenses had been £50 5s., leaving a balance in hand of 13s. 1d.   Mr. J. Millar nominated Mr. R. Acutt as people's churchwarden, and the Minister proposed Mr. G. Rutherford.   These nominations were accepted, Mr. Rutherford undertaking the office on the understanding that some reliable source of income be established, whereby the present " disgraceful state of the Church " should be remedied, as he held that it was " disgraceful to the congregation " that the Church should remain in its present state.   Mr. Goodricke and other gentlemen insisted that the " disgrace " was due to the Bishop.

Mr. W. J. Haygarth was proposed as organist in place of Mrs. Cubitt, the original and present organist, she not being a Churchwoman, and without a vote.   Strong opposition to this ungracious change resulted in a resolution to let the appointment stand over " till ways and means " had been considered.

In May a Local states that:—" The inside walls of St. " Paul's Church are being plastered—a work much " needed, and the improvement already shown is very great." In this month a Bill was introduced into the Legislative Council by Mr. John Millar to constitute a free Vestry, at which every householder of Durban, being a member of the Church of England, was entitled to vote.   The officiating Minister and four members to form a quorum.   The Vestry having power to adopt, frame, alter, or rescind any rules or orders, or bye-laws, etc., not repugnant to the usages of the Church of England.   To sue and be sued ; let pews and sittings ; collect and spend money for charitable or religious purposes, and generally to establish irresponsible government.

On the 18th June, Mr. Millar, finding the members of the Council indisposed to meddle with ecclesiastical matters, withdrew the Durban Vestry Bill for the session, " and to give time for healing of differences."   A Vestry meeting held on the 30th June concurred in the withdrawal, and determined to open communication with the Bishop with a view to a settlement of the existing disagreements.   Their resolution was acted upon, for on Sunday, 30th August, the Bishop preached in St. Paul's both morning and evening, having met the Vestry, and conceded the offertory collection, except on Sacrament Sundays, and yielded in a conciliatory spirit to the views of the majority of the congregation with respect to matters not repugnant to the principles of the Church of England, and conformable to the usages observed in most of the dioceses at home. His Lordship also consented to promote a general Bill regarding Church of England Vestries in this Colony, but only to come into force in cases where a certain majority of the congregation desires its operation.

There was peace and prosperity until the 17th December, when the Vestry met to consider a circular from the Bishop, together with a draft Bill to regulate Church matters throughout the Diocese, as previously promised. But the Vestry, having repented their weakness, doubted if legislation was desirable for any other parish but their own, and regarded the Draft Bill as an artful trap to secure a dominant power to the Bishop, and stifle the voice of the laity. It was too much for them, since it foreshadowed ecclesiastical penalties for any who dared to carry out the Protestant principle of the right of private judgment in the genial manner they had hitherto done, so the following resolutions were carried by overwhelming majorities:—

"1. That this Vestry is in favour of a Legislative enactment for constituting a legal vestry for regulating the temporal affairs of St. Paul's Church, Durban. 2. That the Draft Bill now presented to this Vestry be rejected, as not meeting the requirements of the congregation—as not fulfilling the promises made—and, as not being in conformity with the laws and usages of the Church of England. 3. That this Vestry objects to a Synod under any circumstances as being contrary to the spirit of the Protestant Church of England as there by law established."

The Churchwardens accordingly advertised on the 26th December that at the ensuing session of the Legislative Council they would apply "for a Bill authorising the appointment of a Vestry and Churchwardens for the management of the temporal affairs of the said Church and Burial Ground thereof." Truly, "a merrie Christmas, my masters!"

Harbour Works. Governor Scott was of opinion that the immediate removal of the Bar was a necessity not likely to be realised under Mr. Milne's plans and administration; though the fact was patent that the Engineer had but limited funds at his disposal, yet the Bar might be induced to give way if some Engineer with a little more activity took it in hand. In these matters brooms must always be new, so the question of stopping the works until some other expert's opinion was obtained was brought before the Legislative Council in April, when Mr. J. Millar ably supported Mr. Milne, and recommended a more liberal policy; but the Legislative Council, after appointing a Committee, and hearing Mr. Milne, C.E., Messrs. G. C. and C. J. Cato, Captain Bell, and others, yielded to the Governor's desire on the 14th May by voting £1,500 for general purposes, and £500 for obtaining competent opinion from England as to Mr. Milne's plans and the prospect of a speedy cure. Accordingly on the 9th July Captain Pilkington and Lieut. Skead, R.N., arrived from the Cape, sent up by Sir George Grey at Governor Scott's request, to report generally on our Harbour, the Bar, and its works. During the year the formation of a Steam-tug Company had been mooted by the mercantile community; but vested interests, want of capital, problematical profit without compulsory towage, and finally a reliance upon the Legislature for a remedy, caused the relegation of the scheme to the limbo of good intentions.

Durban Corporation. The administration of the Police and Gaol was still in the hands of the Government as represented by the Police Board, of which the Town Clerk was Secretary. New uniforms were called for by tenders early in January. As the Government paid, the Gaolers and Police deferred more to the Magistrate, than to the Mayor.

Early in January the Council advertise that, having obtained the sanction of the Lieut.-Governor to raise £800 by the sale of Town Lands, a Block had been laid out immediately above the Botanical Gardens, and would be sold by auction by Mr. A. Clarence on the 13th March, at an upset price of £10 per acre. Terms 15 per cent. cash and cost of survey.   Balance in three instalments 3, 6, and 9 months, with interest at 6 per cent.   The Reporter records:—

"The sale at Mr. Clarence's rooms on Friday last was numerously attended, and the competition for the splendid lots above the Horticultural Society's Gardens was exceedingly brisk, the upper lots fetching from £16 to £18 15s. per acre; and the lower lots £10 5s. to £16. The lots near the Umgeni realised not much over the upset price of £10 per acre. . . . . The amount authorised (£800) was realised, and twenty of the lots advertised remained unsold."

During February, the contract entered into with one Forbes to enlarge the work commenced by Mr. Brickhill, and to cut a ditch up the Western Vlei for its permanent drainage, was completed.   The details as to its price, length, breadth, or depth, are not published, but it was expected speedily to convert that swamp into market gardens.   Some ten years later the alien Coolie successfully undertook the garden enterprise.

The County Councils having been revived, a necessary re-election of Councillors followed, and Dr. C. Johnston, having been requisitioned, resigned his position early in March as Town Councillor, upon his election for the Victoria County Council.   The rejoicings that followed were quickly dispelled—Mr. J. Millar having resigned and other changes taking place, Messrs. Lamport, Goodricke, Hartley, McArthur and Gillespie were chosen as Town Councillors during the year.   The Burgesses soon found that Mr. Lamport's energy and undoubted ability were secondary to his individuality, which checked the progressive business of the Borough, and set the Councillors by the ears.

A majority of the Council persisted in ordering that no road should be left on the ridge between the Town and County Lands.   A public meeting was held in June, when, as usual, the speakers were numerous, but a resolution was carried by a large majority directing that a road be left along the Borough Boundary, details to be left to the Council.

In July, the *Mercury* remarks:—

"STREET IMPROVEMENTS.—Smith Street, from the Congregational Chapel to Field Street, is undergoing great improvement by the filling up of the swampy hollows, and raising the lower part by removing the crown of the upper parts, thus rendering the road nearly level. Excellent footpaths are also being made on each side, and the new drains will effectually keep that part comparatively dry. We hope the Council will continue the improvements eastward along the same street, where either swamps or heavy sand-drifts, and the absence of a footpath, render the passage at all times difficult and wearisome. The trunk drain through Field Street also requires to be completed, with its feeders to drain the Vlei."

Referring to signs of progress the paper adds :—

" We might also notice the growth of substantial buildings for mercantile purposes both at Maritzburg and Durban. The spacious produce warehouse in course of erection by Messrs Evans & Churchill, of this port [in Field Street], exceeds, we believe, in dimensions any other single building in the Colony ; and indicates a just confidence in the increase especially of the wool trade."

In connection with this paragraph it may not be out of place to note that Mr. William Cowey had constructed a new Store in West Street, which he named " Britannia House," and opened for the sale of drapery and boots on Saturday, July 18th.

On the first Saturday in August, Mr. Alfred Winter Evans was elected Mayor, and, on meeting for business, the new Council commenced by working off arrears and granting applications for Leases on the new Maritzburg Road through the Berea, then named Block C—viz., Geo. Russell, 10 acres ;˙ W. Throssel, 5 acres ; W. Stonnel, 5 acres ; J. R. Saunders, 5 acres—for 50 years, at an annual rental of 7s. 6d. per acre, and subject to the erection of a house to the value of £25 before the expiry of the Lease. My choice was the Lots Nos. 1 and 2 (each 5 acres) at the corner of the Umbilo and Maritzburg Roads. I took possession on the signing of the Leases in October, and commenced clearing and fencing with the intention of cultivating. Some of the wild fig trees now growing there were originally posts planted by me. As the majority of the Councillors had no notion where the various Leasehold and other Blocks had been surveyed, the Town Lands Committee were authorised " to expend £10, if necessary, in procuring a complete plan or chart of the Town Lands."

It will be remembered that the first Council sneered at the " prosy " " harmless " letter of the Harbour Engineer, Mr. John Milne, in reference to their utilising Cato's Creek for drainage purposes. The " hard facts " introduced by the Umgeni itself, and now the persistent encroachment of its mouth towards the town, had caused the Corporation to refer again to Mr. Milne for his opinion upon the subject generally. He sent in a report confirming his " prosy " letter (to Mr. Cato when Mayor), and pointed out that cutting a channel or disturbing the surface of the Eastern Vlei, which was but the old vacated bed of the Umgeni itself, might in the event of future floods or overflows, every one of which tended to raise the existing river bed, cause the Umgeni to scour out any drain, and probably resume its ancient course into the Bay, to the detriment of the Harbour. The Eastern Vlei should undoubtedly be drained, but before doing so an embankment might be constructed of a substantial character near the Brickfields. Suitable clay having been found near the suggested site, the Council called for tenders for its construction, and in August, though they believed it to be insufficient, accepted that of Messrs. Gwyn and McAlister for £30. After some little difficulty with the Town Surveyor, they were only too glad to accept the offer of Mr. Milne to superintend the undertaking and the construction of the long drain that bears his name. To accomplish this last, they had to negotiate with the military authorities to allow the passage of the drain through the Ordnance land. Captain Grantham, the officer in charge of the Royal Engineers, acceded, offering valuable suggestions in conjunction with Mr. Milne, together with the services of the military ; so here again, the old 45th has left its mark on the face of the Borough.

At a meeting of Council on the 11th September, an application to lease 1 acre at the Congella for Salt Works was granted, but the same applicants, having asked for a lease of 10 acres of Bush Land (for the purposes of fuel, in connection with the manufacture of salt), were refused, on which the *Mercury* justly remarks, " What was the use of bush land to any tenant until it was cleared."

The remainder of the meeting, which sat from 6 to 11 p.m., was taken up by an attempt on the part of Mr. Mayor Evans to reconcile Councillors Lamport and Goodricke to the unparliamentary language which they had heaped upon one another at a previous meeting over the verbal construction of a resolution.

The complaint of certain Burgesses of the " East End," as to the state of the well in Pine Terrace, and their desire

for its removal into West Street, was referred to the Town
Committee.   Mr. J. A. Rich, having been interdicted from
building on the Admiralty Reserve [on the hill-end of Beach
Grove], the whole question of the Council's power to deal
with that portion of the Town Lands was thereby raised.
But as Mr. Rich was " intemperate " in attributing motives
to a Town Councillor, his letter was ordered to be returned
to the writer.   Mr. Councillor Goodricke succeeded in
giving the following notice of motion :—

" That this Council is of opinion that it is desirable to erect a Town
Hall and suitable offices for the transaction of the business of the
Borough ; together with a Borough Gaol ; and that application be
made to His Excellency the Lieut.-Governor for permission to sell
Town Lands to the extent of £2,000 sterling for that purpose, in
amounts of £500 annually ; and that the Town Surveyor be instructed
to bring up his plan and specifications for the erection of a Town
Hall."

This was followed by a notice by Mr. Councillor Gillespie :—

" That a Committee be appointed to consider the propriety of petitioning Government to place the management of the Borough Police
entirely in the hands of the Town Council, and the extra expense
thereby incurred, if any."

That the Council meant business is shewn by the fact
that at their meeting on the 27th September applications by
Gordge and Quested for Leases of Town Lands at the Congella were refused on the ground that in future it might be
desirable to extend that village, when the land would consequently be greatly increased in value.

An application for Berea Land by Mr. W. Elston was
refused for the reason that it might seriously interfere with
the Maritzburg Road, and the land might also be required
for public purposes. Tenders having been called for keeping
the public drains clean and in repair for 12 months, the
Council was shocked at the tender of a bold man named
Chick, who offered to do the work for £60.   Mr. Councillor
Hartley urged the immediate necessity of the work, which
only could be done by contract ; he thought the tender
highly advantageous to the Borough, there being 5,300
yards of drains and culverts to keep in repair.   Mr. Councillor McArthur opposed it ; they should be kept in order
as hitherto under the direction of the Town Committee ;
the culverts were useless—one being quite too small for a

·man to get in, and the large ones having no manholes what-
·ever; the cost of their repair for the present year need not
exceed £20. A long discussion ensued on drains, or what
were supposed to be such—mud holes, sluits, and bridges at
the "West End" of the Town. Some Councillors doubted
if these were included in the work contracted for, though
Mr. Hartley certified to the fact. The Mayor opposed the
reception of the tender until it could be shewn "that the
work was really adequate to the amount." Motion withdrawn until next meeting, when the tender was gratefully
accepted.

Tree planting was commenced about this time by the
Town Lands Committee. Accounts for Syringa trees,
supplied by Mr. G. Bottomley, Umbilo, were passed, and
the Botanic Gardens were looked to for supplies; the
Council having consented to make a road, ditched on each
side, over the flat from the old Maritzburg Road to the
lower entrance of the Gardens, half-way between the present
St. Thomas' and Sydenham Roads. Goats at that time
were kept for milking purposes; they had the key of the
street, and browsed on young trees, rose and mulberry
hedges, or garden stuff, indifferently. The Council was
appealed to on their behalf to save them from the penalty
of death under the Bye-laws, while the Curator at the
Botanic Gardens, when his mulberries were in fruit
appealed against other "kids."

At a meeting of the Council on the 14th October (Councillors Hartley and Harwin absent) a long and weary discussion, involving several amendments, ensued. Mr. Lamport's motion that all main roads on the Town Lands should
be 99 ft. wide, and bye-roads 66 ft. in width, also that
Blocks of land should be of uniform depths of 660ft., was
carried; Mr. Goodricke being outvoted. He had, as we
now think, properly urged that the matter of cutting up the
Berea and formation of lines of road should be left to the
judgment of the Surveyor and Town Lands Committee.
Mr. Goodricke was not happy under his defeat, consequently
at an adjourned meeting on the 16th October a regular
lingual sparring match took place between him and Mr.
Lamport on the several motions of which the latter had
given notice. 1st, "That 7s. 6d. be expended in purchas-

" ing a Minute Book, to be specially devoted to recording
" all matters connected with the leasing of Town Lands."
Mr. Goodricke considered it needless to expend even so
small a sum for the purchase of a book for Mr. Lamport's
scribbling.

2nd, " That the Town Surveyor be instructed to prepare a
" complete plan of the Town Lands for the use of the
" Council and the public." Carried.

3rd, "For rendering accessible the Lots on the Berea now
" surveyed, £50." Carried.

4th, " For improving certain sandy portions of the Town
" Lands by encouraging vegetable growth, and other means,
" £20." Carried.

5th, " For repairing the lower side of the cutting on top
" of the Maritzburg Road, through the Berea, £10."
Carried, though Mr. Goodricke objected, thinking that
some comprehensive plan should be adopted for improving
that disgrace to the Town, the Berea Road. He suggested
various means of doing this—by passing a Bye-law compelling empty wagons to bring clay or rubble to lay on the
road, by making a corduroy road, by obtaining a loan, or
by selling lands for the special purpose. Mr. Hartley supported this view.

6th, " For making a footpath to the S.W. corner of the
' Agricultural Gardens, £25." Mr. Goodricke seconded this
on public grounds, believing such a path desirable not only
for reaching the gardens, but also as rendering more feasible
a road or promenade on top of the hill, a thing much
desired. Mr. Gillespie thought as the land to the east of
the Gardens would be in request, the path should go to the
Garden gates. Resolved that the vote be for a path to the
Gardens.

At an adjourned meeting on the 21st October, the Mayor
and Mr. Harwin being absent, it transpired that the
Umgeni mouth had elongated itself a mile nearer town.
The Town Surveyor, having been ill, had neglected to report
on this encroachment, which was referred to in a report of
Mr. Milne's in reference to the Embankment. At the
opening of the meeting the *Mercury* reporter states:—

" The usual, and we may say, chronic discussion on the conduct of
the Town Surveyor now ensued, when unanimous censure was passed
on Mr. R. S. Upton, the perplexed, over-worked Surveyor.   Motions
and counter-motions by Councillors Lamport, Gillespie and Goodricke
as to the rent to be charged for Berea Leases, Building Sites or Agricultural Sites, for long or short periods, and ranging from 5/ to 30/
per acre, resulted in exuberance of diction and fluency of personalities.
At Mr. Goodricke's instance, the Chairman (Mr. McArthur)called Mr.
Lamport to order.   Mr. Lamport would not submit to the sneers of
Mr. Goodricke or anyone else ; he would give that gentleman a Roland
for his Oliver.   Mr. G. said he would give Mr. L. a little more if he
did not behave himself.   Mr. Lamport : ' Ridiculous, ridiculous ! '
Mr. Goodricke felt moved to join in under Section 26, and called upon
Mr. L. to apologise.—Chairman thought Mr. L. had been out of order.
Mr. Lamport disclaimed improper motives in a neat speech with a
sting in its tail.   Mr. Gillespie considered the explanation highly unsatisfactory, as Mr. L. had for half an hour been uttering the foulest
imputations, and ought to positively withdraw his words.   If such
language were to be used again he would cease to attend meetings
where a Councillor was constantly and at every stage imputing motives of an unworthy character.   The Chairman concurred, and told
Mr. L. that an apology was really due from him.   Mr. Lamport disclaimed, and if any words had slipped, &c., fully withdrew them.   Mr.
Gillespie said that was sufficient, whereupon the Chairman, with a
twinkle in his eye, and a breath of heather in his voice, remarked that
if such scenes were likely to continue, he should consider it his duty
to move that at least one night a week be set apart for the despatch
of business, and one for the wrangling of those members who had
shown themselves of so pugnacious and disputatious a disposition."

The Reporter agreed and regretted : —

" That we are unable to present our readers with a verbatim account
of the above fracas, but the rapid utterance, and confused spiteful
eloquence of these knights of the sneer and quibble, preclude our
giving anything like a complete report of the episodical duello ! "

" As iron sharpeneth iron, so a (Council) man sharpeneth
" the countenance of his friend," and posterity of to-day
may gather from the foregoing the difficulties experienced
by their fathers during the " Fifties " in dealing with their
inheritance. They had before them a clean sheet, and,
because it was so, were equally divided as to its disposal.
At this time Mr. Lamport and Mr. W. Hartley were the
only members of the Corporation who had definite views on
the subject ; but they were regarded with suspicion, as
daring innovators, toying with a public trust. Mr. Lamport was much too advanced ; his idea being that the Town
Lands should be cut up into small townships or villages in

preference to granting leases promiscuously to any Burgess who might apply. Mr. Hartley was more practical and utilitarian, holding that the leasing of lands meant occupation by the tenant, employment to the Burgesses, or in any case a permanent revenue to the town. In this most of the Councillors concurred, and the Burgesses did not protest; hence it became the practice for a prospector, after looking out a nice locality, to place his thumb on the Town Clerk's plan, and apply for a 5-acre lot " somewhere about here !" The problem was then submitted to the Town Surveyor, who was directed to confer with applicant, and survey " as near as possible."

The perplexed Town Surveyor was of necessity a man of right lines and angles, so sought to establish baselines, and keep within his Block and the road instructions of the Council. He roughly outlined Blocks on paper, marking them A, B, or C., with the result that, as someone applied for a Lot, say, in Block B, to the North of the Gardens, and another had also applied for a Lot in the same Block to the North of the Berea Road, the first Lot surveyed would be numbered, say, 1, while the second Lot might be numbered 30. Applications might be delayed a few months, then the adjoining Lots to 1 and 30 be applied for, and in order of time, surveyed and leased; so it came about that No. 1 might be bounded by No. 60, while No. 30 might be bounded by 61.

The above sketch of part of Block B shows the actual consecutive Lots about a mile and a half apart.

It will be understood that, had the Council credited Mr. Upton with the common sense which they claimed for themselves, he would have laid out the land in Sections, the Lots numbered consecutively, and fitted in his roads according to the contour of the ground, regard being had to haulage and drainage. As the pay was very small, and the work very hard, accuracy of detail was not expected; a yard or two either way did not matter then, though we quarrel over the missing link now.

Imagine a dense semi-tropical forest, choked with undergrowth, stringey and thorny. The Surveyor climbs a large tree as his starting point; his man Friday is induced to do likewise; observation is taken by pocket compass, and another prominent tree selected " somewhere about there "; this is pointed out to the intelligent native, who makes a mental note of it. Descending first for a long sapling and a square yard of calico, which are secured by the Surveyor to the tree as its flag, man Friday is directed to take a similar flag and find No. 2; when found his banner is to be displayed.

Meantime Surveyor lives in hopes that it will come out alright, adjusts his compass bearings, and sets his native path finders to cutting a tunnel through the undergrowth sufficient to let in a little daylight; bowling rods are set up in the way they should go, and he re-climbs tree No. 1 to look out for Friday's banner without a device. On discovery he signals his recognition to the native, who returns to pilot him to the spot. No. 2 is ascended and, if the prospect charms, business is proceeded with; if otherwise, another big tree is selected and the alignment readjusted. When the line has been correctly cut it only remains to drag the chain so many times along it, hammering in a bush peg as the different lots are measured; but care was taken that no more work was done than the orders in hand required. Finding the bush pegs afterwards was always a matter of difficulty; should a tree stump be in the way, what more natural than for the settler to erect his beacon (itself usually a bush pole) a foot or two clear of it?

As all Leases were put up to Auction to fix the rental, the Town Surveyor pointed out the Beacons to the purchasers and obtained a receipt for them; after that we renewed our own pegs, when the white ants or other animals had removed the originals; hence the existing errors in survey, for which neither Mr. Upton or his old-time theodolite are to be blamed, though disrespectful people averred that instrument was capable of shooting round corners!

In November the Council finally advertised the regulations they had adopted : —

FOR THE LAYING-OUT OF PORTIONS OF TOWN LANDS.

FOR SALE AND LEASE.

Are published for general information

1. That blocks of land shall be laid out 660 feet in depth.
2. That in all cases, there shall be laid off a road at the front and back of each lot.

UPSET RENTAL.

Class 1. For all plots of ground with a frontage to either of the two branches of the Maritzburg Road, and for all plots of land on or near the summits of the ridges, which may be designated as Villa lots—

For 21 years, 10s. per acre.
For 50 years, 15s. per acre.

Class 2. For all plots in all other situations not presenting any special and peculiar advantages—

For 21 years, 5s. per acre.
For 50 years, 7s. per acre.

Parties intending to Lease portions of Town Lands are requested to frame their applications in conformity with these regulations.

By Order of the Mayor and Council,

MARK FOGGIT, Town Clerk.

Durban, November 6th, 1857.

In this connection I may observe that the road spaces ordered to be reserved between blocks of leased lots were left uncleared. If the tenant wanted to convey material on to his plot by wagon, he was at liberty to select the easiest route through the thinnest bush, and cut down any tree in his way. If he had not taken the precaution to clear a sufficient space on his ground in which to turn, he had of necessity to effect a retrograde movement, reversing his oxen and hauling out backwards. The price of bricks, water, and sawn timber, was thus much enhanced, but perseverance, aided by the universal hatchet, the wheels of the wagon, and the hoofs of the oxen, soon established a thoroughfare sufficing for the pioneer and his next neighbour.

Fencing was then never thought of ; a particular person might avail himself of the Surveyor's lines to stick in a few Fig-tree posts, Mulberry slips, or young Syringas, just to mark his boundary, or serve as fence standards in after years.

The clearing of the new Maritzburg Road connecting with Smith Street was an exception; being required for traffic purposes it was cleared by convicts and stumped; the fire-wood, not taken away by Limeburners, Brickmakers, Bakers and other Burgesses, was burnt on the spot, root stumps being piled up on either side as a sort of border fence, and there left to the white ants, lizards, snakes, and other oldest inhabitants.

The grand old Fig-tree standing in Mr. Throssel's land, seen from the end of Smith Street, served as a beacon. Mr. Upton, having an eye for beauty and regard for the practical, concluded, like the poet G. P. Morris' "Woodman," to "spare that tree," since its removal from the line of road would be expensive and tedious, its limbs and roots covering quite an acre of ground. He accordingly cut his line a wagon-whip's length from the stem. Beyond a little ageing of the lower limbs, it is to all appearance as verdant and sturdy as when first exposed to the admiration of beholders in 1857. It is equally to the credit of Mr. Wm. Throssel, who, as before noted, acquired a lease of the land on which the tree grows at the first letting of Lots in Block C, that he has ever since carefully conserved this ancient ornament to the Berea; let us hope that his energetic son will adopt the words of the singer, "In youth it sheltered me, and I'll protect it now." The curious in detail may be informed that the alignment or direction of the Maritzburg Road through the Bush was determined by that of the new Umbilo Road, which was ordered to skirt the bush in a straight line until the open flat near the Congella was reached; strict injunctions being given to avoid as much as possible encroaching upon the grazing area. When this was accomplished the idea was originated of joining Smith Street with the Maritzburg Road. The big Fig-tree obtruded itself as a beacon, since its position suggested a possible future junction with West Street, so that point was selected, and a line struck at right angles to the Umbilo Road, it being found on inspection to afford an easy gradient up the hill, while it facilitated the right-angled sub-division of adjacent Blocks or Lots. The roads dividing these Blocks were named after the original resident tenants, Moore, Clark, Davenport, and McDonald.

In consequence of the latent desire of the Corporation to take over the Town Police, and the profits derivable from licences, etc., the Town Committee made special investigation into the Police and Prison organization. On their report the Council memorialised the Government for the construction of a suitable gaol, the removal of the Hospital from the present Tronk, and a separate building for a Lock-up. It was also pointed out in forcible language that the circumstances connected with the occupation of that small Erf by so many and varied persons, the disposal thereon of their refuse and other matters, was perfectly disgraceful and injurious, concluding with a request that the Police and the collection of Licences be handed over to the Borough. While the reforming or progressive spirit prevailed at this meeting, a "good intention" motion was recorded, as to the advisability of taking steps toward the establishment of a Public Market.

The Council on the 15th November considered a reply from the Government as to Gaol, to the effect that the revenue would not allow of the expenditure necessary for a new Gaol, Durban not requiring it more than other parts of the Colony, and offering to take any superfluous prisoners to Maritzburg if desired. Government would also do all in its power to carry out any municipal regulation with regard to injurious deposit of nightsoil, a practice which, being common to the whole town, could not be specially treated in the case of the Gaol. Smarting under this "retort courteous," the Council, after a wordy war between Mr. Lamport and Mr. Goodricke, in which all the Councillors took part without securing an apology from Mr. Lamport, resolved to fine Mr. Sidney Peel and Mr. Edward Snell (ex-Mayor) twenty shillings each for encroaching on town lands at Montpelier, Mr. Goodricke dissenting on the ground of the illegality of the resolution. But, at their next meeting, Mr. Goodricke being absent, they ordered that Mr. Vinnecome, a pianoforte tuner, should be fined for riding on the Market Square footpath. These fines have yet to be collected.

Captain Grantham, R.E., having volunteered a report on the expediency of speedily opening out the mouth of the Umgeni, and offering the aid of the military for that purpose at a probable outlay of £20, a motion was proposed to vote £20 or £30 for the purpose, but a conflict of opinion arose as to the probable cost and possible efficiency. The Council apparently got out of the wrangle by adopting the suggestion of a member, and left the matter to Nature. A resolution was, however, passed, " That the Resident " Engineer, Mr. Milne, be requested to give a plan of the " Embankment, with the necessary modifications, now that " clay has been proved to exist in that locality." At the regular monthly meeting on 30th November, the Council, satisfied with their improved prospects from rents of leased lands, fixed the Annual Rates at 8d. in the £ on the rental of occupied property, and 2d. in the £ on freehold value of unoccupied property.

Attorney-General. On the 12th November the *Mercury* informed us that the *London Gazette* had notified the appointment of Michael Hanney Gallwey, Esq., as Attorney General for Natal. On the arrival of the S.S. *Madagascar* on the 6th December, that gentleman himself put in an appearance, and has ever since been on the record, with the added distinction of knighthood and the merited honour of being Chief Justice of the Colony. That Sir Michael H. Gallwey is indissolubly associated with the progress and history of Old Durban and the Natal of to-day is well within the recollection of the older generation, for in his capacity as Attorney General he was the ruling spirit and leader of the " House " in our first Legislative Councils. He had, in addition to framing new laws, to keep us within old ones. Natal as a Colony has never sufficiently credited him with what he did, much less with what he did *not* do under the trying circumstances of reconciling and guiding the diverse representatives of a very free people, of varied nationalities, with the Native looking on.

Fast Day. December 23rd was set apart by Proclamation as a day of humiliation and prayer for the success of our arms in India. The date was not well chosen if the prayers of the many were to avail. Services were indeed held, but indifferently attended, as Burgesses were preparing for Christmas Day; besides, the Lieutenant-Governor's direction came rather late, for without our aid Delhi had fallen and Lucknow been relieved, while a fair proportion of captive mutineers had been blown from mortal guns, and thus deprived of immortality. What more could pious Christians ask for?

Steam Saw Mills. Among the events of the year should be recorded the opening of the first steam-mill for sawing and grinding by Mr. Wm. Royston. It was situated on the beach end of Field Street, opposite Mr. John Brown's premises. We made capital out of this, and hinted that larger undertakings of a similar character were in contemplation in the town. Our sample steam-mill was built of yellow-wood, having an upper floor supported on either side by lean-to's, one for the boiler and engine, the other for the saw-bench. The capacity of the engine was $2\frac{1}{2}$ horse power; it drove one pair of stones and a crusher; also a circular saw that, with care, would cut a 9 inch deal into planks, and was for a time kept fully employed. It afterwards drove the first Cotton Gin introduced into Durban by Mr. Payne, who endeavoured unsuccessfully to revive the cotton industry.

Crinoline. Ladies may be interested to know that in February appeared the first public notice, taken from the English news, that petticoat hoops had been revived; this was followed in March by the real thing, advertised by Messrs. Wirsing and Acutt as "Crinolines and Corded Petticoats." There was a certain fastness about these things, which, being unsuitable for the Dutch trade, did not "take on" with Colonial customers, as we do not find them stocked by those decent drapers, Richard Harwin and Wm. Cowey, until a year or so later, when the influx of ladies from England with the latest fashions rushed us to the extreme depicted in *Punch*, where the huge tubular-hooped skirts of the passengers are hung like magnified parrot cages round the tops of the London Omnibuses. To the advent of this hideous fashion is to be attributed the loss of consideration, courtesy, and

gentlemanly refinement towards women, which is characterised as "Colonial manners," in consequence of the
inability of the male person to get within arm's length to
cherish and support, without the aid of a "Low-backed
Car." Woman then learnt to walk alone, and she now
claims her emancipation. May an old emigrant hope that
the liberty of the parents will not sanction licence in the
children.

Masonic Hall. Early in March Mr. George Winder advertised that he had taken over McDonald's
"Family and Commercial Hotel," the
arrangement with Mr. Galloway having apparently fallen
through. In December he announces that he has re-named
it, the "Masonic Hotel." Various private meetings of
Freemasons having been called at "Brother Winder's"
Hotel, they decided upon forming a Lodge, and holding
their meetings at that place, Mr. Winder having offered his
new dining-room for that purpose. This room has only
recently been replaced by the large and elegant dining hall
of the "Royal Hotel," as now named.

Building Society. The Durban Building Society No. 1, Mr.
John Gray, President, held its first annual
meeting on the 21st August. Building
Societies No. 2 and 3 were also organised
and started during this year.

News Room and Exchange. An attempt was made by Mr. George
Robinson, proprietor of the *Natal Mercury*,
to open on the 1st October the "Durban
Commercial News Room and Enchange,"
in the premises known to us as Grundy's store on the Market
Square (now the offices of the Natal Land and Colonization
Company) adjoining his residence and the *Mercury* publishing office. All newspapers obtainable on view, and such
samples of national and manufactured products as may be
sent for exhibition; yearly subscribers 20s., occasional subscribers 2s. 6d. a month. This was to fill up a supposed
gap between the Durban Club, the Mechanics' Institution,
and the "Hard Facts" of the Chamber of Commerce. I
hope I may not be doing the enterprise an injustice, but I

have a belief that its conversion to other uses speedily followed.

Horses.   Horses traded in the Free State and reared in the upper districts of the Colony were becoming plentiful, and the possibilities of an export trade to Mauritius and India induced Mr. Gillespie and other merchants to venture a trial shipment, so on the 29th December 42 horses and 1 quagga were shipped per barque *Rydal* to Mauritius.

They were made to swim off to the ship behind a boat, slings were then fitted on, and they were "hove up" by the slow process of the ship's winch, and stowed below on top of water casks in the sand ballast. Hay was not manufactured, so Oat Forage, Mealies, and Bran formed their diet; bedding was considered unnecessary. Prices realised were said to have been satisfactory, but the experiment was not repeated.

Fine Arts Exhibition.   The 31st December, New Year's Day, and the 2nd January were appropriated to festivities, because the Agricultural and Horticultural Society was short of funds. They had advertised that they were unable to offer prizes at their Annual Show on the 1st of January, but hoped farmers would nevertheless send their exhibits. To raise funds they purposed holding a Variety Show extending over three days, which they euphemistically described as a "Fine Art Loan Exhibition," including Ombres Chinoise, Witch's Dance, Christmas Tree, Readings and Recitations, Magic Lantern, and Acted Charades, the opportunity being taken to utilise Messrs. Evans and Churchill's new double-storied wool warehouse in Field Street, it having just been completed. As Fine Arts were exceptionally rare, the chief article of attraction and the most imposing was a full life-size replica of "Diana Hunting," by Rubens, about 12ft. by 8ft., the property of Dr. Julius Schulz. We had to accept family portraits and scenery in oils, or which Mr. Robert Acutt was the chief contributor, also watercolours, chalks, and even pen and ink; the standard engravings of the period by Landseer, Wilkie, and others, framed and glazed; the representations of the Coronation of Her Majesty

Victoria, her Marriage, the Baptism of the Prince of Wales,
the Queen, Prince Consort, and Royal children receiving a
casket from the Duke of Wellington ; Landseer's Newfound-
land Dog worked in wool, and other sampler work, with
curios brought from foreign parts, and natural history curios
found in the Colony.   To make up for any weariness to
the flesh, and as a relaxation to the juveniles, the Christmas
Tree speculation was on the upper floor, which was set apart
as a concert room, where a stage and drop curtain were
extemporised, and Charades and Drawing-room pieces of the
" Box and Cox " order were produced by skilful amateurs,
interspersed with vocal and instrumental music   Thus we
saw the New Year in, and, as Pepys would have recorded,
" all vastly entertaining, and so home and to bed."

CHAPTER XIII.

1858.

JOHN RICHARDSON GOODRICKE, MAYOR.

May 6th.   Re-elected August 7th.

THE year was opened by the arrival on the 8th January of the Screw Steamer *Waldensian*, 350 tons, Capt. W. A. Joss, which was intended to run in conjunction with the *Madagascar* as a Mail Service, the Agency of which had been transferred to Mr. John Brown.   In this capacity, they continued to serve for mails, passengers, and cargo, between Durban, Cape Town, and intermediate ports; Capt. Joss becoming quite a popular favourite, finding plenty of time between arrival and departure for visits with horse and gun to surrounding Planters.

Unfortunately for us the *Madagascar* was lost before the year was out between East London and Algoa Bay.

Wesleyan Church. Another early event was the opening of the new Wesleyan Church in West Street, with the bustle and mild excitement consequent upon the attendant ceremonies.   The long contemplated bazaar, which had been postponed from time to time awaiting expected presents of goods from England per *Waldensian*, was held in Messrs. Evans and Churchill's new Wool Store, kindly lent for the occasion, on the 6th,

7th and 8th of January, with marked success, realising the large sum of £280 9s. 8d. cash.

"This result, considering the pleasure drain of the previous week, the prevailing scarcity of money, and the smallness of the population, is truly astonishing, and must be regarded as an evidence of the elasticity and liberality of the people of Durban."

On Sunday, 10th January, the spacious and elegant building (60ft. by 35ft., 18ft. to the wallplate, then the largest in the Colony) was opened for Divine Service.

In the morning the Rev. C. Spensley preached his first and, we regret to say, his last, sermon in the new Chapel, taking the appropriate text, "Glory to God in the highest, on earth peace and goodwill to men."

In the afternoon the Rev. G. Y. Jeffreys (Independent), and in the evening the Rev. D. Lindley (Presbyterian), preached. The total collections amounted to £51 16s. 3d.

On the following Tuesday the necessary Tea-meeting came off in the old Wesleyan Chapel, where I made one of the numerous company that participated. The Rev. Mr. Spensley and his equally esteemed wife were about to return to England owing to ill health; we never expected to see them again.

The usual addresses and motion, saddened by a "rising vote" of sympathy and appreciation by the meeting, were followed by a tearful farewell by the reverend gentleman, who had laboured earnestly and unselfishly, not so much to make converts as to do any good work among us in a truly evangelic spirit. He was in the Protestant community what Father Sabon was among the Roman Catholics. Their acts were only circumscribed by their beliefs. The meeting was a memorable one, as the giddiness engendered by the Tea was sobered in the almost pathetic farewell handshaking that we one and all sought from himself and amiable wife, before quitting the room. They left the Colony in the *Waldensian* on the 14th January, and Mr. Spensley was succeeded in the Durban pastorate by the Rev. J. Gaskin.

St. Paul's Church. The report of the above events and the full copy of the Address to the Rev. Mr. Spensley occupied so much space in the *Mercury* that the Editor was obliged to cut out the more commonplace proceedings of a Vestry meeting when the reconstructed Draft Bill, to be brought before the Legislature on the lines previously indicated, was introduced. .

The omission may not be our loss, notwithstanding the sublime idea that words once spoken go rippling on for ever, as the adjourned meeting of 18th January, instructive and emphatic as it was, opened with a motion by Dr. Holland, seconded by Mr. Winder :—

"That this meeting be adjourned until this day six months.

"This motion, after some violent language from Mr. Raw, was withdrawn, when four of the members went to the door, under protest, but ultimately returned, interrupted the reading of the minutes, and entered into several arguments and noisy discussions, asserting that the Church of England was not an episcopal church. Dr. Holland was especially earnest in asserting this.

"The Draft Bill was then read by Mr. Churchwarden Acutt. Mr. Baker before moving its adoption made several remarks on the necessity existing for such an Act, referring collaterally to the duties of a bishop and curate. He was much interrupted by the interpolated protests and galvanically delivered remarks of Dr. Holland, and by the laughs, Ho-ho s and Ha-ha's of Mr. Raw. Mr. W. H. Acutt seconded the adoption of the report.

"Dr. Holland and Mr. Winder moved that the Bill be rejected.

"Mr. Goodricke rose to speak to the amendment, as he did not approve of the original motion, and proceeded at some lengh to express his views, but was often stopped by the noise proceeding from the same two gentlemen, who took great umbrage at being styled by Mr. Goodricke the 'Bishop's party.' Dr. Holland threatened to tell Mr. Goodricke to which party he belonged.

"At Mr. Goodricke's suggestion, Mr. Baker altered his resolution to the adoption of the preamble only. On the amendment being put, ten hands were in its favour ; against it appeared likewise ten hands, a fact apparently so astonishing that for some time Mr. Raw refused to credit it, and it was only after several upliftings that this gentleman's loudly expressed doubts were satisfied, or rather, we should say, silenced.

"The Chairman gave his casting vote for the original motion.

"Meanwhile during the progress of this consummation, an episode of a startling, we might say alarming, character was being enacted.

"During the confusion that was prevailing Mr. Goodricke in a significant tone asked Mr. Raw, "what he got for going there?" Mr. Raw, starting back in a melodramatic attitude—'You scoundrel, you villain, you good-for-nothing.' Mr. Goodricke—'Ha-ha-ha !' Mr. Raw, still more excited—'You scoundrel, I tell you you're no gentleman. How dare you insult me so? I appeal for protection to the Chair; I won't be insulted.' The original motion was here put, with of course the same result. Those opposed to it immediately left the Church, and with them Mr. Raw, whose passion seemed to have been either of a dramatic and therefore assumed nature, or of an exceedingly evanescent and vapoury character, for on passing Mr. Goodricke he shook hands with that gentleman most heartily, and in a spirit apparently of the serenest and most genial good humour.

"The clauses of the Bill were then discussed and passed by the remaining members of the Vestry. A petition to the Legislature in favour of the Bill is in course of signature, by which the true state of public opinion among the congregation of St. Paul's Church will be tested and made known."

On the 4th February the Churchwardens gave notice by advertisement that the proposed Bill would be brought before the Legislative Council at the forthcoming session.

On Tuesday evening, 16th March, a meeting of the male members of St. Paul's met, as directed by the Bishop's Pastoral Letter, to elect two delegates to the proposed Church Conference, to be held in Maritzburg, to consider the subject of a Synod. The attendance was more numerous than usual, between 40 and 50 being present. The Colonial Chaplain presided. Mr. Baker led off by condemning the proposed Conference and Synod, but recommended delegates to convey the sentiments of the meeting to the Conference. Mr. Churchwarden Acutt was consistent on the same side. Dr. Holland supported a Synod, and moved that Messrs. Winder and Raw be the delegates; seconded by Mr. Savory. Mr. J. D. Shuter was opposed to a Synod, and declared they would not be overpowered by priestly domination, and proposed an amendment accordingly, which, however, was withdrawn in favour of an amendment by Mr. Baker:—"That whilst strongly protesting against a Synod "and the proposed Conference, this meeting appoint Messrs. "Churchwarden Acutt and Sidesman Gillespie to be its "delegates to represent its views." Mr. Goodricke seconded, adding that they did not want a Synod. The Bill now before the Legislature, he was happy to say, was sure to pass. A division took place on the amendment, when 35 votes appeared in its favour, and only 4 against it. It was afterwards resolved that the expenses of the delegates be paid out of the Church funds. While approving the principle, both the gentlemen nominated declared their intention to defray their own expenses. A vote of thanks was passed to the chairman, who, surprised at the courtesy, congratulated the meeting on its good temper

The Bill Mr. Goodricke had so surely prophesied about was duly entrusted to the Borough member, Mr. John Millar, who on the 24th March moved in the Legislative Council the return of the St. Paul's Church Bill to the Committee of the House, with instructions to allow the promoters to alter the preamble. The ensuing discussion ended in the withdrawal of the Bill, the majority of the Council being against the motion. The *Mercury* reports: —

"Vestry Meeting.

"The usual meeting for the appointment of officers, &c., was held on Tuesday evening, 8th April. Mr. Rutherford, one of the Churchwardens, not wishing to continue in office, Mr. Gillespie was chosen in his place, and Mr. R. Acutt was re-elected. Mr. Goodricke and Mr. W. H. Acutt were re-elected sidesmen. Thanks were voted to the Churchwardens, and also to Mr. Goodricke for his zeal in promoting the Church Bill. A resolution was passed adopting the provisions of the rejected Bill for the government of St. Paul's Mrs. Cubitt was re-elected organist, on condition of acting also as leader of the choir."

The Church Conference suggested by the Bishop of Natal was formally opened in Pietermaritzburg on the 20th April. A full report appears in a supplement of the *Mercury* of 22nd May. His Lordship's charge was of some length and of great earnestness, chiefly urging the necessity of establishing synodical action, and *inter alia* expressing a hope that one result would be the healing of the breach between himself and the Durban Churchmen. The clergy and laity throughout the diocese, and of St. Paul's, were duly represented. It need only be noted here that the Conference rejected the proposal for a Synod, but agreed to a Church Council, also that electors need not be communicants. This dire heresy was carried by the laity vote, after a clerical motion, that on special subjects the clergy should vote together, and on other subjects the laity together, had been defeated.

It was specially noted that Bishop Colenso's conduct throughout seemed to have been liberal and conciliatory; the reporter may have been induced thus to express himself owing to the loss of a motion by Canon Jenkens, to give the Garrison of Fort Napier and heathen Christians *(sic)* the right to send delegates to the Council, and the Canon's subsequent action in solemnly protesting, being joined by Archdeacon McKenzie, Dean Green, and Rev. R. Robertson; these gentlemen shook the Conference dust off their feet, bowed and retired from the meeting, and furnished, in lieu of bell, book, and candle, a written withdrawal from all communication; thus causing the clergy rift in the laity lute, which the Bishop was so zealously striving to attune.

It is gratifying to observe that both Churchwardens of St. Paul's voted in support of their Bishop.

To record the outcome of this first gathering of professing Christians for the promotion of the Church of England in Natal, and to mark the commencement of the so-styled "Colenso Schism," I take over the comments of the *Natal Mercury* of the 6th of May:—

"SCHISM.—We understand that the Very Reverend the Dean of Maritzburg, the Venerable the Archdeacon and Canon Jenkens, constituting (with one exception) the Dean and Chapter, have 'presented' Bishop Colenso to the Metropolitan Bishop of Cape Town, for holding 'heretical' views on certain doctrines of the Church; especially the doctrine of the Eucharist. The Bishop's views on that subject as recently expounded in two sermons, now published, are conformable in the main, with those held by Evangelical Protestant Christians of all denominations; while those of the very reverend, venerable and canonical schismatics, are a close approximation to the Transubstantiation of the Church of Rome.

"Hence their 'presentation' of the Bishop's 'heresy'

"Canon Calloway is no party to this affair."

Unfortunately for their piety, zeal, and consistency, they did not profit much by their pains, for the *Mercury* of the 2nd September reports:—

"It is said that the present mail brings the reply of Bishop Grey, the South African Metropolitan, to the charge of heresy, touching the doctrine of the Eucharist, brought against the Bishop of Natal by the High Church Dean and Chapter of Maritzburg; and that Bishop Grey rebukes the complaining clergy for their interference and recommends them to apologise to their ecclesiastical superior."

As for the Bishop's "Schism," the present generation may be surprised to learn that "Colenso on the Pentateuch" had nothing to do with the case; that able work, which his friend Dean Stanley said would live after we were forgotten, was not then written.

The Rev. W. A. L. Rivett, who had been ordained in the Cathedral, Pietermaritzburg, on the 30th May, officiated for the first time in Durban on Sunday, 6th June. He preached four times; in the morning at 9 o'clock to the Military in St. Paul's Church, in the same Church at the usual morning and evening services; in the afternoon at the Point.

He was to take up his ministry at the Umhlanga, Verulam, and Mount Moreland on the following Sunday. Truth obliges me to quote again from the *Mercury* of the 2nd September : —

"At a very select Vestry meeting at St. Paul's Church yesterday afternoon, Dr. Holland was elected a Churchwarden in the room of Mr. Gillespie, resigned, by a majority of 6 to 4 votes. Under the new regulations of the Church Council it appears that the press is excluded unless its representatives happen to be Churchmen who have subscribed the roll. We understand much unseemly altercation occurred as usual on these occasions, in consequence of which Mr. Acutt, the senior Churchwarden, resigned his office. Affairs do not appear healthy in the Church, notwithstanding the recent doctoring."

As is shown by the previous record, Mr. R. Acutt had no special objection to " unseemly altercations "; the true reason for his resignation was the election of the more submissive Dr. Holland.

The excluded reporter has omitted to note that a new man from England, in the person of Mr. A. M. Barnes (Mr. Gillespie's bookkeeper) was elected or nominated in his place. Both the new churchwardens immediately after advertise their attendance at the church " to receive applica- " tions and to appoint sittings."

Peace seems to have settled for a time on the church; or the absence of the Non-Conformist newspaper man may account for the cessation of all but the barest items relating to St. Paul's during the remainder of the year.

Salt. On the 30th January, Mr. Acutt announces that he will sell on the Market Square four tons of Salt, being the first produce of the Congella Salt Works, of which Mr. Chas. McDonald was the proprietor. Old Colonists can trace the outlines of these salt pans between the Limekilns and the Railway at the present day. But like so many of our "sample" enterprises, the industry failed for want of knowledge and capital. Iron boiler-plate evaporating pans were speedily corroded or burnt through; copper could not be afforded, while the sea water was condemned as lacking strength, attributed to the inflow of river water after the sun had done its best to condense in the open paddocks or pans. Mr. Chas. McDonald was followed by other enterprising men, who, notwithstanding their improved methods and appliances, had like him eventually to compromise with their supporters on finding they could not compete with Liverpool and Algoa Bay.

Town Council. In January the Mayor (Mr. Evans) gave notice that a daily Morning Market for the sale of Colonial Produce would be opened on the 10th February.

"Hours 9 to 11 and 2 to 3 daily near the Market Square. Fees payable to the Market Master—for the present the Town Clerk—as follows:—

"Registry fee of 6d. on all wagons, cattle, horses, sheep or goats
"Grain and produce in bags 3d. per muid.
"Ivory, forage and goods by weight, 2d. per cwt.
"Liquors, per half aum (16 galls.) 6d.
"Charges 2 per cent. on amount of sales, all payable by seller."

In anticipation of the certainty of public support and the success that would attend this new departure "to supply a long-felt want," the Council actually called for Tenders for the erection of a Market House, to be built of wood, 20 ft. long and 10 ft. wide.

Messrs. Harwin and Snell having resigned, they were replaced in the Council by Messrs. H. W. Currie and W. H. Acutt.

At a Council meeting on the 25th of January, Mr. Goodricke resumed the subject of a Town Hall, adjourned from previous meeting. He now produced a plan drawn by the Town Surveyor, comprising Town Hall, Borough and Magistrate's offices, with Court Room, Post Office, etc. This, with the Clock Tower attached, would cost £2,800; without the Tower, £2,000.

Mr. Hartley thought that great credit was due to Mr. Goodricke, but he differed, no provision having been made for the all-important requirements of the gaol. He denied that £2,800 would be very insufficient for an adequately comprehensive building, and moved an amendment that the consideration of Mr. Goodricke's motion be postponed for two months. He was totally opposed to the sale of Town Lands on the sytem hitherto pursued, which was a mere frittering away of that valuable property for current expenses. He would, however, sell lands to the amount of £2,000 for the present object, which would be turning the unproductive sand of the Berea into a valuable brick and mortar freehold that might be mortgaged to a large amount. He believed that many prisons, either in England or at the Cape, would willingly lend the Corporation £1,000 at a cheap rate. The entire annual cost of this loan to the Council would be £120, and since the Government now paid £150 (for their offices), there would be a profit to the Town of £30, though, as he said before, it would really be £180. The remaining £800 he thought would be willingly contributed by the public in an additional tax for two or three years. The Chairman remarked that a motion involving a matter of such magnitude required consideration and should not be too hastily decided. Mr. Currie was utterly opposed to the erection at the present time of a Town Hall. He was surprised at Mr. Goodricke advocating the sale of land when but a month or two ago he expressed himself opposed altogether to such sale. At present the lands would not realize one-fifth of the value they would in a year or two when emigrants had arrived, consequently they would fall into the hands of speculators. He believed the Government would not rent the offices, intending to erect their own if the contemplated loan was obtained, and, unless Government would take the building for a term of 5 or 7 years, it would be useless to erect it. Further the Town had no right to erect a Gaol for the County; the Government should have their own Gaol. He referred to the additional revenue proposed to be derived from renting the Town Hall for public occasions; and he thought it would be a shame to ask the burgesses to pay for the use of what they had built. As to balls, he considered they would prove no source of profit to the

Corporation, as the gentlemen who were in the habit of kicking their legs about generally, he had observed, wanted their rooms fresh coloured, and would only require the hall four times a year. The proposition of its utility as a place of defence was the most ridiculous of all. As to the exchange of Berea lands for bricks and mortar, the former required no repairs, which the latter did. Mr. Currie animadverted strongly on the course pursued by former Councils and thought that, before a Town Hall was erected, the town should be paved and supplied with pure water. He moved that it is inexpedient to erect a Town Hall at the present time.

.Mr. Gillespie was in favour of a Town Hall.

As to water, the inhabitants were far better off in this respect than they used to be, through the greater frequency of slate and zinc roofs. The obtaining of water would be a work of a very complicated and expensive nature, and withal not of a permanent character, such as the Town Hall would be. For current expenses he would never sell Town lands, but for the object in question he would. He seconded Mr. Goodricke's motion. Mr. Goodricke replied at some length. As to water supply he thought it fitter work for a private company than for the Corporation. The streets he also agreed were an important subject for improvement, and in three or four years he hoped to see them macadamised. He differed from the other speakers as to the Gaol, it being of advantage to the town to have the labour of county prisoners. The Town Hall was also much needed for public meetings.

Motion put and carried by 3 to 2

Messrs. Goodricke, Hartley, Gillespie, and Currie, were appointed a committee to report to the Council on the subject. Mr. Currie declining to act, Mr. W. H. Acutt was substituted.

Mr. Gillespie moved that £50 be placed at the disposal of the Town Committee for the repairs of the West End Bridge and Embankment. Amendment by Goodricke and Currie that the Committee report on the subject before any money was expended thereon. Carried.

Mr. Currie's contention as to the necessity for street improvements is justified by a " Local " paragraph in March :

"QUICKSAND.—The low part of Smith Street, opposite Mr. Brown's stores recently filled up with sand, actually became a quicksand, from the heavy rains. A gentleman on coming into town suddenly found his horse sink with him, so that only the animal's neck was visible, and the rider of course in no agreeable situation. The road gave no visible indications of such a condition."

Again in April we read: —

"TOWN PUMPS AND FOOTPATHS.—Some of these useful works are out of order, or unfinished, and need the attention of our municipal administrators."

As many matters of local interest are not reported in the proceedings of the Town Council, I hope to be pardoned for inserting newspaper paragraphs relating thereto; thus in April it is recorded: —

"NEW ROAD.—We hear that the new road to Bellair and Pine-town, commencing on the other side of the western bridge and traversing the Berea, is now open, saving three or four miles in distance, as compared with the old road through Congella."

On the 8th April we have: —

"KAFIR NOISES, ETC.—We have several complaints, which we can also personally confirm as to the horrible noises—both by social shrieking parties and by yells on private account—which the town kafirs are allowed to indulge in nightly, near the habitations of our townsmen, and along the public streets. These unearthly noises last often till midnight, 'contrary to the statute in that case,' etc.

"It is obvious, too, that the regulation against carrying arms is entirely disregarded; assegais and knobkerries being universally and openly borne about the streets.

"A much more stringent system of police surveillance is imperatively demanded."

Mr. Blackwood on proceeding to England, resigned his seat in the Council. Mr. A. W. Evans also resigned his position as Councillor and Mayor, his wife's health obliging her to return to England. He left per *Waldensian* on the 5th June with wife and family, which included his bright little boys, "Bobbie" and "Gus," with whom the town was then as familiar as we are now.

Mr. Pinsent was requisitioned for Ward 1, and Mr. A. Ferguson for Ward 3; Mr. Councillor Goodricke being elected Mayor in May for the remainder of the municipal year.

Prior, however, to his having this dignity conferred upon him he managed to raise a storm by which the Council was by no means dignified, causing much ill feeling, loss of time, and columns of type.

At a Town Council meeting on the 13th April, Mr. Goodricke, without consulting anyone, and on his own responsibility, thought it his duty to give notice of the following questions, which I condense:—

1. To ask the Mayor if the Resident Engineer of the Harbour Works has been dismissed, and if so, if such step was taken on the recommendation of the Harbour Board; or if by the Legislative or Executive Councils, or the Lieut.-Governor; and if so, why had such dismissal taken place.

2. Whether the Resident Engineer ever informed the Harbour Board that the present occurrence, viz., the shutting up of the Harbour, would not be the result of any suspension of works?

3. By whose order were the works suspended?

4. As to the state of discipline of the portboat's crew, and whether it is or is not a part of the Harbour Master's duty to attend personally and take daily soundings, etc.?

5. Whether the present portboat is considered efficient for the service; if she is properly manned; if not, have any steps been taken, etc., etc.?

At an adjourned meeting these notices were discussed at great length, eliciting, as was evidently their object, much important information as to the constitution of the Harbour Board, the position of the Resident Engineer, and the general management of the Port.

Mr. Evans, the Mayor, was absent, but a note from him was read, stating that he declined on his own responsibility to answer the questions, but suggested a direct application to the Harbour Board. By formal resolution the Mayor's suggestion to apply to the Chairman of the Harbour Board for answers to the questions propounded was carried by 4 to 2, the minority being Mr. Pinsent and Mr. Lamport, a nominee member of the Harbour Board.

After all the waste of time and eloquence in getting at the Government, the Council dealt with three matters of grave import affecting the welfare of the burgesses, the first of which I take over in full from the *Mercury* of the 22nd April:—

"SANITARY.—Mr. Hartley, with excellent intention, brought forward at the same meeting a scheme for bettering the sanitary condition of the town, by requiring for every house certain arrangements by which the night soil would be removed every day to a place appointed outside the town.

"However excellent the object we are persuaded it is impracticable, and in the present state of the population unnecessary; and it would also involve a serious interference with the liberty of the subject. in transacting his private business in his own way."

' The proposal of Mr. Goodricke for the appointment of a Borough Registrar of Births, Deaths and Marriages is in every view commendable.

"Government have strangely ignored their duty by refusing to introduce a general measure on the subject," etc.

"Mr. Hartley brought under the notice of the Council the disgraceful condition of the public cemeteries, and the desirableness of the Council's taking under its responsible charge that one which is undenominational in its use.

"He succeeded in obtaining a committee to report on the subject," etc.

At the regular meeting on the 25th April all the members were present, having scented the battle afar off. The Mayor, Mr. Evans, presided, and the *Mercury* reports that on this occasion the Council sat from 7 to 11.30 p.m., which fact of itself explains the absence of anything justifying the name of a report.

As a preliminary measure—in the language of the P.R., a sort of "walk round gents and show yer muscle," to let the Burgesses present see that special regard was paid to the requirements of the Borough—they dealt with a letter from the Government, conveying the Governor's sanction to the sale of two vacant Erven, also to the Mortgage of Leases to raise together the sum of £650 for public works, resolving before taking advantage of this permission to refer the letter to the Finance Committee to report upon the present state of the Corporate finances. Then the Committee *re* Registrar of Births, etc., handed in their report recommending co-operation with the Maritzburg Town Council to obtain a public measure applicable to the whole Colony. The Council disposed of that by referring back the question to the new Committee *(sic)*.

Then recognising the prospective income for public works and the labours of Mr. Upton, the Town Surveyor, they resolved to raise his salary to £70, " under special conditions of service," which I am inclined to think had some reference to the design or construction of the proposed Town Hall.

The decks having now been cleared for action, the reply of the Harbour Board was fired, declining to answer the questions of the previous week, on the ground that the Board was answerable only to the Government, to whom the Board referred the Council.

Mr. Councillor and Commissioner Lamport was keeping his powder dry until his motion ˙ that the reply of the Board be entered on the minutes " was seconded by Mr. Goodricke.

Then casting loose his guns, he thundered and volleyed.

In a sober history, metaphor must be suppressed, though its introduction serves to gild the pill of dry dates, figures and facts, otherwise not of general interest.   I therefore condense from the newspaper's account of the strife.

Mr. Lamport made the motion the occasion of a long and eloquent speech, in which he discussed *seriatim* the questions put to the Harbour Board, endeavouring to show that they were in fact an impertinent interference by the Council with the functions of a responsible and independent body.

He maintained that most of the questions betrayed utter ignorance of the Harbour Works and the Port.

He animadverted strongly on the slanderous insinuations thrown out by the mover (Mr. Goodricke) against the officers and servants of the port establishment, warmly vindicating their trustworthiness and zeal.   He referred to the rapid fluctuation from tidal and meteorological causes of the condition of the Bar, asserting that soundings were taken as regularly and accurately as practicable.

Mr. Goodricke and other Councillors frequently rose to order in consequence of the alleged personal and insulting tone of the speaker, and the Mayor several times ruled Mr. Lamport out of order, as the only question of the Council was their right to ask the questions, or the Board's obligation to answer them.

Mr. Lamport, however, very persistently continued on forbidden ground.

Mr. Goodricke, on seconding the motion, forcibly (note the expression) replied to Mr. Lamport's statements and strictures.

He declared his object fully answered by the publicity now given to, and the interest now awakened on, the subject, etc., etc.

Mr. Goodricke was also several times called to order by Mr. Lamport and Mr. Pinsent for personal allusions or irrelevancy, but the Mayor, while ruling irrelevancy, allowed Mr. Goodricke to reply so far as the statements of Mr. Lamport required that indulgence.

Mr. Hartley, during a lull, called the attention of the Council from their personalities to the real question—"Can the Council ask questions of the Harbour Board?" and said that if the press were admitted to that Board they need not take their present course, as publicity would be secured.

The Mayor spoke decidedly against the right of the Council to put questions to the Baord, and explained at length the position of the Mayor on that Board, declaring he did not represent the Council there, and concluded with the anecdote of "Apelles and the Cobbler," recommending the Council to "stick to their last."

Mr. Lamport replied as mover, and was again severely called to order by the Mayor, who declared that he would leave the Chair (and for a moment actually did so) if he were not obeyed.

Mr. Lamport, flushed with his exercise, continued to explain the difficulties the Board had to contend with from Governmental neglect, and concluded, alluding to Mr. Goodricke's movement in the matter, with a broadside from " Horace " that quite paralysed the Council:—

" Parturiunt montes, nascitur ridiculus mus!" (*)

The motion he had proposed was then carried unanimously.

Mr. Goodricke, in deference to the Mayor's dual position (this being his last sitting), would withdraw his first three resolutions, and only move the other two, the first being that the questions the Board had refused to answer be sent to the

* " Mountains are in labour, a ridiculous mouse is brought forth ."

Government. This found no seconder. Mr. Pinsent moved · that Government be memoralised to allow reporters at the meetings of the Board, and meanwhile that the Mayor afford the proper information. Mr. Lamport seconded; Messrs. Hartley, Goodricke and Gillespie opposed; motion rejected by casting vote of Mayor. Mr. Goodricke then moved his second resolution for the appointment of Messrs. Hartley, Gillespie and the mover, as a Committee to obtain a re-construction of the Harbour Board, which Mr. Gillespie seconded and Mr. Lamport opposed, seizing the opportunity to launch out at the press for having styled him a "Government nominee," and "flung back the insinuation with scorn!" After one or two attempts at adjournment, Mr. Goodricke's motion was carried by 6 to 2, Messrs. Lamport and Pinsent being the minority. Meeting closed after four hours' labour.

The Council met again on the 30th April, when the Mayor formally resigned from the Council, being about to leave for England. Mr. Councillor Goodricke was elected Mayor for the remainder of the Municipal year. Mr. Currie having applied for the lease of a piece of ground behind the Burial ground for the purpose of a Foundry, the Council were disposed to grant it, but, on the motion of Mr. Lamport, Chairman of the Town Lands Committee, which had reported against it on the grounds of annoyance and injury likely to result from such works near the town, the application was refused.

The Council also adopted a recommendation of the same Committee to reserve land at Congella for a contemplated extension of that village.

On the 17th May, the *Monarch of the Sea*, an American ship of 1970 tons, with Rice from Akyab to Liverpool, put in for repairs, having sprung a leak during a gale, and reported about nine feet of water in her hold, in consequence of her steam pump having broken down; she had thrown overboard some 2,000 bags. The ship *Jane Morice*, being here, was chartered to go outside, and load up for England; while all the cargo boats in the port were engaged by Mr. G. C. Cato, the ship's agent, in landing the cargo.

At its meeting on the 24th June the Council agreed to erect a Town Hall to cost £1,200, towards which £400 worth of Town Lands were to be sold at once on obtaining the Lieutenant-Governor's sanction, and the Town Surveyor was instructed to draw up a plan of a suitable building.

In the meantime the damaged rice *ex Monarch of the Sea*, was sold at the Point, a large portion realising as much as 7d. per bag duty paid, Mr. S. Crowder, senior, through his sons, Messrs. S. and B. Crowder, Landing Agents, being chief buyer. The offensive nature of the fermenting grain induced the Town Council during July to prohibit its introduction into town; it was ultimately condemned and consigned to the sea from the Back Beach. Mr. Crowder thereupon demanded £755 10s. for loss and damage.

The alarming prospect of a costly Town Hall and sacrifice of Town Lands, together with the pressing rice nuisance, evoked a public meeting, which was held in Drake's Billiard Room on the 20th of July, and is described as crowded and tolerably quiet. The Mayor (Mr. Goodricke) having when Councillor advocated the erection of a Town Hall, vacated the chair in favour of Mr. John Sanderson, so that he might fully explain and discuss the question.

The principal speakers were Messrs. Tyzack, Campbell, Lamport, Pinsent, and Jacques.

The following resolution by Mr. Tyzack, amended as customary by Mr. Lamport, was carried *nem. con.*:—" That " this meeting, while recognising the necessity for a Town " Hall, are yet of opinion that the present is not the time " to incur any large expenditure in its erection."

The Rice question was brought forward and spoken to by Mr. G. C. Cato and Mr. Lamport, who challenged the meeting to give an opinion on the subject " or for ever after hold their peace."

But the meeting, without voting, seemed inclined to leave the question to the decision of the Town Council.

The Council apparently yielded to public opinion, and concluded to proceed with the more important public works of draining the Eastern Vlei and constructing the embankment to restrain the Umgeni; so called for tenders for a

loan of £400 in amounts of £100, on security of the Freehold of 161 acres of leased lands yielding a rental of £77
18s. 9d.

"Corporation will not pay higher rate of interest than 10
"per cent. per annum. The money must be lent for periods
"of three or five years as required, with liberty to repay
"at any time in sums of £100 on six months' notice."

As for the rice, Mr. Crowder was indicted by the Public
Prosecutor for a nuisance "dangerously noxious to the
public" arising from the stench from the damaged rice
piled near the Custom House wharf. The evidence was
long, scientific, and conflicting, resulting after voluminous
quotations of English precedents in the Resident Magistrate finding the case proved, "but taking into
"account that the act of the defendant had not been that
"of an evil-disposed individual, intending to injure the
"public," fined him five shillings, against which the defendant noted an appeal.

August 5th. The Borough Election resulted in the return
of Mr. G. C. Cato and Mr. Pinsent for Ward 1 ; H. Gillespie and J. R. Goodricke for Ward 2 ; W. H. Acutt and
Archibald Ferguson for Ward 3 ; with William Dacomb
and H. W. Currie for Ward 4 ; who, at their meeting on
Saturday, the 7th, elected Mr. J. R. Goodricke as Mayor.

At its next business meeting the office of Borough Assizer
was established.

Mr. E. Kermode's tender to perform the duties for £12
per annum being accepted, he was duly appointed.

Messrs. W. H. Savory and A. M. Barnes were elected
Borough Auditors.

The burgesses having a grievance against Time, the
Mayor shortly after informed the Council that he had purchased 50 lbs. of gunpowder, and had obtained permission
from the Military authorities to use the only available gun
at the Point (the historical 18-pounder), which for a week
during August was fired at 9 o'clock every morning ; thus
we thought we should be able to keep our appointments, but
it was found that the discharge of this piece, notwithstanding it had seriously shaken the Custom House wharf, could

not always be heard [? noticed] in town, so the **Town Coun-**
cil decided to " cease firing " when they had expended the
powder, unless arrangements could be made for a gun to be
fired at the Camp.

This looseness in dealing with Old Father Time seriously
affected Mr. James Brickhill, who was reputed to have a
mania for clocks, and to whom, as a methodical man of
business, minutes were held to be of much value.   It was
owing to his questioning the accuracy of Mr. Cato's time-
flag that led to its being given up.   Now the futility of the
Corporation's gun fire prompted him to write to the papers
suggesting bell ringing, regulated by a flag from the Bluff.
This was followed by a letter from Dr. Mann recommending a solar time gun on the Bluff, fired by the signalman
on the indication of noon by a self-acting Gnomen and a
Dent's 6 guinea lever watch.

Neither suggestion was taken up by the Corporation.

The only decent bell in the town was a spare Cathedral
bell, lent by the Dean of Maritzburg to St. Paul's Church;
those of the Wesleyan and Congregational Churches being
both cracked and of uncertain sound.

Mr. Cato, having been re-elected on Town Committee,
voluntarily resumed the hoisting of a time ball on his flag
staff at 9 a.m. daily.

Mr. Brickhill's chronometrical tastes induced him to pick
up at auctions any promising time-piece, with the idea of
checking one against the other, and arriving at mean time.

He thus accumulated a large stock, differing considerably
in value and style, until his better half despaired of house
room for them; she, good thrifty soul, having to welcome
the coming guests, resolved to speed the parting ones, who
otherwise wouldn't go, so a selection was privately dis-
patched to the Auction Mart.   Her sense of relief may have
given place to other feelings when a few weeks later her
husband re-introduced, with much sanguine anticipation,
two bargains from the very white elephants she had so
prudently got rid of.

The *Mercury* of the 7th October contained the following
note : —

"The Town Council meeting last night, after another fiery farce, adjourned to this evening. It is suggested that these inimitable performances will bear a charge of sixpence each from the company who attend them, the amount to go towards a lunatic asylum."

This uncalled-for observation arose from an editorial lack of appreciation of the dignity of labour ; of the importance attaching to the office of Councillor, and the right of each individual to express and maintain his own opinions.

He had forgotten that Mr. Lamport taught the Council the necessity of returning a Roland for an Oliver, and that vestrymen had become Town Councillors ; each member of the Council was also suffering from nervous apprehension in consequence of the Mayor having now been served with a writ for £755 10s. at the instance of Mr. Crowder and his damaged rice.

Hence the "tu quoque" practice that now obtained, all of course in the interests of the Burgesses.

It appears that at a Council meeting on the 26th September the Town Lands Committee submitted a report upon which the Mayor brought forward eleven resolutions. The three first having been disposed of, the fourth, for placing on the estimates £30 for a road to the Gardens, was carried, the sum being increased to £50.

Mr. Pinsent, when discussing the resolutions, proposed that only sufficient should be voted to complete a wide footpath ; this the Mayor considered both ridiculous and absurd, a remark which excited Mr. Pinsent's indignation to such an extent that he called the Mayor to order.

The next resolution for £40 to open the Umgeni mouth was opposed by Mr. Cato, as being a waste of money ; South African rivers, he had found, when choked at the mouth, would not burst the barrier till they had reached a certain height, and till there was a kind of lagoon formed behind it, when the stream then swept everything before it.

He did not anticipate any danger of the river again coming down [townwards] for many years, as the islands and other obstructions did not now exist.   Mr. Ferguson agreed.

Mr. Pinsent laid great stress on professional opinions, and moved that £10 should be expended in removing the vegetation on the bank, and that enquiries be made with a view to further steps at an early date. Carried 4 to 3.

The fifth resolution was for £75 for making roads in the Berea, which would enhance the value of Berea Lots.

Mr. Pinsent was of opinion that the maximum of Berea residents had been reached, and that in future these lands would be chiefly required for small farms, and would only make roads where they were urgently applied for. He deprecated spending the Borough funds on spec. Mr. Ferguson would object to both items of expenditure unless included in the general expenditure for a staff of labourers. The Mayor considered it would be a breach of faith if they did not make these roads. Mr. Dacomb differed from the Mayor, having applied for a road to his own lot and been refused. Resolution lost by 4 to 3, whereupon the Mayor did not see much use in proceeding with the remaining resolutions, as he considered they met with "factious opposition." Mr. Pinsent rose, indignantly called the Mayor to order, and moved that he be called upon to withdraw the remark last made. This was seconded with much gusto (sic) by Mr. Dacomb. Several Councillors endeavoured to propitiate the wrath of Councillor Pinsent, but he remained firm, declaring his very common-sense proposition was made under the rule. He was there to do his duty, and never intended to come to a bear garden. He claimed in this to have as much regard for the public interests as the Mayor had. Replying to questions from the Chair, His Worship had plainly indicated that the expression was intended for him.

Mr. Gillespie said it was evident Mr. Pinsent took it to himself. (Cries of "Order.")

Thus encouraged, Mr. Pinsent pressed his motion, and in doing so detailed his grievances graphically and at length.

Mr. Dacomb stirred up matters by doing the same.

Mr. Gillespie kept the ball rolling, by saying he was not surprised at the remark which fell from the Chair, though it might be irregular; Mr. Pinsent had at all events confessed that it pinched him. He moved that business be proceeded with, which Mr. W. H. Acutt seconded.

The Mayor said he did not care a pin about the motion, as he would take care it was not on the minutes.

The proposition, however, was carried by 3 to 2; but the Mayor declared he would not withdraw the expression

Mr. Pinsent thereupon moved an expression of disapproval by the Council of the Mayor's remark. Mr. Acutt thought Mr. Pinsent gloried in this kind of work.

The Mayor, taking the bull by the horns, ordered Mr. Pinsent to sit down. Mr. Pinsent refused. The Mayor thought Mr. Pinsent's conduct to have fully justified his remark, which he originally never intended for Mr. Pinsent. Mr. Gillespie recommended the Mayor to leave the Chair; that dignitary replied that he would not allow the conduct of any member to force him to leave the Chair, or forget his duty to the public; he called on Mr. Ferguson to proceed. Mr. Pinsent declared himself in possession of the Chair.

Mr. Gillespie, overcome by the fitness of things, left the meeting in disgust. The Mayor thought Mr. Pinsent should apologise; that gentleman said he would see the Mayor —— first (this last with a vigorous nod of the head). Mr. Acutt was sorry to see Mr. Pinsent was such a peppery gentleman.

Mr. Ferguson now stepped in with a motion that £200 be placed in the estimates for a staff of labourers for the Town Lands, this to include the Berea Road.

Mr. Cato seconded, and said he should not support an expenditure of £1,100, to bring material for hardening the Berea Road from a distance, when it already existed on the top [apparently this being the next resolution on the list].

The Mayor moved as an amendment, seconded by Mr. Acutt, that £1,100 be expended on the road. Mr. Cato recommended the appropriation this year of £400 for a staff, who, besides executing the roads and other works, should carry out, say, 750 yards of the contemplated road this year, to see how it answered.

The amendment having been lost Mr. Pinsent proposed another—" That the work be postponed for the present "until the Eastern Vlei is completed"; not seconded, so Mr. Ferguson's original motion for £200 was carried 3 to 2. £30 for repairing the Umgeni Road was passed.

Messrs. Ferguson and Pinsent were appointed a Committee to inquire into the cutting of wood on the Town Lands. The Finance Committee were requested to bring up their report for the current year. The Mayor was authorized to take steps for assizing weights and measures.

Here the business was thought to have ended, and the Public groped for its hat, but Mr. Councillor Pinsent's peace of mind was suffering, so instead of a vote of thanks to the Chairman, to which we were accustomed, he seized the opportunity to give notice of a vote of censure on the Mayor, who, however, refused to have any such notice put on the minutes, considering it to be a direct personal insult to himself.

Mr. Acutt jocularly observed that, after Mr. Pinsent's expression towards the Mayor, they would be justified in expelling him (the impression seemed to be that Mr. Pinsent had made use of a certain uncanonical word in replying to the Mayor). He, however, strongly disclaimed any such thing, not being in the habit of using such expressions. The Mayor persisted in his refusal to have the notice entered on the minutes; he knew that it was a concocted thing between Mr. Pinsent and Mr. Dacomb to get him to resign his Mayoralty, but he had got the post and should keep it though they passed fifty votes of censure. I was not present then, but was told that the Councillors and Burgesses "left speaking."

At the next meeting on October 6th, Messrs. Acutt and Currie were absent. The Town Clerk having read the minutes, on a question from Mr. Cato, the Mayor stated that he had had them altered somewhat from those read at the last meeting, to give what he considered to be a fair reflection of the proceedings which then took place, and also that his conduct might be set in a proper light before the Burgesses. The Town Clerk had declared the additions correct.

This course was strongly objected to by Messrs. Cato, Pinsent and Dacomb, who denied the correctness of the version given. Considerable alteration and unseemly recrimination ensued, which resulted in the final adoption by a majority of a resolution expunging the statements and additions made by the Mayor.

Mr. Cato having remarked on the inconvenience of that evening as a time for meeting in consequence of the departure of the Mail, an adjournment till the following night was agreed to, after much time had been spent in squabbling as to whether the vote of censure by Mr. Pinsent should be brought forward or not, the Mayor positively refusing to withdraw the words "factious opposition," which had originated the present dispute.

October 7th. Absent Messrs. Acutt and Currie. The minutes of last night's meeting were read and confirmed.

A letter was read from Mr. Goodricke stating that he had bought his Berea Lot [now Dr. McKenzie's residence, St. Thomas' Road], with the understanding that good roads were to be made to it.

The report of the Town Committee read—It disapproved of any measure restricting the Burgesses from cutting firewood for domestic, or even for manufacturing purposes, as oppressive, acting in fact as a poll-tax, but recommending the careful preservation of the Back Beach bush as necessary for the comfort of the town. The Market Master's report was read requesting to be relieved from his duty, stating the receipts during 18 months had been £6 18s. 6d., and the current expenses £8.

He considered the Market under the present regulations to be an entire failure, a means of dissatisfaction to both buyers and sellers.

Mr. Cato recommended that they should file that day's *Mercury*, which contained a very good suggestion regarding a lunatic asylum. Thus refreshed, Mr. Pinsent moved, and Mr. Cato seconded, the suspension of the rules of order, to enable his vote of censure to take precedence of all other business.

Mr. Cato first wished to know if the Mayor would withdraw the words complained of. But the Mayor interrupted him, by telling him he was not in possession of the Chair, and could not speak.

Mr. Pinsent rose to move his resolution, and did so in full and forcible language, for the space of ten minutes, concluding " with further strong remarks on the conduct of the Mayor in not retracting, and in his improper assumption of "illegal power.' "

Mr. Cato endorsed Mr. Pinsent's brief, disclaiming any personal or party feeling, declared his wish to support the Mayor whenever he could justly do so, and expressed his willingness to resign, so little did he care for the office.

Mr. Dacomb exculpated himself, adding a little oil to the fire.

Mr. Ferguson would vote against the motion, believing it to be at variance with the rule under which he considered the subject had been disposed of long ago. He animadverted strongly on the waste of time caused by these disputes.

The Mayor told Mr. Pinsent that he could reply now, but he should reserve the right of final reply. Mr. Pinsent expostulated. The Mayor said the rule could not be altered.

Mr. Pinsent considered this another instance in which the Chair attempted to overcome the rights of the Council, by putting a forced construction on the rules of order.

The Mayor told Mr. Pinsent he should have his right of reply, and much good might he get by it.

The proceedings of the previous night had been minuted and therefore according to rule 26 nothing more could be said on the subject. He then proceeded to quote observations by Mr. Pinsent. Mr. Cato interposed—" Not any misrepresentation of words." The Mayor continued and argued that as Mr. Cato had said he had come into the Council determined to sink all personalities and support the Mayor, he evinced thereby the existence of a party feeling. The notice of motion was quite irregular, as was the whole discussion, and he endeavoured to prove it by the rule.

Mr. Pinsent said they were getting law, but not common sense. The Mayor said he was glad Mr. Pinsent would grant the law, and continued to read the rules amidst sundry interruptions. He considered Mr. Dacomb's seconding of the motion on the previous evening to have been most indecent. Mr. Dacomb got up very vehemently to protest, but the Mayor continued to read the minutes, and then declared he would not put the resolution to the meeting. Mr. Pinsent then said that he would, whether it was out of order or not, and proceeded to reply at very great length. He adverted in unmeasured terms to the Chairman's abandonment of common sense for what he (the Mayor) called Law. He was unable to understand the Mayor's conduct; if he (Mr. Goodricke) had been pleading in the Court, he could have understood it, but to make such pettifogging remarks in that Council ————. Being called to order, Mr. Pinsent withdrew the last expression, but apparently "played to the gallery," for the reporter says, "he continued in the same strain of strong animadversion." All of which was lost on the Mayor, who refused to put the resolution; when, at Mr. Pinsent's request, the Town Clerk handed him the Minute Book, and he proceeded to read the resolution, notwithstanding the Mayor calling him to order and protesting against his conduct.

Mr. Pinsent having put the motion, there were 3 for it and 1 against it, the Mayor and Mr. Smerdon not voting.

The Mayor said he should not sign the Minutes. Mr. Ferguson left the meeting. The ordinary business was being proceeded with when Mr. Ferguson returned, and wished to know if the Mayor would really persist in not signing the Minutes.

The Mayor answered " Certainly," and reiterated his intention not to resign, and, if necessary, he would move the Supreme Court to expunge the entry altogether. He did not care if every Councillor resigned : they might get a better set of men to do the work. Mr. Cato hoped no reference to him was intended.

Mr. Ferguson, belonging to the Peace Society, wished to make the dispute up by mutual concession, but Mr. Pinsent declined to withdraw the motion on his part. The Mayor knew they wanted him to resign, but he would not. Mr. Cato, for himself, gave a flat denial of any such wish. Mr. Dacomb did the same—"they wanted him to entertain them." The Mayor declared he would sit in the Chair for the whole twelve months. After reiterated refusal on the part of both parties to concede their positions, Mr. Ferguson left the room stating that he would never take his seat there again.

After some further altercations and a vain attempt on the part of Mr. Smerdon to induce mutual concessions, other Councillors left their places until a quorum failed to be present, and of course the meeting was at an end, and so was the ordinary business.

A few days previously, the public mind being agitated by a threatened law suit in reference to the damaged rice, some twenty-eight burgesses requested the Mayor to call a meeting:—" To consider the present position of the Rice " question, and whether any means can be adopted to put " an end to the threatened expensive litigation." The Mayor, in replying, declined to call a meeting of the bur- gesses, or take any part in the proceedings:—"Although " I see no reason why you should not yourselves call a " meeting and discuss the matter in any way or manner you " like, and if it is pretended that my sanction as Mayor is ' necessary to convene a meeting, I most willingly and " readily grant you my authority as Mayor to call such a " meeting."

This nice distinction illustrates the advantages the early burgesses derived from having a lawyer as Mayor, a gentle- man whose favourite axiom in Court was "I admit nothing ! "

In explanation of Mr. Goodricke's conduct as above des- cribed, it may be noted that there were many possibilities in the "Rice Case," that Mr. Attorney Pinsent was on the opposite side, and that he and Mr. Cato were among the requisitionists for the public meeting.

The women of Durban made their influence felt at the meeting of Council on the 3rd November, when:—" A " letter was read from several ladies at the West End " respecting the state of the wells in that locality. Resolved, " That the letter be referred to the Town Committee, and " that they report on the best position for the pumps im- " ported, with a view to their equal distribution throughout " the Town."

At an adjourned meeting on the 9th November, resolutions were proposed by Mr. W. H. Acutt to the effect that £400 be borrowed to make the Umgeni Embankment and drain the Eastern Vlei, his proposal being that as soon as the Embankment was completed, and the plan of drainage decided on by special surveyors, the Eastern Vlei was to be let on lease for 25 years, the tenants to make the drains. Consideration deferred until the 15th November, when Mr. Acutt moved the first of his resolutions; Mr. Ferguson, cn Mr. Hartley's re-election to the Council, having consented to withdraw his hasty resignation, seconded the motion. Messrs. Cato, Pinsent and Dacomb insisted on the whole series being considered simultaneously; and on Mr. Acutt maintaining his intention to put them separately, those gentlemen left the Council table and retired to another part of the room. A quorum being left, the first resolution was carried by Messrs. Ferguson, Hartley and Acutt.

This resolution was to be brought under the review by the dissentients at the next meeting.

The enterprising and much enduring Editor of the *Mercury* makes a virtue of necessity, turns down the editorial thumb upon our local Arena, and lets them have it thus:—

"We shall not have space during the session of the Legislature [opened 18th November] to report the constantly recurring 'scenes' of fun, faction and fury that transpire in our local Council room; but we do sincerely hope that the members will endeavour, by a more yielding and conciliatory spirit, to bring to a final end the disgraceful altercations which have prevailed so long, to the entire obstruction of useful business, and the intense disgust of the whole public."

London Hotel. On the 4th February, Thomas W. Deer, late of the Billiard Room at Drake's, announced that he had taken over Clarence's Auction Store, late Church and Schoolroom, Field Street, for a Billiard Room, where he would provide "refreshments of every description, Good Stabling, Beds, etc."

The place was afterwards converted into the "London Hotel," known first as "Deer's," then as "Bob Smith's."

Zulu Cattle. February 27th. A deputation of Zulu traders having applied to "Ketchwaya'" for compensation for their losses on the occasion of his victory over his brother on the banks of the Tugela, he cheerfully handed over some 1,100 head, with a promise of more when he could get them from the Natal Government, as he claimed restoration of all the refugees' cattle; with these he would make up any deficiency in their losses. Five hundred of these compensation cattle, described as being chiefly slaughter-oxen, with some young beasts fit for the yoke, were now advertised by Mr. Robt. Acutt for sale by Auction "by order of the Committee" of Traders, by whom the proceeds would be distributed to the claimants.

Supreme Court. On March the 6th the *Mercury* announced that, as an outcome of our new Constitution, Mr. Walter Harding was to receive the honour of Knighthood, and be appointed Chief Justice of Natal; Mr. Lushington Phillips, of the Manchester Sessions, to be First Puisne Judge; and Mr. Henry Connor, lately Chief Justice and Acting Governor on the Gold Coast, to be Second Puisne Judge.

Medical. Dr. Best, of the 45th Regiment, who had been long stationed in Durban, and was deservedly popular, both with the ladies and the members of the Durban Club, left the Colony for England, with his wife and family, per S.S. *Waldensian*, on the 5th of March, in charge of 47 invalids of his Regiment.

As the military doctors then had private practice, many young Durbanites made his acquaintance.

Dr. Julius Schulz, late Regimental Surgeon in the British German Legion, Government Notice No 10, 1858, in the *Gazette*, announces his admission to practice as Physician, etc.

He took the opportunity to advertise that he was to be consulted at his farm, "Westville," and that he supplied needful medicines. His *confrères* instructed him in professional etiquette as "made in England." He left advertising to the Chemists, and, failing to earn salt among the healthy hard-working peasantry of New Germany, ultimately removed to Durban, where he established a successful practice, and became Police Surgeon and Health Officer of the Borough. He died in 1891, esteemed and regretted.

Cutter "Herald." News reached us in March that this little vessel with cargo and crew had been captured and detained by the Portuguese at Delagoa Bay. Representations were made to Lieutenant-Governor Scott, who promised to get the Admiral at the Cape to send up a man-of-war to investigate. The *Mercury* of the 1st April states:—

"Information apparently reliable has come in to the effect that the hunters in the employ of British traders have resisted the tyranny of the Portuguese at Delagoa Bay, and made havoc of Lorenço Marques, the miserable capital of the settlement, in revenge for the capture of the *Herald* and her crew. Mr. Duncan is said to be on his way home overland. It will be remembered he was not among the captured, having proceeded inland to the residence of the Chief, with whom he wished to open a trade."

On the 9th June H.M. Steam Sloop *Lyra*, 11 guns, Commander Oldfield, arrived from Mozambique, and landed the first batch of liberated slaves, eleven in number, together with the survivors of the Cutter *Herald*, which, as before noted, had been seized by the Portuguese 150 miles up the St. George's River, in what we claimed to be native territory, on a charge of contraband trading, or, in other words, of not paying duty at Delagoa Bay. After detention and much privation, Mr. Duncan, who had returned to the assistance of his crew, was with them sent as prisoners in a Portuguese Brig to Mozambique for trial, one of the crew dying on the voyage. At Mozambique, several of the party were prostrated by fever, which unhappily terminated the life of their brave Captain Duncan on the 5th March.

The Portuguese authorities, without notice, tried and condemned the Cutter and cargo.

On the arrival there on the 4th May of H.M.S. *Lyra* she took off the survivors of the crew, and Mr. McLeod, the British Consul, and family, that gentleman having regarded the conduct of the Portuguese as justifying the withdrawal of diplomatic relations. During the return voyage the *Lyra* fell in with a Dow, described as a Portuguese coasting Cutter, having on board 11 slaves. The Dow was tried Portuguese fashion without notice, condemned and burnt at sea, and the Captain, mate and crew, together with the rescued negroes, brought here to be forwarded to the Cape. The *Lyra* also brought a report that the Spanish Slaver *Menimtonka* had succeeded in carrying off a full cargo of slaves, and was expected back for another venture.

This satisfied "the Point" that our people "knew a Hawk from a Hand-saw" when they saw it.

The prospect of prize money for the captured negroes was generously foregone by the Officers and Crew of the *Lyra,* who subscribed between £20 and £30 for the benefit of Duncan's widow, and the emancipated crew of the *Herald.* Commander Oldfield and those interested in the Cutter made formal demand upon the Portuguese Government for compensation for loss of that vessel and cargo, as also for personal damages.

- The *Lyra* was returning to Mauritius for repairs, and the editor of the *Mercury* avails himself of the opportunity to point out that :—"This port with improvements would " make an admirable naval station, available both for the " repression of the slave trade on the coast, and the protec- " tion and supply of our eastern commerce."

The generous example of the crew of the *Lyra* was immediately followed by the formation of the "Duncan Relief Fund," championed by Mr. Richard Vause, who advertised for contributions, pointing out the necessities of the widow and six children of our fellow townsman whose life had been sacrificed in endeavouring to open up a valuable trade between Natal and Eastern Africa. The response to this appeal was liberal, considering the value of silver at that time.

In the *Mercury* of July 24th, appears an excellent letter from Charles H. Hilliard, Captain Duncan's friend, ship-mate, and fellow sufferer, confirming the existence of the slave trade, and detailing the circumstances of the arrest and removal to Mozambique, with the insulting and menacing attitude of the Portuguese toward their prisoners, as also to the British Consul, Mr. McLeod, which necessitated the abandonment of his post in order to find safety on board H.M.S. *Lyra.*

Romance finds a corner in the heart of the British sailor, notwithstanding his unromantic surroundings, rough exterior and homely ways.   Chas. Hilliard was but a ship's carpenter; a true gentleman of the guinea stamp for a' that.   He was so much concerned at the loss of his friend, and the disastrous results of their joint enterprise, that he quietly yet persistently devoted the remainder of his life and earnings to the support of the widow and children, himself, when incapacitated, finding with them a home until Mrs. Duncan's death.

Thereafter the old man was comfortably provided for by the children while he lived.   The family is now represented by the eldest son, Mr. W. G. Duncan, of Currie Road.

Free Trade.   During the early months of the year the Free State Boers were engaged in a war with that able Basuto Chief, Moshesh, by whom they were fairly matched.
Business is business, but what would we think now, if a Durban merchant ventured to insert this advertisement:—

To Boers and Others.

For Sale, two new long Four-pounder Guns, on carriages complete, with a quantity of Round Shot and Grape. Apply to
                                                J. D. Koch.
Gardiner St., Durban, May 5th, 1858.

Regatta.   Owing to the insufficiency of water, on the Queen's Birthday, the first Durban Regatta, for public money, was held on the 28th May.   Yachtsmen will possibly obtain some information of interest from the following advertisement:—

DURBAN REGATTA.
FRIDAY, MAY 28TH, 1858.
Judge—W. SMERDON, Esq.
STEWARDS—
C. J. CATO, Esq.		L WILSON, Esq.
WILLIAM DACOMB, Esq.
Treasurer - JOHN GRAY, Esq.

THE ENTRANCE LIST will be closed on the 28th instant at 12 o'clock, when Signal Flags will be hoisted at the Flagstaffs of Messrs. Brown and Cato. The start to take place at gun fire from the bath house at 3 p.m., weather permitting. A gun will also be fired at one o'clock.

Durban, May 27th, 1858.		ALBERT WALSH, Hon. Sec.

My diary briefly records the fact of the half holiday, and the weather permitting, but I hve a lively recollection of the general gathering, and the mixed character of the boats of all sizes. The course was to the Point and back to the Judge's boat opposite the Bath house. The Regatta was confined to sailing boats of all sizes and rigs, simply designated first and second class. They were moored in line with their sails hoisted, hauling up to their anchors and sheeting home as the gun fired, fouling each other in the process.

The smaller boats started about fifteen minutes later.

The wind was light and variable, so by the time the Point was reached few of the spectators could tell " t'other from which."

It should be known that all the boats engaged were ordinarily used for pleasure, and were not in any way designed for racing. There were no Silver Cups on this occasion. The necessary funds were raised by subscription and entrance fees; it is doubtful if the prizes exceeded £12.

The *Mercury* gives the following account of : —

"THE REGATTA.—The day being fine, the spectators last Friday were very numerous, indeed the afternoon was a general holiday. The wind however was scarcely fresh enough for the occasion, and the tide was unusually scant. The boats however presented a beautiful appearance as they gallantly sped their way along the surface of our sunny bay. One or two of the boats in the first race, took the ground before rounding the boat stationed near the Point. . . The *Fog* won by a considerable distance. In the second class race the winner was the *Mongola*, followed by the *Mist*. The want of a rowing match was generally felt. . . . Nearly forty gentlemen

dined together in the evening at Mr. Deer's Hotel, and in friendly
hilarity 'fought the battles o'er again.'   The owner of the first
class winning boat is Mr. S. Reddish, and of the second, James
Proudfoot, Esq., commanded by Mr. Herman Wackernow."

**Manufac-   Two new Industries are noted in the
tures.   *Mercury* of the 10th June, as under:—**

"PINE APPLE WINE.—Mr. Agar of this place has succeeded in
producing a beautiful wine from the juice of the pine-apple, which
bids fair to establish a new product in Natal.

"The flavour and keeping properties of this wine are equal to the
most favourite wines of commerce ; and the fruit being capable of
unlimited production in our soil, a trade of indefinite extent may
be carried on."

This wine was effervescing, and had all the taste and
appearance of champagne, but its production in quantity
was hampered by the Excise regulations and licence re-
striction, consequently the utilisation of our surplus pineapples, oranges, and peaches for liquid consumption, remains
to this day an undeveloped industry.

The fruit being allowed to rot saves labour, earns no
wages, and returns no capital.

The other notice refers to myself:—

"NATAL OIL AND FIBRE MILLS.—We have much pleasure in
directing attention to the announcement of the new firm of Russell
and Co. in our advertising columns, and heartily wish success to an
enterprise already proved to possess abundant capabilities."

Assuming that readers of history, like Mr. Gradgrind,
only require "facts, sir, hard facts," I will endeavour to
restrict the "Painful Story of a Failure" to those narrow
limits by which they are linked to the history of Old
Durban.

Mr. W. Relph, at Merebank, and Mr. W. H. Middleton,
of Snaresbrook, had both grown, produced, and exhibited
the Ground Nut, its oil and oil cake ; certainly in the sample
stage.

The resources of the Colony for the production of Fibres
had often been discussed, and my Javanese Dutch friends,
Van Prehn and Colenbrander, had impressed me with the
usefulness of both the Banana and the Pineapple for fibre
and textile purposes.   A relative in England, engaged in
the paper-making trade, assured me of the demand for the
material.

Fired with the idea of growing the Ground Nut, while the Banana and the Pineapple were maturing, I secured the 10 acre lease from the Corporation before referred to, and commenced clearing and planting, accelerated by the knowledge that there was locally a large demand for lamp oil—Colza and Camphine being then generally in use; also that Mr. Hugh Gillespie had a younger brother (James), and a Mr. A. M. Barnes, a qualified London man of large mercantile experience, coming out to assist him in his increasing business.

Mr. Gillespie accepted the intimation of my desire to start the new enterprise, and kindly offered his assistance, on learning that my London relative would join me by contributing the machinery. Unfortunately, being young and enthusiastic, I "started before I was ready"; bought an Erf in Grey Street, opposite St. George's Street, drained it, and erected a Factory of yellow-wood; procured and fitted mill-stone rollers, steam generator, oil vats, hydraulic press, drying floor with a stable for the mill horse, this absorbing all my little savings, and leaving me heavily indebted to Mr. Gillespie.

The Home Government had (through the usual channels) urged upon Mr. Theophilus Shepstone the advisability of inducing the native population to cultivate Cotton, and pay their taxes in kind; but those good creatures, the native women, scorned the idea of producing an article that was not edible, and one, moreover, requiring so much trouble to harvest. As their lords saw it in the same light—requiring at the hands of their women the Egyptian tale of bricks in the way of food stuffs and beer—the paternal suggestions of the Home Government could not be enforced, though cotton seed with "directions" had been freely distributed.

I thereupon applied to Mr. Shepstone, offering to take "at a price" all the ground nuts the natives would produce in payment of their taxes, relying on finding a market in England for the surplus I might not manufacture, pointing out to him that the ground nut was known to all the tribes along the Coast, and was suitable for native habits of cultivation.

He courteously replied that if the natives could not be induced to cultivate cotton, he might see what could be done with the ground nut.   As I could not await the experiment, I induced the German settlers, and other small farmers, to grow them and had several hundred muids delivered.

Of the so-called Fibre from the Banana and the Plantain grown on my Berea Road Plantation, I found that the cost ·of carting the heavy green stems to the mill, their crushing, washing, drying, heckling, bailing and shipping, with freight to London, resulted in my receiving in return a fraction over the cost of the cartage, and the ship freight.

The fruit did not pay for the growing, so there was nothing left for the manufacture.

My London partner said that the price quoted by the paper makers for my sample lot, would only be realised on condition of receiving a regular supply of from 7 to 10 tons monthly, and he recommended my pulping into "half stuff" rather than drying into fibre.

As the fruit did little more than pay the wages of the native hawker, and only unsaleable vinegar could be made from the surplus, I cheerfully abandoned Fibre, devoting my attention exclusively to oil.

I succeeded in producing a good marketable article at a fair profit on cost of production, and found ready sale for my oil cake.   I even indulged the expectation that Shakespeare's tide was nearing the flood, when some other speculators introduced to the Colony a new-fangled lamp, and a new-fangled product for use in them, called variously "Kerosene, Paraffin, Petroleum, and Rock Oil."   The lamps were described as "Young's"—they were handy and cheap, giving a brilliant light; they soon became popular, and my ground nut oil remained unsold in my vats.

These things, taken together, induced me to conclude that life was not worth living on other people's money; that the tide was ebbing instead of flowing, and that I had now, after two years' hard labour,. to face the consequences of my own inexperience.   The business was pronounced a failure, a voluntary sale held, land and machinery sold, and

the Berea Lots transferred to Mr. Gillespie in part payment.
He allowed me to compound some years later for the balance
remaining due to him.

Shipwrecked once more, I resolved to start again, and " go
slow," a wiser and a sadder man.

The old Grey Street Factory is still standing (proof of
the durability of yellow-wood), converted into cottages.

The pressure of the Oil and Fibre business on my time
obliged my resignation of the Secretaryship of the
Mechanics' Institute.   Mr. John Robinson succeeded me.

Dr. Robert Jas. Mann, the recently appointed Superintendent of Education, made what may be described as his
first public appearance in Durban on the 23rd June, the
occasion being his delivery of a lecture on the " Miracles of
Science," given in aid of the Durban Mechanics' Institute
to a crowded and appreciative audience in Mr. Acutt's
Auction Mart.

45th Regiment. After years of hope deferred, the " Old
45th " got the route for Home, with orders
to proceed to Durban for embarkation on
being relieved by the 85th Regiment.

Accordingly Fort Napier was left in charge of a Barrack
Master and a Subaltern's detachment, while the regiment,
headed by Colonel Cooper, marched into Durban on Sunday
morning, the 5th September, and pitched their tents in the
vicinity of the Camp.

The old mangrove-built thatched barracks, in a state of
ruin, were being demolished to make way for the present
brick barracks; then just commenced. The Officers were
quartered in a new slated building owned by Mr. W.
Dacomb, adjoining Palmer and Blackwood's store at the
corner of West and Union Streets.   The Band, under their
able Bandmaster, Mr. Faccioli, played alternately at the
Botanic Gardens and the Market Square.

In honour of the regiment's arrival and speedy departure,
it was decided to entertain the Officers at a Public Ball.
The Mayor and Mr. H. J. Mellor, the Resident Magistrate;
Mr. George Rutherford, Collector of Customs; Captain

Proudfoot, R.D. Rangers; Messrs. Lamport and G. H. Wirsing, were advertised as stewards, and Mr. Frank Beningfield as Hon. Secretary.

The Ball, which was held on Thursday, the 16th September, like all of its kind when the aid of the Military is secured for its preparation, proved a great success. It was held at Winder's Hotel in the new dining and Lodge room, opened for the first time, and tastefully decorated. The catering and accessories were highly approved. Eighty ladies and gentlemen were present, and the regimental Band provided the music. A sit-down supper was laid in the front building, dancing was thereafter resumed and kept up well into Friday morning.

It was a calm, bright, moonlight night; the outside public in Beach Walk enjoying the spectacle through the low windows opened for air, which, however, was not improved by the tobacco smoke of the spectators, whose behaviour was otherwise unexceptional in grateful appreciation of the fascinating music, and in deference to the many ladies who had gathered in groups on the vacant erf adjoining. The advent of the Military effected quite a social revolution in the town. Mr. Faccioli, himself a proficient on the cornopean, aided by Mr. Haygarth, inaugurated concerts, which were a treat to hear. Balls, picnics, horse and boat races, military parades and the Band, proved specially attractive. Though our morals were somewhat relaxed, yet good fellowship obtained. The patience of both officers and men was sorely taxed, as the exigencies of the Indian Mutiny, calling for military reliefs and transports, delayed the arrival of any available troopship, with the expected 85th Regiment.

Sad it is to record that these fine times and merry diversions had a very demoralising influence upon all ranks, when their hopeful anticipations were dispelled by an order from Head Quarters, to repeat the Old Duke of York's celebrated movement and march up the hill again. Though they were "Down, down, down," they were now to go "Up, up, up," once more to their old quarters at Fort Napier. The barrack room language of the men was pathetic, if profane; while the women and children contributed to the general discontent and lamentation, softened certainly by thoughts for "the poor sick craters in Ingy," equally anxious to return to their homes. "Shure," said a woman, "but the bhoys as wint home wid Dr. Best, were the lucky ones!" However, discipline was maintained and on the hot, sultry morning of the 13th December the regiment trailed out of Durban, very unostentatiously, *en route* for Maritzburg, destined to eat their Christmas dinner there, instead of in the Old Country, as expected. Before leaving, Mr. Faccioli relieved his feelings with the score of a new marching tune, which the band rehearsed in town for our benefit, entitled "We must go back again!"

More Emigrants. A ship which, like the *Lady of the Lake* and *Jane Morice*, became a regular trader to and from England, and is associated intimately with the history of Durban and several of its inhabitants, arrived on the 14th September for the first time. To many the name *Early Morn*, with that of her Captain, Lowry, will be as household words, as the following list of her passengers will show :—Mr. John Acutt, Misses Acutt (4), Master Acutt, Capt. and Mrs. S. Helps, Chas. E. Helps, M.R.C.S., Samuel Crowe, M.R.C.S., Mr. and Mrs. C. W. Payne, Miss Payne, Messrs. Rich and Henry Binns, jun.,[*] all of whom testified to the captain's gentlemanly demeanour, the admirable manner in which the ship was found in every way, as also to the singular fact that "had it not been for baffling winds and otherwise unfavourable weather with which we were troubled the whole passage, her run would have been a remarkably short one." She was only 105 days out, having left London on the 1st June. Her registered capacity was 226 tons, and she had a full general cargo, the particulars of which had been advertised, as customary, for some weeks previously, as "expected shortly."

Freemasonry. Brother Geo. Winder having, at the instigation of certain members of the Ancient and Honourable Fraternity, constructed his large dining room especially with a view to its serving

---

[*] Afterwards Premier of Natal.

the purposes of a Lodge room, the brethren accordingly applied to the Grand Lodge of England for a warrant to meet and instruct persons of good report in the principles of the Craft. The Earl of Zetland, Grand Master, duly signed a Charter for the "Port Natal Lodge," No. 1040, appointing Hy. Jas. Mellor, Resident Magistrate, the first Worshipful Master; Lancelot Newton, Senior Warden; and William Garbutt Taylor, Junior Warden. The Charter was dated 3rd March, 1858, countersigned by Lord Panmure, Deputy Grand Master, and William Gray Clark, Grand Secretary. The first Regular meeting was held at the Masonic Hotel on the 12th of August to make a Tyler in the person of Mr. Geo. Pay. Having at its inception pronounced a favourable opinion of the order, I was initiated at its fourth meeting in October, passed the Chair some years later, and am still a member of this, the first lodge in the Colony, a joint owner with my brethren and fellows in the existing Masonic Hall, Smith Street.

Shipbuilding. Did not develop into a local industry for the reason that the coasting trade offered no encouragement, the risks and the attendant expenses being heavy. The Mail Steamers and Cape coasters meeting more than all our requirements, artificers directed their attention to repairing vessels, and to the construction of cargo boats, lighters, or pleasure boats. Sea fishing as an occupation was not thought of. On the 30th September the newspaper records the completion of the first Iron Lighter built here, omitting, however, to state by whom it was accomplished or to give dimensions. " A new and large Iron Lighter for landing goods [inside " the harbour], imported from England by Mr. Kahts, was " launched at Cato's Creek a few days ago, having been put " together on the adjacent bank; she is capable of receiving " thirty tons of cargo."

Circuit Courts. Chief Justice Sir Walter Harding made his first entry into Durban after his elevation to the order of St. Michael and St. George, for the purpose of holding the Circuit Court on the 18th October, and in accordance with an old English custom, worthily followed by the Dutch in

South Africa, a Cavalcade of burgesses, consisting of His
Worship the Mayor, several members of the Town Council
and of the Bar, with numerous other gentlemen, rode out
to meet his wagon on the Berea Ridge, and escort him down
the Berea Road into town.   On arrival at his hotel, they
presented a complimentary address of congratulation and
welcome, to which he promptly replied, inviting them to
partake of liquid refreshment.   This practice of escort was
maintained for several years, being expected by the Chief
Justice as deference due to a man of his degree; but, as
the Puisne Judges and the Attorney General preferred to
come and go at their own convenience in less demonstrative
manner, the custom fell into disuse by the burgesses, being
maintained by officials and members of the legal profession,
who, finding that the Chief could not always be relied on
for "refreshers" after their hot and dusty rides, gradually
found the time at their disposal limited to a formal call
after his arrival.   Some six years later, when holding the
appointment of Deputy Sheriff for Durban, it was my duty
to wait upon the Judges, and Sir Walter asked me for an
explanation of this falling off.   Being aware that he knew
that I knew that he knew, my ingenuity was taxed to stand
dexterously between the two stools, bench and bar, Mayor
and Burgesses, without reproaching either.   The Address
of Welcome presented to the Chief Justice by the Town
Council on his arrival had a double debt to pay, the Mayor
and Mr. Pinsent being members of the Bar, of which the
Honourable M. H. Gallwey, the new Attorney General, was
the recognised head.   He also had come down to conduct
the Crown cases, and acquaint himself with the Durban
practitioners.   He was not alluded to directly, but, in laud-
ing the recent judicial alterations under the new law "For
"the better administration of Justice within the Colony of
"Natal," the compilers of the Address take care to state
that they are immigrants from the mother country, and
"regard it as an earnest pledge of the dawn of an era of
"progress and advancement in our social state as a Colony.
"In such progress this district has already assumed an im-
"portant position, and we confidently predict a future of
"great prosperity and advancement for Natal."   The first
indictment tried on this occasion was a frivolous breach of
the Customs Law, of which James Mattheson, master of

the schooner *Yarra* was found not guilty. The principal witness was Mr. Edwin Lee, the Chief Landing-waiter, whose official officiousness and nice deportment made a lasting impression on the Judge, for, some years later, George Pearson, a burly, good-tempered Landing Agent, having suspended the snappy little gentleman by the coat collar and seating over the wharf edge, in threat of a ducking for some irritating interference, was tried before the Chief Justice for " assaulting and obstructing Her Majesty's Cus- "tom House Officer in the execution of his duty." On this occasion Mr. Lee, in his evidence, described a scratch he had received on his cheek, in mincing mellifluous terms, as " an elongated abrasion," when the Chief, as an antithesis, brusquely demanded, " Give us the small change of that in " English." There was an audible smile in Court. Much paraphrased, this memorable request has been incorporated in the current literature of the Colony.

Weddings.   The *Mercury* of the 21st October thus announced two marriages, which, in their results, may be claimed by " the parties interested" as a portion of Durban's history.

" On Thursday, the 14th inst., at St John's Church, Pinetown, by the Rev. W. H. C. Lloyd, M.A , Colonial Chaplain, assisted by the Rev. James Walton, H. Ellerton, eldest son of R. H. Stainbank, Esq., of Mitcham, Surrey, to Eliza, only daughter of R. W. Munro, Esq., of London, and niece of B. Munro, Esq., of Pinetown."

" On the 20th inst , at the Congregational Chapel, Durban, by the Rev. G. Y. Jeffreys, Hugh Gillespie, of this town, to Marianne, youngest daughter of the late D. S. Churchill, of Nottingham."

In the language of the " Ancient Mariner," I lent a hand at this last ceremony, being myself a wedding guest, by contributing sets of my Villa signal flags to the decorations. The chapel was well filled, the contracting parties being popular ; business men then having time to accompany their lady friends to such interesting displays. The heathenish practice of rice throwing had not been introduced from the East ; the more Arcadian and symbolical scattering of flowers at the feet of the bridal couple then obtained, though hoydenish spirits were not contented without shooting hands full of petals into the faces, or down the necks, of the victims.

The ordinary mode in which we made "haste to the wedding" was by the dignified ox wagon, the tent and sides decorated with flowers and evergreens; the whole family party occupying the interior. Those, who aspired to a little more style, borrowed a light spring wagon from some friendly Missionary, or local owner, and trotted in behind a smart span of Zulu oxen, decorated as aforesaid, with the front and back curtains rolled up to display the warm and blushing Bride and Bridesmaids inside. The men rode on horseback, but they were usually voted a nuisance, and relegated to the rear, in consequence of the dust they raised. On this occasion the light spring van was dispensed with, as the bridal party had only to walk across the street to Mr. J. R. Goodricke's new residence opposite, where the wedding breakfast was held. This function was of the prevailing fashion, a good substantial repast, ladies and gentlemen seated in pairs, supporting the Bride and Bridegroom in their wedding garments, at the head of the table, on which the regulation frosted Bridecake formed the central ornament. Toasts were drank, speeches made and responded to (more or less tangled), when liberties were taken in the name of the bridesmaids. Some wedding presents were in evidence, but they with their donors were not advertised. Of wedding bells we had none, but the occasion was as merry and as enjoyable as the genial host and hostess or ourselves could have desired. I have often recalled that happy social gathering, with some sentimental reflections, when doing business in the same house, after its conversion to the use of a Club House and then to offices for Accountants and Lawyers.

Harbour Matters. A fine large Port Boat, on the lifeboat principle, constructed at Cato's Creek by Mr. Chas. Povall, under the personal supervision of Mr. G. C. Cato, a Harbour Commissioner, was launched and taken over during October, which gave opportunity to the ever vigilant newspaper man to jibe at the local shipbuilding industry, and to sympathise with our boat builders by magnifying the fact that tenders had not been called for her construction, hinting that this privacy savoured of a *job*. Mr. Cato knew what was wanted, and saw that the Government got it, for this boat, though heavier than the whale boats in use, was highly efficient and safer for crossing the bar and communicating in all weathers with vessels outside. It served the Port for many years, and was the means of restoring Midshipman Prince Alfred to his ship the *Euryalus*, after his visit to Natal overland. It will be remembered by many of our townsmen, as, owing to the fact that it had no home, it was always on view floating between the stone groins in front of the Custom House. D. Leslie and Chas. Spradbrow were rated on the estimates its nominal caretakers, as Customs Boatmen.

The *Anne White*, schooner, 198 tons, E. R. Kersey, master, from London, with general cargo, in being piloted into the Harbour on the 22nd November through what was termed "the new North Channel," lost way for want of wind and anchored for a time, but the wind and sea, increasing, caused her to drift, until she took the ground on the Back Beach, head to sea. Spars were rigged to her stern, and, with the assistance of forty men of the 45th Regiment, all her cargo was ultimately landed in fair condition. She was floated off on the 5th December, and brought inside the next day. This catastrophe was opportune, and not to be attributed to an "ill wind," for that heterogeneous combination, then called "the Point lot"— having averred that the vessel might not have gone ashore if the new port boat, when passing to go to the *Pet* outside, had only towed her head off; also that if the weather held fair until the Mail Steamer arrived, she might easily be towed off the shore unharmed—revived the desire for a steam-tug. The Legislative Council being in session, the question was brought before the House, and although the Lieutenant-Governor had decided to reduce the expenditure on the Harbour Works to £600 for the year, he was moved to send a message to the House, "drawing its attention to " the advantages likely to arise from the employment of a " small Government steamer to keep down the Bar and to " act as a Tug, and that from personal conversation with " a gentleman recently arrived, of much experience on such " questions, he had ascertained that the cost of a steam " vessel of 150 tons, with engines of 40 horse power, would " not exceed £4,000, part of which amount might be paid "this year, and the balance next year." The Colonial Secretary explained that the gentleman of experience was named Robinson, and that he was willing to give every information on the subject. The Legislators jumped at the proposal, and appointed a committee to consider the matter, notwithstanding a Macfarlane characteristically enquired where the money was to come from. Mr. Albert Robinson was a travelling member of an engineering firm, and succeeded in placing our first steam tug and our first railway line, finding a satisfactory solution to the question where the money came from.

Not having much of a harbour to boast of, we made the most of the excellent facilities of our sandy Bay for careening ships and executing repairs; the mode being that of the "good old times" so disastrously followed by H.M.S. the *Royal George*, only in our case we allowed our brigs and schooners to take the ground at the edge of some convenient channel, before heaving them down by their masts to get at their keels.

Early in December the mail steamer *Waldensian* was detained over her advertised time of sailing, in consequence of having been beached in the Bay for cleaning purposes. Her sister ship, the *Madagascar*, was lost on the 3rd of the same month by grounding on a reef of rocks near the Fish River on a return trip from East London to Algoa Bay, becoming a total wreck. Crew and passengers saved.

About this time a large vessel from Batavia called for medical aid, and landed her captain, who was too ill to proceed. As a relative incident the *Mercury*:—

"Understood the Semaphore on the Bluff is out of repair, so that the signalman and Port Captain can only communicate by flags with each other, a practice very confusing to vessels outside watching for signals."

Public Meetings. On Monday, 22nd March, a meeting was held to consider the proposed Grants for Ecclesiastical Educational purposes. The conveners and speakers were all Nonconformists, directly opposed to any Ecclesiastical Grant. The feeling of the meeting being decidedly against the Government, the convention was described as one of "unusual

harmony." In case this should have missed fire, a second
meeting was called for Tuesday, 23rd, when it was unanimously resolved that the £5,000 per annum, reserved by the
Charter for Native purposes, should not be expended without first being submitted to the Legislative Council, as the
speakers declared it was evidently intended for the support
cf schools for native youth, and was clearly an ecclesiastical
grant under another name.   That we could see as far
through a millstone as other people we were assured, and
at a public meeting in September in reference to religious
instruction in schools, appointed a committee to look a little
closer into it.   Instructions having appeared in the Government *Gazette* to the Central Board of Education, directing that religious teaching in schools. if any, and of what
kind, was to be left entirely to the local committees, afforded
a rich field for controversy, and called for a Public Meeting
on Education generally; so one was held on the 17th December, ostensibly to hear the report of the committee appointed
in September.   Mr. John Sanderson was called to the
chair, and the following good men and true took active
parts in the proceedings; their names should be sufficient
to recall to older Colonists their peculiar beliefs and special
styles, a thing nobody out of the family will care for nowa-
days.   Mr. Pinsent moved the adoption of the report,
seconded by Mr. H. W. Currie. This with other resolutions was spoken to by Mr. Geo. Robinson. Rev. J. Gaskin,
Mr. Goodricke, Mr. J. C. Adams. Rev. G. Blencowe (recently arrived on the Wesleyan staff. and received with
cheers), Mr. Tyzack. who questioned him, Mr. P. Lennox,
and the Rev. G. Y. Jeffreys.

**Comets
and Stars.**   A brilliant and long-tailed member of this
erratic and mysterious community made its
appearance in our Western heavens on
Monday, the 10th October.   It was seen
shortly after sunset " going west," as Horace Greeley advised
the youth of the United States, and disappeared behind the
Berea about eight o'clock on this and several nights following   Our only official scientist. Dr. Mann, F.R.A.S., was
appealed to.   He looked up the authorities, and pronounced
the stranger to be an acquaintance which first made its

recorded appearance in 1556, and was thought to have portended the death of Pope Urban IV. It then took a turn into space at the rate of several thousands of miles a day, visiting that inconceivable distance where children are told Heaven is situated, returning to show itself again to this world A.D. 1642, after a round voyage of 292 years, and possibly to supply itself with fresh sun fuel. One Fabricius, the astronomer of the Emperor Charles V., kept it in view and recorded its doings. French, Italian, Dutch, and English astronomers got on its track, or on some other Comet's track, and, as usual with the exact scientist, differed in opinion, as certain others did about a Chameleon. One set declared the Comet was bound West, others said it was going East, but they all allowed it was circle sailing round the sun, and might play the mischief with the planetary system and the Earth's constitution. Mr. Bomme, of the Netherlands, and Mr. J. R. Hind, both distinguished and successful astronomers and mathematicians, between them got upon this particular Comet's trail, notwithstanding he was out of sight, and announced that it would be visible again on Earth on the 2nd August, 1858; as we in Durban saw it on the 10th October, this was tolerably exact figuring for an erratic object after a journey of 216 years. Ignorance and superstition fasten on such fiery portents, seeing omens in the stars; so while we looked in each other's faces to see what it meant, the good and pious among us kindly sought to "improve the occasion." The seed fell on good ground, bringing forth buds, if not fruit, for had we not the authority of the celebrated Dr. Cumming, who by working up sixes and sevens, conclusively proved out of Revelations, in his book called "The End," that all things were to reach finality about the year 1862. (*). Hence we were warned both from the press, the pulpit, and the sky of the time that was certainly at hand. For this many people actually made provision, and saved money by not renewing their leases and other contracts.

Three months later we were visited by a "Star" of another magnitude and nature, in the person of Ali-Ben-Sou-Alle, a Wandering Minstrel, who took the town by

* His work was catalogued in the Mechanics' Institute as "The End Coming."

o

storm and scattered all our aspiration for a higher life, in consequence of his imposing presence and skilful playing on strange instruments with unheard-of names, combined with broken French with an Irish twang, carrying away all the women—figuratively, if not literally, a Sabine rehearsal. Robinson Crusoe would have called him a "Moor" or an "Algerine," while I thought he might be of Alexandria, or that maritime country called the Levant, if he was not, as jealous home-staying youths declared, an Irishman. The newspaper man, however, knew better, and all for less than a quarter-column "ad." designated him "A Concert," thus:

"ALI-BEN-SOU-ALLE.

"It will be seen that this marvellous master of music is to give a concert at the Masonic Hall on Tuesday evening. We know not what is the secret of the universal success that in all parts of the world has attended this performer, but judging from his appearance we should imagine that a legion of fairy genii lie hidden within the folds of his gorgeous turban and his massive forest beard if not also within the broad girdle that encircles his portly person. At all events he is himself *A Concert.*"

Having advertised that he would give only one concert, the success attending his first performance in Winder's Masonic Rooms prompted Mr. W. Hartley (who had just completed an elegant and double-storied house in Smith Street, subsequently known, when he became Mayor, as the "Mansion House," and latterly as the "Athenæum Club") to induce the distinguished individual to give another public display in the new domicile; the spacious drawing-room with folding doors was crowded on the night of the 14th December, when the reporter again chortles:—

"The whole of his performance, both instrumental and vocal, elicited the warmest applause. All Ben Sou Alle's gorgeous and costly dress and commanding graceful presence added to the effect. It is surprising how the lungs of one man can sustain for nearly three hours so continuously, expiration of the vital fluid. We can now understand the universal eclat that has attended the world-wide wanderings of this accomplished professor. We need not say that Mrs. Cubitt discoursed her part of pianist with brilliant effect," etc., etc.

The "par" then censured the ill-mannered youths who had intruded their impecunious persons round the windows of private property, "surreptitiously plucking the fruits of genius and long labour." They were, however, offered opportunity for redemption, by a third concert held at Winder's, after which A. B. S. Alle departed for Maritzburg, leaving, if reports were true, some crushed or otherwise soiled hearts behind him.

Mechanics' Institution. In the Chairman's report to the subscribers for the year, he notes that lectures had been given on behalf of the Institution by E. P. Lamport, Esq., on the "Wit and Wisdom of Fable"; Dr. Mann, F.R.A.S., on "The Miracles of Science"; S. W. Rowse, Esq., on "Knowledge is Power"; Rev. G. Y. Jeffreys on "Oliver Goldsmith"; and the Right Rev. the Lord Bishop on "Electricity," with experimental illustrations; the Rev. W. A. Wilder had also promised "Progress of Modern Science." Net result, £12 7s. 9d.

Among the minor matters of local history for the year may be noted the following:—

Crinolines. On 20th March appears this advertisement:—

"THE STEEL SPRING PETTICOAT.

"This most durable, comfortable and becoming article of ladies' apparel may now be purchased for 18s., 20s., or 21s. at VICTORIA HOUSE."

At the end of the year the newspapers entertained us with a description of Her Majesty's visit to Cherbourg, and her amusement at the struggles of the Empress of the French, on ascending by the side ladder to the deck of H.I.M. battleship *Bretagne*, and the gallant efforts of the Duc de Malakoff in securing and compressing the balloon-like crinoline, which prevented the Empress' dress from being blown to the four quarters of the compass by the unmannerly wind. The awkward efforts of the Marshal-Duke excited the greatest mirth among the members of the procession on the imperial barge. After the visit, on descending to the barge, her dress caught on one of the hooks of the ladder, and she remained suspended, as it were, until Madame de Lourmel came to the rescue. The

Emperor and Queen Victoria were unsparing in their plea-
santries at the expense of both.   (*Court Journal*, abridged.)
The curious in these fashionable garments are referred to
Punch, Vol. 34, 1858.

**Convicts or
Coolies.**
With ample cheap labour within our borders, yet the impracticability and uncertainty of our natives kept us constantly
hankering after something like a modified
slavery, as a possible remedy for our chronic complaint.
Thus the *Mercury* patriotically seizes upon a rumour to
build up a first-class Colony :—

"The King of Delhi is to be located in British Kaffraria as a
convict prisoner under a sufficient Imperial force.   The British
Government would do well to turn their attention to Natal, as
requiring, more than any other South African Colony, a
supply of cheap labour, and if a sufficient force of European
troops were stationed here we believe a large number of Sepoy
rebels might be profitably and safely located in Natal.   The
situation of our port and Colony offer peculiar advantages, and
we do not believe there is another part of Her Majesty's
dominions so favourably circumstanced as a convict depot for
Indian mutineers.   Of course we do not advocate the introduction of any actual participators in Indian outrages, but only of
misguided mutineers."

That was all.

"ALLIGATORS.   April 29th.—A few days ago a large alligator
suddenly seized a horse of Mr. Watson's of the Umgeni, close
to the bank of that river on the Durban side, at the boat
landing-place, while the horse was being led across by a
Kaffir. . . .   Considering the great traffic of cattle, horses,
and men across the Umgeni, near its mouth, it is desirable that
the numerous alligators that infest it should be exterminated,
and we have before suggested the inducement of a sufficient
premium per head to Kaffirs and probably others, to do battle
with them.   As many as five or six of these huge monsters may
frequently be seen basking in the sun on the high sandbank recently formed at the mouth of the river—which is a monument
of the neglect of our Town Council—and they might easily be
reached by guns of sufficient range."

"SPEED .July 29th.—The most rapid journey ever made
between Maritzburg and Durban was accomplished a few days
ago by Mr. Henry Pepworth of the City.   With four horses he

performed the distance, about fifty-five miles, in four hours and three-quarters. This, on an African road, we should think is unprecedented."

The first Bicycle Race, over practically the same ground, took place in 1897. There were several competitors, each one riding his own wheel. The winner, a Durban man, accomplished the distance in four hours twenty-seven minutes. Pepworth avoided the heavy sand of the Berea Road by finishing at the Borough boundary (the present Tollgate), while the cyclist took the old road through Bellair, finishing at Umbilo Road, thus, in the slang of to-day, "beating the record."

Cathedral Bells. I hope to be excused for noting an amusing incident in which the member for Durban took a prominent part. It may prove of interest, especially as it shows how far-reaching was the influence of the Bishop of Natal. The following is from the *Mercury* report of the proceedings of the Legislative Council sitting in Maritzburg on 24th November:—

"THE SOOTHING CHIME.—The cathedral bell having commenced tolling its vesper notes to the discomfiture of the auditory nerves of the members, the Usher was sent to stop the disturbance, while the Speaker commenced to read the despatches, but soon returned and stated the ringer refused submission, whereupon Mr. Millar moved that the Kafir be taken into custody for contempt by the policeman outside. The Attorney General objected to that functionary being employed for that purpose. Mr. Bergtheil spoke vehemently in favour of the motion, while Dr. Johnston said this was not the way the Attorney General acted when putting questions to witnesses on nonsensical subjects in the Magistrate's Office, and was proceeding to state his conviction that the Governor was laughing at the Council, and that he saw certain tendencies—when the Treasurer called him to order. The bell ceased. Mr. Millar dropped his motion, threatening severer measures on a repetition of the gratuitous concert, and then the matter subsided."

Atlantic Cable. The breakage of the first Atlantic Cable between England and America had of course been predicted by those wise ones of Durban (and elsewhere) who always reminded us, after

events, that " I told you so."   The world waited in anxiety
for its repair or restoration, and the year closed with the
announcement to us that:—

    "News had been received from Newfoundland that signals had
been received by the Atlantic cable.   Thus some hope is entertained that this great undertaking will not be an entire failure.
Signals had also been received at Valentia."

CHAPTER XIV.

1859.

J. R. GOODRICKE, SAVORY PINSENT, AND WILLIAM HARTLEY — MAYORS.

With our new-born honours thick upon us, the enfranchised burgesses of Durban were evidently desirous of purging themselves of the accusations of undue influence, and implications of bribery made at the first elections, as the printers found that the settlement of their little bills against Candidates for legislative honours were repudiated, or referred to their committees, and by the committees to the several secretaries, who maintained that the requisitions and addresses had been kindly published as news, thus passing the liability until somebody should be euchred; consequently the first issue of the *Mercury* in January contains the following prudent intimation : —

"THE ELECTIONS.

"We think it right to notify that all Election Addresses will be published only as matters of business, and that immediate payment will be expected."

This in anticipation of a forthcoming contest, as the first Legislative Council of Natal was dissolved by proclamation on the 3rd January, the Government having been defeated (by refusal to pass the estimates) on the question of the £5,000, reserved by the Charter for Native purposes, the Council contending that its expenditure should be left to the Council's direction. In this respect the Legislative Council followed the questionable example of the Town Council of Durban in asking for more than their Charters granted them. The independent, patriotic spirit of those times, when nothing was to be gained by subserviency—the Governor having no good gifts to bestow—fostered self-reliance and a general determination to follow the good old plan of taking as much as they could, and keeping it in possible, at their own disposal, for the use of both town and country.

"L'Imperatrice Eugenie" Barque, 308 tons, Capt. Alex. Airth, arrived from London on the 21st January, 71 days from Plymouth. Passengers: Mr. and Mrs. John Brown, Mr. and Mrs. Turnbull, Mr. and Mrs. Marianne and child, Messrs. McArthur, E. H. Hunt, Primrose, Turnbull and Catto (2). This vessel became a regular trader, and her captain eventually married and settled in Durban, becoming Lloyd's Agent on the retirement of Mr G .C. Cato, having in the meantime acted as Port Captain.

Burns' Centenary. Afforded a happy opportunity for the re-union of emigrants from the land o' cakes. The celebration in Durban took place on the 25th January, and is the first recorded instance of what in these days is termed a " Smoker." In memory of our old townsmen who took a part I just record their names, omitting the lengthy programme, the Scottish songs and the poet's writings so familiar to us all. The young man who attended for the *Mercury* states : —

" Dear's large room, Field Street, was beautifully fitted up and lighted ; the walls were adorned with evergreens with the picture of the poet and his statue on Carlton Hill. At the further end of the room raised seats afforded a view of the platform and remote spectators ; the company was more numerous than on any previous occasion of festivity in this town. Two hundred and fifty tickets were sold, but large numbers beside had sight and audience outside through the open windows. Indeed all the ticket-holders could not obtain admission, and many preferred the cooler atmosphere of the verandah [of whom I was one]. Mr. Goodricke, the Mayor, presided, and opened the meeting with a few appropriate and cordial observations on the occasion. Mr. John Sanderson then read an admirably written dissertation on the life and genius of Burns, displaying admirable taste both in method and style; the other addresses per programme were by Mr. Lamport and Mr. W. Campbell, at different periods of the evening. Mr. Lamport however—doubtless carried away by poetic fervour—substituted two Scotch songs and a humorous recitation, introduced by a few suitable remarks. Mr. W. Campbell's address was chiefly illustrative of the social and moral tendencies of Burns' poetry, and both he and Mr. Sanderson vindicated the poet's character from the aspersion sometimes cast upon it. The remainder of the evening—with a quarter of an hour's interval—was occupied with the following performers:—Songs, Mr. Ramsay, Mr. Haygarth; hornpipe, Mr. McAllister; song, Mr. Barnes; recitation, Mr. Ferguson; Highland Fling, Mr. Andrew Milne; songs, Mr. Jones, Mr. Ramsay, Mr. Haygarth; dance, " White Cockade," Mr. McAllister; songs, Mr. Barnes, Mr. Ramsay; " Gillie Cullum," danced by Mr Milne. . . .

" The audience was highly delighted, and in some instances encored the singers; the national dances by Messrs. McAllister and Milne were executed with wonderful agility in full Highland costume, accompanied by no less skilful musician than Mr. McPherson on the fiddle. . . . At the conclusion ' Auld Lang Syne ' was sung by Mr. Ramsay, with the thrilling chorus of the whole company; the singers on the platform joining and crossing hands in appropriate gestures. The whole was finally concluded by ' God Save the Queen,' and three cheers for Her Majesty and three for the Mayor. Ample refreshments in fruits, cakes, and cooling drinks [I distinctly recognised the 'Mountain Dew'] were provided without expense to the company, and the whole of the arrangements reflected great credit on the committee. . . . After the public entertainment, a large number of ladies and gentlemen remained, and for several hours enjoyed the lighter graces of the dance to long past the ' wee sma' hours ayont the twal,' even until the sun awoke a second century of the apocalypse of Burns."

The Natal Railway. First dawned among the possibilities on the 20th January, when we were informed in a sub-leader of the *Mercury* :—

. " We·are happy to announce that a project is on foot, under the auspices of an eminent practical engineer, at present in the Colony, for constructing a railway, with locomotive steam power, between the Point and the town, through the bush and along the principal street thoroughfares. The great width of our streets renders this practicable without injury to general traffic. We believe it is intended to form a company for this undertaking. . . . It has commonly been thought that the Bay Beach should be the line of any rail or tramway from the Point, but it is wisely suggested that the beach should be reserved for the purposes hereafter of a ship channel to the town, and for wharves and warehouses along its side," etc., etc.

A fortnight later a Prospectus of the proposed Company was printed for private circulation, and the *Mercury* of the 3rd February announced that nearly half of the capital was subscribed for in Durban. The prospectus gave, as usual, an estimate of cost and expenses, showing a modest return of 30 per cent. It further stated that the project was warmly supported by the Government; the railway would pass entirely through Ordnance ground, which it was expected would be granted for use free of charge; the Company is established for constructing and working a railway from the Point to Durban, with wharf, shed, and Plant at the Point to land and ship goods and passengers, and terminus in town from whence goods can be delivered by wagons. That the promoters had secured the able co-operation of Mr. A. Robinson, an eminent engineer, and feel every confidence in launching this the first Railway in Natal (and in South Africa). The Prospectus goes on at railway speed as follows :—

"This railway and the other operations contemplated by the Company, are the more essential now that a steam tug is to be placed on the station, which, whilst obviating a recurrence of the frequent detention of vessels, will combine, when the jetty is completed, to make the harbour the most efficient in South Africa, and bring a large amount of passing tonnage to the port, Natal being situated directly on the route from India. It is contemplated eventually to extend the line beyond Congella to the Umhlatuzan, whence stone for the Harbour improvements can be procured, where wagons to and from Pietermaritzburg can be loaded, avoiding the whole of the heavy pull through the Berea sand, and where the growing sugar estates near the Isipingo, Umlasi, and beyond, promise a large amount of traffic. There is not a member of the community but will benefit either directly or indirectly by the opening up of railway communication in Natal, of which this is but the forerunner."

The Provisional Directors were Messrs. R. Acutt, G. C. Cato, A. Coqui, J. Proudfoot, W. Smerdon (Chairman), and G. H. Wirsing (Secretary). We were nothing unless we were practical, so the *Mercury* commenting on the Prospectus, and with a desire to indicate the benefits to the community, announces : —

"The Directors had already made a purchase of wood for the purposes of the railway, a favourable opportunity having offered, and they are preparing to have the line cleared without delay. There was no need to wait for the Act of the Legislature, as there can be no opposition, and the capital will be readily subscribed."

The Town Council does not appear to have been consulted.

A general meeting of shareholders was held on the 28th February, when the Trust Deed was adopted and the following gentlemen elected Direcors : W. Smerdon, J. Millar, R. Acutt, A. Coqui, J. Proudfoot, E. Snell, and G. H. Wirsing. Messrs. J. Henderson, J. Bergthiel, and C. Behrens were elected for Maritzburg. A special vote of thanks was passed to Mr. A. Robinson "to whom the Directors have wisely entrusted the entire management and control of the works. The line of the railway is already staked off, and active operations are proceeding." The Directors appointed Mr. Edmund Tatham secretary.

As I have already shown, public meetings had become a necessity, on any questions of general interest. The Railway Company having applied to the Corporation for a site for a terminus, we felt ourselves called upon to give the Town Council our directions and support, accordingly, a meeting was held early in April, when we : —

" Were almost unanimous that the Market Square ought not to be appropriated in view of the prospective requirements of commerce and health ; and the meeting recorded its opinion that the most eligible site for a terminus is in front of Pine Terrace, north-west of St. Paul's Church, or near the old town pound.".

" At a meeting of the Town Council, on the 28th of April, a reply was agreed to the application of the Railway Company, to the effect that the Council, bowing to the declared will of the burgesses at the late public meeting, declined to lease or sell any portion of the Market Square for a terminus. Mr. Cato wished to add an offer of ground at the entrance of the east end of the town, thus depriving the town of a central terminus.

This very selfish and unfair proposal was frustrated by the judicious interposition of the Mayor. We understand the Directors of the Railway have fixed upon the site north-west of St. Paul s Church, within the Ordnance Ground."

The burgesses of Durban had never willingly taken " No " for an answer, while, as characteristic Britons, they did not know when they were beaten. The Town Council might seek to enforce its authority upon the Company, but it was not quietly allowed to interfere with the enterprising speculations of so promising a concern. Accordingly a petition, emanating from the shareholders, set out their grievance to the Legislative Council, pointing out truthfully that the terminus site sought to be forced upon them was " outside the limits of the town." The Bill before the House was accordingly altered in Committee, bringing the terminus within the Market Square. On this fact becoming known a counter-petition was hurriedly drafted, and signed by some fifty burgesses conveniently caught during an afternoon, and despatched to Maritzburg. The ire of the townspeople was roused and a Public Meeting held on the 11th June in the Masonic Rooms. Mr. Robert Acutt, one of the Directors of the Company, was chairman of the meeting. Mr. Lamport and Mr. Currie moved the first resolution. Mr. Snell, another Director, seconded a subsequent one. In substance the meeting, with the exception of three hands, declared the site previously selected by the burgesses was " central and advantageous," and that the alteration in the Bill without notice to them, " being a gross invasion of the rights of the burgesses, was illegal, unjust, and impolitic.' A petition embodying the views of the meeting, consisting of 250 burgesses, was ordered to be signed by the Chairman and handed to Mr. Goodricke (now member for Durban) for presentation prior to the third reading of the Bill. This petition was duly presented to the House on Monday the 13th June, and rejected by 11 votes to 1, in consequence of the disrespectful words " illegal and unjust." This lesson in language has never been lost upon Durban. Early in August the *Mercury* informed us that advices had arrived stating : —

"The whole working plant had been supplied considerably below the estimate of the Engineer. The permanent way will be constructed entirely of iron, the rails being laid on iron sleepers, supported by iron boxes, on a new plan which had been found to answer perfectly in India, Egypt, and other countries, being much safer and more durable, and in the end more economical than the old plan of wooden sleepers. . . . The whole would be shipped during the last month. . . . We trust the favourable aspect of the undertaking, under the present circumstances, will help to facilitate an amicable settlement regarding the terminus. The line of way being now levelled the whole distance, and the wharf near the Custom House being in a forward state of progress, the only remaining difficulty is the question of the terminus, which certainly was not settled by the Act of the Legislature, but may be easily adjusted by local common sense and mutual concession."

The reference to local common sense came before the Town Council on the 15th August, but without mutual concessions, the Railway Company having applied for information as to the rent required by the Corporation for various sites named, viz., Block A, about 4 erven on the Market Square fronting the Masonic Hotel and Gardiner Street; Block B, the corner on which the present Town Hall and Market House now stands; and Block C, five erven in Pine Terrace opposite "Drew's Corner" (West End Hotel). A stormy discussion ensued, in which all the Councillors participated. Mr. Councillor Cato was of opinion the Railway Company might be willing to pay £60 a year rent for Block A. Some of the Council thought £15 a year for Block B a fair rental, while Mr. Lamport objected altogether to establishing a new principle of cutting up fresh erven in the town for Block C. Mr. Cato virtually represented the Railway Company, and in the course of the contention stated that the Railway Company could not extend the line beyond the town. The Government would very likely have a branch line from Congella joining the trunk near the bush, outside the town. He further explained that the Company intended to erect four Blocks of 1,200ft. of bonded store-room, in which the whole cargo of a ship could be stowed and conveyed by horse tramways to each store. He was so convinced of the utility of the railway that he would sacrifice anything or everything in order to promote it. In five years he was sure no man would be found to have an objection to the Market Square as a site for the terminus. . . . The Company would probably take the four erven in the Market Square at a rental of £60, so as to carry out the provisions of the Bill, and then take the terminus out of the town, erecting meanwhile valuable stores in the Market Square which would not only yield a handsome rate revenue, but on the expiry of the lease revert to the Corporation. Mr. Lamport, in a long motion, informed the Company that Block A was reserved for a Town Hall, that Block C could not be granted because the reservation of fresh erven was sound legislation for the future, but that Block B was at their disposal at the upset price of £15 yearly. He was particularly incisive in speaking to the motion and the various amendments proposed, also upon the Mayor's suggestion that a site opposite Dacomb's Corner be offered. He joined issue with Mr. Pinsent upon the legal aspects of the Bill, and dissected Mr. Cato's statements regarding the erection of buildings, rates accruing, etc. The former were merely castles in the air, the actual buildings a probable blotch, and the whole line of argument a gilded pill. He protested against Mr. Cato's attempt to pin his (Mr. L's) assent down to his preposterous estimate of £60 for Block A. It was ridiculous to talk of fixing a price for the land when by the Ordinance of 1854 all leased lands were bound to be submitted to public competition. Mr. Cato, seldom at a loss, could only retort that Mr. Lamport's knowledge of the law was utter nonsense.

The Mayor (Mr. Hartley) showed the disadvantage of having the terminus upon the Ordnance Reserve, whereby all the actual benefit would go to the Government Chest. He was desirous of postponing the discussion, as in his opinion this was a most important motion, and one the effect of which would be felt fifty years hence. He was over-ruled; amendment after amendment put and lost. The original motion selecting Block B was also lost by the Mayor's casting vote. Then came in Mr. Councillor Ferguson, familiarly known to us as "Bailie Ferguson," with a common-sense motion, " That the land applied for marked C, or any along Pine Terrace, can be leased in the usual way provided by ordinance." Mr. Arthur seconded. Mr.

Cato, with the seaman's axiom, 'One hand for himself, t'other for the owner," feared from their proceedings to-night that the Company would be disheartened and give up the project. He therefore moved as an amendment, "That the Company be informed they can have four erven where the Pound stands, or any Corporation land near Stanger Street." For the amendment 2, against it 4. For " Bailie Ferguson's " motion 3 for and 3 against. The Mayor gave his casting vote in its favour, whereupon both Mr. Cato and Mr. Lamport protested. The hour being late the Council adjourned.

A meeting of the Directors of the Railway Company was held early in October to decide the vexed question of the terminus. The Chairman (Mr. Smerdon) and another Director were absent. The opinion of the Attorney-General was read, and distinctly laid down the absolute necessity, under the Bill of Incorporation, of placing the terminus upon the Market Square. A strong minority, Messrs. R. Acutt, Proudfoot, and Kahts were for having the terminus on the Ordnance land opposite St. Paul's Church. The majority, having respect to the highest legal opinion, voted for the Market Square. It was accordingly settled that the line was to curve from the Ordnance land at the rear of the present Police Station, cross West Street on the curve, and finally terminate on the Market Square proper, on the original block A opposite the Masonic (now Royal) Hotel. A storm was raised outside by this cool appropria-tion of the Borough property, and those burgesses who had ordinarily discussed " the thin end of the wedge," now saw a " white elephant." The resulting agitation led to a reconsideration by the Directors, and, on the recom-mendation of their Engineer, they applied to the Town Council on the 30th November to fix a rental for an area equal to four erven in the Market Square, west of St Paul's (Block B) for a terminus. The Council on a division, fixed the rental at £200 per annum for 50 years. The Company, in anticipation, had requested that the Town Surveyor be instructed to point out to the Surveyor of the Railway the position of the crossing of the wagon road. It is not clear what was meant by this, possibly the present Church Street, but to ensure a correct ruling Messrs. McArthur and Ferguson were appointed a committee to assist them . My readers will see that the day of small things was not to be despised, especially in our enterprising Colony, accordingly the announcement in the *Mercury* of the 1st December was of serious import to us, and should be now received with becoming gravity :—

"THE RAILWAY.—A large portion of the plant for this undertaking, not less than 130 tons weight, is shipped on board the *Lady Mona*, now fully due. The *Clansman, Selina* and *Oak*, which sailed subsequently, have the remaining portions on board; so that if the Directors do not still further cause delay by a bootless pertinacity respecting the site of a terminus, the railway will be opened for traffic early in the year."

This was followed by an equally interesting announcement, which to modern readers may savour of grandmotherly instruction, but at that time the use of concrete in the Colony was a novelty, while the public mind had been exercised as to the manner of wharf the Railway Company would construct :—

"ARTIFICIAL STONE.

" Square blocks of stone are being manufactured for the facing of the new railway wharf, by means of rubble from the Bluff, consolidated in moulds, with a fluid composition of cement and sand, which speedily hardens into a solid mass, having all the appearance of a tooled block, and, we are assured, equal in hardness and durability to any stone in the neighbourhood. The expense is said to be less than one-half of stone brought from a distance and hewed into shape."

By the end of the month we were told :—

"The prospects of this undertaking are now bright and cheering. The larger portion of the plant has arrived, and the permanent way will now very shortly be laid. The line is levelled and fenced along Pine Terrace to the site of the terminus, and we are now most happy to report that the question is now finally settled by a resolution of the ·Board (unopposed) to have the terminus on the Ordnance Ground, the site recommended at a public meeting of burgesses held last April, and all along contended for by us."

Were it possible for modern Natalians to
S.S.Waldensian. revert to "the good old times" of this
history, when we deemed ourselves blessed
with one mail steamer a month, they would have some conception of the dismay that fell upon us upon hearing that the
Waldensian, with the homeward bound mails and passengers to the number of sixty (mostly military invalids) when
crossing the Bar on the 5th February, had struck on a
rock, injuring her stern post and unshipped her rudder,
obliging her to re-enter the harbour at once, to repair
damages. In a leading article the *Mercury* thus explains :

"There was a somewhat heavy swell and surf on the Bar, so
that the port-boat could not take soundings, but, the tides being
full, Captain Joss considered that he would not be justified in
delaying departure beyond the contract time. The steamer
therefore proceeded to the Bar, but the water was found not
sufficiently deep to cross, and the recently opened side-channel,
opposite the back beach was tried. Owing to the lift of the
sea the stern of the steamer unfortunately touched heavily
upon the ledge of rock that lies in that part of the channel, the
rudder was unshipped and the stern-post damaged. As the
wind was blowing fresh on the land, the anchor was immediately dropped to hold the vessel in the channel. . . .
On getting her head to sea the cable was slipped and she
steamed safely out of the channel to the outer anchorage. The
mails and passengers were trans-shipped next day on board the
clipper barque *L'Imperatrice Eugenie*, belonging to the same
owners. The barque was hastily discharged of her remaining
inward cargo on Sunday, and sailed out that afternoon, leaving
for Cape Town on Wednesday the 9th, and it is confidently
believed she will reach the Cape in time to save the mail for
England and return punctually with the January mail. . . .
We trust this untoward event will awaken the Government to
a sense of the vital importance of resuming the harbour works.
We have no hesitation in affirming, on evidence which defies
refutation, that if the works had not been suspended two years
ago, but had proceeded even at their former slow rate of
progress, an effect ere now would have been produced on the
Bar by which the water would have been permanently deepened
at least two feet, and the new and intricate lateral channel
recently used would have been effectually stopped, as it must
be before the Bar itself can be permanently reduced by means
of the full force of the outward current of the waters of the Bay.

At present the water has two outlets, and the scouring current over the Bar is consequently seriously diminished in volume and force."

Readers will recollect that the *Annabella* contributed to this state of things. In a " Local " of the 7th April we are informed :—

" The *Waldensian* mail steamer has completed her repairs with perfect success. A new iron rudder and false stern post have been made and fitted, and the steamer was floated off the beach to her berth in the channel on Sunday, when her screw was found to work admirably. The chief work has been done by Mr. Gavin of this place, but a casting was by Mr. Booklass at his new foundry. This is the first instance of extensive repairs of an iron vessel being effected at this port, but from the perfect success of the attempt, and the now ample facilities for such works at this port, we may anticipate an increasing demand for the talent and energies of our mechanics."

The steamer left for Cape Town and Coast Ports with mails and passengers on the 17th April.

Evangelical Alliance.   A public meeting was held on Thursday, the 10th February, at the Wesleyan Chapel. The Rev. Geo. Blencowe occupied the chair. Proceedings were opened by hymn and prayer by Rev. G. Y. Jeffreys. Rev. Chas. Scott, of Pinetown, moved the first resolution approving the principle, seconded by the Rev. P. Huet, Dutch Reformed Church, in an earnest and eloquent speech. Resolution carried unanimously.

The Rev. W. Ireland, of the American Mission, moved the appointment of a committee of officers, comprising Episcopalians, Presbyterians, Wesleyans, Independents, Baptists, Dutch Reformed, Lutheran, and three ministers of the American Mission in Natal, which was seconded by Mr. Geo. Robinson and carried unanimously. Result:

President, Rev. H. Pearse; Vice-Presidents, Rev. W. Campbell, A. W. Evans, Esq ; Secretaries, Rev. C. Scott, Rev. G. Y. Jeffreys; Committee—Mr. Robert Acutt, Mr. J C. Adams, Mr. Blackwood, Dr. Blaine, Rev. G. Blencowe, Mr. William Campbell, Mr. Henry Cowey, Mr. E. R. Dixon, Mr. Ferreira, Rev. J. Gaskin, Rev. Aldin Grout, Mr. Harwin, Rev. P. Huet, Mr. Kahts, Mr. Lennox, Rev. W. H. C. Lloyd, M.A., Colonial Chaplain, Mr. Martin, Mr Solomon Maritz, Rev. F, Mason, Rev. J. Possett, Mr. T. Platt, Rev. J. Rood, Mr. Wade, Rev. H. A. Wilder, Mr. Wheeler.

The organization, thus successfully established, continued its useful and active operations for some years, dying eventually from lack of opposition and interest.

The Rice Case. As a necessary prelude to the Borough Elections, and the trial of the great Rice Case, I must here, in the order of time, introduce a matter that properly appertains to the Town Council. The trial of the "Rice Case" was set down for the 8th March in the Supreme Court, Pietermaritzburg. The Mayor had £200 placed at his disposal for the expenses of witnesses, etc. (by whom is not recorded). Some prudent burgesses, however, after due consideration, made up their opinions and placarded the town with :—

BURGESSES OF DURBAN.

RICE QUESTION.

We, the undersigned burgesses, impressed with the practical importance of the above subject to the interests of the town, both in respect to the large amount about to be subjected to the glorious uncertainty of the law, and the strong feelings of exasperation and dissension which any failure on the part of the Council would probably give rise to, hereby invite the burgesses to meet at Winder's Masonic Hotel, on Wednesday evening next, February 23rd, to decide whether they will recommend the Council to proceed with the action, and if not, to consider the best means of bringing about a compromise of the question without prejudice to the position of the Council in case such compromise should be declined on the part of the plaintiff, or to take such other steps in the matter as may be deemed desirable. Chair to be taken at 8 o'clock precisely.

W. Palmer, S. Pinsent, J. J. Chapman, J. Brickhill, J. Sanderson.

Accordingly, at this eleventh hour, the burgesses met, and, considering the time for compromise past, rejected by an overwhelming majority the following resolution, proposed by Mr. Councillor Pinsent, who had been unanimous with the other Town Councillors in concurring in the original cause of action :—

"That it is desirable, in order to prevent the pecuniary loss to the burgesses attendant on the possible contingency of an adverse decision on the rice question, that a compromise should be attempted, on the principle that the plaintiff should be indemnified from all loss, and that a Committee be appointed to negotiate with the plaintiff on this subject. That in making this proposition the meeting expresses no opinion on the legal part of the question, or on the propriety of the conduct of the Council."

Borough Election. The general elections for the Legislative Council were set down for the 15th and 16th March for Durban County, and the 16th and 17th March for Durban Borough. The question of the day being the £5,000 reserve, it became necessary to have a public meeting on which to impale and prove the candidates. Accordingly, on requisition, the Mayor called us together at Winder's Masonic Hall on the 28th February, when Mr. Geo. Robinson discovered that the seat of the censor was more congenial than that of a chairman. Mr. Goodricke (Mayor) being himself a candidate, after opening the meeting, vacated the chair, into which the editor of the *Mercury* was at once voted. Mr. John Millar wrote apologizing for unavoidable absence. The other candidates were Mr. S. Pinsent and Mr. William Hartley. Mr. Pinsent, who a week or two previously had convened a meeting on his own account, where he expressed his belief that the opposition to the £5,000 reserve was not so much a matter of principle, as a suspicious jealousy of certain ecclesiastical bodies, was first called upon. He was received with cheers, and after making a very candid statement proceeded to answer questions which amid much uproar were put to him. To Mr. Kermode he replied that if he were offered the Speakership he should decline it, unless no one else could be found. (Hear, hear). This question propounded as a jest, was a cruel one. Mr. Pinsent, though a sound lawyer, a deep thinker, and zealous burgess, the donor of a handsome legacy to our Public Library, was a man of small stature, with an unfortunate spinal curvature. He had a halting hesitating delivery, which, coupled with a prominent head, and the absence of one of two front teeth, gave him in debate a snappish manner that encouraged irreverent wits to nick-name him "Quilp."

Mr. Currie asked if Mr. Pinsent would maintain the right of the Council to control the reserve, even if the Home Government refused that right. It was some time before Mr. Currie got what he thought a satisfactory answer, and the question was put and repeated amid much amusement, uproar, and snuff (then a general and popular refection). Mr. Jeffels asked Mr. Pinsent to reconcile his present statement with his conduct at the County Meeting on labour, and the celebrated case Mellor v. Buchanan was brought on the carpet amidst much uproar. Mr. Goodricke rose, and was duly cheered. He thought Mr. Pinsent had considerably shifted his ground; he, Mr. Goodricke, had never looked on the reserve as a monetary question, but had always maintained the inexpediency of Government controlling the £5,000. . . . Why was it, then, that the people of England were led to believe the Colonists were such a harsh and oppressive community? He ascribed this result to the misrepresentation of such men as Bishop Gray and others, whose pet schemes were to be fostered by the £5,000 reserve. . . . . The elective members should strive might and main to obtain the control of that reserve, which would otherwise be spent in bolstering up the Locations. (Great cheering). In answer to questions by Messrs. Kermode and Tyzack, Mr. Goodricke stated that he should not accept the Speakership, Mr. Tyzack was proceeding to give his private views on the Port, but was stopped by the meeting. He therefore plunged into the labour question, and asked Mr. Goodricke whether he would be for collecting statistics regarding the available kafir labour in the country. Mr. Brunton asked Mr. Goodricke whether it was true he had advised Mr. Snell to go to law with the Corporation. The question was received with immense uproar, in which Mr. William Crowder took a prominent and lively part. After the commotion had in some degree subsided, Mr. Goodricke explained. Mr. Pinsent, having conquered his constitutional nervousness and acquired a second thought, wished to express his views on the subject of kafir voters, and recognized the danger in the present sate of things. In his opinion the adoption of civilized usages and acquirement of civilized education would form a barrier between the barbarian and civilized natives. Mr. Kermode enquired if Mr. Pinsent considered that top boots and kid glooves would form the barrier spoken of. (Laughter).

Mr. William Hartley, on rising, was greeted with prolonged and deafening cheers. He said that after his published address any further remarks would be quite superfluous, and accordingly proceeded to contradict his assertion for a good quarter of an hour, in a well-chosen practical address on the general questions of the day, which was applauded throughout. It was at this meeting that his cognomen, "The Great Fact," was first publicly applied to him. In answer to Mr. Kermode, Mr. Hartley said he would not accept the Speakership. ("You're a brick"). He would stop polygamy. Some confusion arose about a question put by Mr. Kermode as to whether Mr. Hartley would make any distinction between the rights he would confer on a white immigrant and a black refugee.

The Rice question was then introduced, and various questions, altogether irrelevant, were put on the subject.

The meeting now became very noisy, and the unhappy Chairman had considerable difficulty in maintaining anything like order. A great number of questions were asked by various persons, most of which, however, referred to Mr. Hartley's statements. Thus the reporter :—

"The self-willed factiousness of the meeting compelled every interrogator in his turn to take his turn on the platform, which they accordingly did, to the hilarious amusement of those present. Messrs. Mason, Salmon, Brunton, Currie, Maythan, and others respectively put questions. Some of them were of a decidedly ludicrous character, as, for instance, that of Mr. Kershaw, who, mounting the dais in his professional toga [Butcher], asked Mr. Hartley if he would appoint him Speaker, and again, that with which Mr. Kermode closed the business of the meeting by asking Mr. Hartley for a song. Notwithstanding the prevalence of a rather uproarious hilarity the meeting passed off without any occurrence of a disagreeable nature. The large assembly dispersed about 11 o'clock after a cheer for the Chairman, and indifferent cheers for the different candidates."

The polling took place on the 16th and 17th March. With the exception of Mr. Pinsent, who had no organised committee, the usual procedure was followed as to posters, flags, favours, stump speeches, committee meetings in convenient rooms at public houses, and partizan canvassers. The authorities on this occasion made due allowance for any little playfulness on our parts, evidently trusting the burgesses to look after themselves, as they appointed the Chief Constable Polling Officer, thus obliging him to remain within the Market House for the two days of the election, there to maintain order outside to the best of his ability. The polling throughout was very even, resulting, without over-excitement or openly pronounced "undue influences" in the return of Mr. J. Millar, 138 votes, Mr. J. R. Goodricke, 130 votes, as members for the Borough. Mr. W. Hartley received 86 votes and Mr. S. Pinsent 40. The total voters on the roll were 291, and 218 polled. After the customary cheers and congratulations, the candidates were invited outside to the hustings, to return thanks to the assembled hilarious burgesses on the Market Square. The *Mercury* in a supplement states :—"We have not time for a report. The most noticeable and yet characteristic thing was said by Mr. Hartley, who declared that *the loss was theirs.* It was said good-humouredly, at the end of a manly straightforward address, and fairly "brought down the house," testified by laughter, cheers, and cries of "A Great Fact." After the speeches Messrs. Millar and Goodricke were forced into a cart gaily dressed out with flags ; the rustic vehicle was pulled along by the jubilant voters for some little distance, until checked by the Market Square sand, and the prayers of the honourable members to be released from their hazardous position before reaching the Club. It was on this occasion that Joe Harris, a butcher's slaughterman, ascended the hustings in blue smock and apron, and taking off his greasy cap introduced himself to the electors (awaiting the close of the poll) as a future candidate ; alluding to the return of Mr. James Kinghurst for the County, and making a very witty burlesque speech of the Cheap Jack order, replying smartly to questions put to him, and keeping us well amused until an invitation to "liquor up" brought him down. His aptness at repartee, fluency of language, and power of absorption, made him quite a Durban celebrity; so much so that on one occasion the threat was held out of running in Joe Harris for the County, if some unpopular person were requisitioned.

The Masonic Hotel. For reasons which will hereafter appear, it is necessary to mention that on the 10th March Mr. William Wood announced that he had taken over this Hotel and business from Mr. Winder, who was about to proceed to England. It thus comes into our history as Wood's *Masonic Hotel.*

Natal Land and Colonization Co. On the 17th March the Port Natal Company advertised their intention to apply to the Legislature for a Bill of Incorporation, the object being "the more effectual colonization of this Colony, combining also the opening up for that purpose of land now unavailable, in private hands." This new and important undertaking was originated by some of the most influential citizens of Maritzburg. The notice was signed by Richard Vause, Maritzburg, 12th March, 1859. The Editor of the *Mercury*, in a sub-leader, suggests that a more intelligible and expressive title would be, say, "The Natal Land and Colonization Company," the "Port" being the obsolete designation of the Colony, which is now, by the Queen's Charter, the Colony of Natal We are all aware that the suggestion, although made in Durban, was adopted, and that the Natal Land and Colonization Company, when established, fixed its head office in Durban, under the management of the late Mr. Carl Behrens, and still transacts its business in the same place.

Natal Bank. The same issue of the *Mercury* contains a notice signed by Mr. Carl Behrens as Secretary of the Natal Bank, that application would also be made for the Bank's incorporation.

On the 10th April the steam transport *Himalaya,* Captain Seacombe, 3,750 tons, arrived from Portsmouth *via* Algoa Bay, with the head quarters and 450 rank and file of the 85th Regiment from the Cape Colony to relieve the old 45th, who were at length to return home. They were to march out from Fort Napier, their own creation, on Monday, the 18th April. The Rev. W. Nesbitt, the Military Chaplain in Durban, having removed to Fort Napier, the Mastership of the Government School, Field Street, was vested in Mr. G. Thomson on the 1st March, and in April the Commander of the Forces at the Cape appointed the Rev. W. A. L. Rivett " Officiating Chaplain to the Troops of the English Church at Durban and Port Natal " *(sic).* The advent of the 85th Regiment under the command of Major Williamson gave us an opportunity, pending the arrival of the 45th, of enjoying the strains of their fine band under the conductorship of Herr Wiesbecher, which played on the Market Square for an hour and a half each day. Very little time was lost after the arrival of the *Himalaya* in putting the 45th on the road down the hill again. They entered Durban in detachments, escorting a train of thirty wagons, and as the leading companies arrived they were shipped without delay. In these hurrying steam-driven days entire regiments may come and may go without the average Durbanite being aware of the fact until he " saw it in the paper." A few staff sergeants, a commissariat mule wagon or two, some additional uniforms, is all that we see in the streets. Landed dryshod on the wharf, refreshments served out, their baggage packed into trucks, themselves into cosy railway carriages, an exchange of salutes between officers, a nod to the railway guard, a whistle from the engine, cheers from spectators and troops, and the train moves off to land them within twenty-four hours at the limits of the Colony. It was not so in our day. Durban then presented a lively spectacle, the Camp surrounded by tents, wagons, camp fires, cattle, and natives, while scarlet thronged the streets and bye-ways. The echoes were awakened with fun and frolic, and every canteen budded as a music hall ; the police became invisible, discreetly leaving the duty of picking up the stragglers to the armed pickets that brought a halo of

repose after their return to Camp at 10 o'clock each night.
I infer that money must have been plentiful, since the
credit of the 85th Regiment had been duly "cried down"
by a sergeant with drum and fife at each canteen door,
a ceremony I witnessed on this occasion for the first time,
so conclude the publicans referred the sinners to their tap-
room labels, "No. credit given," or announced, "Terms
cash," and got it.   Not the least interesting were "the
women on the strength," those representatives of Mrs.
Bagnet, with their respective daughters Quebec and Malta,
as they bumped along on the baggage wagons, each
hugging a bundle or an infant, while young Woolwich and
their other cropped-headed brothers, mostly barefooted,
kept company with their chums the regimental natives,
who, with characteristic disregard for time, and love of
display, to say nothing of their childlike affection, constituted, with many native women of varying shades and
apparel, a motley crowd of camp followers, all of whom
had come to see the regiment return to the great water
from which most believed they had originated.

The last Company reached Camp on the morning of
Wednesday, the 20th April. A general muster was made,
the last farewells taken of old comrades and civilian friends,
and a brave departure organised. Bag and baggage,
women and children, officers, ladies, servants, and animals,
had mostly preceded the head quarters and nominal rear-
guard to the Point, so early in the afternoon the strains of
martial music announced a movement, and we saw the
soldiers, preceded by the band of the 85th Regiment,
debouch into the Market Square by St. Paul's.   Genial
Colonel Cooper on horseback, the officers and men in
buovant spirits and light marching order, with the colours
in the centre, stepped out gaily down sandy West Street
in the direction of Cato's Creek and the bush road to the
Point, their band playing alternately with that of the
85th, those tear-compelling equivocal tunes, "The girl I
left behind me," and "Auld Lang Syne." Of a certainty
many of their comrades who had taken their discharge and
remained to become burgesses and good colonists, together
with the girls left behind them in the "old country," now
unrecognizable matrons, would know them no more. They

were escorted by the "Royal Durban Rangers" in full uniform, and a cavalcade of civilians Durban made holiday, and followed to the Point to contribute a final cheer to our friends of the "Ould 45th," whose residence in Natal of fifteen years preceded that of the majority of the emigrants and townsmen. I am unable to say if on this brief march to the sea they played "We must go back again," being myself prevented from accompanying them. The *Himalaya* proceeded, as soon as the embarkation was effected, to Algoa Bay, to take on board the second battalion of the regiment and sail direct for England.

A story was told of the time when the officers of both regiments messed together at the Masonic Hotel, and Colonel Cooper of the 45th, being anxious to show the new arrivals (who were interested in the ability, or oddity of the native waiters) his familiarity with the Zulu language, gave the memorable order to "Foetsack the beef, and osalappa the pudding." Six months later we learnt that the regiment was quartered at Preston, Lancashire, where they were inspected and complimented by Sir Harry Smith, who had fought with them at the Cape, and was now General of the District. We seldom realize when we are well off, and are apt to entertain doubts whether "it is better to bear the ills we have than fly to those we know not." Thus, in a letter to an old comrade in Durban, a non-commissioned officer says, "We have all much more to do here than in Natal, and many of us are wishing ourselves back again."

The Great Rice Case Headed a special supplement of the *Mercury* of the 15th April reporting the trial of the action in the Supreme Court before Mr. Justice Connor and a Pietermaritzburg jury, occupying five entire days and a crowd of witnesses. The action was brought by Mr. S. Crowder, sen., against the Corporation of Durban, for damages for the alleged destruction of 1,660 bags of damaged rice *ex Monarch of the Seas*. The defence was that the rice had been destroyed as a nuisance, and to prevent its being sold as an article of food, and that the plaintiff had been convicted and fined in respect of the nuisance; that, as regards 1,000 or 1,200 bags, the defendant Corporation did not destroy them, but merely interfered to prevent the rice being brought further into the Borough.

The Attorney-General and Mr. D. D. Buchanan appeared for Crowder; Mr. Advocate Goodricke appeared in person as Mayor of Durban on behalf of the Corporation.

The Plaintiff relied mainly on the evidence of his son, Mr. William Crowder, a consulting analytical and manufacturing chemist, who showed that he could have converted the rice into very good starch at a profit, when properly manufactured, of £1 4s. per bag, had he been allowed to remove it to the banks of the Umgeni. Dr. R. J. Mann deposed that though the rice was in an extremely disagreeable state owing to the stench, that had nothing to do with the case. He considered the danger to health was not proportionate to the smell, but rather the reverse, and gave scientific and practical reasons for this opinion. Mr. G. C. Cato, subpœned by the Plaintiff, was in the position of the proverbial toad under a harrow, as he diplomatically gave his opinions as Lloyd's Agent, American Consul, agent for the ship, Landing Agent, owner of the *William Shaw*, ex-mayor and present Town Councillor, and a Burgess of Durban. Finding the sale of the rice did not pay expenses of the landing, he recommended the continued lightening of the ship, and 3,000 bags were consequently thrown overboard at the anchorage. His friend Captain Bell deposed that he was not troubled with the stench, as the Port Captain's house was beyond the range of our prevailing winds over the wharf. When surveying the ship with Captain L. Wilson he didn't notice it much, though there had been seven feet of water in the hold and the lower tiers of rice were black. He was most inconvenienced by the heat. Mr. G. Rutherford, Collector of Customs, Mr. R. Dawney, Chemist and Druggist, Messrs. R. Acutt, Auctioneer, and John Gray, storekeeper at McArthur's, considered the starch made by Mr. W. Crowder worth one shilling per lb. It was superior to much that was used in the bleachfields of Glasgow.

During the second day the Attorney-General privately offered to accept £250 and costs, which Mr. Goodricke declined. Mr. Sam Crowder, jun., deposed that he had

offered to sell all or any quantity of the damaged rice at
1s. 6d. per bag. Judge Connor, seeing the point, asked if
defendants would compromise at 1s. 6d. per bag. The Mayor
thought this question hardly fair before a jury, so the case
was resumed.

Dr. P. C. Sutherland, M.R.C.S., deposed to the damaged
rice at the Custom House. He rather liked it, would have
had no objection to take a comfortable sleep by the side
of it ; he had slept five months in a guano ship, where the
smell was much worse. A considerable portion of the rice
was fit for human food, if manufactured. This was the
last conclusive link in the plaintiff's case.

Mr. Goodricke opened his case to the jury, and took
the usual exceptions to everything debatable, which
however, the Judge and the Attorney-General, between
them, speedily put straight He called Mr. Lamport, who
deposed to the very offensive smell of a large stack of rice
near the Custom House about which Mr. Raw, the chemist,
had complained to the Town Council as being likely to
engender cholera and disease. Some of this stack was a
mass of putridity, black, emitting gases, wet, steamy,
mouldy, and exceedingly hot, quite unmerchantable. Many
bags were burst. He would not have taken the whole of
them at a gift. He had dealt in starch in Manchester,
and had scientific knowledge of its manufacture and use.
The consumption of starch in the Colony did not exceed
six tons a year, and he believed there would be a certain
loss to attempt to manufacture starch here from heated
paddy rice for the English market, even at 7d. per bag.
Sixteen witnesses from Durban and Pinetown were examined, cross-examined, and re-examined on behalf of the
Corporation, Mr. A. K. Murray deposing that the rice was
not worth carting out for manure, and he would not take it
as a gift. A wordy passage took place as to the Point
being within the jurisdiction of the Borough, but it was
conceded that Brunton's, on Wheeler's Creek, where a
portion of the plaintiff's rice had been landed and was
there seized and destroyed, was without question within
the Borough. Mr. Justice Connor, in a long and careful
summing-up, showed that the Corporation had prevented
the Plaintiff from making what use he could of the damaged
rice, and left the assessment of damages to the jury. The

jury retired for more than an hour, and returned with a verdict for the plaintiff, damages £150. Recorded accordingly, and, although Mr. Goodricke made an appeal as to costs, in consequence of the Plaintiff having brought them to Pietermaritzburg the Judge said Plaintiff was within his rights, and the Court could not do otherwise than let the costs follow the verdict.

The faces of the burgesses were proportionately long when the result of their defended action reached them, so a meeting was held in the Masonic Rooms on Friday the 15th April, to consider the best course to be taken to provide payment of damages and costs. The Mayor, in opening the meeting, referred to different plans mooted, *i.e.*, by special rate, by sale of certain leases, or by sale of erven along the Market Square on the north side of West Street. In reply to questions by Mr. Currie, the Mayor thought the legal liabilities would be about £500. Mr. Lamport was opposed to town lands, either Berea leases or Market Square erven, being sold for such an object as the present Permanent revenue should not be alienated for any but permanent improvements, neither would he make posterity pay for their present party squabbles. He moved the exercise of unusual economy, the sale of their working stock of oxen and carts, worth £150, the dismissal of the labour gangs and temporary cessation of footpaths. Mr. G. Robinson seconded the motion, though disagreeing as to the sale of carts and oxen, and cessation of needful improvements. The rates that were in arrear would have been collected had the Council spent more time in business than in quarrels. (Cheers.) The Mayor thought the proposal undesirable, as likely to embarrass the Council, as the dismissal of the labour gang would render the convict labour useless. He suggested selling the leased lots at Montpellier, allowing the present lessees the right of fifteen years' purchase. He calculated that £1,100 might thus be raised by the alienation of not more than 20 acres. Mr. Kermode moved (not seconded) that the present year's rates should be put aside to pay the law expenses, any deficiency to be raised by sale of lands. Mr. Hartley expressed his utter astonishment that Mr. Lamport or any other man should put forth so ridiculous a proposition, one

which he looked upon is perfect nonsense. The public of
Durban had determined to defend the case; they had been
proved by high legal authority to have been right, and if,
through some little technical mistake, the case had been
lost, then let them pay as men, and not in a fiddle-faddle
spirit talk about selling the trousers to pay for the coat.
(Cheers). . . . He moved an amendment, "That the
"Council do take such steps as that body may deem desir-
"able for payment of the debt incurred, and when some
"plan is determined on, that they submit the same to a
"public meeting." Mr. Steel, for the sake of promoting
discussion, seconded. Mr. Currie observed it was evident
they would have to pay the money, and the only question
was to find out the most agreeable way of doing so. After
condemning Mr. Lamport, reprimanding the Council, and
criticising Mr. Hartley, bringing both the Mayor and Mr.
Hartley to their feet, Mr. Currie retracted some of his
statements and moved in a second amendment:—" That
"the Council sell as much of the Market Square on the
"north side of West Street as might be required."
Seconded by Mr. C. Povall. Mr. Lamport said, however
theoretically desirable to get rid of the burden in such an
easy way, yet the details of the scheme were not practicable. A Bill would have to be specially obtained, and he
thought it unlikely the Legislative Council or the Governor
would consent. Mr. Gillespie, holding it was not desirable
to levy a rate, hardly thought it reputable, respectable, cr
needful to show to the world that they were in such a
wretched position as to sell their carts and oxen. The
conjunction of so many rates would prove highly oppressive,
and he thought the liability might be settled by the passing
of Promissory Notes, which he was sure many people
would willingly accept, and he, for one, would be willing
to append his name as guarantee to such a document.
(Cheers.) Mr. W. H. Acutt hardly thought anyone would
have anything to do with a Council who were held to be
such a peculiarly queer lot.

Mr. Jos. Mason moved a third amendment. The plans
already proposed were impracticable, unfeasible, and illegal.
To extricate themselves from their difficulty the Council
had simply to levy say 7d. or 8d. in the £ on rental and $\frac{3}{4}$d.
on freehold, and moved "That the Corporation lay a

"further rate to the extent required." Seconded by Mr. Gillespie. Mr. Pinsent supported, as he considered the burgesses were undergoing a course of medicine, and thought the bitterness of the pill would prevent future litigation. Mr. Lennox had thought the Council wrong from the very first. He favoured a special rate. Though only a poor man, he would sell his spare shirts to pay his quota; the rice was a stinking question to begin with, and it had stunk in their nostrils ever since.

Mason's amendment put and lost by a great majority.

Currie's amendment put and lost same way.

Hartley's amendment put and lost by a greater majority.

Lamport's motion put and lost by a corresponding majority.

The result was received with great amusement, repeated cheers and loud laughter, with which we all went home, after an evening well enjoyed, shabbily leaving responsibility with the Town Council, whom we had originally instigated to fight for us.

Town Council. The first reported meeting took place on the 6th April after the trial of the Rice Case.

"The meeting was again the scene of disgraceful personal altercation. It was resolved to convene public meetings of the burgesses, on Saturday evening [see *ante*], on the rice case, and on Monday or Tuesday to decide on the application of the Railway Company to lease a portion of the Market Square as a site for the terminus. The Mayor announced that he should immediately resign, and that he would never enter the Council again, in consequence of the insults he had received since August last, and especially that evening. Mr. Hartley also resigned his office on the Town Lands Committee, in consequence of the insults he had received from his colleague."

"An attempt at a meeting was made on the 21st April [the public meeting of the Rice case was on the 15th]. A quorum was present, but one of the members objected to an allusion to him in the minutes of the previous meeting, and left the room, thus destroying the quorum. A special meeting is to be held next Tuesday evening, *in re* the Mayoralty. As to general business it is entirely at a stand."

"On Tuesday evening, 3rd May, at a special meeting the
resignation of the Mayor was received, but a piece of advice
from his Worship to the effect that the Council were bound to
pay back within their year of office the £400 raised as a loan
for the Eastern Vley, and the £150 raised for the drain in Field
Street, which sums had been applied to ordinary expenditure
instead of to their original object, was rejected. Provision
had been made for paying the verdict to Mr. Crowder (£150),
but not the larger amount of the costs. Several accounts were
passed. Mr. Hartley was requested to withdraw his resignation.
On the following evening Mr. S. Pinsent was elected to the
Mayoralty for the remainder of the year."

At what should have been the regular monthly meeting
on the 2nd June a communication was tabled from Capt.
Grantham, R.E., to the Mayor and Council, intimating the
intention of the Board of Ordnance to lease the whole of
its property near this town, including the barracks or
" Camp," and stating that if the Corporation had any offer
to make it would be transmitted by the next mail to headquarters, " but," says the Mercury :—

"Mr. Goodricke, the late Mayor, sent in his resignation as
Mayor and Councillor about a month ago. His resignation as
Mayor was at once accepted, and without waiting the appointed
interval of three weeks, with a haste and in a spirit, that
seemed, to say the least, indecorous; the Council then and there
proceeded to elect a new Mayor for the remainder of the year,
on the ground that members of the Legislative Council are not
obliged to serve as Councillors without their consent, and Mr.
Goodricke's resignation was held to imply his dissent, and
therefore immediate action was taken. Mr. Goodricke himself
and other parties demur to this view, and hold that as three
weeks' notice is required in all cases, by another clause, the
electing a new Mayor was illegal. Under the doubt thus
introduced it was privately determined to re-accept Mr.
Goodricke's resignation at the regular monthly meeting on
Wednesday, and to re-elect Mr. Pinsent as Mayor, thereby
virtually acknowledging the illegality of the former election.
It was nearly an hour and a half after the time of meeting
before a quorum was constituted; various by-plays and
personal passages between members who played at bo-peep in
and out of the room having transpired, at length a bare quorum
being assembled the minutes of last meeting were read and
confirmed. Mr. Goodricke's resignation was read *de novo*,
an act tantamount to the confession that till then he had been

P

the Mayor. Mr. Pinsent asked the Council to re-elect him,
Mr. P., and a motion to that effect was then hastily made by
Mr. Cato, seconded by Mr. Dacomb, another virtual admission
that the office was then vacant. But now in rushed Messrs.
Acutt and Hartley, and the latter claimed to be heard on the
motion, whereupon Mr. Dacomb rose to order and referred the
Chair to the rule which forbids members coming in after, or
during the mover's reply, to take part in the discussion. The
mover had not replied, and Mr. Hartley claimed to be allowed a
hearing, but Mr. Dacomb persisting, the Chair ruled that Mr.
Hartley could not be heard, and ordered him to sit town. Mr.
H. refused to do so, maintaining that when a point of order
ruled by the Chair was disputed, any member had a right to
demand that the sense of the meeting be taken on the Chair's
ruling. Mr. Pinsent, however, declared that if Mr. H. did not
obey his order he would leave the Chair, and Mr. Hartley
maintaining his position, the Chairman vacated his seat, and
after a series of scenes inside and outside the Council room, the
lights were extinguished, and the Council separated without
doing anything but declaring themselves a body without a
head; and it is even doubtful if they are a body still, since it is
questioned by some whether, with an incomplete Council, Mr.
Goodricke's seat not having been filled, any legal act can be
done. There is now no person authorised to call a meeting, the
act of the Council having plainly ignored the former election of
Mr. Pinsent, and meanwhile debts overdue are pressing, and
the work of the town is standing still."

An editorial grumble at the end of June states that for
all practical purposes the Town Council was defunct,
several spasmodic efforts having been made to convene a
meeting, but they had failed, the whole body being in a
state of helpless anarchy. So they remained, no business
being done, until the 20th July, when they were galvanized
into life, owing to the near dissolution of their term of
office, and in consequence of the acts of Mr. W. Wood of the
Masonic Hotel, who had sued the C rporation for payment of
expenses of public meetings on his premises, and obtained
judgment; the Council thought it necessary to curb any
tendency of its future Mayors to convene public meetings
on requisition, in terms of the Ordinance, so passed the
following resolution, which was duly carried out :—

"That in view of the recent decision in the case 'Wood v.
Corporation,' this Council consider it necessary to declare that
they will not for the future pass or pay any account for the

expenses of public meetings called by the Mayor, unless the calling of such meetings has been previously authorised by the Council.

"That the above resolution be advertised in both the local papers, for the information of the public."

At the end of July a "Local" informs us:—" The dignity of Town Councillor has this year literally gone a-begging, and it was not till very late on Saturday night (23rd July), that the number was made up. A number of our respectable fellow townsmen positively declined the honour, and some of those who ultimately accepted, did so only to save the Borough from non-representation."

The Candidates, who thus would necessarily be returned, were: Ward No. 1, G. C. Cato and Pinsent. Ward No. 2, Lamport and Ferguson. Ward No. 3, W. H. Acutt and John Gavin. Ward No. 4, Hartley and McArthur. The new Council met in terms of the law on Saturday, the 6th August, for the election of Mayor. Mr. Pinsent in the chair. Voting by ballot was agreed to on the motion of Mr. Cato. Result: McArthur 4 votes, Hartley 4 votes. The Chairman gave his casting vote in favour of Mr. W. Hartley who, with brief preface and thanks, said, "I take the Chair as I find it." His election and remarks were received by the burgesses present with cheers. A vote of thanks was passed to Mr. Pinsent, the late Mayor, and by him feelingly acknowledged.

The first regular meeting was held on the 15th August, when the Town Clerk apparently worked off arrears by reading sundry letters and reports all more or less dreary, referring chiefly to overdue rates, Borough debts and demands for payment, Slaughter house sites or "Currie's Kraal" (Old Pound) all of which having been disposed of, a letter from the Governor was read enclosing documents relating to a proposal to erect Barracks on the Berea for the troops Following this was a letter from Captain Grantham, R.E., who, apparently impressed by the neglect of the Town Council to mind its own business, stated in reference to his former letter " that he did not consider the Corporation would be thought eligible tenants for the ground belonging to the Ordnance Department." This imputation brought Mr. Lamport to his feet, and he was about to say in his haste, as did King David of all men, when Mr. Cato—who was currently believed to have a

friend at Court—enlightened the meeting on the historical
aspect of the question, and showed that the leasing of the
Ordnance Reserve bore indirectly on His Excellency's
communication regarding the lease of Berea lands for
Barrack purposes by way of exchange. As the new committees were about to be appointed, no action appears to
have been taken. Much time was absorbed in selecting
the several committees, Police Board, etc., members not
readily agreeing to sort themselves and work together;
this accomplished, they settled down to the question of the
day, the Railway terminus site, and fought over Blocks A,
B, and C until midnight, when Mr. Ferguson's motion
settled the question, as previously related in connection with
the Railway Company

The following meeting (August 23rd) yielded an able
report from Mr. Pinsent in reference to renting the Ordnance land, suggesting several courses for obviating the
difficulties which would follow the indiscriminate leasing to
private parties by the War Department, unless restrictions
were imposed by the Corporation. Mr. Cato suggested the
periodical sale of Corporation leases, and moved, "That
" the sale of Leases be held on the first Saturday of every
"October, January, April, and July." Mr. McArthur
moved as an amendment, " That the sales be held whenever
"the land for six applications is surveyed." Original motion
carried. Mr. Jee, Poundmaster, was allowed three months
grace before he vacated the interesting locality of " Currie's
Kraal" Mr. Cato recommended the slaughter places should
be removed from the West End of the town to the Bayside.
In this he was alone, Mr. McArthur's proposal, " That they
remain as at present situated," being carried. Early in
September the pinching of the shoe induced Mr. Pinsent to
move (without a seconder), " That a special rate be laid to
" pay off the liabilities of the Council in re the Rice case,
" and to replace the £400 raised on mortgage for special
" purposes, but applied for general purposes." The Council,
having, with a guilty conscience, considered the subject in
Committee, finally resolved:—" That the Town Clerk pre-
" pare the Valuation Roll (with the assistance of the
"Town Surveyor) with a view of laying a rate at as early a
" date as possible, and that the Town and Town Lands

"Committee be instructed to prepare their reports
"on the understanding that the Council are prepared to lay
"an increased rate this year in view of the outstanding
"liabilities."

At the ordinary meeting on the 7th September a letter
was read from Captain Grantham with reference to an
exchange of property with the War Department. Referred
to the Town Lands Committee to report.

The Town Solicitor forwarded taxed Bill of Costs *in re*
Corporation *v.* Snell amounting to £11 4s. 11d., and
requesting a cheque, but, there being no present means of
payment, it was referred to Mr. Lamport to report.
Accounts were, however, passed, viz. : —

G. Robinson—on account of £43 0s. 8½d. for printing
and advertisements, £20.

Inspector of Meats—one quarter's salary, £5.

For burying dead cattle—£1 6s.

Mr. Stonnel, Town Foreman—one month's wages, £6
13s. 4d.

The Umgeni, or "River of Entrance"* in the native
tongue, was always a *pièce de resistance* on the Municipal
Bill of Fare. Some unusually timid individual
having reported the closing of the river's mouth, and its
divergence towards the town, the newspapers suggested in
flattering terms to the new Mayor, that this presented an
opportunity for his unbounded energy and ability. Mr.
Hartley performed a pilgrimage accordingly; inspected, and
reported to the Council in a very exhaustive minute, the
substance of which was that the bed of the river had risen
since the last flood, and that the circumstances were loaded
with dire possibilities of the house-that-Jack-built order.

* This name confirms the opinion that the ancient Umgeni
flowed into the sea by way of the Eastern Vlei, since the early
discoverers of the Bluff and Bay so described it. It is
therefore more than probable that the river, through a fresh
water lagoon, enabled Vasco Da Gama to replenish his water
without going far from his vessels. Since the time of Farewell
the ships obtained their sea-going water at the Umbilo, though
the spring in Smith Street supplied occasional wants. In
my opinion Salisbury Island is the creation of the ancient
river.—G. R.

A sand dune blocked the direct outlet; the river had turned
to the right; that it was eating away the Back Beach bush;
that it might reach a thin place; that it might trickle into
the Eastern Vleî (if it entered below the Embankment);
that a flood might follow; that the town might be
inundated ; that the Bay would be silted up some, and that
the Harbour Bar might be moaned for.

The question submitted to the Council was, who should
bell the cat. The general opinion was that the duty
devolved· upon the Government.   Mr. Lamport (at that
time) "expressed unbounded and undiminished confidence
in the reactive processes of nature, and deprecated immediate action of any kind."   Ultimately the Council
resolved to get the burgesses to memorialise the Government
to see to the matter, and, I presume by way of giving force
to their petition, passed another resolution, "That the
Town Surveyor be instructed to take levels of gorge A and
the top of the barrier of the Umgeni mouth."

At a meeting of Council on the 30th November prior to
the general discussion and · conclusion *re* the Railway
terminus, Mr. Isaac Cowley's tender to construct a brick
drain across Central West Street for £50 was accepted.
This drain was intended to carry the water from Pine
Terrace under West Street at an angle, connecting with
Adlam's ditch and delivering into the open sewer by the
side of Drake's Hotel, the bridge drain having become
inoperative in consequence of Mr. Paul Henwood and Mr.
John Prince, farrier, having built upon their erven, while
Mr. Marchant Penfold was engaged in primitive fashion in
raising his erf adjoining.   The Council being unable to
conclude its business, met on the following day, when we
had a renewal of energy and that display of warmth
incidental to public meetings at this time of the year.   The
dullness of figures as reported by the Finance Committee
(Mr. Cato) elicited no emotion, though he informed the
Council that if the Rice debt of £400 was to be paid, the
Corporation was virtually insolvent, and recommended a
more equitable rating of Town and Berea lands.   The
Cemeteries of the various religious denominations having
been under consideration of a committee, it was resolved
on the motion of Mr. McArthur that the land be vested
in a committee of the Mayor and two Trustees to be

nominated by the general subscribers. The Mayor's inspection and report on the Umgeni mouth resulted in his preparing a memorial to the Government for public signature. Mr. McArthur moved that it be read that day six months; in any case the paragraph calling His Excellency's attention to the Mayor's Minute and Captain Grantham's report should be expunged. The Mayor informed the Council they must not do any such thing as shelve it; he would memorialise His Excellency and set the Council at defiance. . . . . They might cut and carve it, but memorialise they must. Of course he was not a perfect man, neither could his production boast perfection; were they afraid that the memorial would do too much credit to the Mayor, or too much discredit to themselves? Mr. McArthur thought that the Mayor would take very good care he got no lack of credit. His Worship agreed with that remark and declared that he had, and he would take care that the Mayor got all the credit. Mr. Ferguson moved, if the objectionable references be expunged, that the memorial be prepared for signature. Mr. Pinsent took exception to certain assertions it contained which were not facts; the statement that Borough property was being carried away, was utter nonsense. Mr. Cato was proceeding to prove that many of the allegations were unfounded, when the Mayor declared that he would not allow Mr. Cato to lord over the Council in this way; these proceedings must and should be put a stop to, or he would leave the Chair. Mr. Cato denied *in toto* that Borough property was being destroyed, the land trenched upon being Admiralty Reserve. He could prove by science and by fact, that, even in the event of a great flood taking place, there would not be sufficient current even to carry away a rush, neither would the outflowing stream affect the Harbour. He objected on principle to calling on the burgesses to sign memorials on every trivial subject. . . He was quite in favour of the memorial being read that day six months, as they would have time to see what Government might intend doing. Mr. Ferguson held that any portion of the burgesses, however small, had a right to be heard. His amendment was ultimately carried by three to two, and the Council adjourned. No further proceedings of the Council during December appear to have been of sufficient importance to be noted.

Alligators. While on the subject of the river, I may here note that in consequence of the frequent accidents and narrow escapes the editor of the *Mercury* writes in a sub-leader on the 21st April:—

"ALLIGATORS or rather Crocodiles as we believe the Natal variety are more properly designated, continue to imperil the lives of passengers, and impede the traffic over the Umgeni. No proper means have yet been taken for destroying them; and meanwhile they literally swarm in their breeding grounds, and will be an increasing pest if no effectual means of extermination are resorted to. . . : It is a matter of public importance, and the Government ought to take it up as the protector of the lives and property of the community." . . .

November 24th we have :—

"ALLIGATORS AGAIN.—The rainy season has again drawn these monsters out of their hiding places to infest the frequented parts of the Umgeni. At all seasons Mr. George at the Lower Drift has them more or less under his eye, one of their chief breeding places being the lagoon north of his residence, which formed, until the recent deviation, the outfall of the river, and from which they issue to bask in the sun on the bank formed seaward of the stream. He has killed several at different times for his own amusement, and for the safety of the drift; and he assures us that he could easily clear the river of them if reasonable inducements were offered; but the work being expensive, whether done by shooting or by poison, it is not likely that any private person will undertake it. Last week a large Alligator 13 feet in length was killed near the Springfield Sugar Mill, and the passage of the river, now that it is frequently high from the rain, is rendered unsafe by the presence of these huge and ravenous reptiles. It is not creditable to the Government that one of the most important thoroughfares in the Colony," &c.

Harbour Works. Several letters appeared in the early part of the year signed by Mr. John Milne, C.E., going minutely into the position of the works, the object, aim, and intention of his plans, and dealing minutely with the objection raised against them. These letters contain very valuable details and declarations as to the tidal area, the width of entrance, mode of construction, and the objects sought to be secured to ensure a depth of 26 feet at half-tide by natural means. Subsequent Engineers have "plowed with his heifer," hence it is almost forgotten that an integral part of his design was to extend a North Pier until it reached as far as a short South Pier run out from the end of the Bluff. The opinions of the Press and the Public as to the injury likely to arise to the Port is expressed in a "Local" of the 28th July :—

"The *Good Hope* with horses on board for the Mauritius market, and the *Reliance* have both been detained in our harbour a protracted period, for want of sufficient water on the bar. The state of the port for the last few months has offered a serious impediment to commerce; and if nothing is done speedily, it will be difficult to induce ship owners to send their vessels here. But for the uncalled-for suspension of the works two years ago, the permanent depth of water would by this time have sufficed for all the needs of our present commerce."

At that early time when Governor Scott found fault with the Harbour Works, captious critics were assured that he had some training as a Marine Engineer, or at least sufficient knowledge to justify his opinions as a qualified amateur. As a new arrival in an out-of-the-way unheard-of Colony, it was not likely he should find any up-to-date Engineer; what was a poor old Scotch body—who was but a Civil Engineer at the best, without any Colonial Office lords at his back—likely to know on so abstruse a subject as Marine Engineering? His past efforts had not shown any marked improvement in the depth of the Bar. His plans must be defective, they were evidently too cheap and too slow; conceived in a narrow spirit; stopped they must be, and were.

In this he was justified by those least able to know anything on the subject; "when the Gubernatorial dog barks, let no man speak."

Some 450 burgesses of Durban with other colonists, anticipating the advent of a steam tug, the building of a railway line and wharf, with the possible silting up of the bar in the meantime, if the Harbour Works were not continued, petitioned the Government for their resumption. This was the self-sufficient reply they received; our dismay may be imagined:—

Colonial Office, Natal,
October 3rd, 1859.

SIR,

In reply to your letter of the 1st inst., I am directed by the Lieutenant Governor to acquaint you for the information of the gentlemen who signed the memorial therein enclosed on the subject of the prosecution of the Harbour Works, that this document has been received too late to be forwarded by the present English mail; it will however be transmitted by the next mail steamer.

His Excellency directs me to add that a decision has recently been received from the Secretary of State on the plans for improvement of the Harbour, and that the plans recommended for adoption wholly differ from, and condemn the works formerly proposed and commenced.

I have the honour to be, Sir,
Your obedient servant.
JOHN BIRD,
For the Colonial Sec.

James Proudfoot, Esq., Durban.

The useless pier of a certain Captain Vetch, Royal Engineer, was the result, adding some £36,000 to the public debt of the Colony. All that now remains of that costly job of timber staging and Umgeni rubble stone, is the dismantled crescent-shaped "barrier reef" visible at half-tide, running out from the Back Beach opposite the Sewerage Works. Being all of us inclined to dogmatise over our opinions, it is only just to the memory of Mr. G. C. Cato to exonerate him from the blame of this undertaking. He was convinced that all the sand forming the bar came down the coast from the north. With his usual energy and emphasis he pointed this out to the different Marine and Admiralty surveyors employed, and, as a conclusive proof, put in the *Annabella* bank and the *Waldensian* rock as evidence.

Vetch's pier was to us stupendous in design, embracing as it did an outer steam basin, (*) meaning a large local expenditure and a certain cure for the Bar, if Mr. Cato's deductions were correct, and, being the oldest inhabitant, he was supposed to know.

---

* Copies of the plans were filed at the time in the Mechanics' Institute,

This vessel had been ordered by the Government for the use of the Port. She arrived on the 14th November under sail, having left London on the 26th July, and was named the *Pioneer*. She had proved herself a first - class sea boat, and sailed into the Harbour without anchoring. She was a paddle boat of 9¾ tons register, with two engines working to 40 horse power, built of iron and drawing six feet of water, reputed to be the first steam-tug in South Africa. The *Mercury* was so surprised at the unexpected realization of our ;wildest hopes, that the flowers of fancy were scattered in her praise, from her appropriate name, to her construction and capabilities, even for passenger traffic and mail carrying on an emergency : —

"Her size being quite large enough to cope with the heaviest seas which may disturb our Bar, while her light draught renders her ingress and egress at all times and in all weathers a matter of certainty. . . . For beauty of proportion and gracefulness of lines competent authorities admit that the *Pioneer* is probably unexcelled, and looking at her as belonging to the tug genus she is unusually elegant," etc., etc.

Followed by a panegyric in favour of Albert Robinson, Esq., M.I.C.E., "to whom the Colony is indebted for the "general design and specifications of the vessel." We were promised that her paddles would be shipped immediately, and she would get to business in a few days, but it was not until the 26th December that

"The beautiful little Port Steamer having had her machinery put in working order, and her paddles fixed, went under steam for the first time in these waters. Mr. Albert Robinson, to whom the Colony is, etc., etc. . . . gave an impromptu invitation to a number of ladies and gentlemen to witness the performance of the steamer, and enjoy an aquatic trip. The party included the Mayor and Mayoress, Major Williamson, and other officers in garrison here, A. Coqui, Esq., M.L.C., and family, the Collector of H.M. Customs, W. Smerdon, Esq., etc., etc. The company would have been larger, but for the numerous absences from town during the Christmas holidays. At half-past two o'clock the *Pioneer* moved gracefully from her berth near the Custom House, passed swiftly down the Bluff Channel across the Bar and out to sea, where she disported for some time in gallant style. Returning into the Bay, she steamed several times round the shipping in Port, and at half-past four returned to her position, when His Worship the Mayor made some appropriate congratulatory and complimentary remarks, and then called for three cheers successively for the *Pioneer* and Albert Robinson, Esq., the Engineer. Three cheers were also given for W. Smerdon, Esq., who had acted on this trip in his old capacity of Captain, and whose skilful steering was the theme of general admiration." . . .

The rest is laudatory of the trip, the vessel, her machinery and Mr. Albert Robinson, but nothing is said of those brave men Dick, Tom, or Harry—Skipper, Mate, or Engineer—who sailed her out and fitted her up. Though it was Boxing Day and a Public Holiday, among all those kind sentiments, there were no signs of cakes and ale.

St. Paul's Church. The constitution of the Church Council as an administrative body, seems to have relieved this Vestry of most of its scruples and much of its responsibility, for I do not find in my notes reference to any special conflict of the scenic order during the year, while the *Mercury*—occupied more legitimately with the Legislative Council, the political changes of the period, and questions of more general interest to the Colony—supplies but one meagre report. Deeming this an oversight I made careful search, but failed to find any fiery letters or abusive correspondence having an ecclesiastical garb, the facts being that the more zealous Vestrymen were now concerned about their own temporalities, and concluded to leave the Bishop of Natal severely alone; while the less strenuous spirits were content to follow either Paul or Apollos under the direction of their representative, the Church Council. The newspaper reports:—

"The annual Easter Vestry Meeting was held on Tuesday [26th April] when the accounts were presented, showing a debt of some sixty pounds. No churchwardens were elected, the office, under present circumstances, not apparently having attractions. Dr. Holland was proposed for re-election; but the nomination was not seconded. A resolution was passed urging on the next Church Council the necessity of promoting a legislative enactment for giving powers to churchwardens, similar to those possessed by other bodies under trust deeds or other legal instruments."

Remembering the position of Diocesan affairs, this resolution recalls the story of the virago, threatened if again using "crooked words," who shouted "Ram's horns, if I die for it!"

More Emigrants. The barque *Kahlamba*, Captain G. Markwell, 350 tons, arrived on the 13th May, 85 days from London, bringing the following passengers, who, notwithstanding their long voyage, presented the Captain with an appreciative testimonial:—Richard Acutt and family; Leon Isabelle and family; Charles D'Almaine, Marguerite D'Almaine; John Smith, Charlotte Smith, Christina Bell, W. H. D'Almaine, Alfred J. Sharpe, Thomas Macadam, J. B. Taylor, James Willis, John Bellis, Richard Draper, William Darby.

The regular trader *Early Morn* arrived on the 7th August, and in the *Mercury* of the 11th appears the following:—

"TESTIMONIAL

"The undersigned passengers take this step publicly to express their thanks to Captain Lowry for the uniform courtesy of his behaviour towards them, and for his considerate attention to their comfort during their voyage from England by the 'Early Morn.'

"(Signed)

"W. Eastwood, M. Eastwood, M. Atkinson, George Smith, Harry Escombe,* G. Atkinson, F. Atkinson, C. Elgie."

On the 2nd of November, per S.S. *Waldensian*, arrived the Rev. John Reynolds, whose ministrations among us for many years as the Vicar of St. Thomas' Church, Berea, cannot be forgotten. A prominent marble tomb marks his resting place in the Churchyard. He came here, accompanied by his wife, from Port Elizabeth in connection with the Congregational body, and I had the pleasure of hearing his first sermon in the Congregational Chapel on the 6th November, prior to his departure to take up his pastorate of the Congregational Church in Pietermaritzburg.

---

* Afterwards Attorney General, Premier of Natal, and member of the Queen's Privy Council.

He subsequently conformed to the Established Church, and, admitted to priest's orders by the Bishop of Natal, was appointed to the vacant cure of St. Thomas', Berea, which had been constituted a parish, with a Vestry of its own.   Patient, self-denying and zealous, he baptised, married, exhorted and buried in a broad and liberal spirit; he was universally esteemed, and died regretted in 1889.

Durban Rifle Guard. Major Erskine, the new Colonial Secretary, having revived the Volunteer spirit in Maritzburg, we of the "Old Guard" found an answering echo in Durban, so though both busy men, my friend John Robinson and myself agreed on the 10th September to " take measures," which resulted in a general muster on the 21st of the month, and is thus reported : —

"At the meeting held last evening it was unanimously resolved to establish a Volunteer Rifle Corps for Durban.   The worthy Resident Magistrate presided, and takes a lively interest in the measure.   The corps is called the ' Royal Durban Rifles,' and as soon as 100 names are enrolled another meeting will be held and officers elected.   Nearly 200 persons were present, and about 40 names were enrolled.   His Excellency, through the gallant Colonial Secretary, has promised the Corps not only rifles, but belts, pouches and powder, and four shillings per day to each man when on drill or duty."

The requisite number of names having been obtained, a meeting was held on the 30th September for the election of officers.   Henry James Mellor, ·Esq., Resident Magistrate, credited with being one of the originators of the movement, presided.   The various officers were chosen by open nomination and vote, amidst much hilarious merriment, resulting as follows—

Colonel in Command . . Henry James Mellor, Esq.
Major . . . . C. Joseph Cato.
Captains . . . . . A. W. Evans, John Brown.
Lieutenants . . . . G. Rutherford, J. F. Kahts.
Sergeant Major . . . .
Sergeants F. Towning, Walters, Thomas Green, A. Curle.
Corporals E. Kermode, J. Forsyth, R. Jones, A. S. Cockerell.

Staff nominated by Colonel—
    Paymaster . . . .   John   Davies.
    . Surgeon. . . . .   Dr.   Holland.
    Adjutant. . . . .   George   Russell.
To this intolerable quantity of Sack, a poor pennyworth
of Bread, for the numerical strength of the Corps was only
110, yet the *Mercury* assured us:—"Under the shadow
of immediate protection of Fort Napier the martial fever
does not seem so virulent as in our more lively and
essentially British little Borough."   The voice of the
people is not always heaven directed, for the "jolly good
fellow" nominated may be utterly unsuitable, or may
decline the honours thrust upon him, consequently the
above list of officers was never confirmed, neither was the
proposed name of the Corps, for as the initial letters
"R.D.R." stood also for "Royal Durban Rangers," the
designation "Royal Durban Rifles" was changed to
"Durban Rifle Guard."   To the best of my recollection
Captain Brown was replaced by Mr. William Brickhill;
while Lieutenants Rutherford and Kahts were exchanged
for Mr. John P. Cato and Mr. Francis Collinson; Pay-
master Davies (clerk to the Resident Magistrate) by Mr.
G. W. Bancroft, while Adjutant Russell, who knew nothing
about the duties, begged to be excused, and received
instead a Commission as Lieutenant and Quartermaster.
The duties involved my taking charge of all the Stores,
in my own quarters, from whence I issued same on requisition.   The uniform was ordered from England and
consisted of regulation drab tunic and trousers with black
cordings and cloth Kepi to match.   Officers had silver
braid.   Arms, the Enfield Rifle (muzzle loader) with
sword bayonet.   Black leather waist belts and pouches.
Officers carried swords with steel scabbards, patent leather
waist belt and slings, with shoulder belt adorned with
silver whistle and chain and ornamental pouch (large
enough for a cigar case) at the back.   We also obtained
from Home a serviceable set of musical instruments,
and organised a small but efficient band, the principal
instrument in which (the big drum) was manipulated by a
very stolid, rotund individual, attached to the Magistrate's
Court as its Constable, who was named by the natives
from his instrument, and was in consequence known to

the boys ever after as "Bum Bum." He fills a place in Durban's history as a local character; the late W. Dick of Maritzburg, in his "Prophet Ignoramus," burlesquing certain legal calamities that befel the Durban Corporation, observes, "And a wise man named Bum Bum said he saw it from the beginning." Stout Sergeant Curle became Drum Major in white gloves and Malacca cane, his place being supplied by Sergeant Kenneth Packman, a newly arrived English Volunteer well up in the drill.

It may not be generally known that the present Excise and Stamp Office on the Market Square, was built by the Government for our accommodation as a Magazine (inner room), Armoury and Orderly room. Unfortunately all my records of the Corps have been digested by white ants, and I am unable to replace them. The Corps increased, flourished and acquired considerable proficiency, taking part in several public functions, giving off a branch to the Artillery, but ultimately vanished under the financial crisis of 1864-5 and the attractions of the Diamond Fields. Mr. B. W. Greenacre became Senior Captain under Major Evans, while Mr. Robert Jameson was promoted Quartermaster on my resignation.

Commercial and Agricultural Bank of Natal — Published a prospectus on the 6th October, proposing a capital of £25,000 in 500 shares of £5 each. It was, in this early stage, of Colonial banking enterprise, to "supply a long felt want of an Institution "whose head and management shall be at "the Port." In other words, to run in opposition to the Natal Bank, because, says the *Mercury* of the day, "Durban, the Port of the Colony, ought to "have a banking establishment of its own, and not remain "a more appanage and dependency of Maritzburg," kindly suggesting to the shareholders of the Natal Bank, "There "need not be, and therefore ought not to be, any hostile or 'jealous feeling on the part of the old, towards the new "institution. . . . The general public will, of course, "benefit," etc., etc. . . . . "It will be seen the under- 'taking is put forth under auspices of the highest respec- "tability, and a large portion of the Capital is expected to "be taken up at the Cape and in England."

To those old Colonists who have followed my local history and politics, the names of the Provisional Committee will remind them that the opposition was not so much to Maritzburg, as to the exclusiveness of the Durban Branch of the Natal Bank, of which "King Cato" was managing director.

Directors: Robert Acutt, W. H. Acutt, John Brown, James Blackwood, J. F. Churchill, A. W. Evans, H. Gillespie, W. Hartley, R. Harwin, J. P. Hoffman, E. P. Lamport, A. McArthur, James Proudfoot, E. Snell, W. H. Savory, G. H. Wirsing; Solicitor, J. R. Goodricke; Hon. Sec., Hugh Gillespie.   The Bank was floated and opened the following year.

MINOR EVENTS.

January. **Aerated Waters.** The progress of our civilization was marked by the announcement by Andrew Welch, West Street, Durban, that he was now able to supply Aerated Ginger Beer, Soda Water and Lemonade, "manufactured from the most approved machinery imported from England.   Orders from Maritzburg punctually executed."   These waters first came into public notice on the occasion of Burns' Centenary on the 25th previously noted, and to the experimental use of these "cooling drinks" (in combination with other liquids) was attributed the early morning hours to which that function extended.

May. **Umgeni Bridge.** Mr. John Milne, C.E., having recommended the construction of a weir and roadway over the Umgeni at Durban, Mr. John Millar moved in the Legislative Council that the Surveyor-General (Dr. Sutherland) report upon the cost and practicability of a bridge to connect Durban with Victoria County.   Reported accordingly, condemning a weir as a costly experiment, and recommending Bishop's Drift as the most suitable site, with approaches sufficiently elevated to be out of the influence of floods; the length of the bridge would be 1,100 feet built on five piers; the cost being, for masonry £12,500, and for the roadway of American pine £4,000. The total estimate £16,500." An iron bridge was not recommended in consequence of the corrosive action of the sea air in a climate like ours.

June. Two notable advertisements appear, quot-
Treacle. ing prices of articles in constant demand:

"Private families can be supplied with molasses of best quality at one shilling and threepence per gallon, also for Kafir use ninepence per gallon, at the Springfield Sugar Mill.

"June 13th, 1859. _____ GEORGE POTTER."

NOTICE.

BRICKS.—We, the undersigned, beg to inform the public that in consequence of the scarcity of Kafir labour, and exorbitant wages now demanded by them, and also the difficulty of procuring wood for burning bricks, we have been obliged to _raise_ the _price_ of _bricks_ to 25s. per thousand at the Brickfields, or 35s. per thousand delivered in Durban.

F. BELL, Umgeni Brickfields,
J. VINCENT, Umgeni Brickfields,
T. WHITTAKER, Berea Brickfields.

Durban, June 10th, 1859.

AUGUST. DARING FEAT.—On Monday, prior to the departure of the barque _Jan Van Brakel_ from the outer anchorage, one of the crew jumped overboard and swam ashore, a distance of three miles, carrying with him a bundle of clothes. He succeeded in accomplishing this great distance, and escaping sharks and all other perils landed safely on the back beach. We have not heard what motive impelled this bold sailor thus perilously to escape from his duty.

Rental   As showing the value of business sites and
Value.   rent producing property in Durban at this
time, I take over the following advertisement, referring to that portion of the Erf
now occupied by Messrs. Ferguson and Co. and Mr. A. A. Smith:—

NOTICE.   NOTICE.

THE BEST BUSINESS POSITION IN DURBAN.
FOR SALE BY TENDER.

The undersigned is open to receive Tenders until _Saturday, August 13th_, at four o'clock p,m., for the purchase of the premises known as

GEE's CORNER

now occupied by Surtees, Robinson and Brown, being portion of the Erf No. 24, Block E, measuring 50 feet frontage to West Street, and 66 feet to Field Street.

These premises will be sold subject to a lease expiring on the 1st day of December, 1862, and yielding a rental of £42 per annum.

Tenders must distinctly state the terms required for payment of the purchase price.

Further particulars, if necessary, may be ascertained at the office of the undersigned in West Street.　MARK FOGGITT.

SEPTEMBER.—The *Mercury* published the following Market Price List, but gives no authority for the quotation :—

COLONIAL PRODUCE.	DURBAN, PORT NATAL.	
DESCRIPTION.		PRICES.
Arrowroot	per cwt.	30/- to 37/-
Sugar	,,	25/- to 32/-
Coffee	,,	85/- to 95/-
Butter	per lb.	1/3 to 1/6
Wool	,,	1/- to 1/3
Boers' Meal	per muid	45/-
Mealies	,,	8/- to 10/-
Mealie Meal	,,	13/- to 17/-
Oats	,,	13/- to 15/-
Oat Forage	p. 100 lbs.	5/- to 6/-
Potatoes (English)	per muid	12/- to 14/-
,, (Sweet)	,,	2/6 to 4/-
Beans	,,	25/-
Bread	p. 2lbs. loaf	6d.
Meat—Beef	per lb.	3d. to 5d.
Mutton	,,	6d. to 7d.
Pork	,,	7d.
Veal	,,	6d.
Bacon	,,	1/- to 1/6
Fowls	each	1/- to 1/6
Ducks	p. pair	6/-
Turkeys	each	7/6
Geese	,,	10/-
Live Stock—		
Draught Oxen	,,	£5 to £8
Cows, Milch	,,	£4 to £6
Sheep	,,	15/- to 20/-
Pigs	,,	10/- to 60/-
Horses	,,	£15 to £25

Fruit—

Bananas	per doz.	3d,
Pine Apples	each	3d.
Lemons	per 100	1/-

EARLY CLOSING.   Durban, Port Natal.

October 18th, 1859.

We, the undersigned Storekeepers of Durban, hereby agree to close our respective Stores on and after the 1st November next at Five p.m., except on Saturdays, on which date they will remain open until Seven p.m. The time to be regulated by Mr. Pulleyn.

W. H. Savory, John Gray q.q., A. McArthur, G. E. Robinson, Palmer and Blackwood, Henry Cowey, George Goodwin, William Grant, J. F. Baumann.

Time.   A local paragraph in the *Mercury* of the 10th November is as follows :—

"We announce with no little satisfaction that Mr. Pulleyn, under arrangements with the Corporation, has undertaken to ring the bell of St. Paul's every morning, precisely at nine o'clock—correct solar time.

" The bell begins to chime exactly at the hour, and continues for two minutes. We hope this simple arrangement will ensure the recognition of some uniform standard by which we may all regulate our watches and time pieces."

Government School.   Mr. Thompson, the Headmaster, having announced that an examination of pupils would take place on the 20th December, parents and all interested were invited to attend.   Junior Division between 10 and 12 a.m., Senior Division between 12 and 2 p.m.   This first public examination was pronounced as being highly satisfactory.   The Mayor and several ladies and gentlemen were present at intervals during the day.   Prizes were given to the most prominent and best conducted children, consisting of books purchased by subscription of a few friends, and a handsome writing desk and work box were also separately contributed by Mr. J. F. Churchill and Mr. A. W. Evans, the latter gentleman at the request of the Master presenting the prizes, with a few appropriate words to each pupil.

Holidays. Christmas Day falling on a Sunday it was announced that "Monday and Tuesday the 26th and 27th December, and 2nd and 3rd January, will be kept close holidays." Quoting again from the newspaper : —

"As usual, our town populations will enjoy two days' holidays during each of the next two weeks. The festivities of the season commence on the 27th with the Festival of St. John, at the Masonic Hall ; but the mysterious joys of this Feast are for the initiated only. On Monday, the 2nd January, the Annual Show of flowers, fruit, and produce will take place at the Gardens of our Agricultural and Horticultural Society. . . . On Monday evening, the 2nd January, our Scotch friends of the Caledonian Club [D. A. L. Buist, Secretary] hold their first gathering in the Masonic Hall. . . .

" On Wednesday evening, the 4th, a grand Amateur Concert will take place in Mr. Acutt's new and spacious Auction Mart on the Market Square for the benefit of the Widows and Orphans' Fund established two years ago. On that and the previous evening, the Natal District of Odd Fellows will hold social and musical meetings at Maritzburg. On the former occasion, after tea, Dr. Mann will deliver a lecture, and other gentlemen addresses. On the latter occasion, a concert will take place, followed by dancing, and vocal and instrumental music."

Christmas Numbers. On the 29th December the *Natal Mercury* burst upon us with its first four-page Christmas Supplement (one-half, paste and scissors contributions, and advertisements) containing a local article of a topical character, entitled "Mrs. Miffin's Experiences" and signed J.R., also an historical summary of the preceding ten years entitled, "Retrospect and Hope," also signed J.R., and further adorned with an original poem entitled, "The Old Country," or "A Colonist's Song," also signed J.R., " all vastly entertaining."

I was not aware that my friend John Robinson, at that time sub-editor of the *Mercury*, was given to poetry ; if so, he speedily relinquished the habit. It is my assumption that the initials are his. For my own part ignominious failures in my salad days have soured my poetic taste, and disposed me to side with the immortal Tony Weller in his expressed opinion, "Poetry's unnat'rl, no man ever talked poetry 'cept a beadle on boxin' day or a Warren's blacking or Rowland's oil, or some of them low fellows; never you let yourself down to talk poetry, my boy. Begin again, Sammy."

Nevertheless the number conveys to its readers the kindliest wishes of the season and desires for an all-round Happy New Year.

CHAPTER XV.

1860.

WILLIAM HARTLEY AND ALEXANDER McARTHUR, MAYORS.

Judge Phillips. The year opened on the 5th January with a public meeting to remonstrate against the suspension of Judge Phillips (Second Puisne Judge) for having expressed from the Bench his disapproval of an act of clemency shown by Lieutenant-Governor Scott in remitting the sentence of a recently convicted criminal, without having first referred the case to the Judge who tried him; in this case Mr. Justice Phillips was himself the presiding Judge. The attendance was large and influential, and, though it followed so closely on the holidays, it was observed that there had never been a meeting in Durban characterised by so much order, moderation, and respectability. Many and forcible were the condemnatory resolutions passed, supported by speeches, clear and radiant reflections of the British Constitution, Trial by Jury and Bill of Rights. The Mayor (Mr. Hartley) presided and led off well, his remarks being received with cheers. Mr. A. W. Evans proposed the first resolution (cheers), seconded by Mr. A. Coqui, M.L.C., (also cheers). Motion put and carried unanimously. Mr. E. P. Lamport then took up the running, and kept himself going with many apt quotations in prose and verse; his resolution was seconded by Mr. R. Acutt. Mr. Pinsent raised a doubt on a legal point, which was badly received,

and brought down on himself crushing condemnation from
Mr. J. D. Shuter and Mr. Goodricke, M.L.C. Mr.
McArthur supported Mr. Lamport's resolution, which was
carried *nem. con.* Mr. Gillespie moved another, which Mr.
R. Harwin seconded (carried unanimously). Mr. P.
Lennox proposed another in a terse yet homely speech,
received with cheers and laughter. Mr. Shuter in seconding the motion expressed his admiration of the propcser's
moving virtue and righteous indignation. (Carried unanimously).

The meeting closed with a vote of thanks to the Mayor,
and we dispersed in the happy consciousness of having done
our duty by the country. We had reason to believe that
our voice was heard.

Mr. Lushington Phillips having gone to England to
plead his own cause, returned in the *Waldensian* on the
2nd June, duly reinstated by the Secretary of State, his
suspension by the Lieutenant-Governor having been set
aside as illegal. A congratulatory address of welcome had
been prepared by the Town Council and signed by about
150 burgesses.

The Mayor and a deputation of townsmen intended to
present the Address at the Point, but the *Pioneer* being
especially expeditious, landed the mails and passengers two
hours before they were expected (*i.e.*, at high water);
consequently His Worship and Escort met the Judge on
his way up to town, and accompanied him to the Masonic
Hotel, where the Address was presented to " the unflinching
defender of our hereditary rights, etc.," and by him acknowledged in cordial but modest terms, followed by the usual
chatty and social ceremonies practised at a public bar.

**Acutt's
Auction Mart**
Had been removed to a temporary site in
West Street, pending the enlargement of
his premises and erection of a more pretentious Mart on the Market Square
Business was resumed there at the commencement of 1860
and for some 36 years the inhabitants of Durban regarded
as a landmark the somewhat Toy-Box order of architecture
that constituted the building. The frontage consisted of
two double-storied square towers connected by a triangular

cornice, in the centre of which was a large clock with a flagstaff overhead. A recess underneath formed a deep porch to the main building, which was entered by three arched doorways, and through these both town and county, their wives and families, natives and Indians mingled and crowded by day, and even by night, when there was "anything on." This old Durban building became historical, being intimately associated with the acts of the burgesses, their good and bad deals, their market-day gatherings, merry jests and friendly intercourse, despite at times the stifling heat and malodorous surroundings.

Commercial expediency and the obliterating hand of progress has demolished the old Mart, and left but a name behind. I therefore feel comforted in recording from the *Mercury* :—

"A QUADRILLE PARTY was given by Mr. and Mrs. R. Acutt in the new premises in the Market Square on Friday evening [6th January]. The company comprised all the élite of Durban and the neighbourhood, and the arrangements were of the most complete description. The music, by Messrs. Haygarth and Taylor, was unusually excellent, and inspired terpsichorean achievements until a late hour. There has seldom been a re-union in this town which afforded so much pleasure to all who had the felicity of being present. Mr. Acutt's new hall is a splendid apartment, equally well adapted for social festivities as for business requirements."

Steam Tug. Jan. 19th.—"When last outside our Port Tug carried away her mainmast by running foul of the *Selina*, whose bowsprit was also broken. Her machinery is evidently not in good working order, rendering her at present useless, and complaints are made of her general management. We cannot say where the blame lies, but it is obvious that a better system must be established if her cost and maintenance are not to be a dead loss to the Colony." . . .

Thus the *Mercury* in consequence of a public meeting having been requisitioned to consider the state of the Bar and the cause of the detention of eight vessels outside. The meeting was accordingly held during the succeeding week. The Mayor opened the proceedings, and a long wait followed, no one apparently knowing where the shoe pinched; whereupon His Worship requested the meeting to appoint a Chairman *pro tem.*, and allow him the opportunity of speaking on the subject and moving a resolution.

Mr. J. F. Kahts was accordingly elected, and Mr. Hartley proceeded to give the history of the Harbour Works to the present time, taking the Government to task in trenchant terms, ultimately moving a sapless resolution " to call the attention of the Government to the present " dangerous and shallow condition of the entrance to our " harbour," etc., etc., seconded by Mr. Paris. Mr. George Potter endorsed unreservedly the statements of the Mayor with reference to the influence of the Umgeni on the Bar. He believed that eventually, if not counteracted, it would block up the Harbour.

Mr. Pinsent rather supported the Government, and would like to hear the views of the Chamber of Commerce as to the purposed expenditure upon Captain Vetch's plan of £300,000, involving a yearly interest of £27,000. Mr. Tyzack supported Mr. Pinsent. Mr. Goodricke, not being prepared, spoke to the subject generally, informing us that the community had been libelled as a radical and noisy set, and he hoped they would redeem their characters and not let the meeting end in smoke; so by way of warming up the meeting he attacked Captain Bell " who had done " an important duty to his country in earlier days. The " right man in the right place was necessary in any office " of this nature, but his experience was not such as to fit " him for the mastership of a steam tug. He might in " that capacity be humbugged at any time by the Engineer. " There was no doubt the tug had not yet done her duty. " . . . . . Captain Bell was too kind-hearted a man " to insist on discipline, or to ensure the execution of his " orders. Seafaring men had told him (Mr. G.) that if " they had the tug in their hands they would have brought " the vessel in "—Mick Wall, a boatman, interjected a bass "No weather to bring her in!" Mr. G. admitted that fact, but suggested Captain Bell should be retired on a pension, concluding with the comforting assurance, " If his Excellency would not listen to Durban radicals, Her Majesty no doubt would attend to their prayers." (Cheers.) The Mayor resumed the chair, withdrawing other condemnatory resolutions touching the New Harbour plans, and called upon Mr. Goodricke to adopt and move his (the Mayor's) last resolution to the effect that six gentlemen prepare a memorial on the Harbour Question for signature in Durban

and Maritzburg. Mr. Goodricke, regarding his position as
a member of the Legislative Council, declined, whereupon
the gauntlet was taken up by Mr. Tyzack, who in moving
the resolution reviewed the subject generally in very emphatic terms.   He was seconded by Mr. Kermode, who took
the opportunity to express his conviction that Milne's
plans would outdo Vetch's altogether. He wished to know
why the latter were considered superior; the outer basin
was only for the benefit of the Admiralty and Men-of-War ;
he believed that neither could the Port boat live in the
present sea, nor that the steam tug, if outside, could ever
come in The meeting broke up after the Mayor had congratulated himself and the meeting on the facility with
which he had been extracted from a dangerous dilemma.
About 200 were present.

Wisdom advises that it is unsafe to prophecy unless you
know ; it was consequently very humiliating to the newspaper writer, who praised the *Pioneer* on the first occasion
of its disporting itself outside, to have to announce at the
end of January, in consequence of the reputed misbe-
haviour of the Steam Tug, Port Establishment, Bar and
weather, that His Excellency John Scott with the Colonial
Secretary, Major Erskine, had paid a protracted visit to
Durban personally to superintend and direct the refitting
of the *Pioneer* and test the effect of her stern rake upon
the Bar : —

   "The immediate cause of the steamer's defective working
was the spindle of the throttle valve being broken, which
occasioned one of the engines to be cut off from steam . . . .
The *Pioneer's* machinery however still requires considerable
outlay to enable it to perform its work properly. None of her
valves are air or steam tight ; the paddle wheels are not rightly
put together, and other matters affecting her efficient working
require attention. The *Pioneer* seems better adapted for river
service than for the rough work and weather of a port like ours.
. . . The rake provided for the tug has been tried on the bar, but
is found insufficient in size and otherwise unsuitable.   The
Lieutenant-Governor has therefore ordered a new one to be
made forthwith, and there is every ground for hoping that by
this means the direct channel over the bar will again be rendered practicable. . . .   When the tug raked the bar on
Monday morning there were seven feet of water on it at quarter
ebb.   The refitting of the tug was entrusted by His Excellency

to Mr. C. Joseph Cato, the Governor himself personally super-
intending and forwarding the work; resulting in the tug successfully bringing in the *Rothay* schooner, and *Selina* brig,
and taking out the barque *Good Hope* all in one day."

The article terminates in a " now we are happy " style,
and the thanks of the mercantile community are directed
to the Lieutenant-Governor under this head; at the same
time his approval of Captain Vetch's scheme is " damned
with faint praise."

The Commer-
cial and
Agricultural
Bank of Natal
Commenced business on Saturday the 11th
February in a wing of Mr. R. Acutt's new
Auction Mart on the Market Square. Mr.
John Brown chairman, Mr. Richard Vause
general manager, Mr. H. Lochee Bayne,
recently arrived from the Colonial En-
gineer's Office, Capetown, cashier, Mr. Joseph A. Jackson
accountant; the Bank afterwards removed to premises in
Central West Street, known as Breede's Store, or Ted
Smith's Store, between what is now D. McDonald's London
Warehouse and T. Alcock and Co's Hardware Store.

They issued neatly engraved Bank Notes from Ten
Shillings upwards (*). Notes for £1 were in greatest
demand, while £5, £10, and £20 were also current. The
Bank started on progressive lines, with liberal discounts
and encouraging advances, in the interests of the Sugar
Industry. Money was easy, hence we no longer hesitated
to accept Buyer's Bills in settlement, provided they added
the discount, for the reason that the more exclusive Natal
Bank found that if they declined " to oblige a customer,"
the rival institution would accept both the customer and
his bills.

To such a pass had the system of accommodation paper
reached that Promissory Notes were given for the most
trivial amounts and transactions, usually at short dates,
seldom exceeding three months. There was scarcely any
expectation that these Promissory Notes would be taken
up with cash, the prevailing idea being to pay, or set off,
something on account and renew for the balance. Small

---

* This is a mistake. I find that the credit of introducing Ten
Shilling Notes is due to Mr. W. Hartley when he opened the
" Durban Bank " about two years later.

farmers had running accounts with the storekeepers and Auctioneers on these lines, each transaction yielding its P. Note; these approved Bills were duly discounted, while the Auctioneer passed his Bill to the seller, which the seller passed to the Merchant, who himself obtained discount and credit at the Banks for his "trade bills." In this simple manner was Capital created and accounts settled, while Notaries did a profitable business by daily attendance at the Banks to present and protest.

Though the story has become a common joke, yet I have myself heard an unsophisticated victim. of these financial complications and many protests exclaim with a sigh of relief after signing a long-term promissory note for the totals and costs:—" Thank God, that's settled ! "

The commercial stability of the period was eventually proved in Court to the dismay of the Judges, and as the fruit of the "Pagoda tree" began to fail, culminated in the financial disasters of 1865-6. The position was thus shown in evidence.

A hunter and trader retiring from business disposed of his wagon and span of oxen. They were sold by Auction for say £150; the Auctioneer passing his bill to the seller (1st £150). One man having bought the wagon for £100, and another the oxen for £50, both passed their bills to the Auctioneer (2nd £150). The buyer of the wagon sold it at a profit to two men in partnership and took their partnership bills in favour of each other (each a moiety) for say £125. The buyer of the oxen retailed them to three men and took their bills collectively for £75 (total £200). These Promissory Notes the sellers passed as trade bills, consequently for one transaction represented by the wagon and oxen, the Banks would hold the paper made by eight men, necessarily endorsed by other eight or more, deeming the several makers and endorsers sufficient security for £500.

This might have been considered good business at the time, but it ultimately absorbed not only the Capital of the Bank, but the money of the depositors, and as much as could be squeezed out of the shareholders by Mr. John Millar on his appointment by the Supreme Court as Official Liquidator some five or six years later.

Stage Coaches. The projection of the Natal Railway, stimulating the idea of accelerated communication, prompted a citizen of Maritzburg to originate a rapid passenger traffic with the Port, by the good old means of Coach and horses On the 15th March we were startled by the following advertisement :—

"THE ROAD. THE ROAD.

"On Easter Monday the ' Perseverance ' will leave Maritzburg at six o'clock precisely, calling at Camperdown, Clough's and Pinetown, arriving in Durban the same day, and starting from thence at the same time on the following Friday. By running the above omnibus to and from Durban (down on Tuesdays after first week, and back on Fridays) JOHN DARE will afford an accommodation to the travelling community which has been long wanted. He therefore trusts that by strict attention to the comfort of his passengers—a safe, easy and neat conveyance, together with the best possible supply of horses, to merit the support of the public generally.

"Fare: Up or Down, £1. Children under twelve, Half Price."

So important and hazardous an undertaking over unmade roads, or tracks cut on the face of the country by wagon wheels and hoofs of cattle, demanded special observation. On Thursday the 12th April it is recorded :—

"The Perseverance Omnibus did not leave Maritzburg on her first trip until Tuesday morning, the arrangements not being sufficiently completed to admit of her departure on Monday. In spite of the unfavourable weather, and the contingent drawbacks of rain and mud, the vehicle with a full freight of passengers, progressed rapidly and comfortably as far as Pinetown. After leaving McNicoll's, however, one of the horses swerved to one side and dragged the bus into a rut. This mishap resulted in a snapped spring, which necessitated a stoppage for the night. Yesterday morning the horses were again harnessed, and the pioneer of rapid locomotion drew up finally about three o'clock at the Masonic Hotel Mr. Dare drives himself and the passengers were well pleased with a pleasant and very easy trip."

On May the 3rd we are told :—

"The Omnibus is doing her work well. On Friday last she accomplished the up-journey through, arriving in the City about a quarter past seven. On Tuesday she left Maritzburg about six o'clock and reached her destination at Wood's Masonic

Hotel on the same day, just as the six o'clock dinner bell was sounding, Mr. Dare has increased his team, and has every anticipation that his present success will prove a permanency."

Meantime he had announced the "Crown" in Maritzburg and the "Masonic" in Durban as his starting places. Passengers were allowed 10lbs. luggage, extra 1½d. per lb. Parcels carried and delivered, 6lbs. for 1s., above 6lbs. 1½d. per lb. Before the end of the month, while Dare was driving the Perseverance down Botha's Hill, both its hind wheels locked, completely upsetting the coach, with its legs in the air, the tent rolling in one direction, the horses and harness tearing off in another, a stout gentleman underneath with some of its weight on the small of his back, and two ladies roughly landed, owning a cut lip and a black eye between them. The other passengers righted the uninjured 'bus recaptured the horses, spliced the harness and proceeded to McNicoll's, where things were made comfortable; the 'bus finally arriving "safely and satisfactorily" in Durban, a little late for dinner. The later historian will tell how John W. Welch of Pinetown, a burgess of Durban, succeeded Dare, establishing a daily Omnibus service both ways; how, encouraged by his success, one Jessup vainly endeavoured to run him off the road; and how the Murrays of Pinetown cut into his passenger traffic on obtaining a contract to carry the mails by postcart. On the retirement of Welch he was succeeded by his sons, one of whom, possessing as many lives as the proverbial cat, continues Postcart Contractor for the Colony outside the limits of the Natal Government Railways.

Beningfields. Mr. Samuel Beningfield, after a lengthy visit to England, returned in the *Oak* on the 3rd February, and announced himself on the 15th March as having resumed business as an Auctioneer, but without defining an office, the well-known site on the Market Square not having been acquired. His first sale was to be held at the store of A. Jacques, Field Street. "Tattersall's" was to be held at Deer's stables, and the Masonic Hotel was constituted "The Garraway's of Natal," for the sales of landed property.

For the rest of the year his racy and descriptive advertisements afford highly coloured pictures of both town and country properties as they were, or should be.

Hospital and Gaol. About the end of March, as the result of endless representations and complaints, the Government engaged the well-built brick residence of Mr. James McKnight in St. George's Street, for the use of the sick, pending the erection of a proper Hospital, which it was understood the Government contemplated building on its Beach Erf, Smith Street, (now occupied by the Government Primary School for Boys) out of the £5,000 reserved for native purposes. It was found that the Gaol accommodation was becoming a scandal, and that some separation of patients and prisoners, including lunatics, was essentially necessary, the old " Tronk " being wholly inadequate for both, apart from its use as a Police Station, notwithstanding Mr. T. Dand's good management, and the transfer of long-term convicts and their clanking chains to Pietermaritzburg and the Government Brickyards.

The Natal Commercial Advertiser and Agricultural Reporter, Under the editorship of Dr. W. H. Ludlow, announced that it would appear as a weekly newspaper on the 20th March, price 6d. per copy; its object being "rather to guide than to lead or be led by public opinion." Publishing office West Street, Durban. As it offered special inducement for all classes of the community to ventilate their grievances, it was favourably received and supported, though its advertising charges were the same as those of the *Mercury.* Unfortunately its career was brief in consequence of the lamented death of its editor and chief proprietor in July following.

Legislative Council. In consequence of the resignation of Mr. John Millar as the Borough member, requisition was made to and accepted by Mr. A. W. Evans; there being no opposition he was declared duly returned in April, without affording us any opportunity to cultivate our Election tactics. The Council met in June, and the voluminous reports of its proceedings contain much interesting matter relating to Durban, the Borough being represented by Messrs. Goodricke and Evans.   The senior member, having transferred his abilities from the Town Council to that arena, speedily came to an issue with the House on such fertile subjects as "Treasury balances"; the Estimates and Votes of Supply; opposing all Ecclesiastical grants. Valuing the services of the Port Establishment including the Collector of Customs and his staff; condemning the formation of Addington without the consent of Durban's burgesses; urging the removal of his old antogonist the Resident Magistrate of Durban to Maritzburg "by way of a change"; receiving at last his quietus from the Attorney General, not so much for opposing an increase of the latter's salary, as for the comparisons and malicious insinuations that accompanied his opposition, on what Mr. Gallwey characterised as "low grounds of spite and utter falseness" and he "regretted that the honourable gentleman belonged to a profession which he would not exercise in England, and still more regretted that so many years of experience at the Colonial Bar had not cured him of such innate vulgarity."

After this it was only to be expected that Mr. Goodricke's commendable motion, made a few days later and seconded by Mr. Evans, to devote £1,000 to the erection of a Government House at Durban, should have been rejected.

Town Improvements   No better record can be had than that of the writers of the period who spoke as they knew, so I save myself from disinterring them from Town Council records; thus I find at the end of January that:—

" We are happy to notice that two gangs of labourers have latterly been at work upon our long-neglected footpaths. The road through the Berea, for which we are indebted to our present Mayor, is a very great improvement on the old road; but it is to be regretted that it had to be done at the expense of necessary works within the town. The drain in central Smith Street is still uncommenced, and the drainage of the Eastern Vlei seems to be as far off as ever from 'an accomplished fact.' Meanwhile a handsome revenue lies buried in swamp and malaria. The Umgeni still pursues the crooked tenor of its way towards the town, unchecked by Government or Municipal interference, inflicting incalculable injury on the Port, and threatening the destruction of the town."

This was followed by the announcement that Mr. G. C. Cato and Mr. E. P. Lamport, "in consequence of protracted `absence from the Colony," had resigned their seats in the Town Council. Mr. Lamport advertised that his business would be conducted by his manager, Mr. Stephen Wasserman. This quiet and unobtrusive gentleman was for many years a Burgess of Durban, and is better remembered by his long association with the Natal Bank, which he joined after Mr. Lamport's return. He was ultimately appointed Manager of the Pilgrim's Rest branch in the Transvaal, which he opened. He returned to Durban on the outbreak of hostilities with the Boers, and at an advanced age found a resting place in our General Cemetery.

St. Paul's Church.—"The annual Vestry meeting was held in St. Paul's Church on Tuesday [11th April] at which a number of matters were adjusted, and Messrs. R. Acutt and John Hunt appointed churchwardens for the ensuing year. These meetings which used to be scenes of so much excitement are now conducted in as quiet and peaceable a way as the ordinary meetings of any other religious community."

This favourable record comforted the afflicted until a Vestry Meeting was held on the 18th June to elect a Delegate to represent Durban parish at the Church Council, in the place of Dr. Mann, resigned. Mr. George Winder and Mr. William Brickhill were both nominated, and on its being put to the vote Mr. Winder was declared elected by 10 votes to 5. Mr. Robert Acutt never yielded gracefully to a majority, so raised a convenient storm by denouncing in language, unsuited for a love feast, the unfitness of Mr. Winder in consequence of his holding—as he expressed it—extreme High Church principles. He supported Mr. William Brickhill, who (on his own showing) had been a good and happy Churchwarden in England, and was consequently more suitable as a delegate from this parish. Remonstrance was unavailing, so Mr. Acutt demanded a poll of the members of the Church on this important question.

Result: election confirmed on a subsequent polling, 27 being for Mr. Winder and 18 against, so the "Ayes" had it, and the Church still stands on its foundation.

Christ Church. On the 11th April a meeting, at which both the Rev. W. H. C. Lloyd and the Rev. A. W. L. Rivett were present, was held at the Point, consisting of boatmen, pilots, sailors and other residents in that quarter, " to devise means of providing the community with settled religious advantages." About £40 was immediately subscribed by those present toward the erection of a sailor's church, and very gratifying resolutions were adopted in furtherance of the object. These good resolves were at once carried into effect, and the *Mercury* of the 26th April publishes a List of Subscribers from the Lieutenant-Governor downwards, making a total subscription to that date of £123 8s. 6d. To Mr. Rivett is due the merit of originating and successfully carrying out this extension of the Church of England. He states in his *Ten Years' Church Work in Natal,* " the " number of houses between the Point and Durban could " not exceed forty, and these were chiefly inhabited by " Port Officials, landing agents, and boatmen. The popula- " tion did not amount to more than one hundred and fifty." As Military Chaplain, his first services to the soldiers stationed at the Block House were held in a small chapel which had formerly belonged to the Wesleyans, and was bought of them by the Bishop for £10. It would not hold more than fifty persons, and was of advanced age; a strong " Sou' Wester " ultimately demolished it. Mr. Rivett relates, " This disaster took place in the winter when " the weather is warm and dry. I first secured the loan of " a small room in a private house, and I found it so well " attended, that the next step was to hold a service in the " open air near the Custom House, under a Euphorbia " tree. On the stump of another close by was placed a " basin of water, where on more than one occasion I ad- " ministered the rite of Holy Baptism to infants after the " second lesson. A large number attended the services " and it was the beginning of a better state of things. . . " The approach of summer interrupted this arrangement.

"A large store was being erected by Mr. L. Wilson near
" the Custom House, and he kindly permitted me to occupy
" the upper room till a better arrangement could be made."
. . . .   "I lost no time in applying to the Governor for
" sufficient land on which to build a Church, School, and
" Parsonage.   In due time the request was granted and
" land set aside for that purpose."   He went to Maritzburg on a collecting tour and raided the Military.   "Every
" officer connected with the 85th Regiment in the City
" from the Colonel to the Ensign contributed a guinea or
" half a guinea.   Several of the civilians also assisted, and
" at the end of the week I had collected and a few promises,
" amounting in all to £70. . . . .   Another plan was
" also set on foot to augment the fund.   Mr. William
" Hodge, one of the pilots, worked energetically and he
" never lost an opportunity of soliciting every Captain and
" Officer on board the ships in Port to do something for
" the Church.   And to his praise be it said under God's
" blessing, he raised in eighteen months, not far short of
" £150.   The zeal and heartiness which he displayed on
" behalf of the New Sailors' Church (and the help he
" rendered to me afterwards as my Churchwarden) will
" never be forgotten by me. . . . .   As soon as there
" was a prospect that sufficient funds would be forthcoming
" I engaged a number of kafirs to clear the trees and bush
" to make a space on which the Church was to be erected.
" I superintended the work.   The spot chosen was close to
" the line of railway facing the beautiful Bay of Durban,
" [corner of Shepstone and Bell Streets, Addington].   A
" building   committee   was   appointed. . . . . .   A
" church without a school was an anomaly and there was
" not one in existence at the Point."

He made a house-to-house call to ensure support to a
schoolmaster for a mixed school, and have the assistance
of a sewing mistress.   He called a public meeting, formed
a committee of management and resolved that the school
should be called the "Point Port Natal School."

Mr. J. R. Scott was nominated secretary, and Mr.
Archibald treasurer.   A temporary school-room was engaged and the services of Sergeant Richardson, formerly
master of the military school at Fort Napier, were secured,

while his wife taught the sewing. The Society for promoting Christian Knowledge made a grant of books. The Bishop furnished maps and apparatus. The School was soon in a position to obtain a grant from Government; a large number of children attended it daily, and it was in every sense successful and prosperous. The stray ceremony of laying the foundation stone of a wooden church, as given with chapters and verse by Mr. Rivett, is too long for quotation and is thus condensed from the newspapers :—

" SAILORS' CHURCH, POINT.

"On Monday evening [24th September] the ceremony of laying the foundation stone of this edifice was performed by the Rev. W. H. C. Lloyd, Colonial Chaplain, who, after the service was over, and the stone had been laid, delivered an able and appropriate address. . . . The Rev. A. W. L. Rivett, Military Chaplain, and the zealous minister of the parish, to whose unwearied and arduous exertions the erection of the building is principally due, conducted the service in a very impressive manner.

"A company of about seventy were present to witness the proceedings. Amongst them were the children of the school under the charge of their new master Mr. Richardson, who sang the National Anthem after the ceremony was over. Both the juvenile and the adult portions of the assembly were afterwards regaled with suitable refreshments at the residence of Mr. Upton. The occasion was both a pleasing and interesting one. When completed the church will consist of a wooden edifice on brick piers measuring 50 feet by 29 feet, with a small tower, chancel and arched windows. It will form quite an addition to the architecture of the Point," etc., etc.

The building was ultimately completed, painted, and suitably furnished and seated. At Mr. Rivett's special request it was named " Christ Church." It appears to have been consecrated by the Metropolitan Bishop of Capetown during his visit in 1864, when the same office was performed for St. Paul's and the then recently erected St. Thomas', Berea. The march of progress has demanded this ground, and it is probable that before this is in type the site will be occupied by the Railway, and a new Church erected elsewhere in Addington.

Town of Addington.

The *Natal Star* having the good fortune to forestall the *Mercury* in proclaiming a piece of real news, the fact is kindly announced in the *Mercury* of the 24th May as follows:—

" That comparatively small portion of our readers, who are in the habit of reading the *Star*, would be surprised by the announcement of that self-constituted Government organ, that a new township to be called 'Addington' is being laid out in the Back Beach bush between the Point Road and the sea, beyond the boundary line of the Town Lands, and on lands formerly granted to the Harbour Board for the purposes of the Port. We find the fact is so ; and that a whisper of the intention had for some time previously oozed out in certain quarters. Moreover, it is affirmed that from 20 to 30 allotments, or erven, have been already assigned to persons in the secret of the Government's intentions. The lots are half-an-acre in extent, and are leased for 50 years at a ground rent of £3 per annum.

We are informed that some of the details thus pompously announced are not correct, but substantially it is true that the Government—that is to say His Excellency, Lieutenant-Governor Scott, the present despotic ruler—so far as he can or dare to be—of Natal, has directed his officers to lay out and survey a new township in the locality stated, without consulting or so much as intimating his intention to the inhabitants of this town, whose interests are thus arbitrarily compromised, without giving the public a chance by fair open competition, of securing lots in the new township; and without the consent or even the cognizance of the Harbour Board whose property is thus despotically appropriated. . . . It is a wanton insult offered to the Harbour Board and the town of Durban, and a wanton injury inflicted on the owners of property in the town. The very bestowal of a separate name, whence derived we know not, unless it be in honour of Mr. Addington, afterwards Viscount Sidmouth, a statesman famous, or rather infamous, in the annals of bigotry. . . . Isolating Durban from the Point by the allocation of a town with a new name, our town of Durban will cease to be the seaport town of the Colony, but the ' Point Addington' will take the place of the 'Point Durban,' Natal, in mercantile transactions.'

Having thus sufficiently sharpened up his readers and himself, the writer is enabled to "go one better" than the *Star* and see through the millstone.

"The real secret of this Addington scheme is well known, notwithstanding the 'policy of concealment.' Certain parties, having the secret ear of the Government, have long been bent, by hook or crook, on diverting the centre of business from the locality where, in consequence of their own grasping shortsightedness, it long ago became located—namely, west of the Market Square, and forcing it back to the eastward, towards *Cato's Creek*. Having signally failed in their manifold and tortuous efforts, they have tried this new dodge, and found too ready a response in the Executive. It now remains to be seen whether the Corporation of the town, including the burgesses, will sit down quietly under this aggressive insult. Our fellow-townsmen have latterly shown a strange falling off from the spirit that characterised them a few years ago," etc., *da capo*

Town Council. In January the Council proclaimed an assessment of 1s. 6d. in the £ on the Rental Value and 2d. on the Freehold. In February a requisition for a public meeting on the alleged inequality of the Rating was presented to the Mayor, who declined to call a meeting. It was then proposed to appeal to the Supreme Court to set the Rate aside. The burgesses apparently contented themselves by protesting before paying. At a meeting on the 20th March, Mr. Jas. Brickhill, who had been elected a Councillor, was appointed on various committees, and moved that the ground between Church Street and Gardiner Street in the Market Square (where the present Town Hall stands) be surveyed for sale. It was also resolved that the application of the Railway Co. for a lease of the land (as already laid out) between the Ordnance land and the Harbour Board [Addington] be granted subject to a rental of £5 per year, with reservation of the right to make culverts and drains under the railway, and on such other terms as the two parties may agree, the period not to exceed 21 years. An adjourned meeting for the consideration of a lengthy Minute by the Mayor, and other business, was held on the 25th of March, when several letters were read from Mr. Goodricke complaining *inter alia* of having been summoned for Arrear Rates and mulcted in a sum of 12s. 6d., "about a matter which would have at once been paid had the Town Clerk had common courtesy and been correct in his accounts."

Also in reference to the Town Solicitorship, he touched on the Rice Case as illustrating the ingratitude displayed by the Council towards one who had earned at least their thanks, instead of being made the subject of unmerited abuse. The revision of the Bye-Laws engaged the spare time of that meeting, as the Mayor's Minute was altogether too debatable a subject to be entered upon lightly, and in haste. It contained many practical suggestions regarding the sanitary improvements of the town, and boldly pointed out the liabilities of the ratepayers. The following category of common nuisances, enumerated by His Worship in these good old times, was enough of itself to scare away sensitive persons from the precincts of such a place. The Mayor complains that our streets are incommoded by heaps of stones, empty cases, ploughs, machinery, piles of unprotected bricks, exposed drains, rolls of lead, offensive smells, butchers' refuse, manure heaps, dirty stables, pig-styes and decayed vegetable matter; the careless cracking of whips, the cruel and torturous lashing of oxen, the inspanning of wagons, the stopping of street crossings, are additional causes of annoyance. He asserts the Bye-Laws are a by-word, and recommends the appointment of a street-keeper under the Town Surveyor, who himself should be employed in laying out the town on a defined plan of levels and system of drainage, regulations for building and oversight of public works, etc.

On the 12th April practical action was taken on the recommendations of the Minute, accelerated by a letter of demand from the Attorney-General for £559, minus the moiety for licenses, on account of Police Expenses. Resolved on Mr. Pinsent's motion that the Mayor inform the Government that the Council are desirous either of relinquishing any responsibility connected with the Police, or of accepting the entire control of the constabulary, provided they have also the entire revenue now, or to be by any reformed system, derived from the licences. Also that he communicate the general desire that the Gaol should be removed, or otherwise rendered more secure. Mr. Pinsent also gave notice of his intention to move that the Council make provision for the endowment of a High School and Library. Councillor McArthur resigned his seat for Ward No. 4.

At the following meeting a sub-committee recommended that the Eastern Vlei be not leased, but only drained to become pasture land; also to avoid its falling into the hands of speculators who would sublet, and because the Western Vlei, having but a single drain, now yielded good herbage in place of rushes. The meeting terminated, however, "rather abruptly in the midst of a ' scene ' which bid fair to realize the lively occurrences of former days." The Mayor declared that, according to the Bye-Laws, he was authorised to set aside the work of any committee, and he persisted in his dictum with so much vehemence, that one of the Councillors took up his hat and left the meeting. As a quorum then ceased to be present, the Councillors returned to their homes with a conviction that their chairman's behaviour had been more pointed than polite. The *Mercury* in commenting on this circumstance sapiently remarked:—"His Worship will do well to remember that the dogged maintenance of a fanciful prerogative has proved the bane of greater men than even the Mayor of Durban."

On the 2nd May the Council received intimation from the Government that Mr. Brickhill's proposed sale of erven in the Market Square could not be entertained until the burgesses at large had signified their approval

On the 8th May resolutions were carried, " that the gang and carts be employed in carting ballast from the pit now opened in Pine Terrace in order to form a road from Field Street to Aliwal Street." The reason for this was that Mr. Upton had claimed the discovery of what he called a "ballast pit" in Pine Terrace (we were talking railway at this time) and suggested its being eventually converted into a catch water reservoir to enable him to flush future drains. This scheme was never carried out, my belief being that the "ballast" in question was lost as soon as found, unless it consisted of the sandy clay underlying Commercial Road. Another resolution was, "That the ground between Church Street and Gardiner Street be surveyed and a portion offered for sale, the proceeds to be applied to ballasting the streets." Mr. Ferguson was also desirous of leasing lots in the Market Square, east of the Church, but was outvoted. But on the 2nd June Mr. F. C. Salmon proposed the leasing of lots at the "East End," extending the town as far as Cato's Bridge. On the 20th of the month a resolution was carried, on the motion of Mr. Pinsent, to set aside a portion of the Town Lands for the endowment of a college; in the meantime the revenue from leasing same to be applied to education generally; of whom, or in what mode, is not recorded, but a public meeting was to be called to settle these little and knotty points. Mr. Salmon was delegated to supervise the drainage of the Eastern Vlei.—At the following weekly meeting a Fire Engine and apparatus were thought necessary for the Borough, so a Committee was appointed to report on same.—On the 26th July it was announced that the complacency of the Council was ruthlessly dispelled. by the refusal of the Acting Lieutenant-Governor, on the advice of the Attorney-General, to allow the north side of the Market Square to be cut up into erven and sold, as such course would be a breach of faith with the purchasers of the original erven in the town. The *Mercury* devotes a leader to the subject in support of the justice of the decision of the Executive.

On Wednesday, 1st August, the unopposed elections for Town Councillors resulted in the return for

Ward 1. F. C. Salmon and Wm. Palmer.
Ward 2. A. Ferguson and S. Beningfield.
Ward 3. Richard Gelder, and John Sanderson.
Ward 4. Alexander McArthur and John Hunt.

At the meeting of Councillors on the following Saturday (in terms of the Law) Mr. McArthur was elected Mayor.

Mr. Wm. Hartley closed his year of office with Mayor's Minute No. 7, particularly detailed and interesting reading at this advanced period of our lives, having a strong family likeness to the private cash accounts recorded by the virtuous youth of the Sandford and Merton age. He, however, grasps the situation, dashes boldly into figures, and to emphasize the position of the Borough shows items of the Assets and the Liabilities, leaving " Balance to good of Estate £72." The Town Treasurer, Mr. W. C. Humphreys, gives a statement of Receipts and Expenditure for the year; receipts from all sources being £987 19s. 11d., while the Expenditure absorbs all but a balance in his hands of £23 5s. 7d. This is vouched for by A. M.

Barnes, Auditor, and A. Ferguson, Councillor. These transactions were evidently becoming involved, a re-organization of accounts was ordered, and the Treasurer instructed to open a new set of books.

Mr. Hartley, before vacating the chair, acceded to the requisition of the Burgesses, and convened a public meeting for the 1st August, to consider four engrossing subjects: The anticipated visit of Prince Alfred and Sir George Grey, at the invitation of the Colony; the disposal of the "Addington" land; the sale of ground in the Market Square; and the erection of Coolie Barracks at the Point. The public discussion of so many subjects occupied two evenings in succession till past 11 o'clock. On the first point the stumbling-block, having regard to the present state of the town's finances, was: Who should pay for the Royal entertainment? Resolved: That the subject at its present stage was premature. The meeting voted that the Harbour Board should be reinstated, and the Addington Lands set apart for its use or otherwise for the use of the Town Council; that another site be selected for the Coolie Barracks instead of at Addington, while the sale of the Market Square was left to the consideration of the incoming Council.

The new Council set to work in a business-like way to re-organize the various Borough offices and departments. The poor pay and other insufficient inducements had encouraged the Corporation's servants to "pick up" any little jobs offering. The Town Clerk himself carried on a separate agency and conveyancing business, the preparation of Borough Leases being a profitable portion; while the Town Surveyor was at every body's call as Surveyor and Architect, leaving him but scant time to engineer the borough. Consequently the Mayor (Mr. McArthur) called for tenders on the 12th September from persons willing to accept the office of Town Clerk devoting their whole time, etc., or otherwise to be Town Solicitor, or Town Clerk and Solicitor in one, and also for the post of Town Surveyor. On the 4th October the Corporation advertised the sale of certain leases by Mr. R. Acutt, including the proposed extension at the East End of the town; also that a new street was named Alfred Street (afterwards changed to Prince Alfred Street), and the Blocks O. and P. would be leased for 50 years at an upset rental of £5 and £3 per lot, those in Block O being 103 feet by 75, and those of Block P being 103 by 67½.

The *Mercury* of the 18th October announces that "Harry Fisher, Esq., a gentleman recently arrived in the Co'ony," had been appointed Town Clerk under the new regulations.*

At their meeting on the 7th November a very valuable discussion took place on the report of Mr. Councillor Sanderson, in reference to the endowment of a Grammar School; unfortunately it grounded on the vexed questions of religious instruction, magisterial or clerical supervision, and was ultimately shelved for a more convenient season.

Mr. Salmon, prior to tendering his resignation as a councillor, vividly depicted the evils arising from the non-existence of a Coroner for the Borough. The Council consented to apply to the Government to share in the pay and appointment of the same officer to serve the entire Colony. The Council also accepted the tender of Alfred Moore to construct wattle fences round the Market Square, and round a drifting sand patch on the Maritzburg Road, between the Botanical Gardens and the town, at an estimated cost of £90 each. On the 13th December a sub-committee was appointed to enquire what compensation the Government will allow for the transfer of the site for the new Gaol, which it was proposed to erect outside the present limits of the town (that is to say on the town lands where it now stands). William Petty was admonished to complete his contract for cutting the drain in the Eastern Vlei; this stimulated him to employ good conduct men of the 85th Regiment at 18d. per diem, by whom the main work was satisfactorily accomplished. Financial provision was also made for widening the Smith Street embankment by 10 feet and replacing the timber bridge over the Western Vlei drain with a brick culvert. A brick culvert was also ordered in place of the sod covered post and faggot crossing at the old [Dutch] road at the

* See *Early Morn.*

head of the swamp near the Gardens.   Business was
concluded by fixing a rate of 3d. in the £ on Freeholds
and 1s. on the Rental Values.

Earthquakes, About 10 o'clock in the evening of the 15th
June Durban was shaken to its foundations
by two shocks of an earthquake following
each other in rapid succession.   The evening had been still, clear and warm for mid-winter, when
suddenly there came a rushing, rumbling sound and vibra-
tion, as of a violent squall of wind with heavy vehicles
passing over a hard road.   The ground trembled, causing
doors and windows to shake violently, leading to the belief
that the rising gale had burst doors open or tumbled over
loose property in back yards.   Rushing out the inhabitants found everything secure within and calm without;
realising they had survived an earthquake, they were proportionately alarmed.   It was felt to a considerable
distance around us, and in some places over the Berea,
where people go to bed early, more severely than we experienced it.   However no physical damage was reported,
but the souls of the nervous were awakened to the fact
that, as shocks had in previous years been experienced in
other parts of the Colony, we might be living on a volcano;
in any case it behoved us to take heed to our steps and
"The End" predicted by Dr. Cumming.   These words of
wisdom were lost; strayed sheep returned to their brows-
ing, content to let the morrow take care of itself, until the
evening of the 21st September, when another earthquake
shock was felt throughout the colony, apparently sharper
in Maritzburg than in Durban, where some people out of
doors failed to notice the phenomenon which seemed by
other reports to have confined itself principally to the
Beach erven; be that as it may, the lightness of the blow
was insufficient for the regeneration of the community; we
talked ourselves into the belief that we were out of the
sphere of influence of earthquakes with their attendant
tidal waves, and I never knew of a builder who considered
either contigency.   The Rev. J. L. Crompton, of Pinetown, was the only person who regarded the possibilities,
and informed me he preferred investing on securities above
Durban's level and the long-range guns of a hostile cruiser

Government School. The annual examination took place on the 18th and 19th June, when the scholars to the number of 170 were examined in reading, writing, history, grammar, and geography. The results, though "Rithmetic" is not referred to, were reported as most satisfactory and reflected the highest credit on the Head-Master, Mr. Thompson. The number of pupils had almost doubled during the past two years. Mr. Winder and Mr. Churchill addressed the pupils and afterwards distributed a number of handsome prizes.

"The Railway" It was to us, and so I continue to write of it. The official title was "The Natal Railway Company"; the Directors, however, feeling themselves flattered by public opinion, speedily advertised it as the "Natal Railway." The *Mercury* of the 12th April describes the situation:—

"Under the energetic superintendence of Mr. Tatham, aided by the co-operation of the Chairman, this work is rapidly progressing towards completion. The line is already laid half the distance, and in a fortnight, if circumstances continue favourable, the rails will have been laid up to the final termination near the Church. . . . Six or eight trucks and two travelling cranes are already mounted and in use. The locomotive is in the *Cadiz*, so that all the materials will soon be received." . . .

The Directors invited applications for the requisite executive staff. Having closed my Oil and Fibre Mills, I was in need of employment, so tendered my services for any responsible office. On the 16th May Mr. John Beard received the appointment of Manager and "Station Agent" at the Point at a salary of £250, while I was appointed "Station Agent" (the Directors apparently requiring no "Masters") at the Market Square terminus at a salary of £150. It was understood that Mr. E. Tatham the secretary would by his own desire retire on the opening of the line, but would continue to act as Resident Engineer of the Company whenever his professional services would be required. On assuming office Mr. Beard found he was expected to take over the duties of Secretary; the Board consequently relieved him of his

Agency by appointing the next approved candidate in the person of Mr. Henry William James (who held a ship master's certificate) to the office of Station Master at the Point, where a good man was absolutely necessary, a man fertile in expedients and with a command of seasonable language. I found in him a sterling friend, ever ready to "lend a hand," so that, during our service, there were but few "Reports"; while any differences between Departments were speedily righted. I am proud to say the friendship, then originated, strengthened on acquaintance and continues unimpaired. I am also indebted to my friend for many notes and recollections of that interesting period of our lives and Durban's history.—I assumed duty about a week after my appointment. Almost my first act on behalf of my employers was overcoming an armed sentry. At the angle of the Ordnance land and facing Gardiner Street Sergeant Major John Adams had acquired from the Board of Ordnance a pensioner's lease of about an acre, and erected a substantial brick cottage thereon; the Railway terminus being upon this land abutted on these premises, to which the line had been laid, and if extended would have passed close in front of his door, but out of consideration for the old veteran the terminus stopped at his boundary. Immediately by the side of his house passed one of the recognised roads to the Camp. On the 26th May I found that in accordance with ancient custom, to maintain their privileges and prevent the establishment of all rights of way, the military-authorities had posted sentries at every road to stop all traffic for one day in the year.

Material was being carted on to the Railway Ordnance land for the construction of platform, engine shed, etc., the passing of which the sentry said was "agin his orders," until I persuaded him by a species of Marine story that the Railway Line was the new boundary of the Ordnance land; that as he allowed people to cross the line which his Sergeant had wrongly pointed out to him, to get to Adams' house, I would say nothing about it, and take care no carts crossed the rails while he was on duty, etc. These and other reasonings enabled us to resume work in peace.

Whether the shipment of so much valuable railway material was not to be entrusted to one bottom I cannot

say, but certain it was that it came by several vessels.   In
April when the greater portion of the rails were laid—the
guage being about 3ft. 6in.—a carriage, six trucks and two
cranes were landed and put together at the Point, which
in consequence was declared to have quite a civilized appearance, with the two cranes overhanging the wharf.   It may
be of interest to state that the trucks were large sized
ballast trucks on four wheels, having wooden buffers, the
sides to fold down.   They were controlled by wooden
brakes attached to long iron levers or handles, hooked up
when running.   Trucks were connected by loose links, and
had coupling chains in addition.   The carriage, or as
conservative railway men called it the " Coach," was a
substantial affair made apparently for the Colony, of three
compartments ; the centre for the First Class, having elegant
cane seats and back, with a strip of floorcloth for the feet,
capable of seating 8 to 10 ; the two end compartments were
of varnished oak, with curved seats and backboard,
intended for the Second Class, and would together hold
20 ; all fitted with practicable glass windows, with scarlet
silk blinds.   The doors, however, could not be locked.
As the journeys would be short hat racks were dispensed
with.   Smoking was only restricted by good manners and
the voice of the ladies.   No provision was made for a
Third Class, as it was never expected the natives would
pay for a ride.   The cranes were the ordinary rotating
wooden jib crane with winch, having a loaded cast-iron
box as a counterpoise, fitted on small four-wheeled trolleys,
to move up and down the line.   One was reputed as of
6 tons capacity, the smaller one of 3 tons.

On the 13th May the brig *Cadiz* arrived with the locomotive which with careful ostentation, notwithstanding it
was reduced to the smallest possible proportions, was duly
landed after the brig came inside.

These packages were forwarded to the Market Square
Station in trucks propelled by the aborigines, arriving
there about the time I entered the service.   The fitting
up to the locomotive was in the hands of our Chief Engineer, Mr. Henry Jacobs, who combined in his own person
the duties of Loco. Superintendent, Fitter and Driver.

He was certainly assisted by Mr. Alexander Davidson, lately Marine Engineer of the *Waldensian*, who became Chief Smith, Fitter, Spring Maker, and head of the Repairing-shop, including a little platelaying, and ultimately a Freehold Burgess of Durban. They were both skilled reliable men and made their own time, which averaged about 12 hours daily, (Sundays off). They were however, not paid extravagantly, yet did not strike for overtime. A smart young seaman was taken on as cleaner and greaser, and under Mr. Jacobs' special training was ultimately promoted Stoker.

An Engine shed of tarred timber was planted across the line about 80 yards from the Market Square Station shaped like an expanded letter A on four legs. The centre was the engine stable, in which was a brick Ash-pit; one lean-to served as a store room, the other as Smith's shop. Firewood and coals were piled up outside under a scaffolding supporting an iron tank into which water from a well had at first to be lifted by hand. Within a temporary erection at the rear of Mr. D. Hull's store [Parker, Wood and Co.], screened from wind and drifting sand by tarpaulins, the Engine was reconstructed, polished and painted, the body being green, the wheels copper colour, with its name "Natal" on a burnished brass plate. It will be best understood if described as a Contractor's engine on four wheels, of 24 horse power, having a new fashioned American pattern funnel, the wide mouth of which was covered by a wire basket to keep in sparks or fragments of wood fuel. It carried water in a tank underneath, and had a sort of open locker on the footplate, for coal, to which was attached a small donkey-engine operating a pump, and connected in some way with the gearing (we were told for "guiding and regulating purposes"). When this little engine was at work, its fly wheel being visible, a keen interest was taken in its pulsation; the untutored spectators regarding it as evidence of the sentient character of the demon Locomotive that gave out such terrifying yells.—The official opening of the Railway was fixed for the 26th June, but the real opening took place on Saturday the 23rd. The Races were held during the week. The Band of the 85th Regiment had come down from Maritzburg to attend them and take part in the Railway Opening. It was performing on the Market Square between three or four o'clock in the afternoon, to the usual gathering of spectators of both sexes and colours, when three prolonged agonizing shrieks from the end of Aliwal Street proclaimed the shrill locomotive whistle, heard for the first time in the Colony.

Mr. Jacobs, like all expert workmen, desired to prove, not only his own work, but that of others, so invited Captain Smerdon and Mr. Tatham to accompany him up and down the line to test it by bringing up a loaded train. The "Natal," had been erected with her head to the Point, and as there was no turntable or "triangle" she had to retain that position, returning stern first. After much smoke and rushing of steam she forged ahead a few dozen yards with slow deliberation, then backed again in the opposite direction. For the first time in the annals of Durban a military Band was forsaken for a greater attraction than even a dog fight could afford. Space having been found on the footplate for the Chairman and Secretary, three prolonged whistles again announced a forward movement; steam was turned on and the engine moved off sedately amid the cheers and handkerchiefs of the breathless spectators, the clicks and smothered "wows" of the half frightened native. With an occasional shriek she ran at moderate speed to the Point, awaking not only the echoes, but every living creature within reach, returning in about half an hour with five trucks in tow (wonderful sight) containing some 40 tons of sugar mill machinery and groups of standing passengers. A good deal of noise, steam and smoke accompanied the laboured breathing and stately arrival of this first Goods Train. A large crowd, inhabitants and visitors, including natives, had assembled at the terminus to witness the advent of "Puffing Billy," which was lustily cheered. These salutations were re-volleyed by the jolly tars, boatmen and other Point constituents who had manned the trucks to share in the honours of a first ride, and help in unloading; while the face of genial Engineer Jacobs beamed with satisfaction as he received the congratulations of the Chairman and Directors, and utilised a pocketful of "waste" before shaking hands all round.

he Opening, June 25. Saturday and Monday we were employed in erecting flag posts and triumphal arches, decorating them and the Engine shed with evergreens and getting things in order for ıe ceremony. The Market Square Station was not ·ected; it consisted at that time of an open timber plat-ɾm on piles, about 4 feet high 25 feet wide and 60 feet ng, to which access was had by wooden steps at one end, here a sort of pay box had been temporarily erected to ɾve as a Station Master's Office, and here the "Booking" ıd also to be done; this did not lend itself to decoration, ıt we made the best use of flags from corner poles. These had hoisted shortly after sunrise when all was bright and ailing in the sunshine. The Point Station of corrugated ɔn was nearly completed; this was also erected on a atform, some of the supports of which were standing in ıe water at high tide, the site being a few yards shore-ards between the modern Sheds B and C. For this :casion it had been fitted up and decorated internally to ɾve for a luncheon given by the Directors, it having been tended that those visitors who desired to extend their lmiration to the *Pioneer* might have the opportunity to ake a tour of the Bay under steam. A ball in the asonic Hotel in the evening was to conclude the events of ıe day. The opening or inauguration was to take place 11 o'clock by His Excellency, Major Williamson 85th ʹegiment, ¡Acting Lieutenant-Governor and Staff; the xecutive Council, the Bishop, the Legislative Council and ɐds of Departments had been invited, also the Mayors of ʹaritzburg and Durban and the Consuls, represented by ɾr. G. C. Cato. By 8 o'clock when the Bluff signal ation dressed itself in a double string of colours and gave ıe time for all the shipping and town flagstaffs to follow ưit, it became evident that we were likely to have a rong breeze from the S.W. By ten o'clock this had so ıcreased as to interfere sadly with our decorations. The rogramme arranged was for the first train to start with ıe Governor and Officials for the Point, where the line ʹould be declared open and the luncheon held. For this ưrpose I had to extemporise a second carriage by veiling a truck in drapery, bunting, and evergreens, having a light awning for shade, and planks nailed across from side to side for seats.

The Royal Durban Rangers in full uniform were to escort His Excellency and party from his quarters at the " East End " and take up a position between the Church and the platform. The children of the various Sunday Schools had standing room reserved for them within an enclosure at one end of the platform ; while the Guard of Honour and Band of the 85th were placed in front, and the general public left to find outspan and foothold on the adjacent sands as inclination prompted. After the first train had left, the public were to be privileged to purchase second class return tickets at one shilling each, " seats not guaranteed." The Bishop and Clergy, Railway Directors, Municipal and other officials who came on foot, were the first to arrive on the platform, where they occupied them-selves exchanging courtesies, holding their hats on, and clustering round my " pay here " window as the only shelter from the increasing gale. About 11 o'clock the Rangers and the brilliant cavalcade escorting the Lieutenant-Governor down West Street wheeled round by the newly erected Mechanics' Institute and halted.

His Excellency and Staff, with the guests invited by the Company, ascended the platform steps ; the Rangers " dressed up to the gutter " and with the 85th presented arms, while the band played the national anthem, the " Natal " blowing off steam meantime in fretful impatience.

The platform company formed a circle, while Bishop Colenso invoked the Divine blessing on the enterprise which had so far been brought to a successful issue. Very simple and suitable was the ceremony and well chosen were the words ; nothing there which could excite a scruple or create a sneer. I have been unable to discover who were the guests invited by the Company to occupy the first train, but I gather from the record at my disposal that, in addition to His Excellency Major Williamson and Officers of the 85th Regiment, there were present the Hon. — Allen, Colonial Treasurer ; the Hon. Theophilus Shepstone, Secretary of Native Affairs ; the Bishop of Natal and Reverends W. H. C. Lloyd and Rivett ; W. Macfarlane, Speaker of the Legislative Council ; Messrs. Boshoff and

W. Evans, M.L.C.; H. J. Mellor, Resident Magistrate;
ı. Rutherford, Collector of Customs; John Ackerman,
yor of Maritzburg; W. Hartley, Mayor of Durban;
J. Cato, U.S. Consular Agent; Captain Athorpe and Dr.
ward, 85th Regiment, Lieutenant Lyons, R.A., Captain
udfoot, R.D.R., Captain Joss, *Waldensian*; Captain
ırdon, Chairman, and the Directors of the Company,
ɼn Councillors with other visitors, including "our own
espondents," who subsequently enlarged and adorned
inauguration and after - dinner speeches in reports
ı one to five columns in length.

he Bishop having concluded, the children took up their
; in the programme, the singing of "God Save the
en," which they essayed to do, led by a cornet and other
ıdly instruments; unfortunately their efforts were
ırbed by the wind, and lost to the majority of the
:tators, but I am enabled to recover the last verse
:h some local poet had very appropriately added to the
onal anthem for the occasion.

> "Oh, Lord our God! behold
> One more free race enrolled
> Under our Queen.
> Bless this new land, we pray;
> Guard well its onward way;
> Speed on our work this day;
> God Save the Queen!"

xpectation stood on tip-toe; the snapping of flags, the
ying of poles and bamboo arches, with their palm leaf
ɔrations out of twist; the rude flutterings of veils and
inine draperies, the skying of hats and other fragments,
" Rangers' " restless horses, tho gaping crowd of
ıketed natives, and the gusty stream of all-pervading
ł, made the scene both memorable and unpleasant.
ıtographs were taken with more or less success by Mr.
Lloyd of Durban, and Mr. Hodgson of Maritzburg.

:veryone was thankful for the Chairman's bow to His
:ellency, with the prolongation of his hat in the direction
:he First Class Compartment in the Coach, whereupon
rest of the guests ɼoon seated themselves, in number
ut sixty. They good-humouredly made the best of
circumstances, and the Chairman having declared they
ɼe "all right" I gave the signal to start. With a pro-

longed wailing shriek Jacobs turned on the steam, and the first train moved off amid the deafening and prolonged cheers of the assembled spectators. Gathering speed as he cleared the Engine House, he ran smartly down to the Point, which he reached in about five minutes. The crowd of natives hurled back a defying yell, and started in pursuit, while a number of well mounted young Dutchmen, who knew a thing or two, decided to test the bottom of the iron horse, so put spurs to their quadrupeds and successfully headed the train until it reached Stanger Street, when it was declared to have bolted round the corner into the bush screaming at them as it ran.

The Guards of Honour were dismissed, and the Band brought on to the platform, where, with their backs to the wind, they entertained us with lively tunes, whilst I marshalled the plank seated trucks for their reception and the next train. Jacobs speedily returned swearing badly at the wind and sand. I left him and my men to shunt the carriages, while I opened my ticket office to the impatient public. I find it noted in my diary that I issued more than 250 return tickets without stopping.

The Band and the public squeezed themselves into all the available trucks, and a kind Providence with Engineer Jacobs watched over their departure when full up. After this first rush the traffic assumed a more deliberate form, but we continued to run up and down all day as fast as circumstances admitted, and it was computed that we conveyed fully 800 people to the breezy delights of the Point on this memorable occasion. The state of the weather prevented a visit to the *Pioneer* whose cruise was abandoned; so the trippers disported themselves about the wattled sand hills and Back Beach; visiting the rudimentary structure called the Harbour Works, and admired the *Waldensian* in the Bluff Channel contributing a Royal Salute of 21 minute guns. Others preferred lingering in the vicinity of the Railway Station listening to the clinking and cheers that followed inaudible speeches, and the occasional merry tunes of the band, while a goodly number sought the friendly shelter of Barker's Anchor Tavern which stood close to the beach, under a big fig tree still standing in the yard of the N.G.R. Point Station.

[t was a matter for congratulation that they all returned
town without accident; the blowing away of the extem-
ised carriage awning, a few flags and decorations,
ether with the downfall of one or two triumphal arches
oss the line, to say nothing of the blinding sand and
irting eyes, added zest to the entertainment of the
gesses. The cold collation in the Point Station was
a success owing to the rattling of the iron structure, the
ping of tarpaulins, the noise of the wind and waves,
arrival and departure of trains; however, the usual
gratulatory and complimentary toasts were drank,
le speeches were made and responded to by most of the
:ial guests, all recorded in brief but proper order by the
ndly reporter.

hough the *Mercury* in its next issue announced that the
ns continued to run regularly after the opening day,
i was not the fact, for that evening Driver Jacobs, with
·s almost in his eyes, appealed to himself as head of the
omotive Department, and a sympathetic committee of
;er and Smith Davidson, the Stoker and the Station
iter, in reference to the Engine, on the ground that it
ild be "positively cruel to run her in the filthy state
was in." Owing to the fact that all the cuttings were
llow and through drift sand dunes, the excavated soil
been thrown up either side of the line, the wind con-
iently carrying the loose top drift right into the heart
he machinery, and the engine was found to be literally
:ed, coated so thickly with sand and dirt, that very
ə bright metal could be seen. Resolved (with adjec-
;) "as she was just grinding herself to pieces" to stop
ning until she was thoroughly overhauled and cleaned.
m blown off accordingly. In this connection I may
tion that Old Durban was not dusty, there was no need
water carts, we had sand simply, clean sand, varying
juality from fine coral white, to heavy Umgeni grit;
density and gravity was regulated by the wind, but
le not in itself dirty, its effect on correspondence, store
ls, and domestic economies was decidedly inconvenient,
in heavy gales the face and eyes needed protection from
fragmentary rocks.

We resumed business on the 29th and ran irregular
holiday trains for two days, as we were to commence with
goods on the 2nd July.   Some amusing incidents came
under my notice during this initial period; space will only
allow my referring to two.   Mr. S. Beningfield, having
many friends among the Dutch farmers, entertained some.
leading men for the occasion.   He invited a portly elder
and his family to the Station to inspect and try the steam
wagon which stood quietly at the platform; the mother
and young people were soon comfortably seated in the
carriage, the head of the tribe stood listening to the
persuasions of Mr. Beningfield, critically eyeing the Engine
and appointments while he revolved in his own mind the
propriety of entrusting himself on board.   Steam began
to escape, the boiler grumbled ominously, and sudden jets
of water and steam were given off in unexpected places.
These signs behoved caution, and notwithstanding I held
the door persuasively open, he replied in Dutch, his countenance beaming with simplicity and benevolence, "Nay,.
nay, I shall ride down on my horse, and then I will come
up in it, because if 'the thing' runs away, it will go into
the sea water and I shall be made dead.   But " (more
cheerfully) "if it runs away coming up, then it will be
stopped by the Berea yonder."   The wife and children
could be spared to take the risk; they looked very grave
when the train started without him.   They all returned
bold and happy later in the day.

On another occasion I with a friend, a master of the Zulu
tongue, overheard the comments of a party of natives
gathered to inspect and possibly to report upon the Locomotive.   Their remarks were in substance as follows:—
"Wow! but it is a strange beast.   Its belly is full of fire
and vapour; they feed it with water and wood logs.   It
is like a Rhinosceros, but it blows smoke and sparks through
its horn.   (Click).   Truly it is stronger than the Elephant,
for it pulls many wagon loads.   It has wheels for some
of its legs, yet it runs faster than the Eland.   It isn't.
asleep now, look at its rump, see it wagging that little
wheel that says 'Goo-goo, goo-goo.'   And it is a rude
and savage beast, for it belches inside like a witch doctor,
and voids hot water and embers when people only look at

When the Inkosi pats its back it screams, and when
holds its little tail, it rushes off.   Beyond doubt it is
ıde by witchcraft of the white men.   Those two who
le on it must be brave men, and have been powerfully
ctored.   Certainly they can control it, and make it
ı this way and that.   Woh! it is beyond our under-
.nding.   (Click)."

The following extracts from my diary condense and
ıstrate the initial difficulties of the Railway Enterprise.

uly 2nd. Commenced receiving and delivering goods.
Contractors' carts more than we could supply.

23rd. [About this time the Station platform was
enclosed and roofed with corrugated iron,
having large doorways as on the existing
N.G.R., at which wagons loaded and discharged.]
Cold drizzling day.   Strong S.W. wind.
Expected Jacobs would not run the train, but
he did, and earned 11/- with passengers.

25th. A great railway event to-day.   For the first
time trucks came up from the Point empty,
with news that the Point was "cleaned out."

27th. Steamer arrived.   Trains running irregularly all
day to bring up mails, passengers and their
baggage.

30th. Very busy all day.   Trains not running
regularly on account of passengers from
Steamer *Sir G. Grey* and ship *Early Morn*.

31st. Hands well employed all day.   Trains running
regularly.   Passengers and goods in profusion ;
luggage in confusion.

ɔ Time-table published for July was :—

assenger trains will leave the Durban Terminus as under :

9 a.m.	returning at	9.30 a.m.
12 a.m.	„ „	12.30 p.m.
Fares, First Class	1/-	each way.
Second Class	6d.	„ „

ιs a matter of fact if there was a demand, we ran
:tra passenger," but goods trains ran at convenience,
ɔn Second Class tickets entitled the holder to the best
t he could find on a truck.

The manner of working was simple, practical and effective; nearly all the men employed as labourers at both stations were seamen, than whom there is no better class for the handling of heavy goods of all descriptions.   They are full of expedients and devices for slinging, hoisting or rolling; parbuckling heavy machinery, securing damaged packages with deft hitches, rigging a Spanish windlass or using a handspike.   The getting of heavy goods into the trucks with the 6 ton crane was easy enough, the getting them out again with the 3 ton crane was a matter of ingenuity and time.   Attached to the cranes were clamps by which they could be fastened down to the rails.   In some instances the weight of the article lifted, when "pinched" out of the truck, would overtilt the crane and tear the rails up; when if time admitted, a soft place in the sand was selected by the man at the brake, on which to drop the cumbrous article, without waiting for orders; once landed clear of the rails it could be "manhandled." In the case of heavy boilers, a timber packing was rigged, on which deals were laid, so that the boiler might be rolled from the truck to the ground at a spot convenient for reloading on to a bullock wagon.   The crane could only be trusted to lift it alternately by the ends, until sufficient packing raised it high enough for the deals to be inserted beneath it.   A stout rope wound round it; the crane applied to the parbuckle, three or four men with levers and a "Yo heave ho!" and over she went, with the result that the staging usually settled or shifted with the weight, and the truck itself half overturned until the boiler rolled clear, followed with as many cheers as a launch.   Sugar mill rollers were similarly disposed of.   The large crane would of course have saved all this, but owing to the height of its jib, it could not pass the Engine Shed without being partly taken to pieces.   It was only used on rare occasions with particularly long and heavy Cornish boilers occupying double trucks.   Each end of the line forked like a $\bigvee$; this for the purpose of shunting and off-loading, or receiving goods about the yard, distant from the platform.   The operation of shunting, though primitive and hazardous, was effectual; the train consisting of engine, carriage and one or more trucks with goods, would draw up at the platform in state and the passengers land; such light

ıds as could be easily disposed of were discharged into
Station at once, from there to be passed into the town
tractor's wagons at leisure.   The train then backed out
ow the "points" and the heavy goods truck would be
ıooked.   A stout hawser with links spliced into each
ι was hooked on between the engine and the carriage;
ıts would be set over and the engine would dash up the
ng, towing the carriage and empty trucks, the active
ıtsman smartly reversing the points directly the engine
. cleared them, so directing the carriage and trucks up
main line to the platform.   Engine would come down
siding; again the points once more reversed; the tow
ə hooked on, and go backwards up the platform line
ing the machinery truck; the points again operated and
truck passed on as far as necessary up the siding to
:harge; the engine would then be at the head of the
ın train ready to start.   The art and the hazard, in
ch our men grew proficient, was to unhook the moving
n or truck when the engine was checked sufficiently for
purpose, carrying the rope clear of the wheels, and
:rwards in overtaking and operating the lever brakes
ı controlled the moving trucks.   As may be imagined,
ı system of unloading soon blocked up all the available
ɔe adjacent to the Station, with heavy machinery.   As
·age was not charged the articles laid there until planters
ɔonsignees found it convenient to send for them, when·
resources were again taxed to get the machinery on to
ir bullock wagons and away.   The increasing traffic
n rendered it impossible for me to manage alone, so
John Ogg Brown, familiarly known as "J.O.B." was
ɔ to me from the Manager's office as Booking Clerk
ι Accountant.   As a boy he had been something on a
ı "Aberdeen way," so was recommended to me for his
·erience, which developed itself chiefly in making out
ɣ bills for the goods carted by the town contractors, and
cking the tickets issued, with the cash taken.   He
ıgned within a year in consequence of the death of his
ther-in-law, Mr. J. A. Wilson, Stationer, whose business
took over in the premises adjoining Messrs. Evans and
urchill's, West Street, known to us now as Murchie's
al store.   I believe he eventually disposed of his stock-

in-trade to Mr. B. Hampson, and became a lawyer's clerk. He was brother to Mrs. Geo. Buchan and Mrs. Archibald McNeil. He married a granddaughter of that old colonist Mr. R. Pollyblank, who survives him. I shall have occasion to refer to another of my assistants later on.

The Band of Hope, Or more correctly the "Durban Temperance Band of Hope," of whose existence I had no previous knowledge, apparently made its first public appearance on the memorable 26th June, and communicated the fact to the *Mercury* as follows : —

"Amidst the general desire to make the day on which our Railway was opened a memorable one, we would mention the above society held their first annual fête in the Wesleyan Schoolroom, kindly lent for the occasion. The children, to the number of sixty, after partaking plentifully of 'the cup which cheers but not inebriates,' plum cake, etc., betook themselves to various amusements, after which Mr. Garland, of Verulam, gave them an appropriate address; the children then dispersed, well pleased with the evening's entertainment."

General Cemetery, The prevailing spirit of liberty and desire for freedom of conscience prompted a large section of the community to bury their dead beyond the pale of the Churches, either Episcopalian or Roman Catholic, according to their own rites and observances; they accordingly obtained from the Corporation a similar block of land adjoining the Church of England burial ground, which it was proposed to place in the hands of Trustees as a Town Cemetery. A public meeting was accordingly called for the 10th July for the purpose of electing Trustees and securing funds to defray the expense of enclosing the Cemetery, "which is open to the use of all without reference to Religious Persuasion. Subscriptions payable to Mr. E. J. Challinor, West Street."

The meeting was duly held and subscriptions promised. Messrs. J. F. Churchill and John Sanderson were elected Trustees; Messrs. John Hunt, John Gray, Wm. Cowey, J. Brickhill, J. Blackwood, and Joseph Adlam to be the

ard of Management for the ensuing year; the Mayor of
rban, the Trustees and the Minister of the Congregational
urch being members *ex officio;* the Rev. G. Y. Jeffreys
ing as Secretary *pro tem.*

The orm Queen. On the 14th July the schooner *William* part of the crew of the ship *Storm Queen* *Shaw* arrived from St. John's, bringing of 1,022 tons, from London to Kurrachee h railway iron, abandoned at sea with 8 feet of water in hold. The crew took to the boats and headed for Natal, t N.E. gales drove them back. The two boats parted npany the same night; the long boat in which was the ptain and major part of the crew was supposed to be t. The pinnace with the chief officer, five white men l seven lascars, after being adrift seven days, effected a ding in St. John's river; the *William Shaw* being re at the time, brought on all but three, who found ployment at the river. Among those landed here was . Frederic Leonard Jonsson, described as a midshipman. e pressure of work at the railway station necessitated ra supervision in the goods department, so some few ys after landing Mr. Jonsson was placed under my ection as checker and general assistant. Being a Swede birth with a tolerably extensive London experience for age, he proved himself smart and exceedingly service- e, notwithstanding his English education having been newhat restricted. He was a man to be trusted. I ld rely upon him to "mind the shop" when I was off ty. The confidence and friendship then engendered s never been misplaced. His self-reliant independence, ewdness and unlimited energy, induced him before the r was out to start business on his own account in a y modest way in Field Street. He has ever since nained a loyal burgess of Durban, and possibly done re than any other man for the adornment and advance- nt of the Borough. As the proprietor of the "Royal tel" (the old "Masonic") on the Market Square, the lexandra Hotel" at the Point, the "Princess Cafe," merly the "Hole in the Wall," and many other valuable properties, he has become a very large, if not the largest, individual rate-payer of the Borough, for which he has also rendered personal service as Town Councillor.

The German House. About 9 miles from Durban on the road to the City, was intimately associated with the lives or experiences of the British Emigrants, and being the first "house of call," establishes a claim in Durban's history.

In Memoriam I take over from the *Mercury* of the 26th July :—

"This scene of olden reminiscences is now, we regret to say, a thing of the past. On Saturday last the whole of the buildings were literally burnt to the ground. A child connected with the family had died, and a large number of the relatives had congregated in the house to celebrate the national observances attendant on such an event. Some of the children, thus collected together, had obtained possession of a box of matches and incautiously set fire to some dry banana leaves, which hung in dangerous proximity to the house. The flames, fostered by a sultry atmosphere and fanned by a westerly breeze, almost instantaneously passed from the leaves to the thatch roof. The house speedily became ablaze. The adult inmates, surprised at the alarming accident, directed all their efforts to the extinction of the flames by the use of wet blankets and other damping agencies. So busily were they engaged in this way, that they neglected the precaution of removing the furniture and chattels, and such goods as there might be in the house at the time. The fire meanwhile spread with quenchless rapidity and fury, and all attempts to extinguish it were utterly futile. In comparatively a few minutes the roof fell in, the wattled walls ignited, the wood work began to blaze, and without the possibility of saving anything, the whole house was a ruin. The group, which was gathered together outside the charred and smouldering embers about half-an-hour afterwards, presented a melancholy spectacle. The women bemoaning with tearful lamentations the losses they had experienced, the children looking wonderingly unconscious of the real effect of the disaster ; the men, grimed and sooty, walking about vacantly as if they could not realize their position ; the stout old landlady herself weeping like a Roman matron over her household gods.

"This roadside establishment was, we believe, the oldest hostelry on the road. In former days many a tired emigrant has hailed its modest roof and recruited his inner man from those inexhaustible stores of bread, eggs and bacon for which it used to be famous. Since the formation of Pinetown, its popularity as a place of public entertainment for man and beast has somewhat waned, but nothing can efface the recollection of its 'fleas and fitches' which most of us number amongst our earliest experiences. We understand that a subscription is being raised with a view of assisting the Langes out of the difficulties in which the late accident has involved them."

More Emigrants. The regular trader *Early Morn* arrived at the outer anchorage on the 23rd July, bringing as passengers, Mr. and Mrs. R. H. U. Fisher and family; Mr. and Mrs. H. Finlayson; Mr. and Mrs. G. S. Miller and child; Mrs. Dillon and two children; Mr. J. Frampton; Mr. F. T. Cookesley; Mr. R. Wilkins, and others in the steerage, who presented our old friend Capt. Lowry with the usual testimonial.

Mr. Fisher Eventually succeeded Mr. Mark Foggett as Town Clerk, and became incorporated in Durban's history. Possessed of marked force of character and strong common sense, he reduced things to order and systemized the Town Office in all its departments, acquainting himself by personal supervision with every requirement of the Borough, directing the Mayor, Councillors and sub-committees in their respective duties, until they learned that it was wiser to leave him a free hand in the affairs of the town rather than interfere in matters they did not understand.

To him belongs the credit of those initial steps which have brought the Borough to its present proud position, the commencement of which—as no half measures ever satisfied him—was a substantial debt of £60,000 borrowed money, for the repayment of which all the Leasehold property and Town Lands between the Berea Road and the Umbilo were hypothecated. His name will be held in affectionate

remembrance, especially by the holders of the Corporation
Debenture Bonds at 6 per cent. interest, passed for this
Loan and repayable in 1906; since his signature is appended
to thousands of interest Coupons, still current.   Like Mr.
Jonsson he subsequently resigned, to join Mr. R. W.
Dickinson in the firm of Dickinson and Fisher.

**London
and
South African
Bank.**

A prospectus was published here on the
9th August, announcing that this institution had been formed in London principally by Cape Merchants, with a Capital
of £400,000 in 20,000 shares of £20 each,
"to afford an increased and much wanted
banking accommodation to the Cape of Good Hope and its
sister Colony of Natal," it being intended to establish
branches here. The Bank was eventually floated, and a
branch afterwards opened in Durban at. the corner of
West Street and Field Street in the enlarged premises now
occupied by the Bank of Africa.

**Public
Health.**

Having learnt that H.R.H. Prince Alfred
had arrived at the Cape, the Legislative
Council in July requested the Lieutenant-
Governor to invite the Prince to visit
Natal with Sir George Grey, the Governor of the Cape, and
voted expenses.   On the 16th August the Mayor, the
Railway Company, Port Office, and Masonic Hotel received
official notification to hold themselves at the disposal of
H.R.H. who was expected overland.   It is, therefore, certain
that we are indebted to the absence of all telegraphic
communication at that time for the visit of Prince Alfred
otherwise the state of things disclosed by the *Mercury* at
this date would have effectually checked, or diverted his
advances; to wit:—

"The measles prevail extensively in this Town and
neighbourhood ; indeed, scarcely a single family is exempt
from the visitation, and many of the kaffirs in service have also
had the disease. Fever likewise prevails to some extent. No
doubt the long dry weather and the peculiar state of the
atmosphere have had some effect in producing this general
sickliness.   But the sanitary condition of this town has
been disgracefully neglected of late ; and now the rains have

set in with no provision for preserving the health of the place. Indeed, no attention whatever has been paid to the state of our drains, which are mostly choked up, fallen in, and utterly useless, or worse than useless, for they have become cesspools of stagnant filth and hot beds of disease. The inhabitants are allowed to throw garbage of all sorts on unoccupied plots ; and these even in dry weather have emitted horrible stenches. We may mention particularly the low, central part of West Street, especially the south side ; and other places are nearly as bad. Pig-styes, manure heaps, and open surface privies are allowed without check ; and in fact our bye laws, which provide powers for the removal of all nuisances, are literally and entirely a dead letter.

"It is high time, if not already too late, for the Council of the Borough to bestir themselves, and we trust the new *régime* will mark its advent by prompt and vigorous measures to protect the public health. The footpaths and fences are in ruin ; but every other improvement should give way to an instant effort to improve the drainage and abate nuisances."

The Natal Mercury and Durban and P.Maritzburg Advertiser. On the 31st March, Mr. George Robinson, the printer, publisher and proprietor, announced that the state of his health necessitated his partial retirement from active life, and that he had accordingly taken into partnership his son John Robinson, and that the imprint of the firm would in future be George Robinson and Son.

On the 1st September, John Robinson and Richard Vause informed the world that they had become the purchasers of the *Mercury,*, Copyright and Printing Office, and acquired also the Press, type and materials of the defunct *Commercial Advertiser.* Promising to be independent and impartial; to adhere to the maxim "Audi alteram partem," and to keep pace with the progress of the Colony, maintaining the re-named *Natal Mercury and Commercial Advertiser* as the leading journal of Natal, under the auspices of the new firm of Robinson and Vause.

R

Prince Alfred's Visit. Sir George Grey, K.C.B., Governor of the Cape Colony, accompanied by H.R.H. Prince Alfred, his Governor Major Cowell and suite, arrived in Natal *via* the Free State and Van Reenen's Pass on Friday, 31st August. The crushing importance and dignity of His Excellency the Governor was quite secondary to that of the Midshipman. The only excuse offered was our fervent loyalty, and desire to honour our Queen in the person of her little son. All the newspapers published Prince Alfred editions, that of the *Mercury* running into ten closely printed columns, ending in a "small cap" benediction, "God Speed Prince Alfred."

The latent craziness, inherent in us all, had gone to our heads in consequence of the kindly intimation at different times from the Cape Colony papers and correspondence of how much they enjoyed the Prince, and how much he enjoyed them (their naartjes especially), that it was more than probable he would never reach Natal; that he was not likely to go overland, but possibly might look in by sea, weeks hence, or not at all.

Undoubtedly we gushed, and were hysterically abject; we hung upon the lad's words and glances, enlarging upon every triviality with fulsome praise. We tortured him with addresses which it is a happiness to think he may never have read; to these his Governor duly replied. The faithful historian must record that as Colonists we made patent our vulgarity; we wallowed in titles and dignities, rubbed up our stars and garters, tacking on all the leading marks we could command, from H.R.H. to a simple "Esq.," and under this inflation we felt ourselves "all honourable men," and obtruded ourselves on the young Prince's attention with enquiries similar to those of the Circus Clown to the Queen of the Ring: "What will your Royal Highness please for to come for to go for to want, that Old Joey may have the honour of presenting it?"

The Viceregal party were entertained on the road by native war dances, School Children and Deputations, and heads of the people, arriving in Maritzburg on the 3rd September, where propitious Fate ordained that they should be received by our early emigrant acquaintance James Archibald, Esq., in his capacity as Mayor of that City. Cæsar had come to Rome, so all Maritzburg threw up their hats and rent the air with acclamations, professedly better for having seen and jostled a live prince, the son of England's Queen. On the following day, with much ceremony and loyal effusion on the part of the citizens, the Prince laid the hastily prepared foundation stone of their new Town Hall; for thirty-one years thereafter that stone placidly laid, like a lost lamb, in the long grass of their Market Square undisturbed, to be carted away in modern times to form part of an elaborate Town Hall erected on another site.*

The Prince hurried away from this function to lunch with his Excellency Major Williamson at Government House, and at 2 p.m. presented new Colours to the 85th Regiment L.I., drawn up with the rest of the Garrison, the "Royal Durban Rangers" and "Natal Carbineers," on the site of the present Railway Station, Camp Hill. The Colours blessed by the Bishop of Natal and handed by the Prince to Ensigns Ramsbotham and Cooper, Captain Boyle on behalf of the Regiment returned thanks in brief and soldier-like words. After presentation there was a march past, which I conclude was a short one, as at 3 o'clock the Royal party and escort reviewed some 4,000 Zulu warriors in full feather and paint, on the slope then reserved for the present Park. The Prince told them truly, through Mr. John Shepstone, that he should never forget the sight he had that day seen. The day closed with a Ball at Government House, which was kept up till four in the morning of the 5th September. The Royal party started for Durban at 8 o'clock, a detachment of the "Rangers" acting as additional escort. Once over the newly erected Victoria Bridge, no time was lost on the road. The Prince headed the cavalcade, and exhilarated by the air and scenery rode "ding-dong, as they cantered along," barely drawing rein until Clough's Sterk Spruit Hotel was reached, where a halt was made for a sumptuous luncheon, for which an hour sufficed. Spare horses were

* Re-laid by Governor Sir C. H. Mitchell, 5th Feby, 1891.

mounted, and another steeple-chase scamper followed
down Botha's and Field's Hill until Pinetown was
reached. Here the panting and dusty party were merci-
fully halted by Messrs. the Reverend J. L. Crompton,
John Walton, and W. A. L. Rivett, in their robes, to
receive an address from the inhabitants, who had been
presented by the Resident Magistrate of Durban in the
persons of Capt. G. Bishop, Messrs. A. K. Murray, P. J.
Payn, and S. Greathead. "Captain Bishop, R.N., then
advanced," says the reporter, "in his naval coat, and read
the address." The train had been reinforced at Clough's
by the strong Pinetown troop of the " Rangers " under
Captain Bennett*; here the entire corps fell in, Cornet
Frank Beningfield carrying the regimental colours. The
Prince read his reply, exchanged salutations with the
inhabitants, smiled on the ladies, and, to quote an old
English ballad:—

> Old Bible-faced women through spectacles dim,
> With hemming and coughing cried "Lord, it is him!"
> While boys and the girls who more clearly could see,
> Cried " Yonder's Sir Dilberry Diddle, that's he!"

"Forward" was the word, and they are reported as
having galloped round Cowie's Hill, on the summit of which
the heavy weights advised the Prince to admire the view.
He is said to have enjoyed the ride and scenery without
signs of fatigue. At the German House in course of
reconstruction, rustic bamboo arches of evergreens and
oranges had been thrown across the road by the German
community. Old Mr. and Mrs. Lange, their stalwart
family and neighbours, greeted the Prince with hearty
cheers and national gutturals. H.R.H., struck by the
reception, spoke for himself in feeling terms, remarking
that he was very pleased to see his father's countrymen
living so peacefully and pleasantly in an English Colony,
A trooper told me they took the opportunity to " look to
their girths," and that the atmosphere thereafter was
strangely flavoured with Geneva, as most of them had
asked for Milk. Groups of well-dressed people gathered
on the roadside to see and salute as the party hurried past

---

* Better known to Durban as " Major Bennett " when
Superintendent of Police.

Rooi Koppies, over the rise and down to the swampy crossing by the Sydenham Road, thence up the incline, now almost obliterated, to the Berea cutting, from which they were able to see the frigate *Euryalus*, 2,500 tons, at the outer anchorage awaiting them.

Here they entered the Borough under a "Sylvan arch" inscribed "Welcome Royal Tar," where the Mayor, Mr. McArthur, Town Councillors S. Beningfield, A. Ferguson, J. Hunt, R. Gelder, W. Palmer, J. Sanderson, and F. C. Salmon, with the Town Clerk, welcomed the Prince, and were respectively rewarded with a handshake. They fell in to the greatly enlarged procession, now estimated at 400, and speedily wished themselves out of it (for sailors on horseback are worse than the proverbial beggars), as the party immediately broke into a canter, and continued the pace to the bottom of the hill, down the Berea Road, recently cleared by the convicts; over the Vlei Embankment into Smith Street. Here the Cape Corps Escort and the Rangers formed up a bit, and wiped their eyes and faces, while the Burgesses assumed some appearance of squad formation, though crowding the roadway when they moved. The Mayor led the procession across into Grey Street and West Street, which were gay with bunting, evergreens and population. The reporter says:—"The acclamations of a people proud of their Britishism greeted him on every side."

At Field Street crossing, a fine four-sided Arch was erected, covered with coloured cloth and festooned with evergreens, "Welcome Prince Alfred," and "God Save the Queen," being the prominent mottoes. As they rode down the sharp incline to low-lying central West Street, the view I had from the Market Square was certainly imposing and spectacular.

The slight youthful figure rode in advance on a spirited horse, followed by His Excellency Sir George Grey, Sir Walter Currie, Major Cowell, General Wynyard, and Capt. Tartleton, R.N., and other officers. The blaze of scarlet, blue and gold, black, white and green, the flashing arms and crimson banner of the Escort, together with the dark mass of mounted burgesses and visitors in hats of all shades and styles, on horses of all sizes, slowly streamed out of the dust cloud of distant West Street, while what served for footpaths were crowded by the gentler sex, in all the beauty of holiday apparel.   The sun was low, but kindly contributed to the final grandeur and glitter of the scene as the Royal Party, on reaching the Market Square wheeled under another evergreen Arch opposite the Masonic Hotel. Here it was received by a Guard of Honour of the 85th L.I., and final cheers from all of us, and dismounted.   The reporter   said :—"On   reaching   the Market   Square the Prince's attention was attracted by the first South African Railway, the locomotive of which might here be seen quietly smoking."

Princes are not permitted, like *bona fide* travellers, to take their ease at their Inn.   The Mayor and Council followed him   and   Sir George Grey   into   the Hotel, having to disburden themselves of addresses to each ; so they crowded into the little Drawing Room, where the infliction was conferred.   The Courtly Reporter noted the effect and records :—"Prince Alfred now seemed to be rather tired with his journey, as no doubt he was, like everybody else who had the pleasure of riding in his train.   Sir George Grey appeared very much gratified by the Address which had been presented to him."

For once we had been praying for a bad Bar, that we might have time to do the honours suitably to the visitors. But Sir George Grey, notwithstanding his gratification, insisted upon immediate departure.   I was instructed to send the train (engine and carriage) down to the Point to bring up Port Captain Bell to confer with His Excellency as to time and tide ; and subsequently got my orders to have steam up and train ready by daylight next morning. This unexpected decision prostrated the ladies, and paralysed their gay cavaliers.   But the Prince, having appeared on the balcony and bowed gracefully and repeatedly to the groups of fair faces in the Hotel grounds amid the cheers of the populace, promised his presence if the projected Ball was held.   A rush was accordingly made to complete the arrangements.   Invitations in the Prince's name had been sent round to a semi-state dinner at the Masonic.   In addition to Sir George Grey, General Wynvard and the Prince's personal suite, there were present, His Excellency Major Williamson, Acting Lieut.-Governor, A. McArthur,

Mayor, the Colonial Secretary and Treasurer, Collector of Customs, J. R. Goodricke and A. W. Evans, M.L.C.'s for the Borough, the Resident Magistrate, Capt. Proudfoot, R.D.R., Lieut. Beadon 85th L.I., Aide-de-Camp, Captain Smerdon, Chairman N. Railway Co., with other, officers of the staff and H.M.S. *Euryalus.*

For music they had the melodious voices of Nature's own children in the persons of the "natives of the country," who had been held in readiness for a dance and display the following day.   About seven in the evening a large bonfire was made on the Market Square, lighting up the palms and other trees with the floral arch and still flying flags.

An ox was killed for roasting, and " a joyful noise " in well kept time and true native fashion, entertained the visitors until a late hour.   Meanwhile Mr. Acutt's new Mart was being prepared, and the Commercial and Agricultural Bank having placed their offices at the Prince's personal disposal, communication was made with Messrs. Acutt and Leslie's Store for use as a supper room, while the Court House and Government Offices were set aside for the ladies.   I take the following from the " Prince Alfred Edition " of the *Mercury :—*

"About half-past nine o'clock the Prince and his suite arrived, with His Excellency Sir George Grey, General Wynyard, and a distinguished company of guests. His Royal Highness was very much fatigued by the labours of the week, and his medical adviser refused to sanction his staying at the ball for a longer period than the opening dance. The Prince, therefore, distinctly expressed his wish to open the ball with the Mayoress, Mrs. McArthur, who was accordingly honoured by the hand of His Royal Highness in the first quadrille. After having thus shown a graceful act of courtesy towards the town, the Prince and Sir George Grey left. Our space will not permit us to dwell further over the varied attractions of the ball, which was one of the best Durban has yet seen."

Mrs. McArthur (Mrs. Fielden's " pretty lady ") became the most envied woman in town and country.   For years after her name was seldom mentioned in society circles, without linking it with this event.   Her just pride did not detract from her genial good nature; she was merciful to her subjects.

By dawn of the 6th I had the train made up, with the addition of a couple of trucks for baggage or chance passengers, and a few candle lanthorns on the platform. Shortly after a Government mule wagon was driven up to the platform with luggage, and a couple of youngsters in reefer jackets in charge. The Governor of the Cape and party walked over from the Hotel, followed by the Mayor, some of the Directors, military officers, and a few townspeople. The Prince was lost to me in the shadowy groups, my functions being usurped by the Directors present.

As no tickets were issued for this "special," I turned my attentions to the baggage and the two middies passing it on, to one of whom—the Prince's chum, Mr. Joscelyn—I heard peremptory quarter-deck orders given to "bear a hand." Somebody said everything was stowed, while many others said *they* were all ready. The platelayer had reported the line clear, so with an easy conscience I gave the order to Engineer Jacobs to start.

It was clear daylight now, and a rush was made for the moving trucks by a few enthusiastic townsmen, as I sprang on, amid the cheers of the assembled bystanders. Jacobs must have perceived his opportunity, or been instigated by the Directors, for on clearing the engine-shed we spun along at a racing pace that became truly alarming as we entered the Addington Bush, but before I could make up my mind if the Dutchman's "dingus" was running away or not, he pulled up gracefully in the Point Station. The reporter who was with us says the time was "2 minutes and 40 seconds, a speed of something less than 40 miles an hour, the fastest journey that South African soil has yet seen."

Proceeding at once to the Jetty, where the Port Boat and other boats awaited them, His Royal Highness, who was in naval uniform, shook hands very heartily with the Mayor and expressed himself very much gratified by the reception he had met with and by what he had seen in the Colony. It is said he regretted at the same time that he was not allowed to make a longer stay. The sun had now risen, the Bay was full, the water a dead calm, with the grey coat of morning still in sight, lingering about the swarthy Bluff, as the boats pulled off to the *Pioneer* in the Bluff Channel, bearing the Royal youth, whom the ladies had pronounced "nice," "a dear," and a "noble little fellow," all too diminutive for a man of war 16 years of age.   The Royal Party was accompanied by the Acting Lieutenant-Governor and other Colonial officials and gentlemen, to H.M.S. *Euryalus* at 'the anchorage, and the reporter adds:—"So amidst the cheers of all who happened "to be present our illustrious young visitor vanished from "our sight like a beautiful dream."   The frigate fired a proceeded on her voyage about 6 o'clock the same evening. That salute promoted a controversy among the Old Salts, conundrum-like in its character, that I have not heard Royal Salute as the steam-tug left her side to return, and determined to this day:—Was it in honour of the Royal Midshipman rejoining his ship, the Governor of the Cape, the Lieut.-Governor of Natal, or Port Natal itself?   In the afternoon the Entertainment Committee carried out a part of the Sports designed for the Prince's amusement.   They were held at the Botanic Gardens; foot and wheel-barrow races and other diversions in which the natives were allowed to participate.   Two of the men of the 85th Light Infantry won the long running race, while the young townsmen, Dickens and Ledson, Lutman and Cuthbert, were winners in their respective ' events."   A. W. Evans, Esq., M.L.C., presided.   The Regatta was postponed to "next springs."

Natal Bank.   On the 13th September the Bank advertises for "Drawings and Specifications for "building to be erected at corner of West "and Gardiner Streets, in accordance with "a rough design at the Bank.   The usual allowance of "2½ per cent. on the estimates will be paid for the draw-"ings, etc., which may be accepted, and the others ": returned to the owners." (*sic.*)   The "rough design" I have heard attributed to Mr. John Milne, C.E., but believe Mr. James Brickhill co-operated considerably.   The existing corner building of the Natal Bank is the result.   The wings are a later addition.

Coolies. Early in the year the Bill for the introduction of East Indian labourers, or Coolies, had become law, as, to the astonishment of most Colonists, it had been confirmed by the Home Government. Mr. W. H. Collins, formerly, Postmaster-General, was appointed Commissioner to proceed to India for the purpose of their selection and shipment. He left bv the *Waldensian* on the 15th March, *via* Cape and Mauritius. In June Captain William Smerdon was appointed Protector of Immigrants or Coolie Agent at Durban, at a salary of £400 per annum. Being a sugar-planter, and himself an applicant for labourers, he resigned at the end of October in favour of Mr. Edmund Tatham, late Secretary of the Railway Company. On the 16th November arrived quite unexpectedly the barque *Truro*, 694 tons, Duggan Master, from Madras, with 341 Coolies on board imported by the Colony more especially for the benefit of the sugar industry. This ship was the first to arrive of four that had been despatched by Mr. Collins, one, the *Belvidere*, having left Calcutta eight days before the *Truro* left Madras, the total number of labourers Mr. Collins was authorised to engage being 1,000. Consternation prevailed; the only thing in readiness was a store of fish in pickle, the *Pioneer* having been employed outside for some time in securing this, believed to be the staple article of Coolie dietary. The Indian Barracks, Addington, were not ready for occupation. Planters were without funds to enable them to pay dues upon the men indented for. Whatever contracts had been made with the Coolies on their engagement as to wages, etc., were not forthcoming, having, it was said, gone to Maritzburg.

Mr. Tatham, the newly appointed "Protector of the Poor," was away on private business, as an economical Government had stipulated that his pay and his duties should begin on the arrival of these Indian Immigrants. The public and the newspapers expressed their sentiments.

Idolatry, Cholera, and other epidemic and contagious evils were at our door. Skilled thieves, Dacoits and Indian mutineers more or less sanguinary, were certain to infect our native population, and things generally would be bad with us. However, Dr. Holland, the Health

Officer, granted them a clean bill of health; they were duly
landed and located in the Barrack Compound, and before
the week was out, most of them had been assigned to
planters, and marched off into the country, there to develop
their peculiar virtues and vices.   Their reception by our
natives was at once antagonistic.   The latter professed to
look upon the strangers with a kind of righteous horror,
expressing a most intense contempt for their meagre
physical development.   They would ask, pointing, " What
thing is that without legs, that cries ' Mi-arry-ah '? It is
not ' abalungo,' certainly not ' abantu,' just ' Ma Coola '
goopellah!" the flavour of cocoanut oil and other essences
obliging them to spit.   At first they openly laughed at
the Coolie, never with them. "Sammy," Natal Rum and a
paternal government have changed all that, for now the
native fraternises with the Indian and willingly works for
him, regardless of caste or condiments.

On the 25th November the man in the street said, "I
told you so!" when the news flew over the town that the
expected Coolie ship *Belvidere* had arrived, that twenty-
four deaths had taken place on the voyage, and that Dr.
Holland had placed her in quarantine outside, until the
decision of the authorities could be ascertained as to the
disposal of her passengers.   Then it was that we learnt
that the Government, in anticipation of such a contingency, had selected a site on the Bay side of the Bluff for a
Lazaretto, and gone so far as contract for the erection of
the necessary building, the construction of which had
indeed been commenced.   But nobody was anxious for
the location of the infected people contiguous to the Bluff
Channel, in daily use by small craft and natives.   After
much anxious deliberation, it was ultimately decided to
form a Quarantine Camp at the back of the Bluff, utilizing
Mr. Milne's tram line to transport their stores and water
to the terminus opposite the Cave Rock.   From there a
rough-hewn goat's path over the sharp rocks, led to the
open sandy site selected, where temporary wattled huts
were constructed covered with old sails.   The Coolies were
brought ashore in a cargo boat, also quarantined, and
landed on the Bluff near the leading marks; special constables, European and Native, being employed as guards,

With this precaution we were mollified, but insisted
upon their " filthy rags " being burnt, and new raiment
issued, after their persons had received the benefit of sea
bathing, and their personal effects had been disinfected.
And it was so.

British Colonists, with insular indifference, accepted the
natives' baptism of " Ma Coolah " as a generic designation
for all Her Majesty's Indian Subjects.

When shops were first opened here for the sale of Indian
goods to the new Coolie population, they became " Coolie
Stores," and their owners " Coolie Storekeepers."   On
the later advent of Aboobaker Amod and other Bombay
merchants and shipowners, educated, intelligent men, with
cargoes of rice and condiments for sale, the only concession
prejudice would make in their favour was to designate
them   " Arab " merchants, though still " Coolie " storekeepers, who spoke " Coolie."   To the natives, however,
this section has now become " Mooselmaan."

The class term " Coolie " is a proper designation for a
low caste man, a simple, unskilled labourer, a hireling ;
there are Chinese, Japanese, Malayan, and East Indian
Coolies, therefore to designate all our Indian fellow-colonists, merchants, storekeepers, traders and mechanics as
" Coolies " is as misleading and insulting as to call all
natives ' Kafirs," all European artizans " labourers," a
wrong that arises from our local ignorance and want of
discrimination.

	Was rapidly increasing in value, since
Town	in April Mr. R. Acutt sold the " Star and
Property	Garter " property in West Street (between
	Jameson and Co. and Woodroffe and

Cato) for £710, two or three years previously the same
house and grounds changing hands at £250.   Part of an
Erf at the west end of West Street measuring 28 ft. by
100 ft. realized £235.   An extensive sale of Berea Leases
took place about the same time and realised very high
prices.   " The Leases are for 50 years, and some of the
Lots put up at 15s. per acre, per annum, brought upwards
of 40s., and all were largely in excess of the upset rental.
The Berea will rapidly become the seat of a numerous

suburban population." Mr. Upton had also received instructions from the Governor to proceed with the erection of a Public Hospital on the Government Beach Erf before referred to. This was estimated to cost £2,500, to be paid out of the Native Reserve Fund.

In October "Kahts' Corner" was advertised by Mr. S. Beningfield for sale by auction, having a frontage of 75 ft. to the Market Square and 50 ft. to West Street. It was sold to Mr. J. F. Churchill for the large sum of £700, which we were told was at the extraordinary rate of £4,000 per acre. That piece of ground is to-day rated by the Corporation as worth more than £7,000, but, as a financial agent, I doubt if £10,000 would purchase it.

Cricket. The flame of intertown rivalry, which hitherto had but flickered, was rekindled by the following:—

CHALLENGE.

" ELEVEN of the MARITZBURG CRICKET CLUB are OPEN TO PLAY ELEVEN GENTLEMEN OF DURBAN.

2nd April, 1860. SAM WILLIAMS, Hon. Sec."

The gauntlet thus thrown down was promptly picked up by Durban, though no organised Cricket Club existed. A preliminary field day was held, followed by an evening meeting at Deer's London Hotel, under the Presidency of Mr. John Hunt, when eleven players were elected as Champions for Durban. Mr. A. Moore, the Acting Curator of the Botanic Gardens, had a nice "pitch" mown on the flat by the Race Course, while arrangements were made for a public dinner to the Maritzburg team, to be held, after the contest, at the Masonic Hotel. "Tickets, wines included, 10s. 6d."

The Match was held on Wednesday, 2nd May, and as a "score" is the essential part of our National Game, I shall feel safe in taking over the *Mercury's* narrative:—

" Most of the Maritzburg eleven arrived on Tuesday. Their anticipations of success were very confident, having the advantage of their opponents in point of practice. Nevertheless, as a matter of course, the Durban players with their ' backers' and fellow-townsmen had a strong impression that the chances lay on their side. Yesterday the stores and other places of business closed about noon, and the town turned out *en masse* to witness the fight. The cricket ground was on the grassy flat near the Gardens, and through the kindness of the military authorities several marquees had been erected. Refreshment stalls were also provided by private speculators, and the scene with its horsemen, flags and wagons was a very gay and inspiriting one.

" Wickets were pitched about half-past ten o'clock, and the playing continued with much spirit and animation until half-past four. The challengers had the first innings. From beginning to end the match was well contested, and the playing on both sides was admirable. When we remember that the Durbanites have had hardly any practice at all, some of them not having played for months past, everyone must admit that their laurels are bravely won. They had a formidable foe, a hard struggle, and we are bound to add, a glorious victory. The great crowd of by-standers seemed to take a keen interest in the progress of the game, and the final result was hailed with loud cheers.

" The following is the scoring :—

PIETERMARITZBURG.

FIRST INNINGS.			SECOND INNINGS.		
Trenouth	2	b Hornby	Taylor	1	b Allington
Maxwell	2	b Allington	Mesham	1	c Hornby
Pepworth	0	run out	Ellis	3	c b Allington
Starr	13	b Allington	Trenouth	6	c b Landsdell
Button	6	b Hornby	Maxwell	4	b Landsdell
Williams	1	b Hornby	Button	5	b Allington
Shepstone	0	b Allington	Campbell	10	b Allington
Campbell	3	b Hornby	Starr	15	b c Hornby
Ellis	1	c Spencer	Williams	1	b Landsdell
Taylor	2	run out	Pepworth	2	not out
Mesham	0	not out	Shepstone	6	stumped
	30			44	
Byes	4		Byes	8	
Total	34		Total	52	

DURBAN.

FIRST INNINGS.			SECOND INNINGS.		
Blundell	0	b Ellis	Allington	5	b Ellis
Landsdell	6	b Starr	Landsdell	0	b Ellis
Burton	6	c Trenouth	Burton	21	not out
Allington	6	b Ellis	Downard	14	b Starr
Downard	13	lb wicket	Walters	5	not out
Walters	1	b Starr		6	wickets to go down
F. Spencer	1	c Shepstone			
Hornby	0	b Starr			
H. Palmer	3	c Williams			
Binns	1	b Starr			
Escombe	3	not out			
	40			45	
Byes	2		Byes	8	
Total	42		Total	53	

TIME.—"A great boon has been conferred on the town [October 11th] by our energetic fellow townsman Mr. R. Acutt, who has just had attached to his new premises, in the pediment of the portico, a large turret clock. This will be one step towards securing an uniform and absolutely correct standard of time, which, notwithstanding Mr. Pulleyn's diurnal and praiseworthy labours with the Church bell, is very far from having been yet attained."

Curfew Bell. In this connection I may mention that the venerable and useful institution, the Curfew Bell, was not brought into operation until the Borough had taken over the entire control of the Police, a year or two later. All good niggers were supposed to have gone to their respective places when the Camp bugles recalled the military to their quarters at 9 p.m. As a rule superstition and custom operated favourably in restraining them from being abroad after dark, though on moonlight nights open-air dances in backyards were frequent and vociferous; but these festive gatherings, like feline concerts, were usually dispersed by projectiles and bad language, perpetrated by the suffering and testy neighbours, about bedtime.

Cutter "Herald." We were in the habit of expressing ourselves strongly at what we deemed the neglect of the Colonies, and this young Colony in particular, by the Home Government; animadverting on red tape and routine of the Circumlocution Office, and the conduct of the Barnacle family, as I have already shown in our threats to pass by the Lieutenant-Governor, and appeal to the Secretary of State direct. It was firmly held that no grievance against the Administration would be redressed, unless the matter was represented in England " to the proper quarter." That quarter, however, was a vague and indefinite one. Some placed their faith in the Archbishop of Canterbury, others in the *Times*, the House of Lords, or a Member of Parliament. When, however, the grievance had been properly represented, and really merited redress, the Home Government could not justly be accused of delay; it was all a matter of Departments. It was, therefore, with complacent satisfaction that we learnt on the 1st November, that the Lisbon Chambers had voted £2,700 to the owners and shippers of the Cutter *Herald*, represented by our townsman Mr. J. D. Koch, as compensation for the seizure and confiscation, at Delagoa Bay, of that bold little craft and her cargo. Whether the parties interested ever got paid. I am unable to say.

The Electric Telegraph. Was not a local institution in 1860; though it was reported that Mr. Edmund " Coolie " Agent, was actively employed in Tatham. just prior to his appointment as organising preliminaries of a Company to establish a Telegraph line between this town and the City. It was thought the capital required would not exceed £2,000, and that the returns would be very large. I believe it was eventually constructed by the Government, but have no data at hand as to time, cost, or particulars. My recollection is of a single wire, carried on bush poles, the instruments used being dials with needles and double handles.

The first public announcement in reference to this Church appeared on the 6th December, notifying that subscriptions were on foot for the erection of a Church on the Berea Ridge. The history of this Church is peculiar. Mr. C. Joseph Cato, the owner of the farm "Brickfields," on cutting off that portion he named "Catoville" (Overport), reserved and gave to the Bishop of Natal, in trust for the Church of England, a portion of the farm on the Borough boundary, which had formed, as previously mentioned, the original Mission Station of Capt. Allen Gardiner, and which he considered additionally hallowed as being the burying place of Capt. Gardiner's young daughter, to whose memory a mutilated marble tablet exists in the Church, rescued by Mr. William Hartley from total destruction as a doorstep, in Mr. G. C. Cato's backyard at the Creek. The Rev. Mr. Rivett, who interested himself in the matter, gives in his book, under date January 18, 1864, a copy of a letter written by him to a lady patron in England :—

"By the outgoing mail I am writing to Mrs. Admiral Harcourt, of Swinton Park, Masham, in Yorkshire, who generously gave a little church for the Congella, to Mr. and Mrs. Daggett. Mr. Daggett, as I have told you, died within a short time after he returned from England. Mrs. Daggett and her little child (who stayed with us before they left) have gone back to England.*

"The church has arrived and is at the Custom House, but there is no one to take any interest in the matter now Mrs. Daggett is gone. The Congella inhabitants are very few in number, and most of them are Nonconformists, so that I question whether it be practicable to place the church in that neighbourhood. The Berea is a thriving suburb of Durban, and a church is needed there, as the people are both able and willing to support a clergyman. I am deputed [? by Mrs. Daggett] to ask Mrs. Harcourt whether she will transfer her munificent gift to the Berea.†

---

* The lady died on the voyage.
† He writes in another place, "I hear it cost over £500, but it includes all the internal fittings, pulpit, reading-desk, seats, etc."

"If she does we shall lose no time in rescuing it from the damage which it must sustain by lying at the Point. I fear a portion of it has already received injury. I feel somewhat assured the lady will comply with the request. Had Mr. and Mrs. Daggett been at Congella, I do not think it would have been used by many beyond their own family."

The generous donor consented, and during 1864 the foundation stone of this little iron church with its prominent spire, was laid by the wife of that zealous Churchwarden, Mr. Robert Raw, who now owned and resided on the adjoining land, and had especially interested himself in the acquisition of this cheap addition to the Church temporal.   The Rev. Mr. Rivett officiated on the occasion.

This structure, in all its essentials the same, still stands, and serves those more worthy people of the Berea for the worship of the Almighty, though as a building it is admitted to be on its last legs.

Public Houses. In addition to the Hotels previously referred to, I may note those houses now existing which had their origin as "Canteens," and afforded refreshment and entertainment in the Fifties. In West Street we had the "Phœnix," a wattle and daub building enclosed by a tall reed fence, kept by an ex-military man.

On the opposite side of the way resided Widow Quested with her two industrious daughters from Kent—passengers ex *Minerva*—in a pretty thatched cottage, standing back from the street, with neat palings and flowers in front. To add to her means she commenced the manufacture of Ginger-beer, setting aside a comfortable room for its quiet consumption. John Gavin's foundry was adjacent, business throve, and she was induced to add the brewing of Hop or Sugar Beer, and ultimately to apply for a canteen licence, christening her enlarged establishment the "Kentish Tavern."

Round the corner of Grey Street (there was no "European" then) we came to "Drew's" or "West End Hotel," a house much frequented by the military; music, dancing, skittles, and use of the gloves, with cheap board and lodging. I believe the main building was of brick; it had

green palings along its front.   Proceeding up Pine
Terrace, we arrived at the " Trafalgar Hotel," taken over
from Platt by Baynes, afterwards by Arnold.   Though the
" Bodega Bar " now stands on this Erf, it will possibly be
recollected as the site of the Trafalgar Theatre.

The " Travellers' Rest " was another military house :
gable-ended and thatched, at the corner of Field Street and
Pine Terrace (Dacomb's corner), the last house of call on
the way to the Camp, or for the traveller by wagon to
Maritzburg or Zululand.   It has changed its name with
changing tenants to the " Jerusalem " and the " Globe."

The " British Banner," in distant St. George's Street,
kept by a man named Robertson, was frequented chiefly by
the artizan class as a sort of social club room, where their
evenings were spent in amusements and the discussion of
local politics and prices.   Bagatelle and cards were general.
Not being a frequenter of canteens, I can recall no pronounced cases of gambling at these houses.   The Magistrate
was rarely troubled with " drunks."   Roysterers usually
saw each other home, or were entrusted to the seclusion of
the nearest bush, to " think of their head in the morning ! "

Street Noises.
The history of Old Durban would be incomplete without recalling that time when
the constant voice of the locomotive was
not heard on the hill; when our over-
cultivated nerves were not strained by the rise and fall,
rumble and squeak of tramcars in macadamized streets,
the dash of smart waggonettes and cabs, the clatter of
horsemen, the thundering roll of trolleys, the sudden telephone bell, and snappy " Are you there?" the dull subdued
throb of numerous machine driving engines, with an
occasional volley from steam hammers, or the sledge's
musical clang cutting iron rails or girders in the streets;
the voices of the capering Ricksha boys and coloured
newspaper urchins, soliciting custom by day, and the
Salvation Army's Band by night.   No! with us in the
Fifties, we had other grievances to which we yielded until
Time and the Bye-Laws substituted our present possessions.

My readers might reasonably conclude that, Durban being built on a sandy flat, our streets would be silent highways. The sand on the contrary was the cause of half our woe, for though the slow lumbering ox wagon made no noise, beyond the clatter of the yokes, as the feet of the uncomplaining cattle sank into the roadway, it was the vile man who drove that "raised Cain" with his infernal yells and screaming abuse, accentuated by pistol-shotlike detonations of his long wagon whip, the cracking of which was a fine art, not so much in its application to some lagging "England," "Holland," or "Blueberg," as to crash it down dexterously by the side of the plodding span, between them and the side walk. The hero who could at the same swing reverse his instrument of torture and make a "back clap" considered himself the admiration of the street.

It was the people on horseback who raised the loudest objections, for even "shooting ponies" could not be expected to stand this invisible fire. Remonstrances, if listened to, only varied the performance, for the usually hilarious outward-bound driver would swing his lash in serpentine coils from one side of the street to the other (no telegraph or telephone wires existed) and freshen up his span by running up their whole length and dexterously flicking in succession every ox, right and left, with the buck skin thong at the end of his whip, finishing up with a screaming "Yaak" long drawn out. Should he then resume his throne on the "fore chest" and restore his bamboo whip stick to its rack, he would give out from time to time, the excruciating yells "Treck"! "Yaak"!! with variations and abjurations in the best "Taal" mixture, comprehensible alone to the souls of the lower animals. At all times of the day the swish of the whip and the cries of wagon or cart drivers could be heard, varied as I have said before, by the diversion and pandemonium of a 'stick fast." In this respect, the Umgeni Brickcarts were, as might be expected, the greatest sufferers, since it required 10 to 12 oxen to bring in a load of 500 bricks. When bricks had to be delivered anywhere on the rise of the Berea, it was the custom to "off load" 250 at the first stick fast, persuade the poor oxen to deliver the

rest, and return for the balance.   Wagons seldom entered
or left the town after dark, and then with no more noise than
necessary to keep the cattle up to the yoke, and let
pedestrians know they occupied the road.

In the absence of a daily press, we had to avail ourselves
of that ancient advertising medium, the Bellman, to
announce public meetings, auction sales, or coming events.
Great interest was always shown in the possible news
conveyed by the leisurely passing native with a placarded
board hung to his neck, his person usually attired in an
old scarlet coatee, a discarded white hat on his head, and
a cow-bell in his hand, which he duly jangled in response
to the invitations of the public to "let's bona," or "foet
zack." It savoured to me of affectation to condemn this
musical news-agent as a nuisance, until after they had
increased and multiplied. A street noise that *did* constitute a public nuisance, an added suffering to the sick
and a hindrance to business, arose out of certain native
customs, one of those few things King Solomon declares he
did not know, "The way of a man with a maid."

Native girls visiting the town (always under male escort)
for business or pleasure, to sell or to buy, more frequently
bearing pots of native beer from their country kraals to
their male friends in service, would come adorned with
well greased limbs, their best beads and red ochre raddle,
conforming to the law by a cotton sheet knotted round
their necks, but, like their veiled sisters of Turkey, contriving to display such charms as never failed to kindle the
amorous sparks in the streets. The sharp-eyed store boy,
house servant or labourer, always quicker to perceive
things farthest from his work, would detect at the street
end the advent of any wandering party. If unable to see,
he was certain to hear the jubilant crowing of the young
men in the distance, which duly prepared him for the
advent of the fair sex. Only the stern sense of duty
imposed by the unsympathetic "Boss" prevented his
running off to see and participate for himself. We might
be in the midst of the most difficult operation, loading,
unloading, sorting, packing, but the moment a party of
lusty wenches came within range and could be distinguished
from married women, a grunt or ejaculation sufficed for

every fellow to drop his employment on the spot, and bolt off to join in a smirking, pleading cordon in front of the steadily advancing girls; offering themselves for selection with such blandishments and promises as are the ways of men, shouting the while "Koma! umtanatu! !" (Choose, my dear one) dancing backwards as the stolid maidens advanced with even pace, as though intending to walk through them. A few paces gave time for the display of a becoming modesty and indifference, and a hasty glance at the boys, then one by one they would indicate their choice with a jerked chin or a moved finger. The encircling ring would at once break up, returning to their respective Bosses, leaping, yelling, laughing, and gesticulating, clapping this one on the back in compliment for his having received more than one vote, and strutting around and chaffing the unfortunate who could not boast of a single "Koma."

Their noisy comments would occupy much time and prevent the resumption of work at the point they left it. To add to the sins for which the unfortunate white soul will have to answer, the girls would scarcely have progressed another hundred yards, when the operation was repeated by the "boys" of that quarter, who retailed their successes to the first gang, those again shouting back their views and experiences, and so every one was cheerful, except the unconsidered whiteman, whose gnashing of teeth was both loud and deep.

As fishing was not an industry, owing to the dislike of our natives to handle or eat fish of any kind, no fish were cried in the streets. Native hawkers of firewood, reeds, grass, brooms, mats, fruit, or vegetables contrived to announce their wares without shouting.

Emigrant Plagues. It was Artemus Ward, I think, who in his "American Showman" observes:— "Monkey's ain't no use except to look at, an' wonder what on 'arth they'll do next!" We have been wondering all these years—without a solution—what on earth was the use of the Durban Mosquito, aborigines of both the swamp and bush; the bush fleas, and the assorted ticks of the grassy flats.

These were the first plagues with which the Emigrants were smitten. Blooming maidens, chubby children, and the darling infant would be put in their little beds in all the beauty and freshness of an English complexion to awake next morning blotched, swollen, and distorted, having served in the hours of darkness as tender, juicy pasturage for the ever voracious mosquito and all the hungry members of his tribe within call.

The daily occupations of the new settlers obliged them to walk through the long grass, and at night curious dwellers among tents might see shapely shadows cast upon the canvas and hear from time to time feminine voices exclaiming "My! Oh! here's another," "Keep still," "Hold up your arm," or "Mind the candle."

Experience came early, and the deduction was sure that the inmates were, in light attire, engaged in tick-hunting, with the probability that the tweezers in father's or brother's many-bladed jack knife were requisitioned to remove the minute red ticks, whose habit it is to cluster on the grass tops and insist on flesh and blood when they obtain the opportunity. These tiny creatures invariably climb upwards, and seek the most inaccessible places on the human body; when they have feasted to repletion they drop off, leaving an irritant poison in the wound lasting for many days with people of tender skins. The Bush Flea on the contrary is more of a gay cavalier, he loves and he rides away; his tickle is worse than his bite; he is quite content to share your camp blanket if you do not resent his liberty of action. If you smear him with cow-dung and purge him with a broom of wormwood he will leave you in peace. Not so the Mosquito and the Tick, who appear to defy most of the offensive unguents applied to your person, and contrive to leave their sting behind. The natural remedy for this intolerable irritation is enjoyed alike by men and monkeys in the form of a hasty scratching; this luxury, if over indulged, causes the skin to break, and in most cases a sore ensues. With the new comer this wound rapidly enlarges itself into a species of malignant ulcer that takes the name of "Natal-sore," confining itself generally to the legs or arms, frequently obliging the patient to relinquish his occupations for a season. For the cure of this evil Mr. James Brickhill compounded an ointment and lotion, afterwards advertised and sold as "Brickhill's Specific," when its healing and cleansing properties came to be recognised. Its chief ingredient was believed to be the fleshy triangular-leafed plant inhabiting the Back Beach, and known to us as the "Hottentot Fig." This plant, pulped or bruised, the early settlers applied as a cold wash or poultice to both men and animals.

The next visitation was caused by the absence of shoe leather and the practice of going barefooted, especially by young people; it was popularly known as "Sand-worm," and found lodgment in the sole of the foot or between the toes. making daily progress in well defined tracks under the surface skin, setting up much inflammation and violent irritation. With the measurable evidence before us, the Doctor's assertion that this "microbe" was not a creeping "worm" was generally discredited, while the violent measures taken to remove it usually resulted in establishing a genuine Natal sore. The cure most in favour was that of counter irritation by rubbing with coarse salt before puncturing the skin over the supposed body of the prostrate foe. In my own case I found speedy relief after rubbing a handful of Liverpool salt into the boarded floor with my bare foot.

Serving to corroborate ancient history, these afflictions of the flesh are still in evidence to the pure-blooded European visitor; the old Colonists—toughened and inoculated —have learnt to regard them with complacency or indifference.

Advertisements. Since the age of Newspapers, the history of the time has been accentuated by its advertisements. To the future Colonial historian, or the casual writer, a large field of instructive and amusing subjects will be found in the Advertising Columns of the early Colonial Newspapers. I have availed myself of a few local advertisements, since they marked our habits as we lived, and the fashion of the time in 1860.

PRIVATE TUITION.
EAST END, WEST STREET, DURBAN.
MR. J. R. YARNOLD

Proposes commencing his select establishment for young gentlemen as above, on Thursday, January 12th, 1860.

Mr. Yarnold met with such encouragement that he was induced to remove to Pinetown, where he erected a suitable building and established a successful boarding-school.

In 1863 the Rev. W. H. L. Rivett and Mr. W. S. W. Blathwayt sought to found a Grammar School in Stanger Street, " For the sons of English Merchants (Gentlemen)." Mr. Rivett on leaving for England tranferred his interest to Mr. Blathwayt, who continued it for some years until the Government made provision for a high-class school in Durban. Mr. Rivett however claims, "Mr. Blathwayt and myself were the pioneers in establishing the first gentleman's school in the seaport of the Colony."

EXCURSION TO ENGLAND AND BACK ! ! !
LADY OF THE LAKE.

In consequence of numerous applications for a trip home and back, notice is hereby given, that, should a sufficient number of applications be received on or before the 15th October next, the above ship will be laid on as above.

Passages through £70, viz. :—

Chief Cabin, Home   £35.

     ,,   Back   £35.

Second Cabin, through, £50, viz. :—

Home, 2nd Cabin   £25.

Back   ,,   £25.

Application to be made to

June 7th, 1860.   Edward Snell & Co , Agents.

LIME.

We, the undersigned, hereby give notice that in consequence of the high rate of cattle and scarcity of labour are compelled though reluctantly, to RAISE the PRICE of ROUGH LIME from 3s. 6d. to 4s. per muid.

W. Brunton.

J. W. Harris.

W. Tunmer & Son.

Congella, August 1st, 1860.

To be Disposed Of.

Half an Erf of Land in Smith Street, with a strong stone foundation.

Apply to E. Pickering, Cooper, East End of West Street."

On the 16th August appears an advertisement by **Mr. Matthew Barr** announcing that in consequence of ill health he is obliged to give up his Butchery Business. This is followed by

THOMAS G. BROWNE,
BUTCHER,
FIELD STREET AND WEST STREET.

T.G.B having taken over the Butchering Business from Mr. Barr begs to inform the Public that he intends carrying on the same in connection with the Business in Field Street, and hopes by strict attention to merit the favour which has been so liberally bestowed both on him and his predecessor.

In consequence of the Long Price of Cattle, and as the following prices are calculated on the lowest scale of Profit, only One Month's Credit will be given.

Boiling Beef	4d.	Mutton	7d.
Prime Joints	5d.	Sausages	7d.
Beef Steaks	5d.	Black Pudding	9d.
Rump „	6d.		

PRIME TRIPE EVERY SATURDAY.

All orders will meet with T.G.B.'s utmost attention and endeavours to give a general and lasting satisfaction.

A Constant Supply of Vegetables.

NATAL RAILWAY.
NOTICE TO THE PUBLIC.

On and after this day the Trains will run at the hours stated in the Company's Time Bills.

John Beard,
Manager.

December 19th, 1860.

The so-called "Time Bills" announced in October that there would be four passenger trains each way on week days only, viz.,

Down . 9 a.m., 11 30 a.m., 2 30 p.m. 4 p.m.
Up . . 9 30 a.m., 12 30 p.m., 3 p.m., 5 p.m.
Fares, First Class 1s. Second Class 6d.
Return, First Class only, 1s. 6d.

They continued to run more or less up to time, influenced of course by the reasonable expectation and convenience of any Director having a belated water picnic, or fishing party, or leave - taking visit to the Mail Steamer. As Christmas was coming I conjecture the Manager desired to acquaint the Public that greater regularity could be expected. But there was a lack of moral courage somewhere, for the Directors did not announce any special trains for Christmas, leaving it for me to bear the blame of any desecration, while the Shareholders pocketed the proceeds. We were informed that as the Public must be considered, Tuesday the 25th was *not* to be a Public Holiday for us,, and passenger trains only would run at the discretion of the Stationmaster.

I cannot do better than quote the poetical correspondent of the *Mercury* in reference to this first adoption of the Railway for excursion purposes by an appreciative Public.

"For a wonder the day was bright and sunny. , . . All the vessels in harbour had branches of evergreens stuck about them, and a few flags hung out. The Railway reaped a fine crop of sixpences and shillings from Point-going townspeople. Twelve trains ran during the day, and all of them were crowded ; the two last especially being crammed with smiling ladies, fat babies, clamorous children, indefinite hobble-de-hoys invading the mysteries of tobacco in its various phases, blushing demoiselles haunted by familiars in the shape of amorous youngsters, with a posse of attendant natives, besprinkled with a few cachinatory Coolies, and wedged in by a heterogeneous mass of hampers, baskets, boxes and fish lines. All these came pouring out of the carriages and trucks on to the Point platform, to be thence deported per sundry boats to the Bluff or the Island. How a Durban Picnicker pities his City Brethren shut out from all these locomotive and nautical privileges.

"Please the Good Fates, who watch over the destiny of this Christmas Colony, we shall have a Maritzburg Railway soon, so that the citizens can rattle down overnight and participate in all these pleasures."

Natal Pioneers. Mr. James Brickhill originated the idea of preserving a memento of the pioneer British Settlers of Natal, that is to say, settlers prior to the year 1851, so he induced, about one hundred and seventy-four of them to subscribe to a photographic scheme by which we were each to receive so many , carte-de-visite copies of our physiognomy, and so many full-plate copies in which the whole of the subscribers were grouped. This was successfully carried out in 1872, the grouping and printing having been done in England. Now that the greater number of these old-time settlers have gone over to the majority, this photographic picture (of which copies are in Durban's Museum) forms a touching and interesting record. I have endeavoured, and I think successfully, to include in the foregoing reminiscences the names of the major portion of those Natal Pioneers, though many were not burgesses of Durban. It is to be regretted that certain superior people declined to subscribe on the ground that they either were here before " The Emigrants," or, being gentlemen and first class passengers, could not be classed or grouped with Emigrants.

It will be noticeable in this Photographic Memorial that none of the Cato family appear, neither do Messrs. John Millar, Hugh Gillespie, Edward Snell, Hy. and T. Milner, Sidney Peel and several others who were alive at the time, and whose names otherwise figure in Durban's History.

Ghosts. Notwithstanding the Lares and Penates which the British Colonist supposed that he brought with him, I am satisfied the good old family Ghost objected to Emigration, and either remained behind or discovered on landing that the Englishman's home as constructed in Durban was not a castle of sufficient permanency to afford a self-respecting bogie decent shelter and occupation, gave up the ghost and returned whence he came ; or otherwise finding that he or she had to consort with coloured spooks unable to speak English removed Overberg, where they are said to enjoy due recognition and amusement among the Dutch farmers. Our Natives certainly admit the existence of the spirits of their ancestors, who usually assume the shapes of harmless brown snakes frequenting their huts, living upon field mice, and drinking milk when propitiated. But, so far as the settlement of Durban is concerned, I have only actual evidence of one disembodied spirit in the shape of " Will o' the Wisp " frequenting our swamps with fitful searchlights when nights are dark and still.

In the "Fifties" one ghost was reputed to haunt a certain dwelling house in Durban after dark, but it was left to a prudent maiden to discover this ghost in the dire shape of a pair of ammunition boots protruding from under her bed. A strong father and a violent mother succeeded in embodying this lonely spirit in the person of a stalwart Artilleryman, who pleaded being overcome by other spirits as the cause of the disaster. Being a friend of the family and otherwise a good fellow he was let off with a caution, and not officially reported.

One ghost set up in business at the Point, frequenting the Bush path, and the grounds of a house where several charming young women resided. His advent scared the natives and the household. The seafaring father kept a club handy, and being himself startled one moonlight evening gave chase, and used his club so skilfully that he laid the sheet-covered ghost to his bed for several days, and the Magistrate was not troubled to investigate the cause.

A few years later, as the Berea lots became occupied, a turnip or pumpkin-headed ghost with candle and skirt caused considerable fright to lonely females and native servants at uncertain intervals. This apparition was reported to the Police, who, unable to patrol that distant locality, recommended a Vigilance Committee, which quickly dispersed the joker by the aid of a material shot gun and a live dog. Spooks then gave up business in Durban, even Churchyards forgot to yawn, the only sounds there after dark being the voices of the night, to which the resident "Bush Babies," Bats, Owls, Toads, and rodent-hunting cats contributed, though on sultry summer nights a shrieking ghost clothed in a green pea pod flies abroad, entering the habitations of the living in the guise of an inflated grasshopper.

Imagination and superstition may secure a revival, especially as our advancing civilisation tends to encourage emigrating spirits to find homes in our drains and water pipes, our reverberating street wires and electric connections.

We need have no anxiety that our children will develop a belief in ghosts, the healthy open-air lives they lead, the absence of ignorant story tellers in the household (Indian and Native bogies obtaining no credit), together with a too familiar intercourse with their seniors—the daily peeps behind the domestic scenes—foster a disrespect for the powers that be, an irreverence for pastors and masters, godfathers and godmothers, the puling infant or the slippered pantaloon, so that a respectable immaterial ghost has little chance of recognition or obedience in their Pantheon.

CONCLUSION.

If the fanciful idea, with which I commenced, has not resulted in a superstructure calling for the admiration of my neighbours, it must be attributed to the fragmentary nature of my materials, and the time that has passed since I set out to collect and piece them together; time snatched from my private leisure after the hours of business, and subjected to all the vicissitudes of social and domestic cares.

Convinced that the idea of a complete superstructure was fallacious, I concede the weakness of my execution, for as Time passed he disclosed the fact that old things were passing away and that as I wrote, the very landmarks of Old Durban were daily yielding to the progress of the age. The niches into which I have fitted them are themselves vanishing, so that the eye of Durban's future citizen may fail to distinguish, or the mind to imagine, the primordial scenes in which my work has been built.

If I have not realised all my expectation, yet I take infinite pride as a Burgess in having successfully raised a foundation, reducing rude matter into due form from " the Year One," carrying it up consecutively for the first ten years of our existence, and ceasing my labours at a point when the Durban of to-day started, with all its institutions fairly developed, on its career of progress and prosperity.

To the first Emigrant Burgesses, the real founders of this truly British Colonial town, must be conceded the honour of having " begun at the beginning," devoting time, labour, thought and much self-sacrifice, for the good of themselves and that posterity of which they were so careful. Posterity can to-day point with pride to their flourishing Borough, and bestow a kindly thought on their industrious, much - enduring progenitors, learning themselves to carry on to grander development and fruition the possibilities now within their reach, so constituting the " Port Natal" of the ancients the most important and progressive seaport town of South Africa, a fitting replica of the Carthage of the North.

Looking back across the short space, within the memory of living men, when Durban was the shelter of wild beasts and birds, the hunter and the savage, who shall predict in this electrically driven age the possibilities of its future development ? May the time never come when the old British stock shall have yielded to climatic influences and lowered itself to an equality with the civilized ' coloured citizen "—native or alien—within our borders, and by affinity engendered a whitey-brown people, subjects of some greater Britain, speaking the language of Volapuk, and ruling the destinies of this borough.

Though I may have awakened some sad and sorrowful memories, yet I trust I have succeeded in rekindling the hopeful aspirations of our early hardy youth, have helped to bring to mind the promises of our speedy fortune and return to the Old Country we called Home; have recalled our struggles with the inevitable, which, overcome, fostered an attachment to our new country and surroundings, prompting us to more vigorous efforts to advance the happy time when we could really pray that ' girl we left behind us ' to share our lives in the Durban we had created, with the liberty we loved and the laws we respected.

If in the sunset of our lives I have brought a ray of brightness, a blush of pleasure, a gladdening of the eyes, and a softening of animosities tending to forgiveness, to my associates the early emigrants, or to those children who survive them, I shall not have toiled in vain, or deem that I have lived unworthily of the principles of Christianity and the teachings of Freemasonry. "Hence we should learn to be meek, humble and resigned, to be faithful to our God, our Country and our Laws, to drop a tear of sympathy on the failings of a Brother, and to pour the healing balm of consolation in the bosom of the afflicted."

FINIS.

L'ENVOY.

It was a shock to my gentlemanly instincts, or what I have considered as such, to be told by an irreverent person that no one would care to know where I gathered my facts, so long as they were facts; yet in the fitness of things I cannot adopt the rude suggestion, or let old acquaintances be forgot, though were I to attempt to enumerate and thank all those from whom I have obtained valuable information and assistance, I should need to add another chapter.

I should deem it an act of ingratitude were I not to acknowledge my indebtedness to the "Annals of Natal"; to my talented namesake's "Natal and its Story"; to the works of "Isaacs," "Gardiner," and others; to Mr. P. Davis of Maritzburg for the loan of the first numbers of *The Natal Witness*; to Mr. F. W. A. Watson, J.P., Clerk of the Legislative Assembly, and Mr. H. E. Stainbank, J.P., the late Speaker, for access to the Parliamentary Library; to Mr. W. Osborn, Librarian, Durban Public Library, for references to many authorities, especially the early newspapers; to Sir John Robinson and the proprietors of *The Natal Mercury*; to Mr. T. L. Cullingworth for access to *The Times of Natal* and *The Star*, published by his father; to my old friends S. W. B. Griffin of Willow Grange, Thos. Cook, of Durban, Thos. Groom, M.L.A., and that veteran colonist Mr. Thos. Green, both of Verulam; to the Honble. Geo. Rutherford, C.M.G., late Collector of Customs; Mr. J. S. Steel, founder of Durban's Museum; Mr. J. B. Cottam, Secretary of the Church Council; Messrs. John P. Cato and Orlando Cato; Mr. James Baxter, all of Durban. To Mr. W. H. Dyer and other Corporation Officials, in addition to many other kind personal friends, fellow passengers, old Emigrants or their children of both sexes, not otherwise directly named in my work; to all of whom I tender my grateful acknowledgments and hearty thanks, in the full assurance that their contributions will bring their own reward to them by the renewed interest they will experience in the history of the days which are past.

G. R.